Rudolf Mrázek

SJAHRIR:
POLITICS AND EXILE
IN INDONESIA

STUDIES ON SOUTHEAST ASIA

Southeast Asia Program
180 Uris Hall
Cornell University, Ithaca, New York
1994

Editor in Chief
  Benedict Anderson

Advisory Board
  George Kahin
  Stanley O'Connor
  Takashi Shiraishi
  Keith Taylor
  Oliver Wolters

Editing and Production
  Donna Amoroso
  Audrey Kahin
  Roberta Ludgate
  Dolina Millar

Cover Design
  Deena Wickstrom

I acknowledge with thanks the support I have received in writing this book from the following institutions: Cornell University Southeast Asia Program and Modern Indonesia Project; the Rockefeller Foundation, the Social Science Research Council (SSRC) in New York, the Toenggoel Foundation in Jakarta, and the Netherlands Institute for Advanced Studies (NIAS) in Wassenaar.

Cover photo: Banda Neira. From the photo and print collection of the Koninklijk Instituut voor Taal-, Land- en Volkenkunde, Leiden (KITLV), Afd. Documentatie Geschiedenis Indonesië (DGI) #8589.

Studies on Southeast Asia No. 14

© 1994 Cornell Southeast Asia Program
ISBN 0-87727-713-3

To George McTurnan Kahin

Contents

Preface: Effort at Biography 1

1. The Homeland 5

   1. The World of Minangkabau and Sjahrir's Mother 5
   2. Sjahrir's Father and the Notion of Rantau 9
   3. Sjahrir's Sister and the Culture of Nationhood 16
   4. Medan and the First Period of Sjahrir's Life 23

2. Bandung, 1926–1929 33

   1. The City and the School 33
   2. Jong Indonesie 39
   3. The Youth and Sukarno 49

3. Holland, 1929-1931 56

   1. Amsterdam and Leiden 56
   2. Perhimpoenan Indonesia 65
   3. The Return Home 75

4. The Return to Java, 1931-1934 82

   1. Chairman of the Pendidikan Nasional Indonesia 82
   2. The Confrontation with Sukarno 87
   3. The Return of Hatta and the Minangkabau Base 95
   4. The Dutch Reaction 105

5. Prison and the Internment Camp, 1934–1935 118

   1. Cipinang Prison 118
   2. Almost an "Ethical" Village 128
   3. Sjahrir at Boven Digul 138

6. Exile in Banda Neira, 1936-1941 154

   1. Politics without Sjahrir 154
   2. Closer to the World 164

3. Flowers, Officials, Nationalists, and the Bandanese 175
4. Juffrouw Cressa, Oom Bing, and the Bandanese Children 189
5. The End of Exile? 197

7. The Japanese Occupation, 1942–1945 209

1. Sukabumi 209
2. Sjahrir's Pemuda 219
3. Network of Power 231
4. Nationalist Mainstream 243
5. Proclamation of Independence 253

8. The Revolution, 1945–1949 269

1. Perdjoeangan Kita 269
2. Prime Minister 283
3. Tan Malaka 302
4. Road to Linggadjati 321
5. The End of Sjahrir's Cabinet 332
6. Adviser to the President 346
7. Madiun 361
8. The End of Revolution 376

9. The Fifties, 1950–1959 402

1. The Fluidity of Power 402
2. Oracle of Delphi 417
3. General Elections 430
4. Civil War 443

10. The Death 459

1. Prison 459
2. Last Writings 473
3. The Death 489

Epilogue: On Memory 497

Bibliography 501

Index 517

Illustrations

Banda Neira	Cover
Sjahrir as a Young Man	x
Sjahrir's Family House in Kota Gedang	8
The Pass between Kota Gedang and Bukittinggi	15
Hotel de Boer	25
Bioscoop Preanger	36
"Poetri Indonesia" of Bandung with Sjahrir	41
Jef Last	60
Leiden University	67
Map of the Netherlands	75
PNI Congress in Bandung	85
Hatta in 1934	98
Sjahrir	119
Boven Digul	129
Leaving Boven Digul	150
Soewarni Pringgodigdo and Soewarsih Djojopoespito	155
Map of the Eastern Archipelago	164
Postcard of Banda Neira	167
Banda Neira	177
Sjahrir	193
Map of Java	208
Japanese Drawings (1)	213
Japanese Drawings (2)	222
Japanese Drawings (3)	246
Premier Sjahrir	284
The Bridge	294
Tan Malaka	303
Sjahrir on the Radio	325

The Linggadjati Signing Ceremony 333
Sjahrir leaving by air 359
Sjahrir under Arrest 381
Five Stamps (Sukarno, Hatta, Maramis, Hadji Agoes Salim, Sjahrir) 398
Bual Bang Betjak 404
Stamps with Sukarno 433
Bual Bang Betjak 461
Hatta Speaking at Sjahrir's Grave 495

These days young people read stories only because they love to hear their melodies; some of them listen to stories only to laugh.

           Hikayat Pancha Tanderan, 1965[1]

---

[1] "Kebanyakan orang muda-muda pada zaman ini membaca hikayat itu sebab suka mendengar lagunya sahaja; ada pula yang mendengarkan hikayat itu sebab hendak tertawa sahaja." Quoted and translated in Hendrik M. J. Maier, *In the Center of Authority: The Malay Hikayat Merong Mahawangsa* (Ithaca: Cornell Studies on Southeast Asia, 1988), p. 83.

Sjahrir as a Young Man
(Photo courtesy of Mrs. Maria Duchâteau-Sjahrir)

Preface: Effort at Biography

This is a study of schools and exile, politics and integrity: more of exile than schools; much more of integrity than of politics. Some who have read a part or the whole of the book in manuscript suggested that this was a biography of a man who failed. I can not disagree more. But I hope that what follows may help our understanding of what a failure really is.

I do not know where this story originated. Perhaps not in Indonesia at all. Perhaps as far back as in my boyhood fascination for the Jewish community in Prague, and, some years later, in my reading of Franz Kafka, a writer who came to manifest this community to me better than anybody else.

Kafka never mentioned the word "Jew" in his literary work. He was a Prague Jew, and a stranger among Prague Czechs, Prague Germans, and even other Prague Jews. He loved Prague, planned to escape the city to Jerusalem, and died in between. After his death, some Czechs, some Germans, and some Jews came to treasure Kafka as an arc, a trembling bridge, that might help them attempt a passage from one narrow tradition to another, and maybe beyond:

> I was stiff and cold. I was a bridge. I lay over a ravine. My toes on one side, my fingers clutching the other, I had clamped myself fast into the crumbling clay. The tails of my coat fluttered at my sides. Far below brawled the icy trout stream....[1]

It is generally accepted that each personality is formed by childhood experience and then by the cultural barriers erected across its path through life. The cultural barrier is a line at which a man is challenged to defect, to strengthen, or to reinterpret some of the fundamental values of his philosophy and behavior. Writing a biography should be a mapping of the checkpoints where cultural barriers are crossed or evaded.

By encountering the barriers one is changing oneself, and one is changing the landscape through which one passes: one builds a bridge for oneself and for others; one builds a bridge of oneself. That is, I believe, what Franz Kafka had in mind: there is unfortunately and repeatedly nothing but a search for integrity in front of every checkpoint. Or ideally that is how it should be.

Sutan Sjahrir was born in May 1909 in Padang Panjang, in the Minangkabau region of West Sumatra. Educated in Medan, Bandung, Amsterdam, and Leiden, he became a leading spirit behind the Indonesian emancipation movement of the 1930s,

---

[1] Franz Kafka, "The Bridge," in Franz Kafka, *The Complete Short Stories* (New York: Schocken, 1976), p. 411.

spent eight years in colonial prisons and in exile, was thrice prime minister of the independent Republic, and died in exile again. Some call him "one of the great figures of the Asian Renaissance."[2]

According to an American intelligence report of 1945, he was five feet and six inches in height and weighed one hundred pounds.[3] His face, described by a Dutch friend, was "very expressive, but it lacked the stereotypical strikingness which leads to 'good photos'."[4] This description probably is just another sort of stereotype.

Sjahrir is generally presented as aloof from everything that seems "traditional," "primordial," or "parochial." Conspicuously missing, indeed, are childhood memories and the reassuring asylum of home culture—features so prominent in the public images of Sjahrir's great contemporaries, Sukarno, Mohammad Hatta, Amir Sjarifoeddin, Soetomo, and Tan Malaka.[5] Just as Kafka never used the word "Jew" in his literary works, Sjahrir hardly ever used the word "Minangkabau." Sjahrir is portrayed as restless and rootless, or, often by the same people, as extraordinarily fast and fluent in his release from traditional Minangkabau or Eastern spheres of thought and morals into the intellectual and ethical sphere of the West.

Sjahrir passed from childhood to maturity through Sumatran, Javanese, Indonesian, Dutch colonial, Dutch metropolitan, and various prison and exile cultures. He lived intensively in each of them and left behind accounts of his experience. There are letters to kin and friends, published and unpublished. There are articles in political and literary journals. There are speeches, deeds, and thoughts. There are photographs and his body language, preserved in the memories of those who knew him. All this, if handled with care, may stand for Sjahrir's own text, a sort of autobiography of Sjahrir. In writing about politics, economy, women, poetry, or whatever, when expressing one's opinions, one is, in a sense and essentially perhaps, writing about oneself. To unearth this "autobiography" in its entirety and to read it with concern—this was the principal ambition with which this book was written.

Any autobiography is intelligible only if the peculiar sequence of its narrative is taken into account. Every autobiography, I believe, progresses backwards, from a point at which the autobiographer is surveying his life, explaining it to his present self, and restructuring it so as to fit the requirements of the moment—of current ethics and aesthetics, of the experience one has accumulated until then.

There are many observation points in Sutan Sjahrir's autobiographical texts. The texts were written over a span of decades, under the spell of different places, cul-

---

[2] Herbert Feith in *Nation* (Sydney), April 30, 1966, quoted in *Perdjalanan terachir Pahlawan Nasional Sutan Sjahrir*, ed. H. Rosihan Anwar (Jakarta: Pembangunan, 1966), p. 64.

[3] Quoted in St. Rais Alamsjah, *10 orang besar Indonesia terbesar sekarang* (Jakarta: Bintang Mas, 1952), p. 134; elsewhere it was 1.47 meters and 54 kilos.

[4] Jacques de Kadt in *De Baanbreker* (1946), p. 4.

[5] Bernhard Dahm, *Sukarno and the Struggle for Indonesian Independence* (Ithaca: Cornell University Press, 1969); John D. Legge, *Sukarno: A Political Biography* (New York: Preager, 1972); Sukarno, *An Autobiography as Told to Cindy Adams* (Indianapolis: The Bobbs-Merrill, 1965); Mohammad Hatta, *Memoir* (Jakarta: Tintamas, 1978); Benedict Anderson, "A Time of Darkness and a Time of Light: Transposition in Early Indonesian Nationalist Thought," in *Perceptions of the Past in Southeast Asia*, ed. Anthony Reid and David Marr (Singapore: Heinemann, 1979), pp. 219–48; Harry A. Poeze, *Tan Malaka, Strijder voor Indonesië's vrijheid: Levensloop van 1897 tot 1945* (The Hague: Nijhoff, 1976); Rudolf Mrázek, "Tan Malaka: A Political Personality's Structure of Experience," *Indonesia* 14 (October 1972): 1–47; Frederick Djara Wellem, *Amir Sjarifoeddin: Pergumulan Imannya dalam Perjuangan Kemerdekaan* (Jakarta: Sinar Harapan, 1984).

tures, epochs, and moods; with lesser or greater courage. Not one but a multiplicity of matrixes served as the foundation upon which the autobiography was built.

The urge to write an autobiography in this sense, may be the most dramatic manifestation of an interaction between the social and the individual. A self-evident way to study this interaction, therefore, is to compare the social and the individual texts available—what Jonathan Culler called "to naturalize" a particular text, which is to confront it with

> a general cultural text: shared knowledge which would be recognized by participants as part of culture and hence subject to correction or modification but which none the less serves as a kind of "nature."[6]

A method like this is convenient, as it helps to organize amorphous material and to distinguish its "elements" and "motifs."[7] The fact, however, that rather than comparing two sets of texts, we are "reading an autobiography," should be contantly kept in mind.

"General cultural texts" and the "individual texts" by Sjahrir could never be analyzed simply as "values" running parallel or cross-cutting each other in a Euclidean paradise. "Perceptions"[8] have to be studied. While an autobiography may originate from the most varying sources, it is always molded into a definite shape and meaning by the sheer power, or weakness, of its author's individuality. Sjahrir's will to write an autobiography and his decision to remain silent will be the principal themes to be studied.

The texts I read never allowed me to accept a stereotype of Sjahrir as moving, fast, fluently, and headlong, into the Western cultural orbit, leaving behind, obscure, insignificant, and meaningless, the culture from which he had started. Neither did Sjahrir appear to me as a solid bridge safely anchored in the two worlds. As my reading progressed, a different picture of Sjahrir's experience emerged: if it was a structure, then it was an immensely elusive, loose, and tenuous one; if a bridge, then a bridge arched between a multiplicity of uncertain riversides, kept above ground and water not by moorings and pillars but by the vastness of the space to be crossed.

This study of Sutan Sjahrir is a personal story in more than one sense. Manifest in it I want to be my fascination with those men and women, in Indonesia and elsewhere, who out of courage, arrogance, or fear, climb the barriers of cultures. Their traces, if they get far enough, disappear as a rule into the vastness of the unknown. Thus, I believe, the universes for mankind are created and Angels of History are moved to march on.

I was lucky to meet on my way to Sjahrir a number of good people who were willing to share their time and knowledge. They were with me, talked and wrote to me about Sjahrir, and led me through mazes of libraries, archives, and private collections in Prague, Ithaca, Jakarta, Bandung, Medan, Bukittinggi, Leiden, Amsterdam,

---

[6] Jonathan Culler, *Structuralist Poetics: Structuralism, Linguistics and the Study of Literature* (Ithaca: Cornell University Press, 1975), esp. p. 140.

[7] For "elements" and "motifs" see V. Propp, "Morphology of the Folktale," *International Journal of American Linguistics* 24, 4 (October 1958): 11–19.

[8] For a contrast between the study of values and perceptions see e.g. Els Postel-Coster, "The Indonesian Novel as a Source of Anthropological Data," in *Text and Context: The Social Anthropology of Tradition*, ed. Ravindra K. Jain (Philadelphia: Institute for Study of Human Issues, 1977), p. 148.

The Hague, and Paris. Some will find their names in the text, others know how they helped without being mentioned. They often manifested more than merely an intellectual curiosity. Their strong feeling about Sjahrir and about my project has been a continuous inspiration. Four of them, Ben Anderson, Jim Siegel, Ruth McVey, and George Kahin to whom this book is dedicated, I respected most throughout, and they became, so I hope, an inseparable part of my life. Am I grateful to them? I don't know. If it was not for them, I might still be sitting in Zizkov, Prague, counting my beads.

1

THE HOMELAND

En satoe en satoe en satoe dat is een
En batoe en batoe en batoe, dat is steen
En roti en roti en roti, dat is brood
En mati en mati en mati, dat is dood.

A song from a *komedie stambul*[1]

1. THE WORLD OF MINANGKABAU AND SJAHRIR'S MOTHER

The Minangkabau of West Sumatra are described as belonging to "probably one of the largest matrilineal societies in the world."[2] The smallest genealogical unit in Minangkabau is formed, according to *adat*—"custom," by a mother together with her children and is called a *samandai*—"a mother." Several close *samandai* (close in terms of matriliny) form a *parui*—"a womb." One *parui*, traditionally, dwells in a common house, with several *parui* composing the lowest territorial unit, a *kampuong*—"a village" or "a town ward," and several *kampuong* agglomerating in a *nagari*—"a community." At the head of each of these groups there is one (or, in the larger units, a council of) *mamak kepala waris*, shortened to *mamak* usually, "a maternal uncle" who guards the *waris*—"the legacy." Each Minangkabau is defined by adat as a member of a *kamanakan*—"a mamak's sisters' group of children."[3]

The house of one's mother (and of her eldest brother, i.e., the *mamak*'s house) was considered in traditional Minangkabau to be the focus of an "inward looking, stability and security searching tendency."[4] This *rumah adat*—"customary house," or *rumah gadang*—"great house," often referred to by the name of a female house member, was supposed to become at birth and to remain for the rest of each Minangka-

---

[1] A. Th. Manusama, *Komedie Stamboel of de Oost Indische opera* (Weltevreden: Favoriet, 1922), p. 22.

[2] Tsuyoshi Kato, "Change and Society in the Minangkabau Matrilineal System," *Indonesia* 25 (April 1978): 1. Tanner and Thomas refer to Minangkabau matriliny as the "cultural centrality" and "decision-making mode." Nancy Tanner and Lynn L. Thomas, "Rethinking Matriliny: Decision-Making and Sex Roles in Minangkabau," in *Change and Continuity in Minangkabau: Local, Regional and Historical Perspective on West Sumatra*, ed. Lynn L. Thomas and Franz von Benda Beekman (Athens: Ohio University Press, 1985), p. 69.

[3] See, for instance, P. E. de Josselin de Jong, *Minangkabau and Negeri Sembilan: Socio-Political Structure in Indonesia* (Jakarta: Bhratara, 1960), pp. 10–13.

[4] P. E. de Josselin de Jong, *Social Organization of Minangkabau* (Leiden: University of Leiden Institute for Cultural Anthropology, 1975), p. 152.

bau's life the *rumah tunjuk*—"a house he could point to as his house of origin."[5] As late as the 1920s, when Sjahrir was in his teens, if a man became seriously ill, every effort had to be made to move him from wherever he fell, be it his wife's or his children's house, into his *rumah tunjuk*: whether or not his mother was still alive, he was supposed to die where his "real house" stood.[6]

The *mamak*'s place, the mother's house, was traditionally supposed to stand for the center of Minangkabau solidarity—"sharing slights, sharing shames." It was the Minangkabau nucleus—but a strikingly vaporous one.

A typical *rumah tunjuk* was a rectangular wooden structure from twenty-five to more than a hundred meters in length, divided crosswise into compartments—*bilik*—with the number of compartments and the length of the house growing as the *parui* group grew. In each of the compartments lived either a *samandai*—a mother with her young children—or a single (unmarried or widowed) female member of the *parui*.

> Every evening a group of strange men, the husbands, entered the house. It may be imagined, what a bustle the house became; each of the men brought with him his own mood, character and will. . . . It may be said of me,

a Minangkabau notes regarding his *rumah tunjuk*, "that I was born into a sort of barracks."[7]

Children, when at home, spent most of their time, day and night, in the front "reception hall," a common area which ran lengthwise through the house in front of the compartments. Any disagreement in the *rumah tunjuk* threatened quickly to become public property; any member had to be extremely cautious not to spark the flame. The whole structure was held together by its components not being allowed to come too close to one another.

Through *rumah tunjuk* life, through *adat*, customs, myths, and legends, a distinctive kind of motherhood was passed down by generations of Sjahrir's ancestors.

Sjahrir's mother, Siti Rabiah—we do not know the year of her birth, only of her marriage, 1898,[8] and death, 1922—had about three-quarter Minangkabau blood and was born of a Minangkabau who lived "abroad." She was born in Natal, South Tapanuli, north of Minangkabau proper. Both Rabiah's mother and perhaps even her grandmother were also born of Natal or Natal-Minangkabau mothers and Minangkabau fathers.[9]

---

[5] Kato, "Change and Society," p. 8.

[6] Muhamad Radjab, *Semasa kecil dikampung, 1913–1925: Autobiografi seorang anak Minangkabau* (Jakarta: Balai Pustaka, 1974), p. 102.

[7] Ibid., p. 7.

[8] According to one source, she married Sjahrir's father in Bonjol, Minangkabau, in August of that year; see Tamar Djaja, *Rohana Kudus, Srikandi Indonesia: Riwajat Hidup dan perjuangannya* (Jakarta: Mutiara, 1980), p. 62.

[9] The materials available contain various names and spellings for Sjahrir's mother. "Rabiah" is the most frequent, and it is also used in Sjahrir's personal documents, such as those presented at his first wedding. See, e.g., *Secret Mail Report* 1937, no. 704. She is listed in Sjahrir's family records as a daughter of Soetan Soeleiman from Kota Gedang, Minangkabau. I have also used information from Muhammad Akbar Djoehana, Sjahrir's nephew; interview in Prague, August 16 and 17, 1983.

Rabiah, with her husband and children, lived in the land of Minangkabau itself for only a very short time. Most of her married life was spent at various places on the Minangkabau fringes, traveling where her husband did. Never did she and her family live side by side in an orthodoxly traditional *rumah tunjuk* with other "mothers" in a "womb."

A quarter of Rabiah's blood was Natal, Mandailing Batak in all probability. *Putri Siti Rabiah*, she was called, suggesting she was in her mother's line a direct descendant of a *tuanku besar*, a local "bigman" in South Tapanuli. Rabiah proudly kept her Mandailing title and carried herself with an aristocratic *esprit*. So effective was she that a favorite family story still relates how the oldest son of Siti Rabiah, Sjahrir's eldest brother, might have risen to become a Mandailing *tuanku besar* himself—if only he had not become (like Sjahrir) an ardent nationalist and "antifeudal" at that.[10]

A native pride in Natal alone, however, would never have made Rabiah and her children complete strangers to Minangkabau. Natal had never been a complete "elsewhere" to Minangkabau culture. Its tradition, including the role of women—more pronounced than among other Bataks—had made Natal a civilization very close to its neighbors to the south.[11] Merchants and other Minangkabau wanderers had come there from times immemorial, adding mightily to the mutual proximity of Natal and Minangkabau. Intermarriages between these wanderers and Natalese women, especially women of noble blood, such as Rabiah's marriage with Sjahrir's father were common and accepted by tradition.[12]

Rabiah is remembered by her kin as a strong-minded woman. Strong character is reflected in the beautiful face under tightly combed black hair, portrayed in a faded photograph of Rabiah in Sjahrir's family album.[13] Rabiah liked immensely to travel, and often went "abroad," not infrequently alone. She got as far, informants say, as Madiun, Java.[14]

---

[10] In the document listed in the previous note Rabiah's mother is also mentioned as "Puti Djohor Maligan, a granddaughter of Tuanku Besar Sintan from Natal." ("Riwajat Hidup Soetan Sjahrir," n.d., n.p. typescript in the *Archives Siti Wahjunah Sjahrir*.) Also interview with M. A. Djoehana, Prague, August 16 and 17, 1983.

[11] On similarities between Mandailing and Minangkabau perceived at the time, see especially M. Joustra, *Batakspiegel* (1910. Leiden: van Doesburgh, 1926); and C. Van Vollenhoven *Het Adatrecht van Nederslansch-Indië* vol. 1 (Leiden: Brill, 1918), pp. 228–29, 238–39, 244.

[12] This did not exclude a strong mutual suspicion of both cultures. According to a Dutch official's impression of 1919—i.e., the time of Sjahrir's childhood—"the West Sumatrans (Minangkabau) feel themselves as 'endlessly higher' than the Tapanulese and, on the reverse, the Tapanulese consider themselves elevated compared to the former; they think of the Minangkabau as, other than the Acehnese, their worst enemies." See G. A. J. Hazeu, "Het eerste Congres van de Jong Sumatraan Bond, 1919," quoted in Hendrik Bouman, *Enige Beschouwingen over de Ontwikkeling van het Indonesisch Nationalisme op Sumatra's Westkust* (Groningen: Wolters,1949), p. 31. Another, more recent, observer tells of a Minangkabau girl living in Tapanuli who "from her early school days was always forbidden to mix with her Tapanuli (Batak) schoolmates on the ground that 'they weren't religious'" (i.e., too emancipated), although actually they were Moslems, too." Istulah Gunawan Mitchell, "The Socio-Cultural Environment and Mental Disturbance: Three Minangkabau Case Histories," *Indonesia* 7 (April 1969): 133.

[13] I was shown the album, while visiting Sjahrir's house, by Siti Wahjunah, Sjahrir's wife, in Jakarta, March 5, 1982.

[14] Interview with Siti Wahjunah Sjahrir, Jakarta, March 3,1982; according to the informant, these were Sjahrir's recollections.

8   *Sjahrir: Politics and Exile*

Sjahrir's Family House in Kota Gedang

Reportedly well-educated, though there is no record of her attending a Western-type school, Rabiah radiated her own particular blend of culture. She is remembered as reciting at family gatherings. Her all-time favorites were *The Arabian Nights Entertainments*; which were also the evergreens throughout Minanangkabau at the time.[15] As family lore has it, Rabiah chose Sjahrir's name and the names of several of her other children under the spell of Scheherazade.[16]

Rabiah especially loved *komedie stambul*, a craze in the 1910s and 1920s in the urban centers of the East Indies, a theatrical form, performed mostly by Eurasians, with a most peculiar mixture of Western and Eastern language, music, and dramatic plots;[17] Scheherazade's tales, again, were often performed, along with Shylock and Sherlock Holmes. The genre hit Malaya and Indonesia after allegedly traveling from "Istanbul" (thus the *komedie*'s name). Siti Rabiah is said to have been in the audience

---

[15] Radjab, *Semasa kecil dikampung*, p. 127.

[16] Interview with Siti Wahjunah Sjahrir, Jakarta, March 5, 1982. (Note also that the Dutch spelling of Scheherazade is Sjaharazad.) A particularly popular figure in *komedie stambul* was "Sharyar, the king of India and Great Tartary"; Manusama, *Komedie Stamboel*, p. 15.

[17] A typical text of *komedie stambul* as performed on Bali at roughly the same time is summarized in Beryl De Zoete, *Dance and Drama in Bali* (London: Faber and Faber, 1938), p. 215. On *komedie stambul* or *komedie bangsawan* see also Manusama, *Komedie Stamboel*; Bronia Kornhauser, "In Defence of Kroncong," in *Studies in Indonesian Music*, ed. Margaret J. Kartomi (Clayton: Monash Papers on Southeast Asia, 1978), especially pp. 131–32; and Burhan Piliang, "Tentang teater baru Indonesia dan perkembangannya di Medan," *Budaya Jaya* 9, 100 (September 1976): 561–67.

whenever a *komedie stambul* troupe stopped in town. Then, at home on her accordion, she would play the newly learned songs.[18]

Other highlights of Rabiah's repertoire included German romances; one source of these may have been Lutheran missionaries who were very active in South Tapanuli at the time young Rabiah was there.[19] Apparently, nothing fundamentally anti-traditional was seen in Rabiah's tastes. It is still a cherished story in Rabiah's family, for instance, that the family had a "lighter complexion." A stranger may even be told a story about "an ancestor with definitely blue eyes."[20]

There were certainly echoes of tradition and matrilineal traits in Rabiah's behavior. She did not merely give names to her children, she bestowed titles: *siti* for her daughters, *sutan* for her sons—traditional and identical in Minangkabau and Natal. Rabiah's house, while far, of course, from being a truly orthodox *rumah tunjuk*, was famed for always being wide open to all the children of Rabiah's relatives and of the neighborhood. No distinction, it is said, was made between Rabiah's own ten children and the other youngsters who happened to appear in the house.[21]

Rabiah's affection, evidently, was widely extended and low keyed. I have found not a single piece of writing in which Sjahrir mentions his mother at any length. Only during his last years, when he was sick (and tired, and less resistant to sentiment, perhaps), did he like to tell his wife a story about Rabiah and himself. On a train once, the story went, Sjahrir's mother tenderly stroked the boy's head. He had been ten years old, he said, and something like that had never happened before.[22]

Rabiah's behavior was hardly ever thought unbecoming by her family, her community, or Sjahrir. Rather, she appears to have been respected as a manifestation of the best in the culture, time, and place. Sjahrir's relation to his mother was not distracted. It was, rather loose—and, thus, in terms of her culture and his, it was meaningful. Later in this book, whenever we run across Sjahrir's "strange" behavior toward his homeland, his family, and, in particular, women—and whenever we reject terms like "aloof" or "harsh" or "unfeeling" as inadequate for describing it—the culture and the image of his mother will always be part of the argument.

2. Sjahrir's Father and the Notion of Rantau

A newborn girl in Minangkabau traditionally was "more valued" than a baby boy.[23] A mature Minangkabau man was termed a *sumando*—an "in-marrying male." He was described in various Minangkabau epithets as being "like a bull buffalo bor-

---

[18] Interview with Mrs. Sjahrizal Djoehana Wiradikarta, Sjahrir's sister, Bandung, March 12, 1982; interview with M. A. Djoehana, Prague, August 16, 1983.

[19] The most detailed report yet on the Rheinische Mission and other German cultural activity in the area is J. G. Warneck, *Fünfzig Jahre Batakmission in Sumatra* (Berlin: Warneck, 1911); for other important information, rather critical of the Germans, see the valuable M. Joustra, *Van Medan naar Padang en terug; reisindrukken en ervaringen* (Leiden: van Doesburgh, 1915).

[20] Interview with M. A. Djoehana, Prague, August 17, 1983.

[21] Interview with Sjahrizal Djoehana, Bandung, March 12, 1982. Rabiah had ten children altogether, in the following order: Soetan Noer Alamsjah, Hafil Datoek Batoeah (Halil), Lalifah, Sjahrizal, Soetan Sjahrir, Azran Soetan, Marah Alam, Soetan Sjahsam, Mahroezar and Idahar Sjah. See Alamsjah, *10 orang besar Indonesia terbesar sekarang*, p. 124; Leon Salim, ed., *Bung Sjahrir: Pahlawan Nasional* (Medan: Masadepan, 1966), p. 12; interview with Violet, the wife of Djohan Sjahroezah, Sjahrir's nephew, Jakarta, March 8, 1982.

[22] Interview with Siti Wahjunah Sjahrir, Jakarta, March 5, 1982.

[23] Hamka, *Merantau ke Deli* (1941. Jakarta: Djajamurni, 1962), p. 103.

rowed for impregnation," "like a fly on the tail of a buffalo," "like a spot of mud on one's forehead," "like ash on a tree stump—a soft wind blows and it will fly away."[24] According to an observer of the Minangkabau scene of the early twentieth century, a child sometimes did not recognize its own father on the street.[25] Mohammad Hatta, a Minangkabau, and Sjahrir's friend and contemporary, recalled from his childhood that at the time "the Minangkabau people used to believe that if a son closely resembled his father, one of them would quickly die." "I don't know if that is true," Mohammad Hatta commented in 1981. "We are at the mercy of God."[26]

If motherhood in Minangkabau served as the culture's vaporous nucleus, then fathers moved around, loosely attached to the nucleus. Men might obtain a divorce over the most trivial matter. They did, and often; polygamy was a custom.[27] While motherhood and the maternal uncle, the *mamak*, were thought crucial in matters "governing strictly lineage affairs"[28]—and were tied by this, most men were allowed to be rather free on the fringe of the community. Inheritance laws definitely favored, and still often favor, the mother's line: the *harta pusaka*—the house, the rice fields, the treasures of the clan—stayed with mothers. But a wide space was left open for fathers to earn their own wealth and to leave it to their children, even their grandchildren occasionally; afterwards, according to custom, however, the wealth had to be appropriated back into the mother's line.[29]

Fatherhood and the male element were pushed towards the fringes in Minangkabau culture. But thus the fringes, the contours, and the meaning of the culture as a whole were made more visible and, to the culture's participants, more real.

The fringes are called *rantau* in Minangkabau: "outward regions" or "areas adjoining the heartland" (which, in turn, is called the *luhak* or *darak*). *Rantau* is any place to which a Minangkabau may migrate, whether it be immediately outside his village, Sumatra beyond the Minangkabau borders, Malaya, the Indonesian archipelago or even a wider world. *Rantau* is a place in which Minangkabau culture's loose elements or excessive tension may be released. But *rantau* is meaningless without "the heartland." It has always been acceptable for an adult man in Minangkabau to go to *rantau* at a certain point in his life.[30] But it was, and is, very

---

[24] Kato, "Change and Society," p. 6; see also G. D. Willinck, *Het Rechtsleven bij de Minangkabausche Maleiërs* (Leiden: Brill, 1909), pp. 525–26. On the residence pattern of Minangkabau males see also *Change and Continuity*, ed. Thomas and von Benda Beekman; Mitchell, "The Socio-Cultural Environment," p. 128.

[25] Hamka, *Adat Minangkabau Menghadap Revolusi* (Jakarta: Tekad, 1963), pp. 56–57.

[26] Mohammad Hatta, *Indonesian Patriot: Memoirs* (Singapore: Gunung Agung, 1981), p. 11.

[27] On the traditionally high rate of polygamy among the Minangkabau as compared to other Indonesians see Mochtar Naim, *Merantau: Causes and Effects of Minangkabau Voluntary Migration* (Singapore: Institute of Southeast Asian Studies, 1971); Josselin de Jong, *Social Organization of Minangkabau*, p. 16 and *passim*.

[28] Elizabeth E. Graves, *The Minangkabau Response to Dutch Colonial Rule in the Nineteenth Century* (Ithaca: Cornell Modern Indonesia Project, 1981), p. 136; see also Josselin de Jong, *Social Organization of Minangkabau*, p. 17.

[29] Thomas and von Benda Beekman, eds., *Change and Continuity*; on the matrilineal ancestral property rules as complicating accumulation of capital among the Minangkabau still in the 1970s see Kato, "Change and Society," pp. 12–13.

[30] Early in one's life is usually the time for going to *rantau* —"before you are needed at home," as a Minangkabau proverb suggests; *Kerantau buyang dahulu, dirumah berguna belum*.

bad for the *perantau* (the man going to *rantau*) to become "destitute in *rantau*," *melarat di rantau*, to be lost in *rantau*, forgotten by those staying home.[31]

A true Minangkabau felt he had been sent (or forced out) to *rantau* by his matrilineal community and he took great care, and sometimes great pains, to fulfill his "obligation" to that community—an "obligation" not rarely described as a burden or shame.[32] He thought it his greatest attainment to return home from *rantau* as a success.[33] And he was aware all the time, remembering the low-key, wide-ranging maternal affection, the ambiguous nucleus of the "house he could point to," that there was actually no absolute safety for him to return to.[34]

Rantau was essentially a male business. Moreover, fatherhood became much more pronounced when a man moved to *rantau* and when he married there, which happened often and was not against Minangkabau custom. A "little family," emerged, with the father more in charge than could ever have been the case in the heartland. A fatherhood-centered kind of power appeared to the Minangkabau as residing in *rantau*.

One perception of *rantau* was of the Minangkabau encountering the non-Minangkabau and essentially male-dominated world. Royal power, according to tradition, came to Minangkabau that way. Prince Adityawarman arrived from Java in the dim past and carved out a patrilineal kingdom for himself. But because all the land had already been divided among matrilineal *nagari* communities, the new ruler's domain had to be placed, and to remain until its demise in the nineteenth century, on the Minangkabau fringes—in *rantau*.[35] Islam also came to Minangkabau in a *rantau* way. It had become the dominant religion of the Minangkabau by the nineteenth

---

[31] Radjab, *Semasa kecil dikampung*, p. 72.

[32] Keeping that balance between *rantau* and *rumah tunjuk* can be very demanding and even leads sometimes to serious mental disturbance. It is telling that a sickness caused by a migrant feeling torn between the strange community in which he lives and his attachment to his place of origin, manifest and studied in Jakarta in particular, is generally called "Padangitis" in Indonesia (a Minangkabau is often called a man of Padang), and Minangkabau are most numerous among those suffering from it. See Istulah Gunawan Mitchell, "Points of Stress in Minangkabau Social Life," *RIMA* 6, 2 (1972): 97, 114. A vivid description of the difficult and actually "shame-full" relation of a Minangkabau in *rantau* to his home matriline is given in Hamka, *Merantau ke Deli*, especially p. 47 and *passim*.

[33] It was obligatory for a *perantau* to bring what he earned back home, and it was done, often theatrically, mostly during *puasa* festivities each year. See Josselin de Jong, *Social Organization of Minangkabau*, p. 16. A delightful description is found in Radjab, *Semasa kecil dikampung*, pp. 172, 206.

[34] It is remarkable how much bitterness and how little sentimentality or nostalgia is involved in *perantau* memories of home. See, e.g., Radjab, *Semasa kecil dikampung*, p. 172; Hamka, *Merantau ke Deli*, pp. 107–8. The geographical definition of *rantau* is extremely vague; it is, I think, correctly described as a rite of passage, and the communal houses in the village where boys are supposed to spend their life after about 8 years of age are seen as a kind of *rantau*, too. Taufik Abdullah, *Schools and Politics: The Kaum Muda Movement in West Sumatra (1927–1933)* (Ithaca: Cornell Modern Indonesia Project, 1971), p. 231; for a description of the essentially *rantau* atmosphere in such a communal men's house see Radjab, *Semasa kecil dikampung*, pp. 26–27.

[35] For the legend see Josselin de Jong, *Minangkabau*, p. 14. "In a sense," Abdullah says, "the royalty could be considered as the representative of the male-principle and the commoners of the female principle, both principles being integrated by a 'sacral marriage'." Taufik Abdullah, "Adat and Islam: An Examination of Conflict in Minangkabau," *Indonesia* 2 (October 1966): 4. See also Kathirithamby-Wells, in *Change and Continuity*, ed. Thomas and von Benda Beekman, pp. 121–30.

century, but it remained, throughout, a paradox, distinctly patrilineal and in a sense marginal: most respected men of Islam were wanderers in the land of Minangkabau with extremely loose ties to the matrilineal communities.[36] When the Dutch appeared, and when, at the turn of the present century, they were about to become the dominant power in the area, "typically those who responded most enthusiastically [among the Minangkabau] were the social and geographic groups traditionally associated with the *merantau* process."[37]

Sjahrir's father came directly from the tradition of *rantau*. Mohammad Rasad *gelar* Maharadja Soetan was born on November 29, 1866[38] in the very heart of Minangkabau proper, in the Padang Highlands, in view of the holiest Minangkabau mountain, Marapi, in the *nagari* Kota Gedang, famous among all the Minangkabau communities for its gold- and silversmiths, for its tenacious adherence to matrilineal tradition, and especially for the number of its men who distinguished themselves in *rantau*.

Gold and silver, probably, gave Kota Gedang its pride and made it rich enough to switch easily to other businesses when late in the nineteenth century times changed.[39] "Goldsmiths," Josselin de Jong writes of Minangkabau tradition,

> were neutral, and in the days of the Minangkabau kings they or their envoys could stop the battle at will by planting a royal yellow umbrella on the *tanah radjo* ("royal land," a veritable no-man's land).[40]

The tenacity of Kota Gedang's adherence to matriliny was as famous as its jewelry. According to a report from the 1910s, the village enforced endogamy to such an extent that Kota Gedang was coming close to biological exhaustion.[41] As late as in

---

[36] According to Abdullah, "Although the position of the religious teacher was not included in the official *adat* hierarchy, his influence went beyond that prescribed by *adat* for a *penghulu* (matrilineal extended family's head). In his own *nagari* a religious teacher could often command the loyalty of the people outside his own *suku* (matrilineal clan). In the supra-*nagari* sphere he stood outside the *nagari adat* communities." Taufik Abdullah, "Modernization in the Minangkabau World: West Sumatra in the Early Decades of the Twentieth Century," in *Culture and Politics in Indonesia*, ed. Claire Holt et al. (Ithaca: Cornell University Press, 1972), p. 202. Or by the same author: "The fascination with the definition of the world rather than the structure of the society, both in terms of its arrangement and its religious validity, was to remain one of the most dominating themes of the history of Islam in Minangkabau." Taufik Abdullah, "Islam, History and Social Change in Minangkabau," in *Change and Continuity*, ed. Thomas and Benda-Beekman, p. 149.

[37] Ibid., p. 77.

[38] As in Sjahrir's mother's case, there are several different spellings of the Sjahrir father's name. Again, this is the spelling as it stands on Sjahrir's marriage certificate; see *Secret Mail Report* 1937, no. 704. For the date of birth and sketchy genealogy see Tamar Djaja, *Rohana Kudus*, p. 62.

[39] K. A. James, "De Negeri Kota Gedang," *Tijdschrift voor het Binnenlandsch Bestuur* 49 (1915): 189, 193–94; for the still lasting fame throughout Indonesia of Kota Gedang goldsmiths and silversmiths see Mochtar Lubis, *Het land onder de regenboog: De geschiedenis van Indonesië* (Alphen: Sijthoff, 1979), p. 183.

[40] Josselin de Jong, *Minangkabau*, p. 83; see also p. 60.

[41] "The centuries-long traditional marriage-network, through which the desirable blood-exchange and selection are so much been restricted, had already left its mark. In general, the type of *Kotagedanger* is slender and tuberculosis is spreading." James, "De Negeri Kota Gedang," p. 189.

1920—and in a case that stirred all of Minangkabau—a Kota Gedang girl was "proclaimed dead" by her family and community because she dared to "marry outside."[42]

But Kota Gedang was most famous for its *rantau*. According to the *nagari* historian,

> In Kota Gedang, the *perantau* life was pursued by almost all males. Village families had numerous slaves and retainers who tended to daily agricultural tasks, and the women provided whatever general supervision was needed over the fieldwork. Men were free to practice their *perantau* occupations unburdened by domestic obligations.... *Perantau* life was idealized and a stigma was often attached to a youth, even the heir to a *penghulu*-ship [extended matrilineal family head], who stayed home.[43]

The power and wealth of gold and silver, it seems, first brought the men of Kota Gedang to *rantau*. Then came the business in coffee. During the 1820s, Kota Gedang had already "opted for the Dutch side,"[44] and during the following decades it expanded into the *rantau* of the new colonial epoch more effectively than any other *nagari* in the land. A story which became proverbial throughout Sumatra told of Kota Gedang children traveling each day along the steep path to the Dutch schools at Fort de Kock (Bukittinggi) on the opposite slopes of the valley.[45] Soon no prestigious "Dutch-colonial" school nearby was without a few Kota Gedang students. By the second decade of the twentieth century, young men from Kota Gedang were studying as far away in *rantau* as Batavia on Java, or even Holland.[46]

Many of Kota Gedang's men soon found employment in the new Dutch colonial justice and financial departments, in schools as teachers, and in topographical and medical services.[47] By general consent, one of the most advanced and promising of

---

[42] *Adatrechtbundels* XX, 144, quoted in Josselin de Jong, *Minangkabau*, p. 67. The girl's name was Daena, and she married a Javanese in Medan, where they both worked. Discussion about the affair can be found in *Soeara Kota Gedang* 5, 13 (October 1920); "Perkawinan Daena," ibid., p. 14; "S.M.A.A.L. Boeangan Si Daena," ibid., 5, 17 (December 1920); "Bagaimana Pikirankoe tentangan Vrijheid perampoean berhoeboeng denga perkawinan Daena," ibid., 5, 3 (February 1921); "Penoetoep dari perkawinan Daena," ibid., 6, 4 (March 1921).

[43] Graves, *Minangkabau Response*, pp. 132–33.

[44] The fact of early pro-Dutch loyalties/affinities, according to Graves, "is charged by outsiders, and accepted by some Kota Gedang villagers themselves." See ibid., p. 133.

[45] For example, see James, "De Negeri Kota Gedang," p. 185; Mohammad Hatta, *Memoir* (Jakarta: Tintamas, 1978), pp. 23–24; Roem, *Bunga Rampai*, vol. 2, p. 51.

[46] Of 160 pupils at the Fort de Kock government school ninety were from Kota Gedang; in the European Elementary Schools (ELS) designed primarily for Dutch children on the West Coast and elsewhere, sixty-nine Kota Gedang children studied, in the Dutch-Native Schools (HIS) fifty-three young Kotagedangers sat, twenty-six (!) girls among them; at the model colonial School for Training Native Doctors (STOVIA) founded in Batavia in 1902, fifteen Kota Gedang youths were enrolled in 1915, while one Kotagedanger studied in the even more prestigious Koningin Wilhelmina School also in Batavia. In 1910, the "Studiefonds Kota Gedang" were established and two boys from the *nagari* were sent to Holland to study at the Technische Hooge School in Delft. See James, "De Negeri Kota Gedang," pp. 186–88, 193–94.

[47] By 1915, 165 Kotagedangers, at a time when the village had a few thousand people, were listed as well advanced and successful in *rantau*. Seventy-two were said to be proficient in Dutch, and seventy-nine worked outside the West Coast of Sumatra. Thirty-five worked as non-*adat* (i.e., colonial) bureaucrats of whom eighteen held positions in justice departments,

these *rantau* positions was that of *jaksa*, public prosecutor at the colonial civil and criminal court.[48]

A *jaksa* served "with foreigners" and was therefore respected at home as a man opening the way for his kin into a wider world. To prevent the abuse of this access, the Dutch took care not to post any *jaksa* directly in his home area: thus *rantau* was opened still wider to a *jaksa*. At the same time, a *jaksa* was supposed to advise the Dutch on "traditional native law" and therefore should not be pushed too much by the Europeans into "non-native" preconceptions. A *jaksa* was not to be too close to either side. A *jaksa* was to be a sort of bridge. That was the profession of Sjahrir's father.

Sjahrir's father came from one of most ancient of Kota Gedang's matrilineages, the Datoek Dinagari branch of the *suku* (matrilineal clan) Kato. He paid endogamy its due by accepting a Kota Gedang girl as his first wife, with whom he had three daughters and three sons—Rohana, Ratna, Roeskan, Radena, Bajoeng, and Noerzamhariz. Mohammad Rasad and his first wife never divorced. The wife and, after she died, the oldest daughter maintained the family's "house one may point to" in Kota Gedang throughout Mohammad Rasad's life.[49]

In 1915, Mohammad Rasad was listed as one of ten *jaksa* who were natives of Kota Gedang.[50] It was a tradition for men in the family, evidently: Mohammad Rasad's grandfather, Datoek Dinagari, had been a *jaksa*; he had served as the first official of that rank in Fort de Kock in 1833-1868. Two of Datoek Dinagari's other sons, one of them Mohammad Rasad's father, were *jaksa*, too. Both Mohammad Rasad's father and grandfather, probably, had also married Natal women; both, like Mohammad Rasad, left their first wives, Kota Gedang women, in charge of their houses back home.[51]

Mohammad Rasad never served in or near Kota Gedang. His first post, probably, was in Padang Panjang, a Minangkabau town at a "junction point between the *darak* [the heartland] and the *rantau*."[52] Then he moved deeper into the *rantau*, to Jambi, south-east of Minangkabau.[53] By that time he had already married three other "*rantau*" wives, all of whom he later divorced—in 1889, 1909, and 1914 respectively. After Jambi probably came Bonjol, where he met Sjahrir's mother, Siti Rabiah, then Padang Panjang, again, and in 1910 again Jambi. After another four years, in 1914, he moved still deeper into *rantau*—to the cosmopolitan city of Medan on East Sumatra's

---

thirty-one in finance departments, thirty-eight as teachers, six in topographical services and six in medical services. Ibid.

[48] On *jaksa* in the Netherlands East Indies see, e.g., Daniel S. Lev, "Judicial Institutions and Legal Culture in Indonesia," in *Culture and Politics*, ed. Holt et al., pp. 266, 276, 317.

[49] Alamsjah, *10 orang besar*, p. 137; interview with Sjahrizal Djoehana, Bandung, March 12, 1982; Tamar Djaja, *Rohana Kudus*, pp. 62–63.

[50] James, "De Negeri Kota Gedang," p. 193.

[51] Datoek Dinagari's other son who was a *jaksa* was the father of another important Kotagedanger and the grandfather of the famous Indonesian politician Hadji Agoes Salim. Interview with Sjahrizal Djoehana, Bandung, March 12, 1982; interview with Mrs. Violet Sjahroezah, Agoes Salim's daughter, Jakarta, March 5, 1982.

[52] Here, the goods changed hands from *rantau* caravans to the merchants of the Minangkabau heartland. See Muhammad Saleh's autobiography (1850–1914), quoted in Tsuyoshi Kato, "Rantau Pariaman: The World of Minangkabau Coastal Merchants in the Nineteenth Century," *Journal of Asian Studies* 39, 4 (1980): 743, n. 37.

[53] Tamar Djaja, *Rohana Kudus*, p. 62.

The Pass between Kota Gedang and Bukittinggi
(KITLV, Afd. Documentatie Geschiedenis Indonesië [DGI]) #11.235

coast. There, he retired in 1924, served for a short time as a legal adviser to the Sultan of Deli, and died in 1929.[54]

Sjahrir's father never cut his ties to Kota Gedang. In 1922, the year his last *rantau* wife, Sjahrir's mother, died (Mohammad Rasad's first Kota Gedang wife had died in 1897), fifty-six year old Mohammad Rasad—clearly to accommodate his village's custom—was married one more time in Kota Gedang, and again to a Kota Gedang woman.[55] He was listed, throughout, in the village journal *Soeara Kota Gedang*, "The Voice of Kota Gedang," as a distinguished member of the community. His contributions to the village were carefully noted in the journal and during the village's public meetings. His debt to the matrilineal community—the debt of shame—was mentioned, in exact figures, as often, and as prominently as his contributions.[56]

---

[54] Interview with Sjahrizal Djoehana, Bandung, March 12, 1982; interview with M. A. Djoehana, Prague, August 17, 1983. A different sequence and some different places where Mohammad Rasad stayed—Alahan Panjang, Simpang Tonang, Rao, Simpang Tonang TaloeTaloe, Padang, and Toengkel—are listed in "Kartini Ketjil dari Minangkabau: Sitti Rohana binti Maharadja Soetan dari Kota Gedang sebagain perintis djalan bagi poetri di Minangkabau," *Pandji Islam* 12 (May 19, 1941): 9054.

[55] Tamar Djaja, *Rohana Kudus*, p. 62, gives her name as Kiam.

[56] For example, see *Soeara Kota Gedang* 4, 7 (April 1919), on Mohammad Rasad promising 100 fl. for the fiscal year 1920; ibid., 4, 13 (July 1919) congratulating the *nagari* on Idul Fitri celebration; ibid., 6, 9 (July 1921) and ibid., 6, 13 (November 1921), where he is listed as paying only 40 fl. between 1919 and 1921. A property dispute between Mohammad Rasad and Kota Gedang over a horse, which dragged on for four years between 1904 and 1908, is described in "Kartini Ketjil dari Minangkabau," p. 9055.

Medan was where the photograph I saw at Sjahrir's house was taken. Mohammad Rasad was already a *hoofddjaksa*, "head *jaksa*," by then. He was at the peak of his career. He had gotten as far as any man of his *nagari* could hope to, and he commanded adequate respect for his success. But, through the same process, an unpaid debt to his matriliny had accumulated. In the photograph, he is a proud old Minangkabau in a Moslem cap and European clothes. A Star of the Knight of the Oranje Nassau Order is pinned on his jacket. His grandson told me that the occasion for the photograph was the Dutch Queen's birthday.[57]

3. Sjahrir's Sister and the Culture of Nationhood

History seemed to accelerate in Minangkabau towards the beginning of the twentieth century. Western economic penetration into the colony became highly visible.[58] After half a century of enterprising optimism, double-faced liberalism, and hesitant philanthropy in Dutch colonial policy in the East,[59] a new Dutch Christian-Social Democrat coalition in 1901 proclaimed an "ethical course" as the new official guidelines. The "ethical policy" would "provide the Netherlands with a proper moralistic foundation [and] inspire Hollanders towards a more glorious colonial future," and, mostly through the spreading of Western education, "also ope[n] the way for Indonesians to share in the glory of their own future."[60]

In the words of *The History of Minangkabau*, "the hammers of modernization were beating upon almost every place in the social organism, upon each of its veins and nerves."[61] In 1908, a year before Sjahrir was born, scattered rural uprisings took place in Minangkabau against the efforts by the Dutch administration to tighten its control over the region through the introduction of a new system of taxation.[62] According to one view, the uprisings were a

> nostalgic struggle ... directed against the unintelligible outside forces that increasingly dominated people's lives.... [The uprisings] ended in despair.[63]

---

[57] This, again, is a picture from the family album of Sjahrir that I was shown by Mrs. Siti Wahjunah Sjahrir in Jakarta on March 5, 1982; interview with M. A. Djoehana, Prague, August 17, 1983. Mohammad Rasad was awarded the medal in 1923; Tamar Djaja, *Rohana Kudus, Srikandi Indonesia*, p. 62. According to "Kartini Ketjil dari Minangkabau," p. 9054, Mohammad Rasad got, during his service, "five medals, small and big, gold and silver ones."

[58] The best survey of the colony's economic development of that time is still J. S. Furnivall, *Netherlands India: A Study of Plural Economy* (Cambridge: Cambridge University Press, 1939), pp. 174–427.

[59] On the 1850s and 1860s as the "pre-history" of the "ethical course" see M. K. (D. M. G. Koch), "Prof. Boeke over de ethische richting in de Nederlandsch-Indische politiek," *Kritiek en Opbouw* (February 16, 1940), pp. 20, 36.

[60] Robert Van Niel, *The Emergence of the Modern Indonesian Elite* (The Hague: van Hoeve, 1970), p. 9.

[61] M. D. Mansoer et al., *Sedjarah Minangkabau* (Jakarta: Bhratara, 1970), p. 173

[62] On that act as a "break with tradition" see, e.g., Bouman, *Enige Beschouwingen*, pp. 18–19. In 1914, the provincial administration was reorganized; a merit civil service was installed—the *demang*, who, much more than his predecessors, distanced himself more from the matriliny and got closer to the Dutch administration nexus. Abdullah, *Schools and Politics*, p. 23.

[63] Abdullah, "Modernization in the Minangkabau World," pp. 209–10.

"Despair" may be the correct word, but only if what is meant is that the Minangkabau became aware (in Freud's terms) of the "intolerable burden of culture." This despair did not incapacitate the Minangkabau in responding to the outer world in their particular and genuine way.

Minangkabau *rantau*, even after 1908, functioned as a buffer, softening the Dutch impact on the Minangkabau heartland and on the heart of Minangkabau tradition. *Rantau* itself kept its peculiar character as a culture of the fringes—a place where the culture of Minangkabau proper, as well as the culture of the actual Holland or the actual West beyond the seas, resounded only in a muffled way. Not only the Minangkabau *perantau* but also some of the Dutch, who had wandered so far, absorbed, and accepted, many of the perceptions of the culture in-between.

"Association" was the proclaimed official ideal of the new "ethical course" in the East Indies. For the mainstream ethical system proponents it was an ideal of *gelijkstelling*, "the equalization," of the best of the "natives" with the Dutch,[64] the building up of a group of "brown Hollanders," who would speak "almost faultless Dutch." For other proponents of the "ethical policy," however, it seemed too simply like a conquest. These Dutchmen, for whatever reason, were repelled by the "soul-of-clay . . . golden-calf . . . ultramaterialistic" society of Europeans in the colony.[65] They saw themselves and their race, in relation to the "natives," as more complex: they were "first, exploiters, second, guardians, and third, partners in distress."[66]

Their views may have been religious,[67] or socialist,[68] but they almost invariably also had a distinctly romantic flavor.[69] These Dutchmen's intentions were often lofty and thus, sooner or later in the colony, proved to be unrealistic. More than others, these proponents of the "ethical policy" were prone to venture too far from the Dutch colonial mainstream and, thus, were "bound for exile."[70] Because the colonial

---

[64] "Indonesians who had attained a Western education and maintained a basically Western life style could apply for classification as Europeans." C. L. M. Penders' note to Hatta, *Indonesian Patriot*, p. 58.

[65] Henri Borel, "Indië van de Europeanen," quoted in Robert Nieuwenhuys, *Oost-Indische spiegel; wat Nederlandse schrijvers en dichters over Indonesië hebben geschreven, vanaf de eerste jaren der Compagnie tot op heden* (Amsterdam: Querido, 1972), pp. 321–22.

[66] J. H. W. Veenstra, quoted in E. B. Locher-Scholten, "Kritiek en Opbouw (1938–1942). Een rode splinter," *Tijdschrift voor Geschiedenis* 89, 2 (1976): 215.

[67] On the connection between the associationist ideas among the Dutch and the Theosophical movement see, e.g., Van Niel, *The Emergence*, p. 129.

[68] Theodore van Deventer, a father of the ethical course was, by his own confession, a man of "socialistic leaning" (letter to parents in 1886, quoted in Nieuwenhuys, *Oost-Indische spiegel*, p. 319), the co-sponsor of the ethical policy was H. H. van Kol, at the same time "the colonial authority for the Social Democratic Party" (Van Niel, *The Emergence*, p. 9). J. E. Stokvis, another leading socialist in the colony was called, and not without reason, *"ethicus"*; see D. M. G. Koch, *Batig Slot* (Amsterdam: De Brug, 1960), p. 101. Augusta de Wit, a foremost "ethical" writer and one on rather the romantic if not the sentimental side of it, was from 1916 a member of the social democratic party, too, and, according to Nieuwenhuys, "her entering the party was due less to her political insight than to her ethical attitude" (Nieuwenhuys, *Oost-Indische spiegel*, pp. 327–28).

[69] Beekman writes suggestively on the strong trend of romanticism among Dutch colonial authors in general. E. M. Beekman, "Dutch Colonial Literature: Romanticism in the Tropics," *Indonesia* 34 (October 1982), especially pp. 17–39.

[70] The term is used in the context of British in India, where comparable streams among colonials might be detected; quoted in John A. McClure, *Kipling and Conrad: The Colonial Fiction* (Cambridge: Harvard University Press, 1981), p. 17.

relationship was an injustice, one of them said, every European had "to work so as to make himself superfluous as rapidly as possible."[71] These proponents of the "ethical policy" were characterized by their "strange-ness from home," and it was fitting when a well-known "ethical" novel of the period was sub-titled *"Indrukken van een zwervelinge,"* "impressions of a wanderer."[72]

There were very few businessmen among this vanguard group. There were some government officials. But the group was mainly composed of journalists, scholars, and teachers. They often got very deep indeed into the body of the indigenous society and culture. They seemed able to cross the line between "colonial" and "native," but they were scattered in the process. Because they thought of their role in terms of affinity, they would be successful, they believed, if they could articulate this affinity to the indigenous people, and to themselves. Their conquest, to a very large extent, proceeded by way of translation.

A process of dissident proponents of the "ethical policy" going astray could be detected in many parts of the colony. Minangkabau perceptions and the tradition of *rantau*, however, seemed to be exceptionally effective in fostering the phenomenon. The spread of Dutch-style and Dutch-language schools in Minangkabau at the time had no equal anywhere else in the colony.[73] Schools became a striking new feature of the Minangkabau landscape. They were built—the buildings in "classical style," in "colonial style," in "traditional" Minangkabau style are still there—mostly, in the places reached first by the Dutch roads and railways, on the fringes of the Minangkabau world.

The "ethical"-Minangkabau "translation" emerged at the turn of century and soon became a new language of *rantau*. *Perantau* and *zwervelingen*, Minangkabau and Dutch wanderers, came together in an ambiguous mixture of cultures, or a new culture, perhaps. A culture off the mainstream, bound for exile, and loose.

In that translation the Minangkabau *perantau* became *"dynamisch,"* "dynamic." They moved, in the "ethical" image, forcefully around their culture's traditional matrilineal nucleus which was translated and imagined as *statisch*. *Intellect met energie*, "intellect with energy," *nuchterheid*, "matter-of-factness," *wilskracht*, "willpower"—these were the terms which the Dutch vanguard proponents of the "ethical policy" liked to use in describing themselves, and into which they also translated "the best of Minangkabau."[74] A Dutch author describing the *rantau* qualities of Kota Gedang exclaimed in 1915: "Yes, the pulse of the evolution in the East is unmistakably felt here."[75]

---

[71] J. E. Stokvis in *De Locomotief* (March 12, 1923), quoted in Dahm, *Sukarno and the Struggle for Indonesian Independence*, p. 47.

[72] This was the subtitle of a book by Marie C. van Zeggelen published in 1910 in Amsterdam by Scheltema and Holkema, *De Hollandsche vrouw in Indië: Indrukken van een zwervelinge*.

[73] In 1912 there were twenty-three "ethical" schools in Padang alone, with a total of twelve-hundred pupils, compared with only fifty-three such schools for the whole island of Java plus Madura. XY, "Het Inlandsch Onderwijs te Sumatra's Westkust," *Koloniaal Tijdschrift* II, 1 (1913), p. 398; quoted in Graves, *Minangkabau Response*, p. 141.

[74] James, "De Negeri Kota Gedang," pp. 187–92. Even authorities who were not exactly charmed by Minangkabau style, real or imagined—like Willinck, for instance, one of the founding fathers of modern Dutch colonial scholarship—believed that "the laws of the (Minangkabau) people are . . . the most remarkable of all the Archipelago." Willinck, *Het Rechtsleven*, p. 1.

[75] James, "De Negeri Kota Gedang," p. 187.

The looseness of the Minangkabau cultural nexus was highly praised—and translated as *democratie*. According to an influential Dutch study of the time,

> It is sufficiently well-known that in Minangkabau-Malay society there is no place for aristocracy. *Tagak samo tinggi, doedoek samo rendah* ("raise to the same height, fall to the same depth") is one of the foremost principles on which the society is based, and each matter is naturally and under all circumstances handled according to this principle.[76]

"*Moepakat*," a Minangkabau term for decision making in a *nagari* village community, was "translated" as "*referendum*." The Minangkabau world as a whole became, in this translation, "a federation of small native republics."[77]

At the turn of the century, after decades of bloody struggle and politics, the "Dutch East Indies" emerged, at least in Dutch eyes, as one, compact colony covering the whole Indonesian archipelago. In the perspective of this new whole, Minangkabau and the island of Sumatra gained the transparent quality of the fringes. Minangkabau became a very visible and often representative part of the *buitengewesten*, the "outer regions," as against "central" Java.

Set against the Dutch image of Java—as the land of rice fields, palaces, and temples, the purest manifestation of the ancient "Orient"—the "outer regions" represented "newness."[78] Mohammad Hatta heard it explained early in the twentieth century by his Dutch teacher: "the Sumatrans and the Javanese are different—the Javanese are servile, humble and patient, while the Sumatrans are courageous."[79] And also: "The Moluccas [the spice islands where the Dutch appeared first, in the seventeeth century] are the past, Java is the present and Sumatra is the future."[80]

---

[76] "Maleische democratie en padangsche toestanden," *Sumatra Bode* (March 27 and 28, 1907), p. 115. Ten years later, the statement was almost verbatim repeated ("*zeer republikeinsche,*" "very republican," "*een federatie van dorpsbonden,*" "a federation of village unions," etc.) in the most influential book of the time and of Dutch colonialism perhaps. Van Vollenhoven, *Het Adatrecht*, pp. 256 ff. The "*Tagak samo tinggi*" quote with the same "democratic" interpretation appears also in another classic of the time, L. C. Westenenk, *Acht dagen in de Padangsche bovenlanden* (Batavia: Javasche Boekhandel, 1909), p. 43. See also the "translation" reappearing in various forms in standard Dutch studies such as B. J. Haga, *Indonesische en Indische democratie* (The Hague: Den Ster, 1924), esp. pp. 24 ff; J. C. van Eerde, *Koloniale volkenkunde* (1914. Amsterdam: De Bussy, 1926), esp, pp. 123–24, 159.

[77] Van Eerde, *Koloniale volkenkunde*, pp. 116, 121. Other Dutch scholarly treatises of the time, depicted the Sumatrans' "*republikeinsche vrijheidszin,*" "republican sense of freedom," and "*dorpsrepublikanisme,*" "village republicanism." C. Lekkerkerker, *Land en volk van Sumatra* (Leiden: Brill, 1916), p. 205.

[78] Even a man rather biased against the Minangkabau, G. D. Willinck, wrote in his classical study, in many ways a standard for Dutch scholarship of the whole prewar period, about the "autocratic rule of princes in Java," and the "image of Buddha with closed eyes," having "no spirit of initiative," and contrasting it with the Minangkabau, where there was a "completely different spirit: a great concern with the future ... a great amount of contradiction and individual as well as social energy." G. D. Willinck, *De Indiën en de Nieuwe Grondwet: Proeve tot vaststelling van normale staatsrechterlijke verhoudingen tusschen het moederland en de koloniën* (Zutphen: van Belkum, 1910), pp. 23–24.

[79] Mohammad Hatta, *Bung Hatta Antwoordt* (Jakarta: Gunung Agung, 1979), p. 113.

[80] See Hatta, *Indonesian Patriot*, pp. 33–34. "At that time," Hatta remembered, "I did not realize that this was the motto of the Dutch colonialism which was then poised for the full scale exploitation of Sumatra ... and I interpreted the motto 'Sumatra is the future' to mean that the future 'golden period' of Sumatra was very much in the hands of the Sumatra youth." See also

Statistics show that the Minangkabau actively responded to this effort at "ethical" translation.

> The demand to learn Dutch became so great among the Minangkabau that anyone with the slightest knowledge of the language would establish a backyard school giving crash courses to aspiring civil servants and professionals.[81]

"Almost every day" petitions from Minangkabau citizens were published asking for more Dutch-style schools.[82]

This did not mean that Dutch suddenly and solidly became "the inner language"[83] of the "modern" Minangkabau. The language of the new *rantau* had to be, like the *rantau* culture itself, a language in-between. For the Minangkabau there had been a long-established vehicle of communication in *rantau*—a simplified Malay used by native and foreign merchants and travelers throughout the archipelago. As colonialism progressed, the Dutch used a modified version of this "bazaar Malay," and established a *"dienst,"* or "service" language for the lower levels of the colonial administration and business. It was the mutilated language, now, that was to express the new transition. The merchant and civil-servant Malay was pushed toward becoming a cultural vehicle. Clumsy, and crowded with as "yet" untranslatable Minangkabau and Dutch phrases, it served the purpose well.

De Oostkust, "The East Coast, " a journal of the Djaksa Bond, "Jaksa Union, " to which Sjahrir's father in all probability subscribed, was a perfect example of a text in the trembling "service" Malay.[84] *Soenting Melajoe*, "The Malay Ornament," a journal published at the same time by the *jaksa*'s daughter and Sjahrir's half-sister, Siti

---

Mrázek, "Tan Malaka A Political Personality's Structure of Experience," pp. 34–35 on the concept being widespread in Minangkabau. Also Lekkerkerker, *Land en volk van Sumatra*, pp. I, VII: "Among the progressive great islands of the Dutch Indies, Sumatra stands in the forefront. It is the island of the upcoming future." *Statisch*, "static, unmoving, passive," became, in the large body of the Dutch journalistic, scholarly, and political literature, a code for the Javanese nucleus of the colony. When a prominent Dutch "ethical" writer, G. A. J. Hazeu, in 1918, reviewed a new Minangkabau youth journal, he used exactly the same vocabulary as another Dutch author, three years before, when describing *rantau* qualities of *nagari* Kota Gedang. The journal, Hazeu said, is "in general written in a very matter-of-fact [*nuchter*] and down-to-earth way," in "a healthy critical spirit.... The young men and women who can discuss the evolution of their society in such a way, are, in their spiritual freedom, in no way inferior to their Western contemporaries." Then the Dutchman turned to another "native" journal, published this time by Javanese youths. This he found "quite the opposite" to the Sumatran paper, full of "sorely deep speculations," and "occasionally wholly unreadable." See G. A. J. Hazeu, Adviser for Native Affairs, commenting on Jong Java and Jong-Sumatranen Bond journals in 1918; quoted in Bouman, *Enige Beschouwingen*, pp. 60–61.

[81] Graves, *Minangkabau Response*, p. 140.

[82] "Director of Education to Governor General, March 17, 1913" in *Verbaal*, May 21, 1913, No. 50.

[83] The term is from Benedict Anderson, "The Language of Indonesian Politics," *Indonesia* 1 (April 1966): 102.

[84] It was a two-dimensional, administration-business language; see, e.g., "Verslag dari keadaan dan perdjalanan," the "Union's activity report," read, at the Union meeting first in Malay and then translated by the chairman of the Bond into Dutch, as the journal put it: *"dengan setjara divertaling oleh Voorzitter kita." De Oostkust* 9, 9 (July 9, 1927): 190.

Rohana Kudus, was already being written very much in the still more trembling language of the new *rantau*.

Even during her lifetime, Siti Rohana became a celebrated woman, with epithets applied to her like "the first woman educator in Minangkabau" or even the "Kartini of Minangkabau," being thus compared with Raden Ajeng Kartini (1879-1904) who in turn was called "the mother of Indonesian nationalism." Rohana was born to Mohammad Rasad and his first Kota Gedang wife in September 1884. She had no formal education, and her father was her teacher.[85] When her mother died and her father married again, Rohana returned to the family's house in Kota Gedang.

She is remembered as having designed the costumes for a theater she organized in the village—mostly Minangkabau legends reportedly were performed. Rohana founded, in the first years after her return to Kota Gedang, a small girls' school, and in 1911, the village's Keradjinan Kaum Ibu Setia, "Association of Industrious Mothers." At the same time, she started and helped to build up the Vereenigingen Studiefonds, a community scholarship fund for sending Kota Gedang youngsters to schools in the wider world.[86]

She was, for a woman, remarkably exposed to the *rantau*. Some time in 1911, she approached Datoek Soetan Maharadja, an editor of *Oetoesan Melajoe*, "The Malay Messenger," and asked him to give her a women's page in his paper. Datoek Soetan Maharadja, called sometimes the "father of Minangkabau journalism," was a prominent voice of the new translation. "*Kemadjuan* [progress]," he wrote, "should be understood not as an imitation of the outside world but rather as the unfolding of ideals inherent in Minangkabau *adat*."[87] Maharadja's first journal, *Insoelinde*, "The Archipelago," founded in 1901 and written in Malay, was filled with Dutch words like *dynamisch, nuchterheid, wilskracht*, or their Malay and respectively Malay-Minangkabau "equivalents." *Adat*, the Minangkabau ethos—as Maharadja, in affinity with the vanguard proponents of the "ethical" policy, understood it—was "democratic," and the traditional Minangkabau mechanism for decision making, *moepakat*, proved it.[88]

Rohana got the women's page in *Oetoesan Melajoe*. The next year, 1912, again with the help of Datoek Soetan Maharadja she became an editor of *Soenting Melajoe*, the first women's magazine in Malay.[89]

Although a passionate voice for women, Rohana never lost contact with the world of fatherhood. According to one report, it was Rohana's father who introduced her to Datoek Soetan Maharadja. Some surviving letters, all written in Malay, suggest that Rohana and her father always maintained a warm relationship. She often signed her name in *Soenting Melajoe*, as "*Rohana Kuddus binti* [daughter of] *Maharadja Soetan*."

---

[85] Interview with Rohana published in *Api Pantjasila*, May 22, 1962.

[86] For details on Rohana's life see especially Tamar Djaja, "Sitti Rohana," *Buku Kita* 1 (September 9, 1955): 387–90; and I. Djumhur and H. Danasupata, *Buku peladjaran sedjarah pendidikan* (Bandung: Tjerdas, 1956), pp. 128–29. Rohana's interview in *Api Pantjasila*, May 22, 1962; Claudine Salmon, "Presse féminine ou féministe?" *Archipel* 13 (1977): 164, 166; "Kartini Ketjil dari Minangkabau."

[87] Datoek Soetan Maharadja quoted in Abdullah "Modernization in the Minangkabau World," p. 222.

[88] The quotations are from 1917 and 1915 respectively. Ibid., pp. 222, 235.

[89] Rohana was named as a member of the board already in volume 1, no. 2 (July 1912).

It was, most probably, also through her father that she got to know her Dutch friends. Professor Ph. E. van Ronkel was one of them, a former teacher at the Dutch Gymnasium in Batavia, Java, who served in Minangkabau at one time. The other was L. C. Westenenk, the Dutch assistant resident in Minangkabau and a prominent "ethical" authority on Minangkabau.

Rohana and her students made "traditional Minangkabau" *sarong* and *selendang*, shawls or stoles, and "Europeans often came to Kota Gedang just to buy one of Rohana's products as souvenirs"; her merchandise went "as far as Paris, to *Co. Au Bon Marche*, Maison Aristide."[90] In 1913, Mr. Westenenk and his wife invited Rohana to Holland to participate in a woman's exhibition in Brussels. She did not go because her in-laws did not give her permission.[91]

Rohana became, at one time in her life, a Singer sewing-machine representative, *"agen Singer,"* in Kota Gedang.[92] She composed *syair*, poems in a traditional Minangkabau style, on themes such as *Kemajuan*, "Progress,"[93] and *Koningin Wilhelmina*, "The Dutch Queen."[94] She wrote about "progressive women's fashion,"[95] and once listed the "top ten" most beautiful women in history—Helena, Cleopatra, Scheherazade, Dante's Beatrice, Elizabeth of England, Wootvillie[?], Maria of Scotland, Nelli Gwinne [Nell Gwynn?], Madame Pompadoure, and Mrs. Siddone [Sarah Siddons?].[96]

Besides her many other engagements, one report says that Siti Rohana Kudus bought a dispensary in Medan in 1915 as an additional source of income and as a way to disseminate her views further. This information is not entirely clear, and some other sources deny it.[97] Certainly, however, Rohana moved to Medan in 1920 and stayed there for four years, before she moved to Padang and then back to Kota Gedang. She remained in Medan, as everywhere, a highly visible and active personage. She served, together with another well-known Sumatran journalist, Parade Harahap, as editor of a local magazine *Perempoean Bergerak*, "An Active Woman," and she also taught at a Medan school called *Dharma*, "Duty."[98] Between 1920 and 1924, Rohana must have seen almost daily her father's "little family," also living in Medan. This is an important fact, because these years in Medan, were the crucial years of Sjahrir's early life.

---

[90] Tamar Djaja, *Rohana Kudus*, p. 54.

[91] On Rohana's planned trip there is an article in *Soenting Melajoe* 2, 12 (March 13, 1913); on her not going she wrote a letter to her father ("Rohana is crying"); the letter is reproduced in Tamar Djaja, *Rohana Kudus*.

[92] Ibid., p. 47; photograph is ibid.

[93] *Soenting Melajoe*, 2, 22 (May 23, 1913). For Rohana on *"kemadjuan"* see also ibid., 1, 30 (August 30, 1912).

[94] Ibid., 1, 30 (August 30, 1912).

[95] *Soeara Kaoem Iboe*, 1, 3 (September 21, 1924).

[96] *Soenting Melajoe*; n.d., quoted in Tamar Djaja, *Rohana Kudus*, p. 56.

[97] On Rohana Kudus' shop in Medan see James, "De Negeri Kota Gedang," p. 190; Hazil Tanzil, Sjahrir's relative and a man, as a rule, very knowledgeable about Sjahrir's family, doubted the information. Interview with Hazil Tanzil, Jakarta, March 8, 1962.

[98] Salmon, "Presse féminine," p. 176.

4. Medan and the First Period of Sjahrir's Life

Possibly, Sjahrir did not retain even the vaguest memory of his birthplace, Padang Panjang. Sjahrir was born there on March 5, 1909, in the *jaksa*'s house on Air Matakucing, the main street of the town. A Moslem school, a *surau*, stood next to the house, and the street led down to nearby Matakucing Lake. Besides Sjahrir's parents, an older brother and a sister also lived in the house—Soetan Noer Alamsjah, born in 1900 in Bonjol, and Siti Sjahrizal, born in Padang Panjang two years before Sjahrir.

Only a year after Sjahrir was born, the family moved to Jambi. Sjahrir's other two brothers were born there—Soetan Sjahsam in 1911 and Mahroezar in 1913. Sjahrir grew to the age of four in Jambi. He quickly learned, as his older sister remembers, to walk, to talk, even to read a little, because she often took him with her when she went to school.[99] If Sjahrir remembered anything from Jambi—the "native" civil servants' quarters where his family lived, the occasional European dressed all in white, the rubber plantations around the town, the wooded hills on the horizon—it would easily have merged in his mind with Medan, which came next.

As far as we know, the family lived on Gang Mantri, in a part of Medan called Kampong Aur.[100] They were not rich, but they were well-off enough to send the most intelligent of their children to "modern" schools.[101] Sjahrir is said to have been "the cleverest of the boys." In the tests given regularly by their father, Sjahrir usually got nine to ten points out of a possible ten. Only for handwriting did he rarely get more than five points.[102]

In 1915, at the age of six, Sjahrir enrolled in the best school available in Medan—the Europeesche Lagere School, ELS, the "European Lower School."[103] At the time, only 4,631 "natives," in contrast to 26,817 European children, attended Western-style primary schools in the colony of 60 million.[104] History classes in Sjahrir's school as

---

[99] Interview with Sjahrizal Djoehana, Bandung, March 7, 1982.

[100] Letter to the author by H. Mohammad Said, Medan, dated December 28, 1983. Compare with *Medan Area Mengisi Proklamasi* (Medan: Biro Sedjarah Prisma, Badan Musjawarah Pejuang Republik Indonesia, 1976), p. 752, n. 55.

[101] A *Hoofddjaksa* in 1927 got on average between fl.300 and fl.450 per month which was high on the official native pay scale; the monthly wage for an *assistent wedana* of the police, a sub-district level official, was between fl.175 and fl.250. See "Geschikt dan ungeschikt," *De Oostkust* 9, 9 (1927): 184–86; a new Ford car in Medan in the spring of 1926 cost fl.1,740, with a starter fl.200 extra; *Sumatra* 3, 11 (March 13, 1926). On the standard of living of another Minangkabau *hoofddjaksa* at that time, comparable to Sjahrir's father, see Salim, *Limabelas tahun Digul*, pp. 510–11.

[102] Interview with Sjahrizal Djoehana, Bandung, March 7, 1982.

[103] H. Rosihan Anwar, ed., *Mengenang Sjahrir* (Jakarta: Gramedia, 1980), p. 18; Subadio Sastrosatomo, "Sjahrir: Suatu perspektif manusia dan sejarah," in ibid., p. xl. There were two ELS in Medan at that time, see S. van der Plas, *Memorie van Overgave*, Sumatra's East Coast (July 2, 1917), pp. 119–22.

[104] The data are for HIS and ELS schools. *Encyclopaedie van Nederlandsch-Indië* 8 vols. (The Hague: Nijhoff, 1917–1939), 3: 94; on the colony's population being about 60 million at that time see ibid., 1: 299. Just a year before Sjahrir entered ELS, in the colony a new system was invented of Hollands-Indische Scholen, HIS, seven-year primary schools with Dutch as the medium of instruction to relieve the Indonesians' pressure for Western education and to avoid lowering the ELS's standards by popularizing it too much. There were four HIS in Medan by 1916. Van der Plas, *Memorie van Overgave*, pp. 119–22; also Simon L. van der Wal, ed., *Het Onderwijsbeleid in Nederlandsch-Indië, 1900–1942* (Groningen: Wolters, 1963), docs. no. 27–29, 51, pp. 244–57; also Penders in Ali Sastroamijoyo, *Milestones on My Journey* (St. Lucia: University of Queensland Press, 1979), p. 385, n. 8. The best studies available on the subject of

well as in all the others, began with "One day in 1596, four [Dutch] ships from afar appeared before the town of Bantam."[105] The pupils sang, on festive occasions, "Because of the Dutch blood in our veins, our song rises so high."[106] They were expected to wear trousers and jackets,[107] to speak Dutch among themselves in class and to their teachers; they switched to Malay, whenever they were among the "natives" or the Dutch in a mixed crowd.[108] Their textbooks were exemplary examples of "ethical" translations:[109] ABC books about "Isa the tea-plantation worker," for instance, a native girl too timid to complain when overlooked on a pay day ("you must be more daring," a white master, who has discovered the error, urges her);[110] more advanced textbooks, with chapters on Multatuli, a Dutchman of the late nineteenth century who risked his official career to help the "natives"; textbooks with portraits of C.Th.van Deventer, the "father of the ethical system."[111]

The Meer Uitgebreid Lager Onderwijs, "MULO," "The Advanced Elementary School," to which Sjahrir graduated in 1923 and where he spent the next three years, was again the best school in Medan. It was more "ethical" than the *Hogere Burgerschool* "HBS," "Citizen's High School," a possible alternative which existed in some of the other cities in the colony.[112] While the HBS was virtually identical with schools of the same name in Holland, MULO was "designed for the Indies." Any subject of "no use in the Indies" was supposed be replaced by "topics relevant to the culture of the Indies."[113]

---

the Indies colonial education in general are still I. J. Brugmans, *Geschiedenis van het onderwijs in Nederlands-Indië* (Groningen: Wolters, 1938), and C. L. M. Penders, "Colonial Education Policy and the Indonesian Response, 1900–1942" (Ph.D. thesis, Australian National University, 1968).

[105] The "main historical personalities" (*hoofdpersonen*), in the textbooks, were listed as follows: "(1) Columbus; (2) Cortez; (3) Charles V; (4) Martin Luther; (5) Calvin; (6) Ignatius de Loyola; (7) Willem of Orange; (8) J. P. Coen; etc. See F. van Rijsens, *Hoofdpersonen uit de Algemeen Geschiedenis*, vol. 1 (12th edition; Groningen and Batavia: Wolters, 1928), p. 26; for the "1596" beginning see, e.g., G. van Duinen, *Geschiedkundig leesboek voor de lagere school in N.I.* (Batavia: De Veurnadig, 1919), p. 8 (the Dutch ships also appear on the textbook's cover).

[106] Roem, *Bunga Rampai*, vol. 2, pp. 97–98.

[107] M. Manggis Dt. Radjo Panghoeloe Rasjid, "Bung Hatta: Sepanjang yang saya kenal sampai menjelang remaja" in *Muhammad Hatta: Pribadinja dalam kemanusian*, ed. Meutia Farida Swasono (Jakarta: Sinar Harapan, 1980), p. 209.

[108] Interview with Beb Vuyk and her husband, Leonen, June 8, 1983. Beb Vuyk, a Eurasian, attended that kind of school in the Indies at the same time as Sjahrir did.

[109] Most of the textbooks were printed in Holland by J. B. Wolters: Groningen, The Hague, but were specifically designed for the colony.

[110] A. M. de Man-Sonius and M. Mendel, *In en buiten Zonneland. Een drietel leesboeken*, vol. 2 (Groningen, The Hague: Wolters, 1925), pp. 5–9.

[111] A. M. de Man-Sonius, A. J. Schweitzer and J. van der Wateren, *Nieuw leesboek. Bloemlezing ten dienste van voortgezet lager en middelbaar onderwijs in N.O.I.* (Weltevreden: Visser, 1922), pp. 40–51, 59–67; A. J. Eijkman and Dr. F. W. Stapel, *Beknopt Leerboek der Geschiedenis van N.I.* (1919. Groningen, Batavia: Wolters, 1937), p. 86.

[112] A HBS was not opened in Medan until 1928. C. J. van Kempen, *Memorie van Overgave*, Sumatra's East Coast (September 10, 1928), p. 292; also *Hoogere Burgerschool met 5 jarigen Cursus en Algemeene Middelbare School ... te Medan: Programma van de Cursus 1929–1930. Tweede Schooljaar* (Medan: Deli Courant, 1930), pp. 43–48.

[113] From the correspondence on the subject exchanged between the Minister for Colonies, the Directorate for Education and the Adviser for Native Affairs between 1913 and 1917; see van der Wal, ed., *Het Onderwijsbeleid*, docs. no. 51, 54, 55, 56, pp. 244–57; see also ibid., *bijlage*, p.

Hotel de Boer
KITLV (DGI) #19.744

We still know little about Sjahrir at the time. He played soccer. He was a fast center-forward, fast as lighting, a friend says.[114] He played the violin. A lady who met him later says he played horribly, but the young Sjahrir seems to have been good enough at the time to play fox-trots, for a little pocket money, at Medan's fashionable, *echt* colonial, and, except for servants and musicians, all-white *Hotel de Boer*, "Farmer's Hotel."[115]

---

698. See also a review of the MULO textbook of history in *Mededelingen van de Vereeniging van leerkrachten bij het M.U.L.O. in N.O.I.* 1, 9 (May 12, 1928).

[114] Interview with Burhanuddin, Jakarta, March 6, 1982. According to a report on the Minangkabau Association in Medan, *Minangkabau Saijo*, "Minangkabau men coming *merantau* to Medan are very fond of soccer, a sport from Europe"; there was a heated debate at the Association's general meeting about a possible Association's soccer club ("M.S.V.C.—Minangkabau Saijo Voetbal Club"), the worries being about "Minangkabau men having hot blood, thus the good name of the nation might be blemished." Also, the meeting suggested a compromise, the European sport should be combined with the traditional Minangkabau sport, *silat/pentjak*. *Andalas* ("Sumatra"), November 27, and again December 25, 1923.

[115] Interview with Siti Wahjunah Sjahrir, Jakarta, March 12, 1982. His Master's Voice was offering the following music sheets in Medan in 1925, all fox-trots: "What Do You Do Sunday, Mary?," "Indian Pawn," "Peter Pan," "That's What I Will Do," and "Alabamy Band," besides "Stars and Stripes Medley" ("a one-step") and "Poem" by Fibich described as a waltz. *Deli in Woord en Beeld* 3 (November 11, 1925). On the Medan hotels of the Hotel de Boer level being all-white see, for instance, Ladislao Szekely, *Tropic Fever: The Adventures of a Planter in Sumatra* (Kuala Lumpur: Oxford University Press, 1979), p. 46.

In 1915, just when Sjahrir entered the first grade of his ELS, a new "ethical" *Bibliotheek voor Nederlands-lezende Inheemsen*, "Library for Dutch-reading Natives," began to publish and distribute in the colony, especially among ELS and MULO students, cheap editions of its choice of juvenile reading. Dutch children's classics, were prominent on the list: *Puss In Boots*, Oltmans' *Little Shepherd*, Malot's *Alone in the World*, Burnett's *Little Lord*, Karl May's American Indian novels, *Don Quixote*, *Baron von Munchhausen*, a popular History of Java by Mrs. Fruin-Mees, books about exotic areas like Netherlands-Ambon, Netherlands-Menado, and Nova Zemlja, "ethical" stories from the Indies by Marie van Zeggelen.[116] Sjahrir later mentioned the "hundreds of [Dutch] children's books and novels" he had read in his "early youth."[117]

One would be surprised if the soccer- and violin-playing Sjahrir had been left untouched by another craze of the time, the movies—with Tom Mix or Buffalo Bill or d'Artagnan. At least the last of these characters also appeared in a *komedie stambul* version at the same time.[118]

Much of the story of Sjahrir's childhood may be told through the way his clothes and costumes changed. Sjahrir got an elementary Islamic education from his father, and one can picture the boy's tiny white-garbed figure at the *jaksa*'s feet. Did Sjahrir's father change for the occasion, or did he leave on his official uniform as an *ambtenaar*, civil servant? Between the ages of six and twelve, each day after classes in his Dutch-style school, Sjahrir changed from the prescribed trousers and jacket and stepped across the street to attend Koranic courses.[119] And there was a soccer uniform, too, and a dinner jacket, probably, prescribed for the *soirées dansantes* at the *Hotel de Boer*. (Somehow, any description of Sjahrir's "ordinary" clothes remain out of the picture.)

---

[116] Minister for Colonies to the Queen, 26.2.1926 in *Verbaal*, February 26, 1926, no. 45. Advertisements for some of the literature in Malay—Gulliver Travels, the Story of Napoleon Bonaparte, Buffalo Bill—can be found even earlier in Rohana's journals in the form of traditional Minangkabau *syair*. See, e.g., *Soenting Melajoe*, 9, 6 (February 6, 1920), p. 3. These were also some of the books that Hatta and Sjahrir gave later to their pupils as good reading. See Des Alwi, "Oom kacamata yang mendidik saya" in *Muhammad Hatta*, ed. Swasono, p. 324. On Karl May being popular among the Sumatran youth in the 1910s and 1920s see Hatta, *Memoir*, p. 67.

[117] Sjahrir (Sjahrazad), *Indonesische Overpeinzingen* (Amsterdam: De Bezige Bij, 1945), August 28, 1937. The Amsterdam edition of *Indonesische Overpenzingen* was in part translated into English by Charles Wolf, Jr. as *Out of Exile* (New York: John Day, 1949), and into Indonesian by H. B. Jassin as *Renungan Indonesia* (Jakarta: Poestaka Rakjat, 1947). I have greatly profited especially from Charles Wolf's translation and I gratefully acknowledge my debt.

[118] On Tom Mix being a fashion in Minangkabau at that time see Radjab, *Semasa kecil dikampung*, p. 123; Douglas Fairbanks was d'Artagnan in the famous movie version of 1921; see Jerzy Toeplitz, *Geschichte des Films*, vol. 1 (Munich: Rogner und Bernhard, 1988), p. 130. On the Three Musketeers being played by *stambul* troupes see Nieuwenhuys, *Oost-Indische spiegel*, pp. 387–88. In *Andalas* journal for 1926 we find "Joseph" (of Egypt) being played at *Oranje Bioscoop*, "Tom Mix" at *Deli Bioscoop*, "Jack Dempsey" in *Tjong Koeng Bioscoop* and *Politie Setan* ("The Police Devil") at *Royal Bioscoop*. There is an interesting letter by one W. L. Leclercq from Medan dated January 1928 about the movie culture in the city; reprinted in *Orientatië* 1, 7 (April 1948): 54.

[119] Interviews with Sjahrizal Djoehana, Bandung, March 7, 1982, and with Siti Wahjunah Sjahrir, Jakarta, March 12, 1982. L. F. Tijmstra, "Zoeklicht op Sjahrir"(January 16, 1946) in *Collection J. W. Meyer Ranneft*, no. 497. On the usual parallel education in *surau* and Western school for the Minangkabau boys of that level and generation see Hatta, *Indonesian Patriot*, p. 99.

Sjahrir lived in a colorful household. Indies journals in Dutch and Malay were spread on the coffee table. Yet, the *jaksa*'s house was very much ruled by women. Three more children were born to Rabiah in Medan: Boejoeng Oeki in 1915, Abdoel Gafoer in 1917, and Idharsjah in 1918. For a while at least, another daughter of Mohammad Rasad, Radena, lived in the house together with Rabiah and her children and Radena's own four little boys, Djohan Sjahroezah, Djazar, Djazir, and Hazil Tanzil.[120] Before Rabiah died, in 1922, a family legend has it that she told her sons, "Don't dare to disobey your older sister: it is she who is responsible for your future."[121]

Sjahrir was thirteen when his mother died, and the oldest of the three boys living in the house.[122] But it was Sjahrizal, Sjahrir's eldest sister, fifteen years old at the time, who took charge of the little family's affairs. Her father, she told me later, "did not have much interest in the children except for their education."[123] It would have been difficult for him to do so—Sjahrir was his eighteenth child, and, by 1923, the *jaksa* had become a happy father, with various wives, twenty-five times.

For young Sjahrir, to experience the Medan of the 1910s and 1920s was to experience *rantau*, and the new "ethical"-Minangkabau translation of *rantau*, in a most exemplary case.

The three dozen petty rulers surviving in and around Medan—the Malay, Simelungun Batak, and Karo Batak sultans—were wasting their power and prestige largely in intrigues against one another.[124] They offered the "ethical" Dutch, and the "modern" Minangkabau as well, a flagrant illustration of a feudalistic anachronism and a perfect argument for the future to belong to *democratie*.

Medan might easily have been taken as an exemplary city of "matter-of-factness," "evolution" and "progress." Non-existent before the 1860s,[125] the city emerged in the two decades over the turn of the century: Medan's European population became six times larger in those twenty years, and its Asian population grew thirty times.[126] By the mid-1920s, Medan was acknowledged as the most "urban" settlement in Sumatra, and—besides Batavia, Surabaya, and Semarang—the most

---

[120] *Canang* [special edition], January 18, 1987, p. 40.

[121] Interview with Sjahrizal Djoehana, Bandung, March 3, 1982.

[122] One brother, Sjahsam, was born in Jambi, January 16, 1911. (See the Dutch Embassy in Brussels to the Foreign Ministry in The Hague, 26.11.1948; in *Archief Buiten. Zaken*; A.G. no. 7283, 1949.) The younger brother, Mahroezar, was born 1913 in Medan; see *Prisma Medan* 1976, p. 752.

[123] Interview with Sjahrizal Djoehana, Bandung, March 7, 1982.

[124] Van der Plas, *Memorie van Overgave*, p. 174. See also Michael van Langenberg, "Class and Ethnic Conflict in Indonesia's Decolonization Process: A Study of East Java," *Indonesia* 33 (April 1982): 3, n. 2, for the list of the principalities and the literature on the subject.

[125] In Medan histories, 1862 is described as Year One, the year of the treaty (*Acte van Verband*) between the Sultan of Deli and the Dutch representative E. Netscher which opened the area to colonial exploitation and made Medan the center of the new world. *Limapuluh Tahun Kotapradja Medan* (Medan: Djawatan Penerangan, 1959), pp. 35, 48. Medan officially became the center (through its establishment as the seat of a Governor and a Law Council among others) in 1909; see *Encyclopaedie van Nederlandsch-Indië* 2: 691–92.

[126] According to *Encyclopaedie van Nederlandsch-Indië* 2: 691–92, in Medan, in 1915, there were two thousand Europeans, fourteen thousand Chinese, and seventeen thousand "natives." Ibid. Between 1920 and 1930, again the Medan population increased by 69 percent; Michael van Langenberg, "North Sumatra under Dutch Colonial Rule: Aspects of Structural Change," *RIMA* 11, 1 (1977): 110.

real city in the whole archipelago.[127] In 1913, instead of prisoners, "free coolies" began to be employed to clean the city streets, and, in 1928, motor cars were assigned to the task. In 1924—and Sjahrir must have witnessed this—the main racecourse of Medan was selected as the first stop in the archipelago for the first-ever Holland-Indies trans Euro-Asia flight; the landing occurred amidst great celebration throughout the city, on November 21.[128]

The region was known throughout the East as a "Deli miracle." Coffee, tobacco, and rubber plantations, symetrically arranged and connected by train, surrounded Medan. Officials, merchants, planters, and coolies, more than 250 thousand of them, populated the place.[129] There were waves of capitalist booms and bankruptcies, but a postwar depression had just been overcome by the mid-1920s, during Sjahrir's time in Medan, and optimism reigned.[130]

There were still, in the mid-1920s, fresh memories of Medan being "a half wilderness,"[131] a "Wild West." "Every Dutch loafer was a potential *grand seigneur* in Deli."[132] Street singers in Medan still sang that someone who had murdered in Java could find a new life here.[133] The "men of Deli" still were pictured as "cutting down and burning the primeval forest."[134] The land of Medan was still "the Gold Land" of the planters, the *perkeniers* (from *perk*, "flower bed," "garden"). The planters had settled down a bit in the 1920s; they bet on horses, played soccer, tennis, cricket, sailed (in that scale of priorities),[135] and drank *bols*, especially. But for many, and for themselves, too, they were still seen as *"een nieuw mensentype,"* "a new kind of men"[136] ("the irrepressible race who stride booted into the council-halls of kings," in

---

[127] Legge, *Sukarno: A Political Biography*, p. 36.

[128] In *Gemeente Medan 1909–1934* (Medan: Deli Courant, 1934), n.p.; there are photographs of some of these occasions. In the entry "Medan" in the second volume of the encyclopaedia of the Dutch East Indies, published in 1918, we read: "This city has a very special character, it appears neither European nor typically Indies-like. Its orderly layout was kept from the beginning according to a plan, and its neatness [*netheid*] distinguishes this city favorably from most other bigger places in the Indies. . . . It has also a voluntary firebrigade, which is unique in the Indies. . . ." *Encyclopaedie van Nederlandsch-Indië*, 2: 691.

[129] Based on the reports of *Handelsvereeniging Medan* quoted in J. Weisfelt, *De Deli Spoorweg Maatschappij als factor in de economische ontwikkeling van de Oostkust van Sumatra* (Rotterdam: Handelshogeschool Dissertatie, 1972), p. 171. Compare H. J. Grijzen, *Nota van overgave*, Sumatra's East Coast (February 1921).

[130] See, e.g., (Sjahrir?), "Kapitaal dan Boeroeh di Deli," *Daulat Ra'jat* 2, 26 (May 30, 1932); a sharp increase in production, especially of coffee (which was was principally from the Medan-Deli area), is clear for the 1920–1925 period as compared with 1915–1920, in Furnival, *Netherlands India*, p. 316.

[131] Grijzen, *Nota van Overgave*, pp. 1–2.

[132] This is in Tan Malaka's letter to the League for Civil Rights, dated February 1933; the letter is published in Poeze, *Tan Malaka, Strijder voor Indonesië's vrijheid*, p. 566.

[133] Grijzen, *Nota van Overgave*, p. 2.

[134] Ann Stoler, "In de schaduw van de maatschappij: een geschiedenis van platage-vrouwen en arbeidsbelied op Noord-Sumatra," in *Feminisme en antropologie* (Amsterdam: Sara, 1981) quoted in *Excerpta Indonesica* 25 (July 1982), p. 13.

[135] M. J. Lusink, *Kroniek 1927: Oostkust van Sumatra* (Amsterdam: Oostkust van Sumatra Instituut, 1928), p. 92.

[136] Leopold Szekely-Lulofsz, quoted in Nieuwenhuys, *Oost-Indische Spiegel*, p. 351.

Kipling's fitting description of their British-Indian counterparts[137]), true embodiments of "the passion of enterprise, and the spirit of the vanguard."[138]

The planters provided an influential personality model in Medan during those years—a Karl May's Old Shatterhand or a Tom Mix of sorts. They were also men defined by a manifold frontier and a pluralist inheritance. Undeniably of Medan, and still "all were strangers."[139] What "struck one first" was that these men had "almost no noticeable connection with any community."[140] "None of them 'belonged': They came from elsewhere and were looking forward to going elsewhere."[141]

It may seem absurd to make a connection between the Medan *perkeniers* and the vanguard proponents of the "ethical" policy in Medan. As one might expect, the *perkeniers* typically were rough, and frequently brutal toward one another and toward "the natives." And the proponents of the "ethical" policy might be expected to be sensitive, and occasionally sentimental (toward one another and toward "the natives"), living for their *jours* where "men and their wives talked about philosophy and theology between playing music."[142]

But absurdities were possible in the sphere of in-between. A booted planter might even be seen at the piano, in an "ethical" *salon* (or, for that matter, at one of the monthly concerts of Beethoven or Schubert at the Muziekkorps Sumatra Oostkust, "Orchestra of the East Coast" of the Delische Kunstkring, the "Deli Art-Circle").[143] Proponents of the "ethical" policy existed on the plantations, such as the famous Dr. C. W. Janssen, a director of the Senembah plantations, and at the same time a philanthropist, a director of the Oostkust van Sumatra Koloniaal Instituut, the "Colonial Institute of Sumatra's East Coast," who built model schools for coolie children, each with a playground and a hall for gymnastics.[144] Also, women built the bridge. Not a few of the "ethical" writers, known through the colony, who lived in or wrote about Medan were women—Annie Salomons, Carry van Bruggen, Madelon Szekely-Lulofsz, Jo Manders, Dana Tscherning Peterson.[145] Some, indeed, were the planters' wives.

---

[137] Quoted in McClure, *Kipling and Conrad*, p. 22.

[138] Nieuwenhuys, *Oost-Indische Spiegel*, p. 346.

[139] Ibid., p. 347.

[140] Van der Plas, *Memorie van Overgave*, p. 252.

[141] Lily Clerkx, *Mensen in Deli: een maatschappijbeeld uit de Belletrie* (Amsterdam: WU University Press, 1962), p. 103.

[142] H. Veersema, *Delianen van de tafelronde* (Medan: Köhler, 1936), p. 141, quoted in ibid., pp. 20–21.

[143] Lusink, *Kroniek 1927*, pp. 84–87; the "Muziekkorps S.O.K." concerts did not come to an end until 1927. On January 7, 1926, a new Sumatra Oostkust Orkest had its premiere in *Deli Bioscoop*; there also was, in Medan, "Het ensemble van het Grand Hotel." See *Sumatra* 3, 3 (January 16, 1926), p. 9.

[144] See a long eulogy on Dr. C. W. Janssen in Lusink, *Kroniek 1927*, p. 5. Enlightening information on Dr. Janssen, and on Minangkabau reaction to him, can be found in letters by Tan Malaka (a teacher in the Janssen schools and a Janssen protégé); see the letters and other sources on Dr. Janssen in Poeze, *Tan Malaka*, pp. 78, 81, 83, 101–2, 566. See also Tan Malaka, *Dari Pendjara ke Pendjara* (Jakarta: Widjaya, n.d.), 1: 56, 59, 62–63; translated in Helen Jarvis, ed., *From Jail to Jail* 3 vols. (Athens, Ohio: Ohio University Southeast Asian Series, 1991), 1: 35, 48–49, 55–59; and Mrázek,"Tan Malaka," p. 15.

[145] Nieuwenhuys, *Oost-Indische spiegel*, pp. 342–48. See also Reid's introduction to Szekely (*Tropic Fever*, pp. XII–XIII). On the influence of, perhaps, the most important of them, Szekely-

Let us try again to imagine Sjahrir's family house in Medan. Dutch "Happy-Home" magazines were sold through the colony, and the *jaksa*'s family surely read them, too. A "fresh-air house" was advertised in them and became a must; also "a bedroom with a still life on the wall," "a modern kitchen, naturally," with "a *Perfection* petroleum cooking range."[146] A *hoofddjaksa* had to have "an advanced household" to keep in step with the place; sometimes even a local Dutch official might visit him.[147] *Jours* were held in the house, where Rabiah played her accordion and Sjahrir his violin, in between light conversation, and recitations from *The Arabian Nights*.

Sjahrir lived very much in a tropical *art nouveau* world during the early period of his life. Absurdly at first glance, it was almost a world of nostalgia for over-there-back-home—which was Holland! Sjahrir-the-boy moved through almost-Dutch interiors—the ELS and MULO classrooms, his father's office, his home and the homes of his friends and relatives of the same *niveau*, of a few Dutch classmates, perhaps, and of some Eurasians. The real world of the colony came to him through the doors and windows of these interiors. Naturally, thus, the world came, as often as not, in the form of either exoticism or petitions.

To his father's office in the Dutch colonial criminal court (and Sjahrir was often there), "native" coolies, if courageous enough, came to complain about the harassment and brutality of their supervisors. Later, to the office of Sjahrir's older friend and brother-in-law, Dr. R. M. W. Djoehana—a graduate of the best school in the colony, and a medical doctor at the main Medan *Gouvernement Polikliniek* (Sjahrir was a frequent visitor at this office, too)—coolies and rickshaw drivers, prostitutes, tuberculosis sufferers, and opium addicts streamed, complaining, again, and looking to the "ethical" doctor and his "modern" medicine for help.[148]

Medan was a "bizarre" place. There were Chinese, Japanese, Minangkabau, Bataks, Eurasians, and Europeans, many of them non-Dutch; English was widely spoken in Medan.[149] Virtually all of the coolies on the plantations, the "scum of the bazaars," were from Java.[150]

It was easier in Medan than anywhere else to see the Javanese as a true manifestation of the "pre-modern," "passive East."[151] A well-known "ethical" writer described them:

Lulofsz, on the Indonesians see, e.g., M. Ullfah Santoso, "De Indonesische vrouw en het Passief Kiesrecht," *Kritiek en Opbouw* (June 1, 1938), p. 126.

[146] From contemporary magazines quoted by Nieuwenhuys, *Oost-Indische spiegel*, pp. 342–43. The most popular magazine in Sjahrir's family, his sister told me, was *Andalas*.

[147] *Jaksa*, even *hoofddjaksa*, however elevated in Indonesians' view, were held in rather low esteem by Dutch officials. Letter from H. Mohammad Said, December 28, 1983. Still, Sjahrir's sister told me the Dutch district officials visited the house occasionally. Interview with Sjahrizal Djoehana, Bandung, October 22, 1987.

[148] Interview with Prof. Dr. R. Mohammad Djoehana Wiradikarta, Bandung, March 7, 1982. There were three departments in the hospital: (1) general department—this was where Dr. Djoehana worked, (2) a mental hospital, and (3) a Chinese section.

[149] There had to have been some "bridge language" between Dutch and English in Medan, too. See, for example, spring horse races being called "*de voorjaarraces;*" *Sumatra* 4, 16 (April 17, 1926).

[150] In 1920, out of 238,336 workers coming to Sumatra under a previously negotiated contract, 212,395 were Javanese (and 23,868 were Chinese); see Weisfelt, *De Deli Spoorweg Maatschappij*, p. 171.

[151] In 1920 only 12,162 of 250,462 plantation workers in the area were "free workers." Ibid. The rest, the "contract coolies" were legally forbidden not only from striking or invoking other

They walked, they ate. They slept. They had, sometimes, a woman. If they spoke, they might speak of the same topic: a far-away village on Java.[152]

Given the image of the Javanese, when the Dutch proponents of the "ethical" policy and the planters had to decide who was the "modern," "dynamic" element of "native" Medan society, the choice seems to have been equally easy for both groups. The conclusion was general: "the Minangkabau."[153]

After the turn of the century, Medan became a model for the Dutch colony's new frontiers. But also, for some, Asians as well as Westerners, it became a melting pot out of which a new, modern nation might emerge. A prominent Minangkabau wrote in a novel about the Medan of the time:

> They came here as contract coolie laborers from Java, as merchants from Minangkabau, Tapanoeli, Bawean, Bandjar and Betawi,[154] and from other places, too. After they endure the most varied kinds of hardship, a new assimilation (by which I mean a synthesis, a blending together) takes place. Its result is called a Child of Deli. And this Child of Deli, he is a bud, the richest flower in the bouquet of the emerging Indonesian nation.... His manners are free, his Malay is fluent, the accents of different places of origin vanish into a new Language of the Great Indonesia.[155]

Not unlike the Dutch planters in Medan, thus, the indigenous crowds of the place were also seen as "*een nieuw mensentype,*" "a new kind of men," emerging in the East. The Minangkabau *perantau*, by general acclaim and by their own conviction, were the most dynamic element of the new kind of "Indonesian" in Medan. They were where the future pointed. By logical extension, the Minangkabau *perantau* were seen, and saw themselves, as the most dynamic element of a new nation. In the mid-1920s many of the Minangkabau in Medan were looking forward, with a growing intensity, to fulfilling the role.

By the mid-1920s, Sjahrir's father was approaching retirement age and was hardly likely himself to move dynamically into yet another era. But two of his cousins, for instance, sons of other Medan *hoofddjaksa*, did so dramatically, and in a manner easy for Sjahrir to see. In Java, one of them, Hadji Agoes Salim, had become by the early 1920s, a major figure in the new militant and mass Indonesian nationalist movement Sarekat Islam, the "Islamic Union." His brother, Abdul Chalid Salim, had left for Java, too, and by the mid-1920s was well on his way to becoming an Indonesian Communist leader and an outcast.[156]

---

workers' rights to strike, but even moving from the plantations without their employers' consent or changing their contract (which was a long-term, several-year contract). In many aspects, actually, it was only a slightly modified form of slavery.

[152] Madelen Szekely-Lulofsz Rubber quoted in Clerkx, *Mensen in Deli*, p. 46.

[153] Minangkabau and Mandailing, S. van der Plas wrote in 1916, "form the most intellectually developed part of the native population. It is among them that one finds awakened associations." (Van der Plas, *Memorie van Overgave*, p. 66.)

[154] Bawean is an island in the Java Sea close to Madura; Banjar is a place in West Java; Betawi is Batavia (now Jakarta).

[155] Hamka, *Merantau ke Deli*, pp. 5–6.

[156] For the early political years of Hadji Agoes Salim see Van Niel, *The Emergence*, pp. 118–19 (based on the author's interview with H. A. Salim). For the younger of the brothers see the

In 1923, Dr. Djoehana moved to Java, too, for a better job and eventually a brilliant medical career. With him went his wife—Sjahrir's sister, the woman who had taken care of the *jaksa*'s little family until then. In the succeeding months, it appears, the rest of the family in Medan began to gravitate toward her new place of residence. In the summer of 1926, Sjahrir finished his schooling at the MULO, and it was, naturally, his turn to go.

---

man's memoirs, Salim, *Limabelas tahun Digul*, especially pp. 38–42. On Chalid Salim's first arrest in July 1927 see Lusink, *Kroniek 1927*, pp. 34–35.

2

BANDUNG, 1926–1929

> Sukarno and his friends lived in a house in Regentsweg (now Jalan Kabupaten), which I had to pass when I went from our school in Tegalreja, to the centre of the city. I still remember vividly how in passing the abode of those young intellectuals, I felt pride, sympathy and solidarity with them in a struggle which promised a new era for the Indonesian people. They indeed, symbolized at that time the awakening of a new Indonesia.
>
> Soetan Takdir Alisjahbana[1]

1. THE CITY AND THE SCHOOL

Mohammad Hatta once explained why he—a Minangkabau teenager going to Java early in the century—decided out of all the "ethical" schools available, upon a commercial school and, thus, the career of "a merchant." It could not be otherwise, Hatta said, because "in our family there was not one person who ever held a civil service position."[2] Seventy years after the event, this old friend of Sjahrir could imagine but two alternatives for a *perantau*—either that of a *handelaar* (merchant) or of an *ambtenaar* (civil servant). Both were clearly family careers, that of his father and of his uncle. "Not for a single moment did I ever think of becoming an *ambtenaar*," Hatta added, as if not sure if the explanation he had given was clear enough.[3]

Sjahrir chose the *ambtenaar*'s path. The MULO diploma he obtained in Medan qualified him to become a lower official, in the state railways or pawnshops, for instance, or a government secondary school teacher. But the MULO had been designed mainly as a "substructure for the AMS,"[4] the Algemene Middelbare School, "General Intermediate School," which, in turn, was to provide an opening for its graduates to go yet higher, to college either in the colony or in Holland. The

---

[1] S. Takdir Alisjahbana, *Indonesia's Social and Cultural Revolution* (Singapore: Oxford University Press, 1966), p. 138.

[2] Hatta, *Bung Hatta Antwoordt*, p. 116. Mohammad Hatta chose the Middelbare Handelschool in Batavia, and then higher commercial studies in Holland up to the Handelshogeschool (at the university level) in Rotterdam.

[3] Ibid.

[4] Director for Education to Governor General, March 16, 1914 in van der Wal, ed., *Het Onderwijsbeleid in Nederlandsch-Indië, 1900–1942*, pp. 248–53; and Nota of W. H. Bogaardt to Governor General, May 18, 1917 in *Verbaal*, March 13, 1918, no. 44.

division of the AMS in which Sjahrir enrolled, the "Westerse-klassiek," "Western-classical," division, was expected to prepare students "for juridical examinations" and for college law studies.[5] Sjahrir, as this choice of school suggests, was sent to Bandung to carry on his father's profession, becoming a *jaksa* in a wider *rantau* and at a higher level.[6]

A new AMS was to be opened in Medan in 1927. Nevertheless, Sjahrir went on to Java. The AMS in Bandung, founded in 1920, was at the time one of the most expensive schools in the colony and the second most expensive in the city, surpassed only by the Technische Hoogeschool, "Technical College."[7]

Anda Murad, a scholar and a Minangkabau herself, points out in her thesis how often young Minangkabau *perantau* tended, if possible, to wander into areas where their sisters or other women of their families had already settled.[8] The presence of sisters or other substitute mothers, waiting in a male-defined *rantau* and prepared to take care of the new coming men, was a sort of perverted tradition in itself. Or was it a heightened tradition perhaps. The young Minangkabau, even in the freer and looser sphere of *rantau*, was made constantly aware of his unceasing dependence on women.

This might be one reason why, in Sjahrir's own recollections and in the memoirs of his friends, images of female relatives waiting in Java and caring for Sjahrir are so subdued. Hamdani, Sjahrir's schoolmate in Bandung, remembered that Sjahrir "lived *in de kost* [bed and board], in the house of a Minangkabau man on Dr. Samjudo Street."[9] Maybe, Hamdani—himself a Javanese—did not know, and was not told by Sjahrir, that the "Minangkabau man on Dr. Samjudo Street" was the husband of Radena, Sjahrir's half-sister who had moved from Medan to Bandung a short time before Sjahrir did.[10] And Sjahrir's full sister was in Java, too—Sjahrizal Djoehana who lived with her husband in Serang, five hours by train from Bandung. It was too far, the lady complained to me sixty years later, to keep tight control over Sjahrir, except during vacations.[11]

---

[5] Ibid. According to a report from 1929, 96 percent of the 133 students of the Bandung AMS continued their studies after graduation. *Algemeen Verslag van het Onderwijs in Nederlands Indië* XXX 1 (1929): 114.

[6] Interview with Sjahrizal Djoehana, Bandung, March 7, 1982.

[7] According to the available figures (for the late 1930s) the average expenses for a pupil (student) for one school year were:
People's schools: ca. 5 f. (guilders)
Native MULO: ca. 65 f.
Technical School: ca. 169 f. to 202 f.
AMS: ca. 260 f.
HBS: ca. 174 f.
MULO: ca. 213 f.
Technische Hoogeschool: ca. 345 f.
Director for Education to Governor General, February 27, 1940, *Secret Mail Report* 1940, no. 341; also in van der Wal, ed., *Het Onderwijsbeleid*, p. 666. Hamdani, Sjahrir's classmate at the AMS, says that tuition was fl.25.- per month; interview with Hamdani, Jakarta, October 30, 1987.

[8] Anda Murad, *Merantau: Outmigration in a Matrilineal Society of West Sumatra* (Canberra: Australian National University, Department of Geography, 1980).

[9] Hamdani, "Sutan Sjahrir di masa mudanya," in *Mengenang Sjahrir*, ed. Anwar, p. 72.

[10] Interview with Sjahrizal Djoehana, Bandung, March 7, 1982.

[11] Ibid. and interview with Sjahrizal Djoehana, Bandung, October 22, 1987.

The family was spreading from Kota Gedang and Medan. Mahroezar, Sjahrir's younger brother, also left for Bandung in 1926 in the middle of his ELS school years and at the same time as Sjahrir.[12]

For Sjahrir the change from Medan to Bandung did not seem to have been particularly radical or painful. Bandung was a city located at a higher altitude than Medan, and much cooler, but its cultural landscape was very similar. It was surrounded by an almost identical kind of "advanced," "twentieth-century" country. By the 1920s *Preanger* (Priangan), the region of West Java around Bandung, was, like Deli, the site of some of the colony's largest coffee plantations. Bandung was much closer to Batavia than Medan, but it was still marginal. The "real" center of the colony, Batavia, was a five-hour ride by train, and its people were very conscious of the distance. Bandung and the *Preanger* region contrasted sharply with Java proper, the real mainstream of Javanese civilization.[13] The *Preanger* was "far less Indianized [than Java proper] and more strongly Islamicized"; thus, in many ways, it was "an intermediate zone between Java and the Outer Islands."[14]

Bandung was more metropolitan than Medan. It had more schools, including several of Indies-wide importance,[15] and quite a few of the colony's central offices. It was also the seat of the Dutch Indies central military command. The houses in Bandung were more fashionable than those in Medan, and the gap between current European and colonial architecture was smaller; there were some functionalist buildings in Bandung, already in the 1920s, and even a trace of *Bauhaus*.[16] In February 1928, the first radio conversation took place between Bandung and Berlin: it lasted five minutes and the "quality was very good."[17]

The Bandoengsche Kunstkring, "Bandung Art Circle," was, definitely, more *à jour* than the Kunstkring in Medan. It had 848 members in 1928, a symphony orchestra, and a theater company. It organized, in that year, thirteen concerts (with the Viennese Trio and the Dresden String Quartet, among others), nine theatrical performances (with the London Musical Comedy Company for instance), three film evenings, five exhibitions (all of Western art), three public lectures, and a special night of Javanese dance by dancers from the royal court in Solo.[18] There were regular youth concerts, and a lecture series in which AMS professors were prominent figures—on history, on literature, on philosophy, and on the spirit of the

---

[12] There is a report on Mahroezar finishing his Medan ELS by 1929 in "Politiek Verslag Oostkust van Augustus '34" in *Secret Mail Report* 1934, no. 1137.

[13] Java proper is usually understood as the area in Central and East Java between Banyumas and Malang with its nucleus in the Yogyakarta-Surakarta area.

[14] Fritjof Tichelman, *The Social Evolution of Indonesia: The Asiatic Mode of Production and its Legacy* (The Hague: Nijhoff,1980), p. 154.

[15] The Technische Hoogeschool of Bandung was founded in 1920 (Dahm, *Sukarno and the Struggle for Indonesian Independence*, pp. 43–44), the HBS in 1915 (*Encyclopaedie van Nederlandsch-Indië* I: 139, where the Bandung schools in general for 1915 are listed). For the development of Bandung schools during the 1920s and 1930s see the Director for Education to the Governor General, February 27, 1940 in *Secret Mail Report* 1940, no. 341.

[16] Djefry W. Dana, *Ciri perncangan kota Bandung* (Jakarta: Gramedia, 1990).

[17] *Onze Courant* 13, 5 (March 1, 1928), p. 3.

[18] *Jaarverslag v.d. Bandoengsche Kunstkring* (Bandung: Kunstkring, 1928), *passim*. See also ibid., 1926, listing concert trios from Paris and Rome, and ibid., 1927, reporting on a German operetta with *"Schwarzwald mädel,"* for instance, and a lecture by Rabindranath Tagore on art. See also *Bandoengsche Kunstkring, 1905–1930. Gedenkschrift, passim*.

Bioscoop Preanger
KITLV (DGI) #11.887

East.[19] Advanced "natives," especially students of the better schools were much more versatile than in Medan and were seen, occasionally, among the audience.[20]

Bandung soccer matches were on a higher, inter-island level, and teams came from as far away as Singapore.[21] Although the better clubs were still all-white, tennis was the fashionable game for all races to play.[22] Movies reached Bandung almost instantly, on their way from the West. Late in the summer of 1926, when Sjahrir arrived, a screen version of Conrad's *Nostromo* was shown in the Bioscoop Preanger in Bandung at practically the same time as it appeared in London, Amsterdam, and Leiden.[23]

---

[19] See, e.g., J. C. de Haan, "Het Grieksche Epos. Homerus," in J. C. de Haan et al., *Zeven Artikelen over Grieksche Kultuur* (Bandung: Vorkink, 1923), pp. 15–23, and J. C. de Haan *Geschiedenis* (Amsterdam: Bat. Versluys, 1933), on the activities of Sjahrir's professor of history.

[20] Compare with Tan Malaka: "When the economy was at its peak (1926–1927) it was relatively easy to make a living, workers could get employment easily, and some of the younger generation had the opportunity to learn to speak Dutch and to get rather soft jobs as clerks. Furthermore, there were all kinds of light diversions like cinemas, soccer, and hula dancing." Tan Malaka, *Dari pendjara ke pendjara*, 1: 150; *From Jail to Jail*, trans. Jarvis, 1: 140.

[21] *Kaoem Moeda* (Bandung), 1926–1927, *passim*.

[22] Ibid.

[23] Ibid. (September 1926, *passim*).

There were 15,937 Europeans in Bandung late in the 1920s, ten times as many as were in Medan when Sjahrir was there.[24] As in Medan, however, they formed only about one-ninth of the city's total population.[25]

Sjahrir's school in Bandung, not unlike the MULO in Medan, was conceived as an examplary "ethical" school. Like the MULO, the AMS was multiracial—in Bandung's AMS, in 1927, out of a total of 107 students, 56 percent were "natives," 13 percent Chinese, and 31 percent Europeans.[26] Like the MULO in Medan, the AMS in Bandung was "Indies-centered."[27] The school's aim was, in the Dutch view, to exemplify

> the right and duty of the youth of the Indies to study their culture, to find, in the culture, a place for themselves, and to carry on, later, responsibilities of leadership.[28]

Dutch, Malay, English, French, Latin, Ancient History, History, Geography, Civics, Botany, Gymnastics, Physics, and Chemistry were subjects taught at the school.[29] And for the students there Western knowledge was to be "not an ultimate object but a means."[30]

Sjahrir appears to have been a perfect AMS scholar: swift, alert, and bright. He was not exactly "a diligent kind of a student."[31] He was rather a debater, also courageous enough to ask his Dutch professors "pertinent questions." Dr. de Haan, a well-known and distinctly "ethical" figure in Bandung and throughout the colony,[32] and

---

[24] *Bandoeng 1906–1931. Officieele jubileum uitgave . . . van gemeente Bandoeng op 1.April, 1931* (Bandung: Gemeente Bandoeng, 1931), n.p.

[25] Ibid.

[26] *Algemeen Verslag van het Onderwijs in Nederlandsch Indië* 28, 1 (Batavia: Landsdrukkerij, 1927): 165–66; in the AMS in Yogyakarta 60 percent of the students were "natives," in Solo 93 percent, in Batavia 82.8 percent, and in Malang 51 percent. Ibid. In 1929 Europeans made for only 27 percent of the students in the Bandung AMS, but still this was the highest percentage found in any of the AMS schools in the colony. *Algemeen Verslag van het Onderwijs in Nederlandsch Indië* 30, 1 (1929): 99.

[27] See, e.g., Nota W. H. Bogaardt, in *Verbaal*, March 13, 1918, no. 44. In Bandung in 1925, there were five HBS with 1,603 Europeans and 123 "native" students and two AMS with seventy-four European students and 154 "natives"; in addition, there were twenty-eight Chinese in the two AMS. Van der Wal, ed., *Het Onderwijsbeleid*, appendix, p. 698.

[28] Ibid.

[29] Ibid.

[30] Nota W. H. Bogaardt, in *Verbaal*, March 13, 1918, no. 44.

[31] Soewarsih Djojopoespito, "De thuiskomst van een oud-strijder," *Tirade* 21, 221 (January 1977): 40–41.

[32] See, e.g., J. C. de Haan, *Schets van de Westeuropeesche Letterkunde* (Batavia: Wolters, 1932). For a review of one of de Haan's MULO textbooks see *Mededelingen Mulo* 1, 9 (May 12, 1928). See also de Haan, "Het Grieksche Epos." De Haan, especially, is well recorded in the history of the colony and may well serve as an example of the "ethical" teacher. A comparison of the "Eastern spirit" with the "Greek spirit" was part of his Bandung public lecture series; when he wrote about Goethe, his great favorite, for instance, he gave a general introduction, twenty lines on Faust and seven lines on other works; all the rest, ninety lines was given to an analysis of Goethe's "Paria" ballads. de Haan, *Geschiedenis*, pp. 148–52.

Miss Dr. Katwijk, Sjahrir's teachers of history and classics respectively, are mentioned by name.[33]

Sjahrir in Bandung, it seems, was no Kipling's Trejago who "crosses the border only in disguise."[34] Sjahrir's categorical insistence that there were "no ghosts and spirits"—rather a minority view in Java of the time—his repeated emphasis that everything was "logical," became proverbial and even a subject of anecdotes among his Bandung friends.[35] But indeed, "matter-of-factness" and "rationality" were exactly what was expected, in Bandung, of a boy "from Minangkabau." Sjahrir soon became a star, so his friends' memoirs say, in his AMS classes, as well as in Patriae Scientiaeque, "Motherland and Science," the AMS students' debating club.[36] The *rantau* widened this way and sometimes contracted strangely; translation kept the culture of *rantau* alive; the name of the debating club was in neither Dutch nor in Malay, but in Latin.

As in Medan, Sjahrir sometimes played soccer in Bandung, still as center halfback. Friends say that he was "expert, fast, and clever" in the sport.[37] He belonged to the neighborhood club, *Voetbalvereeniging Poengkoer*, "Soccer Association Rear End," but he played more often with a team composed largely of AMS students, in a club called *Luno* an abbreviation for *Laat U niet overwinnen*, Dutch for "Don't let yourself be conquered."[38]

As in Medan, theater in Bandung was very much a part of the city life. Sjahrir played in the—AMS-connected—*Batovis* which was an abbreviation of the Dutch *Bandoengse Toneel Vereeniging van Indonesische Studenten*, "Indonesian Students' Bandung Theater Company."[39] *Batovis* toured Bandung and places nearby. The students played *toneel* not *komedie stambul*—a more purely Western form of drama. (An article in Medan's *Deliana* in late 1928 commented that high-school and college students in Java were more advanced that those in Medan, which was proven, the article stated, by the fact that students in Java were playing *toneel* while those in Medan still stuck

---

[33] Mangandaralam Syahbuddin, *Apa dan Siapa Sutan Syahrir* (Jakarta: Rosda Jayaputra, 1988), p. 65.

[34] Rudyard Kipling. *Beyond the Pale*, quoted in McClure, *Kipling and Conrad*, p. 9.

[35] One of Sjahrir's friends in Bandung tells a story of one of the group's excursions, when Sjahrir insisted on spending a night among the holy tombs of Salek. Sjahrir left the place in the middle of the night and explained his desertion in the morning by complaining of "clapping doors, chilling wind, and an abominable odor of flowers." "We mocked him and laughed," the friend remembers. "Through your logical reasoning," they teased him, "how would you explain all these invisible things?" Soewarsih Djojopoespito, "De thuiskomst van een oudstrijder," p. 41.

[36] Hamdani, "Sutan Sjahrir di masa mudanya," p. 74. Hamdani says about twenty people participated in average. Interview with Hamdani, Jakarta, October 30, 1987.

[37] Hamdani, "Sutan Sjahrir di masa mudanya," in *Mengenang Sjahrir*, ed. Anwar, p. 72; Burhanuddin, "Sjahrir yang saya kenal" in ibid., pp. 48–69; interviews with Hamdani and Burhanuddin, Jakarta, March 5 and 6, 1982.

[38] Ibid.

[39] Among Sjahrir's soccer friends in Bandung Hamdani lists Ma'mun, Soemantri, Siwojo, Wiwi, Soebagio, Lagimoen, Boediono, and himself; among Patriae Scientaeque members, Sjahrir's AMS colleagues Boediono, Samsoeddin, Roesbandi, Santoso, Ongko G. (there was a Chinese Ongko family with three boys, Ongko E, Ongko F, and Ongko G, all close to Sjahrir then in various groups), Harsono, Imam Soedjahri, and Hamdani again; among the Batovis members, Tjutjun (Rusni), Hardjan, Inoe Perbatasan, Soebagio, Dipo Ling. Hamdani, "Sutan Sjahrir di masa mudanya," pp. 72, 74, 76–77; interview with Hamdani, Jakarta, March 5, 1982.

with *komedie stambul.*)[40] Sjahrir, in *Batovis*, was a "director, a writer, and sometimes an actor, but only in roles of intellectuals."[41] *Batovis* played almost every month, in Dutch, and "many Dutch people came to see the plays."[42]

During the three years that Sjahrir spent in Bandung he travelled only occasionally to see his sister in Serang and to Batavia, where his half-sister's family had moved; once during this time he might have visited the house in Medan. He traveled more with his AMS schoolmates and his *Luno* and *Batovis* friends. In old family albums of his friends photographs are treasured of picnics, bicycling, and boating. It is clear from the photographs that all this was done in an almost purely Western style. The young people traveled around Bandung, on the *Dago* Road or the *Grooten Postweg*, "Great Post Road," with their breathtaking views of the nearby mountains; or they made trips to nearby Girijaya, Situ Aksanto, Pengalengan Lake, or to the volcano of Tangkubau Perahu, for the day and during weekends.

They wandered through the country, stayed overnight in empty cabins or in the open, once even in a graveyard. One memory from this period is of Sjahrir entertaining his friends during a picnic on a violin;[43] another is of Sjahrir singing "folksongs mixed with Western classics and Strauss waltzes."[44] He was "perhaps the only one among us," a friend says, "who could sing these Western songs correctly, even their mostly German texts."[45]

Instead of performing for the planters in the *Hotel de Boer*, Sjahrir, in Bandung, was dancing himself; waltzes, fox trots, and charlestons. Sjahrir now attended more fashionable and more multiracial *soirées dansantes*. If it was a sign of daring among some of Sjahrir's generation to be "bold enough to get close to the Dutch girls,"[46] then Sjahrir, as he is recalled, was in the vanguard.[47]

2. Jong Indonesie

In Bandung's city center, on what is today called the "Street of Asia and Africa," in a window of the *Algemene Indische Dagblad* (*AID*), "General Indies Daily," a news bulletin was displayed each day at about six o'clock in the evening for the Dutch-reading public. According to a friend of his, Sjahrir was seen at the journal window "almost every evening."[48]

---

[40] *Deliana* (September 1, 1928), pp. 3–4; see also on student *toneel* in Java, ibid. (August 1, 1928), pp. 11–12.

[41] Soewarsih Djojopoespito, "De thuiskomst van een oud-strijder," p. 40.

[42] Syahbuddin, *Apa dan Siapa Sutan Syahrir*, p. 6. Interview with Murwoto, Jakarta, December 6, 1987.

[43] Soewarsih Djojopoespito, "De thuiskomst van een oud-strijder," pp. 40–41.

[44] Hamdani, "Sutan Sjahrir di masa mudanya," p. 72.

[45] Ibid.

[46] Abu Hanifah, *Tales of a Revolution* (Sydney: Andus and Robertson, 1972), p. 30.

[47] Hamdani, "Sutan Sjahrir di masa mudanya," p. 71; L. F. Tijmstra, "Zoeklicht op Sjahrir"(January 16, 1946), in *Collection J.W.Meyer Ranneft*, no. 497; Subadio Sastrosatomo, "Sjahrir: Suatu Perspektif manusia dan sejarah," in *Mengenang Sjahrir*, ed. Anwar, p. XII; interview with Subadio Sastrosatomo, Jakarta, March 4, 1982. Rusni in Syahbuddin, *Apa dan Siapa Sutan Syahrir*, p. 5.

[48] Burhanuddin, "Sjahrir yang saya kenal," p. 48; interview with Burhanuddin, Jakarta, March 6, 1982.

At about the time Sjahrir arrived in Bandung, the AID bulletin reported the arrival in the Indies of a new governor general—A. C. D. de Graeff, a close friend, it was said, of many prominent "ethical" proponents.[49] Alarming reports of an attempted Communist uprising—with centers in Batavia, West Java, and in Sjahrir's homeland, Minangkabau—appeared in the news bulletin shortly afterwards, late in 1926 and early in 1927.[50] Six months thereafter, and a year after Sjahrir arrived in Bandung, another report appeared in the AID window. The Perserikatan Nasional Indonesia, "Indonesian National Association," was founded on July 4, 1927, in Bandung by Mr. Sukarno C. E., a graduate of Bandung's Technical College, a school just a few blocks from Sjahrir's AMS.

Sjahrir's friends later claimed that Sjahrir, on February 20, 1927 in Bandung, was among the ten boys who decided to start the young people's nationalist association Jong Indonesie, "Young Indonesia."[51] No contemporary record of his participation could be found.[52] However, he is mentioned in a police report in February 1928 as the chairman of one of the association's meetings.[53] In August 1928, "Soetan Sjahrir, student of the AMS" was already known to the Bandung police as "the chairman of the editorial board" of the young association's journal.[54]

By late 1928, Jong Indonesie had spread far beyond Bandung. The association already had branches in Batavia, and in Yogyakarta and Surabaya in central and eastern Java. There were branches of the girls' division of the association, Poetri Indonesia, "Daughters of Indonesia," in Bandung, Batavia, and Surabaya. Three journals, at least, were published by the association—*Jong Indonesie* in Bandung, *Kabar Kita*, "Our News," in Surabaya and *Soeara Kita*, "Our Voice," in Yogyakarta.

---

[49] On this governor general see, e.g., Koch, *Batig Slot*, p. 38; H. Sneevliet, "De nieuwste explosie van koloniaal machtsmisbruik in Indonesië," *De Nieuwe Weg* (Amsterdam) 5 (1930). See also John Ingleson, *Road to Exile: The Indonesian Nationalist Movement, 1927–1934* (Singapore: Heinemann, 1979), esp. pp. 40–41, 94–97, 105.

[50] For detailed information see Harry J. Benda and and Ruth T. McVey, eds., *The Communist Uprisings of 1926–1927 in Indonesia: Key Documents* (Ithaca: Cornell Modern Indonesia Project, 1960). What was prominently to be seen in the Vorkink publishing house window, it seems, were mostly lists of Dutch contributors to the fund "for the victims of the communist *keri* [sickle] violence"; see, e.g., *Kaoem Moeda*, November 15, 1926 ff.

[51] On the beginning of Jong Indonesie see *Politiek-polititioneel overzichten van Nederlandsch Indie* (hereafter *PPO*), February 1927. (For the years 1927–1930 of the central reports, the edition by Harry J. Poeze is used: Harry J. Poeze, ed., *Politiek-politioneele overzichten van Nederlandsch-Indië*, vol. 1 [1927–1928] [The Hague: Nijhoff, 1982], p. 6); *PPO*, April 1927 (Poeze, ed., *Politiek-politioneele overzichten* 1: 145).

[52] Sjahrir was a member of the *Jong Indonesie* central board according to *Dossier Sjahrir* in Collection Meyer-Ranneft, no. 497. Hamdani, "Sutan Sjahrir di masa mudanya," p. 75; and Burhanuddin "Sjahrir yang saya kenal," p. 49, spoke of Sjahrir as the Bandung branch chairman (*ketua* and *voorzitter*, respectively). Sjahrir, however, is not mentioned, as far as I know, in any police or press report (*PPO* or *Overzicht van de Inlandsche en Maleisisch-Chineesche Pers*, (title varies) hereafter *Overzicht van de IMC pers*) until February 1928, including a rather detailed report on the organization in *Overzicht van de IMC pers*, 1928, no. 1, pp. 16–17.

[53] *PPO*, February 1928 (Poeze, ed., *Politiek-politioneele overzichten*, 1: 248–49). On Sjahrir being among the founders see Sastra (not very reliable regarding this as he came to know Sjahrir only in 1932), Sastra, "Sjahrir untuk Sastra dan Sastra untuk Sjahrir," *Mengenang Sjahrir*, ed. Anwar, p. 82; also Tijmstra, "Zoeklicht op Sjahrir." See also Murwoto, *Autobiografi selaku perintis kemerdekaan* (Jakarta: Departemen Sosial, 1984), p. 9, who says Sjahrir was the chairman of the organization's congress in 1927.

[54] Ibid., July 1928 (Poeze, ed., *Politiek-politioneele overzichten*, 1: 358).

"Poetri Indonesia" of Bandung with Sjahrir, seated third from left.
(Collection Hamdani, Jakarta)

The Bandung branch remained the strongest; it had 300 members in early 1929, and there were seventy girls in the Bandung branch of Poetri Indonesia.[55]

There was a clear connection between Jong Indonesie and the "ethical" schools of Bandung and other Javanese towns. Burhanuddin was perhaps the only one, among the Bandung Jong Indonesie inner circle, who had not had a significant Dutch-style school experience.[56] Soebagio Mangoenrahardjo and Raden Mas Soemantri, two other prominent Jong Indonesie leaders and friends of Sjahrir were, respectively, a student and a former student, of the Technical College.[57] Boediono,

---

[55] *PPO*, October 1927 (Poeze, ed., *Politiek-politioneele overzichten*, 1: 145); see also ibid., July 1928, (Poeze, ed., *Politiek-politioneele overzichten*, 1: 358); August 1928, (Poeze, ed., *Politiek-politioneele overzichten*, 1: 389); November 1928 (Poeze, ed., *Politiek-politioneele overzichten*, 1: 469); December 1928 (Poeze, ed., *Politiek-politioneele overzichten*, 1: 493). Compare with J. Th. Petrus Blumberger, *De nationalistische beweging in Nederlandsch-Indië* (Haarlem: Willink, 1931), pp. 393–94. An attempt to form a branch of the organization in Semarang by October 1928 did not succeed; see *PPO* October 1928 (Poeze, *Politiek-politioneele overzichten*, 1: 441). *Fadjar Asia*, May, 19, 1928 in *Overzicht van de IMC pers*, 1929, 1: 371; *Pemoeda Indonesia* 1, 10–12 (July–August 1928) in *Overzicht van de IMC pers* 1928, 2: 45.

[56] Burhanuddin attended Sarikat Ra'jat secondary school. For information on Burhanuddin's educational background see "Interrogation of Burhanuddin" in *Secret Verbaal*, November 28, 1934 L33.

[57] *PPO* July 1928 (Poeze, ed., *Politiek-politioneele overzichten*, 1: 358); for Soebagio's biodata see Benedict Anderson, *Java in a Time of Revolution: Occupation and Resistance, 1944–1946* (Ithaca: Cornell University Press, 1972), p. 442.

the first chairman of Jong Indonesie,[58] Hamdani, the Jong Indonesie's secretary and treasurer,[59] and also Samsoeddin,[60] were Sjahrir's classmates at the AMS. Murwoto came from AMS Yogyakarta. And one finds the same names among the members of the Luno soccer club (Soebagio, Soemantri, Boediono, Hamdani, and also Burhanuddin), the *Batovis* theater (Soebagio, Hamdani, and Samsoeddin), and Patriae Scientiaeque (Boediono, Hamdani, Samsoeddin).[61]

The mood and style of the AMS permeated Jong Indonesie. The association's activity in Bandung appeared to be almost equally divided between its cooperative shop—where "souvenirs" and "traditional artifacts" were made and sold for charity and for financing other undertakings—its soccer and tennis clubs, club house, theater company, and its library with "120 books—in Malay, French, English, German, and Dutch."[62]

One field of Jong Indonesie activity should be especially mentioned: the youth association's own school, Tjahja Volksuniversiteit. The school was another way of translation, as its very title suggested: "*tjahaja*" is Malay for "radiance"or "gleam" or "ray of light," and "*volksuniversiteit*" is Dutch for "people's university."[63] Jong Indonesie organized other Tjahja Volksuniversiteit schools in Batavia and Yogyakarta, but Bandung's school was considered to be the most advanced and the model.[64]

Soebagio Mangoenrahardjo, Sjahrir's very close friend at the time, was the Bandung school's founder and director. Sjahrir is listed among the top leaders.[65] According to a Bandung report of 1928,

---

[58] Sastra, "Sjahrir untuk Sastra," pp. 80, 82.

[59] Hamdani, "Sutan Sjahrir di masa mudanya," p. 73; see also Anderson, *Java in a Time of Revolution*, p. 436.

[60] "Police report on Hamdani," in *Secret Verbaal*, November 28, 1934 L33.

[61] *PPO* July 1928 (Poeze, ed., *Politiek-politioneele overzichten*, 1: 358); Hamdani, "Sutan Sjahrir di masa mudanya," pp. 74–75; another important Jong Indonesie leader at that time was Soedarsono, two years behind Sjahrir at the AMS ("Dossier Sjahrir" in *Collection Meyer-Ranneft*, no. 497).

[62] *Fadjar Asia*, May 19, 1928 in *Overzicht van de IMC pers*, 1929, 1: 371. On Sjahrir at that time "active in building people's cooperatives" see "Riwajat Hidup Soetan Sjahrir," n.d., n.p. typescript in the *Archives Siti Wahjunah Sjahrir*.

[63] There was also a Volksuniversiteit Indonesie, with its center in Batavia, organized by Parade Harahap, the journalist whom we already met as the co-editor of the Medan's women's journal *Perempoean Bergerak*; for more details on this school system see its journal *Volksuniversiteit*, nos. 1–6.

[64] In Batavia, the *Tjahja* was established by a meeting in November 26, 1928; on both this and the establishment of Yogyakarta *Tjahja*, see *PPO* November 1928 (Poeze, ed., *Politiek-politioneele overzichten*, 1: 466–67). In Bandung on January 31, 1928, the journal *Volksuniversiteit* emerged from the Bintang Timoer press (*Overzicht van de IMC pers*, 1928, p. 292); I was not able to locate any issues of this journal. On *Tjahja* being discussed at the Jong Indonesie meetings see, e.g., *PPO* May 1929 (Poeze, ed., *Politiek-politioneele overzicht van Nederlandsch-Indië*, vol. 2 [1929–1930] [Doordrecht: KITLV, 1983], p. 117), and ibid., July 1929 (Poeze, ed., *Politiek-politioneele overzichten*, 2: 161). For the Yogyakarta *Volksuniversiteit* of the youth organization see *Soeara Kita* 3, 1(November 1928): 8.

[65] Tijmstra("Zoeklicht op Sjahrir") says that Sjahrir was the "*directeur*" of *Tjahja*, a claim which, given the other sources, is improbable. On Soebagio founding the *Tjahja* in Bandung with one Adang, Dadang and R. Moeso among others, see *PPO* November 1928 2: 415. In "Police report on Hamdani," Hamdani is said "to have established here, on the initiative of the

this university is designed not merely to teach reading and writing, but also to give instruction in foreign languages, economics, mathematics, physics, and other study subjects. All lectures are given to Indonesians of every age and to women as well as men, free of charge by high school and college students. . . . Six hundred persons are already registered as "pupils." There are coolies, peasants, and workers among the registered, and also a few dozen women and old people over forty.[66]

There are other reports of Tjahja Volksuniversiteit teaching "Dutch, Indonesian, English, German, and French and in law, anthropology, sociology, stenography and history."[67]

Sjahrir's friends from Tjahja Volksuniversiteit recalled how they "traveled around Bandung," how they taught the common folk in the villages "for a simple dish of rice," and how they "wore sarongs."[68] According to one account, "Sjahrir himself hung a board above the entrance of his 'university' which read 'Free English Lessons by Mr. Soebagio from New York'."[69]

It, evidently, was the quality of the time—this belief that the essentially AMS syllabus the students used at the Tjahja Volksuniversiteit, stenography, or French, might somehow, in the future at least, be useful for a peasant or a fifty-cent-a-day coolie.[70] Actually, the real "common people" seem to have been rather the exception in the Tjahja Volksuniversiteit classrooms. They knew hardly any languages except Sundanese, which, in turn, was unintelligible to most of the Tjahja Volksuniversiteit teachers, Sjahrir included. Pupils from the city in fact prevailed at Tjahaja Volksuniversiteit, and the lectures were given either in Malay or in Dutch.[71]

According to Jong Indonesie's statutes of 1927, it was the aim of Jong Indonesie to promote the idea of Indonesian national unity through a boy scout movement, sports, journals, and booklets, and through holding meetings.[72] Jong Indonesie, one of the association's leaders stated, "is not based on politics"; it "studies politics as a

---

known Soetan Sjahrir and Soebagio, the so-called Volksuniversiteit Tjahja." (*Secret Verbaal*, November 28, 1934 L33.)

[66] Inoe Marto Kusumo in *Pemoeda Indonesia* 1, 10–12 (May–August 1928), quoted in *Overzicht van de IMC pers*, 1928, 2: 45.

[67] Ingleson, *Road to Exile*, p. 65. Soebagio's report on the school is summarized in *PPO* II, September 1929 (Poeze, ed., *Politiek-politioneele overzichten*, 2: 209).

[68] The picture is based on Tijmstra, "Zoeklicht op Sjahrir," and especially on the interviews with Hamdani and Siti Wahjunah Sjahrir, Jakarta, March 6. and 12, 1982; the latter recalling what Sjahrir had said. See also Hamdani, "Sutan Sjahrir di masa mudanya," pp. 74–75.

[69] Sutrisno Kutojo, ed., "Inventarisasi Data Biografi Pahlawan Nasional Sutan Sjahrir," typescript, n.d., *Archives Siti Wahjunah Sjahrir*, p. 4.

[70] There were educational systems in Indonesia at that time which emphasized developing practical skills, too: Taman Siswa for instance; see Ruth T. McVey, "Taman Siswa and the Indonesian National Awakening," *Indonesia* 4 (October 1967): 128–49; Tjahja Volksuniversiteit, it seems, did not belong among them.

[71] Hamdani, "Sutan Sjahrir di masa mudanya," p. 75; interview with Hamdani, Jakarta, March 6, 1982; Soewarsih Djojopoespito, "De thuiskomst van een oud-strijder,"p. 40; Burhanuddin, "Sjahrir yang saya kenal," p. 49; interview with Burhanuddin, Jakarta, March 6, 1982.

[72] *Jong Indonesie* (Bandung), October 1927 in *PPO* October 1927 (Poeze, ed., *Politiek-politioneele overzichten*, 1: 146); see also Petrus Blumberger, *De nationalistische beweging*, pp. 393–94; also *PPO* July 1928 (Poeze, ed., *Politiek-politioneele overzichten*, 1: 358).

scholarly subject."[73] Most of the "political" debates of Jong Indonesie took place, and, possibly, most of the "political" decisions were made, at the Patriae Scientiaeque debating club. A great deal of the group's politics was also made in the theater.

Tjahja Volksuniversiteit, as well as Jong Indonesie itself, received support from various sources,[74] but mostly, it seems, from donations at *Batovis* theatrical performances.[75] Some of the most successful *Batovis* evenings were organized on Bandung's bright *Braga* street, in a house rented from the Dutch, a clubhouse called *Ons Genoegen*, "Our Pleasure," with the name changed for the occasion to *Thons, Tot Heil Onzer Nationale Strijders*, Dutch for "To Celebrate Our National Fighters."[76]

Perhaps, the most heatedly debated "political" issue in the AMS, Patriae Scientiaeque, and Jong Indonesie, was "anti-feudalism." Looking closer, it was almost exclusively an issue of fathers. Boys and girls belonging to the association themselves believed that 80 percent of their fathers came from "feudal civil service" and thus from "aristocratic" families.[77] Moving against "reaction" entailed in large part, lamenting that "many of our members" were obliged to leave the association "obeying the will of their elders,"[78] as well as bewailing the fact that "a great number of pupils were forbidden by their fathers to attend the school."[79]

Ningrat, a Javanese term commonly used to describe the aristocracy, became for the young, "modern," "nationally conscious" Indonesians—often themselves sons and daughters of "aristocrats"—a word provoking disrespect.[80] Jong Indonesie journals sneered at aristocrats as:

> ambitious, climbing, nonchalant nobodies. . . . What a row of portraits; the noblest figures of the "native" elite! What splendor and what regal dignity.[81]

---

[73] The chairman of the organization at a Surabaya meeting on January 29, 1928, quoted in *PPO* January 1928 (Poeze, ed., *Politiek-politioneele overzichten*, 1: 224–25), and at a Yogyakarta meeting on July 29, 1928, quoted in *PPO* July 1928 (Poeze, ed., *Politiek-politioneele overzichten*, 1: 358).

[74] Very probably the Indonesian National Association (later Party) was one of the sources of support. On Jong Indonesie's cooperation with the Association Party see below.

[75] Soewarsih Djojopoespito, "De thuiskomst van een oud-strijder," p. 40; Subadio Sastrosatomo's introduction to *Mengenang Sjahrir*, ed. Anwar, p. XII.

[76] Soewarsih Djojopoespito, "De thuiskomst van een oud-strijder," p. 40; *PPO* November 1928 (Poeze, ed., *Politiek-politioneele overzichten*, 1: 469). She uses the abbreviation Thonis instead of Thons.

[77] Interview by George McT. Kahin with Sjahrir, Jakarta, February 15, 1949. I am indebted to Professor Kahin for providing his interviews with Sjahrir to me. Sjahrir in that particular interview described the revolutionary leaders as coming 80 percent from the "feudal civil service," 20 percent from the "middle class."

[78] *PPO* December 1928 (Poeze, ed., *Politiek-politioneele overzichten*, 1: 496). For similar cases in another group of youth at that time see Hatta, *Indonesian Patriot*, pp. 90, 96 (the cases of Rasjid and Arnold Mononutu).

[79] *PPO* February 1929 (Poeze, ed., *Politiek-politioneele overzichten*, 2: 14).

[80] *Ningrat* in Poerwadarminta's dictionary means "nobility," "noble," "sublime" or "lofty," as well as "bourgeois"(!). See W. J. S. Poerwadarminta, *Kamus Umum Bahasa Indonesia* (Jakarta: Balai Pustaka, 1976), p. 677. It is a common suffix at the end of noble names (Djajadiningrat, Woerjaningrat, Hendraningrat) meaning, actually, "of the world" or "of the universe" (Anderson, *Java in a Time of Revolution*, p. 203n.).

[81] *Pemoeda Indonesia* 3, 1 (April–May 1929).

It was no accident that some of the bitterest articles written on the anti-feudal theme were signed *Si Piatoe*—Malay for "The Orphan."[82] Nor was it accidental that highly emotional images "Mother Indonesia" and "Fatherland" appeared so frequently in the youths' writings on what they described as "politics."[83]

As part of a Jong Indonesie meeting held in early 1928, of which Sjahrir was the chairman, a play was performed on the theme. In the plot, an aristocratic official, ignorant about progress, forbade his *"zeer vooruitstrevend,"* "very progressive," daughter to invite Dr. Tjipto Mangoenkoesoemo to their house, because Dr. Tjipto was a people's leader. The daughter in a long fierce speech, pleads for the idea of Indonesian freedom, convinces her father to receive Dr. Tjipto, and even to shake hands with him (applause). Another aristocrat emerges at that moment, however, still higher and still more "reactionary." He censures his subordinate, the newly enlightened father, for being patriotic, and makes an effort, besides, to force the girl into marriage with a native policeman. "How could I be faithful to a police official, who is old-fashioned and reactionary," the girl asks. After she again strongly pleads her case, even the higher official is won over to the youth's cause, and the drama climaxes with police official even being ordered to stop spying on the activities of the people's leader Dr. Tjipto.[84]

Politics, for these people, was an issue of growth and maturing, of transition, and of translation.

In December 1928, the Second All-Indies Youth Congress took place in Batavia. Some of the Bandung group traveled to Batavia, and several reports say that Sjahrir was in the audience.[85] The youth at the congress made a pledge to "One Country," "One Nation," and "One Language." *Indonesia Raja*, "Great Indonesia," a song to become the future national anthem, was played for the first time at the congress, in the rhythm of a waltz, on a violin, a guitar, and a ukulele.[86]

The country, nation, and language to which the young people pledged was Indonesia and the Indonesian language.[87] In a geographical and demographic sense,

---

[82] *Soeara Kita* 1, 2 (October 1928): 2.

[83] See, e.g., Inoe Marto Koesoemo's poem *Weeklacht van mijn vaderland* (Lamentation of my fatherland) or another poem by "somebody in Bandung" to Mother Indonesia in *Pemoeda Indonesia* 1, 10–12 (May–August 1928), quoted in *Overzicht van de IMC pers*, 1928, 2: 44–45.

[84] PPO February 1928 (Poeze, ed., *Politiek-politioneele overzichten*, 1: 249). For another text see "Op het drempel van het leven (Toneelspel uit het Indonesische studentenleven. Fragment)" in *Pemoeda Indonesia* 2, 1 (April–May 1929).

[85] Hamdani says that Sjahrir went to the Congress as a member of the Bandung delegation (Hamdani, "Sutan Sjahrir di masa mudanya," p. 74). This is not supported by any document on the Congress accessible to me. See, e.g., *Empatpuluhlima Tahun Sumpah Pemuda* (Jakarta: Gunung Agung, 1974), especially pp. 61–85. Idham, Sjahrir's relative living at that time in Batavia, told me that he remembered Sjahrir was at the Congress and also visited Idham's family on the occasion; Idham was ten at the time. Interview with Idham, Jakarta, January 6, 1988.

[86] Abu Hanifah, *Tales of a Revolution*, p. 62, and the same author in *Bunga Rampai Soempah Pemoeda* (Jakarta: Balai Pustaka, 1978), p. 340. See also *Empatpuluhlima Tahun*, p. 68; for the complete text of the song see ibid., p. 71–72. A Dutch observer at the Congress commented on the song: 'This is, with its banal European melody and crippled rhyme, an example of degeneration of taste, but it is not politically dangerous." (van der Plas to Governor General, in *Secret Verbaal*, May 24, 1929 Ir 10). For other memoirs of the event see in *Serasi*, November 1, 1987, memoirs by Ibu Sud.

[87] "Poetoesan Congres Pemoeda-Pemoeda Indonesia," in *Empatpuluhlima Tahun*, p. 69.

this was the Dutch East Indies; the language was "Indonesian," bazaar and service Malay, modified once more to perform yet another historical function.

Sjahrir and his friends worked hard to accomplish this. Already a year before the congress, in December 1927, the Dutch name of "Young Indonesia," Jong Indonesie was translated into Indonesian, Pemoeda Indonesia. Speaking "Indonesian" was encouraged repeatedly in the Pemoeda Indonesia meetings as the principal task of any patriot.[88]

Indonesian was attractive to the youth because it was free of mystical "feudal" traditions. The language's appeal, in a sense, lay in its flatness. Indonesian, as bazaar and service Malay before, lacked the sonority—and perhaps the disturbing quality—of a mother tongue. Decades later, Indonesian was still said to have "something curiously impersonal and neuter about it."[89] Sjahrir and his friends might have felt liberated by the fact that they had "acquired their language second hand."[90]

A scene often repeated was of a youth, at a public meeting of Pemoeda Indonesia, who began a speech in Indonesian and, after few words or sentences, muttering an excuse, fell back into Dutch again.[91] A Pemoeda Indonesia journal was forced to compromise with its prospective contributors:

> if you are afraid to express your thoughts in Indonesian because you are not proficient enough in it, write to us in Dutch; step by step, certainly, we all will learn.[92]

It is clear that this was not an easy time for many members of Pemoeda Indonesia. Not everybody was exposed to Malay as intensively as Sjahrir had been in Medan. Also, the native tongues of most of the boys and girls in Pemoeda Indonesia, generally Javanese and Sundanese, differed far more from Malay-Indonesian than did either Minangkabau or Mandailing, the languages Sjahrir heard at home.

It might have been a *déjà vu* for Sjahrir. Language, translation, and progress again seemed strikingly similar. Indonesian was a school subject, as we have seen, in Tjahja Volksuniversiteit—the same way that it was a school subject at the AMS.[93] Dutch was, in both cases, a language next in kin. Some issues of the Pemoeda Indonesia journals were still written wholly in Dutch; others, partly in Dutch and

---

[88] A. K. Pringgodigdo, *Sedjarah Pergerakan Rakjat Indonesia* (Jakarta: Pustaka Rakjat, 1950), p. 119, Hamdani, "Sutan Sjahrir di masa mudanya," p. 73. According to some reports, it was a rule that one should speak Indonesian at the Pemoeda Indonesia meetings (*Fadjar Asia*, May 19, 1928, quoted in *Overzicht van de IMC pers*, 1928, 1: 371).

[89] Anderson, "The Language of Indonesian Politics," pp. 105-6.

[90] I am using here a formulation of Franz Kafka to Max Brod about Jews and Germans; translated in Frederic V. Grunfeld, *Prophets without Honour: A Background to Freud, Kafka, Einstein and Their World* (London: Hutchison, 1979), p. 192.

[91] Such a case is quoted, e.g., in *Overzicht van de IMC pers*, 1928, 1: 371. On the youth speakers and youth journals' contributors asking forgiveness for "not yet" being able to speak their national language see, e.g., *PPO* December 1928 (Poeze, ed., *Politiek-politioneele overzichten*, 1: 495); *Soeara Jakatera* 1 (April 1930), quoted in *Overzicht van de IMC pers*, 1930, 2: 127; *Indonesia Moeda* 1 (March 1930), quoted in ibid., 1930, 2: 5–6.

[92] *Soeara Kita* 1, 1 (September 15, 1928): 4. On the "difficulties, the efforts to speak and to write Malay cause for the youth leaders," see, e.g., "Adviser for Native Affairs to Governor General, October 25, 1928" in *Secret Mail Report* 1928 no. 1083.

[93] *PPO* November 1928 (Poeze, ed., *Politiek-politioneele overzichten*, 1: 466).

partly—mostly the simpler pieces and very occasionally poetry—in Indonesian.[94] The statutes of Pemoeda Indonesia in 1929 were published in an Indonesian "translation," and the Dutch "original text" was printed, too.[95]

Sjahrir's group was fierce in its nationalism. Bandung police regularly judged articles in *Jong Indonesie* and *Pemoeda Indonesia* to be "influenced by extremism."[96] Some theater performances were banned.[97] The governor's office informed the principal of Bandung's MULO and the rector, Dr. Bessem, of the AMS of the undesirable activity of his students.[98] Still, there is no sign of any disciplinary measure having been taken against Sjahrir or, as far as we know, any of his Pemoeda Indonesia friends at the AMS. One story was later narrated by Sjahrir himself: He was called to the AMS rector's office to explain something he had done. The "explaining," as Sjahrir describes it, happened in something like a scholar-to-scholar or father-to-son talk: "What is freedom?" the Dutch rector mused both to Sjahrir and to himself. Nobody is free!"[99]

---

[94] "Van der Plas Report" (*Secret Verbaal*, May 1,1928 IrC9) commented on this. On the ease at switching from Dutch to Indonesian and back (in *Pemoeda Indonesia* journal) see, e.g., *Overzicht van de IMC pers*, 1928, 2: 298. The same switching is recorded at the Pemoeda Indonesia Bandung Congress of December 1928; see PPO December 1928 (Poeze, ed., *Politiek-politioneele overzichten*, 1: 495). This remained a practical arrangement until at least the early 1930s; see, e.g., *Indonesia Moeda* 1 (March 1930), quoted in *Overzicht van de IMC pers*, 1930, 2: 5–6.

[95] This, as stated in the journal, was done "because the youths of the 'generation 1928,' alas, have difficulties with their own language"; see *Pemoeda Indonesia* 6–7 (August–September 1929), quoted in *Overzicht van de IMC pers*, 1929, 2: 79.

[96] E.g., PPO October 1927 (Poeze, ed., *Politiek-politioneele overzichten*, 1: 146).

[97] E.g., on September 8, 1928 and in November again, see PPO August 1928 (Poeze, ed., *Politiek-politioneele overzichten*, 1: 390); ibid., November 1928 (Poeze, ed., *Politiek-politioneele overzichten*, 1: 469).

[98] "Van der Plas Report, August 29, 1927," *Secret Verbaal*, May 1, 1929 IrC9.

[99] Sjahrir (Sjahrazad), *Indonesische Overpeinzingen*, October 4, 1934. On Sjahrir being asked to the headmaster's office to explain his extramural activities see also Hamdani, "Sutan Sjahrir di masa mudanya," p. 71; even Hamdani, an associate of Sjahrir in politics, does not claim that any disciplinary measures were taken by the AMS against Sjahrir throughout his stay in Bandung. Sjafruddin Prawiranegara, who says he entered the Bandung AMS just when Sjahrir passed his final exams, spoke of Sjahrir as of someone "more than anybody else at the AMS known and *respected* by both students and the teachers." This is an interesting remark by a man who later himself became a prominent nationalist, even if we admit this may be in part a myth of a later origin (Sjafruddin actually is wrong: when he entered the AMS in 1928, Sjahrir still had another year to go, unmentioned, it appears, by the other student). See Mr. Sjafruddin Prawiranegara, "Bung Sjahrir Pendekar Kemerdekaan dan Pendekar Demokrasi" in *Mengenang Sjahrir*, ed. Anwar, p. 128. Another of Sjahrir's later famous school-mates at the AMS Bandung, Mohammad Natsir, says the rector of the school was "much more broad-minded than other colonial officials," he let Natsir's own student organization, Jong Islamieten Bond, for instance, "lest the watch-dogs of the regime notice," meet in the AMS building "as if it was an evening class." Natsir's reminiscences in Siti Wahjunah Sjahrir's private file were graciously provided to the author. Also interview with Natsir, Jakarta, November 30, 1987; Hamdani, again, Sjahrir's classmate at the AMS, repeatedly stressed that the professors at the AMS, namely Dr. de Haan and the rector were *bebas*, "broad-minded." Interview with Hamdani, Jakarta, October 30, 1987. The rector of the AMS, Dr. E. Bessem was a respected figure in the colony; he was also very close, as a lecturer in Latin, to the Law College in Batavia. (*Boemipoetra* 1, 1 (September 1, 1924): 5. See also for a short biographical sketch of Dr. Bessem on the occasion of planning his retirement for 1929 *Onze Courant* 13, 23 (December 1, 1928): 5.

Pemoeda Indonesia voiced sarcasm against the then famous Dutch colonial authority, official, and scholar, H. Colijn—"Father Colijn" as the youth called him.[100] It may seem an excessive act of daring by the young nationalists. But H. Colijn was also a favorite target for many "ethical" Dutchmen in the colony, including, in 1928, the governor-general himself. Governor-General de Graeff—"the last 'ethical' governor-general" as he was often described—at the same time as Pemoeda Indonesia, criticized Colijn for "being oblivious to the national consciousness of educated young Indonesians."[101] Instead, de Graeff said, the Dutch should view Indonesian nationalism as

> a movement, which is in itself perfectly natural and which for the last decennia has been made possible and advanced by our colonial policy.[102]

Pemoeda Indonesia challenged the Dutch, indeed, on the basis of a culture built "over the last decennia" by the Dutch themselves. The "educated young Indonesians" complained about the efforts by the Dutch to weaken the "critical spirit," and to perpetuate the idea of "race supremacy."[103] If the proponents of "ethical" policy were explicitly attacked, it was because they did not seem to be "ethical" enough. They were accused—not unlike fathers often are—of telling "lies" to the youth, of being "vague" in their "promises about the future," of "not being serious enough in what they set out to do."[104]

In a 1928 issue of *Pemoeda Indonesia*, one "Katja S." wrote a poem, published on the front page and in flawless Dutch, "To Jean-Jacques Rousseau": "Thy name, O Master, like the sound of bells, echoes from the past."[105] These were boys and girls of a generation defined by their classrooms. Their models, like the language of their "politics," were acquired secondhand.

This was an "ethical" school generation, however they might hate the word. "Can you give anything to your Fatherland, if you yourself do not possess a harmonious soul?" asked a hero in another Pemoeda Indonesia theater performance in 1929. Another student on the stage answered: "I try to enspirit my life. . . . A fight for freedom is a search for happiness."[106]

This was a generation which perceived the world of the colony through the windows of their classroom, and articulated this reality on the stage. They spoke the flat language of the sphere in-between.[107] They played soccer and tennis, so far from Amsterdam or The Hague. They moved by keeping themselves distant from their "reactionary" and "feudal" fathers. They were driven by a mission to help peasants,

---

[100] E.g., *Pemoeda Indonesia* 3, 1 (1929).

[101] De Graeff in April 1928. See Simon L. van der Wal, ed., *De Volksraad en de Staatkundige Ontwikkeling van Nederlands-Indië*, 2 vols. (Groningen: Wolters, 1964/1965), 2: 47–48.

[102] "Government Secretary to Governor of Central Java, January 5, 1929," *Collection Gobée*, no. 5 secret; used translation by Ingleson, *Road to Exile*, p. 81.

[103] *Jong Indonesie* 2 (August 1927) in *PPO* August 1927 (Poeze, ed., *Politiek-politioneele overzichten*, 1: 97).

[104] *Pemoeda Indonesia* 3, 1 (April–May 1929).

[105] *Pemoeda Indonesia* (Congress Number) 6–7 (January–February 1928), quoted in *Overzicht van de IMC pers*, 1928, I, p.16.

[106] *Pemoeda Indonesia* 3, 1 (April–May 1929).

[107] See, e.g., Takdir Alisjahbana, *Indonesian Language and Literature. Two Essays* (New Haven: Yale University Southeast Asian Studies Cultural Reports Series, 1962), p. 14.

but they were drawn away from the villages by what they saw as the village communities' "oppressive silence" and "taciturn reservation."[108] They might have written, with Kafka, of their affection for "my people, provided I have one."[109]

3. THE YOUTH AND SUKARNO

Sukarno's "Indonesian National Association," which was founded, as we have already mentioned, in Bandung in July 1927, soon changed its name into the Partai Nasional Indonesia, PNI, "Indonesian National Party." Almost immediately it came to dominate nationalist politics not only in the city but throughout Java and beyond. This was the beginning of the meteoric career of Sukarno and, according to many, the true beginning of the modern Indonesian nationalist movement as well.

While in Bandung, Sjahrir, as far as we know, was never a member of Sukarno's party,[110] but some of his friends were.[111] Sukarno's party colleagues acted as "advisers" to Pemoeda Indonesia.[112] Boys and girls from Sjahrir's circle attended Sukarno's public party conventions, and some of them, including Sjahrir, sometimes visited the debates of Sukarno's inner-circle.[113] Sukarno himself occasionally spoke at Pemoeda Indonesia meetings. In March 1928, he defined Pemoeda Indonesia and his party as a "one and an indivisible whole."[114] Police reports at the time described Pemoeda Indonesia as "a nursery of leaders for [Sukarno's] organization."[115] Not rarely, Sjahrir's Patriae Scientiaeque debating club met in the garden pavillion of Iskaq Tjokrohadisoerjo, a close friend of Sukarno and a member of the Sukarno party's top leadership.[116]

Sukarno was a little older than the youth—he was Sjahrir's senior by nine years—and of similar status and educational background as most leaders of

---

[108] *"Beklemmend stil,"* and *"zwijgende terughouding"*; see Suwarsih Djojopuspito, *Buiten het Gareel: Indonesische roman. Met een inleiding van E. du Perron* (Utrecht: de Haan, 1940), pp. 208-9.

[109] Quoted in Grunfeld, *Prophets without Honour*, p. 186.

[110] For instance, see Tijmstra, "Zoeklicht op Sjahrir."

[111] Soebagio, most significantly, was quite important, it appears, even in Sukarno's party decision making.

[112] This was, by late 1927, namely Mr. Soenarjo (see *PPO*, October 1927 (Poeze, ed., *Politiek-politioneele overzichten*, 1: 146).

[113] Boedijono (Boediono), "chairman of the central committee of Jong Indonesie," was mentioned as present at a meeting of Sukarno's inner circle in Tjipto Mangoenkoesoemo's house (together with Sukarno, Iskaq and Sartono) late in 1927; see *Sin Po*, November 26,1927 in *PPO* November 1927 (Poeze, ed., *PPO*, October 1927 (Poeze, ed., *Politiek-politioneele overzichten*, 1: 170). Also, there was a Pemoeda Indonesia delegation at the first PNI's congress, Bandung, May 27–30, 1928; see ibid., May–June 1928, 1: 329. On Sjahrir "frequently" being a guest on Regentsweg where Sukarno lived see Takdir Alisjahbana, "Sjahrir dan sikap dan struktur politik yang diperlukan untuk dunia yang sedang tumbuh," *Ilmu dan Budaya* 3 (July 1981): 263–78. Soetan Inoe Perbatasari, three years older than Sjahrir, is mentioned as someone in 1927 on the executive committee of the Jong Indonesie and in the same year a propagandist for the PNI and presiding occasionally over its debating club. B. B. Hering, ed., *The van der Most Report: A P.I.D. View of Soekarno's P.N.I.* (Townsville: James Cook University Press, 1982), p. 57.

[114] This was the meeting of Pemoeda Indonesia on March 10, 1928 which was chaired by Sutan Sjahrir; see *PPO* February 1928 (Poeze, ed., *Politiek-politioneele overzichten*, 1: 248–49).

[115] Ibid., October 1927 (Poeze, ed., *Politiek-politioneele overzichten*, 1: 145–47). Also ibid., May 1929 (Poeze, ed., *Politiek-politioneele overzichten*, 2: 117).

[116] Hamdani, "Sutan Sjahrir di masa mudanya," pp. 74–75.

Pemoeda Indonesia. Coming from a "lesser aristocratic" family, Sukarno went through the best "ethical" schools in the colony. He attended the ELS and the HBS, and he graduated in Bandung in 1926 from the most prestigious Technical College.[117]

Sukarno was as fierce in speaking, writing and acting as his younger friends. When Sjahrir came to Bandung, Sukarno was already preaching a radical policy of non-cooperation with the Dutch colonial government.[118] "Only natives might be members of the executive" of the Algemeene Studieclub, "General Study Club," that Sukarno and his friends founded in Bandung in November 1925.[119] Two years later, when the PNI was founded, non-cooperation principles were incorporated into the new party's statutes in uncompromising terms. "All efforts to narrow or to eliminate the line between *sinis* [ourselves] and *sanas* [them] are bad for our movement," Sukarno declared in August 1928. "Everything that perfects the division between us and them is good for our struggle."[120]

Non-cooperation was formulated by Sukarno fiercely, dramatically, and in virtually absolute terms. Its fierceness, dramatic effects, and absoluteness, however, were part of the period, and not fundamentally different from the culture of the young people in Pemoeda Indonesia.[121] Sukarno's articles and speeches of the time, with

---

[117] Dahm, *Sukarno*, pp. 28–30, 43–56. On Sukarno presenting his origins as noble (royal even) see Sukarno, *An Autobiography as Told to Cindy Adams* (Indianapolis: Bobbs-Merrill, 1965), pp. 17–20.

[118] Sukarno, of course, did not invent non-cooperation. Hatta, for instance, remembers discussing the idea (with Hadji Agoes Salim) in 1918, adding that the idea, then, did not appeal to him yet. (Hatta, *Indonesian Patriot*, pp. 36–37, 148.) The idea of an emotionally charged and absolute non-cooperation did not appeal to many others; for example Tan Malaka in 1921 was still listed as a candidate for *Volksraad*, the colonial council. (Poeze, *Tan Malaka*, p. 93.) According to Van Niel, non-cooperation became the policy of the Indonesian students' organization in the Netherlands, Perhimpoenan Indonesia, sometime in 1922. (Van Niel, *The Emergence*, p. 225.) In 1923 the police reported that "whites are never admitted" to the Perhimpoenan Indonesia meetings (Report to Minister for Colonies, December 17, 1923 in *Secret Verbaal*, December 28, 1923 Ir218.) From then on the non-cooperation policy spread quickly throughout the nationalist organizations, with Sukarno and his Bandung group the most active and important among its proponents.

[119] *PPO* March 1927 (Poeze, ed., *Politiek-politioneele overzichten*, 1: 21) on rejecting Tjipto Mangoenkoesomo's proposal that this be changed.

[120] Sukarno in August 1928, quoted in Dahm, *Sukarno*, p. 95; Dahm describes Sukarno's non-cooperation as not tactical but "absolute." (Ibid, pp. 55–56.)

[121] *Massa actie*, for instance, "mass action," the frequently used maxim of Sukarno's program—mobilization of the Indonesian people against colonialism—does not seem to be taken from the orthodox Marxism of Rosa Luxemburg as is sometimes suggested, but rather from "*Tante* ['Aunt'] *Jet*," Henriètte Roland Holst, a Dutch poet turned politician, a Calvinist turned Communist, a lady who based her "revolution" on harmonizing principles of socialism, humanism, and Christian faith. On Roland Holst's book, *De revolutionnaire Massa Actie* (Rotterdam: Brusse, 1918), see, e.g., J. de Kadt. *Uit mijn Communistentijd* (Amsterdam: van Oorschot, 1965), pp. 198, 322; Tan Malaka wrote on Roland Holst, e.g., in *Sumatra Post*, July 24, 1920 (quoted in Poeze, *Tan Malaka*, p. 86). (Tan Malaka, author of a book on *Massa Actie*, too, is most often connected with the concept in Indonesia.) On Roland Holst being close to the Tachtigers, the Dutch generation of the 1880s, the poets influential, also, among the Dutch proponents of the "ethical" system in Indonesia and among the young Indonesians early in the twentieth century as well; see J. de Kadt, "Onze Multatuli," *De Nieuwe Kern* 3 (1936): 220. On Henriètte Roland Holst as "one of the greatest poets of Holland," and "a socialist with a deep and fine feeling," see, e.g., Sjahrir's history professor de Haan in de Haan, *Geschiedenis*, p. 164.

their endless quotations and lists of names, and with their quotations in foreign languages, resounded with strong echoes of "ethical" translation.[122]

Conflicts were reported between Sukarno and the young people. At one of the youths' meetings, Sukarno is reported to have been censured publicly by Suwarni, the chairman of Poetri Indonesia and a close friend of Sjahrir, for praising his party too much.[123] According to Sjahrir's friends, Sjahrir himself also confronted Sukarno. On this occasion, when acting as the chairman of the Pemoeda Indonesia meeting, Sjahrir, so his friends relate,

> banged his gavel and reminded Sukarno, in a businesslike way [*zakelijk*], not to use Dutch language excessively during a nationalist meeting, and not to talk coarsely [*kasar*] to the women present.[124]

Both incidents, if real, remembered, or fantasized about, are similar in a way: young people—Sjahrir was in his late teens at the time—tried to reassert themselves against an older man. Sukarno was, no doubt, regarded by the young people as the principal nationalist leader. But the respect was based on uncertainty. Under a colonial regime based on political, economic and military power as well as on cultural domination, Sukarno preached "psychological revolution," in which "the achievement of spiritual freedom came first."[125] He appealed to the youths' own evident sense of an empty space around and inside themselves. His dramatic ferocity made it easy for the young people to perceive the older leader as a man moving himself precariously through the same sphere as they did. A later description of Sukarno as a "dramatically delinquent father"[126] may well also fit the relation between Sukarno and Sjahrir's circle in this time.

---

[122] In spite of his "absolute" non-cooperation, Sukarno also easily fitted into the mixed company which met at the house of Marcel Koch—an imposing figure of Bandung society, a Dutchman who had been living in Java for years, the most prominent heir in the colony, perhaps, of the receding tradition of the socialist wing of the "ethical" movement. According to his friends, Marcel Koch was "the socialist of 1907 . . . his marxist socialism was thoroughly an element of belief and of the eschatological expectations which formed him during his childhood . . . he remained a man of the pre-1914 time." See Locher-Scholten, "Kritiek en Opbouw," pp. 209–21. There were, e.g., lectures by Koch's circle (by Stokvis for instance) organized in the Ons Genoegen clubhouse and sponsored by Sukarno's organization. (*Kaoem Moeda*, November 4, 1926).

[123] Soewarni was reported as telling Sukarno: "Sir, this is not a place for making PNI propaganda." See Blumberger, *De nationalistische beweging*, p. 380.

[124] Burhanuddin "Sjahrir yang saya kenal," pp. 49–50. See also S. Pringgodigdo in *Sikap* 4, 34 (1951): 6, and H. Algadri, "Soekarno dan Sjahrir sesudah proklamasi," "Memoirs" (unpublished typescript, ca. 1987), p. 90; also interview with Hamid Algadri, Jakarta, December 2, 1987, for the (unspecified) tension between Sukarno and Sjahrir allegedly already existing in Bandung. For a colorful description of the critical attitude of some Batavia students to Sukarno, see also Abu Hanifah, "Revolusi Memakan Anak Sendiri: Tragedi Amir Sjarifuddin," *Prisma* 6, 8 (August 1977): 86–90.

[125] Ingleson, *Road to Exile*, p. 64.

[126] Willard Hanna later described Sukarno as "the dramatically delinquent father of an overgrown, underdeveloped, adolescent nation." Willard A. Hanna, *Eight Nation Makers: Southeast Asia's Charismatic Statesmen* (New York: n.p., 1964), pp. 1, 92; quoted in Legge. *Sukarno*, p. 6. A father indeed, see *Soeara Pemoeda Mataram* 1, 1 (April 1929): 12: "*Bapa dan pahlawan kita jang maha moelia, Ir. Soekarno*."

Sukarno was born in Java. Although he was already in his late twenties when Sjahrir came to Bandung, he had never been outside the island.[127] He described his nationalism as a "return to ourselves."[128] He tried to make "an appeal at once to modernity and to tradition, or perhaps more exactly a mediation of tradition through modernity."[129] He believed in the power of the indigenous culture to "absorb" the impact of Marxism.[130] He spoke of "turning off Islam."[131]

Sukarno was proud of being "popular among all, from *kromo* [Javanese for common folk] to *bupati* [Javanese for regent]."[132] For Sukarno, as he wrote in 1928, *kromo*, the common folk, did not mean a "thoughtful mind," but "a temperamental heart";[133] he saw himself as a *"burgervader,"* "citizen-father," to the common folk.[134] He heard the Indonesian future as "a voice of promise, like the far off music of the *gamelan* [a traditional Javanese orchestra] on a clear moonlight night."[135] "True nationalists," to Sukarno,

> whose nationalism is not merely a copy or imitation of Western nationalism but is based on a feeling of love of man and humanity—nationalists who receive their nationalist feeling as a divine inspiration [*Wahju*] and express it as an act of devotion [*bakti*] are free of all pettiness and narrowness of thought. For them, the love of country is great and wide, giving space to other views, just as the air is vast and spacious and offers all living things a place and all they need for life.[136]

Sukarno, in style and thought, was strikingly different from the "ethical" culture as it was translated in Minangkabau and in Medan. He was different from Sjahrir in this sense, too. Bandung, however, was, at the time, culturally almost as distant from Java proper as it was from Medan. The "native people" of and around Bandung

---

[127] By June 1929 it was reported that Sukarno was denied the passport which each Javanese needed, by law, to leave the island; Sukarno wanted to go to Sumatra's West Coast to Minangkabau. *Nieuwe Rotterdamsche Courant*, June 28, 1929, quoted in *Indonesia Merdeka* (Perhimpoenan Indonesia) 7, 3 (July 1929): 57.

[128] Sukarno, January 1928, quoted in Dahm. *Sukarno*, p. 139; see also ibid., p. 104.

[129] Anderson, "The Idea of Power in Javanese Culture," p. 16.

[130] On Sukarno paying "scant attention" to urban labor and peasant questions see, e.g., John Ingleson, "Revolutionary Ideas and the Secular Non-Cooperating Nationalists in Indonesia," *RIMA* 8, 1 (January–June 1974): 20, 25. Regionalism also, McVey notes, was "not raised" in Sukarno's platform of 1926–1927; see McVey, "Nationalism, Islam and Marxism: the Management of Ideological Conflict in Indonesia," introduction to Soekarno, *Nationalism, Islam and Marxism* (Ithaca: Cornell Modern Indonesia Project, 1969), p. 3. McVey writes of "the ambivalence of those balancing psychologically between two worlds," meaning the "national elite" and the "new metropolitan culture," including Sukarno.

[131] This was what also Gobée noted in Sukarno's propaganda; see "Deputy Adviser for Native Affairs to Governor General, July 19, 1928," in *Secret Mail Report* 1928 no. 751.

[132] Editorial by J. M(anoppo) in *Matahari Indonesia*, November 12, 1928, quoted in *PPO*, December 1928 (Poeze, ed., *Politiek-politioneele overzichten*, 1: 494).

[133] Sukarno's letter to Tjipto Mangoenkoesoemo, October 5, 1928, quoted in Ingleson, *Road to Exile*, p. 88.

[134] Ali Sastroamijoyo (a prominent leader of Sukarno's party himself) in his memoirs; Sastroamijoyo, *Milestones on My Journey*, p. 80.

[135] Quoted in Legge, *Sukarno*, p. 116.

[136] Sukarno in 1926, translated and quoted in Dahm, *Sukarno*, p. 68.

were not Javanese *kromo*, but Sundanese, a group with a distinct culture, and suspicious of the "true Javanese" often to the point of open animosity.[137] Sukarno himself, who came from Blitar and Surabaya and was a native of East Java, was a stranger to Bandung, too. His speeches had to be made in Indonesian, if he wanted to be understood and did not want to speak Dutch; sometimes, what Sukarno said had to be translated into Sundanese.[138] There might have been a feeling of wanderers' affinity between a Minangkabau and a Javanese in Bandung.

Just at the time when Sjahrir and Sukarno were in Bandung together, H. Colijn— the symbol of extreme Dutch colonial reaction, the "Father Colijn" so hated by the youths—published a pamphlet describing "Indonesian unity" as "an empty concept."[139] The individual islands and regions of the archipelago, Colijn wrote, were separate entities, and the future of the colony was not possible except region by region.[140] Some other Dutch authorities liked to point out at the same time how the Indonesian nationalist movement in general and particularly in Bandung was "dominated by the Javanese" or about to be "torn apart" by tensions between the Javanese and the Minangkabau.[141]

This was a mighty cause creating an affinity between Bandung nationalists, however Minangkabau, Javanese, or Sundanese they might be. Sukarno reacted promptly against Colijn's views, and Pemoeda Indonesia joined him most vocifer-

---

[137] Many of them, like Suwarsih Djojopoespito, were deeply Sundanese; Suwarsih's distance from the *kejawèn* kind of Javanism is clearly manifested in her *Buiten het Gareel* book; often she was, like Sjahrir, described as a sort of non-Eastern who was "of clear and critical outlook" (etc. etc.) "almost Western,"[*bijna Westers*]. (Du Perron's Introduction to Suwarsih's novel; Suwarsih Djojopuspito, *Buiten het Gareel*, p. 8.) Another of the group, Javanese Soejitno Mangoenkoesoemo, became almost notorious (later) among his fellow Javanese for his disrespect towards such consecrated Javanese values as "Borobudur, Arjunawiwaha, Panji tales, etc." and for his conviction that the "West could give us at the moment much more than that." See for example Soejitno Mangoenkoesoemo in *Kritiek en Opbouw*, March 16, 1939, pp. 41–42.

[138] Sukarno is, for instance, described as "from Surabaya" in "Van der Plas Report 1927– 1928," *Secret Verbaal*, May 1, 1928 Ir C9. On Sukarno's speeches in Indonesian being translated into Sundanese during some meetings of the Indonesian National Party see report on Madjalaja meeting in *PPO* October 1928 (Poeze, ed., *Politiek-politioneele overzichten*, 1: 438); Sukarno's second wife was Sundanese and she devoted most of her time to helping Sukarno in his political career.

[139] H. Colijn, *Koloniale vraagstukken van heden en morgen* (Amsterdam: De Standaard, 1928), pp. 59–60.

[140] Ibid., *passim*. On Colijn's administrative reform proposals along those lines see Harry J. Benda, *Continuity and Change in Southeast Asia* (New Haven: Yale University Press, 1972), pp. 246–47.

[141] According to a secret Dutch analysis of 1927 there were "two facts of importance for fighting revolutionary propaganda" in West Java, particularly in Bandung. The first was the aristocratic origin of the nationalist leaders; the second was the fact "that the top and even the second-echelon leadership almost exclusively consists either of the Javanese or of the Minangkabau." "Van der Plas Report 1927–1928," *Secret Verbaal*, May 1, 1928 IrC9. Another internal Dutch report, a year later, considered Sukarno's all-Indonesian PPPKI federation as "about to fall under Javanese domination."Van der Plas Report 1928," *Secret Mail Report* 1928, no. 1083. According to the same report, the most influential activists in the PPPKI were *echte Javanen*, "thorough Javanese," two of the "thorough" Javanese listed were 'Tjokroaminoto and Sukarno"; "the Sumatrans," the report added, "are completely ignored"; ibid. Some important streams of the youth movement, too, were found—at the same time and by Dutch observers again—to be "Great-Javanist"; e.g., G. F. Pijper's Report on the Jong Java Congress," *Secret Mail Report* 1928, no. 619.

ously. More frequently than before, the *Batovis* theater now presented *tableaux vivants* on *persamaan soekoe*, "the unity of ethnic groups."[142] Efforts to push the Indonesians back into separation one from another, as Javanese, Sundanese, or Sumatrans, Sjahrir wrote in his journal in August 1927, were a mischievous, *divide-et-impera* plot—a deceit typical of *colijnialism*.[143]

"With the Indonesian National Party we are going to spread the idea of unity through the whole of Indonesia," a young author, possibly Sjahrir himself, wrote in Pemoeda Indonesia in mid-1928.[144] Pemoeda Indonesia applauded a broad federation of Indonesian nationalist organizations (the Permoefakatan Perhimpoenan2 Politik Kebangsaan Indonesia, PPPKI), put together by Sukarno primarily, in Bandung again, in December 1927.[145] A week after the birth of the PPPKI, a Pemoeda Indonesia congress was held in Bandung, with Sukarno attending, and Sjahrir as the congress chairman. National unity was the main theme.[146]

The next month, delegates of *Jong Java*, a Javanese youth organization, and Jong Islamieten Bond, an organization of Moslem youth from Sumatra, attended a Pemoeda Indonesia meeting, again to work out the idea of unity. Pemoeda Indonesia took the initiative, and Sukarno's actions were clearly a model. In opposition to Colijn's statements, various regional youth organizations were to be merged into one all-national body.[147]

On March 10, 1928, Sjahrir is on record as presiding over still another meeting of Pemoeda Indonesia with the same aim.[148] At a meeting on April 23, 1929—it was the time of final exams at the AMS, and this is perhaps why Sjahrir is not mentioned in the records—Pemoeda Indonesia and another youth organization, Pemoeda Sumatra, decided to merge.[149]

This unity was articulated in "flat" Indonesian. It was a unity happening in the sphere in-between, mostly on the stage or in the classroom. It was a brightly costumed unity as it was a brightly costumed revolution. Debates, indeed, mostly took place in schools, and political meetings as a rule took place in movie theaters.

---

[142] Interview with Hamdani, Jakarta, October 30, 1987.

[143] *Jong Indonesie* 2 (August 1927) (an article by 'Rumondor'). On J. E. Stokvis warning "against the desires of Colijn who wishes for territorial representative bodies and thus a splintering of popular Indonesian influence" see Erik Hansen, "The Dutch East Indies and the Reorientation of Dutch Social Democracy, 1929–1940," *Indonesia* 23 (April 1977): 70.

[144] S.S. (Soetan Sjahrir?) in *Pemoeda Indonesia* 1, 10–12 (May–August 1928), in *Overzicht van de IMC Pers* 1928, 2: 44.

[145] See, e.g., the *Pemoeda Indonesia* meeting of February 18, 1928 with speeches excerpted in *PPO*, February 1928 (Poeze, ed., *Politiek-politioneele overzichten*, 1: 247).

[146] On the Pemoeda Indonesia Congress see the report in *PPO* December 1927 (Poeze, ed., *Politiek-politioneele overzichten*, 1: 192); on Pemoeda Indonesia as the pivot of the youth-unifying efforts see, e.g., *PPO* January 1928 (Poeze, ed., *Politiek-politioneele overzichten*,1: 232).

[147] This was a January meeting in Batavia and another followed in February in Bandung; *PPO* February 1928 (Poeze, ed., *Politiek-politioneele overzichten*, 1: 248–49).

[148] Ibid.; see also Blumberger, *De nationalistische beweging*, pp. 393–94.

[149] *Pemoeda Indonesia* 1, 2–3 (September–October 1928) in *Overzicht van de IMC Pers*, 1928, 2: 298; *PPO* December 1928, in Poeze, ed., *Politiek-politioneele overzichten*, 1: 495–96; Blumberger, *De nationalistische beweging*, p. 394. On the Weltevreden April meeting see *Pemoeda Indonesia* 3, 1 (April–May 1929) in *Overzicht van de IMC Pers* 1929, 2: 20); nobody from Bandung is mentioned as officially present. Also *PPO* December 1929 (Poeze, ed., *Politiek-politioneele overzichten*, 2: 271–72). See also *Soeara Pemoeda Mataram* 1, September 4, 1929, p. 3.

The Pemoeda Indonesia and Pemoeda Sumatra merger took place just when Sjahrir was about to graduate from AMS. Early in May, he did so, and his *rantau* widened still further. In June 1929, Sjahrir packed some woollens, stopped for a while to see the now almost empty "house one may point to" in Medan, visited Kota Gedang for a day or two, and boarded a ship bound for Holland.

3

HOLLAND, 1929-1931

> Nothing much was strange to me when I came to Holland, and the first months were a continuous remembering.
>
> Sjahrir 1937[1]

1. Amsterdam and Leiden

Sjahrir reached Holland sometime late in the summer of 1929.

> The climate and society there can enervate us easily. The life behind the walls, in these stuffy rooms, the restlessness among this people, all this works on us excessively.[2]

This was not a complaint, but a piece of advice Sjahrir wrote to his younger brother later, after experiencing Holland for two years. It was a warning against what might happen if one came to Holland unprepared. "He flowered in the climate of the West," a man who knew him intimately in Holland wrote about Sjahrir during those two years.[3] Sjahrir seemed to pass from the Indies to Holland even more easily than he had passed from Medan to Bandung. "Nothing much was strange to me when I came to Holland," he himself wrote, "and the first months were a continuous remembering."[4]

As had been his family's wish, Sjahrir registered at the faculty of law at the University of Amsterdam.[5] Sjahrir's sea fare, in all probability, had been paid by his father. And—as in Bandung—Sjahrir had a female relative awaiting him in Holland. Sjahrizal Djoehana, the sister whom Sjahrir's mother had always told to take care of the boy, had lived in Amsterdam for a year when Sjahrir arrived. She had come with her husband, who had won a state scholarship to upgrade his "native" diploma and

---

[1] Sjahrazad (Sjahrir), *Indonesische Overpeinzingen* (Amsterdam: De Bezige Bij, 1945) (hereafter IO), August 28, 1937.

[2] Ibid., April 20, 1934.

[3] Salomon Tas, "Souvenirs of Sjahrir," *Indonesia* 8 (October 1969): 136.

[4] IO August 28, 1937.

[5] This was Gemeentelijk Universiteit in Amsterdam according to "Dossier Sjahrir" in *Archief Proc Gen*, no. 262; thus also in "Riwajat Hidup Soetan Sjahrir," n.d., n.p. typescript in the *Archives Siti Wahjunah Sjahrir*.

was taking courses—at the University of Amsterdam, too—in surgery and gynecology.[6]

Medical students were an especially well-established Indies group in Holland. They received one of the highest paying state scholarships. Their homes, large and well-equipped as a rule, were gathering places for the larger Indies community in Holland. The Djoehanas lived in a recently built "skyscraper" in a middle class neighborhood of South Amsterdam. There were many visitors, and there were many opportunities for Sjahrir to meet influential Indies people who might open the door wider into Holland.[7]

A Dutch visitor, a student of Indology, described the spirit of the Djoehanas' apartment shortly after Sjahrir arrived in Holland:

> I soon understood why it was [Sjahrir's] sister who had rented the flat. I was confronted in real life with what I had till then known from books: the tradition of the Minangkabau matriarchate, which places property right in the hands of the female line. Sjahrir's sister, as small and beautiful as he—but in whose face her character had drawn a harsher line—ruled not only over her husband, a gifted physician, but over everyone in the extended family who came within her reach ... my visit occasioned a small panic, which manifested itself in much giggling and slamming of doors.... In the end I was directed to a room which Sjahrir identified as his own but which seemed to me intended for multiple use. He made the statement, to be sure, with a smile that had more self-depreciation than embarrassment in it.[8]

Sjahrir's sister much later told me a story, which, no doubt, the guests at the apartment, and in Sjahrir's presence, also must have heard many times: Sjahrir had come to Holland as "a helper" for the family; each of the Indies doctors under a government scholarship had been permitted to take one "helper" with him on the trip. She further told me that Sjahrir had never actually studied at the university; he had "just moved around." She had carefully screened Sjahrir's friends and had suggested her own favorites as Sjahrir's companions, but—as she said—she could not do everything.[9]

From the Djoehanas' apartment, Sjahrir explored Holland, moving in wider and wider circles. Sometimes he was away for a night, sometimes for a week. His nephew Aki Djoehana, at that time four years old, remembers how, going to the bathroom at night, he occasionally stumbled over Sjahrir "bivouacking" on the kitchen floor, with a friend or two.[10] Soon after Sjahrir came to Holland, his father died, and thus the most significant source of financial support for Sjahrir dried up. There are some re-

---

[6] Interview with Sjahrizal Djoehana, Bandung, March 7, 1982; for R. Moehammad Djoehana Wiradikarta listed in the University files see Harsja W. Bachtiar, "The Development of a Common National Consciousness among Students from the Indonesian Archipelago in the Netherlands," *Majalah Ilmu-Ilmu Sastra Indonesia*, 6, 2 (May 1976): 34 n.

[7] Interviews with Maria Ullfah Subadio, Jakarta, March 4, 1982; and with Sjahrizal Djoehana, Bandung, March 7, 1982.

[8] Tas, "Souvenirs of Sjahrir," p. 136.

[9] Interviews with Sjahrizal Djoehana, Bandung, March 7, 1982; the helper preferably was to be a relative. Also interview with Maria Ullfah, Jakarta, March 4, 1982—one of Sjahrizal's favorites, whom Sjahrir also liked.

[10] Interview with M. A. Djoehana, Prague, August 17, 1983.

ports, even, that support from his father ceased earlier, as the old *jaksa* was disappointed by his son's way of life in Holland, his politics in particular.[11] Early in 1931, Dr. Djoehana finished his courses and the family returned to the Indies. Sjahrir was free at last! And he had virtually no money left.[12]

There were three mail deliveries per week between Java and Holland at that time; letters and journals took only five days to arrive. The names of the streets were almost the same in Amsterdam as in Bandung. Modern buildings, also, were *art nouveau* and functionalist, some with traces of *Bauhaus*.

The students from the Indies might be called *"Hoi, pinda Chinees,"* "peanut Chinaman" or *"niger,"* "negro," on the street but that was a "lower-class vulgarity" or something done by "naughty children," and it did not get under one's skin much.[13] There was *Tehuis voor Indische studenten,* "Home for Indies Students," in The Hague, funded by Ministry for Colonies, for those who needed some help. Not many did need it, Mohammad Hatta commented later. Hatta also described the institution:

> Anybody who ever stayed in this home will admit how spoiled we Netherlands Indies students actually were. Board including three meals a day was only three guilders. There was always rice for the evening meal and fried rice for lunch on Sundays. For the other meals we had bread like the Dutch.[14]

According to a friend of Sjahrir at the time, a Dutchman,

> The racism that was characteristic of colonial relations in the Netherlands Indies and which was an unavoidable consequence of the power relationship there—for a tiny minority had to keep an overwhelming majority under its thumb—found little echo in the Netherlands itself.[15]

It was a racism of a subtler kind. The fashion and food of the Indies invaded Holland during the early twentieth century. *Rijsttafel*, a dish of tropical ingredients arranged on plates with a colonial opulence, almost became a national meal in Holland. There were traditional Indies textiles called by a hybrid Dutch-Malay name—*dubbel ikat*—adorning the walls of the Dutch salons, side by side with Dutch paintings of windmills or of the North Sea. The imposing building of the Colonial Institute in Amsterdam was just three years old when Sjahrir arrived. On Sundays, "sweet" *gamelan* music was performed, or "more dynamic" *rabana-pupui*.

In a matter of days after his arrival in Amsterdam, Sjahrir wrote to a student organization in the city—the Sociaal Democratische Studenten Club, "Social Democratic Students' Club"—asking for information about the youth movement. When he received Sjahrir's letter, the club's chairman, Salomon Tas, as he recalls, jumped on his bike and went to "look him up."[16] Sjahrir and Tas became friends easily, and, after the Djoehanas left, Sjahrir moved to Tas' small house nearby. There they lived,

---

[11] Attorney General to Governor General, May 3, 1948 in *Archief Proc Gen*, no. 262.

[12] Interview with Sjahrizal Djoehana, Bandung, March 7, 1982.

[13] Interview with Maria Ullfah, Jakarta, March 4, 1982.

[14] Hatta, *Indonesian Patriot*, p. 62.

[15] Tas, "Souvenirs of Sjahrir," pp. 136–37.

[16] Ibid.; see also Salomon Tas, *Wat mij betreft* (Baarn: Ten Hare, 1970), p. 148.

Sal Tas with his wife Maria Duchâteau and their two small children, Maria's friend Judith, and Sjahrir.[17]

Salomon Tas was a baker's son, of modest origins, but a cultured man with an interest in literature, music, and politics. He was a graduate of the very good Dutch secondary modern HBS school, as were also Maria and Judith. A fifth member of the intimate circle, Jos Riekerk, a Eurasian born in the Indies, had an advanced elementary school MULO diploma from Padang, West Sumatra, and an HBS diploma, also, from Amsterdam.[18]

It was still largely a school-defined community. Sjahrir's Indies colonial "ethical" secondary school AMS was not thought of as any different from the Dutch HBS. Years later, Tas was still convinced that Sjahrir was an HBS graduate, like the rest of the group.[19] They thought of Sjahrir as an equal: "He laughed a good deal," Tas wrote,

> but it was not the laugh of so many Indonesians, an expression of shyness, a barrier against the need to reply. Sjahrir was open, direct . . . his temperament came to its natural maturation [in Holland]. I never found in him anything which resembled the "stereotype" of the "Oriental mentality." He was direct, hated circumlocution and stood uninhibitedly open to the ideas of others.[20]

Sjahrir went out each night, with Sal, Maria, Judith—and Jos Riekerk sometimes—to a café, a theater, a concert, or a political meeting. There were other people around of the largely artistic *avant-garde* community. Another Eurasian, namely, the painter Salim—born near Medan half a year after Sjahrir, an adopted child in a planter's family—had lived in Holland from the age of twelve and was a graduate of the Gymnasium in Arnhem.[21] There were others, going to the *Tuschinski* movie house, to the *Stadsschouwburg* municipal theater, meeting in the bar *Americain* or in the popular restaurant *Bohemien* on the Lange Leidse Dwaarstraat, where, reportedly, Sal Tas' Social Democratic Students' Club had been founded.[22]

Occasionally, Sjahrir seemed even faster than the rest. "I lost track of Sjahrir for some time," Tas remembered,

> later I gathered from his stories that he, in search of radical comradeship, had wandered further and further left, coming to rest at last with a handful of anarchists, who had managed to keep themselves free of all capitalist taint

---

[17] Interview with Judith, who later became Tas' wife, The Hague, October 25, 1983; interview with Jos Riekerk, Utrecht, October 15, 1983.

[18] Tas, *Wat mij betreft, passim*; interview with Jos Riekerk, Utrecht, October 15, 1983; J. de Kadt, *Politieke Herinneringen van een randfiguur* (Amsterdam: van Oorschot, 1976), pp. 90–91, 131; interview with Judith Tas, The Hague, October 25, 1983.

[19] Tas, *Wat mij betreft*, p. 148.

[20] Tas, "Souvenirs of Sjahrir, p. 136.

[21] Interview with Salim, Paris, February 2, 1988; L. P. J. Braat, ed., "De brieven van Soeleiman," *De vrije Katheder* 6, 1 (May 3, 1946), pp. 1–3; Yazir Marzuki, *Pelukis Salim* (Jakarta: Djambatan, 1983), p. 51. I heard also of Salim being very much a part of Sjahrir's circle at the time in an interview with Maria Duchâteau-Sjahrir, Lorques, February 13, 1988.

[22] D. de Vries, "Twee vaderlanden," *Orientatie* 5 (February 1948): 22–23.

Jef Last
Painting by P. A. Berger in Letterkundig Museum, The Hague

by avoiding any profitable work, and who survived by sharing everything with each other except for tooth brushes (insofar as there were any) but including contraceptives. He re-emerged from this rather quickly and without damage, and afterwards his interest in socialism took more practical form.[23]

Sjahrir was still a debater rather than a diligent student. His systematic course work at the university "soon petered out."[24] His sister was probably right about this. Politics, even more than in Bandung, were part of Sjahrir's moving fast and keeping loose.

One source suggests that in Amsterdam, and implicitly under Sal Tas' influence, Sjahrir's vague, "social" ideas changed into a more distinct "socialist" conviction.[25] Sal Tas qualifies what kind of change it might be:

> Against the vague, sentimental, ethical views which were then current in Dutch social-democracy in the guise of "religious socialism," we placed the clear courageous, virile—and naturally scientific!—teaching of historical, dialectical materialism. Viewed from the present, it was a bit of Friedrich Engels dressed up as Cyrano de Bergerac—what a fine time we had![26]

The Tas group, the Social Democratic Students' Club, was a youth organization loosely attached to the mainstream Dutch Social Democratic Labor Party, the SDAP. The student group published its own journal, *De Socialist*, and Tas' portrayal of its views were often reflected in the journal's pages. Except that the young radicals were not completely free of "ethical" and "religious socialism" either. The compassionate *Tante Jet*, "Aunt Jet," Henriette Roland Holst, was as influential among the *De Socialist* group as she had been among the students in the Indies.[27] Exoticism also flourished. A prominent member of the group, Jef Last, a poet, and later Sjahrir's friend, too, defined his socialist ideal as the "socialism of the kind-hearted lady *Boddhisattva Kwan-yin*"—the creed of those who "refuse to enter *nirvana* as long as the last man is in grief and wanders in grief through the world," or as socialism of "wrathful Buddhas."[28]

Sjahrir, according to Tas, was one of the "very few among us" who took the trouble not just to talk about socialism but "really to study it." Among Sjahrir's reading at the time Hilferding is listed with Rosa Luxemburg, Karl Kautsky, Otto Bauer, Hendrik de Man, and, of course, Marx and Engels.[29] In order to find out more about socialism—and to make some money, no doubt—Sjahrir, went as far as to attempt real labor union work. The job was with the secretariat of the International Transport Workers' Federation (ITWF).[30] Even this was not wholly real, actually. There was no

---

[23] Tas, "Souvenirs of Sjahrir, pp. 139–40.

[24] Ibid; see also *Het Nieuws van den Dag*, February 27, 1934 in *Collection Gobbée* no. 37.

[25] Tijmstra, "Zoeklicht op Sjahrir."

[26] Tas, "Souvenirs of Sjahrir, p. 139.

[27] See, e.g., article on *Tante Jet*, Henriette Roland Holst in *De Socialist* [Amsterdam], January 3, 1930. (On *Tante Jet* see above chap. 2, n. 121.)

[28] Jef Last, "Wij zijn niet anders," *De Nieuwe Weg* [Amsterdam] May 1930, p. 133.

[29] Tas, "Souvenirs of Sjahrir, p. 139.

[30] Tijmstra says, instead of or besides the ITWF, Sjahrir worked for Metaalbewerkersbond, the Union of Steelworkers. Tijmstra, "Zoeklicht op Sjahrir."

daily routine in the ITWF. The Federation was also absorbed in high-flown and rather abstract politics. Its "radical Marxist" chairman Edo Fimmen, a man also very close to the Social Democratic Students' Club, was

> a Danton-figure with a Beethovenesque visage and hairstyle but with the gentle temper of a Salvation Army recruit.... Fimmen had in fact belonged to the Salvation Army in his youth, and he remained a part of it at heart his whole life long.[31]

Tas describes Sjahrir's socialism at the time as an urge "to embrace all humanity, above all the common people, or at least the workers"; it was a "spiritual plunge into the proletariat," Tas says, a "pure pilgrimage."[32]

There were striking similarities to Bandung—to Pemoeda Indonesia, Patriae Scientiaeque, and the *Batovis* theater, and to Tjahja Volksuniversiteit. Maria Ullfah, an Indies student in Leiden at the time, who met Sjahrir at the Djoehanas' apartment, remembers how Sjahrir took her to a lecture by Jef Last in a movie theater in Leiden, and how, after this ("to enjoy the universal language of music," Sjahrir explained to her), they went to a *Volksconcert*, "People's Concert," where classical music was performed for Dutch workers. Another time he took her to theater matinées, where working-class children were the directors, writers, and actors; *The Merchant of Venice*, Maria Ullfah recalls, was one of the plays they saw. Other days they went to Volkshuizen, she says, "People's Clubs,"

> where young workers and workers' children improved their knowledge and skills in classes of English and of other languages, as well as in courses in sewing and in dramatic arts.[33]

There were picnics, too. So called "Socialist Weekends" were organized by *De Socialist* journal. Young people—a multiracial community on principle—went to Amersfort, Arnhem, Assen, or to Kijkduin on the sea. There were debates at the Café Bellevue and camping in the dunes. On a Kijkduin weekend, for instance, at the end of the summer of 1929—just after Sjahrir's arrival—a "stylized fight dance" was performed by Roesbandi, Sjahrir's friend from Bandung and a former member of Jong Indonesie and Patriae Scientiaeque, dancing with Abdoelmadjid, a future leader of the Indonesian Communist Party. There was another dance that weekend, a dance creation by one Florrie Rodrigo, nationality unspecified: "With each next move," as *De Socialist* reported,

> the dancer liberated her art from the bourgeois individualism which has dominated dance through the capitalist era. She danced as if in a quest, and she reached close to a new form of art, to new potentialities of expression which are based on the value of labor. This gave her dance a proletarian and a revolutionary character.[34]

---

[31] Tas, "Souvenirs of Sjahrir," p. 140.

[32] Ibid., p. 139.

[33] Maria Ullfah Subadio, "Bung Sjahrir" in *Mengenang Sjahrir*, ed. Anwar, pp. 92–93; also interview with Maria Ullfah, Jakarta, March 4, 1982.

[34] *De Socialist*, October 5, 1929, p. 5; on Abdoelmadjid, see Anderson, *Java in a Time of Revolution*, pp. 411–12.

At the time Jef Last published a series of small books of poetry with titles such as *Partai Komoenis Indonesia, Digoel-Wilhelmina,* and *De poenale sanctie,* on the Indonesian Communist Party, on the first internment camp, Boven Digul, in the Indies, where the Communists were sent, and on the exploitation of coolies on the plantations in Sumatra. Each of the booklets was sold for only ten cents, "so that the poor can buy it."[35] There was virtually not one issue of *De Socialist* where the problem of the Indies was not very visibly present.

Naturally, the group denounced everything which smelled of "colonialism." To "ethical colonialism," the young people were especially sensitive. "First of all," *De Socialist* wrote in October 1929,

> it is neither philanthropic nor "ethical" motives, that make us stand on the side of the Indonesians and make us support their struggle.[36]

"Ethically romantic methods," Jef Last wrote, should be rejected. This was in the same article in which he proposed his Kwan-yin and angry Buddha socialism instead.[37]

Sjahrir's closest friends among the Dutch knew the Indies from textbooks. Many of them were "Indologists," studying some subject or other concerning the Indies at a Dutch university.[38] Both Jos Riekerk and Sal Tas, when Sjahrir was in Holland, studied "Indies law" at the University of Leiden. Sjahrir himself, after the Djoehanas left, switched his highly irregular studies to Leiden and also to Indies law.[39]

Leiden was just an hour by train from Amsterdam. Compared with Amsterdam—and not unlike Bandung compared with Batavia—it was a proud place pushed towards being provincial. It was also a college town where teachers and students were the elite. The Direct bookshop, on Leiden's Brijstraat, the main avenue of the town, displayed the widest imaginable choice of exotic Oriental, colonial Indies, and nationalist Indonesian literature.[40] The famous Leiden School of Indology, the cradle of the most noble and authoritative "ethical" thought at the turn of the century, was still the town's jewel.

"It was disastrous," Bernhard Dahm wrote,

> that at this time the School of Leiden—Snouck Hurgronje, van Vollenhoven, Hazeu, and others—could exert no influence on policy in the colony. The warning by these leading authorities on Indonesia against underestimating the [Indonesian nationalist] movement, and their proposals of greater concessions to the Indonesians, accomplished only one thing: the establishment

---

[35] Reviews of the books are in *Indonesia Merdeka* (Perhimpoenan Indonesia) 8, 3 (May 1930): 54.

[36] *De Socialist*, October 5, 1929.

[37] Last, "Wij zijn niet anders," p. 135.

[38] J. de Kadt, "Sjahrir: Poging tot plaatsbepaling. Benevens een paar persoonlijke herinneringen," *Tirade* May 1966, p. 464.

[39] Sjahrizal Djoehana says "maybe." Jos Riekerk felt that Sjahrir enrolled "perhaps." Given the Dutch system, Sjahrir might quite easily have enrolled and felt free to be as diligent as he wanted until the first *tentamen* examination, which usually did not take place before the second year of study. The *tentamen*, all interviewed agree, Sjahrir never took. Interviews with Sjahrizal Djoehana, Bandung, March 7, 1982; Jos Riekerk, Utrecht, October 15, 1983; Judith Tas, The Hague, October 25, 1983.

[40] Maria Ullfah Subadio, "Bung Sjahrir," p. 92.

of a Faculty of Indology at Utrecht, in obvious competition with Leiden. In this way, business circles sought to prevent the influence of the School of Leiden from becoming too great in the colony . . . this was the voice of those who made policy.[41]

Ch. Snouck Hurgronje, C. van Vollenhoven, and G. A. J. Hazeu were still teaching in Leiden when Sjahrir registered. The venerable professors were increasingly alienated from the colonial mainstream. They were ridiculed as dreamers. "The gentlemen of the Leiden Faculty of Indology see apparitions," M. W. F. Treub, a very influential colonial expert of the time wrote, "and if those are something more than apparitions, then they are the children of their own imagination."[42]

The "ethical" professors of Leiden were immersed in "native cultures" so deeply that sometimes even their Dutch acquired a distinctly foreign accent.[43] They moved through the space in-between. And even the most venerable among them were frustrated. Snouck Hurgronje, for instance, wrote in 1928 about "Father" Colijn almost as bitterly as Sjahrir's *Pemoeda Indonesia* did in Bandung—and as the young socialists in Holland did.[44] The same professor lectured in Leiden at that time:

> As long as our system is not radically changed, as long as we keep on manifesting that we are not prepared ever to end our rule, so long will the evil remain undiminished, men be made into our enemies, and Digoel [internment camp in New Guinea] remain the only tool of our policy.[45]

Sjahrir's friend Jos Riekerk went to the Leiden School of Indology because it was cheaper than the College of Engineering in Delft which, originally, he would have preferred. But once in Leiden, he decided to become a progressive official in the colony. He graduated from Leiden in 1931 and served in the Indies during the following decade. He served well, "with heart and spirit," as Sjahrir later wrote; he was one of those, in Sjahrir's words,

> who believe that their ideals are realistic, and that there [in the Indies], in colonial policy, there is still a place for their moral ideals.[46]

Riekerk's writings in *De Socialist* during 1930 prove how Marxist and anti-colonialist he believed himself to be[47]—and how he believed that his radicalism went "morally" well with his mission. It was Riekerk, most probably, who convinced Sal

---

[41] Dahm, *Sukarno*, p. 92; a similar view is given by H. Feddema and O. D. van den Muijzenberg, "Was de Utrechtse Indologie-opleiding een petroleumfaculteit?" *Amsterdam sociologisch tijdschrift* 3, 1977, pp. 465–77.

[42] M. W. F. Treub quoted in Dahm, *Sukarno*, p. 92. On Treub's prominence in the Utrecht versus Leiden controversy see Feddema and van den Muijzenberg, "Was de Utrechtse Indologie-opleiding een petroleumfaculteit?" pp. 105–18.

[43] E.g., Hatta, *Indonesian Patriot*, p. 91.

[44] C. Snouck Hurgronje, *Colijn over Indië* (Amsterdam: Becht, 1928).

[45] Quoted in Bouman, *Enige Beschouwingen*, p. 99.

[46] IO July 8, 1937.

[47] See, for instance, Riekerk's letter to the journal in "Discussie rubriek," *De Socialist*, January 24, 1930, p. 7.

Tas also to enroll in Leiden Indology. And when Tas did not have money for the school, Riekerk took him to the most eminent "ethical" professor, van Vollenhoven: the professor reportedly arranged for the young socialist Sal Tas to study Indies law for free.[48]

Sal Tas spent two years in classes in Leiden and got as far as his preliminary (*tentamen*) examination. Throughout the time Sjahrir was there, Sal Tas also wanted to be a progressive colonial official. He later (in 1932) left the school, not because he lost confidence in his radical-socialist progressive-official vision, but because he came to the conclusion that "the reactionary colonial government, as developed now," would not give him the job.[49]

Sjahrir made his way to Indies law in Leiden primarily through these two friends. The textbooks which Jos Riekerk had used first, and then Sal Tas, went to Sjahrir. At the same time, Indies law in Leiden was a natural next step. Bandung AMS was designed as a stepping stone for an Indies law career. This also was what Sjahrir's father, if still alive, might have liked to see. Except that Sjahrir was a bit too fast and a bit too loose. Jos Riekerk told me that he did not know if Sjahrir ever read the textbooks he had borrowed from him: "It was difficult to keep track of him," Riekerk said. And because I too was evidently trying to keep track of Sjahrir, the old man looked at me as if I might help:

> Many of the books Sjahrir did not return at all. At my post on Sumba island, I still was bombarded by notes, recalls from the University Library in Leiden asking me either to return the books, or to pay the fines. And the books are not back yet![50]

2. Perhimpoenan Indonesia

Mohammad Hatta was born in 1902 in Aur Tanjungkang, on the outskirts of Bukittinggi, West Sumatra. His family home stood on a street carrying today the name of Sutan Sjahrir. Hatta's father was a prominent Minangkabau *ulama*, a Moslem scholar; there were some almost saints in Hatta's ancestry, as well as merchants famed for the wealth they had amassed in *rantau*, the fringes, the outward regions.[51] Hatta attended ELS, European Lower School, and the advanced primary school, MULO, in West Sumatra. He graduated from Prins Hendrik School—from its commerce section—in Batavia. While still in Sumatra, he read a lot of Heinrich Heine, "who apparently had quite an impact on me," he said; once he wrote a patriotic-religious sonnet himself.[52] At Prins Hendrik School, Mohammad Hatta became active in politics and served as the treasurer of the student Jong Soematranen Bond, "Young Sumatrans' Union."

Hatta's studies were financed by a distant relative, "uncle" Max Etek Ayub, a Minangkabau merchant living in Batavia, who liked to be called the "first Indonesian broker." It was Max Etek Ayub who gave Hatta the six-volume *De Socialisten* by H. P.

---

[48] Interview with Jos Riekerk, Utrecht, October 15, 1983.

[49] Interview with Judith Tas and Jos Meyers, The Hague, October 25 and 12, 1983.

[50] Interview with Jos Riekerk, Utrecht, October 15, 1983.

[51] Hatta, *Indonesian Patriot*, p. 5; Rasjid, "Bung Hatta" in *Muhammad Hatta*, ed. Swasono, p. 207; Abdullah, *Schools and Politics*, pp. 169–70.

[52] Hatta, *Indonesian Patriot*, p. 80; the sonnet mentioned can be found in A. Teeuw, *Modern Indonesian Literature*, vol. 1 (The Hague: Nijhoff, 1967), p. 11.

Quack, an opus which Hatta says also influenced him strongly. In 1921, a group of Minangkabau merchants around "uncle" Max Etek Ayub provided five hundred guilders to send Hatta to study in Holland. Additional money came via the prominent "ethical" socialist J. E. Stokvis, who helped the young Sumatran student to the "Van Deventer Foundation." (Van Deventer, as the reader may recall from the first chapter, was the "Father of the Ethical System.") Stokvis, Hatta wrote, "gave me some advice on how to study and what to do besides, like going frequently to see theaters, operas, concerts, etc." Mohammad Hatta took some money also from a Dutch branch of the Theosophical Society, a New York founded eclectic church preaching the unity of Eastern and Western beliefs; this debt, Hatta says, he did not repay till 1952.[53]

In 1929, when Sjahrir arrived in Holland, Hatta had been there for eight years and was still a student at the "Business School" in Rotterdam. By 1929, Hatta was already a man well known in the Dutch world of politics, even a celebrity of a sort. He was the chairman of Perhimpoenan Indonesia, "Indonesian Association," a Holland-based organization of patriotic students from the Indies. With several other leaders of the association, Hatta was accused in 1928 of subversive activity against the colonial government. The students stood trial and, to the great acclaim of liberal and socialist circles in Holland, were acquitted. Hatta later described the event as displaying the fair attitude of the Dutch and the correctness of the Dutch legal system. It was another experience that, according to his biographer, "made a profound impression on Hatta personally."[54]

Hatta in 1929 was a man increasingly restless to get his degree finally, and to return home. "At that time," Hatta remembers,

> I had made it clear that I was going to resign as chairman [of Perhimpoenan Indonesia].... And so I began to train new cadres to replace me, such as Abdullah Sukur, a law student who had passed his first stage examination ... he originally came from Ambon, Rusbandi, a law student at the University of Leiden, and Sutan Sjahrir.[55]

Under Hatta's auspices, Sjahrir moved through Perhimpoenan Indonesia as smoothly as he moved through the Dutch young socialists' world and through the university quarter in Leiden. In 1929, Hatta stepped aside, as he said he would, and Abdullah Soekoer "was duly elected."[56] At a meeting convened by Perhimpoenan Indonesia on February 4, 1930, just about half a year after he arrived in Holland, Sjahrir was already listed in a police report as the meeting's main speaker.[57] A fortnight later, he was elected secretary of Perhimpoenan Indonesia, the third highest position in the organization, with Roesbandi as chairman.[58] In May 1930, Roesbandi

---

[53] Hatta, *Memoir*, pp. 67–69, 84, 98–99; Hatta, *Indonesian Patriot*, pp. 86–87, 91.

[54] Mavis Rose, *Indonesia Free: A Political Biography of Mohammad Hatta* (Ithaca: Cornell Modern Indonesia Project, 1987), p. 43.

[55] Hatta, *Indonesian Patriot*, p. 125. According to *Indonesia Merdeka* (Perhimpoenan Indonesia), Hatta's process of leaving the leadership already began early in 1929.

[56] Hatta, *Indonesian Patriot*, p. 127. On the elections see also *PPO* February 1929 (Poeze, ed., *Politiek-politioneele overzichten*, 2: 58).

[57] *PPO* February 1930 (Poeze, ed., *Politiek-politioneele overzichten*, 2: 296, 317)

[58] *PPO* March 1930 (Poeze, ed., *Politiek-politioneele overzichten*, 2: 336).

Leiden University

resigned, and Sjahrir became, in Perhimpoenan Indonesia, a man second only to the new association's chairman.[59]

There were hardly two more different characters among the Indonesians in Holland than Hatta and Sjahrir. As in Bandung, Sjahrir was known for his "swift dippings into science";[60] Hatta was "studious."[61] Yet, besides their both being freedom fighters, naturally there was a strong, classroom kind of affinity between them—an understanding based on their both having graduated from the same Dutch-colonial "ethical" schools in the Indies, an understanding deepened by their both advancing, now, to the top of the Dutch colonial "ethical" educational system, in Holland itself.

There was another affinity between Hatta and Sjahrir. Both had exceedingly uncertain relations with home. Sjahrir's father was dead, and there is no report of any significant support still coming to Sjahrir from his family. Hatta felt an obligation to his family, a debt to be paid to his "uncle" especially, much more strongly than Sjahrir did. Still, like Sjahrir, Hatta clearly believed that for a young man of the Indies, late in the 1920s, being modern was equal almost to being fatherless. "To the sons is left the choice," Hatta said in a speech in 1928, either to join the nationalist cause, or

---

[59] *Indonesia Merdeka* (Perhimpoenan Indonesia) 8, 1–2 (January–February 1930): 30; ibid., 8, 5 (October 1930): 91. *PPO* June 1930 (Poeze, ed., *Politiek-politioneele overzichten*, 2: 403).

[60] Tas, "Souvenirs of Sjahrir," p. 143.

[61] Abutari in *Bung Hatta Mengabdi pada tjita-tjita Perdjoeangan Bangsa* (Jakarta: Panitia Peringatan Ulang Tahun Bung Hatta ke-70, 1972), p. 68

to imitate the fathers in their dull routine, comfortably and willingly and slavishly carrying out orders from above, renouncing the promotion of any ideals and only thinking of a career.[62]

There were some important Minangkabau friends around Hatta and Sjahrir in Holland. As Hatta promoted Sjahrir in Perhimpoenan Indonesia, so he himself, eight years earlier, had been promoted by another prominent Minangkabau student leader, Nazir Datoek Pamoentjak.[63] As at home, in Perhimpoenan Indonesia the Javanese and the Minangkabau were the two ethnic groups which clearly dominated politics. But what had been strong in Bandung seemed even stronger in Holland. "From the vantage point of Europe," a historian of Perhimpoenan Indonesia wrote,

> the particularistic, ethnic and regional differences that had once loomed large were now placed in a different perspective.[64]

To the patriots, the Indies appeared even more as one entity from afar. The distance felt in Holland made being Indonesian and speaking Indonesian even more categorical.

Perhimpoenan Indonesia was an elite organization—it apparently never had more than fifty members.[65] Any member of the association, when he returned home—a man exposed to Holland, and sometimes with a Dutch degree—was thought to be qualified to become a leader.

By the late 1920s, former members of Perhimpoenan Indonesia held leadership positions in Indonesian parties such as Boedi Oetomo, Sarekat Islam, or Sukarno's Indonesian National Party. The association's journal, *Indonesia Merdeka*, "Free Indonesia," was smuggled into the colony, and romantic stories are still eagerly retold of how the Dutch customs officers were tricked.[66] Hatta, out of the country for eight years, a name sounding from a distance—especially as it became known, in 1928, that he had been acquitted by the Dutch court—came close to equaling Sukarno himself in popularity. In April 1929, by a decision of the federation of nationalist parties PPPKI of which Sukarno's party was a prominent member, Perhimpoenan Indonesia was acknowledged as the "official and plenipotentiary representative" of the Indonesian movement abroad.[67]

It was still a loose network. Perhimpoenan Indonesia sounded strong in the Indies, in great part because its voice came from a distance.[68] What appeared as wis-

---

[62] Hatta's defense speech of 1928 quoted in Rose, *Indonesia Free*, p. 25.

[63] Hatta, *Indonesian Patriot*, pp. 62–63; Hatta, *Memoir*, p. 105.

[64] Ingleson, *Road to Exile*, p. 3.

[65] Bachtiar, "The Development." In August 1927, for instance, there were 109 students from the Indies in Holland, twenty of whom were members of Perhimpoenan Indonesia; see "Adviser to Students Annual Report," in *Verbaal*, August 17, 1927, no. 39. According to Rose, *Indonesia Free*, p. 50, "[Perhimpoenan Indonesia] membership had begun to decline in 1928 due to Dutch policies to upgrade the tertiary institutions in the Indies and to discourage Indonesians from studying in Europe." This might have made the association even more exclusive.

[66] Interview with Maria Ullfah, Jakarta, March 4, 1982.

[67] *PPO* March 1929 (Poeze, ed., *Politiek-politioneele overzichten*, 2: 64).

[68] Rose, *Indonesia Free*, p. 30 quotes Hatta's speech from 1927: "As the mountaineer, at the top of a hill, has a better view of the landscape than the people who live in that landscape, so the Indonesian students in Holland are in a better position to take a view of the colonial situation

dom might have often been judgement based on a lack of information. Hatta himself remembers how badly informed they, in Holland, had often been. He regularly read, he says, only one Indies journal, a Malay version of the Javanese *Darmo Kondo*. He did not receive even *Soeloeh Indonesia Moeda*, "Torch of Young Indonesia," a journal to which he occasionally contributed![69]

In the summer of 1929, just at the time of Sjahrir's arrival, the loose network was charged with a new vitality. Hadji Agoes Salim paid a long visit to Holland. The older son of the other Medan *hoofddjaksa*, Sjahrir's cousin, Hadji Agoes Salim was one of the most prominent Indonesian national leaders and one of the most impressive Minangkabau of the period.

Hadji Agoes Salim was already forty-five at the time and a respected leader of the nationalist movement in the Indies. He came to Europe, some time early in 1929, as a "technical adviser" to the Nederlandse Verbond van Vakvereenigingen, the "Netherlands Trade Union Federation." He attended an International Labor Organization conference in Geneva,[70] then came to Holland and spent a little less than a year there.[71] He met Dutch labor leaders during his visit, among them Edo Fimmen, Sjahrir's employer at the International Transport Workers' Federation.[72] Hadji Agoes Salim moved quickly through both the Dutch and the Indies worlds in Holland; he made public appearances, including several at Perhimpoenan Indonesia meetings.[73] He attended at least one of the young socialists' picnics and published a long two-part article in *De Socialist*.[74] It might have been Hadji Agoes Salim, actually, who introduced Sjahrir to Edo Fimmen, and Salim might have acted as Sjahrir's sponsor in Holland on other occasions as well. Sjahrir's articles in *De Socialist*, on the other hand, paid respect to Salim's political acuteness.[75]

---

than their countrymen, who lived under the colonial hypnosis." Compare with Hatta, *Memoir*, p. 244.

[69] Moh. Rasjid's interview with Hatta published in *Daulat Ra'jat* 2, 34 (August 20, 1934).

[70] On the mission see Salam Solichin, *Hadji Agus Salim: Hidup dan Perdjuangannja* (Jakarta: Djajamuri, 1961), p. 63. Ahmad Subarjo Djoyoadisuryo, *Kesadaran nasional; sebuah otobiografi* (Jakarta: Gunung Agung, 1978), p. 153 says Salim went to Europe in April 1929.

[71] In December 1929 Salim was back in Batavia. *PPO December 1929* (Poeze, ed., *Politiek-politioneele overzichten*, 2: 275.

[72] Salim was present at the NVV Labour Congress; see *PPO* October 1929 (Poeze, ed., *Politiek-politioneele overzichten*, 2: 244); on Salim meeting Fimmen see Attorney General to Governor-General, July 23, 1930 in *Secret Mail Report* 1930, no. 727.

[73] *PPO* October 1929 (Poeze, ed., *Politiek-politioneele overzichten*, 2: 241); ibid., November 1929 (Poeze, ed., *Politiek-politioneele overzichten*, 2: 260).

[74] *De Socialist*, October 10, 1929; ibid., October 19, 1929.

[75] One story that Sjahrir told Jef Last in Holland was about Sjahrir and some other of his Pemoeda Indonesia friends trying to disrupt one of Salim's speeches in Bandung by booing. Salim, Sjahrir told Last, reacted marvellously. He stopped in the middle, began to talk about how pleased he was that even sheep came to listen to patriotic speeches, sent the sheep to graze for a while while the speech would go on in the human language, but invited the sheep to come back and promised, as he was fortunately very gifted linguistically, that a special meeting would be organized in which he, Salim, would speak sheep language, too. "We did not leave," Sjahrir said to Last, but "blushed and listened till the end. We still did not agree with Salim in everything, but we never tried to boo him again," Sjahrir concluded. Jef Last, "In Memoriam," in *Seratus Tahun Haji Agus Salim*. ed. Hazil Tanzil, pp. 110–11; see also Jef Last, *Zo zag ik Indonesië*. (The Hague: van Hoeve, 1954), pp. 74–75.

Hadji Agoes Salim, while in Holland, worked hard to present Perhimpoenan Indonesia not just as the principal representative of the Indonesian movement abroad, but as *geestdrager*, "the inspirer," of the movement.[76] "There is a sufficient number of mature men in the association," Salim wrote,

> leaders who went abroad late enough in their lives, and who had lived in Indonesian society for a long enough time for neither them nor their association ever to become "uprooted." ... There is a real difference between Perhimpoenan Indonesia on one side, and the nationalist movement in Indonesia itself on the other side.... Perhimpoenan Indonesia, first of all, stands outside of the day-to-day political struggle, beyond immediate contact with the authorities of the government, justice, and police.... The greater freedom they enjoy here [in Holland], the impossibility, indeed, of practical action, allow them to manifest themselves more keenly and intensively than the parties back home ever can.... All that also leads to [Perhimpoenan Indonesia's] greater discipline.... Thus, we can safely state, that Perhimpoenan Indonesia serves the movement at home as a representative, as a reproducer and as a restorer.[77]

Hadji Agoes Salim thus emphasized the role of Perhimpoenan Indonesia as a force working on the fringes and from a distance. It was Mohammad Hatta, Salim reportedly repeated throughout his visit in Holland, who was "the man of the future ... of Indonesian nationalism, of the future Indonesian state."[78] According to a Dutch offficial back in Batavia who watched the Indonesian movement at the time very closely,

> Above all, and this is perhaps the most important element [of the present movement in the Indies], strong personal ties have developed between Mr. Salim and Mr. Hatta—both from Minangkabau, both by their inclinations ethical and yet, by their set up, of very critical minds, almost to the point of destructiveness....[79]

On December 29, 1929, while Salim was still in Holland, the colonial authorities in the Indies acted on their belief that the Indonesian nationalist movement had crossed the limits and was an intolerable danger to colonial law and order. Four top leaders of the Indonesian National Party, including Sukarno, were arrested in Bandung. The shock jolted the movement. Eleven days after the arrest, those party leaders who had not been arrested issued an order to the branches and to individual members of the Indonesian National Party to cease all political activity in the party's name.[80] The center of nationalist politics suddenly became hollow.

---

[76] Hadji Agoes Salim, "De Perhimpoenan Indonesia en de Indonesische Nationalistische Beweging," *De Socialist*, October 19, 1929, pp. 2ff.

[77] Ibid., p. 3.

[78] de Kadt, *Politieke Herinneringen*, p. 53.

[79] Kiewit de Jonge, "Inlandsche beweging op Java: Politieke mededeeling II (strictly personal), November 11, 1931, pp. 17–19; in *Collection Gobée*, no. 34.

[80] For the text see for instance *De Socialist*, February 2, 1930, p. 2.

Sjahrir reacted slowly to Sukarno's arrest. Eventually, in a series of articles published in *De Socialist*, in November 1930, he wrote about Sukarno, now, as about a man who

> has been waiting for four months already, and still shall wait for months, in a prison cell of 1.48 meters in width and 2 meters in length, for whatever decision might be taken.[81]

Onmacht—"lack of power," "impotence"—was the catchword in Sjahrir's articles. And *toneel*—"theater"—appeared to be the metaphor through which he tried to convey the meaning of what had happened. Sukarno's trial, Sjahrir wrote, would be *toneelstuk*, "a show." "Several leaders of the Indonesian National Party out of thousands" were picked up "to play a role." The Dutch decided upon everything, according to Sjahrir—the stage, the opening day, "the plot, or better the moral of the piece"; they did it in order to impress the audience.[82]

The stage in Bandung, as Sjahrir remembered it, crashed, with Sukarno, the principal actor, going down with it, and with the Bandung youth in the audience watching with awe. Bandung's limelights went out, and Sjahrir's reaction read almost like relief or even liberation.

"With Sukarno in prison," Sjahrir wrote, "one period of the Indonesian people's movement is at its end." Sjahrir cited three examples of when something like this had happened before, all three, in his presentation, certainly not glorious events in the history of the movement; rather manifestations of grave mistakes and embarrassing experiences—the so called Garoet Incident in 1919, when a part of nationalist Sarekat Islam allegedly let itself be provoked into an act of violence; the crippling split in the movement in 1923 between the Islamic and Communist wing; and the stillborn Communist rebellions of 1926 and 1927. "And now," Sjahrir went on,

> the Indonesian National Party is also destroyed, and Sukarno goes to serve his term in prison.... The example of Sukarno, too, is a lesson to the Indonesian people.... We are going, now, towards a new period in front of us.[83]

Writing of the movement at the moment of the crashing blow, Sjahrir wrote of a "standstill," rather than of a "dead end."[84] He himself even seemed to move faster after the disaster. "Indonesian politics so far," Sjahrir wrote in *De Nieuwe Weg* early in 1931,

> have been dominated by a group consisting, first, of the feudal nobility, second, of the extremely insignificant and still embryonic liberal bourgeoisie,

---

[81] Sjahrir, "De vervolgingen in Indonesië: het proces Soekarno c.s.," *De Socialist*, November 8, 1930, p. 6.

[82] Ibid.

[83] S. Sharir (Sjahrir), "De vernietiging der P.N.I: Het slotstuk," *De Socialist*, April 24, 1931, p. 6.

[84] Sidi (Sjahrir), "De Indonesische beweging op een dood punt," *De Nieuwe Weg* 6 (August 1931); 237, 239. For some reactions to the article see Attorney General to Governor-General, May 10, 1933 in *Secret Verbaal*, April 29, 1933-T9; *PPO* September 1931, p. 12 (Poeze, ed., *Politikpolitioneele overzichten*, 3: 111; *Secret Mail Report* 1933, no. 490. On Sjahrir admitting this was an article written by him see *Secret Verbaal*, November 28, 1934-L33.

and, third, of well-paid and well-positioned intellectuals born out of one of the two.

The Indonesian National Party, Sjahrir continued,

> was permeated by the influence of those "enlightened" groups, who, because of their descent and education, were stuck in bourgeois and feudal worlds and were not fit to become leaders of a mass movement. Even Sukarno did not disentangle himself from this.[85]

After Sukarno's arrest the style of the Indonesian movement visibly changed.[86] In 1931, the Indonesian National Party, inactive since Sukarno's arrest, was formally dissolved by its leaders, and in its place the same group of men established a new party—Partai Indonesia, abbreviated to Partindo, "Party of Indonesia." Partindo's inaugural meeting was described as being "in sharp contrast with the PNI's [Indonesian National Party] meetings in its heyday."[87] There was now

> noticeably greater emphasis on self-help, cooperatives and *swadeshi* [the production and purchase of indigenous products]. . . . All but two of the *Partindo* leaders were dressed in sarongs, which was to be a regular occurrence at subsequent meetings. Sartono [the party leader] spoke at length on the need for Indonesians to wear clothing made in their own country and promised that the promotion of *swadeshi* would be one of the major tasks of *Partindo*. . . . Sartono warned that those who were not dressed in *swadeshi* clothing, or at least did not wear a headcloth made locally, would in future be refused entry to *Partindo* meetings.[88]

Already in 1928, and speaking almost like Sjahrir in 1930, a prominent Dutch civil servant and expert opined that there was hardly anyone around Sukarno, including his party leadership, "who does not originate from the highest aristocratic

---

[85] Sidi (Sjahrir), "De Indonesische beweging," pp. 238–39.

[86] After Sukarno was arrested, and only two days before his trial began in Bandung, on August 18, 1930, the new Partai Ra'jat Indonesia, "Party of the Indonesian People," was founded by Mohammad Tabrani in the Indies. Tabrani came from Madura, an island adjacent and culturally very close to eastern Java; he tried to attract the membership of the crippled Indonesian National Party, and especially its "culturally conscious" East Javanese following. *Overzicht v.d. IMC pers*, 1930, 1: 299–300; 2: 150, 286. On November 11 of the same year, Dr. Soetomo established Persatoean Bangsa Indonesia, "Union of the Indonesian Nation," also a distinctly Javanese organization, based in East Java, as well, with some representation in the center and west of the island. According to Ingleson, the PBI "began life as a Surabaya party and despite efforts to extend its organization into Central and West Java remained a regional East Java party." Ingleson, *Road to Exile*, p. 125. In spring of 1931, rumors were heard of a possible alliance between the almost exclusively Javanese Persatoean Bangsa Indonesia, the Boedi Oetomo, and also the regionalist West Java Pasoendan. Ibid., p. 139. On the rumors see also, e.g., *Aksi*, March 30, 1931.

[87] This is Ingleson paraphrasing a Dutch report on the Partindo meeting (Ingleson, *Road to Exile*, p. 143); for the original see *Secret Mail Report* 1931, no. 794. For similar reports on the new style in Partindo see *Aksi*, February 11, 1932 or *Overzicht vd IMC pers* 1 (1932): 102.

[88] Ingleson, *Road to Exile*, p. 143.

circles in Java," and who was not of an "aristocratic-intellectual spirit."[89] He exaggerated—with the exception of Sartono, Sukarno's comrades were essentially of lower *ningrat* circles. Now, however, Sartono, who, indeed, was of the highest Javanese royal rank,[90] became the top Partindo leader.

By 1930, it was rumored that Sartono's Partindo was contemplating closer cooperation—or perhaps even an organizational unity—with Dr. Soetomo's newly established and almost exclusively Javanese Persatoean Bangsa Indonesia, "Union of the Indonesian Nation," and some other distinctly Javanese political parties and groups.[91] Sjahrir and Hatta watched this very closely and reacted sharply. Sjahrir reprimanded Sartono for being so "timid" as to approach people like Soetomo. To ally with Soetomo!—Sjahrir wrote in emphatic disbelief—"the famous *Raden Mas* [His Highness] Doctor"! And to befriend "Soetomo's party," "that Javanese-aristocratic association"!![92]

It was as if Sartono's flirtation with Javanese cultural nationalism awakened a new sensitiveness in Sjahrir. The people of Indonesia, Sjahrir wrote, were being made into "an object, a toy in the hands of 'the enlightened,' a horse for the intellectual cavaliers," "a parade horse." As for the "glorious history of Indonesia before the Dutch came," Sjahrir wrote with irony, "all that boasting about the old greatness of the land and the culture, all that feudal-bourgeois nationalism—it is empty talk and impedes progress."

> For the subjected, there had never been any freedom and greatness; the freedom and the greatness of the time did not belong to them. . . .[93]

Ningrat, the aristocracy—and in the whole context of his writing *Javanese* aristocracy—was clearly the determining notion in Sjahrir's perception of what was wrong

---

[89] Van der Plas' report, 1928, in *Secret Mail Report* 1928, no. 1093; see also van der Plas' report for 1927–1928 in *Secret Mail Report* 1928, no. 90. According to Rose, *Indonesia Free*, p. 47, one of the points on which Sukarno did not accept Hatta's advice regarding the Indonesian National Party's program in 1928 was "the concept of 'universal suffrage,' the right of the ordinary person to a strong voice in government [that was] so central," Rose says, "to Minangkabau *adat*. . . . Without this concept, there would be no firm basis for a breakdown of the 'aristocratic' principle, so strongly entrenched in Java." On a similar omission of the word "*ra'jat*," "people," also suggested by Hatta, from the party's name in 1927; see ibid., p. 40.

[90] Daniel Lev, for instance, believes that Sartono's royal rank, which put him on the level of Europeans in criminal proceedings, was one of the reasons why Sartono was not arrested in December 1929 together with Sukarno. See Daniel S. Lev, "Origins of the Indonesian Advocacy," *Indonesia* 21 (April 1976): 163.

[91] de Jonge, "Inlandsche beweging op Java," pp. 15–16.

[92] For Hatta's reaction see Hatta, *Memoir*, p. 241. Hatta later wrote that Sartono's following was 75 percent *ningrat* or bourgeois and that he and his friends "in their innermost hearts paid homage to the ideas of Boedi Oetomo." See Hatta in *Moestika*, February 5, 1932, summed up in *Overzicht v.d.IMC opers* (1932), 2: 103. For Sjahrir's reaction, see Sidi (Sjahrir) "De Indonesische beweging," pp. 238, 237; (Sjahrir), in *Indonesia Merdeka* 9, 74 (1932) quoted in de Jonge "Inlandsche beweging," p. 6; Sjahrir in *Daulat Ra'jat* 1,1 (September 20, 1931). It should be noted that Soetomo actually was not "Raden Mas" and, as far as I know, never used the title. A Minangkabau, Mohammad Jamin, a rising star in the Indonesian movement, was also attacked by Sjahrir on this occasion. But this was because the Minangkabau tried to adjust the movement to what Jamin himself described as "Great-Java ideals." Ibid., p 238. (Jamin's father was Minangkabau; his mother was Javanese.)

[93] Ibid., pp. 238–39.

and weak in Indonesia. As for the location of the creative, powerful center, however, "where the urge for action [*actie-drang*] dwells," as he himself defined it, he remained strikingly vague.

At this time, Sjahrir used Marxist terminology freely and vehemently. But he applied the categories with certain and rather consistent imprecision. The force that was to be the basis of the Indonesian revolution was to him "peasants, workers, small tradesmen and the poor middle class."[94] "Class struggle," as Sjahrir defined it at that time, was "freedom struggle."[95] He appeared almost to take the step that his imprecision often suggested was logical: a step that Hatta took.

Looking, indeed, for where "the urge for action dwells," for something clearly opposing *ningrat* aristocratic culture and *ningrat* aristocratic power, Hatta began to use extensively the term *daulat* (or *kedaulatan* as a derivation of *daulat*). *Daulat* or *kedaulatan* is a word of Arabic origin and, according to a current Indonesian dictionary, it means happiness or welfare under a sovereign authority, or the exercise of such an authority.[96] While *daulat* was rather rarely heard on Java with this meaning,[97] it was widely used as such in the Malay- and Islam-influenced cultures of the Indies, including very importantly Minangkabau.

It was probably in Holland that Hatta first wrote about the *kedaulatan* concept. He would be developing it for the rest of his life. It was to be a democratic concept, Hatta wrote, "the people's sovereignty," thus *kedaulatan ra'jat*. *Ra'jat*, "the people," would be the sovereign. *Ra'jat* for Hatta, meant all the social groups of Indonesia except *ningrat*. The *Ra'jat* was to be the sovereign and would be organized into self-governing communities. The state would be built out of these communities on the principle of the highest possible decentralization. The self-governing, fundamental communities of *ra'jat* would be the power center of the structures of the state.

Hatta never made a secret of the models he had used for his concept. The first of them was G. D. H. Cole's "guild socialism"—an influential theory of the time, referring to the self-governing guilds of artisans and merchants in late medieval Europe. Hatta's other model was what he saw as the traditional Minangkabau system of a federation of village republics, a system made up of self-governing *nagari*, "communities." The reader may recall this from the first chapter, when an effort was made to define the early twentieth-century Dutch colonial "ethical" translation of Minangkabau culture. Hatta described his model as *"demokrasi asli Indonesia,"* "Indonesian indigenous democracy."[98]

Sjahrir, in Holland, also began to use the term *kedaulatan ra'jat*. But he never elaborated upon the concept. Sjahrir was oblique whenever Hatta was explicit in his approach to the "traditional" *nagari* phenomenon—or rather apparition. The word *asli*, "indigenous," so freely used by Hatta is not found in Sjahrir's vocabulary as he

---

[94] Ibid.

[95] "Het vonnis van Bandoeng: Een rede van Kam. Sjarir" *De Socialist*, January 30, 1932, p. 13.

[96] W. J. S. Poerwadarminta, *Kamus Umum Bahasa Indonesia* (Jakarta: Balai Pustaka, 1976). In Dutch, on one siginificant occasion at least, *daulat (ra'jat)* is translated as *Heil des Volks*, "welfare of the people." *Collection de Jonge* no. 64, p. 71.

[97] On one meaning of *daulat* which became important in Java during the mid-1940s, see Anderson, *Java in a Time of Revolution*, pp. 87, 334–35.

[98] Mohammad Hatta, "Demokrasi asli Indonesia dan Kedaulatan Ra'jat," *Daulat Ra'jat* 1, 7 (January 10, 1932); see also Mohammad Hatta, "Gilden-Socialisme," ibid., 4, 87 (February 10, 1934).

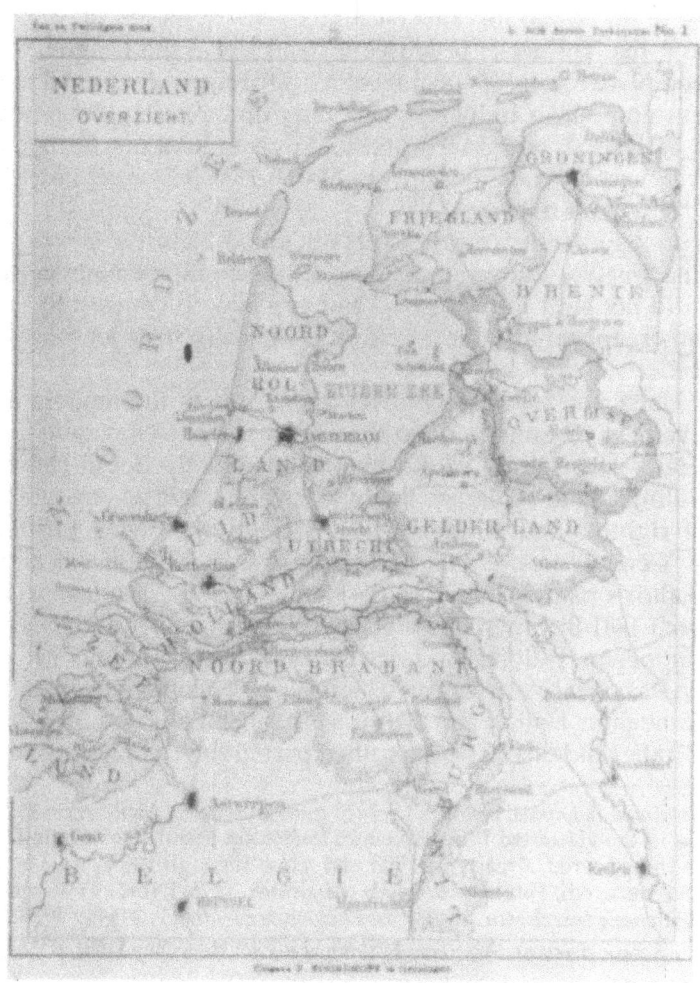

Map of the Netherlands
(from the *Bos Atlas*)

stayed in Holland. Neither did he ever use at this time, as far as we know, the word "Minangkabau."

3. THE RETURN HOME

Its distance from the day-to-day politics in the Indies, as Hadji Agoes Salim put it very clearly, made for much of Perhimpoenan Indonesia's coherence and power. Distance from Dutch and European reality might be equally important. The socialist movement in Europe, however, just at the time, was leaving less and less space for bystanders and wanderers.

In the summer of 1929, just when Sjahrir arrived in Holland, Hatta attended the Frankfurt congress of the League against Imperialism and Colonialist Oppression as an Indonesian delegate. As on several previous occasions Hatta went to the radical left-socialist League's convention and he considered it—for a freedom fighter—a natural thing to do. When he came back this time, however, he was already complaining about the "influence of Moscow," and about the League being less than before "a good place for us."[99] Later meetings in Holland continued to be organized jointly by Perhimpoenan Indonesia and the "Communist-dominated" League—indeed until early 1931, and Sjahrir presided over at least one of them.[100] Through 1930, however, tensions rapidly grew. In March 1931, Hatta was expelled from the League as a "bourgeois reformist."[101]

It is a curious experience to trace Hatta's and Sjahrir's moves on the newly sharply defined map of European politics. Both men, increasingly oppressed on the left, clearly did not shift to the right. Their reaction, in contrast to what might be expected, rather, appeared to be an effort to intensify their looseness and to keep their distance.

Neither Hatta nor Sjahrir were ever very close to the moderate wing of the socialist movement in Europe, or to the Dutch Social-Democratic Labor Party in particular. Hatta consistently voiced his irritation at the Social-Democratic Labor Party's unwillingness to recognize the Indonesian people as "mature enough" and deserving a right to independence.[102] As Hatta was being pushed out of the increasingly "Communist-dominated" League against Imperialism, also the warmth of his and Sjahrir's relationship with the moderate socialists dropped to its lowest level. In March 1931 Sjahrir was secretary of Perhimpoenan Indonesia—and at the time Perhimpoenan Indonesia described the Social-Democratic Labor Party leadership, in its official statement as "champagne drinking hypocrites."[103]

At the same time, Hatta's and Sjahrir's connection with *De Socialist* and Sal Tas' Social Democratic Students' Club intensified perceptibly.[104] There is no climax to the

---

[99] Hatta in *Persatoean Indonesia*, October 15, 1929 quoted in *Secret Mail Report* 1929, no. 1016. An uneasy feeling in the Hatta-led Perhimpoenan Indonesia about the League being under the control of Stalin appeared already in 1928 and grew through the spring of 1929; see *PPO* February 1928 (Poeze, ed., *Politiek-politioneele overzichten*, 1: 267); ibid., September 1928 (Poeze, ed., *Politiek-politioneele overzichten*, 1: 433); and *Indonesia Merdeka* 7, 2 (May 1929): pp. 39–40.

[100] This meeting took place on February 4, 1930; see *PPO* February 1930, p. 26; March 1930, p. 37.

[101] See *PPO* August 1929 (Poeze, ed., *Politiek-politioneele overzichten*, 2: 196 97) for a report on the Frankfurt meeting. See also *PPO* May–June 1931, p. 29; a report on the Perhimpoenan Indonesia meetings where this was discussed, late in May and early in June 1929, is in Attorney General report on Perhimpoenan Indonesia, August 17, 1931 in *Secret Mail Report* 1931, no. 813.; see also *Secret Mail Report* 1934, no. 287; for Hatta's comments (he gives the date incorrectly as 1930) see Hatta, *Memoir*, pp. 240–41 and Hatta, *Indonesian Patriot*, p. 129.

[102] See Dahm, *Sukarno*, pp. 96–97. In 1931, while the SDAP colonial program spoke carefully of the "development of self-government under native leadership leading to a preparation for independence," Sjahrir demanded the "right to self-determination"; while Sjahrir declared the need for "nationalization" in Indonesia, the SDAP went no further than a suggestion for the "expansion of state enterprise." Sidi (Sjahrir), "De Indonesische beweging," p. 240; the SDAP's colonial program is quoted and commented upon by Hansen, "The Dutch East Indies," pp. 69–70.

[103] Statement of the Perhimpoenan Indonesia executive printed in *De Socialist*, March 27, 1931, pp. 8–9.

[104] The pages of *De Socialist* also bore witness to this. The Club's representative, P. J. Schmidt, left the League against Imperialism just a few weeks before Hatta was expelled. P. J. Schmidt, early in February 1929, explained why he thought it was inevitable that he would leave the

story of growing oppressiveness, however. There was little radical change among the young men around the Social Democratic Students' Club and *De Socialist*—Sal Tas, Jos Riekerk, Jef Last, and others—from the time Sjahrir first came to Amsterdam, and met Sal Tas in Djoehanas' apartment. Like Sjahrir and Hatta themselves, these young people merely grew more disenchanted with the Socialist establishment and Communist establishment, and they merely drifted even more, and yet faster than before, into an unmapped space.[105]

It is possible that, in spite of the changes in the European socialist movement, Sjahrir and Hatta—moving with the Social Democratic Students' Club and *De Socialist*—might have managed to stay much longer in Holland, and in largely the same style. Through 1930, however, and especially by the spring of 1931, the political map of the Indies also appeared to be drawn in radically sharper lines. Watching their motherland and feeling their responsibilities, Sjahrir and Hatta also in this repsect had much less space to breathe and to move than they might otherwise wish. The distance between them in Holland and their homeland in the East narrowed uncomfortably.

There was disenchantment in the Indies among the nationalists after Sukarno was arrested and other leaders failed to respond purposefully. Hatta's and Sjahrir's articles, written in Holland, further fueled the disenchantment. As a result, pressure grew to get both men much more involved.

In March and April 1931, two "study clubs" of a new type were established in the Indies, one in Batavia, the other in Bandung, to express the increasing dissatisfaction and to overcome the uncertainty in which the movement found itself.[106] Some of Hatta's and Sjahrir's friends were in both "study clubs"—Abdoel Karim Pringgodigdo, for instance, who had shortly before returned from Holland and knew Hatta well, Inoe Perbatasari and Murwoto, who were friends of Sjahrir from the time of his high school studies in Bandung. Neither Hatta nor Sjahrir were widely mentioned at the outset. The movement of dissent, which called itself the *golongan merdeka*, "free groups," was described by the Dutch police in Batavia still in October 1931 as "less developed radical elements including some old communists," "merely individual clusters not tied in any coherent network."[107]

League; *PPO* February 1929 (Poeze, ed., *Politiek-politioneele overzichten*, 2: 58–59). Edo Fimmen announced that he was leaving the League in October. See *PPO* December 1930 (Poeze, ed., *Politiek-politioneele overzichten*, 2: 488). Both the Club and *De Socialist* were vitriolic against the Social-Democratic Labor Party's colonial policy. See, for instance, *PPO* June 1929 (Poeze, ed., *Politiek-politioneele overzichten*, 2: 153). See also a booklet by P. J. Schmidt published sometime around April 1931, *Het koloniaal gevaar* ("The colonial threat") as commented upon in *Secret Verbaal*, April 27, 1931-Z7. At the same time, both the Club and *De Socialist* were increasingly sensitive lest Hatta and Sjahrir should change their moves and fall back either on the Communists or on the moderates. P. J. Schmidt, "De Perhimpoenan Indonesia en wij" *De Socialist* January 30, 1931, pp. 2–3; "De Perhimpoenan Indonesia en wij: Repliek," ibid. March 6, 1931.

[105] See especially Jef Last who left the group because his friends were not "consistent" and "radical" enough. "Jef Last treedt uit de Partij: Zijn afscheidsbrief aan 'De Socialist'," *De Socialist*, January 17, 1930, p. 10.

[106] "Riwajat Ringkas dari PNI: I," *Kedaulatan Ra'jat* 6 (August 1934); Secret Report on PNI in *Secret Mail Report* 1932, no. 830; Ingleson, *Road to Exile*, p. 144.

[107] *PPO* October 1931, pp. 4–6. See also "Verslag van openbare vergadering van de golongan merdeka op zondag 1 Nov. 1931 te Batavia belegd," in *Secret Mail Report* 1931, no. 1148.

As months passed Hatta in particular—older and better known than Sjahrir—was pressed to return. On occasion, Hatta appeared almost alarmed by the prospect. In April, just when the first *golongan merdeka*, "free groups," were being established, he published his plan

> to leave politics for a time in order to concentrate on his [academic] courses and to pass, at last, his doctoral examinations at the Rotterdam Business School.[108]

Hatta had been in Holland for nine years. He had been sent there with the greatest hopes by "uncle" Max Etek Rais and his community. He had yet to pay his debts, and he had not yet even reached the *doctorandus*, "candidate," level.[109]

The return of both Sjahrir and Hatta was to be highly hesitant Their debt to their motherland, also, might be perceived as a debt of guilt.

In June 1931, Hatta wrote to his friend Soedjadi, an activist in the *golongan merdeka*, and told him that when he came back from Holland, he would not join Sartono's Partindo. This implied, at last, that Hatta was willing to involve himself with the "free groups" movement. Still, he did not set any definite date for his return. And the activity he wanted to engage in, after he went back to the Indies, so he wrote to Soedjadi—was "social pedagogic work"![110]

Being a Minangkabau, being educated in "ethical" schools, being still a student, indeed, explains much of this otherwise very curious emphasis. The connection between education, power, and freedom was direct.

Already in 1927 Hatta had written:

> According to my plan, the people, through the improvement of education, must gradually be brought to the stage of development which can lead to an independent existence.[111]

Sjahrir was not much different from Hatta in that sense. He is remembered as telling a friend, in Holland: "I really feel that teaching is the greatest work there is."[112]

Hatta, in his letter to Soedjadi, in July 1931, suggested that the "free groups" start their action by publishing a journal, that the name of the journal be *"Daulat Ra'jat,"*

---

[108] *Aksi*, April 15, 1931; also *Persatoean Indonesia*, April 10, 1931 quoted in *PPO* March 1931, p.15.

[109] Hatta, *Memoir*, p. 242. (The degree of "doctor" in the Dutch system required still at least two years beyond that.)

[110] *Overzicht v.d.IMC pers*, 1931, 2: 494; see also Ingleson, *Road to Exile*, p. 146.

[111] Quoted in ibid., p. 27. This, of course, was not a wholly exceptional attitude and certainly not one without precedent. Tan Malaka, for instance, remembered how Hadji Busro, a prominent Sarekat Islam leader in Semarang, told him in 1921: "Don't speak at public meetings. Let other people do that for the time being. It's best if you devote all your energies to education. After three or four years there will be people who can take your place if you get involved in politics and get exiled." "This is," Tan Malaka commented, "what I did first. Indeed it was sound advice. But because there was a real shortage of people in all fields, I was forced to immerse myself in public meetings.... Now I was stepping onto the slippery ground of politics and once your foot is on it, it is hard to pull back." Tan Malaka, *Dari pendjara ke pendjara* 1: 73; in *From Jail to Jail*, trans. & ed. Helen Jarvis, 1: 67–68.

[112] Tas, "Souvenirs of Sjahrir, p.147; see also ibid., p. 145 and Tas, *Wat mij betreft*, p. 148

and that the journal's mission be the "education of the masses."[113] Sjahrir, at the same time, also, highlighted "education of the masses" as the main task of political leaders. The aim of this education, Sjahrir wrote, should be to make the masses aware of themselves (*sadar*). *Keteguhan*, "firmness," and *pengabdian*, "devotion," according to Sjahrir, were qualities that should especially be taught.[114]

Late in August 1931, the "free groups" from several cities met and acted on Hatta's and Sjahrir's advice. A sort of a common structure was established, and it was decided that it would be neither a *partai*, "party," nor a *perserikatan*, "association," but a *pendidikan*, "education,"—Pendidikan Nasional Indonesia, "Indonesian National Education."[115]

The new journal of the "free groups" was called *Daulat Ra'jat*, as Hatta had suggested. The journal's first issue came out on September 20, 1931. Six men were listed on the editorial board, among them Hatta and Sjahrir, as "residents" of Rotterdam and Amsterdam respectively. An editorial in the first issue declared "social pedagogy" to be the basis of the movement.[116]

Indonesia seemed closer to Holland with each passing day. Hatta and Sjahrir, through their new involvement in Indies politics, were increasingly under attack in the Indies as well as in Holland, namely for not being respectful enough to Sukarno and for needlessly endangering the unity of the Indonesian nationalist movement.

At a Perhimpoenan Indonesia meeting on July 19, 1931, Hatta was for the first time publicly criticized by some other Indies students in Holland for statements he had made about the current situation back home.[117] Sjahrir, at the time serving as the secretary of Perhimpoenan Indonesia, was not able to stop the growing opposition to his older friend.

The attack was joined by those among the Indies students who were close to, or getting closer to, the Dutch Communist Party. At a Perhimpoenan Indonesia meeting on November 8, Hatta was accused formally of "acting against Perhimpoenan Indonesia discipline, which binds all members to consult the executive before they express their views in public." After a debate, at the same meeting, Hatta was expelled from Perhimpoenan Indonesia. Sjahrir cast the only dissenting vote and then announced that he was leaving the organization together with Hatta.[118]

Sal Tas described the scene immediately after the expulsion:

---

[113] *Overzicht v.d.IMC pers* 1931, pp. 266–67.

[114] Sidi (Sjahrir), "De Indonesische beweging," p. 239; Sjahrir, "Kaoem intellectueel dalam doenia politik Indonesia," *Daulat Ra'jat* 1 (November 10, 1931), p. 6.

[115] *PPO* November 1931, p. 5. Other names were suggested, like Partai Indonesia Merdeka, "The Party of Free Indonesia," or Partai Daulat Ra'jat. On discussions about the name, see also *Daulat Ra'jat* 1, 5 (October 10, 1931); *PPO* October 1931, pp. 4–6; *Banteng Ra'jat* (Djokjakarta) 1, 15 (June 25, 1932).

[116] *Daulat Ra'jat* 1, 1 (September 20, 1931).

[117] S., "Perhimpoenan Indonesia mentjela Hatta-Soedjadi," *Daulat Ra'jat* 1, 4 (October 20, 1931).

[118] Attorney General to Governor-General, December 12, 1931 in *Secret Mail Report* 1932, no. 26; see also announcement in *Daulat Ra'jat* 1, 7 (November 20, 1931); a comment "Perhimpoenan Indonesia sekarang dipakai oleh Partai Indonesia sebagai pandji boeat kelawan kita," *Daulat Ra'jat* 1, 8 (November 30, 1931); and Sjahrir's own reaction in ibid., 1, 9 (December 12, 1931).

I took the first train for Leiden in search of my friends. In a large room at the residence of a wealthy Indonesian, Hatta was sitting in a chair, his hands on his knees, staring out in front of him. Behind stood a couple of Indonesian students, nervously chatting.

Hatta began to tell Sal Tas about what had happened, and how concerned he was, especially about the reaction in Indonesia.

His story was interrupted by a burst of laughter. It was Sjahrir, who sat on the piano, his legs dangling. His laugh had a sarcastic tone. Now Sjahrir was younger than Hatta and that counts in a student milieu and doubly in an Indonesian one. But he could not conceal his annoyance at all that despair. "What difference does it make?" he broke out. . . . "We are not going to protest the decision of the PI [Perhimpoenan Indonesia] executive. We'll let it be known we'll have nothing to do with the PI." His outburst stopped Hatta's keening.[119]

In the Indies, at the same time, the lack of leadership grew with each day increasingly disturbing for the "free groups."[120] In September 1931 a Dutch informant, watching for every threatening sign from the nationalist movement, still saw "no leader of a greater style" among the "free groups."[121] Friends and "free groups" leaders urged Hatta "to return as quickly as possible."[122]

Hatta believed fervently that he was just a few months short of his graduation. Sjahrir, on the other hand, was clearly more flexible—to put it mildly—in his university course work. The fact that he was looser made Sjahrir the one to enter actual Indies politics first. The two decided that he would sail home immediately. They thought that six months should be enough time for Hatta to get his degree. Then he would take charge of matters in the Indies, so that Sjahrir could return to Holland "to finish his studies."[123]

In mid November 1931, Sjahrir began to take leave of Holland. The departure was a hasty one, and he told his friends that he was leaving for "a danger zone."[124] Yet, there was a clearly visible eagerness. Sjahrir told Judith, a young woman from the Sal Tas circle, when saying good-bye, that he was leaving "to teach his people

---

[119] Tas, "Souvenirs of Sjahrir, p. 142.

[120] On the lack of leadership as the main problem felt by *golongan merdeka* through late 1931 see X, "Setahoen dalam organisasi," *Banteng Ra'jat* 1: 32–33.

[121] Gobée's report to Governor-General September 6, 1931 in *Secret Mail Report* 1931, no. 1148; for the same impression see, e.g., the police report on the *golongan merdeka* meeting in Batavia on November 1, 1931, ibid.

[122] Letter by Soedjadi reported for instance in *Secret Mail Report* 1932, no. 830, encl., pp. 2–3.

[123] Burhanuddin, "Sjahrir yang saya kenal" in *Mengenang Sjahrir*, ed. Anwar, p. 52; interview with Burhanuddin, Jakarta, March 5, 1983; interview with Sjahrizal Djoehana, Bandung, March 7, 1982, and with M. A. Djoehana, Prague, August 16, 1983; Hatta's interview with Ingleson quoted in Ingleson, *Road to Exile*, p. 155. Sjahrizal Djoehana says lack of money and weakened health ("because of bad living in Holland") played a part in Sjahrir's decision to return. Lack of money is given as the reason in "Sjahrir Personalia" and Attorney General to Governor-General, June 2, 1948 in *Archief Proc Gen*, no. 262. Another Dutch source, however, states that politics were definitely the reason for Sjahrir's hasty return. *Secret Mail Report* 1932, no. 830.

[124] Tas, "Souvenirs of Sjahrir," p. 145; de Kadt, "Sjahrir: Poging tot plaatsbepaling,"pp. 464–65.

and to have a political influence at the same time."[125] He was going home with an apprehension, busily gathering everything he believed had enriched him abroad. He was confident, evidently, that he would be able to take a great part of what was good in the Dutch *rantau* with him.

Some time near the end of Sjahrir's stay in Holland, a romantic relationship had developed between him and Sal Tas' wife, Maria. Now, Sjahrir was arranging for Maria to join him later in the Indies—she would marry him and/or work as an instructress in the Indonesian women's movement.[126] At the same time, according to Sal Tas,

> Sjahrir brought up the suggestion that I should accompany them [Hatta and Sjahrir] to the Indies, in order to take part in the formation of a cadre school. Hatta would [later] teach economics there, Sjahrir and I would somehow divide sociology, politics and organization between us.[127]

Jos Riekerk was already in the colony, serving as an official in the island of Flores east of Java. Jacques de Kadt, another of the *De Socialist* circle and brother-in-law of Sal Tas, was approached by Sjahrir, a few days before his ship sailed. Sjahrir and Maria invited de Kadt for a cup of coffee (as usual, de Kadt says, Maria did the greater part of the talking). Sjahrir told de Kadt that he was returning home to raise the self-awareness of the Indonesian people and that de Kadt should be a party to the effort. De Kadt's role, Sjahrir suggested, would be to publish "articles and pamphlets on the Indonesian movement" in the Dutch socialist press abroad. "I saw him off," de Kadt recalled, "with a deep feeling of respect, and of helplessness."[128]

---

[125] Interview with Judith Tas, The Hague, October 25, 1983.

[126] When interrogated in the Indies four years later, Sjahrir denied having any political motivation for inviting Maria; she was to follow him, he said "on account of their personal relations." Cabinet to Minister of Colonies, June 1938, *Secret Verbaal*, July 8, 1938-U22 out of *Secret Mail Report* 1934, no. 1290 in *Secret Verbaal*, November 28, 1934-L33. Mrs. Maria Duchâteau-Sjahrir also remembers her plans to join Sjahrir as involving "no politics"; they were strictly personal: "we were in love." Interview with Maria Duchâteau-Sjahrir, Lorques, February 13, 1988.

[127] Tas, "Souvenirs of Sjahrir, p. 145.

[128] de Kadt, "Sjahrir: Poging tot plaatsbepaling," p. 465.

4

THE RETURN TO JAVA, 1931-1934

> For a couple of weeks, a European lady has been seen on Medan streets attracting some attention as she has evidently decided to wear a sarong and kebaya and appears to be married to a native.
>
> *De Sumatra Post*, April 16, 1932.

1. CHAIRMAN OF THE PENDIDIKAN NASIONAL INDONESIA

Before he left Holland, Sjahrir convinced Salim, his friend the painter, to go with him to the Indies to see what his land of origin really looked like. Salim had been away from the East for years and, as he remembers, he based his images of the Indies very much on what he saw in the Colonial Museum in Amsterdam and what he heard from visitors or from the students of Indology in Leiden. Salim left Holland at about the same time as Sjahrir. He was deeply shocked by what he found, "arriving from free Amsterdam to the officials' Batavia where even art was narrowly restricted by law."[1]

Salim tried but did not succeed in entering the Bataviase Kunstkring, "Batavia Art Circle," of rich and established artists, who just "rode their two-seaters" and to whom "Picasso, Chagall and Braque were just names." He was pushed back towards the "poor huts of the Indonesians," but, as he then knew "about three words in Malay," he found, besides a few of Sjahrir's friends,

> merely a most dumb *kampong* population.... What did they know about Cubism and Surrealism? Who among them had read Gide's *Voyage au Congo* or Malraux' *Voie Royale*?

Salim earned a living designing advertisements—some made of neon, some for Coca-Cola, others "with leaping tigers [for Tiger Balm] and still others with giant glasses of Heineken Beer."[2] Salim also made a little money working for Sjahrir's movement.

Sjahrir himself got off the ship in Singapore. He spent two days in the British colony in search of Soebagio, one of his good friends from Bandung, a fellow soccer

---

[1] de Vries, "Twee vaderlanden," *Orientatie* 5 (February 1948), pp. 22–30.

[2] Interview with Salim, Paris, February 2, 1988. Excerpts from four letters from Salim to a Dutch friend, L. P. J. Braat, written from the Indies between March 1933 and April 1934, are published in L. P. J. Braat, ed., "De brieven van Soeleiman," *De vrije Katheder* 6, 1 (May 3, 1946).

player and a classmate and comrade from Pemoeda Indonesia politics. Sjahrir found Soebagio self-exiled from the Indies and—so the story goes—"disguised as a blind sailor," and tried to convince him to return home with him to "renew the interrupted struggle."[3]

In the last week of December 1931, Sjahrir stepped ashore in Batavia. He just missed the *golongan merdeka*, "free groups," convention which took place in Batavia on December 25. He did not get a seat in the executive of their new organizational structure—Pendidikan Nasional Indonesia, "Indonesian National Education"— which was elected at the convention and he was not even mentioned in the convention's records.[4]

After returning from Holland, Sjahrizal Djoehana, Sjahrir's sister, lived with her husband in the Central Javanese city of Semarang. Sjahrir visited the family a few times during the next two years, and his sister began supporting him again, but, as she says herself, gave him money only very occasionally.[5] More often Sjahrir seemed to visit his half-sister Radena, who lived in Batavia with her sons Djohan Sjahroezah, Djazar, Djazir, and Hazil Tanzil; the father of the family was working outside Java at the time.[6] Sjahrir had another home in Batavia where he "spent nights and shared daily meals," the house of his Medan cousin Hadji Agoes Salim with whom he had recently experienced such a crucial time in Holland.[7]

Soewarni and Soewarsih, two young women Sjahrir had known well in Bandung, were in Batavia and met Sjahrir during the first days after his return. Soewarsih later remembered that Sjahrir wore "huge, clearly borrowed slippers, a stained sarong, a jacket and a skullcap."[8] He—so it seems—impressed his young friend as a politician in disguise. Certainly, his outfit reminds one strongly of the colorful costumes from the Bandung *Batovis* theater student-company times.

In a matter of days, Sjahrir took over the leadership of the "free group" in Batavia. This was significant for the group was working, at the same time, as "a tem-

---

[3] Burhanuddin, "Sjahrir yang saya kenal," pp. 48–69; interview with Burhanuddin, Jakarta, March 5, 1983.

[4] *Aksi*, December 31, 1931. In *Daulat Ra'jat* 1, 9 (December 30, 1931), Sjahrir was still listed as a "correspondent from Europe."

[5] Interview with Sjahrizal Djoehana, Bandung, March 7, 1983.

[6] Interview with Hazil Tanzil and Violeta Sjahroezah, Jakarta, March 8, 1982. Radena's husband worked at that time with the oil company, NKPM in Palembang, South Sumatra. Interview with Hazil Tanzil, Jakarta, March 8, 1982; see also John D. Legge, *Intellectuals and Nationalism in Indonesia: A Study of the Following Recruited by Sutan Sjahrir in Occupation Jakarta* (Ithaca: Cornell Modern Indonesia Project, 1988), p. 82.

[7] Sjahrir, "Hadji Agoes Salim sebagai diplomat," in *Hadji Agus Salim*, ed. Solichin, p. 171.

[8] Suwarsih Djojopuspito, "De thuiskomst van een oud-strijder," pp. 41–42. Compare Soewarni's slightly different description of Sjahrir's costume: "When I saw him in such a pitiful state, I had to hold my tears back. The sleeves of his jacket were too long, it was difficult to guess its original color." Soewarni Pringgodigdo, "Over du Perron en zijn invloed op de Indonesische Intellectuellen (1936–39)," *Cultureel Nieuws* 16 (January 1952), p. 145. Soewarsih's husband, Soegondo Djojopoespito, had also been a prominent youth leader before Sjahrir left for Holland. Soewarni's husband, Abdoel Karim Pringgodigdo, had studied in Holland and was a member of Perhimpeonan Indonesia; he had returned a few months before Sjahrir and had helped to found the "free groups" in Batavia.

porary committee for establishing a branch of the Pendidikan Nasional Indonesia."[9] Djohan Sjahroezah—Radena's son, Sjahrir's nephew, and a student at the Batavia Law School at the time—was made the committee's secretary.[10] On January 10, 1932, Sjahrir also took over as chairman of the editorial board of the movement's journal *Daulat Ra'jat*.[11] The painter Salim, among others, was commissioned to write overviews of events abroad and to recommend articles from European journals to be translated.[12]

From Holland, Hatta appeared to be working at a distance to keep the movement loose. He sent a cable to the Pendidikan's December convention (realizing perhaps that Sjahrir would not make it in time to be present) and asked the convention again to "refrain from forming a party [and to] uphold the club structure . . . with its essentially informative character."[13]

Sjahrir developed the same theme in a series of articles he wrote for *Daulat Ra'jat* in January and February 1932. Each political structure, Sjahrir wrote,

> should consist of individual parts, and each of the parts should have its own way of life. The lives of the individual parts might be organized under a larger group, but only if the parts do not have a strong enough wish to lead a free life of their own.[14]

Change is necessary, Sjahrir wrote. Permanent change reflects "social dynamics," and, thus, it is natural and progressive that change should break, "into two or more parts, what once had been a whole."

> Only a structure which is able to live fully, to struggle and to provide space for all of its parts to live fully as well, is a perfect structure.

Any unity could only be "tactical," "temporary," and, therefore, "incidental." An effort to force parts together could only produce a transvestite (*anak bantji*). Such a unity would be "sick, misguided and harmful to the movement."[15]

Both men believed that only education could make sense of this organizational looseness. The Pendidikan Nasional Indonesia, Sjahrir said at a public meeting in Batavia, early in March 1932, "wants first to educate, and thus to map the path which leads to freedom." This was the difference, Sjahrir said, between the Pendidikan, and the political parties. Each Indonesian patriot, Sjahrir said, was free "to choose among the already existing political parties." Even so, one could still be a faithful follower of

---

[9] Sjahrir's letter to *Bintang Merah*, January 18, 1932; *Daulat Ra'jat* 1, 13 (January 20, 1932). See also Mohamad Bondan, "Tjatjatan tentang Pendidikan Nasional Indonesia," n.p., May 22, 1971, a typescript in the *Archives Siti Wahjunah Sjahrir*, p. 1.

[10] Subadio Sastrosatomo's introduction to *Mengenang Sjahrir*, ed. Anwar, p. xviii.

[11] *Keng Po*, January 21, 1932 in *Overzicht v.d. IMC Pers* 1932 1: 63. *Daulat Ra'jat* 1, 12 (January 10, 1932): "Our editorial board is now under the leadership of Sdr. [Comrade] Sjahrir."

[12] Braat, ed., "De brieven van Soeleiman," p. 4.

[13] Reprinted in *PPO* December 1931 (Poeze, ed., *Politiek-politioneele overzichten*, 3: 131); also *Aksi*, December 31, 1931.

[14] Sjahrir, "Faham persatoean," *Daulat Ra'jat* 2, 14 (January 30, 1932).

[15] Sjahrir, "Faham Persatoen," *Daulat Ra'jat* 2, 16 (February 20, 1932); 1, 17 (February 29, 1932); see also "S." (Sjahrir), "Barisan persatoean baroe, *Daulat Ra'jat* 2, 17 (February 29, 1932).

PNI Congress in Bandung. Sjahrir is seated at extreme right.
(Collection Murwoto, Jakarta)

the Pendidikan. It was not the aim of the Pendidikan, Sjahrir said, "to make agitation." Its aim was "to bring clarity."[16]

It was later remarked that the movement's journal had a "didactic character."[17] The topics in *Daulat Ra'jat* indeed were predominantly educational with very little news and few reports. Long lecture-like treatises explained the laws of history, capitalism, the labor movement, Marxism, democracy, and other subjects. A major part of the promotional section of *Daulat Ra'jat* consisted of advertisements for new textbooks, evening schools, and correspondence courses. "*Daulat Ra'jat*," Hatta wrote,

> is not a journal for agitation but a journal for education.... The journal sharpens an understanding and a consciousness. With a sharpened understanding and consciousness, a sense of obligation also grows in the movement and, thus, the meaning of the path we are moving along becomes clear. Because of this ... the journal is the leader."[18]

---

[16] Sjahrir's speech at a Pendidikan Nasional Indonesia meeting in Batavia on March 6, 1932 as recorded by a police agent. *Secret Mail Report* 1932, no. 303.

[17] John D. Legge, "Daulat Ra'jat and the Ideas of the Pendidikan Nasional Indonesia," *Indonesia* 32 (October 1981): 160.

[18] Quoted in Hatta, *Memoir* (Jakarta: Tintamas, 1978), pp. 326–27.

According to Sjahrir, "this journal is here to put the people's movement back in order."[19]

"It is unclear," a Dutch historian has written, "how Sjahrir, on January 4, 1932, could write that he had taken on himself chairmanship of the Pendidikan."[20] But at least one of the large newspapers in the Indies also reported in January that the movement "is now under the leadership of Dr. [sic] Sjahrir."[21] Without accepting any formal function in the central Pendidikan executive, merely, so it appeared, through making speeches, and writing and editing the journal—through teaching, indeed—Sjahrir moved fast towards the top position in the movement.

Sjahrir lived in Batavia, but the center of his life and his politics gravitated back to Bandung. He traveled from Batavia frequently, and most often to Bandung.

In December 1931, before Sjahrir's return, it had been decided that the first congress of the new Pendidikan would be held in Bandung.[22] The central Pendidikan executive was made up largely of Bandung activists and predominantly of Sjahrir's friends. Familiar names appeared especially in the Pendidikan's "commission for courses." Out of the commission's five members, three—Hamdani, Murwoto, and Inoe Perbatasari—had been part of Sjahrir's most intimate circle in Bandung before he left for Holland.[23] The experience they, together with Sjahrir, had acquired as young teachers at the Bandung students' Tjahja Volksuniversiteit, "People's University," between 1926 and 1929 evidently made them particularly well qualified for the positions of leadership in the Pendidikan.

As planned, the Pendidikan Nasional Indonesia's first congress met in Bandung between June 23 and June 26, 1932. Burhanuddin—another close friend of Sjahrir from pre-1929 Bandung—welcomed the guests. Present at the congress were delegates from Pemoeda Indonesia, Sjahrir's pre-1929 youth organization, from the Tjahja Universiteit, and from Istri Sedar, "Conscious Woman," the newly named sister branch of the Pemoeda Indonesia. Sjahrir's long-time friend Soewarni was Istri Sedar's chairwoman.[24]

The congress elected a new central executive. Sjahrir became the chairman; Soekaemi, the outgoing chairman, became his deputy; Hamdani and Murwoto became the first and the second secretaries, Soeka, who had also been close to Sjahrir in the old days in Bandung, became the second treasurer. Besides Soekaemi, Maskoen was the only one in the new leadership not from Sjahrir's old Bandung student group.[25]

---

[19] (Sjahrir), "Barisan Persatoean Baroe," *Daulat Ra'jat* 2, 17 (February 29, 1932).

[20] Kwantes in R. G. Kwantes, ed., *De Ontwikkeling van de Nationalistische Beweging in Nederlandsch-Indië*, 4 vols. (Groningen: Wolters-Noordhoff, 1975–82); 3: 87n. (This was a remark referring to a letter which Sjahrir wrote after his arrival to Maria Tas-Duchâteau in Holland.)

[21] *Keng Po*, January 21, 1932 quoted in *Overzicht v.d. IMC pers* 1932, 1: 67–68.

[22] PPO December 1931 (Poeze, ed., *Politiek-politioneele overzichten*, 3: 130), pp. 2–4.

[23] Police report on Hamdani in *Secret Verbaal*, November 28, 1934–L33.

[24] On Istri Sadar see, e.g., Salmon, "Presse féminine ou féministe?" *Archipel* 13 (1977): 181–182, 197. Sri Mangoensarkoro, *Riwajat pergerakan wanita Indonesia* (Jakarta: Wanita Rakjat, 1946), p. 4; *PPO* October 1930; Poeze, ed., *Politiek-politioneele overzichten*, 2: 443–44); A. K. Pringgodigdo, *Sedjarah Pergerakan Rakjat Indonesia* (Jakarta: Pustaka Rakjat, 1950), pp. 188–92.

[25] Maskoen had been Sukarno's close associate before 1929 and was one of the three nationalist leaders who had stood trial with Sukarno in 1930. Maskoen, however, had been disillusioned by what Sartono and Partindo had done after Sukarno went to prison; he had become involved with "free groups" and now was elected the Pendidikan executive's first treasurer.

The working committee of the Pendidikan's new executive was also chaired by Sjahrir. Hamdani and Maskoen were committee members, along with Soebagio, who, in the meantime, had evidently let himself be convinced by Sjahrir and had returned from Singapore. Soeka and Murwoto were elected working-committee advisers.[26] The congress decided that, besides *Daulat Ra'jat* as a theoretical journal— an official Pendidikan press organ would be published, *Kedaulatan Ra'jat*. Sjahrir, Soebagio, Burhanuddin, Inoe Perbatasari, and Maskoen made up *Kedaulatan Ra'jat*'s editorial board.[27]

The Pendidikan secretariat had its office in Bandung. The addresses shifted between Kopoweg 53 and Kampoeng Bong 61A-5B, both private residences, of Maskoen and Hamdani respectively.[28] Sjahrir now traveled to Bandung practically each week, and before the end of 1932 he moved there. He was again, and daily, with old friends and often, indeed, in the same houses, halls, and classrooms. He mostly lived with Hamdani, when he was in town, and with Hamdani's family he often went to see movies in the same theaters he remembered from before his years in Holland.[29]

2. THE CONFRONTATION WITH SUKARNO

The Dutch-staged trial of Sukarno had taken place in Bandung in August and September 1930. Contrary, perhaps, to what Hatta and Sjahrir had expected, the trial turned out to be another good performance by the great actor. Sukarno's defense speech on December 1 became a new classic of the nationalist movement. Later that month, Sukarno was sentenced to four years in prison, but his silence appeared as impressive as the trial and his oratory had previously.[30]

After months of flamboyance, Sukarno became a hermit. And this turned out to be a powerful role to many of Sukarno's followers, especially in Java. Some nationalist newspapers now published prayers to Sukarno. Those mystically inclined—and their numbers seemed to be growing—expected Sukarno to emerge from prison as somebody not unlike the Javanese *Ratu Adil*, "Just Prince," the noble savior of Java-

---

[26] On the congress see *Secret Mail Report* 1932, no. 732; also "Riwajat ringkas dari Pendidikan Nasional Indonesia," *Kedaulatan Ra'jat* 6 (August1934); *Banteng Ra'jat* 1, 16–17 (July 5–15, 1932); *Semangat Pemoeda* 1, 5 (July 15, 1932): 8; for memoirs by a participant see Sastra, "Sjahrir untuk Sastra,"pp. 81–91, 183–84. Murwoto, *Autobiografi selaku perintis kemerdekaan* (Jakarta: Departemen Sosial, 1984), p. 18, notes that it was Sjahrir who decided that Murwoto and Hamdani at least would get the posts. See also Bondan, "Tjatjatan tentang Pendidikan," p.1.

[27] *Kedaulatan Ra'jat* 1 (October 1932). Hatta joined the journal editorial board when he came back; see below.

[28] *Daulat Ra'jat*, 2, 35 (August 30, 1932).

[29] Hamdani, "Sutan Sjahrir di masa mudanya," in *Mengenang Sjahrir*, ed. Anwar, pp. 78–79; interview with Hamdani and Suzanna, Hamdani's wife, Jakarta, October 26, 1987; Maskun Sumadiredja, "Mengenang Bung Hatta" in *Muhammad Hatta*, ed. Swasono, pp. 395–405, p. 397. According to Murwoto in interview, Jakarta, December 6, 1987, Hamdani was one of the few in the Bandung group with whom Sjahrir corresponded regularly while in Holland. Hamdani said that all the correspondence was later lost. Interview with Hamdani, Jakarta, October 30, 1987.

[30] Legge, *Sukarno*, pp. 109–17; Suwarsih Djojopuspito, *Manusia Bebas* (Jakarta: Djambatan, 1975). [Translation of *Buiten het Gareel*], pp. 57–58; Roger K. Paget, ed. and trans., *Indonesia Accuses! Soekarno's Defence Oration in the Political Trial of 1930* (Kuala Lumpur: Oxford University Press, 1975).

nese tradition.[31] When a delegation from the Dutch tram- and railway- and steel-workers' trade-union visited the Indies in May 1931 it paid two visits to Sukarno in prison. The trade-unionists were immensely impressed by his popularity and reported back to Holland that they had seen "Sukarno's portraits even in the humblest huts."[32]

In September 1931, the departing Dutch Governor-General announced a shortening of Sukarno's prison term as a sign of good will. On the last day of December 1931, Sukarno was to be released. The Governor-General's announcement, as well as the growing signs of revival around Sukarno, undoubtedly prompted Sjahrir's return home.

Men from the Pendidikan, but not Sjahrir—Soeka, Maskoen, Inoe Perbatasari, Murwoto, and Hamdani—were sent to meet Sukarno at the prison gate. *Daulat Ra'jat*, on January 10, 1932, published a welcome. A portrait of Hatta—besides those of Semaoen, the Indonesian Communist leader, Diponegoro, the leader of the Java War against the Dutch in the 1820s, and, of course, Sukarno himself—adorned the hall where the reception for the leader took place.[33]

Four days after Sukarno's release, Sjahrir wrote, from Batavia, to his Dutch friend Maria in Holland:

> It is now very difficult for us, because the greatest part of those associated with us are fanatical followers of Sukarno and anxious to be united with him as soon as possible, with the danger that they may abandon the principles built up by us with great difficulty.[34]

"It is unwise for the moment," Sjahrir continued, "for the D[aulat] R[a'jat] (and thus Hatta also) to oppose him and bring the situation to danger point." A direct confrontation, now, Sjahrir believed, "will mean the isolation of our ideas and probably the political death of Hatta. . . ."[35]

In an article published in *Daulat Ra'jat* in February, Sjahrir maintained that the differences between the Pendidikan and Sukarno were of "a fundamental character [*Grundcharakter*]." Cooperation might be possible, "fusion even," he wrote, "but only as a tactical, and temporary measure."[36]

Sukarno was invited and spoke to the Pendidikan congress held in June 1932 where Sjahrir was elected chairman.[37] Yet Sjahrir apparently did not doubt—as in January—that Sukarno would "follow the old line."[38] And Sukarno, as months

---

[31] Legge, *Sukarno*, pp. 114, 123; See also, e.g., *Aksi*, April 18, 1931.

[32] *De Strijd*, December 4, 1931, quoted in Peter van Tuijl, "Mijn positie is helaas niet erg benijdenswaardig: Nico Palar en de koloniale politiek van de Nederlandse sociaal democratie, 1930–1947" (Ph.D. thesis, University of Amsterdam, 1985), p. 22.

[33] *Daulat Ra'jat* 2, 12 (January 10, 1932).

[34] Sjahrir to Maria Duchâteau, January 4, 1932 in Attorney General to Governor-General, August 19, 1932 in *Secret Verbaal*, October 19, 1933-O24; I have used John Ingleson's translation; Ingleson, *Road to Exile*, p. 171.

[35] Ibid.

[36] Sjahrir, "Faham persatoean . . . sepandjang strategie I"; and Sjahrir, "Faham persastoean . . . sepandjang taktiek I," *Daulat Ra'jat* 2, 15 (February 10, 1932).

[37] *Daulat Ra'jat* 2, 30 (July 10, 1932); *Secret Mail Report* 1932, no. 273.

[38] Sjahrir to Maria Duchâteau, January 4, 1932 in Attorney General to Governor-General, August 19, 1932 in *Secret Verbaal*, October 19, 1933-O24.

passed by, was proving Sjahrir right. He presented himself even more than before as an actor, an orator, and a Javanese. He portrayed his release from prison as a return from a Javanese hermit's abode, something "equal to the descent of Kakråsånå," "the return of Wasidjåjådårå from his place of penance, Argåsonjå," to save "the princesses Erawati and Banawati from danger."[39] The mythical Javanese heroes were Sukarno himself, while the lofty Javanese princesses to whom he was referring, were to be Sartono's Partindo and Sjahrir's Pendidikan.

In late June 1932, the Indonesian press predicted that Sukarno would have to abandon his plan of placing both the competing movements under his leadership. It was speculated that he would join one of the rival groups.[40] On July 5, Hatta passed his examination in Rotterdam, got his *doctorandus* degree, and let his friends know he might be expected back home in two months.[41] Sjahrir's and Hatta's journal *Daulat Ra'jat* was still recommending Sukarno's writings to its followers.[42] As increasingly expected, on August 1, 1932, Sukarno decided against Sjahrir's Pendidikan and in favor of Sartono's Partindo.[43]

During the following twelve months, the membership of Partindo, now under Sukarno's leadership, ballooned to twenty thousand. The Pendidikan remained at roughly the same level, one thousand members, as in December 1931 at the time of Sjahrir's return.[44] The contrast was striking. Even more striking, however, was the way in which the Pendidikan's smallness and accompanying sense of marginality was incorporated into its style and quest for power.

---

[39] The police stenographic record of the speech is in *Secret Mail Report* 1932, no. 100.

[40] Ingleson, *Road to Exile*, p. 175.

[41] *Daulat Ra'jat* 2, 30 (July 10, 1932); 2, 34 (August 20, 1932). *Semangat Pemoeda* 1, 6 (August 15, 1932), p. 96, wrote that Hatta had already got his degree and departed from Holland on July 20.

[42] *Daulat Ra'jat*, 2, 30 (July 10, 1932). See also another Pendidikan journal *Banteng Ra'jat*, 1, 4 (March 8, 1932); 1,7 (April 5, 1932). At the Istri Sedar congress on July 15 in Bandung, Soewarni Pringgodigdo, the chairman, welcomed Sukarno as a speaker and all present stood up and shouted three times *Hidoeplah Ir. Soekarno!* "Long Live Ingenieur Sukarno!" (*Sinar Deli*, July 25, 1932, p. 2).

[43] Ingleson, *Road to Exile*, p.175. Murwoto, of the Pendidikan executive, tells about Sukarno inviting him for a talk "under four eyes," just before the decision was made. "Sukarno told me in Dutch," Murwoto remembers,"pointing to his head, '*Mijn intellect zit bij Mr.Sartono*,' then he pointed to his chest and said, '*Maar mijn hart zit bij jou*.' Which is translated something like 'My intellect is with Mr. Sartono, but my inner heart (*hati nuraniku*) is with you.' . . . Then Sukarno told me I would get seventy-five guilders a month if I would be willing to become the General Secretary of Partindo. . . . But I told him that I had already given my word: '*Ik zal mijn woord niet terugslikken*'." (Murwoto, *Autobiografi*, pp. 17–18.) Sukarno, at least in his later autobiography, suggests that he was very angry at the Pendidikan intransigence. "In the absence of strong decisive leadership [i.e., when Sukarno was in prison], two Netherlands-educated intellectuals, Sjahrir and Hatta, disagreed with the methods of their confreres," Sukarno wrote. And "I never quite understood this fancy intellectual hairsplitting. Hatta and Sjahrir never created any might. All they ever did was talk. No action, just conversation." Sukarno, *An Autobiography as Told to Cindy Adams*, pp. 117–18.

[44] J. Th. Petrus Blumberger, *Politiek partijen en stroomingen in Nederlandsch-Indië* (Leiden: Leidsche Uitgeversmaatschappij, 1934), pp. 22–23. Pringgodigdo says the Pendidikan had by June 1932 about 2,000 members (Pringgodigdo, *Sedjarah*, p. 128); but he does not seem to be very dependable in describing Pendidikan's size at the time. For instance, he says that at that time the Pendidikan had sixty-five branches, of which thirty-five were candidate branches. A contemporary Pendidikan source, the official journal *Kedaulatan Ra'jat* listed for June 1932 only twelve branches. *Kedaulatan Ra'jat* 1 (October 1932.)

According to some Dutch civil servants' and police reports, the Pendidikan "worked, more than Partindo, among the lower classes," it "consistently spread propaganda among the lowest strata of the population... targeted poor villagers... small peasants [kleinen tani]."[45] The areas that the Pendidikan was reportedly "reaching down into," however, appear actually to have been limited almost exclusively to two regions—Cirebon and Indramayu. Both of these were located on the northern coast of western Java, thus culturally on the margin of Java proper, and both were "atypical" of Java as their "lower class" dynamism had been very much determined by their large sugar plantations.

The Pendidikan's leaders appear to have acutely sensed the frontiers of Java proper, the "real" Java. Repeatedly, the Pendidikan central executive put brakes on the propaganda of its local branches, as if deliberately slowing the process of the individual branch's "reaching down." Some provincial and local branches of the Pendidikan were even dismantled—at the very moment, it appears, when the organization's expansion might have crossed the fine line. The Pendidikan seems to stop, or recede even, rather than come close to using a *Ratu Adil*, "Just-Prince," "Javanese-tradition," "glorious-Java" kind of ideology. In that initial period the Pendidikan seems to halt suddenly whenever *djimat*, "charms" or "mystical thinking" might have come into play—or whatever other manifestations of what could be perceived as "regionalist," "pre-modern" or "cultural-nationalist emotions."[46]

The Pendidikan Nasional Indonesia, in contrast to Partindo, never attracted large crowds to its meetings, not even when its top leaders came to town. In contrast to Sukarno, Sjahrir was considered a bad public speaker, especially given that so many of his speeches had now to be given in Java proper. It was no longer merely Bandung or West Java, where Sundanese was spoken and where Sukarno was also in a sense a stranger. Sjahrir's inability to switch into Javanese, as he headed an all-Indies organization, became flagrant. It sharply contrasted with Sukarno's oratory, which in its intermingling of Javanese was a masterpiece.[47]

As most activity took place in Java, Partindo, in contrast to the Pendidikan, appeared to be more safely rooted in "both worlds" of the Indies—the "genuinely native" community with its strong beliefs in tradition, as well as the "modern" men and women of the colony. University graduates dominated the Partindo leadership, and many of the leaders had degrees from Holland, often owning quite respectable law, or civil engineering, or medical practices in the colony.[48] At the same time, as a historian has put it:

---

[45] Nota Kat Angelino, August 1933 in *Secret Verbaal*, October 19, 1933-O24; also Nota Kat Angelino. September 6, 1933, p. 25. Resident Cirebon Van der Plas to Governor of West Java, November 5, 1932, in *Secret Mail Report* 1933, no. 71. Governor of West Java to Governor-General, December 7, 1932 in *Secret Mail Report* 1932, no. 1226; also in Kwantes, ed., *De Ontwikkeling*, 3: 671. "Conference of the residents of West Java," speech by Resident of Ceribon November 15, 1932 in *Secret Mail Report* 1933, no. 71.

[46] Ibid. The arrogance the Pendidikan exercised towards those in the villages was mentioned in Dutch reports, and also reported was the growing resentment of "customary village heads and traditional Islamic leaders" towards the Pendidikan. Police report on Residency Cirebon for November 1932, pp. 3–4 in *Secret Mail Report* 1933, no. 71.

[47] For an illustration of how the flavoring of public speeches in Indonesian with Javanese was almost a must, see e.g. *Banteng Ra'jat* 1, 21 and 30 (August 25 and November 25, 1932).

[48] This was also true at the branch executive level of Partindo. Ingleson says, "*Partindo* branches were in the main, established and controlled by one or more Netherlands-educated

it does seem that, in general, those who were educated in the Netherlands and led *Partindo*, were the sons of the traditional élite. . . .[49]

The Pendidikan tried and succeeded in being different. Its leadership took pains, throughout 1932 and 1933, to present the movement as clean of any "intellectual-aristocratic spirit." The Pendidikan carefully registered all of the *ningrat*, "aristocratic," characteristics of its opponent.[50] "Noble bearers of degrees" was a favorite term. Indeed, more men and women among the Pendidikan's top leadership possessed a less respectable colonial education and thus, theoretically, faced a less certain future than did their Partindo counterparts. There seemed to be, as far as incomplete records allow us to speculate, a greater proportion of lower school teachers and low paid petty clerks in the Pendidikan—intellectuals often on the brink of subsistence or unemployment.

Sjahrir and Hatta, with their Dutch experience, seemed to attract fewer members of the established intellectual elite on Java than Partindo did. Sjahrir returned to the largely unchanged small group of Indies-educated friends whom he had left behind when he departed for Holland. Hatta remained the exception and indeed a lonely figure in the Pendidikan executive: nobody among his comrades had a Dutch degree.[51] There seem to have been many more "professional revolutionaries" in the Pendidikan than in the lawyers', doctors', and engineers' Partindo—unsettled men dependent fully on the organization's funds.

The colonial police frequently reported that the Pendidikan concentrated its activity in the same regions of Java where the Communist Party of Indonesia had been active before its destruction in 1927.[52] As the reader may recall from the last chapter, as early as October 1931 the police spotted "less developed radical elements including some old Communists" at early meetings of the "free groups" out of which the Pendidikan emerged.[53] Similarly, Soekarto, the editor of *Daulat Ra'jat* before Sjahrir returned, was listed in the police records as a "well-known communist." Suspected as Communists were also other leaders of the Pendidikan, for instance Bondan and Soehadi.[54] Also, according to some contemporary sources sympathetic to the Pendidikan, the difference between Partindo and the Pendidikan, early in 1932, was "like that between the social democrats and the communists."[55] Sastra, after June 1932 sometimes described as a "proletarian" mentor of Sjahrir, was a self-educated man

---

doctor, lawyer or engineer. . . ." Ingleson, *Road to Exile*, p. 194; see also Ingleson, "Revolutionary Ideas," pp. 27–28.

[49] Ibid.

[50] E.g., *Aksi* November 28, 1932 in *Overzicht v.d. IMC pers* 1932 IIA, pp. 353, 357; Sn (Soewarna), "Masih sadja jang kliroe," *Menjala* 2, 8 (January 1933).

[51] See the record on the Pendidikan Nasional Indonesia interrogations in *Secret Verbaal*, November 28, 1934-I33 where there is detailed information on the education of all the top leaders.

[52] *PPO* October 1932, p. 6 (Poeze, ed., *Politiek-politioneele overzichten*, 3: 222).

[53] *PPO* October 1931, pp. 4–6. (Poeze, ed., *Politiek-politioneele overzichten*, 3: 115). Also *Verslag van openbare vergadering van de golongan merdeka op zondag 1 Nov.1931 te Batavia belegd*, in *Secret Mail Report* 1931, no. 1148.

[54] *PPO*, October 1931, pp. 4–6.

[55] *Moestika* January 23, 1932 in *Overzicht v.d. IMCC pers* 1932 IA, p. 66.

living in a suburb of Bandung "truly among the common people." He had spent four years in prison for his participation in the 1926 Communist uprising.[56]

Hatta's and Sjahrir's attitude towards communism at that time was on the surface ambiguous. Both men believed that Hatta's expulsion from the League against Imperialism and Colonialist Oppression and their losing ground in the Perhimpoenan Indonesia in the early 1930s had been very much the doing of the Communists.[57] At the same time, the Pendidikan, as Sastra for instance wrote later, used the Communists as a doctor uses a stethoscope, to listen to what was going on deeper in the national body than it itself could see.[58] The fragmentation of the Communist organization in the Indies, the fact that the party, after the aborted uprisings in 1926 and 1927, was crushed and its members scattered and pushed to the fringes of Indonesian society and politics seemed to build up a curious kind of companionship between the Communists and the Pendidikan—not wholly the powerless affinity of margin.

The essence of the fragmentation of the Indonesian Communists at the time—marginal and, in fact, largely in exile—was the splinter movement connected with a Minangkabau revolutionary and *perantau*, Tan Malaka. Tan Malaka had been the chairman of the Communist Party of Indonesia in the early 1920s, and he served later as a representative of the Comintern in South and East Asia. In that capacity, he disagreed, in 1926, with the decision of the Communist Party of Indonesia to begin the armed struggle. He distanced himself, and was distanced, from the party and from the Comintern as the uprising was attempted and failed. The resulting bitterness between him and the rest of the party lasted for decades.

In 1927, in exile in Thailand, Tan Malaka had founded a new party, the Partai Repoebliek Indonesia, PARI, "Party of the Indonesian Republic." Then and for years to come, Tan Malaka's whereabouts were uncertain. Some copies of his journal, *Obor*, "Torch," were reportedly smuggled into the Indies; some were typewritten; others even circulated in longhand.[59] No copies survive, not even in the police archives, and Tan Malaka's subsequent life in the Indies was largely a rumor. He was marginal in other senses, too: his fame, whatever this may mean, was much greater in Sumatra than in Java.[60]

A certain Gaban and one Iljas Togo, allegedly Tan Malaka's agents in Singapore, are said to have served, in early 1932, as "contacts" between Tan Malaka and Hatta in Holland.[61] Later some connection between the Pendidikan and Tan Malaka's

---

[56] See Sastra, "Sjahrir untuk Sastra," especially p. 85. also Sjahbuddin Mangandaralam, *In memoriam Sutan Sjahrir; perdjuangan dan perderitaannja* (Bandung: Panjasakti, 1966), p. 24.

[57] E.g. Mohammad Hatta, "Perhimpoenan Indonesia dan saja," *Daulat Ra'jat* 1, 14 (January 30, 1932); *Kedaulatan Ra'jat* 2 (November 1932), *Banteng Ra'jat* 1, 16–17 (August 5–15, 1932), ibid., 30 (November 25, 1932); *Menjala* 1,1 (November 1932) and ibid., 2, 6 (January 1933).

[58] Sastra, "Sjahrir untuk Sastra," p. 85.

[59] Leon Salim, "Inspektur Belanda Memanggilnja Tuan," *Fokus* 2, 28 (January 19, 1984). Jarvis, ed., *From Jail to Jail*, 1: lxxxviii.

[60] Occasionally, "agents" of the PARI were detected in the Indies. But by and large, this was a leaderless movement. Soebakat, the most able associate Tan Malaka ever had, was arrested by the Dutch and died in prison in February 1930. Djamaloeddin Tamin, the next best around Tan Malaka, perhaps, was arrested at the same time as Soebakat and, although released, remained under close police surveillance. In October 1932, Tan Malaka himself was put in jail in Hong Kong. Ibid., 2: 33ff ; see also Poeze, *Tan Malaka*, especially chapter X, pp. 354–446.

[61] Ibid., p. 413.

movement was, so the police suspected, maintained through the Perhimpoenan Peladjar-Peladjar Indonesia, PPPI, "Association of Indonesian Students," at the Law School in Batavia. Jahja Nasoetion, a leader of the PPPI, in a Dutch report from 1933 was mentioned as "the most important figure" in Tan Malaka's network in Batavia.[62] Another Law School student and PPPI leader—who repeatedly appeared in the police reports as a follower, contact or agent of Tan Malaka—was Sjahrir's nephew, Radena's son, Djohan Sjahroezah.[63]

True to what Hatta and especially Sjahrir learned in Holland, the Pendidikan declared itself to be a movement intimately close to the Indonesian proletariat. *Daulat Ra'jat* serialized Marx's *Das Kapital*. Hatta wrote commentaries popularizing Marx's thoughts.[64] Pendidikan's journals repeatedly called themselves "proletarian."[65]

Sjahrir was remembered afterwards by other members of the Pendidikan as "a man who moved among workers" and "worked with the labor movement."[66] After Sjahrir took over *Daulat Ra'jat* in January 1932, the number and length of articles on labor problems in the journal markedly increased. Sjahrir himself wrote on the issue extensively. His speeches were increasingly, and with passing months almost exclusively, concerned with labor.[67] By the time of the Pendidikan conference in March 1933, he had become the movement's official labor expert.[68] When in May 1933 the Congres Kaoem Boeroeh Indonesia, CKBI, the "Indonesian Workers' Congress," held a convention in Surabaya, Sukarno, Soetomo, and Sjahrir were the main speakers.[69] As the convention ended, Sjahrir was elected the CKBI chairman.[70]

---

[62] Attorney General to Governor-General, March 16, 1933; Attorney General to Governor-General, November 13, 1933 in *Secret Mail Report* 1933, no. 1106; *PPO* Batavia March 1933, pp. 7–8; Police report to Attorney General in *Secret Mail Report* 1936, no. 446; On Jahja Nasoetion as a leading activist for PARI in Batavia see Nasoetion's younger follower and friend, Adam Malik; Adam Malik, *Mengabdi Republik: Adam dari Andalas* vol. 1 (Jakarta: Gunung Agung, 1979), p. 182 and *passim*.

[63] Another possible link, real or alleged, might have been Roeksodipoetro, a student at the Law School, chairman of the PPPI, and at the same time a member of the Pendidikan's commission for education.

[64] Beginning *Daulat Ra'jat* 3, 58 (April 20, 1933).

[65] See, e.g., *Daulat Ra'jat* 3, 66 (July 10, 1933); or *Banteng Ra'jat* 1, 15 (August 1932) in *Overzicht v.d. IMC pers* 1932 IIA, p. 148.

[66] Iwa Kusuma Sumantri, *Sedjarah Revolusi Indonesia*, 3 vols. (Jakarta: Iwa Kusuma Sumantri, 1969), 2: 110; Adam Malik, "Sambutan untuk peringatan hari lahir 70 tahun almarhum Bung Sjahrir" in *Mengenang Sjahrir*, ed. Anwar, p. 2.

[67] Sjahrir's first public speech in Java on which we have a detailed report was on March 6, 1932, and dealt specifically with labor problems; see "Verslag van de openbare vergadering . . . Pendidikan Nasional Indonesia, March 6, 1932, Batavia," in *Mail Report* 1932, no. 303. On August 14, 1932, for instance, in Sukabumi, Sjahrir spoke on "nationalism and democracy"; on August 22, in Surakarta, on "capitalism and imperialism"; on November 13 and 25 in Purwokerto and Semarang, and on December 4, in Bandung, on "trade unions." *Banteng Ra'jat* 1,21 (August 25, 1932); also *Banteng Ra'jat* in *Overzicht v.d. IMC pers* 1932 IIA, pp. 340, 370.

[68] It was decided that at the movement's planned congress Sjahrir would speak on the problem of labor and Hatta on "merchants and village unions," *PPO* April 1933, p. 17 (Poeze, ed., *Politieke-politioneele overzichten*, 3: 280).

[69] Records of the Congress, "Verslag 1ste Kongres Kaoem Boeroeh Indonesia . . . Soerabaja van 4 tot 7 mei 1933" (included in Gobée report to Governor-General, May 29, 1933 in *Secret*

The CKBI labor federation was confined to Java and its membership was overwhelmingly Javanese. Sjahrir, indeed, as a non-Javanese, was the sole exception in the federation's leadership. Most of the executive's members were politicians from Central and East Java. Soetomo—the man, we may recall, Sjahrir had ridiculed in Holland as "His Highness Doctor Soetomo"—became the federation's secretary and treasurer.[71] The CKBI headquarters, after the convention, were moved from Surabaya—the port and sailors' and workers' city, to Yogyakarta—the heart of Java proper.[72]

Was Sjahrir moving at last from the margin toward the core of the Indonesian movement? Sukarno gave a rousing opening address to the convention in Surabaya, but then excused himself and, still on the first day, left, as he said, to visit his parents.[73] None of the other Partindo leaders made any strenuous effort to become a leader of the federation. Soetomo, who was elected Sjahrir's deputy, did not seem to take his position very seriously. He even let it be known in private at the time of the convention that he "[does] not believe in this federation and [expects] the federation soon to collapse."[74]

The economic depression which hit the Indies in 1930 crushed the modern, and especially the export sector of the colonial economy. A sharp decline in capitalist activity pushed hundreds of thousands of native workers out of factories and plantations. Indonesian society, however, the Javanese peasant community in particular, manifested an impressive capacity to absorb the flood and to cushion the shock. There was little unrest.[75] The "modern proletariat," especially in Java, appeared—in the indigenous society as well as in nationalist movement—more marginal after the depression than it had before.

In a booklet written for labor at the time, Sjahrir quoted statistics extensively. In 1931 there were, according to the statistics, two million workers in the Indies, which was less than 3 percent of the native population. Only about 6 percent of the 3 percent were organized. This tiniest segment's organization was still further fragmented into more than a hundred trade unions.[76]

In a series of articles published at the time, L. N. Palar, a labor expert from the Dutch Social Democratic Labor Party, concluded that the movement in the Indies was "as good as dead."[77] Sjahrir's own federation might have served as a good example of this. The CBKI was a conglomerate of four unions—the Persatoean Kereta Api, "Union of Railway Employees," the Pegawai Drukkerij Indonesia, "Indonesian Clerks in Printers Shops," the Sarekat Chauffeur Indonesia, "Union of Indonesian

---

Mail Report 1933, no. 689. See also *Bintang Timoer*, January 7, 1933 in *Overzicht v.d. IMC pers* 1933 IA, p. 28.

[70] Ibid.

[71] Ibid.; also Attorrney General to Governor-General, August 19, 1933 in *Secret Verbaal*, October 19, 1933-O24. Soetomo was the CKBI's chairman till the May 1933 convention. Ibid.

[72] For a survey of the situation in the Javanese labor movement at the time see also Pringgodigdo, *Sedjarah*, pp. 104, 180–81.

[73] "Verslag 1ste Kongres Kaoem Boeroeh Indonesia."

[74] Gobée report, May 29, 1933, in *Secret Mail Report* 1933, no. 689.

[75] See, e.g., John Ingleson, "Urban Java during the Depression," *Journal of Southeast Asian Studies* 19, 2 (September 1988): 309.

[76] Sjahrir, *Pergerakan Sekerdja* (Batavia: Daulat Ra'jat, 1933), p. 29.

[77] *Vakbeweging*, November 1934 quoted in van Tuijl, *Mijn positie*, p. 44.

Chauffeurs," and the Sarekat Koesir Indonesia, "Union of Indonesian Coachmen." It was, clearly, a curious conglomerate in itself. Moreover, it was a very loose conglomerate and, as far as is known, had virtually no organizational ties to other trade unions in the colony.[78]

As Sjahrir accepted the labor federation chairmanship, and as he became increasingly concerned with labor, he appeared also to become increasingly detached from the Pendidikan itself. He left the chairmanship of the editorial board of *Daulat Ra'jat* late in 1932. In early 1933 he resigned as the chairman of the Pendidikan executive. He was still listed as a deputy chairman of the Pendidikan, but later in the year it seems, he also left that position and afterwards was mentioned merely as a "general adviser to the Pendidikan."[79]

More and more Sjahrir devoted his time "fully to the workers."[80] And, thus, he went further and further to the fringes. In July 1933, he was elected chairman of the Congres Kaoem Boeroeh Indonesia for another term.[81] A few days later, he appeared at a meeting in Semarang of another trade union, the Persatoean Boeroeh Kereta Api Indonesia, "Union of Indonesian Railways Workers." A police report described his function as representing a trade union centrale—so obscure evidently to the police agent, that he misspelled it beyond recognition.[82]

After July 1933, Sjahrir seemed to loosen even his ties with the CBKI he was supposedly the chairman of. The organization itself was disappearing. There are almost no traces in either the very detailed police reports or in the memories of his friends of what Sjahrir subsequently did in the movement. Only an extremely marginal trade union, about which nothing is known but the name—Organisatie Kaoem Boeroeh Penganggoeran Indonesia, "Organization of Unemployed Indonesians"—is mentioned once as, now, the only recognizable focus of Sjahrir as a political leader.[83]

3. The Return of Hatta and the Minangkabau Base

From its beginning, the Pendidikan was a Java-based organization. All twelve of the its branches, and both of its *krings*, "districts," as listed by the Bandung congress in

---

[78] *Verslag 1ste Congres*, and Attorney General to Governor-General, August 19, 1932 in *Secret Verbaal*, October 19, 1933-O24.

[79] Interrogation of the Pendidikan leaders in *Secret Verbaal*, November 28, 1934-I33. Some say Sjahrir still acted as the "deputy chairman for organization" after he resigned from the chairmanship because he was closer to Bandung than Hatta who lived in Batavia; e.g., *Riwajat HSS*, p. 7; Murwoto, *Autobiografi*, p. 19. Bondan, "Tjatjatan tentang Pendidikan, p. 2.

[80] *Sikap*, July 27, 1933, in *Overzicht v.d. IMC pers* 1933, 2: 495–96; also Attorney General to Governor-General, November 22, 1933 in *Secret Mail Report* 1933, no. 1137.

[81] Report by Semarang police, July 25, 1933 in *Secret Mail Report* 1933, no. 946. Soewondo, also of the Pendidikan, became the first secretary; Soetomo remained as the second secretary.

[82] Ibid.

[83] Interview with Hamdani, Jakarta, October 30, 1988; interview with Burhanuddin, Jakarta, March 5, 1982. On Sjahrir's concern for unemployed workers see e.g. his speeches from the time as recorded in *Secret Mail Reports* 1932, no. 303 and 1933, no. 689. No connection is documented between Sjahrir's activity and Surabaya's Comité Werkloozen Front, "Committee of the Front of the Unemployed." On the Committee, with its a headquarters in Surabaya, led by "Jahja alias Pamboedi alias Koesoemardjo," together with a "certain Djawoto," see *PPO* July 1930 (Poeze, ed., *Politiek-politioneele overzichten*, 2: 414). Both Koesoemardjo and especially, Djawoto became, by 1932 at least, important Pendidikan activists.

June 1932, were located on Java. Out of the ten branches registered at the congress as being "in a state of preparation," only one was from outside Java—Pariaman, in Minangkabau.[84] A half year later, when the number of branches had grown to thirty-two, twenty-six of them were still on Java. All the remaining six were on Sumatra; four of them in Minangkabau.[85] There were five Pendidikan or pro-Pendidikan journals published by October 1932: *Banteng Ra'jat* in Yogyakarta, *Daulat Ra'jat* in Batavia, *Api Ra'jat* in Surakarta, *Marhaen* and *Kedaulatan Ra'jat* in Bandung.[86] No Pendidikan or pro-Pendidikan journal was published outside Java.

Java surrounded the Pendidikan and inevitably left its mark. Reading through its journals, one might come across a metaphor out of Javanese tradition; a hero from the *wayang*, the Javanese shadow-puppet play, might occasionally be used as a model for a true nationalist as it had traditionally been used as the model for a true Javanese. Even the *Ratu Adil*, the Javanese savior-prince, might be invoked now and then.[87] What was striking, however, was not the fact, that these "Javanisms" appeared in the Pendidikan journals, but how rare they were.

In the first thirty-five issues of *Daulat Ra'jat*, only six articles dealt specifically with Java. As many as ten articles, at the same time, were devoted to Sumatra, six of them to Minangkabau and one to Medan. In the journal's advertisement section, Minangkabau firms, either in Sumatra or in Java, took almost all the space.

As one reads through the articles in *Daulat Ra'jat* issues of the time, one is struck by a contrast. In the Javanese articles few "Javanisms" were admitted. Articles on Java in *Daulat Ra'jat* appear to have been written generally in a dry political and detached way. Most are, in fact, articles on all-Indonesian matters which just happened to have taken place on Java. The Sumatran articles, on the other hand, and namely the texts on Minangkabau, impress one as very colorful, politically cultural, and distinctly regional in flavor.

In a very long article, for instance, entitled "The Minangkabau Story and the Movement," published in a prominent place in *Daulat Ra'jat* in August 1932, the author signed H.M. (Haroen Moein most probably) wrote,

> Minangkabau was a self-standing domain, in the past, made up of people devoted to their own time-honored values and laws. The Minangkabau did not lag in technological progress, economy, social organization or morals behind the other peoples of the world, either in the West or in the East.

There were difficult times, the article explained, such as when "the Hindus with long noses" came. The Minangkabau, however, were strong enough to react by adhering to their customs (*adat*), to Islam, and to commerce.

To have their way, the Hindus "fathered Adityawarman," the Javanese king, and forced him upon the Minangkabau people. Next, "imperialism and capitalism" came from the West. Again, the intruders "had much less of a free hand in Minangkabau, than they enjoyed in Java and other places...." Again the

---

[84] *Kedaulatan Ra'jat* 1 (October 1932).

[85] Ibid., 1, 2 and 3 (November and December 1933).

[86] This is the list that appeared in ibid. 1, 1 (October 1932).

[87] E.g.*Keinsjafan Ra'jat* 2, 4 (March 1933). *Api Ra'jat* in August 1932 wrote, "People had to strive for the coming of the Ratoe Adil, which is Freedom." Quoted in Nota Kat Angelino, September 6, 1933, p. 29.

Minangkabau "community of custom [*kaoem adat*] stood firm like a sturdy buffalo" and also "Islam remained the faith of the people." In the future also, "the welfare and happiness of Minangkabau" will depend on "the deeds of the Minangkabau themselves."[88]

This attitude was evident while Sjahrir was still chairman of the Pendidikan and editor of *Daulat Ra'jat*. It became much more pronounced after Mohammad Hatta returned from Holland.

It was planned that Hatta would stop in the Middle East on his way home to meet Indonesian students and Egyptian nationalist leaders in Cairo and "to fulfill his Islamic duties" in Mecca."[89] Even when this plan was not realized, for lack of money, it was widely publicized, and gave Hatta's return a specific Islamic accent. Another accent was commercial. When Hatta's ship arrived in Batavia on August 24, 1932, he was welcomed by a Pendidikan delegation but also by an *ad hoc* reception committee of the Dewan Perniagan Persatoean Kita, "Our Unity Commercial Council"—a group of patriotic merchants over which Hatta's "uncle" Ajoeb Max Etek presided. (The council's representative at the welcoming ceremony was its secretary, one Mohamad Roem, soon to be son-in law of Sjahrir's cousin, Hadji Agoes Salim.)[90]

Hatta's first political act was to "associate himself" with the education committee of the Batavia branch of the Pendidikan; at the branch's next plenary meeting, a few days after his arrival, he was elected chairman.[91] Then, however, events took rather a surprising turn. After spending barely six weeks on Java, Hatta left for Sumatra, "to visit family," and "for only a month" as he announced.[92] The top leader, a man generally expected to take over the leadership of the Pendidikan from Sjahrir, a man who had hastened his return and was eagerly awaited, spent the following three months in Minangkabau and returned to Java only when forced to do so—after he was expelled from West Sumatra by order of the local Dutch authorities.[93]

In Minangkabau, this was a period when many *perantau*, "the men going to outward regions," were returning. After years of drowsiness following the crushing of the Communist uprising in 1927, the Minangkabau were in state of deep stirring. In contrast to Java, the response to the economic depression seemed to have a more dynamic effect in West Sumatra; in particular it forced a great number of Minangkabau merchants abroad to return home.[94] Coincidentally, a group of highly gifted and articulate Minangkabau Islamic students was returning from Cairo and Mecca, with

---

[88] H. M. (Haroen Moein), "Riwajat Minangkabau dan Pergerakan, *Daulat Ra'jat*, 2, 35 (August 30, 1932).

[89] *Dewan*, 1 (1932) in *Overzicht v.d. IMC pers* 1932 IA, p. 41.

[90] *Soeloeh Ekonomi*, August 1932 in *Overzicht v.d. IMC pers* 1932 IIA, pp. 169–70; Hatta, *Memoir*, pp. 254–56, 307; Mohamad Bondan, "Mengenal Bung Hatta dari dekat" in *Muhammad Hatta*, ed. Swasono, p. 278.

[91] Bondan, "Tjatjatan tentang Pendidikan," p. 1.

[92] *Adil*, October 3, 1932 in *Overzicht v.d. IMC pers* 1932 IIA, p. 232.

[93] *PPO Sumatra West Coast November 1932* in *Secret Mail Report* 1933, no. 115; *Semangat Pemoeda* 1, 10 (December 15, 1932).

[94] About 60 percent of the Maninjau traders in Minangkabau, for instance, were reported to have come home by the third quarter of 1931 as a consequence of the depression. *PPO Sumatra's West Coast*, 3rd quarter of 1931 in *Mail Report* 1931, no. 1200 quoted in Abdullah, *Schools and Politics*, p. 189.

Hatta in 1934

a new spirit of modernism and a political mission.[95] As teachers and in cooperation with the merchants, the student returnees quickly helped revitalize and politicize Islamic Thawalib and Diniyah school systems throughout Minangkabau.

In May 1930, mainly out of the Thawalib schools, a new political party was founded in Minangkabau, the Persatoean Moeslimin Indonesia, or Permi, "Union of Indonesian Muslims." The Permi's program was made up of ideas of modernist Islam, *kebangsaan*, "nationalism," and *kemadjoean*, "progress."[96] In addition, accord-

---

[95] Ibid., p. 149.

[96] Ibid., p. 131; statements by Permi conference of August 1930 and the party resolution of July 1931 see ibid., pp. 131, 159–61; On Permi at this initial stage see also Kwantes, ed., *De Ontwikkeling*, vol. 3, doc. no. 99.

ing to Permi, *keberanian*, "bravery," was needed to "erase the shame 'etched on [our] foreheads' as the result of humiliation inflicted by a foreign power."[97] A Minangkabau historian later commented:

> A traditional sense of communal shame thus obliged every Minangkabau [in Permi's interpretation as in the Minangkabau tradition] to defend the honor of his world (*alam*).[98]

Hatta visited family and also toured Minangkabau widely. He gave speeches in Pariaman, Maninjau, Padang Panjang, and Bukittinggi, and also in Medan. He campaigned for the Pendidikan and he seemed to be very much at ease doing this: much more certainly than Sjahrir had appeared to be a few months earlier, when he was doing the same in Java.[99]

Hatta clearly moved in the same orbit as the students from Cairo and Mecca, and as the Permi activists. His recruits to the Pendidikan also were clearly chosen from essentially the same pool of Minangkabau men—the Diniyah and Thawalib students and teachers and the merchants were most often mentioned as the people whom Hatta approached, impressed, and convinced to join him.[100] Darwis Thaib, who was to become the top figure in the Sumatra Pendidikan, was a member of the Permi executive before he met Hatta. Chatib Soeleiman and Leon Salim, second and third in rank after Darwis Thaib, were respectively an adviser to and a chairman of the Persatoean Moerid Diniyah School, "Union of Diniyah School Pupils"; both, Chatib Soeleiman and Leon Salim, moreover, remained in the Islamic student union even after they became Hatta's followers and joined the Pendidikan.[101]

While the Minangkabau Permi had 10,000 members, by August 1933, the Minangkabau Pendidikan had only 250.[102] The Minangkabau Pendidikan was surrounded and constantly challenged. It gave an additional Minangkabau (thus also Islamic) accent to the central Pendidikan as *Daulat Ra'jat*, for instance, tried to help its West Sumatra comrades to resist the challenge:

> A member of the *Pendidikan Nasional Indonesia* who dies while fighting for national freedom, is he judged by Allah as a *kafir* [infidel]? To be a

---

[97] Quoted in Abdullah, *Schools and Politics*, p. 164.

[98] Ibid.

[99] PPO Sumatra's West Coast November 1932, in *Secret Mail Report* 1933, no. 115. Report of the *wedana* of the police in Padang, October 18, 1933, in *Secret Verbaal*, April 19, 1934-V9. On Hatta arriving on September 9 in Medan to establish a Pendidikan branch there, see *Semangat Pemoeda* 1, 8 (October 15, 1932): 131. On the nervousness about the split between Partindo and *golongan merdeka* in Minangkabau, see, e.g., *Semangat Pemoeda* 1, 2 (April 15, 1932): 18.

[100] PPO Sumatra's West Coast October 1932 in *Secret Mail Report* 1932, no. 1227. See also a report on later police raids on Thawalib schools and the finding of copies of *Daulat Ra'jat*, along with writings by Hatta and the Pendidikan, *Secret Mail Report* 1933, no. 1518 in *Secret Verbaal*, April 19, 1934-V9; also Abdullah, *Schools and Politics*, pp. 200–206.

[101] PPO Sumatra's West Coast November 1932, in *Secret Mail Report* 1933, no. 115; Abdullah, *Schools and Politics*, p. 193. Both also remained editors of the union's monthly *Kodrat Moeda*. On Chatib Soeleiman see Rifai Abu and Abdullah Suhadi, *Chatib Suleiman* (Jakarta: Departemen Penerangan dan Kebudayaan, 1976), esp. pp. 9–12. On Leon Salim, see Salim, "Inspektur Belanda," and interview with Leon Salim, Jakarta, November 3, 1987.

[102] G. F. E. Gonggryp, *Memorie van Overgave*, Sumatra's West Coast (December 31, 1934), p. 28; also Abdullah, *Schools and Politics*, p. 185.

nationalist such as the *Pendidikan* wants one to be, does not this make a *Pendidikan* follower a *moertad* [apostate] to Islam?[103]

Anyone who dies while under the spell of a passion for his motherland, *Daulat Ra'jat* suggested, is an infidel, indeed, because he has "idolized" his motherland. If, however, this man, fighting for the freedom of his motherland, keeps himself *bertauchid* [acknowledging the Oneness of God], then he will reach paradise. In that case, Pendidikan asserted, "the mercy of Allah is with *Kedaulatan Ra'jat*."[104]

The Pendidikan's "Minangkabau conference," which convened in March 1933 in Padang Panjang, became a major event for the entire all-Indonesian organization.[105] The Padang Panjang branch, according to some estimates, became next in importance only to the central headquarters in Bandung and to the powerful branch in Batavia.[106]

The number and length of articles on Minangkabau in *Daulat Ra'jat* rose, too: in the journal's issues no. 45 through no. 85, in 1933, there were nine long articles on West Sumatra and only five contributions of a comparable length on West, Central, and East Java together.

The new and first thorough articulation of Pendidikan's policies originated in Minangkabau. Hatta enunciated it during his stay in West Sumatra, "in his mother's house, indeed."[107] In November 1932, the Pendidikan leaders in Bandung received Hatta's long letter from Bukittinggi—a text called *Kearah Indonesia Merdeka*, "Toward Free Indonesia."[108] The text was discussed by the Pendidikan executive and its final revision was entrusted to the "education committee," chaired by Sjahrir.[109] Sjahrir and Soebagio were asked to produce a version of the new program in simplified language and in the form of questions and answers. These *150 Tanja Djawab*, "150 Questions and Answers," were to be used for day-to-day practical training of the cadres in the Pendidikan courses.[110]

One does not have to read Hatta's original text in order to see how Sjahrir, with the help of Soebagio, willingly reflected the ideas coming from Minangkabau. *Kedaulatan Ra'jat*, "the people's sovereignty," as presented in Sjahrir's and Soebagio's version of the program, "should be based on collectivism, which formed the pillar of our early-day communal life." The "early day" meant:

---

[103] Dar Tyb (Darwis Thaib) in *Daulat Ra'jat* 2, 48 (January 10, 1933); compare "Sedikit djawaban tentang Pendidikan Nasional Indonesia di Minangkabau sambil memperkenalkan diri," ibid., 2, 46 (December 20, 1932); also ibid., 3, 57 (April 10, 1932). See also Abdullah, *Schools and Politics*, p. 170; PPO Sumatra's West Coast December 1932, in *Secret Mail Report* 1933, no. 227.

[104] Dar Tyb, in *Daulat Ra'jat* 2, 48.

[105] *Daulat Ra'jat* 3, 57 (April 10, 1933). A special "regional secretariat" for West Sumatra was established by the conference. PPO Batavia, April 1933, p. 17 (Poeze, ed., *Politiek-politioneele overzichten*, 3: 278–80).

[106] Interview with Burhanuddin, Jakarta, March 5, 1982.

[107] Rose, *Indonesia Free*, p. 66.

[108] Maskun, "Mengenang Bung Hatta," p. 399. Sjahrir announced in *Daulat Ra'jat* 2, 35 (August 30, 1932), that work was being done on a program, *Kearah Indonesia Merdeka*, "Toward Free Indonesia." See *Daulat Ra'jat* 2, 35 (August 30, 1932).

[109] Ibid. *Daulat Ra'jat*, 3, 56 and 57 (November 20 and 30, 1932).

[110] Maskun, "Mengenang Bung Hatta," p. 399; interview with Burhanuddin, Jakarta, March 5, 1982.

Earlier our people lived in a natural economy without any capitalist exploitation. Owners worked their fields with their own hands and with their own tools. Theirs were both the fruits of their work and the sweat of hardship.

The *kedaulatan ra'jat* "people's sovereignty" should be a type of progress which "conforms to both present-day society and the original Indonesian democracy [*demokrasi asli*]."[111]

Ningrat-pemilik-ambtenaar, "aristocrats-proprietors-officials," as always for Sjahrir, were the main enemy.[112] But this time, being anti-aristocratic and progressive, it was stated explicitly, did not mean being "individualistic." Jean Jacques Rousseau's ideal of individualism and of personal freedom, according to the "150 Questions and Answers," could only make "the people's sovereignty" "lame and crippled." Instead, "communal meetings, the collective voice of the people, and mutual consent," "original democracy" again should be the rule.[113]

Individual rights of ownership were to be limited, according to the "150 Questions and Answers," to "personal clothing and furniture." An individual might have merely a "right to use" (*gebruiksrecht*), and a "right of disposal" (*beschikkingsrecht*), which would allow him or her to use, dispose of, profit from, and even inherit to some extent, some utilities, including "a small business," provided that this was not harmful to the community.[114]

According to Sjahrir's and Soebagio's "150 Questions and Answers," the Pendidikan aimed at a social system in which communities were defined as the "body politic," or as "public legal corporations." The "smallest groups" were to be the most important part of the "people's sovereignty" state, and these were to be mutually equal (*sama rata*). Each of these communities "will govern its own affairs, by its own conviction, its own rules, provided these do not contradict the interests of general government."[115]

---

[111] "De honderdvijftig vraagstukken," in Attorney General to Governor-General, February 24, 1934 in *Secret Mail Report* 1934, no. 300; questions/answers nos. 102-4, 119

[112] Sjahrir, "Faham persatoean...Sepandjang taktiek II"; Hatta in *Daulat Ra'jat* 2, 34 (August 20, 1932); Sjahrir, *Pergerakan Sekerdja*, p. 14; Sjahrir, "Pergerakan Indonesia menempoeh saat jang penting," *Daulat Ra'jat* 3, 66 (July 10, 1933); "De honderdvijftig vraagstukken," no. 14. See also Hatta's speech reported in *PPO* Sumatra's West Coast, November 1932, in *Secret Mail Report* 1933, no. 115. The Pendidikan attacked *swadeshi*, especially *loerik*, the typical home-made striped cloth of Central Java. Sartono, now second to Sukarno in the leadership of Partindo, was called a "butcher of the movement and a dealer in *loerik.*" See, e.g., Sjahrir, "Vaderslandsche Club-Swadeshi-Soekarno," *Daulat Ra'jat* 3, 66 (August 10, 1933). See also on *loerik*, the reaction in *Keinsjafan Ra'jat* 2, 8 (April 1932), and editorial in *Daulat Ra'jat* 2, 35 (August 30, 1932). Glorification of the "Modjopahit" Javanese medieval kingdom, and thus the idea of the glorious Javanese past before the Dutch came, was attacked as "*ningrat* propaganda" and a misleading of the masses. E.g., "Drs. Mohd Hatta dan kaoem Djoernalis. Pidato Drs. Mohd.Hatta didalalm pertemoean djoernalis Padang, October 24-25, 1932" in *Semangat Pemoeda* 1, 9 (November 15, 1932). For opposition to the Madjapahit concepts and against *ningrat*, see also Murwoto at the Pendidikan meeting in Yogyakarta, March 19, 1933 in *Secret Mail Report* 1933, no. 384.

[113] "De honderdvijftig vraagstukken," nos. 56, 58, 102, 121.

[114] Ibid., no. 133.

[115] Ibid., nos. 60, 126, 128, 133, 139.

Some observers considered the Pendidikan's concept of ownership and statehood to be "somewhat contradictory."[116] Others dismissed it as a deviation from correct Marxist thought.[117]

The Minangkabau-Islamic Permi attacked Pendidikan's program as "an affront" against Minangkabau custom (*adat*) and against Islamic law.[118] The Pendidikan's leaders responded vehemently to this criticism. Pendidikan's new program, *Daulat Ra'jat* wrote, was in fact a program of "an enlarged family"; it respected the Minangkabau principles of *tolong-menolong*, "mutual help," and *sama rata-sama rasa*, "equality."[119] The Pendidikan's program, *Daulat Ra'jat* predicted, would have "great success among the Minangkabau people, because it is built on the same pillars as Minangkabau society itself."[120]

Sjahrir, by co-authoring the "150 Questions and Answers," went a long way toward meeting Hatta's convictions about "original democracy" and about the source of dynamism for Indonesia's future lying in Minangkabau. Still, it seems, Sjahrir kept moving around, more at a distance. Breaking Hatta's argument into fragments through the use of questions and answers, Sjahrir effectively evaded being as explicit as Hatta. Explaining the crucial concept of ownership, for instance, while Hatta's argument was carefully constructed and wholesome, Sjahrir, after questions nos. 126 and 128 which dealt with the right of use and the right to occupy, placed the following as question and answer, no. 130, without making any connection:

"What are *oelajat* rights?"
These are the rights of land ownership which one encounters among the people in Minangkabau.[121]

Sjahrir, and Hatta, although to a lesser extent now than in Holland, still moved in the sphere in-between. They—and their organization with them—remained on the fringes of colonial Indies society, and also outside the nationalist mainstream on Java. Nor could they be wholly identified with the Minangkabau regional-Islamic revival. The lasting visible hesitation on the part of both of them to cross the threshold, fully enter the actual, down-to-earth, day-to-day world of politics was a consequence of this uncertainty and looseness.

The Pendidikan journal *Banteng Ra'jat* which was published in Yogyakarta, wrote in January 1933 about the "feeling of uneasiness" among Pendidikan followers "about us being merely a Pendidikan, merely an education." "Some comrades complain," the journal noted, "that we were already too mature to be pushed back into classroom benches."[122] There are people in the Pendidikan who wanted to believe that the school-like structure was conceived as merely a short-term, tactical stage of

---

[116] Ingleson, "Revolutionary Ideas," p. 25.

[117] *Indonesia Merdeka* (Perhimpoenan Indonesia), n. 4–5 (May 1933), p.16; see also a statement by the press bureau of the Pendidikan Nasional Indonesia in *Daulat Ra'jat* 3, 57 (April 10, 1933) for emphasizing the difference between its and the Communist concept of ownership.

[118] For the debate see *Berita*, April 25, 1933 and *Seng Po*, February and April 1933 quoted in Bouman, *Enige Beschouwingen*, pp. 86–87.

[119] Dar Tyb in *Daulat Ra'jat* 3, 85 (January 10, 1934).

[120] *Berita* March 27, 1933 in *Overzicht v.d. IMC pers* 1933 IA, p. 218.

[121] "De honderdvijftig vraagstukken," nos. 126, 128, 130.

[122] X, "Setahoen dalam organisasi," *Banteng Ra'jat* 1, 32–33 (January 1933).

the movement.[123] Neither Hatta nor Sjahrir, however, seemed to submit to this. On his return to the Indies, Hatta stated unequivocally, "Politics in a colonial period may only mean education."[124] As he remembered this period later, he strongly believed that organizing an education was "more difficult" than organizing a party.[125]

Indeed, as the Pendidikan developed, it became progressively less a "real" political party. By late 1932 and in 1933, the main task of its branches was increasingly identified as preparing its members to "pass an examination."[126] Hatta's Bukittinggi program "Toward Free Indonesia," Sjahrir's and Soebagio's "150 Questions and Answers," together with other materials (on nationalism, the history of the "People's University," capitalism, imperialism, the history of Indonesia after 1600, democracy, the history of Holland under Spanish rule, the history of French, Irish, Turkish, Indian, Chinese, Filipino movements) were intensively studied in the Pendidikan courses and often read aloud instead of speeches.[127] The learning "had to be repeated, until the members' knowledge was perfect."[128]

Surprisingly in this context, Sjahrir wrote in late 1932 in *Daulat Ra'jat* that if one word was to express the essence of a truly modern Indonesian quest for freedom, the word should be "organization."[129] Sjahrir penned several long articles on "organization" at this time, and reportedly liked to think of himself as a *Realpolitiker*, a pragmatic man of politics.[130] But Sjahrir saw "organization" in a very special way, indeed. Rather than "respecting a form," he wrote, organization was "a self-awareness, an awareness of others, and a will to participate in struggle."[131] If one had to pick one word to describe what Sjahrir meant by "organization," the word would again be "education."

After months of Pendidikan activity, the Bandung friends of Sjahrir—now the top Pendidikan leaders, Hamdani, Burhanuddin, Murwoto, Soebagio—were still repeatedly and almost consistently described by the police as "the teachers of *Tjahja*," the "People's University" which Sjahrir and they had founded as high-school students seemingly an epoch ago. This may not have been merely a habit of police reports. Sjahrir's speeches, as one reads them now, remained, and perhaps were increasingly "academic." It was typical that as Sjahrir moved closer to Indonesian labor, for instance, his favorite topic and speech theme should become "the history of the labor movement abroad."

---

[123] For instance, according to a police report from mid 1933, the "Pendidikan's leaders do not consider the Pendidikan Nasional Indonesia to be a true [*echte*] party yet...." *PPO* Batavia June/July 1933, pp. 8–9. *Banteng Ra'jat* wrote on October 25, 1932 that if education truly progresses during the next year the Pendidikan might become "a true party [*partai jang sedjati*]."

[124] Hatta in *Daulat Ra'jat* 2, 36 (September 20, 1932), quoted in Hatta, *Indonesian Patriot*, pp. 117–18.

[125] Hatta, *Memoir*, pp. 330–31.

[126] This is clear from the pages of *Kedaulatan Ra'jat*, with its "reports on organization." Regular reports were sent to the central executive; each branch was obliged to send a report once a month.

[127] This is a selection from the Pendidikan syllabus which is in *Secret Mail Report* 1933, no. 490.

[128] Burhanuddin, "Sjahrir yang saya kenal," p. 55.

[129] Sjahrir, "Organisasi," *Daulat Ra'jat* 3, 40 (November 10, 1932).

[130] Interview with Hazil Tanzil, Jakarta, March 8, 1982.

[131] Sjahrir, in *Daulat Ra'jat* 3, 40 (November 10, 1932).

In mid-1933, Sjahrir wrote a text to be used in courses for railway workers.[132] "The struggle by workers to annihilate capitalism," he wrote there,

> is mainly a struggle to enlighten and to educate. The workers' organizations, therefore, while they may have the form of trade unions, must be in their core bodies to educate the workers.[133]

Sal Tas, Sjahrir's Dutch friend, described Sjahrir's thinking as "rationalistic hygiene."[134] According to one of Sjahrir's articles written for *Daulat Ra'jat*, thinking should be "honest (*djoedjoer*) and revolutionary, that is, in agreement with truth and consciousness."[135] Correct thinking, in Sjahrir's formulation, had to be "rational," "matter-of-fact, down-to-earth, involved, but calm." What was definitely wrong, Sjahrir wrote, was "mystical thinking," "thinking in charms," "a heated (*panas*) way of thinking," "ideas on the verge of madness, disregarding norms (*oekoeran*)." To express this, Sjahrir repeatedly used the word *nafsoe*.[136]

Nafsoe, or *nafsu*, is a word of Arabic origin and a very influential concept, especially in strongly Islamic regions of the Indonesian archipelago. *Nafsu* in those areas traditionally means "lustful desire," a passion in which human energy may be expressed, but which may easily cross the limits. The manner in which *nafsu* is controlled can manifest the quality of a man and of a culture. Thus, it also can bring power. Any way of controlling *nafsu* inevitably involves a certain amount of asceticism, of toning down one's passions and also one's connections with the actual world. Modernist Islam especially, and West Sumatra's modernist Islamic schools very significantly, taught the control of *nafsu* through *iman*. *Iman* is loyalty to a body of beliefs, a spirituality, but loyalty always in sharp contrast to mysticism and magic, thus also in sharp contrast to turning off the world completely. *Iman*, in this sense, should remain close to *akal*—"mind, brains, intellect" which works dynamically but in concurrence with the soul.

Both the word and the concept of *iman* were occasionally used in Pendidikan's texts, especially by Pendidikan leaders from Minangkabau. Darwis Thaib, for instance, wrote in *Daulat Ra'jat*:

> We of [Pendidikan] know well that the fundamental principles of our struggle are *iman* and organization. [We got together] to teach *iman*. The [Pendidikan] is a sign of *iman* [*tanda iman*].... It is upon the bond between *iman* and people's sovereignty that the building of the Pendidikan stands. This is the fortress. The power of *iman* may glare strongly or it may fade [*loentoer*] at some moments. At some moments, one may be released [*lepas*] from the fortress. He may descend towards, and disappear [*terdjoedjoen*] into the field of fighting which never ceases.[137]

---

[132] Sjahrir, *Pergerakan Sekerdja*, p. 4.

[133] Ibid., p. 12.

[134] Tas, "Souvenirs of Sjahrir," p. 153.

[135] Sj. (Sjahrir), "Pengaroeh psychologis dalam pergerakan haroes disingkirkan," *Daulat Ra'jat* 3, 73 (September 20, 1933).

[136] Ibid.; also Sjahrir, "Organisasi," *Daulat Ra'jat* 3, 40 (November 10, 1932); Sjahrir, "Faham persatoean, Sepandjang taktiek II, Sepandjang strategie I."

[137] Dar Tyb (Darwis Thaib) in *Daulat Ra'jat* 3, 85 (January 10, 1934).

Hatta wrote in September 1932, "We want to go to school first, to learn about strengthening our spirit."[138] The real power, "the fortress," for Hatta was *kekoeatan roekoen*,[139] again a very Islamic and Minangkabau term and concept, a "power" (*kekoeatan*) rooted in, expressed by, and limited to faith and "harmony with custom" (*roekoen*).

Sjahrir emphasized *sadar*, "awareness of others, awareness of oneself," as the opposite of *ellende*, "misery, distress, or disorder." Anyone who was not balanced spiritually, wrote Sjahrir, was *takoet*, "afraid, unable to act." Being conscientious and being educated was equal to having *kodrat menjoesoen*, "the power to organize." The true *kodrat*, the power itself, was to Sjahrir *tenaga moreel* or *kekoeatan bathin (moreel)*, "the power of spirituality" or "spirituality in harmony with morals."[140]

Sjahrir saw the aim of education, and the power of the movement as making others and making oneself *tegoeh*, "firm," *tetap*, "constant," and *tenang*, "composed."[141] In an article in 1932 he defined the aim of the Pendidikan as *politische Aufklärung*, "political enlightenment."[142] And he wrote that the Pendidikan existed to build *zelvertrouwen*, "confidence in oneself," and to overcome *maloe*, "faintheartedness and shyness."[143]

Sjahrir, as a "*Realpolitiker*," evidently believed already at that time—as he wrote later—that "the first aim of the Pendidikan [should be] the education and teaching of members—thus no direct political action...."[144]

In September 1933, after he had given up most of his functions in the Pendidikan and had moved to work largely with obscure labor unions—outside day-to-day politics, outside the nationalist mainstream, outside "the field of fighting which never ceases," toward the fringes—Sjahrir wrote about what now he evidently believed was his power base. "The power of this organization," Sjahrir wrote,

> is neither in the strength of its membership, nor in the way the organization's frame is put together. The power is inside, in the dynamism which elucidates the pillars, changes the pillars into signs, obligations and promises, and, thus, builds a deeper awareness....[145]

4. THE DUTCH REACTION

The Pendidikan's June 1932 congress accepted *kebangsaan*, "nationalism," as the principle of its policy. Also, according to the congress, the Pendidikan "as an organi-

---

[138] Hatta, *Daulat Ra'jat* 2, 36 (September 20, 1932), as quoted in Hatta, *Indonesian Patriot*, p. 137.

[139] Quoted in Hatta, *Memoir*, p. 331. *Kekoeatan* means "power," and *rukun* "to be in harmony," *rukun iman* being "pillars of faith," and "*rukun sjarat*"—"conditions of *rukun*"—typical Minangkabau phrases for something that must be in harmony with *adat*, "customs."

[140] "De honderdvijftig vraagstukken," no. 147; Sjahrir, "Organisasi," *Daulat Ra'jat* 3, 40 (November 10, 1932); Sjahrir, "Faham persatoean, Sepandjang taktiek II."

[141] Sjahrir, "Organisasi," *Kedaulatan Ra'jat* 1 (October 1932); Sj. (Sjahrir), "Reformisme, opportunisme dan radicalisme," *Daulat Ra'jat* 3, 79 (November 20, 1933).

[142] Sjahrir, "Faham Persatoean ... Sepandjang taktiek II."

[143] Sjahrir, "Organisasi"; Sj (Sjahrir), "Boeroeh dimasa ini," *Daulat Ra'jat* 3, 74 (September 30, 1933).

[144] Introduction to Sjahrazad (Sjahrir), p. 5.

[145] Sj (Sjahrir) "Boeroeh dimasa ini."

zation does not suggest any cooperation [with the Dutch colonial power]."[146] Thus, the Pendidikan declared itself to be a part of the Indonesian radical, "non-cooperative" nationalist movement. There were, however, significant nuances separating the Pendidikan from some other groups in the movement concerning this particular issue. Partindo especially, and Sukarno namely, as Hatta put it, "rejected cooperation in all fields"; according to another Pendidikan leader, they "recognized no truce" and were "dogmatic."[147]

A concept of *sini* against *sana*—"us," the Indonesians, against "them," the Dutch—a concept of an uncompromising and permanent confrontation, was extensively used by Partindo leaders. It rarely appeared, however, in the Pendidikan texts. As far as I know, Sjahrir, at the time, only once used the word *sana* to describe the Dutch and on this occasion *sini* was not used, nor was the categorical theme implied.[148] There were several occasions, on the other hand, when Sjahrir explicitly attacked the *sini-sana* concept. In his booklet on trade unions, for instance, he described it as a dangerous effort to blow the dissimilarities between "East" and "West" out of proportion, to make them into

> "a fundamental difference, into something magically established as fate [*hoekoem hikmat*]—something beyond the capacity of mankind to change."[149]

The *sini-sana* concept, Sjahrir wrote, was in fact a "mythical exhortation [*wasiat*]."[150]

The "temporary" and "practical" nature of nationalism was emphasized in the the Pendidikan's program.[151] The body of argument, both in Hatta's "Toward Free Indonesia," and in Sjahrir's and Soebagio's "150 Questions and Answers," was filled with examples from the Western—the Greek-Roman, French-Revolutionary, Modern-European—stories of progress and wisdom.

Sjahrir and Hatta—to express themselves and their Pendidikan—used both flawless Indonesian and flawless Dutch. There was a striking number of parentheses, especially in Sjahrir's writing: Indonesian, Dutch, sometimes German, English, or French were used. Words from several worlds and two universes—"the East" and "the West"—were interjected and checked each other. This helped to create a distance from matters purely and explicitly Eastern, Minangkabau, Islamic, and purely and explicitly Western, and Dutch at the same time. Upon this vagueness, a bridge might perhaps be built suggesting affinities between the opposite sides. This might have been another stage of the *dienst Melajoe*, "service Malay," which Sjahrir's father, the *hoofddjaksa*, had used. Except that Sjahrir and Hatta now were more anxious,

---

[146] A statement by the Pendidikan executive on the Bandung Congress in *Daulat Ra'jat* 2, 29 (June 30, 1932); *Secret Mail Report* 1932, no. 840; *Banteng Ra'jat* 16–17 (July 5–15, 1932); Sj-h (Sjahrir), "Strategie dan taktiek perdjoeangan," *Daulat Ra'jat* 3, 80 (October 30, 1933).

[147] Hatta, *Memoir*, p.289. Murwoto, *Autobiografi*, pp. 16–17.

[148] Sjahrir, "Faham persatoean, Sepandjang taktiek I."

[149] Sjahrir, *Pergerakan Sekerdja*, pp. 13–14, 18–19.

[150] Ibid.

[151] "De honderdvijftig vraagstukken," no. 7. According to Anderson in his introduction to his translation of Sjahrir's *Perdjuangan Kita*: "In very general terms, the Pendidikan Nasional Indonesia believed that the Dutch would remain in control for the indefinite future, and that in any case, Indonesians were by no means prepared, intellectually and organizationally, for the assumption of power." Sutan Sjahrir, *Our Struggle* (Translated with an Introduction by Benedict R. O'G. Anderson) (Ithaca: Cornell Modern Indonesia Project, 1968), pp. 1–2.

more knowledgeable, and more skeptical; richer by experience, and more deft at covering their growing uncertainty about the possibility of ever building the bridge.

In Holland, at the other end of the bridge, both men's friends, Sal Tas, Jacques de Kadt, Edo Fimmen, and the editor of *De Socialist* Piet Schmidt, after months of hesitating on the fringes of the Dutch social-democratic movement, finally split from the mainstream Dutch Social Democratic Labor Party. Early in 1932, these men in Holland established their own Onafhankelijke Socialistische Partij, OSP, "Independent Socialist Party."[152]

The OSP, in its Struggle Program of 1932, demanded among other things, "full and immediate independence for Indonesia.[153] The OSP's new journal *Fakkel*, "Torch," presented the Indonesian struggle in dramatic colors. Sal Tas wrote about "the active volcano of Sumatra's West Coast."[154] The Pendidikan itself, according to the OSP, was "the revolutionary avant-garde,"[155] "the only truly radical Indonesian party."[156] In particular, its "proletarian" policy and Sjahrir's role in it were praised.[157]

The Pendidikan warmly welcomed it when Sjahrir's and Hatta's Dutch friends finally detached themselves from the "indolent" social-democrats.[158] There was probably an exchange of printed materials between the OSP and Pendidikan, along with occasional letters. In one letter, in December 1932, the OSP suggested that Hatta might stand as one of the party's candidates for the coming Dutch parliamentary elections.[159]

This was, indeed, a situation Sjahrir might have envisioned when he left Holland. The best qualities from *rantau*, "the outer regions," the other side of the bridge, might be used for the struggle in the Indies. Neither Hatta, nor Sjahrir nor the other leaders of the Pendidikan could see any "obstacle as far as principles were concerned" to Hatta running in the election; Hatta was willing to declare his candidacy.[160] At this point, however, a storm was raised by "the true" non-cooperationists, especially Partindo and Sukarno. The Pendidikan's argument that the Dutch Parliament was not a repressive colonial institution but a democratically elected body appeared lame when confronted by the principles of *sana* versus *sini*. There seemed suddenly to be no bridge at all. Hatta declared that he had been

---

[152] *Daulat Ra'jat* 2, 24 (May 10, 1932); Hansen, "The Dutch East Indies," pp. 59–85; Tas, "Souvenirs of Sjahrir," p. 146. Fritjof Tichelman, *Henk Sneevliet, 1883–1942: Een politieke biografie* (Amsterdam: Van Gennep, 1974), pp. 72–73. For the position of the OSP on the very fringes of Dutch political life at the time see J. C. H. Blom. *De muiterij op de Zeven Provinciën: Reacties en gevolgen in Nederland* (Bussum: van Dishoek, 1975), p. 34.

[153] *Fakkel*, December 24, 1932.

[154] Sal Tas, "Indonesië komt in beweging," ibid., January 17, 1933.

[155] Ibid.

[156] Ibid., February 23, 1934.

[157] Sal Tas, "De volksbeweging in Indonesië," ibid. September 26 and 29, 1933.

[158] *Daulat Ra'jat* 2, 24 (May 10, 1932).

[159] See de Kadt's letter, e.g., dated March 13, 1933 in *Secret Verbaal*, November 1934-L33.

[160] On the exchange between the OSP and the Pendidikan regarding Hatta's candidacy, see *Daulat Ra'jat* 2, 46 (December 20, 1932); also *Fakkel*, February 2, 1933, *Stuw*, January 1, 1933; Hatta, *Bung Hatta Antwoordt*, p. 279. Also *Sing Po*, December 10, 1932 in *Overzicht v.d. IMC pers* 1932 IIA, p. 389.

misunderstood and that the discussion about his candidacy had never come close to a definite decision.[161]

During the first half of the 1930s, the growth of colonial education programs in the Indies radically slowed; even the existing Western-style system of education was reduced in size and quality.[162] The main reason was the Great Depression and "the wretched state of the economy" in the colony itself.[163] The frustration and disbelief in democratic systems which accompanied the Great Depression in the West was strongly reflected in the East. The Nederlanden-Indische Fascisten Organisatie, "Netherlands-Indies Fascist Organization," and the Nationaal-Socialistische Beweging, "National Socialist Movement," expanded rapidly.[164] The Vaderlandse Club, "Patriotic Club," founded in 1929 by the Dutch in the Indies as "a reaction against the ethical policy," grew as well.[165]

While Sjahrir was still in Holland, early in September 1932, the new Dutch Governor-General, Jhr.B.C. de Jonge, arrived in the Indies. A horoscope published by a Dutch Indies newspaper as a welcome saw in de Jonge's stars that by his strong hand "the extremist movement shall be crushed."[166] To historians, de Jonge was "an unashamed conservative,"[167] "a die-hard colonialist of the pre-'white-man's-burden' vintage."[168] To Marcel Koch, a socialist of the "ethical" vintage, watching this from Bandung, the arrival of de Jonge marked the outset of "the most reactionary and the worst government in the Indies we have ever had."[169]

The new Governor-General was "determined to tolerate no nonsense from upstart Indonesian political agitators," and he called even a man like Soetomo ("His Highness Doctor" to Sjahrir) "simply a Communist."[170] It was, in a sense, a perfect setting for the passionate confrontation between *sini*, "us," and *sana*, "them." De Jonge watched for an opportunity to prove himself, and Sukarno and Partindo never felt so justified in their uncompromisingly non-cooperationist views. Both courage and hysteria grew; crowds were excited, and myths of race were invoked on both sides. On August 1, 1933, Sukarno was arrested for the second time.

---

[161] Ibid.; also *Oetoesan Indonesia*, December 10, 1932, in *Overzicht v.d. IMC pers*1932 11, p. 13; *Sikap*, April 13 and 15, 1933, in *Overzicht v.d. IMC pers* 1933 IA, p. 246.

[162] Susan Abeyasekere, *One Hand Clapping: Indonesian Nationalists and the Dutch, 1939–1942* (Clayton: Monash Papers on Southeast Asia no. 5, 1976), p. 37; C. L. M. Penders, "Colonial Education Policy and the Indonesian Response, 1900–1942" (Ph.D. thesis, Australian National University, 1968); Teeuw, *Modern Indonesian Literature*, p. 32.

[163] Report by Governor of West Java December 17, 1932 in *Secret Mail Report* 1933, no. 71; Kwantes, ed., *De Ontwikkeling* 3: 673.

[164] Elsbeth B. Locher-Scholten, "De Stuw, tijdtekening en teken des tijds," *Tijdschrift voor Geschiedenis* 84, 1 (1971), pp. 36–65, 100.

[165] Pieter Joost Drooglever, *De Vaderlandse Club 1929–1942: Totoks en de Indische politiek* (Franeker: T.Wever, 1980), p. 347. In 1930, 30 percent of the adult male Dutch population living permanently in the Indies, were members of the "Patriotic Club," "a strikingly high degree of political organization," a Dutch historian comments,"within a group in which traditionally politics were held in very low esteem." Ibid., p. 348.

[166] "Redactie Horoscoop van de maand: Jhr. Mr. B. C. de Jonge. Gouv. Gen. van Ned. Indië. Zuiderkruis," pp. 3–5, in *Collection de Jonge* no. 63.

[167] Ingleson, *Road to Exile*, p. 158.

[168] Penders's introduction to Sastroamijoyo's *Milestones on My Journey*, p. 90n.

[169] Koch, *Batig Slot*, p. 42.

[170] Ingleson, "Revolutionary Ideas," p. 15.

A special decree by the Governor-General, issued at the same time, made it extremely difficult to organize any public meeting whatsoever in the Indies. On August 14, the Governor-General warned even advisory bodies to the colonial government that "open debates of a political nature" were "undesirable."[171]

The Pendidikan acted as if it were trying to suggest that it might stay out of the mounting hysterics. It again challenged Sukarno's and the Partindo's concepts of *sini* against *sana* as irrational and harmful. It attacked Dutchmen like de Jonge in essentially the same way, and often with the same words. Sjahrir wrote in September 1933 that the Dutch policies of the de Jonge style "urge passion [*nafsoe*] and greed," and "are unable to bring about perfection [*kesempoernaan*] in society."[172]

Governor-General de Jonge, besides all the other characteristics mentioned, was a man of the "Utrecht school," thus easily incensed by anything smelling of "Leiden."[173] He certainly could not be expected to tolerate flamboyant nationalists of Sukarno's type. Yet he felt, as he later wrote in his memoirs, that

> "the danger was not being carried in the womb of this nationalism but in the mentality of certain Europeans; if there was to be a revolution, it was about to come not from down there [in the Indies] but from the opposite direction."[174]

Reading the Governor-General's memoirs, one can easily see how most of the time he was angered not actually by Sukarno, but by "the haughty theoreticians," "those café socialists," "those has beens." De Jonge took real pleasure in chasing the "soft" officials, the journalists, the men of "Leiden stuff."[175] It was, in a paradoxical sense, a feat of "ethical" schools. The colonial programs of education, as it appeared now, indeed created a meaningful affinity between some of the Dutch and some of the natives: as de Jonge moved against the remaining Dutch "ethical" eggheads, the natives in the Pendidikan emerged as de Jonge's very real enemy.

Through their "ethical" education, the Pendidikan leaders had entered the Western cultural universe. Or in a way they had. The phrases and concepts which Sjahrir, Hatta, and their colleagues used seemed now perfectly intelligible to the Dutch officials who were chasing them. It appears even that no translation was necessary. The Dutch and Dutch-trained indigenous officials, police agents, and informers reporting on the Pendidikan invariably found its journals and statements "very clear and coherent."[176] The Dutch around de Jonge accepted Pendidikan's image of itself at face value. In police reports—almost exactly and word by word as in Sjahrir's and Hatta's

---

[171] The government declaration of August 1, 1933 is in *Aneta*, August 1, 1933 also in *Collection de Jonge* no. 64, p. 43. The August 14 directive was aimed especially at the *Volksraad*, a body of moderate deputies from the Dutch, indigenous and "foreign Oriental" population. Drooglever. *De Vaderlandse Club*, p. 130.

[172] Sjahrir, "Sekedar tentang so'al kapitalisme," *Daulat Ra'jat* 3, 74 (September 30, 1933).

[173] On the Utrecht school see above Chapter 3.

[174] B. C. de Jonge, *Herinneringen van Jhr. Mr. B. C. de Jonge* (Groningen: Wolters, 1968), p. 105.

[175] Ibid., pp. 79–80, 137, 169, 236 *passim*; also Locher-Scholten, "De Stuw," p. 37. Also de Jonge to Minister of Colonies, August 29, 1933 in *Secret Verbaal*, October 19, 1933-O24.

[176] For example, see Kiewet de Jonge, Adviser for Native Affairs, "Inlandsche beweging op Java (eigenhandig en strikt persoonlijk), Weltevreden (Batavia) November 18, 1931, *Collection van Gobée* no. 34.

own texts—the Pendidikan appeared as "more radical" than Partindo and "distinctly revolutionary"; Sjahrir according to that language "belonged to revolution."[177]

In perfect agreement with Hatta's and Sjahrir's own view of themselves, the Dutch police saw them as penetrating deep down to "the lowest layers of the population." In accord with Sjahrir's own perceptions, Dutch experts and policemen viewed his wander toward the fringes of colonial politics—his focus on disunited, minute, obscure trade unions and on the opaque world of the unemployed—as a most daring, most noteworthy, certainly meaningful, and certainly dangerous journey.[178]

Like the Pendidikan's leaders, and in sharp contrast to the views of Sukarno and his party, the Dutch saw in Hatta's initial willingness to stand for the Dutch elections as an OSP candidate not a compromise, but a shrewd and potentially effective tactic—as the Surabaya police put it, "a short cut on the path toward Indonesian independence."[179]

The Dutch colonial administration, most significantly, shared the Pendidikan's view of education as the principal source of political power. Like the Pendidikan itself, Dutch reports on the organization made no clear distinction between "education" and "political education."[180] The Dutch police firmly believed, and reported with growing alarm that, through education, the Pendidikan "slowly but surely" was moving toward its revolutionary aim.[181] In the same vein, logically and naturally, Sukarno was seen as "dangerous but stupid."[182]

It was, to the Dutch around de Jonge, a most damaging piece of evidence against the Pendidikan that both its top leaders, Sjahrir and Hatta, had "studied in Holland" and "lived in Europe." The Pendidikan, the colonial police reports warned and emphasized, was "quite comparable to Western organizations."[183] The police scrutinized the Pendidikan's teaching materials, syllabi, and examinations with almost grotesque care.[184] "Surprisingly they are quite clever," Batavia police reported regarding Hatta and Sjahrir in November 1933.[185]

---

[177] Gobée, Adviser for Native Affairs, to Governor-General, March 12, 1932 in *Secret Mail Report* 1932, no. 303; also in Kwantes, ed., *De Ontwikkeling* 3: 618; Attorney General to Governor-General, February 10, 1933 in *Secret Verbaal*, April 29, 1933-T9, also in Ingleson, *Road to Exile*, p. 210, n. 75.

[178] See, e.g., the exchange between Gobée, the Attorney General and the General Secretary's offices on the Pendidikan's labor activity in *Secret Mail Report* 1934, no. 287 and Attorney General to Governor-General, February 10, 1933 in *Secret Verbaal*, April 29, 1933-T9. See also Attorney General to Governor-General, January 12 1933, and Governor of East Java to Governor-General, July 22, 1933 in *Secret Mail Report* 1933, no. 893. On the sensitivity of Dutch officials to the Pendidikan's activity among the "proletarians," especially "the unemployed hit by the depression" in Surabaya, see *Secret Mail Report* 1933, no. 71.

[179] A Surabaya police report, July 15, 1933 in *Secret Mail Report* 1933, no. 893.

[180] E.g. Gobée to Governor-General in *Secret Mail Report* 1932, no. 303.

[181] "Voorstel tot interneering," December 22, 1933 in *Secret Mail Report* 1934, no. 287.

[182] Koch quoted in Dahm, *Sukarno*, p. 173.

[183] "Voorstel tot Interneering," December 22, 1933; Attorney General to Governor-General, February 10, 1933 in *Secret Verbaal*, April 29, 1933-T9.

[184] See, e.g., *Overzicht v.d. IMC pers*1932 12: 18; ibid.1933 2: 6.

[185] The report was written in Dutch, but some words were in Indonesian, for instance *akal*; the phrase was *"wel akal's hebben." PPO* November 1933, p. 11 (Poeze, ed., *Politiek-politioneele overzichten*, 3: 336–37).

Four months after Sjahrir left Holland, Maria, his friend from Holland, according to the plan they had made together, followed him with her son and daughter (both were children of Sal Tas). Sjahrir travelled from Batavia to Medan and met Maria when her ship arrived from Colombo. On April 10, 1932, in a Medan mosque, they were married.[186]

Sjahrir and Maria had exactly five weeks to live as husband and wife. They stayed in Medan, in the house where Sjahrir used to live before going to school to Java, together with Sjahrir's older brother, Soetan Noer Alamsjah, and his family; a younger brother, Soetan Mahroezar, stayed in a house nearby. Sjahrir and Maria traveled little around Medan; they did not go to Kota Gedang "because there was not enough money for this."[187] They soon expected to move to Java. They went shopping in the new *Kesawen* market. They walked, so I was told,

> hand in hand, on the streets, and even in front of the Grand Hotel, which was still at that time closed to "natives," even if the "native" happened to be a sultan.[188]

Sjahrir had been back from Holland for only four months. He might not necessarily have thought of his actions as a provocation. Or—as one of his Pendidikan friends later put it—he might have been willing to demonstrate by showing up with a white woman "that the Indonesian nation was as human as the Dutch nation."[189]

Medan was an even more fashionable Indies city in 1932 than it had been when Sjahrir left it six years earlier. The Italian Opera had just came to town to give a series of performances in the *Empress Bioscoop*, beginning May 14—*Troubadour, Rigoletto, La Bohème, Carmen, Il barbiere de Sevilla, La Traviata, Tosca, Cavagliere Rusticano, Faust,* and *Madame Butterfly*. Hollywood hits were shown with great success—*New Moon* at the *Oranje* theater and *Two Fisted Justice* at the *Orion*.[190] Sjahrir, it appears, became an equally great attraction.

"The news spread quickly through the Dutch as well as the native community. Local papers made a big issue of it and urged the Government to take action against Sutan Sjahrir and his wife."[191] Maria was stopped on the street by "other whites" and asked if she did not "need some help."[192]

Four days after Sjahrir and Maria were married, an article appeared prominently in the *Sumatra Post*, the biggest Medan paper:

---

[186] Nota by the resident of Moluccas, February 20, 1936 in *Secret Mail Report* 1937, no. 704; Maisir Thaib, *Sjahrir Pegang Kemoedi* (Bukittinggi: Penjiaran Ilmoe, 1946?), p. 12. The arrival of the ship "S.S. Saarbrucken" on March 28, 1932 is announced in *De Sumatra Post*, March 24, 1932.

[187] Interview with Maria Duchâteau-Sjahrir, Lorques, February 13, 1988.

[188] Letter by Mohammad Said to the author, October 1987; Interview with Maria Duchâteau-Sjahrir, Lorques, February 13, 1988.

[189] Salim, *Bung Sjahrir*, p. 14.

[190] *De Sumatra Post*, April 16 and May 13, 1932.

[191] Letter by Mohammad Said to the author, October 1987.

[192] Interview with Maria Duchâteau-Sjahrir, Lorques, February 13, 1988.

The Lady in a sarong and kebaya
Under police surveillance

For a couple of weeks, a European lady has been seen on the Medan streets attracting some attention as she has evidently decided to wear a sarong and kebaya and appears to be married to a native.

The night before last, when this married couple was about to enjoy a movie, several Europeans inquired of the lady why she was clothed in the native fashion.

Why not, anyway. But another issue is that the above mentioned lady is married, in Holland, to a certain T., who has made quite a name for himself in the world of revolution. It was in Holland that she met her present husband, the son of a former hoofddjaksa in Medan. . . .

As far as we know, the lady is under police surveillance.[193]

It was quickly discovered that Maria, indeed, had not formally divorced her first husband, Sal Tas, before leaving for the Indies. There were legal ways to straighten out the formalities. Maria had become a Moslem in Medan, and her marriage with Sjahrir was Islamic, not Christian. Sal Tas, also, would probably have agreed to release her since they had not lived together for some time. (It was also the epoch of free-love among the European avant-garde.) Neither the local Islamic officials nor the government in Batavia, however, were thinking about how to please the two young unorthodox people. On May 5, 1932, Sjahrir's marriage was declared void by an Islamic official, and, on May 14, the Dutch authorities put Maria on a ship leaving the colony.[194]

The incident was a warning of what might come. De Jonge's government was eagerly watching for any opportunity to act against anybody connected with the Pendidikan. And the occasion was seen as especially propitious if a white person was involved.

On February 4, 1933, Indonesian and Dutch sailors, in a common action, mutinied on the Dutch warship *Zeven Provinciën*. The ship was, at the time, off the northwestern coast of Sumatra. Four days after the mutiny started, Governor-General de Jonge cabled to the minister of colonies in The Hague. There was, he reported, "no sign of special activity by the Pendidikan Nasional Indonesia."[195] But, two days later de Jonge had obtained the information that he evidently expected:

> At the headquarters of the *Bond van Inlandsch Marine-personnel* [Union of Native Marine Personnel] in Surabaya, a number of blank membership cards of the Pendidikan Nasional Indonesia have already [sic] been found.[196]

"This, naturally, makes it plausible," the report went on,

---

[193] *De Sumatra Post*, April 16, 1932.
[194] Letter by Attorney General, June 25, 1936 in *Secret Verbaal*, July 8, 1938-U22.
[195] In *Secret Verbaal*, April 29, 1933-T9.
[196] Attorney General to Governor-General, February 10, 1933 in *Secret Verbaal*, October 19, 1933-O24.

that this labor union was, in fact, a cell of the Pendidikan. Thus, also, it is logical to suspect that the activity of the Pendidikan is related to the present mutiny.[197]

No Pendidikan involvement in the mutiny on the *Zeven Provinciën* was ever proven. But the suspicion was also never allowed to die. All the government's reports on the Pendidikan's "involvement" concluded that the proof had not "yet" been found.[198] It was thought "logical," "plausible," and "natural" for the Pendidikan to be involved in an affair such as this.

De Jonge acted on this conviction. On February 8, 1933, while the mutiny was still in progress, de Jonge's department of justice informed various sections of the administration, that "in a short time," it "shall move to forbid all government officials, not only those in the military branches, to be members of the Pendidikan Nasional Indonesia."[199] On June 27, the decree was issued.[200] Two weeks later, the police raided the Surabaya branch of the Pendidikan for an alleged press offence. The event was made more ominous by the fact that the next Pendidikan congress was to be hosted by this branch.[201]

"It would take many people to stop the rain," Sjahrir wrote on de Jonge's restrictive decrees of June 1933.[202] The last occasion on which we have a report on Sjahrir is at a labor union meeting in Semarang in late July. The police reported that the size of this union was being rapidly reduced, that the membership was demoralized by the June decrees, and that the union generally was "passive." Sjahrir is recorded as saying in his speech: "Even if we lose our fight, moral victory is on our side."[203]

Hatta, as had already been planned in Holland, took over the chairmanship of the Pendidikan from Sjahrir. But, as Sjahrir before him, Hatta too did not appear too eager to immerse himself in the matters of actual day-to-day colonial politics and in

---

[197] Ibid. It might be logical, in a sense, to look for some connections in Surabaya; the announcement of a 7 percent cut in sailors' salaries at the Surabaya naval base was reportedly the crucial impetus for the mutiny. See Blom, *De muiterij*, pp. 40f.

[198] Attorney General to Governor-General, February 10, 1933; Council of the Indies documents, ibid.; Attorney General to Governor-General, March 9, 1933, and de Jonge to Minister of Colonies, August 29, 1933 in *Secret Verbaal*, October 19, 1933-O24. The suspicion might be further stimulated by excited commentaries on the mutiny in the OSP press in Holland. See, e.g.: "Waarde kameraden," *Fakkel*, February 9, 1933. On the position of the SDAP and other Dutch political parties of the left on the *Zeven Provinciën* mutiny see van Tuijl, *Mijn positie*, pp. 31ff, and Blom, *De muiterij*, pp. 40–53, 176–77, 355.

[199] Minutes of Extraordinary Meeting of the Council of the Indies, February 8, 1933, *Secret Verbaal*, April 29, 1933-T9.

[200] Governor-General's Decision of June 27 in *Secret Verbaal*, July 18, 1933-H17

[201] *Menjala* 2, 21 (July 23, 1933), ibid., 2, 9–10, ibid., 2, 33; *Daulat Ra'jat* 3, 68 (July 30, 1933). On the arrest of some local Pendidikan leaders see e.g. *Stuw*, July 16, 1933, p. 174. On the congress' preparation see Governor of East Java to Governor-General, July 22, 1933 in *Secret Mail Report* 1933, no. 693. This was not first arrest in Surabaya. Already in January six leaders of the branch were arrested for using in their writings the words *haroes berrevolusi*, "have to work toward a revolution." See de Jonge to the Minister of Colonies January 13, 1933 in *Secret Verbaal*, February 15, 1933-B3.

[202] See, e.g., Sjahrir, "Pergerakan Indonesia menepoeh saat jang penting."

[203] Report by the police in Semarang, July 25, 1933 in *Secret Mail Report* 1933, no. 946. See also Semarang police reports dated July 13, 1933, July 17, 1933 in *Secret Mail Reports* 1933, nos. 879 and 930.

organizational work. Hatta continued to live in Batavia, while the Pendidikan's headquarters remained in Bandung.[204] And, just a few weeks after being elected chairman, in April 1933, Hatta left for a visit to Japan, as an adviser to his "uncle," Max Etek Rais, who was in the Far East looking for new commercial connections.

During the trip, Hatta was described in some Japanese papers as "the son of a powerful noble from Padang" and as "the Gandhi of Indonesia."[205] There were rumors, still persisting years later, however almost certainly untrue, that "Hatta had gone to Japan to meet Tan Malaka."[206] Although Hatta was already critical of Japanese imperialism at the time, he was very impressed by Japan's technological progress.[207] He did not return to Java until late in 1933.[208]

Not unlike Sjahrir, Hatta appeared to be moving out of the limelight as 1933 passed. From early September on, Hatta was no longer listed as the head of *Daulat Ra'jat*; he was now merely a member of the board.[209]

From mid 1933 on, not a single public meeting of the Pendidikan was reported. At the same time, the organization appeared, paradoxically, to become increasingly true to its declared aims. A historian of the period has written of the men of the Pendidikan:

> while regretting Sukarno's arrest and criticising the restriction on all non-cooperating parties, [they] nevertheless saw the government's measures as confirmation of the correctness of their arguments over the past two years.[210]

A police report remarked, in September 1933, that *Daulat Ra'jat* was becoming even "more theoretical and scholarly."[211]

As the tension began to grow in the colony, toward the middle of 1933, the Pendidikan executive issued "General Instruction no. 2," requiring all branches and individual members to put yet greater emphasis on education.[212] To make this edu-

---

[204] Bondan, "Tjatjatan tentang Pendidikan, p. 2.

[205] *Osaka Asahi*, April 15, 1933 and *Osaka Jiji* May 9, 1933 quoted in "Bezoek van Mohammad Hatta c.s. aan Japan" in *Secret Verbaal*, July 27, 1933-F18.

[206] Tamin (sic) to Schemmers, a Dutch officer in Columbia Camp in Brisbane, June 1, 1945, in *Collection van der Plas* B-4.

[207] At a Pendidikan public meeting in Yogyakarta, for instance, just before he left for Japan, Hatta's speech was stopped by the police present because he too strongly attacked "imperialism in the Pacific," Japan's policy towards China, the Lytton commission and Western softness toward Japanese imperialism. See report on the meeting on March 19 in Gobée to Governor-General, March 30, 1933 in *Secret Mail Report* 1933, no. 384.

[208] The trip was evidently successful from the commercial as well as the political point of view. In November 1933, the departure for Japan of another representative of the Djohan Djohor Coy, Hatta's "uncle's" company, was reported. On the same ship to Japan was Parade Harahap, a journalist who later became one of the foremost advocates of contacts between the Indonesian nationalist movement and Japan. Attorney General to Governor-General, November 21, 1933 in *Secret Mail Report* 1933, no. 1420.

[209] In *Daulat Ra'jat* 3, 71 (August 30, 1933) still the "editorial board is led by Mohammad Hatta"; in the next issue Hatta is listed merely as a "member of the editorial board."

[210] Ingleson, *Road to Exile*, p. 223.

[211] *PPO* Batavia November 1933, p. 11.

[212] The instruction as it reached the Minangkabau branch is in *PPO* Sumatra's West Coast May 1933 in *Secret Mail Report* 1933, no.848; see also Abdullah, *Schools and Politics*, pp. 201–2;

cation more effective, in late summer 1933, the central executive suggested a "five-man" course as the best form of action. By this time, an instructor's report, bad grades in fact, could lead to the expulsion of an individual, or even a branch, from the organization.[213]

Sukarno's followers suffered a brutal blow in November. After a few weeks in prison, their leader, in several letters to de Jonge, announced that he was resigning from Partindo and that he no longer stood for the principle of uncompromising non-cooperation.[214] Portraits of Sukarno were torn down from the walls.[215] The Pendidikan was proven right once more, or so its leaders believed. It continued steadily on its way. Now, even "two-man courses" were reported.

Hatta remembered later: "The political quiet caused the government and the police to see ghosts in broad daylight."[216] The Pendidikan, as it stayed detached, made the Dutch increasingly nervous. The police again reported an "unmistakenly Communist tendency" in the Pendidikan.[217] Sjahrir's and Hatta's withdrawal from the spotlight of actual politics and the "five-man" and even more the "two-man" Pendidikan courses appeared to the police as nothing but the building of "reserve cadres" and "shadow boards." Once more in accord with the Pendidikan leaders' image of themselves, the colonial authorities saw the Pendidikan's renewed accent on education as a "further effort at the concentration of power"—something that "must not be taken lightly."[218] In November 1933, a police commissariat in Batavia opined:

> Exactly the manifest harmlessness of the Pendidikan, and its conspicuous non-activity, should be taken as proof that the government is justified in its suspicion.[219]

Language and translation, typically, remained a crucial part of the process. Early in 1934, Burhanuddin, who was as we may recall one of the Pendidikan's leaders and Sjahrir's close friend, said—in Indonesian—that the Pendidikan, now, was traveling along *soelit*, "difficult," ways. A police agent translated this phrase into

---

see also on the instruction *PPO* Batavia February 1934, p. 9, and *PPO* Sumatra's West Coast September 1933 in *Secret Mail Report* 1933, no. 1367.

[213] On the five-man and two-man courses, and for the questions and answers which passed between the branches and the center, see *PPO* Batavia January 1934, p. 3; ibid., February 1934, p. 9; *PPO* Sumatra's West Coast September 1933 in *Secret Mail Report* 1933, no. 1367; ibid., January 1934 in *Secret Mail Report* 1934, no. 217.

[214] (Hatta), "Tragedie Soekarno," *Daulat Ra'jat* 3, 80 (November 30, 1933), also reproduced in Hatta, *Indonesian Patriot*, pp. 172–73. (See also Hatta, *Memoir*, p. 335, confirming he wrote the article.)

[215] Dahm, *Sukarno*, pp. 166f.

[216] Hatta, *Indonesian Patriot*, p. 170.

[217] A nota for the General Secretary, September 6, 1933 in *Secret Verbaal*, October 19, 1933-O24, also *PPO* Batavia February 1934, p. 9 (Poeze, ed., *Politiek-politioneele overzichten*, 3: 363–64).

[218] *PPO* Batavia November 1933, p. 10 and *Voorstel tot Interneering*, December 22, 1933 in *Secret Mail Report* 1934, no. 287. This did not mean that shadow committees of a sort were not part of the Pendidikan's method. In 1927, for instance, Hatta reportedly initiated the appointment of two Perhimpoenan Indonesia executives in Holland, "to prevent scholarship holders from being victimized by the Dutch authorities." Rose, *Indonesia Free*, p. 35.

[219] *PPO* Batavia November 1933, p. 11.

Dutch as stating that Pendidikan was traveling along *geheim of duister*, "secret or dark" ways.[220] On another occasion, during the same month, the Dutch police rendered the Dutch phrase in a Pendidikan text, *stille arbeid*, "quiet or inconspicuous work," as *ondergrondse actie*, "underground action."[221]

On October 9, 1933, a ban was declared on all meetings of radical nationalist organizations, including the Partindo and the Pendidikan.[222] At the same time, prominent West Sumatran leaders of the Islamic Permi were arrested.[223] (As if to prove the affinity, at the same time, in Holland, steps were being considered to arrest Salomon Tas of the OSP.)[224]

On November 16, the Batavian Dutch liberal, "neo-ethical" and pro-Leiden journal *Stuw*, "Dam," announced that it could not survive the pressure from the conservative government.[225] On December 16, the last issue of *Stuw* was published.[226] On December 22, Governor-General de Jonge submitted to the Council of the Indies—the highest decision-making body in the colony—a "Proposal to Intern Leaders of the Pendidikan Nasional Indonesia."[227]

On January 24, 1934, De Jonge's Adviser for Native Affairs E. Gobée, a man still not too far from the "neo-ethical" group, had warned the Governor-General not to put "the level-headed leaders" in prison; such an action, he said, might open the field for "thoughtless hotheads."[228] On February 16, however, all was decided. The Council of the Indies admitted that the Pendidikan was not posing "an immediate threat to law and order." But, because the Council believed its duty was to deal with "latent dangers" as well, the Pendidikan leaders were to be arrested without delay.[229]

On Sunday morning, February 25, 1934, the police awoke about thirty members of the Bandung Pendidikan in their homes and took them away for interrogation. Thirteen were detained in custody, including the top leaders, Burhanuddin, Mur-

---

[220] See Adviser for Native Affairs, Gobée writing on the "error" in his letter to the Governor-General, August 22, 1934 in *Secret Verbaal*, November 28, 1934-L33.

[221] *Bahagia*, February 27, 1934 in *Overzicht v.d. IMC pers* 1934, 1: 150.

[222] Circular in *Secret Verbaal*, June 18, 1938-K20 quoted in Ingleson, *Road to Exile*, p. 222.

[223] On arrests on the Sumatra's West Coast see *Secret Mail Report* 1933, no.1108; Abdullah, *Schools and Politics*, p. 195. Also Audrey Kahin, "West Sumatra: Outpost of the Republic" in *Regional Dynamics of the Indonesian Revolution: Unity from Diversity*, ed. Audrey Kahin (Honolulu: University of Hawaii Press, 1985), p. 147.

[224] The Minister of Justice to the Prime Minister, July 20 1933 in *Secret Verbaal*, July 24, 1933-X17.

[225] Locher-Scholten, "De Stuw," pp. 37–38. On Stuw being "neo-ethical" see also G. J. Resink, "Rechtshoogeschool, jongereneed, 'Stuw' en Gestuwden," *BKI* 130, 4 (1974): 428–49; Yong Mun Cheong, *H. J. van Mook and Indonesian Independence, 1945–1948* (The Hague: Nijhoff, 1982), pp. 14–15.

[226] Announcement by *Stuw*, November 16, 1933, pp. 257–58.

[227] *Voorstel tot Interneering*, December 22, 1933 in *Secret Mail Report* 1934, no. 287.

[228] Adviser for Native Affairs Gobée to Governor-General, January 24, 1934 in *Secret Mail Report* 1934, no. 287 as translated by Ingleson, *Road to Exile*, p. 227.

[229] Advice of the Council, February 16, 1934 in *Secret Mail Report* 1934, no. 287.

woto, Soeka, and Hamdani. At the same time, Hatta and Bondan were arrested in Batavia.[230]

Sjahrir was not among the Pendidikan leaders apprehended that day. His whereabouts were uncertain, and some of his closest friends in the Pendidikan, indeed, thought that he had already left the colony, on his way to Holland. They knew that a few weeks before, Sjahrir had received money for the trip, possibly through Maria in Holland.[231] Some time in December 1933, at a secret meeting of the Pendidikan executive, Sjahrir was given permission to "continue his studies in Holland."[232]

Sjahrir had indeed booked a place on the Dutch steamer *S.S. Aramis*, scheduled to depart early in March.[233] He waited in Batavia, in the house belonging to his half-sister Radena, and it was there that the police found him. He was arrested a day after the others, on February 26.[234]

---

[230] *Het Nieuws van den Dag*, February 26, 1934, *Collection Gobée* no.37. Also "PNI dan 25 Februari 1934" in *Daulat Ra'jat* 4, 89 (March 10, 1934); on other reactions in the Indonesian press *Overzicht v.d. IMC pers* 1934, 1: 134–39.

[231] Burhanuddin, "Sjahrir yang saya kenal," p. 59; interview with Burhanuddin, Jakarta, March 5, 1982. The telephone interview with Mrs. Maria Duchâteau-Sjahrir, The Hague, January 10, 1987.

[232] Bondan, "Tjatjatan tentang Pendidikan," p. 2. At the same meeting Hamdani was allowed to leave the organization. Ibid.

[233] Documents of Attorney General in *Secret Verbaal*, November 28, 1934-L33.

[234] *Het Nieuws van den Dag*, February 27, 1934 in *Collection Gobée* no. 37. Salim in L. P. J. Braat, ed., "De brieven van Soeleiman," p. 6; Interview with Hazil Tanzil, Jakarta, October 26, 1987.

5

PRISON AND THE INTERNMENT CAMP, 1934–1935

> Tanah Merah, as a place, appeals to me enormously. Spacious official quarters, and a pretty village [*een mooie desa*] over the great Digoel River.
>
> Van der Plas to van Mook.[1]

1. CIPINANG PRISON

Hatta and Bondan were taken to Glodok prison in Batavia, Burhanuddin, Maskoen, and Soeka, to Sukamiskin jail in Bandung, and Murwoto, to Banceuy prison in the same town. Sjahrir alone went to Cipinang prison in the Meester Cornelis quarter of Batavia, where he was to spend the next eleven months.[2]

"There was no question of ill-treatment in Indies jails for political offenders," a historian writes, "nor were there any extreme pressures placed on those arrested to confess or recant."[3] There were special divisions in some prisons for "Europeans and Communists," and the presence of a Bible in Sjahrir's cell in Cipinang suggests that he might have been put in one of these compartments.[4] Sjahrir was allowed visits from his family, and he could write letters and read books either from the prison library or borrowed from the outside and "censored."[5] He was permitted to get food from friends and order meals from restaurants.[6]

Those were the rules. Actually, in early July, after more than four months in prison, Sjahrir recalled having had a total of merely two visits from the outside.[7] He

---

[1] Private letter from van der Plas to van Mook, April 18, 1943, in *Collection van der Plas* Map B-8, no. 17

[2] Resolution on the internment of Hatta and others in *Secret Verbaal*, November 28, 1934-L33. Early in May another leader of the Pendidikan, Ismoe Hadjiwijaja, went to Cipinang prison; see *Daulat Ra'jat* 4, 95 (May 10, 1934); this is not mentioned by Sjahrir.

[3] Ingleson, *Road to Exile*, p. 220.

[4] Sjahrir (Sjahrazad), *IO*, March 29, 1934.

[5] Ibid. Murwoto has a nice passage about the library in his Banceuy prison, at the same time: for some reason, Murwoto says, the prison library in Banceuy was full of books on "metaphysical science and occultism." Murwoto, *Autobiografi selaku perintis kemerdekaan*, p. 22.

[6] *IO*, September 18, 1934.

[7] Ibid., July 6, 1934.

Sjahrir

had gotten meals from the outside, but this had stopped after a few weeks,[8] and, in mid-June, the friend who had been arranging for his books left Batavia. Sjahrir wrote early in August:

> for the past two months, all contacts with the outside world have been broken. No more books, either from the library or from elsewhere.[9]

His only connection with the outside after this, it seems, were the letters he began to send, intitially once a month and then with growing frequency, to Maria in Holland.[10]

In retrospect, Sjahrir has sometimes been presented as a man who could not stand solitude.[11] He certainly was conscious of the bars in the window of his Cipinang cell. The wisdom of what his "ethical" high school rector had told him in Bandung—"What is freedom? Nobody is free"—now appeared to him as the rhetoric of somebody who had never really had to find out.[12] Nor, however, did Sjahrir give signs of deep depression.

In Cipinang, Sjahrir did not appear to experience much of the hellish feeling one might expect from an endless row of days dragging on:

> For me, in spite of it all, this last month [the first month in prison] has passed fairly quickly. I am not badly off here ... fairly spatial cell ... the bars, the materialization of the idea of coercion ... sharpening the awareness of freedom.[13]

This was prison, certainly,

> Yet, the seclusion does me good. All the time I have been back from Europe, I have never been able to think so calmly [*rustig*].... I have already read a couple of novels here, and I have refreshed the memories of my youth by reading the Bible once more, and thoroughly. I had been wanting to do that for a long time, but something always had prevented me.[14]

Hatta, at the same time, described his prison as a *"pertapaan,"* "abode of an ascetic"; he saw living behind bars as a "strengthening of *iman*"—of loyalty to a body of beliefs, strengthening of spirituality.[15] Sjahrir did not use the "traditional" words

---

[8] Ibid., September 18, 1934.

[9] Ibid., August 3, 1934.

[10] The originals of the letters to Maria sent between 1934 and 1940 exist in four files in Mrs. Maria Duchâteau-Sjahrir's possession in Lorques. Only a part of them, edited by Mrs. Duchâteau-Sjahrir, were published as *Indonesische overpeinzingen* in 1945. A selection of *Indonesische overpeinzingen* was translated into English by Charles Wolf and published, in 1948, as Sutan Sjahrir, *Out of Exile* (New York: John Day, 1949). The letters were sent by air mail, written on two two-sides in very small script.

[11] Hatta's speech at Sjahrir's funeral in Leon Salim, ed., *Bung Sjahrir*, p. 63.

[12] *IO*, October 4, 1934.

[13] Ibid., March 29, 1934.

[14] Ibid. The translator of the letter into English, Charles Wolf, perhaps with Sjahrir's connivance, translated *"rustig,"* "calmly," as "clearly and fully." (Sjahrir, *Out of Exile*, p. 2.)

[15] Letter by Hatta from Glodok prison to Moerad, April 20, 1934, published as "Soeara dari pertapaan," in *Daulat Ra'jat* 4, 95 (May 10, 1934). *Iman*, a traditional Islamic and Minangkabau

pertapaan or *iman*. Yet, as one can see from his letters to Maria, not unlike Hatta, Sjahrir constructed the story of his imprisonment very much as one of continual and growing detachment, not unlike *pertapaan* indeed, as a way of strengthening the spirit, a coming closer to what one believes is the truth.

Food was not a wholly trivial matter in this context. Sjahrir wrote to Maria, after the supply of meals from the outside had stopped:

> I feel myself, also, more like a 'true' prisoner with this prison food, than I did when I was getting meals from the outside. I am forgetting more and more what taste and relish are. I see eating now as a duty, and fulfillment is thus transferred from eating towards the eaten, about the same way in which one feels fulfilled after one has properly acquitted oneself of another task: a spiritual [*geestelijke*] satisfaction of the soul more than a sensual [*zinnelijke*] satisfaction of the stomach, a satisfaction, thus, of a spiritually 'higher' quality. You can see what one can discover over tin-bowl meals![16]

As before, in his letters from prison, Sjahrir declared himself to be strongly on the side of "comprehension [*begrip*]," as opposed to "intuition [*gevoelens*]."[17] However, his distrust of "fashionable wisdom," of "quasi" or "false" scholarship, visibly intensified in prison.[18] It even appeared, occasionally, as if he now regarded much of rationalism itself—not unlike the relish in food—to be part of the discardable superficiality of the world outside. "I feel with growing certainty," Sjahrir wrote in July,

> that the contemporary world is ruled by mere words [*frase*]. I have little trust in what is generally presented as social science. That drifting of scholarship everywhere ... is so strikingly parallel to the drifting of politics, so that one can not seriously believe in either. This is my problem at the moment: the guides have become untrustworthy."[19]

Time, too, seemed to become, to Sjahrir, something of the glimmer of the outside world—also something from which one might find it rewarding to be more detached. "I notice myself getting unconsciously into the habit of thinking in the context of time as little as possible," Sjahrir wrote in Cipinang:

> My notion of time, as my stay in prison is indefinite [no date was set for a release], has become rather objective, so to speak, which means that now I have no interest in appearance [*schijn*]. Events which look like pillars and milestones might lead me along the wrong track....[20]

In his letters from prison, Sjahrir repeatedly, and till the last moment, expressed a hope that he and the other Pendidikan leaders might get "a second-degree sen-

---

notion, as the reader may recall from the last chapter, was also one of the building blocks of the Pendidikan ideology.

[16] *IO*, September 18, 1934.
[17] Ibid., e.g., May 25, 1934.
[18] Ibid., July 6, 1934.
[19] Ibid.
[20] Ibid.

tence," a milder exile, to Flores, for instance, where Sukarno had been sent by the decision of the Governor-General shortly before. Occasionally, even the hope of "expulsion [*externeering*]"—to Holland for instance!—crept in. Sjahrir censored himself, always, and ridiculed such hopes as "naive." The hopes, however, kept coming back. It is as if we can hear a sigh in one of his letters from Cipinang:

> Certainly, I am not a hardened politician [*politieke rot*], and I hardly could be, with my almost exclusively academic training and at my age.[21]

On November 16, 1934, it was decided that five leaders of the Pendidikan, Sjahrir among them, would be sent to the internment camp at Boven Digul,[22] in spite, for instance, of a last minute appeal for pardon by one of the senior and most respected leaders of Indonesian politics, Hadji Agoes Salim, published in the Islamic paper *Pemandangan*:

> Hopefully. . . . Drs. Mohammad Hatta and his associates, who are threatened with exile, will be preserved for their work of education and training.[23]

Boven Digul was the worst possible alternative—a fearful, malarial place at the end of the world. And internment, as a rule, was for an indefinite time, possibly for life.[24] Sjahrir received the news in prison on December 9. "So it is decided," he wrote on the same day,

> and a conclusion is brought to a period of doubts and wrestling in my mind about those whom I have to leave behind. . . . The doubts, the distress [*ellende*] through which I have been dragging myself during these last two years [*sic*!] come now to an end; I do not wish to, and I can not think about them any more.[25]

At the very moment when captivity was set in front of him as a future, when he was preparing to live "in the camp," Sjahrir, twenty-five at the time, felt the contours of his personal integrity more sharply perhaps than he ever had since returning from Holland. He connected calmness with power:

> It is so dark that once some light falls on it, maybe, a new and infinite perspective will open. We must not stare blindly at temporal symptoms, at

---

[21] Ibid., July 6, September 11, November 23, 1934.

[22] Resolution on internment of Hatta and others in *Secret Verbaal*, November 28, 1934-L33.

[23] Hadji Agoes Salim, "Boleh Djadikan Drs. Mohammad Hatta akan Dibuang," *Pemandangan*, October 2, 1934, quoted in Rose, *Indonesia Free*, p. 77.

[24] Leon Salim, an Indonesian political activist and Sjahrir's friend, remembers how in prison in the mid-1930s he had just two wishes, to eat a roasted chicken again and not to be sent to Boven Digul. (L. Salim, "Inspektur Belanda Memanggilnja Tuan," p. 51.) In Cairo at the same time, M. Rasjid Manggis Dt. Radjo Penghoeloe, an Indonesian student and also later a political associate of Hatta and Sjahrir, was busy "writing a scenario for a play with the title 'Boven Digoel'." M. Rasjid Manggis in *Bunga Rampai Soempah Pemoeda* (Jakarta: Balai Pustaka, 1978), p. 81. See also Hatta's article on the camp published in 1929 and reprinted in Hatta, *Portrait of a Patriot*, p. 379.

[25] *IO* December 9, 1934.

actuality; we must strive to see what is greater and move our spirit thereto. This gives calm, and power, and conviction.[26]

Sjahrir did not take part in the campaign which *Daulat Ra'jat* started for their release. Sjahrir's silence in that regard can not be explained merely by prison censorship. Hatta's voice was heard very distinctly from prison: he sent a letter to *Daulat Ra'jat*, which was published, without any retribution from the authorities.[27] With the only exception of Djohan Sjahroezah, his nephew, Sjahrir probably did not even correspond privately with anyone from the Pendidikan on the outside.[28]

In his letters to Maria, Sjahrir listed the books he read in prison—the Bible, novels, no politics whatsoever. He did not complain of being unduly restricted in his reading. Hatta, no more privileged than Sjahrir, evidently was allowed to read freely and was even escorted, once, to his house from prison to check his private library and bring some books back to his cell. Hatta could and continued to read "political stuff." Sjahrir listed the matters most on his mind while in prison: his "family," by which he increasingly meant Maria in Holland, and his "studies," philosophy mostly, psychology, and sociology.[29]

"Our own estimations of ourselves," Sjahrir wrote during his last weeks in Cipinang about "us" Indonesians,

> naturally differ from how the colonial government estimates us. But this does not seem to be as strongly so in my case and, therefore, there is still some layer under the surface of my perceptions, some subconscious expectations based on the standard by which I evaluate myself.[30]

Sjahrir called this sub-layer in his mind "a congenial belief in mankind and its righteousness."[31]

He rejected martyrdom just as he was about to become a martyr himself. The cult of Christ on the cross should not be dogmatized, he wrote, nor should the Evangelist's: "Greater love hath no man than this, that a man lay down his life for his friends." At this moment, it was rather Don Quixote who came to Sjahrir's mind. But even he, so Sjahrir thought, played too much on "fantasy" and "wasted his energy."[32]

What Sjahrir was against was not the principle of martyrdom itself, but pushing the principle too "dogmatically" into a "principle of a complete self-denial." This excess, he warned, is a device to curtail freedom. It could be best seen, he pointed out, in the case of Holland under dogmatic Calvinism—"the native country of individualism" moving towards "compact faith" and "state absolutism."[33]

---

[26] Ibid., December 22, 1934.

[27] Hatta's letter to Moerad, *Daulat Ra'jat* 4, 95 (May 10, 1934).

[28] Interview with Hazil Tanzil, October 26, 1987; interviews with Hamdani and Murad, Jakarta, October 30, 1987 and January 5, 1988.

[29] *IO*, July 6, 1934, and March 29, 1934.

[30] Ibid., November 23, 1934.

[31] Ibid. (The American translator of this passage into English translated "congenial belief [*sympathiek geloof*])" in Sjahrir's text, as "maudlin." (Sjahrir, *Out of Exile*, p. 31.)

[32] *IO*, December 16, and May 25, 1934.

[33] Ibid., December 16, and September 22, 1934.

Sjahrir might come easily to terms with a *pragmatic* Calvinism. He rejected "hedonism" in the same passages. He still clearly thought—in private life and in politics, as well—along a scale remembered from the Dutch "ethical" schools of his youth. He still thought as a bright student. "What they call 'sinful men'," Sjahrir wrote in Cipinang, "is indeed an image of unripe man."[34]

What should at all costs be avoided, Sjahrir believed, were "absolute and sharp rules."[35] In a lengthy passage, he meditated about the case of the Italian anarchists, Sacco and Vanzetti, who had been executed in Boston seven years before. Sjahrir described the two Italians' trust as "naive," and "out of place." At the same time, however, he made it perfectly clear how strong an affinity he felt with the two Italians as he himself sat in the Dutch prison, looking—in disbelief—towards the Dutch judging him.

What Sacco and Vanzetti did, Sjahrir wrote, was what they believed was "good." They tragically failed. There is not the slightest indication, in Sjahrir's text, that the men's ethics were flawed. Sacco and Vanzetti were merely placed "at the wrong time," and they became the "stakes in politics."[36]

When Hatta, Sjahrir, and their friends were arrested and put in jail, as Djohan Sjahroezah, a Pendidikan activist and Sjahrir's nephew, described it later,

> the masses in general were unstirred, despite the fact that they were so close to what had happened. No mass protest, no gathering, no spontaneous demonstration by the people! None of that at all. The [arrested] men were treated as a threat to public law and order, and yet, in real life, nothing happened—totally nothing that one might notice. Public law and order had not been disturbed for a single moment, at least not in the sense one attaches to it.[37]

The main press agency in the Indies, *Aneta*, was quite justified in reporting, in February 1934, on the government action against the Pendidikan, that the "police raids and arrests positively did not attract public interest."[38] There was an interpellation in the Dutch Parliament in The Hague, but it was easily dismissed by a two-line answer from the minister.[39] There were some reports in foreign papers, with the names and facts blurred beyond recognition.[40]

Except for a few articles in the Indonesian press,[41] the people in the Indies were not touched. Sjahrir, as his letters from Cipinang to Maria bear witness, was aware of this.[42] After two years of living and conducting politics "amidst the people," he sensed that he was, for all practical purposes, forgotten. Yet, he did not seem much

---

[34] Ibid., December 16, 1934.

[35] Ibid.

[36] Ibid., November 23, 1934.

[37] Djohan Sjahroezah in *Kritiek en Opbouw*, March 15, 1941, p. 40.

[38] *Aneta* quoted in *Overzicht v.d. IMC pers* 1934, I, p. 136.

[39] Interpolation by Effendi, March 6, 1934, in *Secret Verbaal*, March 8, 1934, no. 6.

[40] Berliner Börsen Zeitung on February 28, 1934 reported the arrest of Hatta as an arrest of "javanischen Gandhi"; copy in *Secret Verbaal*, June 8, 1934-X14.

[41] See on this *Darmokondo*, February 27, 1934; ibid.

[42] *IO* June 24, 1934.

disturbed by this. As he prepared to depart for a place as far from the people as one could imagine, Sjahrir appeared to feel that, now, he could think of his people with more conviction and a deeper intensity than ever before. When he was told about the Digul sentence, Sjahrir wrote:

> "It was as if I were reminded of my people . . . reminded of all that made for bonds between me and my people's fate and grief."[43]

A change was caused, as Sjahrir wrote to Maria, essentially by his new "distance [*afstand*]" enforced by the arrest,

> from the dearest and most beautiful thing a life could bring in this world. . . . My personal happiness was destroyed, and I was torn from those who were most close to me.[44]

Sjahrir was stripped of his most personal, most immediate, and most actual ties with the world, and thus was pushed (or helped) to remember. "Now," Sjahrir wrote in the same letter to Maria,

> all that—the decomposition, the destruction of my personal happiness, the distance from those closest to me -- is claimed by the people. All my grievances have disappeared. All that remains is my feeling of belonging to the downtrodden people, and my feeling of bondage with them.[45]

"We have so often misunderstood each other, the people and I," Sjahrir wrote in the same letter and as if about time past,

> . . . the people were for me, often, too dull; they made me feel hopeless with their obstinacy, their delusions angered me and made me lose my patience with their pettiness. In spite of the fact that the people's fate and the aim of my life were one and the same thing, in spite of the fact that we were tied together, the people even filled me, occasionally, with bitterness.[46]

The actual events in the Indies during and after the Pendidikan leaders were arrested could hardly have been expected to calm Sjahrir's "impatience," "anger," "despair," and "bitterness" towards his people. The people did not lose the qualities which had made Sjahrir despair before. What changed, it seems, was that Sjahrir relegated these qualities—like everyday politics, like the relish in food, like everyday time—to the world outside, to the realm of the glimmer, of actuality and temporality, which should not be allowed to distract him from the essence.

"One of the problems of these times," Sjahrir wrote from Cipinang prison, "is the solitude of the individual amidst the heaped masses."[47] Now, in prison, Sjahrir could remember the masses and, maybe, was less alone.

---

[43] Ibid., December 9, 1934.
[44] Ibid.
[45] Ibid.
[46] Ibid.
[47] Ibid., September 22, 1934.

We are, Sjahrir wrote in Cipinang, "children of an individualistic time." Thus, there are temptations: "Freud, and Fries, and Heymans," and "novels." There are dangers: "self-love and self-presumptions" or "believing in one's accountability to one's God only, without a mediator." Wrote Sjahrir:

> An individual might try to keep his individuality by concentrating on his life; [then] the deepening of self-consciousness might be parallel to the deepening of egocentrism, the seclusion of oneself, and the exclusion from oneself of others. . . .[48]

There is a letter by Sjahrir, written a few weeks after he had mentioned his liberation from the sensuality of eating. The letter describes "recurring dreams, almost nightmares, of most various and most opulent meals, of all sorts of fantastic delicacies."[49] Sjahrir makes other admissions in the letters from Cipinang of coming too close, sometimes, to being "overwhelmed . . . by modern psychological explanations [of ourselves], which are, in essence, pessimistic." "The weaker we are," he wrote, "the more eagerly we try to project our personality onto everything."[50] Whatever one did, there remained an "inner current" in man, Sjahrir wrote; "we remain submissive to blind powers which reside within us, but which we do not know."[51]

"Pessimists, cynics, and egoists, by their nature, are unhappy people," Sjahrir wrote to Maria after seven months in jail; "the highest personal bliss attainable is to be one with the general good fortune of mankind."[52] He still believed, as did the best among his "ethical" teachers, that a better world might be built on compassion:

> Is not, at the end of ends, our personal grief nothing but a very small part of a great, general sorrow? Is not exactly this sorrow [*leed*] of ours the most profound and the strongest bond that keeps us together?"[53]

In his prison letters, Sjahrir attacked many of the qualities of the actuality of Western civilization: "'Bata' shoes and slogans," "Babbitt," "Bergson, D'Annunzio, Mayakovski and numerous others in Germany," the "broken spiritual unity," the "loss of all forms."[54] Three values flagrantly stood against this: *geestelijke eenheid* "spiritual unity," *levenseenheid*, "personal integrity," and *schoonheidsgevoel*, "a feeling for beauty." Those were *de juiste gids*, "the correct guides;" there was, besides, *rustigheid*, "calmness," opposing *ruwheid*, "coarseness or crudity."[55]

Sjahrir, it seems, aimed at a journey from the actual to the real. But this often led him sadly back in time:

> [Take the Bata shoes and slogans, and] compare all that with the personal integrity and the beauty of living in Plato or Kant! All our efforts must aim at

---

[48] Ibid., October 30, 1934.

[49] Ibid., October 31, 1934.

[50] Ibid., October 30 and December 16, 1934.

[51] Ibid., September 22, 1934.

[52] Ibid., July 22, 1934.

[53] Ibid., December 9, 1934.

[54] Ibid., July 22, 1934.

[55] Ibid., July 22, 1934, and January 6, 1935.

finding a spiritual unity and a personal integrity, must strive at a restoration [*terugzoekend*], striving out of our special fields, from leaves and branches, back [*terug*] to the stem, and, then, to the roots.... Rather than throwing old thinkers into a trash bin, and feeding ourselves with 'slogans,' instead we should search, together with those old thinkers, for a universality and real community. Instead of the superficiality and bombastic sentiments of [Bergson and the others], we should turn to the gold mines of true beauty and spiritual harmony that is to be found in the old thinkers....[56]

Sjahrir never mentioned his sister as having visited him in Cipinang. He did write, after half a year in prison, that his younger brother (probably Mahroezar) made one visit.[57] The family of Djohan Sjahroezah, Sjahrir's nephew, helped at the beginning, especially by sending meals. A few months after Sjahrir's arrest, however, Djohan himself became a political prisoner for a press offense, and these contacts also stopped.[58]

There were no true family connections after that. The only person in the Indies, indeed, who was not a prisoner and appeared to be still in touch with Sjahrir, was his new friend from Holland—the painter, Salim. In one letter from prison, Sjahrir recalled how he had lured Salim from "his Bohemian world" in Amsterdam, from cafés and bars like the *Rotonde* and the *Americain*, to see the real East: "to find out" how wrong the Colonial Institute image of the Indies was and "that the wajang [shadow theater] of Jodjana [exotic dancing] or Bali do not give any true picture of Indonesia."[59] Salim remained faithful to Sjahrir. He borrowed books for his friend at the Batavia Museum—a twin institution of the Colonial Institute in fact. He regularly wrote letters to Sjahrir in prison. Yet, in September, Sjahrir noted that Salim

> does not understand much of the colony. [He is not wholly unlike the Dutch] planters with their tropical frenzy [*tropenkolder*] who . . . feel themselves strangers in their own land and are being truly themselves only when dreaming of "the old times in the *rimboe* [forest]."[60]

His friend, Sjahrir wrote, was disgusted by the oppression and by the "Eastern qualities of the natives"—*indolentie*, "indolence," *onderworpenheid*, "submissiveness,"

---

[56] Ibid., July 22, 1934.

[57] Ibid., August 3, 1934.

[58] Ibid., July 6, 1934. Djohan Sjahroezah is called "Djon" in the letters. On Djohan Sjahroezah's trial and sentence see *Daulat Ra'jat*, 4, 95 (May 1934).

[59] Ibid., September 20, 1934. Salim is called "Soeleiman" in the letters. *Raden Mas* Jodjana was a Javanese dancer, initially a student, like Hatta, at the Rotterdam Handelshoogeschool, and married to a Dutch woman. During the 1930s he performed his *"Tari radja-radja"* and was known throughout Europe. Later he established a dance school in Berlin. See, for instance, an article on Jodjana in "Indian Arts and Letters" (London) 10, 1 (1936), translated in *Poedjangga Baroe* 6, 3-4 (September–October 1936), p. 66. See also Beb Vuyk in "Tari Jodjana," *Konfrontasi* 11 (March–April 1956), pp. 11–12, where Beb Vuyk calls Jodjana dancing—as well as a documentary film made of it—"kitsch."

[60] *IO*, September 20, 1934. "*Rimboe*," jungle" or "forest," is left in Indonesian (or Melajoe rather) in the Dutch text. The phrase suggests the language mixture used by Dutch planters who had lived long in the Indies; it might be translated like "in the good old rough times down there."

and *schuwheid*, "shyness."[61] By mid-June, indeed, the frustrated Salim had left the Indies.[62]

To all appearances, only the letters to Maria remained. Sjahrir, no doubt, in spite of what had happened in Medan, considered his marriage to Maria perfectly valid. Separated from politics, from his kin, from the outside world, Sjahrir wrote of Maria, and of her (and Sal Tas') children, as *de mijnen*, "my family."[63] Maria's and her kids' house in Holland became, for Sjahrir in the Javanese prison, *thuis*, his "home."[64] Some time shortly before his arrest, Sjahrir managed to send one of his younger brothers, Sutan Sjahsam, *thuis*, "home," to Maria and to the children. He wrote to Maria from Cipinang, telling her to take good care of Sjahsam.[65]

It might be a new *rumah tunjuk* for Sjahrir—the house a man starts his life's journey from and is destined to return to—if Minangkabau tradition allowed such a blasphemous shift in topography and culture. Maria was a Dutch woman. Sjahrir's letters to her were written in Dutch with only occasional words in Indonesian for notions too specific to the Indies. Maria lived on the other side of the globe. On her way back from Medan she found out that she was pregnant, but the boy that Sjahrir had fathered died three weeks after birth.[66]

There was an extreme looseness and an immense distance. Letters were the only connection and even these were censored. Maria worked for the family's subsistence, her children—a boy and girl—were bewildered by the occasional exotic postcard from a man they hardly knew, and who signed himself "father."[67]

It may be that Sjahrir, in Cipinang, mapped his *rantau*, "the outward regions," more clearly than ever before—the wide-spreading network of low-key affections, the glimmering outside world with the center distant, vague, and addressed in language acquired second hand. Sjahrir wrote in Cipinang that the connection with his *thuis*—the letters to Maria in Holland—became "more significant for my state of mind, at the moment, than my actual release might be."[68]

2. ALMOST AN "ETHICAL" VILLAGE

The internment camp of Tanah Merah was situated almost exactly in the center of New Guinea, the huge jungle-covered easternmost island of the Indonesian archipelago. It was built at the upper reaches of the Digul River—thus it was also commonly called Boven Digul, "Upper Digul."

---

[61] Ibid. Elsewhere in his Cipinang letters Sjahrir wrote about "the famed trilogy: 'Eastern' modesty, 'Eastern' resignation, 'Eastern' patience'." Ibid., March 29, 1934; see also June 24 and December 9, 1934.

[62] Ibid., September 20, 1934. See also L. P. J. Braat, ed., "De brieven van Soeleiman," *De vrije Katheder* 6, 1 (May 3, 1946) and interview with Salim, Paris, February 2, 1988.

[63] *IO* February 11, 1936.

[64] Ibid., October 31, 1934.

[65] Ibid., March 29, 1934. According to Mrs. Duchâteau-Sjahrir, Sjahrir sent Sjahsam to help her at the time of the economic depression; Sjahsam was working at the time, Maria says, with a British company on Sumatra. Interview with Maria Duchâteau-Sjahrir, Lorques, February 13, 1988.

[66] Ibid.

[67] Interview with Josselin Tas, The Hague, October 25, 1986.

[68] *IO*, May 25, 1934.

Boven-Digul
Cover design for *Boven-Digoel* by Dr. L. J. A. Schoonheyt (1936)

The camp came into existence in January 1927 and was initially designed to hold the convicted participants in recent Communist uprisings in Java and Sumatra.[69] Five, and later seven, platoons of Dutch colonial infantry guarded the camp. The highest local authority was a military *gezaghebber*, "administrator," with the rank of captain. The number of internees steadily declined after 1927. Of the original more than two thousand, little more than four hundred remained in 1935, when Hatta, Sjahrir, and their friends arrived.[70]

According to the law, the internees in Tanah Merah were not prisoners. Their banishment to the place was not formally a part of a "criminal proceeding," but was described as an "administrative measure." The internees, inside the camp, according to the Governor-General's directive, were to

---

[69] Governor-General, January 5, 1927 in *Secret Verbaal*, January 10, 1928-Ir Q.

[70] "Boven Digoel Kwartaalverslag," 2nd quarter 1935; *Secret Mail Report* 1935, no. 945, in *Secret Verbaal*, November 6, 1935-V23, *bijlage* A. Exact numbers were 2,100 in early 1927, and 442 in mid-1935.

enjoy the same rights and be subject to the same obligations as all free persons; the Government [should] refrain from doing more, with respect to the internees, than keeping a vigilant supervision over them.[71]

Tanah Merah, officially, was neither a "concentration camp" (this being long before Buchenwald and Auschwitz anyway) nor a "penal" camp. The camp was to be called an *isolatie kolonie*, "isolation colony."[72] There was some barbed wire around, but its purpose was to enclose the quarters of the military and the civilian staff in the camp against the surrounding jungle.[73]

This was a vast jungle. Beyond it, snowy peaks could sometimes be seen in the dim distance towards the northeast. No internee coming from Java, nor even from Sumatra, could ever before have experienced a forest like this. The trees and flowers were largely nameless to the men and women from the archipelago's western islands. Headhunters were the natives of the place. Crocodiles infested the Digul River. Rain was usually heavy, and a long while before it came, the roar of falling water could be heard from afar. Flying ants attacked the camp at regular intervals; they blackened everything, they stormed the huts, the men, and the *Petromax* lamps that were supposed to keep them away.

Twenty attempts at escape were recorded at Boven Digul between 1927 and 1935. About a third of the fugitives—some with the *Bos Atlas* used at the colonial schools of the time—got as far as the Australian western part of the island; one or two of them even reached the Thursday Islands south of the New Guinea coast. All of the escapees, without exception, either came back to the camp exhausted, disappeared in the jungle, or were returned by the friendly authorities of the British Commonwealth.[74]

Letters and newspapers were brought to the camp once a month by the police ship *Albatros*—called by the internees *kapal poetih*, the "white ship," or with a fine sense of history, *taxi kompeni*, "taxi of the [Dutch East Indies] company."[75] Letters and newspapers were censored. No radios were available to the internees; the wireless service in the camp existed only for the authorities. Yet, this was not the kind of solitude as Joseph Conrad described in *Heart of Darkness*:

> solitude—utter solitude without a policeman..., silence—utter silence, where no warning voice of a kind neighbour can be heard whispering of public opinion.[76]

---

[71] Governor-General in *Secret Verbaal*, January 10-1928 Q.

[72] E.g., M. van Blankenstein, 9 October 1928 quoted in Kwantes, ed., *De Ontwikkeling van de Nationalistische Beweging*, 3: 165. For more detail see M. van Blankenstein's series on Boven Digul in *Nieuwe Rotterdamsche Courant*, September 8–11, 3, 15–16, 1928.

[73] Interview with Burhanuddin, Jakarta, March 5, 1982; also Chalid I. F. M. Salim, *Limabelas tahun Digul*, p. 183.

[74] See, for instance, H. Thamrin in *Volksraad*, August 7, 1935 in *Handelingen Volksraad* 1935, pp. 719 and 1026; clippings of the proceedings in *Secret Verbaal*, October 20, 1937-M27; interviews with Burhanuddin, Jakarta, March 5, 1982, and Murwoto, Jakarta, December 6, 1987.

[75] Murwoto, *Autobiografi*, p. 24; a picture of Tanah Merah with the "*Albatros*" in the background can be seen in L. de Jong, *Het koninkrijk der Nederlanden in de tweede Wereldoorlog* (Leiden: Nijhoff, 1984) XIa, p. 323.

[76] Joseph Conrad in McClure, *Kipling and Conrad*, p. 90.

For the camp, the successive waves of new exiles marked the time. Four years after the first, Communist, inhabitants arrived in 1927, waves of arrested leaders of the PARI, Tan Malaka's ex-Communist, almost phantom-like party, reached the camp in 1931, and again in 1933.[77] Afterwards, in early and mid 1934, Islamic leaders were brought in, particularly from Permi—the party which after 1932 was locked in so close a relationship and so tense a conflict with the Pendidikan, especially in the regions of Minangkabau. At the same time some arrested leaders also arrived from the Partai Sarekat Islam Indonesia, "Party of Indonesian Islamic Union," another Islamic party.[78] Early in 1935, Sjahrir, Hatta, and their friends from the Pendidikan Nasional Indonesia were brought to the camp.

With all the waves came news from outside—news, as a rule, of successive failures to change the colonial system. The progression of time outside reached the camp strictly censored and as a series of shocks. Groups of newcomers were thrown into the camp, each coming from a different area of Indonesian politics and culture. To a depressing extent, the newcomers came with experiences which could only with difficulty be shared by those who were there before them. The politics of the outside world echoed in the camp not unlike the endless and nameless jungle.

There were diseases in the camp, as varied and exotic as the animals, flowers, and trees, and as the names, indeed, of the new parties and leaders: *filariasis Bancrofti, ulcera tropica, ichthyosis, elephantiasis cruris, elephantiasis genitalis, framboesia tropica, mengitis cerebra spinalis,* and tuberculosis, of course, and malaria for which Boven Digul became notorious.[79] A Dutch official wrote about the camp:

> Men of twenty-seven, after ten years of internment, are grey and broken, and stricken in years. Complete wrecks turn out to be men younger than fifty.[80]

In 1930, only three years after the camp was opened, another high-ranking Dutch official visiting the camp concluded that about two-thirds of the Tanah Merah internees had had enough: they were harmless enough, so the official concluded, to be released without any longer posing "any danger to public order in the colony."[81]

There were both men and women in the camp. Female exiles were rare at Boven Digul, but wives were allowed—even encouraged—by the colonial authorities to accompany their exiled husbands. In June 1935, when Sjahrir was there, two female

---

[77] In August 1931 there was a major round-up of PARI (Partai Repoebliek Indonesia) in Banjarmasin, Cepu, Wonogiri, and Kediri. The arrested men were sent to Boven Digul all by a decision of September 7 (*Secret Mail Report* 1936, no. 446). One of the Tan Malaka's closest associates, Djamaluddin Tamin, was arrested in September 1932 and sent to the camp with one Djaja bin Joesoef and one Moham. Ibid.

[78] On the PSII exiles see Abdullah, *Schools and Politics,* p. 206 and *Daulat Ra'jat* 4, 103 (July 20, 1934); on the Permi leaders being exiled to Boven Digul see *Daulat Ra'jat* 4, 99 (April 20, 1934) and *Secret Mail Report* 1938, no. 1108.

[79] During the year Sjahrir was in the camp, for instance, during April, May, and June, the number of malaria cases grew according to the camp administrator's report, from fifty-five to seventy-two and eventually ninety-three. "Boven Digoel Kwartaalverslag," 2nd quarter 1935, p. 8; a detailed medical report for 1935 may also be found there, with death statistics, etc.; for the early months of the year and for the previous period of 1934 see "Boven Digoel Kwartaalverslag," 4th quarter 1934, in *Secret Mail Report* 1935, no. 419, in *Secret Verbaal,* May 7, 1935-W8, esp. pp. 3–5.

[80] Van der Plas to van Mook, 18 April 1943 in *Collection van der Plas* Map B-8, no. 17.

[81] "Hillen Digoel Verslag," 22 July 1930 in *Secret Verbaal,* November 1, 1930-K24.

exiles and sixty-eight exiles' wives lived in the camp, among 440 men.[82] This made for a ratio of about one woman for every six or seven men. Not the zero-to-one-thousand ratio of Nazi concentration camps, of prisons, or of mental hospitals. Weddings went on in this perverted normalcy. Among the internees, the lucky ones with wives did not dare to leave their houses "lest blood leads a woman astray." Love charms and amulets were on sale in the camp, as everywhere in the Indies, but here it was a married woman, as a rule, who was to be seduced. There were rumors of polyandry, and the rumors heightened anxieties, stiffened marriages, and crippled normalcy still further. Fortunately, men soon grew impotent in the climate of the camp.[83]

Children were born at Boven Digul: there were 136 children in Tanah Merah when Sjahrir came, 67 of them younger than three years; 6 babies were born in April and May 1935 alone.[84] Some unmarried internees wrote letters from the camp to women "outside," and these are the most disturbing documents of the colonial epoch we can think of. The internees told horrendous lies in the letters, portraying the camp in rosy colors, luring the brides-to-be to travel to New Guinea to start a happy family life.

As on the outside, there were police informants inside the camp. There was also a prison in Tanah Merah. Seven prisoners were serving terms in May 1935, for instance; three of them had seven-year sentences, the others three, two, and one. Not quite a normal prison again: the prison guards might be seen playing cards with the prisoners, the prison gate was often left ajar for fresh air.[85] There was a camp in the camp— Tanah Tinggi, "Higher Ground," still further upstream and deeper in the interior. This was a place to restrain "the incorrigibles" from Tanah Merah—a truly hellish, debilitating, fast killing place. At the time Sjahrir was in Tanah Merah, there were about six dozen "incorrigibles" up at Tanah Tinggi—men, women, and also their children.[86] Even as an outcast, banished as far from the world as Tanah Merah, one could still be exiled.

When the camp at Boven Digul was opened, a secret order from the Dutch Governor-General stated that this should be a place where "current political ambitions are exchanged for interest in matters of a more domestic and social nature."[87] In 1935, when Sjahrir was in the camp, higher authorities strongly reprimanded the camp's administrator for being over-zealous in his supervision of the internees—namely not allowing free circulation and debate sessions on books like Ramsey Mac-

---

[82] "Boven Digoel Kwartaalverslag" 2nd quarter 1935, *bijlage* A.

[83] Salim, *Limabelas tahun Digul*, pp. 182, 302–3.

[84] "Boven Digoel Kwartaalverslag" 2nd quarter 1935, p. 8 and p. 2.

[85] B. J. Haga, "Verslag betreffende den toestand van de interneeringskampen in Boven-Digoel" (medio Mei 1935), in *Secret Mail Report* 1935, no. 853, in *Secret Verbaal*, November 6, 1935-V23 (further "Haga Digoel Verslag" II), pp. 9–10; "Boven Digoel Kwartaalverslag," 2nd quarter 1935: bijlage 3; Salim, *Limabelas tahun Digul*, pp. 192, 324; "much water shall flow through the Digoel River before there will be a new prison," Haga's report complained ("Haga Digoel Verslag" II, p. 9).

[86] Interpolation by Sneevliet of Minister of Colonies Colijn, *Handelingen Tweede Kamer* in *Secret Verbaal*, October 17, 1935-U21, where the number 65 for *"onverzoenlijke"* is given by the minister; see also Nota J. Th. Petrus Blumberger, 15 October 1937 in *Secret Verbaal*, October 20, 1937-M27, also in Kwantes, ed., *De Ontwikkeling van de Nationalistische Beweging* 4: 468–69.

[87] Governor-General to Governor of Moluccas, 5 January 1927 in *Secret Verbaal*, January 10, 1928-Ir Q.

donald's *Socialism Critical and Constructive*, or Firmin Riz' *L'energie Americaine* published in *Bibliotheque de philosophie scientifique*.[88] In the same year, Tanah Merah was described in a secret Dutch report as "trim and neat," with the internees' huts, "on the whole," "neatly painted." "The good examples are spreading," the report cheered, and, in the future, the camp would "look even neater."[89] Still eight years later, another Dutch official visiting the camp—a former member of the "neo-ethical" *Stuw* group in fact—wrote to a friend:

> Tanah Merah, as a place, appeals to me enormously. Spacious official quarters and a pretty village [*een mooie desa*] over the great Digoel River.[90]

There was a "Wilhelmina Hospital" in the camp, named after the Queen of Holland, of course, with more than forty beds available—an incomparably better *ratio per capita* of medical care for the internees than for the free population in the colony on the outside. Patients at the hospital, both internees and staff, were not rarely treated in the same rooms and by the same doctors.[91] According to a man who was interned in the camp for many years, some of the Dutch doctors got naturally closer to the educated patient-internees, than to the often ignorant and vulgar patient-guards.[92]

There were two mission schools, one Catholic and one Protestant, in Tanah Merah. Both were opened to the children—forty pupils in 1935—of the military and civilian staff. A government school worked for the internees' children. A former Communist leader, Soetan Said Ali, was the school's principal; Indonesian and Dutch were the languages of instruction; in 1935, the school operated four classes, with from five to six children in a class. Twelve internees, at the same time, had official permission to teach children in smaller "family schools."[93] "A little Communist school at Tanah Tinggi" in addition, was mentioned in the regular Dutch report in May 1935.[94]

The dismissal of one of the teachers at the government school was reported in 1934: the teacher allegedly had mixed too much politics into his teaching. There were

---

[88] "Haga, Digoel Verslag" II, p. 3.

[89] "Boven Digoel Kwartaalverslag," 2nd quarter 1935, p. 1.

[90] Van der Plas to van Mook, 18 April 1943, in *Collection of Van der Plas*, loc. cit.

[91] The author of "Boven Digoel Kwartaalverslag," 2nd quarter 1935, p. 8, was not quite certain if this was as it should be in an internment camp.

[92] Salim, *Limabelas tahun Digul*, p. 279. It was a "shock" for some exiles, Salim remembered, when one of the doctors published his haughty memoirs in 1936, without any visible compassion for former "friends" in the camp. L. J. A. Schoonheyt, *Boven-Digoel* (Batavia: de Unie, 1936); Salim, *Limabelas tahun Digul*, p. 487. Reportedly, a brochure was published reacting to Schoonheyt's book (Van Munster en Soekasih, *Indonesie een politiestaat; een antwoord aan Dr. Schoonheyt*) but I was not able to locate it.

[93] No more than three families could send their children to such a "family" school at one time.

[94] "Boven Digoel Kwartaalverslag," 2nd quarter 1935, p. 9; consulting Haga's report from August 1934 (B. J. Haga, "Digoel Verslag betreffende de toestand van de interneeringskampen in Boven-Digoel, medio August 1934," in *Secret Verbaal*, May 7, 1935 W8) (further "Haga Digoel Verslag I"), p. 25; it appears that the number of "private" internee-teachers grew in that year from ten to twelve. It was difficult, Haga complained, to control those teachers, as they were teaching small groups of children and, thus, according to colonial law, could not be subjected to the "Toezicht ordonnantie (Order of Surveillance)." (Ibid.)

several complaints from the camp authorities about how difficult it was to control the schools, especially the smaller "family schools." But no school closures for political reasons—in contrast to what was happening in the colony outside the camp—were reported throughout the camp's existence.[95]

The internees in Tanah Merah organized a Kunst en Sport Vereeniging Digoel, the "Digul Arts and Sports Association," mainly a soccer club. There were two soccer fields in the camp, one for the internees, the other for the military; the civilian staff occasionally played with the internees. There had been a tennis court, but it was apparently no longer in use when Sjahrir came.[96]

A Dutch journalist who visited Tanah Merah in 1928 was struck by "how widespread Dutch was in the camp."[97] As the proficiency in Dutch was a sign of being modern in the Indies, then the camp at Boven Digul was very modern indeed. English, besides, played some role—it was "modern" and yet not "colonial." There were signboards on the internee's huts, reading "English Teacher," "Barbershop," "Hairdresser," and "Laundry." When a high Dutch official visited Tanah Merah on a tour of inspection, some internees on the camp's main road called to him, in painstakingly correct English, reportedly: "Good morning, Sir! How do you do?"

Wayang orang, traditional Javanese dance-theater, was performed in the camp. The Digoel Concert Band—nicknamed Digoel Bu-sneert, "Digul Trash-Can," by the internees—played its own version of jazz. At one time or another, there were at the camp the Opera Association Orient and the Music and Opera Association Liberty (both names were in English) and they played *komedie stambul*, the Malay theatrical genre full of sweet songs and romantic action which, as the reader may recall, had been such a craze in Medan during the 1910s and 1920s, and such a favorite of Rabiah, Sjahrir's mother. The camp cinema in Tanah Merah featured Tarzan, Tom Mix, and Douglas Fairbanks; admittance to the movies was 7 1/2 cents for men and 2 1/2 cents for women.[98]

A few photographs from Tanah Merah survive—of internees in their best clothes—usually all-white European suits with ties, and occasionally hats. The men and women before the camera pose stiffly in front of exotic backdrops. Some of the snapshots have inscriptions in English, like *Farewell-Photo Taken For Departure of Family Barani, Boven Digoel*. Others have inscriptions in Indonesian like *Tanda Peringatan Boven Digoel*, "Souvenir of Boven Digul."

One of the photographs shows a dead man, with a board at his head, on which a short poem is crudely carved. This is Aliarcham, top leader of the Communist uprising in 1926, who died at the penal camp at Tanah Tinggi, and who became Boven Digul's best known martyr. The poem above Aliarcham's dead body is by Henriëtte Roland Holst, the "Aunt Jet" mentioned earlier, a Dutch poet who based her

---

[95] Ibid., esp. p. 13.

[96] Salim, *Limabelas tahun Digul*, pp. 167, 206; interview with Burhanuddin, Jakarta, March 5, 1982.

[97] Blankenstein, September 13, 1928 in Kwantes, ed., *De Ontwikkeling van de Nationalistische Beweging* 3: 165.

[98] Salim, *Limabelas tahun Digul*, pp. 168, 179–82; interviews with Burhanuddin and Murwoto, Jakarta, March 5, 1982 and December 6, 1987. See also "Gamelan door geinterneerden gemaakt van kookpannetjes, leege sardinenbliskjes en andere, niet van Java of elders ingevoerde materialen, Tanah Merah, Boven Digoel, Nieuw Guinea," *Tropisch Nederland* 2, 2 (1929).

"revolution" on harmonizing principles of socialism, humanism, and Christian faith.[99]

It is quite possible that, back in 1927, Governor-General de Graeff—a man called sometimes the last "ethical" Governor-General of the Dutch East Indies—truly imagined that Tanah Merah, if handled well, might become a normal village over the great Digul River. An additional stimulus to that idea might have been the fact that since the late 1920s, a colonization of New Guinea—"the land of the future" as it was now sometimes called—had become an idea widespread among the Dutch community in the Indies, and many former "ethical" hopes might have been projected into it.[100]

A secret government communication of January 1927 presented the first exiles to Boven Digul as something not much short of pioneers, indeed as men building the "foundation of a thorough colonization of these new lands"[101] From the beginning and still when Sjahrir and Hatta arrived, the internees at Tanah Merah were encouraged "to open new land." Those who agreed were granted a government subsidy of about ten guilders a month;[102] if they qualified as clerks they might get a job at the camp for as much as eighteen to thirty guilders a month.[103] These were *werkwilligers*, "willing to work." The internees who "declined to work" were frowned upon by the authorities, but they were nevertheless "taken care of." They got "pocket money" (sic) of about 7 1/2 guilders a month and some allowances *in natura*; they were called "*naturalisten*."[104]

At the time Sjahrir was in the camp, in the middle of 1935, 209 men, out of the camp's population of 440 men, were "willing to work." They worked as peasants, carpenters, dyers, painters, masons, forgers, sawyers, gravediggers, or as brickmak-

---

[99] For instance, Salim, *Limabelas tahun Digul*, pp. 360, 491. For more on Aliarcham see Ruth T. McVey, *The Rise of Indonesian Communism* (Ithaca: Cornell University Press, 1965), p. 315.

[100] See, for instance, special journals published in Bandung (Sjahrir's town) and Semarang: *Kolonisatie Nieuw Guinea nieuws: mededeelingen van de afdeeling Bandoeng* 1–35 (1931–1935), and *Onze Toekomst: orgaan der Vereeniging kolonisatie Nieuw Guinea* 1–13 (1927–1939). ("*Onze Toekomst*" is Dutch for "Our Future.") For details see Drooglever, *De Vaderlandse Club 1929–1942*, especially pp. 198, 201–8, 349–50. The Eurasian community was particularly active in creating hopes in this regard. See also M. K. (Marcel Koch)," Problemen de Indo-Europeaan," *Inzicht* 1, 4 (June 28, 1947), p. 5 on the wave of enthusiasm for this colonization being strong especially after the First World War.

[101] First Government Secretary to Governor-General, January 5, 1927 in *Secret Verbaal*, January 10, 1928-Ir Q.

[102] On the basis of a five-hour work day the wage was sixty cents a day. Just before Sjahrir came, on December 1, 1934, the daily wage was lowered from sixty to forty cents. "Boven Digoel Kwartaalverslag," 4th quarter 1934, p. 3. For comparison, the minimum daily wage for male labor on initial contract on East Sumatra's plantations by the mid-1930s was thirty cents. See Anthony J. S. Reid, *The Blood of the People: Revolution and the End of Traditional Rule in Northern Sumatra* (Kuala Lumpur: Oxford University Press, 1979), p. 41. As for prices at the Tanah Merah camp at that time (1934 and 1935), 1 kg rice was 0.065 guilders, 1 kg of smoked meat, one guilder, fish, about a fifth of the price of meat, 1 liter of coconut oil, 0.18 guilders, 1 liter of petroleum, the same price. ("Boven Digoel Kwartaalverslag," 1st quarter 1935, *Secret Mail Report* 1935, no. 731 in *Secret Verbaal*, November 6, 1935 V23, p. 4.)

[103] Salim, *Limabelas tahun Digul*, pp. 269–70; the chief of the inmates' self-governing body, "*hoofd*" or "*lurah*" Boedisoetjitro was getting thirty-nine guilders a month, his deputy thirty-six guilders; the lowest wage for a clerical job, according to resident Haga, being 13.50 guilders. ("Haga Digoel Verslag" I: *bijlage*.)

[104] Ibid.; see also Murwoto, *Autobiografi*, p. 25.

ers. The others were "supported in kind," 120 men altogether; in addition, there were a few invalids and prisoners in the camp.[105] There was also a small group of shopkeepers, moneylenders, and middlemen—"foreign orientals," mainly Chinese— who, not unlike the situation on the outside, were distrusted in the camp, depended upon by the internees and scorned by them at the same time as *burdjuis*, "bourgeois" and "parasites."[106]

It was an open secret that the authorities handled those "willing to work" much more gently, especially when it came to deciding which of the exiles was "mature" enough to be released from the camp.[107] The camp produced truly grotesque "peasants," "workers," and "clerks."[108]

The better educated among the exiles were not expected to forget what they had learned in their "ethical" classrooms—namely the story of the expanding Western civilization, a sense of a mission which might be carried on not only by whites, but by the most "bright" among the "natives" as well.

Imagine these internees, on some of the cooler of Boven Digul's evenings, sitting in front of their huts—there were even some easy chairs at the camp!—resting and watching the trees and plants, some nameless, but some which they themselves had brought to this otherwise barren land—citruses, pineapples, bananas, papayas, jackfruit. . . . The sound of church bells reaches them from one of the mission schools, a muezzin's voice, or "a guitar, a mandolin, a violin. . . ."[109] And imagine a moment— in this "pioneer culture," in this bizarre Kipling-Defoe world—when savages, halfnaked, non-civilized, true children of the forest (true natives), enter the camp.

Kaja-Kaja people, of the tribes living in jungle around the camp, made frequent visits. They came, as a rule, "in close formation and armed" often to see movies, "of which they especially liked," one internee says, "the films about Tarzan."[110] *Kaja-Kaja* might stay in the camp for some time, from one full moon to the next usually, cleaning houses, doing laundry, and cooking for the internees. They were paid in

---

[105] There were sixty-four additional *"naturalisten"* at Tanah Tinggi. See "Haga Digoel Verslag" II: *bijlage* A. In early 1930 the ratio was 380 *"werkwilligers"* to 225 *"naturalisten"* ("Hillen Digoel Verslag," July 22, 1930, p. 463).

[106] There were twenty-three of these "self-employed" persons at the camp in mid-1935. Ibid. On the internees' reaction to them see Salim, *Limabelas tahun Digul*, p. 157.

[107] According to a secret Dutch communications related to Tanah Merah, *"naturalisten"* and *"communisten"* or *"extremisten"* were often almost identical categories. See, e.g., "Boven Digoel Kwartaalverslag," 2nd quarter 1935, p. 5; also "Boven Digoel Kwartaalverslag," 1st quarter 1935, p. 2; in "Haga Digoel Verslag" II: *bijlage* B, also ibid., pp. 4, 6–9 of the report's text. The internees were very well aware of this Dutch attitude, I was told by Murwoto (Jakarta, December 1987).

[108] The Dutch officials themselves soon became aware that the red soil around the camp was "highly unfertile" and that "colonization" as dreamed of could hardly be successful; still, it appears, they often declined to believe what they knew because the whole structure of the colonial concept was built on it. Haga says in May 1935 that "agriculture (had) not yet succeeded," van Langen had it that the situation in that sense was not "propitious"; Wiarda, significantly, was aware that, if the drive at normalcy definitely failed, the camp would appear as just a *"concentratiekamp."* (Haga Verlslag II, p. 8; "Boven Digoel Kwartaalverslag" 4th quarter 1934, p. 3; "Boven Digoel Kwartaalverslag," 4th quarter 1935, p. 4. On the soil of Boven Digul being "extremely infertile" see Van der Plas to van Mook on April 18, 1943, in *Collection of Van der Plas*.

[109] Salim, *Limabelas tahun Digul*, p. 178; Schoonheyt, *Boven-Digoel*, p. 80.

[110] Salim, *Limabelas tahun Digul*, p. 154.

food, "as much as they could eat," and, after their term was over, they might in addition get an ax, a shirt, a pair of shorts, a pack of tobacco, or a combination of these.[111] The savages learned, for instance, a new form of salute from the internees and guards: from the most primitive stage of their habitual greeting, not specified, through raising an index finger upon meeting somebody in the camp, and finally "saluting like the military do, or shaking hands in the Western way."[112]

Boven Digul was a place, where different cultures met—as they should, indeed, according to the ideal "ethical" image. It was almost the same as on the outside. Chalid Salim, a Sumatran and a Minangkabau, believed that the Dutch authorities in the camp strongly favored the Javanese. The Dutch in Tanah Merah, Chalid Salim wrote, clearly showed the greatest interest in Javanese arts. "Whatever their true motives," Chalid Salim wrote,

> we saw, in these friendly approaches by the Dutch, a policy to excite homesickness among the Javanese and to stimulate the Javanese to yearn for their villages.... Thus, we could meet, again in the camp, the Dutch use of traditional Javanese culture and art as a tool to sharpen contradictions between "Java" and "non-Java."[113]

Chalid Salim's description of a man whom the Dutch had chosen as the "representative" of the internees is a caricature of the *ningrat*, the Javanese aristocrat:

> This official, apparently, still held to feudal customs. Wherever he went, he demanded that he be followed by another internee with a parasol to shelter [him]. Often, I was tempted to ask [him] mockingly, if his parasol soon might change into a *"pajung emas"* [golden umbrella] or perhaps a *"songsong kuning"* [state golden umbrella] indicating that a *bupati* [regent], or a man of an even nobler rank was being escorted along.[114]

All the internees came to the camp believing in Indonesia, in a modern civilization unifying all the island and regional cultures and interests. The initial group of internees in Boven Digul came almost exclusively from Java, where the Communist uprisings had started; but rather than from Java proper, they came mostly from the island's western parts. The next wave of internees, still in 1927, came largely from Sumatra, mainly from West Sumatra, where the Communist uprising had broken out next. From that time on, the "Sumatran tendency" at Boven Digul grew steadily. In 1930, most of PARI exiles sent to Boven Digul were Sumatrans, especially again from West Sumatra, with some truly impressive Minangkabau among them such as Djamaluddin Tamin. Early in the 1930s, another Sumatran, and again predominantly Minangkabau wave reached the camp—the leaders of Permi and Partai Sarekat Islam Indonesia, Minangkabau politicians and Islamic scholars like Iljas Jacoeb, Djalaloeddin Taib, Moechtar Loetfi, Sabilal Rasjad, Hadji Oedin Rachmany, and Datoek Singo Radjo. Far fewer Javanese of comparable stature came through the years.

---

[111] Hatta, *Memoir*, p. 352; Hatta, *Indonesian Patriot*, p. 183.

[112] Salim, *Limabelas tahun Digul*, p. 232.

[113] Ibid., p. 297.

[114] Ibid., p. 332.

Sadly, given the idea apparently so important on the ouside, the Tanah Merah internees built separate *kampongs,* "quarters," for themselves, in separate corners of the camp: thus there was *Kampoeng Oedjoeng Soematera,* "Sumatra's End," the Acehnese *Kampoeng Atjeh,* the Central and Eastern Javanese *Kampoeng Djawa,* the West Javanese *Kampoeng Banten,* and another "quarter" for the Ambonese and Menadonese.[115]

There was a *gamelan,* the traditional Javanese orchestra, *wayang* and *ketoprak,* another genre of Javanese theater, all of them ethnically exclusive. There was a *pencak* club, an association for the traditional martial arts; it was wholly Minangkabau. "Modern art" might be expected to transcend ethnic and subnational boundaries. But from what we know about Tanah Merah "jazz," for instance, the bands were "very Sumatran" with some Javanese playing in them. The *Komedie stambul,* reportedly, was Sumatran as well, with an occasional Javanese. As elsewhere in the colony, sports—Western sports of course—came closest to playing the role of a unifier.

The Christians in the camp almost as a rule were Ambonese and Menadonese.[116] The most prominent Islamic figures, again, came from Minangkabau.[117]

The camp administration, in contrast, appeared to be largely patterned on Java. The titles of the "officials" were Javanese or, better, Dutch-Javanese: at the top was the *wedana,* "district chief," whose immediate subordinate was the *assisten wedana.* The same Dutch official who described Tanah Merah as "a pretty village [*een mooie desa*]," also praised the camp's *wedana* by suggesting that the internee in question might easily be mistaken for "a true Soemedang [Javanese] aristocrat."[118]

In New Guinea, at the remotest fringe of the archipelago, the colony, and the nation, at the greatest possible distance from Java, it appeared particularly bizarre to be "keeping Java in the middle," and, certainly, to the self-conscious non-Javanese particularly irksome. "Sumatrans, and chiefly the Minangkabau," a Dutch official wrote in his report on Boven Digul in 1930, "do keep themselves most separate as a group, and they occasionally look down on the others."[119] "The Minangkabau refuse to live with their partners in distress together in a common place," wrote a Dutch doctor in the camp in a book published in 1936.[120]

3. Sjahrir at Boven Digul

On January 28, 1935, Sjahrir was led out of Cipinang prison. He was taken in a police car to the port in Batavia, where he met with the other Pendidikan leaders destined

---

[115] Schoonheyt, *Boven-Digoel,* p. 161.

[116] An exception was Chalid Salim of Minangkabau, and he makes it clear that he was the exception.

[117] *Imam,* "mosque leader," in Tanah Merah was first Hadji Haroem Rasjid, and then Hadji Mochtar Loetfi—both Minangkabau internees, who before their internment were acknowledged throughout Sumatra as among the most important Islamic figures of their time. See Abdullah, *Schools and Politics,* pp. 149, 152, 203–6; Salim, *Limabelas tahun Digul,* p. 177.

[118] Letter by van der Plas to van Mook, 18 April 1943, in *Collection of Van der Plas,*

[119] "Hillen Digoel Verslag," July 22, 1930.

[120] Schoonheyt, *Boven-Digoel,* p. 161. He learned much during his stay in the camp, the doctor said. He believed perhaps more than before in the possibility in the future of "broader brotherhood between East and West." But, at the same time, he became convinced, watching camp life, that the Sumatrans and other Outer Island (non-Javanese) peoples would never, never submit to Javanese supremacy. (Ibid., p. 95.)

for New Guinea. Three of them—Hatta, Bondan, and Burhanuddin—years later remembered their impressions of Sjahrir at that moment. Sjahrir talked and joked the whole way to the ship. He had gotten fat: he explained that these were special bolsters, on his posterior, which he had invented for the hard prison benches. Visibly at least, Sjahrir, twenty-five at the time, was not frustrated by the vision of the camp.[121]

"Sometimes it even looks like a pleasure outing," Sjahrir wrote in a letter to Maria, after they had been three days at sea.[122] With Java's shores out of view, leaving the Java Sea and then Celebes (Sulawesi) behind, Sjahrir wrote:

> It goes here, on the whole, somewhat more kindheartedly than in Java or in Makassar.... It is easy to see that we are already in the eastern regions and, actually, to all effects secluded. This is clear from the fact that, apparently, nobody knows about our arrival; also there is nobody who looks inquisitive or evinces that he has ever heard about our banishment. As a policeman who escorted us from Makassar said: "All that lies east of Makassar is *doesoen dan hoetan*, village and wilderness." Twice a month there is a ship to Makassar, the only connection with Java; once a month a ship for Digul.

And, writing this, Sjahrir—the just banished revolutionary, child of a new Indonesian urban culture, man of recent Amsterdam experience—added, without the slightest change in tone: *Wat is dit Oosten van ons land mooi*, "How beautiful the eastern part of our country is."[123]

As they traveled further, Sjahrir wrote, there was "splendidly blue sea" all around:

> sometimes light and translucent, like mother of pearl, sometimes deep-dark blue, always purely beautiful... white and green petit islands, couched so finely, they rest in the blue of the sea, and they bathe in the golden, and sometimes silver colored, light of the sun.[124]

Buru Island, east of Sulawesi—thirty years before it too was to become a place of internment, and as famous as Boven Digul—to Sjahrir, watching from the ship, "looks like a fairy-tale land."[125] Banda Island, two stops next to the east—Sjahrir did not know at the moment that he was to come back and spend six years in exile in Banda—appeared to him untouched, softly whispering, and dreamy:

---

[121] Burhanuddin, "Sjahrir yang saya kenal" in Anwar, ed., *Mengenang Sjahrir*, pp. 59–60; Hatta, *Memoir*, p. 349; Bondan, "Mengenal Bung Hatta dari dekat" in *Muhammad Hatta*, ed. Swasono, p. 279; on the trip see also Murwoto, *Autobiografi*, pp. 23ff.

[122] *IO*, January 30, 1935.

[123] Ibid., February 11, 1935. The exclamation seems strange indeed. The American translator evidently also had some hesitation in rendering the phrase, adding "And yet" before the sentence: "*And yet*, how beautiful the eastern part of our country is!" Sjahrir, *Out of Exile*, p. 44; emphasis mine.

[124] Ibid. In another letter, against the overcultivated world of the western part of the colony, the eastern islands were projected as providing a virginal promise of healthy development and a dynamic future. Ibid., February 21, 1935.

[125] Ibid., February 11, 1935.

forsaken ... there is, on view, an old fortress of the East-India Company ...,
but there are almost nowhere people to be seen.... All this, again, has
passed away; nothing, here, reminds one of the bloody times, even the old
fortress on the hill has nothing bloody about it any more. It watches us
peacefully and it harmonizes with its surrounding.[126]

People, when they appeared, were, to Sjahrir, natural, pure, and wholesome:

In this part of Indonesia, it is nature which overrules everything. Everything
is splendor of nature, and man is more a piece of nature than of a society. Involuntarily, you perceive him also from that point of view, and judge him
only by his physis, his racial phenomena, and in terms of this natural beauty.
It does not trouble you that he is less civilized, he prompts your mind to no
social queries.[127]

A port of call, a lighthouse of civilization, a trafficking of mankind, some moments of
actuality and some moments of bustle, were noted by Sjahrir. But they were quickly
passed over:

By sunset, we left the bay.... On the sea full of life, many boats sailed; they
were glittering and slim, fast and full of zest for living [*levenslust*], they
played just as the waves did, with the dreamy blue mountains like silent
watchmen behind.... Again, there were millions of magic lights on the sea.
The mountains lost their gloom and became again friendly in their dream. I
sat in front, at the ship's stern, leaning against the flagstaff; I did not think, I
did not even feel, I forgot where I was, I forgot myself, I lost myself in this
beautiful universe.[128]

Thus, on February 20, 1935, Sjahrir with the other exiles sailed into the Digul River.

Sjahrir and Hatta, on their way to Boven Digul, were eligible for special treatment. They belonged, according to law, to a distinct category of colonial subjects
"wholly or partially academically formed," which implied that they had had some
years of Western-style university education. (Islamic education, however high, did
not qualify.) It appeared that Sjahrir and Hatta were to be the only internees of that
category in Tanah Merah.

Both men were given second-class tickets on the ship. They spent "most of their
time," as Sjahrir wrote, on the deck, with their "non-academic" friends. But the privilege was there and, certainly, very visible to the others. There was always a possibility, whether used or not, for the "academically formed" pair to retire into the
comfort of the ship's cabins, reserved otherwise for the colony's well-off and/or
white.[129] It clearly also mattered to other Tanah Merah internees. "*Doctorandus*
Mohammad Hatta and Soetan Sjahrir just arrived at Tanah Merah. They came as
second class passengers," this was how the news reached the camp.[130]

---

[126] Ibid., February 21, 1935.

[127] Ibid.

[128] Ibid.

[129] Ibid., January 23, 1935 written "*in de salon van de tweede klasse.*"

[130] Salim, *Limabelas tahun Digul*, p. 305.

Hatta's and Sjahrir's welcome to the camp was also a privileged one. Their ship was to dock at night, and, out of fear of demonstrations perhaps, the authorities took other precautions to keep their arrival secret. There were no demonstrations. But neither was the arrival kept secret. A special "reception committee," organized by the internees, welcomed the two VIPs at the ship, and, still on the same night, a "banquet" was held in their honor.[131]

Already at the banquet, the issue of *naturalisten*, those "paid in kind," and *werkwilligers*, those "willing to work" was debated, and it was quickly resolved. Both Hatta and Sjahrir decided to join the ranks of those "paid in kind"; they would not voluntarily work on the camp's official projects.[132] This, of course, was in accordance with the well established nationalist principle of non-cooperation. But, the reasoning in this case, as everything in the camp, does not appear to have exactly followed the ways of the outside world. According to Chalid Salim, who was a member of the "reception committee" and present at the banquet,

> Hatta and Sjahrir have thought, in my view correctly, that they, as academicians, were not ready, as *werkwilligers*, to hoe the fields.[133]

Hatta himself remembered later what he had thought about the problem in the camp:

> If I wanted to join the *werkwillig* group, I would have been *werkwillig* in Jakarta where several Government jobs were offered to me.... There, I could certainly have become a *tuan besar* [a big man], there would have been no need to go to Digul to become a coolie on wages of 40 cents per day.[134]

Sjahrir wrote to Maria from the camp on the same issue:

> For us the choice truly was not difficult at all. Forty cents a day for a coolie job through the best part of the day appealed to us very little. After laboring from seven in the morning till noon, the coolest hours, nobody is fit to put his brain to any work.[135]

In the perverted normalcy of Boven Digul, Hatta and Sjahrir remained members of an elite. While other internees ordinarily were expected to construct their own houses, Hatta and Sjahrir found houses prepared for them upon their arrival. Hatta's place was big enough that, for the first few weeks, he could easily take in three of the other Pendidikan newcomers who had nowhere to stay.[136] There was a "kitchen" in

---

[131] Ibid., pp. 145, 306, 346; Hatta, *Memoir*, pp. 346, 350–51.

[132] Others in the Pendidikan group also chose to become "*naturalisten*." Only Murwoto later changed his mind. In "Boven Digoel Kwartaalverslag," 1st quarter 1935, pp. 1–2, there is a report on the Hatta-Sjahrir group arriving at the camp on February 22 and "all of them entering the category of *naturalisten*." Murwoto began to work "voluntarily" for family reasons, which, it seems, the others accepted. (Hatta, *Indonesian Patriot*, p. 184; Murwoto, *Autobiografi*; interview with Murwoto, Jakarta, December 6, 1987.) On Murwoto among the *werkwilligers* see, e.g., "Boven Digoel Kwartaalverslag," 2nd quarter 1935, p. 5.

[133] Salim, *Limabelas tahun Digul*, p. 307.

[134] Hatta, *Memoir*, p. 358 quoted and commented upon in Rose, *Indonesia Free*, pp. 78–79.

[135] *IO*, March 7, 1935.

[136] Murwoto, *Autobiografi*, p. 25

the house, Hatta remembered later, "a spacious room for a library" (Hatta had brought sixteen trunks of books with him), and "also a reception room."[137]

It seems that this house had initially been prepared for both of the "academicians," but that Sjahrir decided to live in his own way and separately from Hatta.[138] Sjahrir moved into an already occupied house with three younger exiles and, after a few weeks, he found a vacant house, which he gradually made his own.

This was "a nice little house," as he described it to Maria, after about five months in the camp: "a box made of zinc," and "when the sun begins to shine truly fiercely, one can not stand it inside." It was a place, he wrote in the same letter, "most charmingly situated high above the river," with a panoramic view of the jungle on the other side, and with "the green little garden plots" built by the exiles on a steep riverbank below the house. "Each morning," Sjahrir wrote, "I think it more beautiful to watch the river, the trees, and the plots."[139] Each morning, he might have added, until a truly bad rain came, which happened regularly, and the swollen river washed away the plots and the terraces, leaving just the zinc hut standing on top of the disaster.[140]

Neither Sjahrir or Hatta complained much about their material subsistence. Hatta was clearly the better off of the two, but this seems to have been partially by Sjahrir's own decision. The authorities, for instance, permitted both intellectuals to write articles for Indonesian or Dutch journals of their own choice and, thus, to earn more money. Hatta made ample use of the opportunity. Sjahrir never did.[141]

Hatta was well enough off to have constantly at least one *Kaja-Kaja*, "children-of-the-forest," helper.[142] Sjahrir, as far as we know, took care of his household himself. Both Sjahrir and Hatta received some money from the outside. Three women—his half-sister Radena from Batavia, his sister Sjahrizal Djoehana from Semarang, and Maria from Holland—sent Sjahrir some money. But—as both Sjahrizal and Maria, and also one of Radena's sons admitted—the mails were very irregular, and there

---

[137] Hatta, *Indonesian Patriot*, p. 183.

[138] This is based on several interviews; Sjahrir says in one of his letters that the house was given to Hatta. *IO*, March 7, 1934.

[139] Ibid. July 24, 1935. Usually the houses at Tanah Merah were built as a communal effort of the inmates, with the camp authorities providing "sheets of galvanized iron while the exiles were expected to cut their own timber from the surrounding forest." Rose, *Indonesia Free*, p. 80.

[140] In February and March 1935, there were "ongewoon hoge waterstanden," "unusually high water levels," reported on the Digul River at the camp; "Boven Digoel Kwartaalverslag," 1st quarter 1935, p. 3. Then and just before Sjahrir wrote the quoted letter, the river was calmer reaching 15 feet at Tanah Merah in April, 11.25 in May, and 13.75 in June. "Boven Digoel Kwartaalverslag," 2nd quarter 1935, pp. 9–10.

[141] *IO*, May 30, 1935; Hatta wrote for *Pemandangan* for fifty guilders a month, according to Burhanuddin, "Sjahrir yang saya kenal," p. 316; Hatta says he was getting five guilders for a column. Hatta, *Indonesian Patriot*, p. 182.

[142] They got on track. Indeed, they were becoming civilized, as Hatta, for instance, suggests in his delightfully humorless way. What they charged him for moving his sixteen trunks of books from the "*Albatros*" ship to the camp on his arrival, and what they charged him for moving the same number of trunks when, a year later, he was leaving the camp, differed distinctly, he says, and with a very perceptible upward turn. Hatta, *Memoir*, p. 352; Hatta, *Indonesian Patriot*, pp. 183, 188.

was never very much to be sent: altogether, a very small sum, indeed, reached Sjahrir in the camp.[143]

The free food rations which Hatta and Sjahrir got as *naturalisten*—those "paid in kind"—seemed sufficient. According to Hatta, they had enough food except for the salted fish and the peas, which were, in the camp, the only source of certain vitamins. Throughout his stay in the camp, Hatta also remembered, he had had enough rice to give some away to whoever came and asked for it.[144]

Sjahrir resisted malaria longer than other internees did. After ten months, however, he also fell ill, and then he suffered more than the average, because he appeared to be allergic to quinine.[145] Sjahrir liked to appear tough. With worried affection, he once referred to the other Pendidikan friends exiled with him as *slappe stadskinderen*, "soft town-children."[146] The same term, however, might not be wholly inappropriate for both him and Hatta as well. The two "academically trained" men were physically unprepared for the camp sort of life. As far as the camp climate and environment were concerned, indeed, the advantage was clearly on the side of these more simple internees, the less privileged, the third-class passengers, more seasoned to what actual life in a colony might be.

Being better educated and having attended colonial schools longer, Sjahrir and Hatta had built bonds which were subtler, but not less restrictive. When these two men observed the world around them, they inevitably thought in scales and looked in directions different from those of "ordinary" internees. When some further privilege was offered to them, one day in the camp, Hatta, as he later remembered, reacted:

> If you want to give me extra, why don't you give me the same allowance as the other educated internees are receiving in other places, like *Dr.* Cipto and *Mr.* Kusuma Sumantri in Banda Neira or *Ir.* Sukarno in Endeh??[147]

Hatta and Sjahrir were made an elite in a perverted way. The more they were dealt with as the elite in the camp, the more exiled they felt.

While still on the ship, one of the men in the Pendidikan group, troubled about the future, asked Hatta for advice and a comforting word. Hatta, the man recalled, had told him:

---

[143] Interview with Sjahrizal and Hazil Tanzil in Bandung and Jakarta, March 7, 1982 and October 26, 1987; and with Maria Duchâteau-Sjahrir in Lorques, February 13, 1988. Sjahrir's half sister in Batavia was not in very good shape to help an exile; one son, Djohan Sjahroezah, was until late in 1935 in prison, too, and there was very little money in the house. Sjahrir's sister, Sjahrizal, and her husband supported Sjahrir through his studies, but they became rather unresponsive when he embarked on the "Bohemian and rebel" path. Maria Duchâteau-Sjahrir, with two children herself, was working as a secretary for low wages.

[144] Hatta, *Indonesian Patriot*, pp. 183, 185.

[145] *IO*, May 30, July 24 and October 19, 1935; Bondan, "Mengenal Bung Hatta," p. 283; interview with Murwoto, Jakarta, December 6, 1987.

[146] *IO*, December 24, 1936.

[147] Hatta, *Indonesian Patriot*, p. 186. Hatta used Dutch designation for academic titles: "Dr." for Tjipto, who was a medical doctor, "Mr." (Meester) for Iwa, who was a lawyer, and "Ir." for Sukarno who had a college degree in civil engineering.

> When the wider world is narrowed by others, you have to build a universe in your own bosom.

Slightly confused, so the exile said, he went to the other intellectual available on the ship, to Sjahrir, and has asked him what Hatta might have really meant by this. He remembered Sjahrir explaining:

> Do not feel remorse, and do not lose hope. By remorse you will punish yourself, and if you lose hope, you will only burden your soul.[148]

Sjahrir spent his first few weeks in the camp with a group of other exiles, planning and building a house for a Pendidikan friend expecting the arrival of his wife with a baby.[149] Besides, very soon, and as earlier in Medan and Bandung, Sjahrir became a star soccer player, the center forward this time, of the *Soetji Hati*, "Pure Heart," club of the Kunst en Sport Vereeniging Digoel, "Digul Arts and Sports Association."[150] Sjahrir also swam laps, regularly, first in the Digul River, and then, after he heard of some fatal accidents with crocodiles, in the smaller and hopefully safer Bening River nearby.[151]

After he settled down a little, he made an expedition to the *Kaja-Kaja* lands upstream. He paddled alone in his small canoe, so he wrote to Maria. He met the savages, saw their huts, and exchanged tobacco for "a fair amount of sago." He was old-hand enough not to barter his ax for a piglet. The trip, one feels, was embarked upon as much to improve a monotonous diet as for the pure pleasure of the almost Defoe adventure.[152]

Hatta organized his time in Tanah Merah with the punctuality worthy of a scholar—"7 am: heat the stove; 8 am: [for instance] Sombart; 10 am: collect the fire wood."[153] Hatta's regimen was sometimes a subject of jokes among other internees. But, mocking aside, it was impressive—amidst the debilitating flabbiness of the camp culture a display of the willpower to observe the norms. One may call this life in an "ivory tower" or one may call it, in Hatta's own words, building a "new universe in one's bosom."

In contrast to Hatta's, Sjahrir's time ran erratically to say at least. He kept moving so much that he earned a nickname, *kelana djenaka*, "comic rumbler." It was recalled that he visited people at all possible and impossible hours of the day or night. He would borrow some sugar or coconut oil, or a banana, or he might come just to chat. He appeared "cheerful and joking," ready at any time for a game of chess or checkers, or for a word game. He might give a helping hand in the kitchen. He was

---

[148] Burhanuddin, "Sjahrir yang saya kenal," p. 61; interview with Burhanuddin, Jakarta, March 5, 1982.

[149] Murwoto, *Autobiografi*, p. 25.

[150] The Pendidikan crowd appears to have been quite an addition to Tanah Merah's soccer history: Hatta and Burhanoeddin played backs and Murwoto was in goal. Ibid., p. 26; Bondan, "Mengenal Bung Hatta," p. 282.

[151] Salim, *Limabelas tahun Digul*, p. 311; Murwoto (*Autobiografi*, p. 26) writes that there were no organized sports except soccer at the time they reached the camp.

[152] *IO*, October 7, 1935.

[153] Hatta, *Memoir*, pp. 357, 371; Salim, *Limabelas tahun Digul*, p. 307; Bondan, "Mengenal Bung Hatta," p. 264; interview with Burhanuddin, Jakarta, March 5, 1982.

also remembered as leaving as suddenly as he came, never sticking in any one of the many place he was passing through.[154]

When asked, Sjahrir explained to others in the camp, that physical exercise, the swimming, the soccer, the wandering around, was a way for him "to keep his spirit healthy."[155] To Maria, he wrote:

> Now, still less than in prison, can I submit to distress. I have to use all my energy to stand up against the climate, nature, the diseases, and, first of all against the demoralizing influence of the life in this community of exiles, with all its petty mindedness, mutual suspicion, and psychic deviations.[156]

Despite the fact that Sjahrir, as we noted, was allowed to send articles to the press, as he wrote to Maria, from Tanah Merah, on May 30:

> I am firmly resolved, the first years, to publish nothing. In no case shall I write political articles, not only because of the danger that they may not pass through censorship—a danger, naturally, great in the case of political publications—but because I took upon myself, for a couple of years, precisely in that field, to keep silent.[157]

Indeed, Sjahrir did not publish a single article while he was in Tanah Merah. But every week, he did write one very long letter to Maria. Each month he packed four or five of the letters in a big envelope, to be ready when the *Albatros* police ship arrived to pick up the mail.[158]

One story by Hatta suggests how significant a role these letters to Holland already played in Sjahrir's life. After a few months in the camp, Hatta remembered, Sjahrir decided to sign a "declaration of political non-activity." He did this, in spite of Hatta's strong advice against it and in spite of the fact that Hatta himself shortly before had categorically refused to sign a similar statement. Sjahrir according to Hatta, was "accused ... by the other *naturalisten* [the non-cooperating internees in the camp] of surrendering to the government." This, however, says Hatta, lasted "only a couple of weeks," until it became generally known why Sjahrir had done it— to get a raise in his "pocket-money" allowance from the government from 2.60 guilders to 7.50 guilders a month "to make up for the costs of correspondence with his wife in Holland."[159]

---

[154] Salim, *Limabelas tahun Digul*, p. 311; interviews with Burhanuddin and Murwoto, Jakarta, March 5, 1982 and December 6, 1987.

[155] Salim, *Limabelas tahun Digul*, p. 311.

[156] *IO*, March 15, 1935.

[157] Ibid., May 30, 1935.

[158] Interview with Maria Duchâteau-Sjahrir, Lorques, February 13, 1988; Hatta, *Memoir*, p. 360; besides these letters, Sjahrir, it seems, corresponded very little. There were only one or two letters to his close political associate and friend in Holland, Sal Tas; there were none to others like J. de Kadt or G. J. Riekerk. Some letters were reportedly written to Djohan Sjahroezah in Batavia and to Sjahrir's younger brother in Medan, Soetan Mahroezar; all were evidently lost. Interviews with Judith Tas, Jos Meier (the secretary of J. de Kadt), G. J. Riekerk, Hazil Tanzil, Violeta Sjahroezah, and Sjahrizal Djoehana, in The Hague, Utrecht, Jakarta, and Bandung, between March 1983 and October 1987.

[159] Sjahrir declared that he did not intend "to overthrow the existing social order by violent means." On the incident see Hatta, *Memoir*, pp. 360–61, and Hatta, *Indonesian Patriot*, pp. 186–

Those who knew him at the camp often described Sjahrir as "boyish," even "child-like." Curiously, this characterization virtually never bore the depreciating connotation one might logically expect.[160] The "childishness," paradoxically, seemed to approximate Sjahrir's being truly himself, truly a man. Never, since the time he left Medan, and never, possibly, since his mother Rabiah died when he was twelve, had Sjahrir talked so intensively to a woman. Sjahrir is also remembered singing in the camp. One of the songs recalled, as it was sung very often by Sjahrir and as it was so very strange to that place, was one, which he could hardly have learned from anyone but his mother, and she, perhaps, from some stray German missionary in her native Natal:

> Das gibt's nur einmal, das kommt nie wieder,
> das ist zu schön um wahr zu sein.
> [It happens once, it never comes back,
> it is too nice for it to be true.][161]

"I do not feel well amidst my people," Sjahrir wrote to Maria after living four months in the camp, "and for the time being, through a great part of a day, I travel [ik trek] back to my books." Sjahrir, the "comic rumbler," was reading John Stuart Mill, at the time, and he wrote:

> I am prepared to consider this not to be ordinary literature, [it is so good that it] may still be used even as a textbook.[162]

As before, and stronger than before perhaps, if there was a single deeply felt, and solid connection between Sjahrir and the others—between Sjahrir and "the people"—it was a roundabout way, through teaching. Hatta organized a sort of a night school in his house, and he lectured regularly, mostly on economics. Sjahrir—again in a much less regular way— taught English, sociology, history, and law. Best remembered, however, and most truly a "school," were Sjahrir's reading aloud to smaller select groups of internees from the letters to be sent to Maria in the next mail.[163]

In a letter of March 7, 1935, Sjahrir described Tanah Merah for Maria:

> Tanah Merah, to all appearances, is like another village [desa], little different from a normal village [behoorlijke desa] on Java or Sumatra. The government

---

87. Also on the declaration see *IO*, May 30, 1935; Sjahrir writes that "we" meaning himself and Hatta, "made an explicit declaration."

[160] This emerges from the interviews I had with Burhanuddin and Murwoto, as well as from various places in Hatta's memoirs and much later in Hatta's speech at Sjahrir's funeral. Hatta quoted in Salim, ed., *Bung Sjahrir*, p. 63.

[161] Salim, *Limabelas tahun Digul*, p. 311.

[162] *IO*, May 11, 1935.

[163] Burhanuddin, "Sjahrir yang saya kenal," p. 63; interview with Burhanuddin and Murwoto, Jakarta March 5, 1983 and December 6, 1987. Neither Hatta nor Sjahrir are in Haga's list of Tanah Merah's *naturalisten* teachers as of May 1935; perhaps because they were mostly teaching adults. There were some children remembered as pupils or students of Sjahrir (the later Communist leader, Lukman, for instance). Haga Digoel Verslag II; interview with Burhanuddin, Jakarta, March 5, 1982.

site, here, may well pass for the European quarter in one or another Javanese town.[164]

Not unlike the "neo-ethical" colonial official quoted in the epigraph to this chapter, to Sjahrir the camp seemed to be in a way like another village and, thus, a sort of a little Indies, the colony in essence—an experiment. In an April letter, Sjahrir wrote:

> I have, here, at Digul, an opportunity to dig deeper into the psycho-physical construction of our people. All layers of our people are represented here, and I have observed that, here, their souls protrude more naked than if they had stayed at home....[165]

In one of his truly gloomy letters from Tanah Merah, he wrote to Maria:

> At the first moment, as I saw the men here mostly as mental ruins, I thought: "I can never let it go so far. When I truly have no hope in the future, and feel that I am about to be spiritually starved, then I will put an end to it."[166]

Sjahrir did find words for the internees as harsh as *ballast*, in English generally a term for any heavy material carried by a ship to provide a proper draft and stability, but in Dutch a word used often to denote something without any value, "padding" or "rubbish." In one place Sjahrir wondered, "why so few of [the internees] had ever thought of that solution." By "that solution," Sjahrir meant suicide.[167]

Sjahrir saw the internees (the little-Indies population? the essence of the colony's people?) as having a "primitive nature," "primitive or half-civilized psychology." This was, he wrote, what (to him) had been "hidden behind," and what now appeared "naked," after the mask fell off:

> learned, "newly-fashioned" habits and would-be "modern," shiny words and phrases of propaganda, mostly misunderstood, but still so handy, and so skillfully made that one may often be misled by them.[168]

Tanah Merah, Hatta wrote in *Daulat Ra'jat* early in 1934, before he knew he himself would go there, might become

> "a Mecca" of the Indonesian progressive movement, a training ground for internees to become leaders of a new type, a boiling pot, where parochial and undeveloped regionalisms might become a modern Indonesian nationalism.[169]

Now, in the camp, both Hatta and Sjahrir found themselves trying to span an abyss.

---

[164] *IO*, March 7, 1935. According to Hatta, "Tanah Merah (was a) pseudo village administered like an ordinary Javanese desa, except that its headmen were detainees rather than local residents." Hatta paraphrased by his biographer, Rose, in *Indonesia Free*, p. 78.

[165] *IO*, April 6, 1935.

[166] Ibid., November 24, 1935.

[167] Ibid. On the use of the word "ballast" see ibid., April 6, 1935.

[168] Ibid.; see also ibid., May 11, 1935.

[169] See, for instance, Hatta's "Diatas segala lapangan Tanah Air akoe hidoep akoe gembira" in *Daulat Ra'jat* 4, 85 (January 20, 1934).

"I do not understand them yet," Sjahrir wrote to Maria about his fellow internees and after spending six months in the camp. Sjahrir tried to find out "what is hidden behind their words and actions." But, as a rule, he paused:

> Perhaps, it is wrong for me to look for things in their lives, which, who knows, may never have existed.[170]

> Did I become a stranger amidst my people? Why am I dejected by the things which make their lives full and which they warmly appreciate; why do I perceive as largely meaningless and ugly what to them is beautiful, pure, and by which they are touched?[171]

Nothing explicitly Minangkabau can be found in Sjahrir's letters from Boven Digul. The very word "Minangkabau" was used by Sjahrir, in the letters, only once or twice. This in spite of the fact—as we know from many hints—that Sjahrir in fact moved in the camp largely among the Minangkabau, or, more broadly, Sumatran, or, broader still, non-Javanese community.

There were the Minangkabau like Hatta and Burhanuddin of the Pendidikan who were political comrades and naturally in daily contact with Sjahrir. Chalid Salim was his cousin, the younger brother of Hadji Agoes Salim; they already knew each other from Medan, and appear to have been very close throughout their time in the camp.[172] Hamid Loebis, to whose house Sjahrir moved when he came to Tanah Merah, was a Minangkabau from Medan and a boyhood-friend of Sjahrir from the time of elementary school. Besides, as we read various recollections from the camp, a Batak, a Menadonese, a Minangkabau, again, were mentioned in the group around Sjahrir; almost never a Javanese.[173]

In matters of religion, namely Islam—in contrast to Hatta,[174] and in contrast to what might be expected of a true Minangkabau—Sjahrir behaved with detachment. In the camp, he was known as *arif*, "sophisticated, pragmatic, scientific." In his letters to Maria, he occasionally criticized Islam. But on a second reading we can see how much he took care to qualify the kind of Islam he then had in mind. He was against the Islam, he wrote, as it was taught by "self-proclaimed quacks [*kwakzalvers*]." He was against the Islam of "hazy and coarse religious notions." He was against "primitive" Islam.[175]

Might there have been, thus, another Islam for Sjahrir? "I am asking myself," Sjahrir wrote in another letter from the camp,

---

[170] *IO*, May 11, 1935.

[171] Ibid., June 20, 1935.

[172] Salim, *Limabelas tahun Digul*, p. 306.

[173] *IO*, April 21 and July 24, 1935; interview with Burhanuddin, Jakarta, March 5, 1982. According to Burhanuddin, Hamid Loebis was a friend of Sjahrir from Medan, and Sjahrir moved in with him first, instead of living with Hatta. After his release from Boven Digul, Hamid Loebis lived in Padang.

[174] Hatta, in contrast, was known as a *'ta'at'* devout Moslem. Salim, *Limabelas tahun Digul*, p. 309; interviews with Burhanuddin and Murwoto, Jakarta March 5, 1982 and December 6, 1987. See, for instance, *kebetulan letak tempat tidurku sesuatu dengan kiblat* "in fact place my bed in accordance with the law of Islam" (Hatta, *Memoir*, p. 357).

[175] *IO* September 10 and June 20, 1935.

whether Islam, with regard to Hinduism, does not play the same role in history that Protestantism did against Catholicism in Europe, viz., articulating a bourgeois view of life against a feudal one. As far as I know, research was never directed that way, and, yet, it is important. For that kind of study, one would, perhaps, have to take the whole Asiatic society into account: a sociology of Islam and of Hinduism in Asia.[176]

When Sjahrir mentioned Hinduism, the contrast with Islam became very clear, and so did—in a roundabout way—Sjahrir's view of Islam. There was no qualification, in Sjahrir's letters, no hesitation, and no question about Hinduism having no progressive role at all:

> The Eastern philosophy of death is not expressed by Buddhism only. The not-be, as the highest ideal, is a sort of general concept of life in this passive East.... The Easterner does not work in trade, he does not fight. Just think of the non-violence and *satyagraha* of Gandhi, who attempted to change that passivity into a means of struggle.[177]

> Here [in the "the passive East"], for centuries, there has been no spiritual life, no cultural life, no progress. What are these famous monuments of Eastern art—nothing but remnants of a feudal culture, in which we, men of the twentieth century, can find no basis for ourselves. What could *wajang* [shadow-puppet theater], with its simple symbolics and mysticism, like the European allegories and wisdom of the Middle Ages, still offer to us, to intellectuals, or to cultural men? Practically nothing.... Culturally we stand closer to Europe and America, than to Boroboedoer or Mahabharata....[178]

How much was Sjahrir aware, when he wrote the letters from the camp, of the similarity between his and Dutch "ethical" vocabularies? "The passive East," "the feudal East," "the mystical East," the East, which "does not work in trade" and "does not fight" were, no doubt, "ethical" *clichés*. At the same time, they were *clichés* of the similar Dutch "ethical" image of contrast—as described in the first chapter of this book—between "Java" and "non-Java" in the Indies. The "non-Java," non-"Eastern," non-"passive," of course, meant, especially Sumatran, and namely Minangkabau.

Sjahrir was truly disgusted by the internees who took part in the feasts sponsored by the camp authorities—on the Dutch Queen's birthday, for instance—wearing Orange royal colors, and singing the Dutch anthem.[179] Sjahrir with deepest conviction rejected cooperation between the Indonesians and the Dutch as he witnessed it in the camp. But he put the "cooperation" he talked about in quotation marks! This was, he wrote, "'cooperation' with morally crippled men," a bond between "morally defective creatures" on one side and "half insane creatures" on the other side.[180] The question arises: what might "healthy" and "normal" in this context have been for Sjahrir?

---

[176] Ibid., February 14, 1935.

[177] Ibid., November 24, 1935.

[178] Ibid., June 20, 1935.

[179] Ibid., October 31, 1936; also ibid., February 9, 1937.

[180] Ibid., October 31, 1936.

Leaving Boven Digul
Sjahrir is standing third from left; Hatta standing second from right

For Sjahrir, the camp was the fruit of an unhealthy mind or a misunderstanding. "Heavens perhaps knows," he wondered, looking at some internees, "what might have made anybody send these young boys into exile."[181] He challenged the "cooperation" in the way one might lament a missed opportunity. Thus Sjahrir wrote to Maria about a dear friend he had made in the camp:

> A splendid fellow, a civilized, and a well developed man. His great humanity grew out of Christian morality; he was a Menadonese by origin, and a Christian. Besides, he was one of the first Indonesian socialists still at the time of Sneevliet and Baars [which is in 1910s and 1920s], and he then was a member of the Douwes Dekker's *Indische Partij* [Indies Party]. What happened to him is dreadful. He had been out of the movement for two years, but they arrested him anyway, in 1926, and they exiled him, just when he was about to get married. He was, at the time, a landowner in Menado; he came from a wealthy family. Also all of his married sisters are well situated, and one of them, younger than he, is now a student at the Law School in Batavia.[182]

Sjahrir might appear over-sensitive, in Tanah Merah, to the letter of colonial law. He wrote to Maria how deeply disturbed he was when told that his internment was an "administrative 'punishment'." This, he wrote, "to me is something that contradicts all in which I believe as juridical wisdom; it is a fallacy, a misconstruction."[183]

Sjahrir challenged the Dutch prison and exile system in the way a reformer might do. To him, Tanah Merah was lower on the scale of values than Cipinang—the prison where he spent the previous year. In Tanah Merah, Sjahrir wrote, the staff was overbearing to the internees and the style of the camp was based on the assumption of the staff's superiority. The director of Cipinang prison, however,

> in contrast to [Tanah Merah], can occasionally see his task as that of the headmaster of a social-educational institution; he can entertain the idea that he, in fact, has to care for socially derailed, psychically unbalanced asocials, so-called criminals. There is some conviction in him, indeed, that his task is a positive one.[184]

"From our talks," Chalid Salim wrote later, recalling his debates with Sjahrir in Tanah Merah,

> it became clear that Sjahrir was truly a Hollandophile.... The student life in Leiden left clearly a mark of Dutch-ness on him ... and Sjahrir's marriage with a Dutch woman had also broadened his world of thinking, which was tainted Dutch. During our discussions, I often thought: "Truly stupid of the Dutch to exile these two intellectuals [Sjahrir and Hatta], so European in

---

[181] Ibid., April 21, 1935.

[182] Ibid., October 31, 1936. Sjahrir called his friend Liantoe. His real name was Najoan; interview with Burhanuddin, Jakarta, March 5, 1983.

[183] *IO* March 7, 1935.

[184] Ibid., April 24, 1936.

their disposition, and to send them to so rotten a place of exile! Truly unclever and retarded these Dutchmen!"[185]

Sjahrir, writing from the camp, emphasized one quality with an increasing conviction: the capacity of man to

> rise above oneself, above one's surroundings, above one's time ... [above] the ideas and ideals of one's own time and land, which are relative and temporary.[186]

Truly great men, he wrote, were always "timeless, above time [*boventijdelijke*], and universally human." Whether Sjahrir was aware of it or not—by the way he construed the qualities of greatness—his time once again was made to float, to hover above the actual world. Or, perhaps, more than that—by Sjahrir's recalling his heroes from the "ethical" classroom and "off" the camp actuality as much as possible—Sjahrir's time was made to proceed towards the past.

A series of great figures appeared in Sjahrir's letters: Goethe, and Beethoven, and Shakespeare, and Dante and Plato; their presence, however, contributed distinctly to the sadness of actuality—"after Dante comes d'Anunzio?"[187] As when Sjahrir came to Holland and nothing seemed strange to him, this, again, seems to be remembering as a way of spiritual survival. "The greats from the past," Sjahrir wrote in Tanah Merah on July 20, 1935, "our spiritual kindred, our contemporaries."[188]

From the moment Hatta and Sjahrir were arrested, in 1934, the Dutch authorities were uncertain about how to handle the two men. Experts repeatedly professed doubts as to whether the Boven Digul internment was not "too harsh, and, besides, whether it might not provoke unnecessary criticism" of the government.[189]

The implication was that Boven Digul might not be suitable "for intellectuals."[190] Early in December 1935, in Batavia, the Director of Justice argued, in a letter to the Governor-General, that

> to be interned in Boven Digoel, means much heavier suffering for an intellectual than for an illiterate; academically trained leaders should be placed in a camp different from that to which their uneducated followers are being exiled.[191]

A plan to establish a special camp, or a secluded place, for "educated" exiles, was repeatedly considered throughout the period.

---

[185] Salim, *Limabelas tahun Digul*, p. 313.

[186] *IO* July 20, 1935.

[187] Ibid.

[188] Ibid

[189] For instance, Adviser for Native Affairs to Governor-General; Documents of the *Volksraad* and the Adviser's office of June 29 and June 24 respectively in *Secret Mail Report* 1935, no. 785 and 1936, no. 12, *bijlage*.

[190] Ibid.

[191] Chief of Justice section to Governor-General December 4, 1935 in *Secret Mail Report* 1936, no. 12, *bijlage*.

There were debates in the highest offices of the colony, in September and again in October 1935, with Hatta and Sjahrir as a special item.[192] Finally, on January 2, 1936, the Council of the Indies and the Governor-General reached a decision. Dutch authorities with jurisdiction over the Eastern part of the archipelago, to which Boven Digul also belonged, were asked to find a more suitable place of exile for the two academically formed natives.[193]

Notwithstanding several months of rumors, the decision came as a surprise to the camp. Hatta says that they were not prepared, and one boat had to leave Tanah Merah without them because packing, his books especially, took a long time.[194]

This was how the "ethical" perversity climaxed. The two men made a last round of visits through the camp. Final photographs of the Pendidikan internees together were taken at a local studio. "Not much was said during the parting," recalled Burhanuddin, who was to remain for another six years: "Sjahrir said only *Hou je taai*, 'Never say die!'"[195] Then, it was not long before Sjahrir and Hatta boarded the *Albatros*, and the white police ship herself disappeared from the internees' view, behind the first turn of the great Digul River.

---

[192] "Interneering van Mohammad Hatta en Soetan Sjahrir elders dan te Boven Digoel," Attorney General document in *Secret Mail Report* 1936, no. 12, *bijlage*.

[193] Documents of the Council of the Indies in *Secret Mail Report* 1936, no. 12.

[194] Hatta, *Indonesian Patriot*, p. 187; Hatta says the first date might have been November, but that hardly could have been so because the decision was not made before January 2.

[195] Burhanuddin, "Sjahrir yang saya kenal," pp. 63–64.

6

EXILE IN BANDA NEIRA, 1936-1941

> One can see nothing at all around, all roads seem blocked, and a feeling of loneliness descends. We are like a man who dreams unlovely dreams.
>
> *Kedaulatan Ra'jat* editorial,
> January 12, 1938[1]

1. POLITICS WITHOUT SJAHRIR

Sometimes, looking at the political scene in the Indies after 1934, one has a feeling that the whole country went into exile. Soewarsih Djojopoespito, Sjahrir's friend from Bandung times, wrote about a "spiritual depression."[2] Tjarda van Starkenborgh, who in 1936 succeeded de Jonge as the Governor-General, and Ch. J. I. M. Welter, who a year later became the new minister of colonies after "Father" Colijn, did not relieve the oppressiveness of the regime. If anything, they were more dreary than their predecessors. Marcel Koch, an old hand in the Indies, a compassionate Dutchman who for years watched all this from Bandung, believed that the regime had finally become "a police state."[3]

Leaders whose names, before 1934, had been identified with the radical nationalist movement quit the scene. Students, who had done so much for the enthusiasm of the past years, as one of them wrote,

> began to disappear one by one, from Djakarta, the centre of national politics and became members of the hardworking masses.[4]

The former party of Sukarno, Partindo, "yielded to *force majeure*" in December 1934 and abandoned its policy of non-cooperation.[5] Two years later, Partindo dissolved itself. Another radical party of the early 1930s, Permi, the mostly Minangkabau "Union of Indonesian Muslims," after also seriously considering self-dissolution, decided in July 1936 to restrict itself to "fields of economic, social, and cultural work."[6]

---

[1] *Kedaulata Ra'jat*, 12 (January 1938).
[2] Soewarsih Djojopoespito in *Kritiek en Opbouw*, March 1, 1939, p. 38.
[3] M. K. (Marcel Koch) in *Kritiek en Opbouw*, March 29, 1941, p. 53.
[4] Hanifah, *Tales of a Revolution*, p. 85.
[5] Dahm, *Sukarno and the Struggle for Indonesian Independence*, p. 173.
[6] *Masjarakat* 1, 9 (June 15, 1936) and ibid., 1, 14 (July 30, 1936).

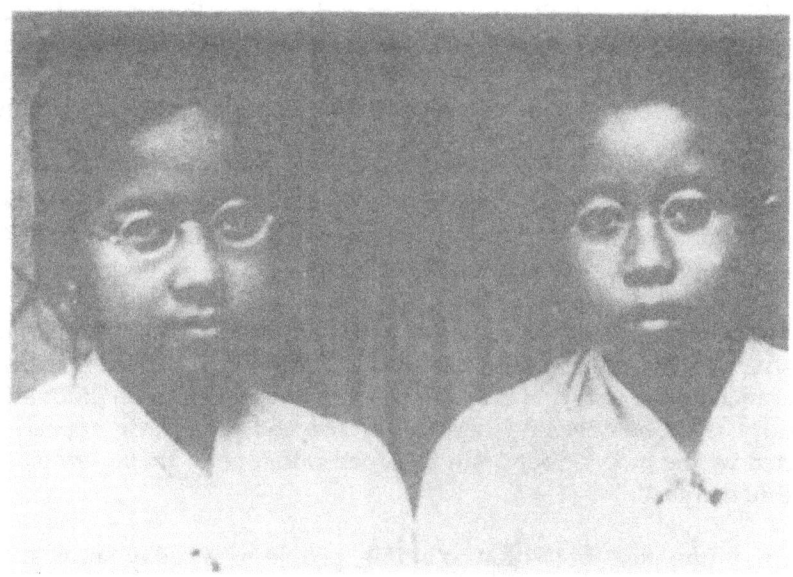

Soewarni Pringgodigdo (L) and Soewarsih Djojopoespito
(from C. H. Snoek, *De Indische Jaren van E. du Perron*)

Parindra, "Party of Great Indonesia"—the conservative political association which, in the early 1930s, grew out of the Javanese semi-aristocratic Boedi Oetomo—dominated the political scene. The most daring of its actions was, in 1936, the "Soetardjo Petition" pleading for an imperial conference to discuss the possibility—in the undetermined future—for self-government in the Indies. The highly polite request was rejected outright by the Dutch.

The threat of fascism and war grew steadily through the period. Gerakan Rakjat Indonesia, or Gerindo, the "Movement of the Indonesian People," was established in 1937, largely as a successor to Partindo. Gerindo offered to cooperate with the colonial government against fascism, if the government was willing to make some concessions. As in the case of the Soetardjo petition, without much hesitation, the government rejected the offer.

Perhimpoenan Indonesia, the "Indonesian Association" in Holland—the organization in which Hatta and Sjahrir were active in the early 1930s—had, by 1937, also distanced itself from the policy of radical non-cooperation and had restricted its aims to those of cultural and social emancipation.[7] In 1937, even the Communist Party of Holland abandoned its radical slogan, "Indonesia free of Holland now!"—a state-

---

[7] In 1939, Perhimpeonan Indonesia even asked the Dutch government to remove the names of its members from the list of those who were not to be employed as government officials: the loyalty of the Perhimpoenan Indonesia now, it was argued, should not be doubted. *Secret Verbaal*, 1940-Y31; also *Secret Mail Report* 1937, no. 388 quoted in Kwantes, ed, *De Ontwikkeling van de Nationalistische Beweging* 4: 430–32.

ment of principle which had made for so much of the excitement and dynamics of the late 1920s and early 1930s.[8]

The connection between nationalism, politics, and culture changed too. In the mid-1930s, a group of Indonesian writers and artists gathered around a new journal, *Poedjangga Baroe*, "New Writer." The "New Writer" declared itself to be the "leader of the new dynamic spirit to create a new culture of Indonesian unity." According to a historian, however, the movement observed rather a "studied neutrality on political affairs," and

> restricted [its] patriotic expression to the lyrical celebration of the beauty of [the Indonesian] islands and to essays which attempted to formulate a culture for the Indonesian nation of the future.[9]

Much of the radicalism of the past had been transformed into nostalgia. Sukarno's moral lapse in 1933 was all but forgotten. Gerindo, in particular, lived very much on the sound of Sukarno's name,[10] and even those Indonesians who, in the early 1930s, had been definitely pro-Hatta and pro-Sjahrir, appeared now to be affected by the mood. Soewarsih Djojopoespito, one of them, wrote, in her novel published in 1940:

> Oh, in the past, in [Su]Karno's time, people who today sneer at us were happy to be called our friends. Today, they feel happy that [Su]Karno can not command them, because it would be bad for their careers. Today they sneer at us.[11]

According to the introduction to the first edition of Soewarsih's novel,

> The "great time of [Su]Karno" is remembered among those [radically Indonesian] circles as a hurricane of enthusiasm, which passed over and away. [Su]Karno himself became almost a legendary figure.[12]

There was a price to be paid for the timidity and the nostalgia. The cooperative blues of the late 1930s were almost the exact opposite of the "ethical" ideal of an increasing togetherness between the two cultures. The Dutch gave Indonesians little for their new willingness to cooperate. Humiliation almost as a rule accompanied an individual Indonesian's successful career in the framework of colonial order. Impotent bitterness accompanied the humiliation. As, indeed, an Indonesian noted towards the end of this period,

---

[8] Susan Abeyasekere, "The Soetardjo Petition," *Indonesia* 15 (1973): 102; George McTurnan Kahin, *Nationalism and Revolution in Indonesia* (Ithaca: Cornell University Press, 1952), pp. 50–51.

[9] Heather Sutherland, "Pudjangga Baru: Aspects of Indonesian Intellectual Life in the 1930s," *Indonesia* 6 (October 1968): 117.

[10] For instance, Attorney General's circular August 19, 1937 in *Secret Mail Report* 1937, no. 714. The Gerindo leadership was made up of Sartono, Amir Sjarifoeddin, Jamin, A. K. Gani, Sanusi Pane, and Wikana. Ibid.

[11] Djojopoespito, *Buiten het Gareel Indonesische roman. Met een inleiding van E. du Perron* (Utrecht: de Haan, 1940), p. 14.

[12] Ibid., p. 8. The introduction is by Eddy du Perron.

The Indonesian national movement is subjective and chauvinistic. In the great struggle which is coming there would be no place for liberalism and tolerance.[13]

There was a visible weakening in the expectations that the archipelago might any time soon become a modern political entity or a unified national state. According to Colijn's successor, the new minister of the colonies, Ch. J. I. M. Welter,

> political reforms must henceforth proceed at a local level, [they must reach] to the masses, and not to the movement of Western-educated, alienated nationalists.[14]

Regional conversion of all-Indonesian groups and movements, as well as cultural fragmentation of Indonesian principles, were complementary to this. Only lonely voices, indeed—like the young lawyer Amir Sjarifoeddin—warned against regional cultures being emphasized again, as in the time of "Father Colijn," at the expense of things Indonesian and modern.[15]

Hatta's and Sjahrir's Pendidikan Nasional Indonesia survived throughout the 1930s. It was never declared illegal by the colonial government.[16] It was, however, subjected to close supervision and to almost incessant harassment. Five successive central boards were exiled to Boven Digul, after 1935.[17] *Daulat Ra'jat*, the Pendidikan's theoretical journal, disappeared with its last issue on September 10, 1934.[18] *Kedaulatan Ra'jat*, the Pendidikan's official press organ, lasted till March 1938; but it was being published clearly with the greatest difficulties; there were gaps of months, and once even a year, between the individual issues.

The number of Pendidikan branches also steadily declined. From thirty-one branches in 1933, the number dropped to twenty-eight in August 1934, and to twenty in December 1937.[19] Members were leaving. According to *Kedaulatan Ra'jat*, in 1937, there were no more than a few dozen activists left.[20]

---

[13] Soeroto in *Kritiek en Opbouw*, April 1, 1939, p. 62. The Dutch repeatedly talked at this time about the distance growing between the Indonesians and the Dutch; see for instance, Meyer Ranneft in 1941 quoted in Kahin, *Nationalism and Revolution*, p. 60; Limburg Stirrum in 1938, quoted in Koch, *Batig Slot*, p. 26.

[14] Welter in March 1938, quoted in Abeyasekere, "The Soetardjo Petition," p. 102.

[15] A.Sj. (Amir Sjarifoeddin) in *Kritiek en Opbouw*, November 22, 1941, p. 327.

[16] See documents of the office of the Adviser for Native Affairs, May 20, 1939 in *Secret Mail Report* 1939, no. 1006.

[17] *Daulat Ra'jat* 4, 92 (April 10, 1934); *Kedaulatan Ra'jat* 6, 7 and 11 (August 1934, June and December 1937); *Masjarakat* 13, and 17/18 (July 15, 1936 and October 23, 1936); *Secret Mail Reports* 1936, no. 1057, 1937 nos. 428 and 2746, 1939 nos. 533 and 1006; Maskun Sumadiredja, "Mengenang Bung Hatta" in *Muhammad Hatta*, ed. Swasono, p. 403; Sastra, "Sjahrir untuk Sastra," in *Mengenang Sjahrir*, ed. Anwar, p. 88.

[18] The end of *Daulat Ra'jat* was clearly abrupt; there was no suggestion in ibid., 4, 107 (September 10, 1934), that this was to be the last issue published.

[19] *Banteng Ra'jat* 1, 32–33 (January 10, 1933); *Daulat Ra'jat* 4, 92 (April 10, 1934), *Kedaulatan Ra'jat* 6 (August 1937). For 1933, in addition, ten "candidate branches" are mentioned, and none in later years.

[20] *Kedaulatan Ra'jat* 8 (July 1937).

These two, and a few other pro-Pendidikan journals, against the grain of the time, tried to keep clear of the new general regionalist trend.[21] Ties within the Pendidikan's organization had always been loose, however, and, with the top well-educated leaders gone, the debates in the Pendidikan also became visibly tainted by "cultural-national" issues. Criticisms of "Great Javanism," "Hindu-Boeddhist cunning," "demoralizing wajang," grew heated.[22] At the same time, those Pendidikan papers published in Java and by Javanese editorial boards, presented Pendidikan principles occasionally in unprecedentedly "Javanist" terms.[23]

By early 1936, the Pendidikan central executive had moved from Bandung eastward to Surabaya, East Java, and it did not return to cosmopolitan West Java until 1942.[24] Pendidikan formally remained a unified and all-Indonesian movement. But the ties between the center and the individual branches grew strained in the extreme.[25] Reading *Kedaulatan Ra'jat* during the period demonstrates how rarely the Pendidikan executive was able to entice even an activity report or a minimal finan-

---

[21] For a few months after the arrest of Hatta, Sjahrir, and other top leaders in 1934, the Pendidikan appeared to be quite successful in keeping itself in shape. T. A. Moerad, a close friend of both Hatta and Sjahrir, a Minangkabau, and a member of the Pendidikan from the very beginning, worked effectively and, mainly through his editorship of *Daulat Ra'jat*, maintained the organization together essentially in the style of the previous period. For Moerad's view of the time immediately after the arrests see his article in *Pikiran Ra'jat* 4, 106 (July 30, 1934). Already, the short, several-week long interregnum of Haroen Moein, however (Moerad was arrested, in August), brought about a visible change for the worse. Haroen Moein, like Moerad, was a Minangkabau. But, in contrast to Moerad, he was also a man known for his aggressive, often dogmatic profession of "the only true Minangkabau" values. (Haroen Moein himself was arrested in October.)

[22] The quotes are from *Kedaulatan Ra'jat* 13 (February 1938) and 14 (March 1938); see also an article against "Indonesia Merdeka dibawah keradjaan Madjapahit " in *Kedualatan Ra'jat* 11 (December 1937).

[23] Indonesia was venerated in these papers as *Iboe Pertiwi*, the Hindu Mother-Goddess of the Earth. Pendidikan's leaders were addressed *Bapa-Bapa*, "Fathers." Pendidikan's aims were "defined" as the "Beauty of *Kedaulatan Ra'jat*." Pendidikan's weapons now were the Hindu-Javanese "charms, *pantja soena* and *tjandrabirawa*." See, for example, *Kedaulatan Ra'jat* 8 (July 1937), and ibid., 7 (June 1937).

[24] Ibid., 9 (September 1937).

[25] Especially the Sumatran branches of the Pendidikan, as we noted, consisted almost or altogether exclusively of the native sons of the area. As the loose organization was hit at its central leadership level, and as the general tendency toward regionalism in the colony grew, this became a fact of much greater importance than before. Already by late 1934, Dutch police reported that the leading Pendidikan figures in West Sumatra were spending an increasing proportion of their "political" time on an Islamic and Minangkabau-cultural-national revival. For instance, PPO Sumatra's West Coast, November 1934 in *Secret Mail Report* 1934, no. 1176. In more remote local organizations of the Pendidikan, and among less educated Pendidikan members, the "use of magic" and the tendency towards "occultism" were repeatedly, and with satisfaction, noticed by the police. PPO Sumatra's East Coast, December 1938 and ibid., 4th quarter of 1939 in *Secret Mail Reports* 1939, no. 222 and 1940, no. 230. Late in October, 1934, an open letter by the Pendidikan branches of Sumatra's West Coast accused the central executive on Java of using "dictatorial methods." In two weeks, an ultimatum followed, in which two of the Pendidikan Minangkabau branches required the center, "no later than December 1," to change the Pendidikan's statutes: the central executive's "commissars"—the main venue for supervising the regions—were either to be abolished or very much restricted in their powers; "Island Councils" were to be introduced, and given full authority to establish and dissolve branches in their respective islands. PPO Sumatra's West Coast, October 1934 in *Secret Mail Report* 1934, no. 1437.

cial contribution from individual branches.[26] In 1936, for instance, a member of the Pendidikan central executive admitted in a secret communication to a comrade:

> We are resigned to the fact that we can not move anywhere. We merely have to stay in Surabaya.[27]

Elementary school teachers, workers, small traders, watchmen, chauffeurs, and the unemployed, now appeared to be leading the Pendidikan.[28] Neither Hatta nor Sjahrir wrote any new texts for the organization. The thorough and incessant police raids uncovered no unpublished text or illegal pamphlet by either of the two exiled leaders.[29] Old texts by Hatta and Sjahrir were read and re-read in the Pendidikan courses. The same old pre-1934 questions were asked and answered in these courses, copied and transported in the strictest, most conspiratorial way and with great risk throughout the crumbling structure. Hatta's and Sjahrir's texts became treasured residues of the past.[30]

Sjahrir, who always maintained a greater distance than Hatta, appeared transformed into merely a name on classics for a restricted circle. There might be some personal contacts: a letter might be exchanged or a messenger might pass through. Almost none of this can be proved in retrospect. Most of the "contacts" existed merely as rumors or as suspicions.

---

[26] *Kedaulatan Ra'jat* 9 (August 1934), ibid., 11 (December 1937), ibid., 13 (February 1938); see also *Masjarakat* 13 (July 15, 1936) and Nota by Attorney General to Governor-General, April 14, 1938 in *Secret Mail Report* 1938, no. 533. Only a highly irregular correspondence was evidently being kept between the center and the branches. See, for instance, a detailed report on raids against the Pendidikan branch in Makassar in "Proces Verbaal Mawengkan November 1936" in *Secret Mail Report* 1937, no. 377.

[27] Letter by Loekman, June 5, 1937, in *Secret Mail Report* 1937, no. 2746. Even the professionally highly suspicious police came to believe, after the mid-1930s, that the connection between the Javanese center and the Sumatran branches was "more or less broken." *PPO* Sumatra's West Coast, March and November 1934, *Secret Mail Report* 1934, nos. 480 and 1176. See also Moerad, *Merantau*, p. 299.

[28] Police report, Surabaya to Attorney General, May 21, 1938 in *Secret Mail Report* 1938, no. 533; "Proces Verbaal Soetidjab alias Tjiptoprawirjo," June 9, 1937, in *Secret Mail Report* 1937, no. 2746. Resident of Celebes to Governor-General, June 19, 1937; "Proces Verbaal Mawengkan cs," November 1936, in *Secret Mail Report* 1937, no. 377. see also *Secret Mail Report* 1939, no. 1006; Police report, Makassar, in *Secret Mail Report* 1937, no. 377; *PPO* Sumatra's East Coast July 1937 in *Secret Mail Report* 1937, no. 1137.

[29] A single new article by Hatta appeared in *Kedaulatan Ra'jat*, in March 1938. But it was a reprint of an article he had written for a non-Pendidikan paper. *Kedaulatan Ra'jat* 14 (March 1938). On a single occasion, Sjahrir's and Hatta's names, with photographs of both men, were printed in *Kedaulatan Ra'jat*. This was in August 1934, in an article on the history of the Pendidikan. Ibid., 6 (August 1934). Thereafter, the two leaders went virtually unmentioned, until, three years later, *Kedaulatan Ra'jat* published another historical survey. This survey featured a photo of Sjahrir, and Hatta was briefly quoted. Ibid., 9 (August 1937). After this, nothing further appeared, not even in the *Kedaulatan Ra'jat*'s manifesto "Free Our Leaders!" which was published in September 1937: the leaders to be freed were neither Sjahrir nor Hatta, but the recently arrested Pendidikan executive of Loekman and Soetidjab. Ibid., 10 (September 1937).

[30] For instance, "Proces Verbaal Soetidjab alias Tjiptoprawirjo," and "Proces Verbaal Mawengkan cs"; Interview with Listyo, Jakarta, November 27, 1987. Listyo, an important activist in Sjahrir's movement after 1942, had studied in 1936 and 1937 in Surakarta, and he remembered the reverence with which *Daulat Ra'jat* and Hatta's and Sjahrir's texts were handled by the local Pendidikan members at the time.

Sjahrir's older brother, Soetan Noer Alamsjah,[31] and his younger brother, Soetan Mahroezar,[32] appeared several times in police reports on the Pendidikan after 1934. Beginning in 1937, however, the two names virtually disappeared. Some of Sjahrir's letters to Mahroezar from Banda Neira reportedly were kept in the family for some time—because of the exotic stamps I was told; both the letters and the stamps, anyway, seem now irretrievably lost.[33] According to Soetan Noer Alamsjah's daughter, there was probably never any serious correspondence between Sjahrir and his older brother during this period.[34]

Djohan Sjahroezah, Sjahrir's nephew, and before 1934 one of his closest associates in the Pendidikan, was released from prison in late 1935.[35] In 1936 (his name

---

[31] In September 1933, as the danger of government action against the Pendidikan grew, the Bandung executive invited Soetan Noer Alamsjah from Medan. Early in 1934, when Sjahrir and Hatta were arrested, Noer Alamsjah returned to Medan "with a task given to him by the central executive to propagate the executive's aims." *PPO* Sumatra's East Coast, February 1934 in *Secret Mail Report* 1934, no. 448; *PPO* Sumatra's West Coast, March and April 1934 in *Secret Mail Report* 1934, nos. 480 and 877. In February 1934, the police reported Sjahrir's brother as the chairman of the Medan branch of the Pendidikan; in April, he was mentioned as "commissar" for the whole island of Sumatra. *PPO* Sumatra's East Coast, February 1934 in *Secret Mail Report* 1934, no. 448; *PPO* Sumatra's West Coast, April 1934 no. 877. Noer Alamsjah, reportedly, was one of the men who signed the letter of October 1934, in which Sumatran branches of the Pendidikan complained about the "dictatorial methods" of the central executive in Java. *PPO* Sumatra's West Coast, March and October 1934 in *Secret Mail Report* 1934, nos. 480 and 1437. Amidst police reports of growing disagreements inside the Medan branch of Pendidikan, Soetan Noer Alamsjah, in August 1936, resigned as the chairman of the branch. In March 1937, he announced his candidacy for the Medan *gemeenteraad*, "city council," on the Parindra ticket. He won and was reported to be sitting on the council by May; in August, he became the vice-chairman of the Parindra branch in Medan. *PPO* Sumatra's East Coast April, August and December 1936, February, March, May, June, and August, 1937 in *Secret Mail Reports* 1936, nos. 125, 575, 1937 nos. 354, 436, 894, and 1093; van Suchtelen, *Memorie van Overgave*, Sumatra's East Coast (April 17, 1936), appendix III.

[32] Mahroezar was also in Bandung at the time of Sjahrir's arrest, and he returned to Medan a few weeks after Soetan Noer Alamsjah. In mid-1934, he was mentioned as teaching Dutch at a Medan school called Taman Pendidikan, "Garden of Education." In August, Mahroezar reportedly became a candidate for the Pendidikan executive in Medan, but it is not known what became of his candidacy. *PPO* Sumatra's East Coast, April and August 1934 in *Secret Mail Reports* 1934, nos. 754 and 1137. In 1936, Mahroezar was mentioned as executive editor of "a new monthly to be published under the name '*Populair*'"; according to this report, "the journal's collaborators are expected to be Drs. Mohammad Hatta and Soetan Sjahrir, who is the brother of Soetan Noer Alamsjah, both presently interned, and Soetan Sjahsam, also a brother of Soetan Noer Alamsjah, who now lives in Holland." *PPO* Sumatra's East Coast, October 1935 in *Secret Mail Report* 1935, no. 1317. No copies survive, as far as we know; a certain "Salim in Paris" was later also listed among the journal's "permanent contributors." *PPO* Sumatra's East Coast, February 1936 in *Secret Mail Report* 1936, no. 315. *Populair*, in all probability, did not survive beyond 1937; police, also, found nothing in it but "articles dealing exclusively with business and sports." *PPO* Sumatra's East Coast, February 1936 in *Secret Mail Report* 1936, no. 315. In 1937, Mahroezar left Medan and went to Natal, the birthplace of Rabiah, his and Sjahrir's mother. There, with some friends, he had founded a further unspecified "Natal Instituut," and a private Dutch-Native School at which he also taught. Mahroezar did not return to Medan till 1939. Then, he became the owner of a service garage in the city, called *Tjahja*, which, reportedly, became a gathering place for Indonesian patriots during the war and into the beginning of the Indonesian Revolution. *Medan Area Mengisi Proklamasi*, p. 752, n. 55.

[33] Interview with Sjahrizal Djoehana, Bandung, October 22, 1987.

[34] Interview with Ida, a daughter of Soetan Noer Alamsjah, Jakarta, January 4, 1988.

[35] Interview with Hazil Tanzil, Jakarta, March 8, 1982.

misspelled by the detective as "Djohan Saharoesa"), Djohan was mentioned as attending a meeting with a Pendidikan "commissar," a certain Moechtar, to discuss how "new life might be breathed into the movement through holding courses."[36] Not much more is known about the event.[37] And, also, it was the last time Djohan's name appeared in the police reports in connection with the Pendidikan.[38]

Two sisters, young women who knew Sjahrir from the time when they had played student theater together in Bandung—Soewarsih Djojopoespito and Soewarni Pringgodigdo—with their husbands, Soegondo and Abdoel Karim, with Soejitno Mangoenkoesoemo, a young law student working in Buitenzorg (Bogor), and some others made up the core of a group where Sjahrir's name echoed through the 1930s.[39] These young people met variously in Bandung and in Batavia. They debated books and politics, largely in the style of the student clubs of the mid-1920s. Only rarely were any of these men and women seen at a Pendidikan event.[40]

In spite of the colonial reaction of the time, they tried to keep themselves "balanced" and, first of all, open to what they called "the universal culture of modern mankind." They read avidly, mainly "progressive" Western authors, and they

---

[36] A police report to Attorney General, October 20, 1936 in *Secret Mail Report* 1936, no. 1057. Compare with *PPO* Batavia, January and February 1936, pp. 13–15. Djohan reportedly proposed that special bodies be established in Pendidikan branches, with the aim of education and of improving inter-branch communication. The police report referred to the new bodies alternately as *badan pendidikan*, "educational bodies," and *geheime schakel dienst*, "secret liaison." Ibid.

[37] A certain Soemarno from Malang, whom we know nothing else about, together with Hamdani and Ismoe, were mentioned by the police as parties to the Sjahroezah plan. "Ismoe," in the report, might be Ismoe Hadiwidjaja, a Pendidikan activist, who spent a few months in Cipinang prison in 1934, at the same time as Sjahrir. *Daulat Ra'jat* 4, 95 (May 10, 1934). Hamdani, of course, had been a close friend of Sjahrir since Bandung. Interviewed about the matter, Hamdani recollected that he had been in contact with Djohan Sjahroezah but nothing more than that. Hamdani was more specific in saying that he did not believe there had been any correspondence between Djohan Sjahroezah in Java and Sjahrir in Banda Neira at that time. Interview with Hamdani, Jakarta, October 30, 1987.

[38] In mid-1936, Djohan Sjahroezah became the editor of a new journal, *Ilmoe dan Masjarakat*, "Science and Society." The first issue of the journal, on September 25, 1936, featured a long article by Mohammad Hatta, "The Outlines and Limits of Economic Science"; another article by Hadji Agoes Salim, "The Dynamics of Customary Communities"; and a "Panorama." The rest of the issue was filled by a long review article by Soetan Sjahrir, "Friedrich Engels of Gustav Meyer." It was the first text published by Sjahrir since his arrest. *Ilmoe dan Masjarakat*, 1, 1 (September 25, 1936). *Ilmoe dan Masjarakat* seems to have been helped into existence by another Batavia journal, *Masjarakat*, "Society," launched early in 1936 by a former editor of *Daulat Ra'jat* and Pendidikan leader, T. A. Moerad. In September 1936, *Masjarakat* announced that *Ilmoe dan Masjarakat*, had just appeared, and it announced, at the same time, that *Masjarakat* itself was leaving the scene. *Masjarakat* 1, 17/18 (September 30, 1936) and interviews with Hazil Tanzil and Violeta Sjahroezah, Jakarta, October 26, 1987. Three years later, another journal, *Negara*, "State," appeared to take over from *Ilmoe dan Masjarakat*. Again, Djohan Sjahroezah was in charge. (Interestingly enough, Adam Malik in his memoirs, thirty years later, described *Negara* as the *majalah partai*, "party journal" of Tan Malaka's PARI. Malik, *Mengabdi Republik* 1: 199.)

[39] Soewarni Pringgodigdo, "Du Perron dan Pengaruhnja kepada kaum intelek Indonesia, 1936–1939," *Sikap* 4 (1952): 33.

[40] Listyo remembers meeting Soegondo at several Pendidikan meetings in Surakarta in about 1936 or 1937. Interview with Listyo, Jakarta, November 27, 1987.

were particularly critical, as they had been in the 1920s, of the "fossilized" native, *ningrat*, aristocratic, traditions.[41]

The gloomy Indies of the time, in the memoirs of one of the group, Soewarni Pringgodigdo,

> was a world which has made idealists out of us, and Sjahrir, although in Banda, seemed very close. It was as if his influence had enfolded our souls and our minds.[42]

It came as something wholly natural that it was a Dutchman, who revitalized the group, in the late 1930s, and who came to epitomize the revitalized group's spirit.

The Dutchman was Eddy du Perron, "one of the leading literary men in the Netherlands"[43] and a well-known figure in the European avant-garde of the 1930s; to him, for instance, in 1934, André Malraux dedicated his *La Condition Humaine*. Du Perron was born in the Indies in 1899, and he spent his first twenty-two years in the colony. Then he left for Europe, and in 1936, after fifteen years of absence, in search of his roots, returned to his "land of origin."

Possibly through Abdoel Karim Pringgodigdo, Soewarni's husband who had studied in Holland and had been a member of the Perhimpoenan Indonesia at the same time as Sjahrir and Hatta, Eddy du Perron met the group. He instantly "charmed" the young women and men. This was, Soejitno Mangoenkoesoemo wrote later,

> something, I had never before experienced with any European.... He re-opened my eyes to the world of Western thought and feeling.... He taught me to look at myself ... he stood by me, while I was overcoming my big inferiority complexes; he taught me, in short, what "human dignity" meant, if, of course, such a thing can be learned.[44]

In words of Soewarsih Djojopoespito, Eddy du Perron became a "guru" to the group. He encouraged his young native friends to write. In particular, he helped Soewarsih to write and to publish her *Buiten het Gareel*, "Free of the Harness," arguably the best novel written by an Indonesian in the pre-Independence period.

Du Perron also introduced Soejitno, Soewarsih, and their friends to the Bandung journal, *Kritiek en Opbouw*, "Criticism and Construction," where he himself worked. *Kritiek en Opbouw*, which presented itself as "an independent and advanced Indies journal," tried, in a sense, to take up where the "neo-ethical" journal, *Stuw*, "Dam,"

---

[41] See especially Soejitno Mangoenkoesoemo, "Nog iets over ons Indonesiers," *Kritiek en Opbouw*, March 16, 1939, pp. 40ff; Soewarsih Djojopoespito, "Naar een nieuwe vrijheid," ibid., October 22, 1941, pp. 340ff. See also Soejitno Mangoenkoesoemo, "Brief van een Indonesiër aan E. du Perron (March 22, 1940)," *Criterium* 8/9 (August/September 1947): 495–98. De Kadt on his meeting with Soewarsih in J. de Kadt, *Jaren die dubbel telden: Politieke Herinneringen uit mijn 'Indische' jaren* (Amsterdam: van Oorschot, 1978), p. 40.

[42] Soewarni Pringgodigdo, "Du Perron dan Pengaruhnja," pp. 34–35.

[43] Teeuw, *Modern Indonesian Literature* (The Hague: Nijhoff, 1967), p. 43. For more on du Perron's influence on Indonesian literature see Subagio Sastrowardoyo, *Sastra Hindia Belanda dan kita* (Jakarta: Balai Pustaka, 1983), pp. 72–94. See also Kees Snoek, *De Indische jaren van E. du Perron* (Amsterdam: Van Ditmar, 1990).

[44] Soejitno Mangoenkoesoemo in *Kritiek en Opbouw* August 16, 1940, pp. 187–88.

had ended in 1933, crushed by Governor-General de Jonge. *Kritiek en Opbouw* was more "progressive" than *Stuw*, and it became, perhaps, the single most articulate Dutch dissident voice in the Indies at this time of repression. It also, however, and by the same token, in the sense of the actual or *real* politics in the Indies, was even more marginal than *Stuw* had been.[45]

Kritiek en Opbouw was close to the Algemeen Democratische Bond, the "All-Democratic Union," the most outspokenly anti-fascist movement among the Dutch in the colony. Writers for *Kritiek en Opbouw* saw the Dutch regime in the Indies as "dictatorial, bureaucratic and autocratic rule."[46] Some of them went as far as to say that they "explicitly recognized the Indonesians' right to be independent."[47]

The fact that the Indonesians around Soewarsih and Soejitno were introduced to this journal, and some of them even accepted as authors, became very important. It meant that this tiny and exclusive group of native intellectuals was suddenly being heard. For not a few among the "progressive" Dutchmen and Dutch-reading public, Soewarsih's and Soejitno's friends became a representative stream of indigenous nationalist thought.

Eddy du Perron, Soewarsih Djojopoespito wrote later, helped the members of the group in their "difficult passage between two worlds."[48] Acording to Soewarni:

> We avidly drank his inspiring words, and his fascinating personality was like a torch enlightening our troubled ways.... With him, we did not feel like beings of another race.... His talk ran smoothly from *Arjuna Wiwaha* [a story from the Hindu epic *Mahabharata*] to Shakespeare, Plato, Socrates, Dostoyevsky, Pushkin, Chekhov, Conrad, Gide, Malraux, Stendhal, or Baudelaire. He conversed in Sundanese, changed suddenly to French, or spoke English, when talking about Shakespeare or Huxley.... He had us read not only politics, Marxism, history and economics, but also *belles-lettres*. He did not hide how much he disliked it whenever our minds appeared not open enough to our own culture; it was not only world literature we were supposed to read.[49]

It is not difficult to see how Sjahrir fitted into this. In this atmosphere, there did not appear to be much need for any actual, direct, or explicit contact. What seemed essential was memory. Soewarni Pringgodigdo wrote later in recollections on du Perron:

> Talking hour after hour, Eddy once asked: "Do I resemble somebody? You seem, sometimes, as if you have known me before, as if you know my

---

[45] On *Kritiek en Opbouw* see Elsbeth B. Locher Scholten, "Kritiek en Opbouw (1938–1942). Een rode splinter," *Tijdschrift voor Geschiedenis* 89, 2 (1976): 202–27.

[46] Quoted in ibid., p. 213.

[47] Nieuwenhuys, *Oost-Indische spiegel*, p. 396.

[48] Soewarsih Djojopoespito in ibid., p. 193.

[49] Soewarni Pringgodigdo, "Du Perron dan Pengaruhnja," pp. 32–33. There is a discussion about du Perron's argument that modern Indonesians should look more towards their own culture. Takdir Alisjahbana argued against this in *Poedjangga Baroe*. Now was the time, Takdir wrote, to look more to Europe. See S.T.A. (Soetan Takdir Alisjahbana), "Sambil laloe. Minat E. du Perron," *Poedjanga Baroe* 7, 1 (July 1939): 18–19.

soul before I speak?" I answered: "You are like Sjahrir. There is the same purity and cleanliness in the way you talk. You are clear, real, and gentle like Sjahrir.... Sjahrir is you, except that you possess the gaiety and effortlessness of a Frenchman, combined with the beauty of Pasundan [West Java]. Sjahrir is a bit slower; he is a man born in Sumatra, with all the traits and faculties that the fact brings with it.[50]

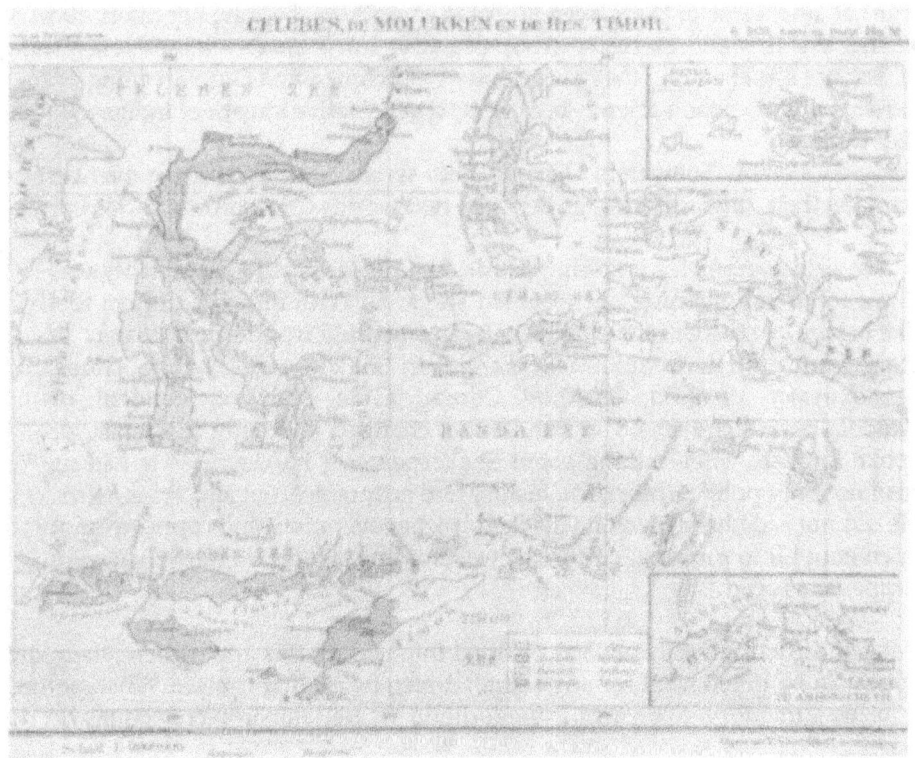

Map of Eastern Archipelago
(from the *Bos Atlas*)

2. Closer to the World

After ten days at sea, Sjahrir and Hatta reached Banda Neira on February 11, 1936. They were told, upon arrival, that the entire Banda archipelago, the islands stretching for "more than two hundred kilometers" across the Banda Sea between Sulawesi and New Guinea, would be their "place of internment."[51] After four months, how-

---

[50] Soewarni Pringgodigdo, "Du Perron dan Pengaruhnja," p. 34.

[51] *IO*, February 11, 1936; Des Alwi, "Oom kacamata yang mendidik saya," in *Muhammad Hatta*, ed. Swasono, p. 319.

ever, the Dutch authorities decided that the two exiles' freedom was to be restricted to Banda Neira, or "Neira," the main island of the Banda group.[52]

Banda Neira is about three kilometers long and two kilometers wide. There were 7,000 inhabitants living on the island at the time, mostly fishermen and peasants. There was no transport, except bicycles.

Five years before Sjahrir and Hatta arrived, the Dutch elementary school, ELS, had been closed in the only town on the island, Kota Neira, and only a seven-year "Dutch-Native" school, HIS, remained.[53] The Dutch *gezaghebber*, "administrator," governed Banda Neira with a staff of five. There was a *Harmonie Club*, near the town, a club for the Dutch community, but no more dances were being held.[54] Marvellous 100-year-old trees still lined the main street (in 1960, they were cut down for firewood).[55] A big church, built in 1825, had replaced a yet older building destroyed in an earthquake.[56]

The Javanese family of the government school headmaster lived in Banda Neira as well as one other family from Java, that of the government doctor. A few retired Dutchmen lived there and some planters in the hills; and the families of the two other exiled Indonesian leaders—Tjipto Mangoenkoesoemo, who had been in Banda Neira since 1928, and Iwa Kusumasumantri, who had come in 1930.

The nearest town of any importance was Makassar (Ujung Pandang today), about thirty-six hours away by ship. A trip to Batavia by plane took thirteen hours.[57] Compared with Tanah Merah, censorship, while still in force, was less strict; or so the exiles believed.[58] Mail arrived by ship from Makassar as often as once a fortnight.[59] In Sjahrir's words, Banda Neira was "closer to the world."[60]

About a hundred of the letters Sjahrir wrote while in Banda Neira were made available to me. Besides these, Sjahrir began in 1936 to write articles again. Most of the names, schools, and problems noted in Sjahrir's texts from Cipinang and Tanah Merah recur in his writings from Banda Neira. There are occasional changes in topic as well as interpretation. But a clear continuity prevails—naturally as now in his late twenties and thrown into still another new world, Sjahrir tries to uphold his structure of experience as a functioning whole.

The other side—the West and naturally the Dutch—still figured prominently in Sjahrir's thoughts and writings. As before, he wrote much about the "bad qualities" of those who had sent him into exile. In his letters from Banda Neira, he singled out the Dutch *kleingeest*, the "pettiness," along with their *bekrompenheid*, "narrow-mind-

---

[52] Government decision, June 5, 1936 in *Secret Mail Report* 1936, no. 12; see also *Secret Mail Report* 1936, no. 548 in *Secret Verbaal*, July 8, 1938-U22.

[53] Iwa Kusumasumantri, "Autobiography dari Prof. H. Iwa Kusuma Sumantri" (typescript dated May 1971), pp. 73–74; Hatta, *Memoir*, pp. 365–66, 374.

[54] Willard A. Hanna *Kepulauan Banda: kolonialisme dan akibatnja di Kepulauan Pala* (Jakarta: Gramedia, 1983), p. 161.

[55] Ibid.

[56] Ibid., p. 4.

[57] Soejitno Mangoenkoesoemo, "Brief van een Indonesiër," p. 489. Compare with Sutan Sjahrir, *Out of Exile*, p. 227.

[58] "No more censorship of my letters, at least no more open censorship," Sjahrir wrote in his first letter from Banda Neira. *IO* February 11, 1936.

[59] Iwa Kusumasumantri, "Autobiography," p. 75.

[60] *IO* February 11, 1936.

edness," and *kortzichtigheid*, "shortsightedness."[61] The "petit Holland," Sjahrir wrote, "is neither noble nor generous."[62] This Holland "would speak in the same spirit about revolutions as about canals in Amsterdam."[63] This Holland is

> so full of fences, field drains, and border lines ... there are, in the lives of the Dutch, more borders than open space ... they want to live their lives—and this is their fundamental principle—without breaking through any of the borders, be they made of religion, custom, or merely fashion.[64]

Statisch, "lacking vigor and dynamism," was another term familiar from his earlier writing, by which Sjahrir now again described what he saw as "bad Dutchness":

> the attachment they feel for rest [*rust*] and order [*orde*], for equilibrium [*evenwicht*], and for a more or less static spiritual life ... there is no nation in the world which uses the word "equilibrium," in thinking and in acting, as often as the Dutch do.[65]

As before, this was not a simple and stereotypical image of the Dutch as stolid cheesemakers. "The Dutch," Sjahrir wrote in Banda Neira,

> talk very much about an authority, power, and prestige, yet they remain largely anarchist petty-bourgeois [*kleinburgers*]. Because they are either painstakingly conscientious [*angstvallig*], or licentiously riotous [*losbandig*], they lack a true feeling for proportion and harmony.[66]

The Dutch, to Sjahrir, were not "politics-minded," but "bureau-minded." They were, more precisely, "mission-minded," and at the same time disturbed by their "conflicting [*tegenstrijdig*] principles, not unlike a Christian who lives in an un-Christian way."[67]

These characteristics strikingly often had something to do with a state of health. Sjahrir overused words referring to health to describe "bad Dutch-ness"; he repeated strong adjectives like *onzinnige* "absurd," *zinloos* "senseless," *ongezond* "unhealthy," *krankzinnige* "insane," *psychopatische* and, even, *sadistische*.[68] Thus, as in Tanah Merah,

---

[61] Ibid., February 21, May 6 and 29, and August 12, 1936.

[62] Ibid., July 10, 1937.

[63] Ibid., August 12, 1936.

[64] Ibid., May 9, 1936.

[65] Ibid.

[66] Ibid., September 2, 1937.

[67] Sjahrir to Iwa Kusumasumantri, August 24, 1939 in *Secret Mail Report* 1939, no. 1215; also *IO* September 5, 1937.

[68] For instance, *IO* August 6 and 28, 1937. H.Colijn, to the youth of Sjahrir's generation a symbol of the worst features imaginable in Dutch colonialism, published his reminiscences, when Sjahrir was in Banda Neira. In them, Colijn professed his warmest fondness for the Indies. Sjahrir commented that to him Colijn's reminiscences were "senseless," and the Indies were to Colijn, as Sjahrir saw it, a "mad little hobby-horse." Ibid., August 6, 1937.

Postcard of Banda Neira
(KITLV [DGI] #6115)

Sjahrir's notion of the "sick" Dutch body, or more precisely the "sick" Dutch-colonial body, kept open the possiblity of healing. It was clearly the image of a body which had been healthy, once, and might become healthy again.

The vision of *afbraak en herbouw*, "demolition and rebuilding"—the demolition of the Dutch system, and the rebuilding of an Indonesian system in its place—occasionally appeared among Indonesians, through the murky years.[69] Such a vision, however, did not seem to appeal to Sjahrir. He might at times become very impatient in Banda Neira with the lingering pace of progress in the colony; but he never painted a catastrophic picture of what might be in store for the Dutch.

Indeed, throughout his exile, Sjahrir never explicitly wrote about a future Indonesia without the Dutch. If a "revolutionary situation" arose in the Indies, he wrote, it would not happen because of the inevitability of history. The catastrophe might come if the Dutch colonial government, "in aggressive manner," penetrated too deeply through the lower layers of the Indonesian people.[70] The catastrophe would come, in other words, only if the Dutch went completely insane.

---

[69] See, for instance, A. Sj. (Amir Sjarifoeddin) in *Kritiek en Opbouw*, November 22, 1941, p. 327.
[70] *IO* December 24, 1936.

"It is not, strictly speaking, my business, to bother with what is good and what is bad for the colonial rulers," Sjahrir wrote in December 1936.[71] Yet his thoughts about possible improvement in the Indies appeared almost as a rule to have been thoughts about changes *among the Dutch*. In Banda Neira, as in Tanah Merah, Sjahrir portrayed progress largely as a process of healing. Sooner or later, he believed, "a period of 'progressive' colonial policy will come again."[72]

This, to him, was "inevitable,"[73] and would mean

> policies conceived in broad outlines and wide perspectives . . . an increase in the number of well-trained and well-educated Indonesians admitted in the colonial management.[74]

It would also, Sjahrir wrote, mean a change from the "aggressive" and "blind" policy of the present, to a policy of understanding what is "just, and good," and "reasonable." It would mean a return to *"raison."*[75]

"In a struggle for power," Sjahrir wrote in Banda Neira in May, 1936, "ethics are never a guide to a calculating brain, and a sensitivity to an enemy's ethics may exist only among men, who live in peace."[76] If Sjahrir believed this, however, he was hardly talking about the kind of struggle he himself was waging against the Dutch. On the topic of the Dutch Queen's birthday celebration in Banda Neira—after he noted how much hypocrisy was evident among the participants—Sjahrir wrote:

> The funniest part was the fact that I, an exile, appeared to have [among all the Dutch and "natives" present] the strongest feeling for the dignity of power.[77]

In his letters from Banda Neira Sjahrir described how eager he was for Dutch journals and magazines, "even for the most trivial news." He preferred, he wrote, the *Nieuwe Rotterdamsche Courant* "even if a month old," to any paper from the Indies.[78] The ease with which Sjahrir talked with a Dutch party passing through Banda Neira one day also sounds peculiar, given the fact that it was an exile—a rebel against the Dutch government—who was talking. The group included

> Captain W., the commander of the garrison and the chief of local administration at Tanah Merah, whom I knew from my Digoel time, and a commissar of the Moluccas residency police, a former classmate of mine.[79]

---

[71] Ibid.
[72] Ibid., July 8, 1937. See also ibid., June 17, July 24 and December 24, 1936.
[73] Ibid., July 8, 1937.
[74] Ibid., February 21, 1936 and July 8, 1937.
[75] Ibid., May 5 and December 24, 1936.
[76] Ibid., May 9, 1936.
[77] Ibid., September 2, 1937.
[78] Ibid., June 17, 1936.
[79] Ibid., August 5, 1937. "Captein W," of course, was the Tanah Merah administrator Wiarda; see above, chapter 5, on Boven Digul.

Occasionally, it might even appear as if Sjahrir were watching his fellow Indonesians from where the Dutch vantage point was supposed to be:

> I care for the Indonesians more than for other groups of the population. It is completely normal, it is a sympathy for the "underdogs."[80]

At moments like that, it becomes clear that Sjahrir, in thinking of healing the Dutch, was thinking, in fact, of healing himself. He wrote in March 1938:

> In spite of the fact that I have now been out of Digoel already for two years, I am not yet altogether normal. I am still too distrustful and not yet in a state to leave behind the bitter experience.[81]

In the letter, he used a medical term to describe himself. He called his condition "a light case of persecution mania."[82]

In a letter dated February 1937 he wrote: "Luckily, not all the officials who were sent over here by the Dutch lost their morality on the way." Striking, again, are the figures Sjahrir decided to use to illustrate that statement: Douwes Dekker (Multatuli), a compassionate Dutch colonial official and writer of the late nineteenth century; G. A. J. Hazeu and Snouck Hurgronje, Leiden men and the architects of the "ethical policy" (as Sjahrir wrote, "they felt all too well" the policy's shortcomings);[83] W. Lefebvre, the former Dutch Resident, a top colonial official in Minangkabau at the time of Sjahrir's childhood, who resigned his position later in protest against what he believed was the insensitivity of Dutch policy towards the native population.[84]

All of these examples of "good Dutch-ness" were either dead, or long ago separated from the centers of actual power. The last of the examples used in Sjahrir's letters was Jos Riekerk, then serving as a low colonial official in a remote post in the Indies not far from where Sjahrir was in exile. As the reader may remember, Jos Riekerk had been one of Sjahrir's student friends in Leiden, an ardent "Marxist" contributor to *De Socialist* at that time; he also was a Eurasian and, thus, even biologically a man in-between. A "soft-boiled child," Sjahrir wrote about Riekerk,

> exactly the type of man who might advance in the colonial service when the "progressive" colonial policy comes up again.[85]

Early in 1938, Sjahrir published one of his very few articles from exile—a long essay for the Batavia Indonesian literary journal *Poedjangga Baroe*, "New Writer." Bourgeois culture," he wrote,

---

[80] *IO* August 28, 1937.

[81] Ibid., March 7, 1938.

[82] Ibid.

[83] Ibid., February 18, 1937 and March 11, 1938.

[84] Ibid., February 18, 1937. Lefebvre became a member of the League against Colonialism and was also very close to the group around the journal, *De Socialist*, in Holland when Sjahrir was there and also close to the same group.

[85] *IO* July 8, 1937.

which also is called Western culture, has already become the universal culture, the culture of the whole world.... The culture of educated men in the East is nothing but this Western culture.... This truth and this reality do not necessarily degrade [Eastern intellectuals]. On the contrary, they are in accordance with the spirit of time.[86]

For the Eastern man, Sjahrir wrote in the same essay, Western culture was an "heirloom [*poesaka*]," which he must "absorb and master."[87]

This was not a suggestion of surrender. Indonesian culture, Sjahrir wrote, was "very young":

But, as a matter of fact, this quality becomes an advantage at the present moment. [Indonesian culture] is still full of joy, and it is not yet scared by the skepticism and pessimism of the aging West. Its spirit can still flare up and strive after an ideal, something which may only amuse the skeptics of Europe. [Indonesian culture] is prepared to attain its ideals in new ways ... together with the spirit and the forces of change which do exist in Europe itself.[88]

It may be illuminating to make an inventory of what Sjahrir disliked in "Eastern culture"—first of all, the "civil-servant mentality," obsession with "hierarchy," "feudal ideology," "slave mentality," and, what grew out of all this: "Eastern inferiority complexes";[89] next, "stagnancy" and an inclination to "tranquility and reflection," "gentleness [*haloes*]-ness," excessive "tolerance," a propensity for "mystics," a "museum-and-incense" style of life, a "disregard for the [real] world and life, a virtuosity in the art of negation."[90]

As in Tanah Merah, Sjahrir, beyond any doubt, was determined not to submit to anything resembling the regional conversion that was taking place in the nationalist politics of the time. Any island, regionalist, or cultural-nationalist bias had to be banned from the thoughts and actions of this man, who saw himself as modern and Indonesian. Yet, sometimes, it seems that while the surface of Sjahrir's mind remained almost unscratched, there were cleavages, and growing tensions underneath.

Sjahrir selected the fifteenth century as the one, when the "bad" qualities overwhelmed Eastern civilization in Indonesia.[91] The fifteenth century, of course, was a time which has no particular meaning—good or bad—for Sumatra, Minangkabau, or most other parts of Indonesia. But it was certainly the most cherished high point for Javanese traditional culture, philosophy, art, and statehood.

---

[86] Sutan Sjahrir, "Kesoesasteraan dan Rakjat (Banda Neira, May 1938)," *Poedjangga Baroe* (*nomor peringatan* 1933–1939) 7, 1 (July 1939); reprinted in Sutan Sjahrir, *Pikiran dan Perdjoeangan* (Jakarta: Poestaka Rakjat, 1947), pp. 79–90.

[87] Ibid.

[88] Ibid.

[89] Ibid., p. 80; see also ibid., p. 93 and *IO*, March 12, 1937.

[90] Sjahrir, "Kesoesasteraan dan Rakjat," pp. 79–80, and *IO* March 12 and June 10, 1937.

[91] Ibid., January 20, 1937.

In the same way, "the vanished land of the Middle Ages,"[92] as described by Sjahrir, the land of

> hierarchic relations, of a feudal society, where a small group seized upon all the material and spiritual riches and kept the majority of poor people in their place through religion and philosophy, instead of feeding them properly ... ,[93]

could hardly be mistaken for anything among the contemporary clichés of Indonesia's past but that of traditional Java. And as if there might be any doubt of what he meant, in the same article Sjahrir challenged the ultimately "bad" Eastern quality of "virtuosity in tolerance" and then elaborated on the theme:

> It is a fact that, above all on Java, there are men who for hours can think of nothing, and—as Westerners may call it—day-dream.[94]

In April 1939, an irritated rejoinder to this particular article by Sjahrir appeared in *Poedjangga Baroe* from a young Indonesian poet, J. E. Tatengkeng. Tatengkeng challenged Sjahrir, because, as Tatengkeng put it, Sjahrir measured Indonesia exclusively by "Western norms [*oekoeran Barat*]."[95]

A revealing discussion followed. In a long reply published in the same journal, in June 1939, Sjahrir first wondered, why Tatengkeng, a man from Celebes (Sulawesi) and a Christian, should have been so provoked:

> Was he, perhaps, influenced by some missionary, who [in turn] might have been searching for a Javanese soul and for that Javanese soul's so "natural" aptitude for mystics?[96]

What Tatengkeng actually manifested by his reaction to Sjahrir, Sjahrir wrote, was a desire

> to attract Indonesian men of letters to travel with him, across the waters of the Hindoestan, as far as the land of the [Hindu epic] Ramayana. [Tatengkeng tries to make young Indonesian writers] cultural heirs of the authors of the Ramayana or the Mahabharata, the [Javanese chronicle] Pararaton or the [Javanese epic] Nagakertagama, or the heirs of [Javanese court poet] Ranggawarsita ... heirs of feudal-mystical ... speculative-mystical, [and] fantastic-mystical ideologies.[97]

---

[92] Ibid., March 12, 1937.

[93] Ibid.

[94] Ibid.

[95] J. E. Tatengkeng, "Kritiek dan oekoeran sendiri," *Poedjangga Baroe* 6, 10 (April 1939): 157–59. For more illustration of Tatengkeng's views at the time see J. E. Tatengkeng, "Penjelidikan dan Pengakoean," *Poedjangga Baroe* 3, 1 (July 1935): 19–26.

[96] Sjahrir in *Poedjangga Baroe* 7, 1 (June 1939): 91–96.

[97] Ibid., especially p. 96.

The prime "good" quality of the Eastern man, to Sjahrir in Banda Neira as before, was "dynamism," a "dynamic spirit," "vitality," a capacity to see one's life "as strife, as a fight, and as a movement."[98] The next "good" quality was "rationality," allied with "sobriety, matter-of-factness," and also "moral responsibility." A man who was "matter-of-fact [*nuchter*]," Sjahrir wrote, could hardly fall victim "to the phantasies of the Ramayana and the Mahabharata."[99]

To such a modern Eastern man, Sjahrir believed, there might be "no cosmic life, but the life of humans, dignifying, enriching, and beautifying man as a species...."[100] This was a belief in a universal man.

Sjahrir still believed, as he had been taught in the "ethical" schools of his youth, that the "good" qualities were capable of "bridging [*overbrug*] the deep cleft between a fact and a notion, [the strangeness] between a subject and an object"; that they were capable of helping a modern man to grasp the world so *geladen*, as Sjahrir wrote, "so full of suppressed anger."[101] "Only rationality," Sjahrir believed, "is powerful enough to rule this world."[102]

There were, however, cleavages under the surface. The bridge—Sjahrir believed in and built his life upon—was not getting steady.

"The last years, especially my stay in Tanah Merah, did something to me," Sjahrir wrote in March 1936,

> which I had never experienced before. In my own skin I found that, with all the manners, all the humanity, all the religiousness and morality we believe we possess, there is a beast in us which can make all the culture, humanity, and religion into something comical....
>
> One may be learned and skilled in sheltering himself by scientific formulae; he may be wrapped in his academic degree and all the shiny garments of civilization and culture—[and yet], the beast in him, unrecognized and unwanted, peeps and protrudes out of every pore.[103]

"Whoever claims that reason can forestall the primary life function is a big liar," Sjahrir wrote in August 1936.[104] "At the moment," he wrote some time later,

> I am of an opinion that emotional life [*gevoelsleven*] is of paramount importance, and that it is, like nature, the most genuine [*oorspronkelijkste*].[105]

And after another while:

---

[98] Sjahrir in *Poedjangga Baroe* (May 1938), p. 96; *IO* December 31, 1936, January 20, 1937; S. van de Garde (Sjahrir), "Friedrich Engels en onze tijd: Een verdediging dialektiek," *De Nieuwe Kern* 3 (1936–1937): 132–34.

[99] Sjahrir in *Ilmoe dan Masjarakat*, November 1936, p. 98. See also Sjahrir in *Poedjangga Baroe*, June 1939, p. 96.

[100] *IO* December 31, 1936.

[101] Sjahrir in *Ilmoe dan Masjarakat*, November 1936.

[102] *IO* December 31, 1936.

[103] Ibid., March 21, 1936.

[104] Ibid., August 14, 1936.

[105] Ibid. December 29, 1936.

Indeed, impulses, urges, passions [*drifts*], as I now believe, can never be eliminated by reason. Exactly the opposite is true—reason always rules only as much as the impulses, the urges, and the passions let it, and, when the impulses, etc. are fully at play, reason is either cut off or placed in the service of the impulses, the urges, and the passions.[106]

These were moments when Sjahrir appeared very uneasy indeed about his exile experience. Or, maybe, they were moments when the bridge he was building by his life appeared in its truest form. He wrote in July 1937:

Wholly consciously, I often try to keep myself superficial [*oppervlakkig*] in order not to be puzzled and not to brood.[107]

To live without "emotions [*gevoelens*]" became for Sjahrir "too positive"; it was inadequate, it was "abstract reasoning" without "experience [*ervaring*]." A "purely rational life" came close to being seen as "merely a life, which appears to be [*een schijnleven*], a life of a self-deception. . . .[108]

Idealistic thinkers, "men like Tolstoy, and even Gandhi, whom I used to look towards for such a long time, departed from me," Sjahrir wrote from Banda Neira in March 1936.[109] Kant, formerly also one of Sjahrir's masters, was losing his appeal as well. Now, Sjahrir referred to Kant with growing disrespect as to "that idealist . . . with all of his so highly esteemed reason."[110] Nietzsche, and his notion of *Triebleben*, appeared now to express Sjahrir better than anybody and anything else.[111]

The Nietzschean *wil*, "desire, wish," became, in Sjahrir's writing, almost identical with what he had previously defined as vitality and dynamism.[112] Engels, as always, was a great man to Sjahrir, but now primarily because—besides "relativism," and "pragmatism"—he taught that life and the world "are moved by wish and will."[113] Marx also kept his place among Sjahrir's great men, it seemed now, mainly because of his "pessimistic realism," and because of "his idea that men are not what they intend [*menen*], but what, as physical entities, as animals, they unconsciously do." "Marx and Freud," Sjahrir came to believe, in Banda Neira, were "geniuses . . . because they were capable of seeing a distinction between conscious and subconscious life."[114]

---

[106] Ibid., March 17, 1937.

[107] Ibid., July 1, 1937.

[108] Ibid., May 29 and December 29, 1936

[109] Ibid., March 21, 1936.

[110] Ibid.

[111] Ibid. We may note that Nietzsche was also a prominent influence for Tan Malaka throughout his life (Mrázek, "Tan Malaka," pp. 7ff). Sukarno, according to Dahm, also experimented with the philosopher: "During his imprisonment (1930–1931) Sukarno had attempted to take Nietzsche's 'Superman' as an example. But he soon gave up and concluded [that] . . . if Nietzsche had tried to have anyone in prison live as a Superman, he would certainly have had no success." (Dahm, *Sukarno*, p. 134, n. 24)

[112] *IO* March 24, 1936 and Sjahrir in *Ilmoe dan Masjarakat*, November 1936, p. 100.

[113] Ibid., p. 307. see also van de Garde (Sjahrir), "Friedrich Engels," p. 143.

[114] *IO* May 5, December 29, 1936; see also Sjahrir in *Ilmoe dan Masjarakat*, November 1936.

Only if we give "a very relative value" to reason, Sjahrir wrote, can we keep our theories "practical."[115] Only if we accept Marx's concept of man as an animal based on subconscious drives, "can we come to terms with historical and social laws."[116]

Words of uncertainty, like "relative," "relatively speaking," and "temporary," appeared with great frequency. Sjahrir wrote in August 1936, for instance:

> We can not expect reason to do even as little as to restore an equilibrium in our spiritual and physical life, once the balance is disturbed. This can be done only through, and in a union with, feelings, sensations, and emotions. This only can grow from the sphere of feeling [gevoelssfeer], etc., from the sphere of instincts...."[117]

In Sjahrir's writing from Banda Neira the word *weer*, "again, once more, once again," appeared it seems, as often as the words "temporary" or "relative." According to Sal Tas,

> Sjahrir, isolated in Banda, had remained with the ideas of his student years. In his ears there still rang the polemics that we as young Marxists had carried on.... For him, to leave Marxism meant... another betrayal of his beloved."[118]

Sal Tas, no more in close contact with Sjahrir anyway, was right only to an extent. Sjahrir disagreed with those of his friends from Holland who later, like Sal Tas, considered their Marxism to have been nothing but a youthful episode in their lives. To Sjahrir, these people, indeed, had deserted their "former comrades in faith."[119] Sal Tas was not right, however, in implying that Sjahrir merely stuck to the memories of his Holland period.

Sjahrir wrote about himself as "not knowing enough," or being "unaware" in the past, and he included in the time of ignorance the years when he was in Holland. He saw himself as "progressing" in Banda Neira—as he put it once—from *onbewust*, the "unconscious," towards a growing awareness of *onderbewust*, the "subconscious."

Sjahrir "progressed deeper," which was as often as not *weer*, towards the "again," the "once more," the "once again." He moved, so he wrote, from *schooltjes*, the "little schools," of the narrow-minded actual Europe *veel dieper*, "yet deeper," through Kant—"the greatest philosopher of Protestantism," to Goethe, and Marx and Nietzsche—the universal geniuses,[120] as far, as deep, as far back, as to where one might believe the true beginnings or origins were—"not the German myths [the Niebelungen]," Sjahrir wrote, "but the Greek heroes...."[121]

Sjahrir "progressed deeper" in Banda Neira than he had in Tanah Merah. Was it as far back as his "ethical" AMS Western-classical school in Bandung? Classical

---

[115] *IO* April 12, 1936.
[116] Ibid., May 5, 1936.
[117] Ibid., August 14, 1936.
[118] Tas, "Souvenirs of Sjahrir," p. 147.
[119] *IO* May 29, 1936.
[120] Ibid., May 9 and 30 and December 31, 1936,
[121] Sjahrir in *Poedjangga Baroe*, March 1939, p. 93.

Greece, indeed, became almost the measure of all things to Sjahrir in Banda Neira. "How strongly my feeling reacts," Sjahrir wrote in May 1936,

> against the pettiness, the Calvinist stiffness, the stubborness, which, as I can see it, is so distant from the generous and free [*ruime*] spirit of classical Greece.... Take Plato, for instance.... Free, full of space, generous, fine at each point.
>
> In this sense, in Goethe there is also a true classical soul, also in Beethoven, also in Marx; but not in Kant, for instance. The best in Goethe's romanticism is, in a way, comparable to the classics. Goethe escaped what romanticism developed later into: a culture of the petit bourgeois; rather, one would find something of Plato in Goethe.[122]

Sjahrir's writing in Banda Neira defined progress as a movement from blindness, madness, and abnormality towards fairness, sensibility, reasonableness, towards the Dutch as well as the Indonesians becoming healthy and ethical, indeed, healthy and ethical again.

What was behind was the beast in us, the impulses, and "uncivilized [*onbeschaafd*] mankind." But what was ahead might easily be "a sham building [*schijngebouw*] of civilization and culture."[123] Upon the urges of the substrata, the *Triebleben*, the oldest, primeval *oer-instincten*, a building might be erected of secondary sensations—"prejudices, manners, ethics, aesthetics."[124]

Sjahrir saw his generation and himself as *sangat moeda (. . .) masih penoeh kegembiraan*, "very young and still full of joy." At the same time, his generation appeared to him *onmondig*, "adolescent," *nog niet geestelijk volgroeide*, "not yet spiritually grown-up," *nog niet geheel rijp*, "not yet fully mature."[125] Sjahrir's anxiety might also have been the fear of growing into a false adulthood.

3. Flowers, Officials, Nationalists, and the Bandanese

In February 1939, Hatta wrote in a letter to Nehru from Banda Neira:

> How long I have to live so, nobody can tell. In my case I have the patience and endurance to defy this severe life of banishment, only one thing troubles me often, i.e. that something is going wrong without a possibility for me to intervene.[126]

Tjipto Mangoenkoesoemo, another of Sjahrir's new fellow exiles in Banda Neira, was reported to be suffering from fits of anger, and these were caused, his family believed, by the man's "feeling painfully alone."[127] Iwa Koesoemasoemantri wrote

---

[122] *IO* May 30, 1936.

[123] Ibid., March 21, 1936.

[124] Ibid., August 14, 1936.

[125] Sjahrir in *Poejangga Baroe*, May 1938; *IO* August 14, 1936 and March 11, 1938.

[126] Hatta to Nehru, February 12, 1939 in *Jawaharlal Nehru Papers* (Nehru Smarag, New Delhi) box IIL, file 96.

[127] The recollections of Donald (a step son of Tjipto) quoted in M. Balfas, *Dr. Tjipto Mangoenkoesoemo: Demokrat Sedjati* (Jakarta: Djambatan, 1952), p. 123.

about his own "unsufferable feeling of boredom" in Banda Neira, and about the "fear of going mad from being so lonely and so worried."[128]

"Our life, in that place of banishment," Iwa wrote later:

> was more saddening than life in prison. In what mental state we were! We were haunted because, unlike any prisoner, we did not even know how long we would have to stay.... The place was so small.... Can anybody imagine how we felt having to go through life like that, each day meeting the same people, staying with the same things, like the waves of the sea, for instance, huge and blowing and thundering waves that would never stop. All that only deepened the loneliness of our hearts. Because of that, we often were upset and desperate, losing hope that we would ever again live amidst our people.[129]

Sjahrir seemed very different. Hatta remembered that, except for the first few weeks when he appeared to brood about the friends he had left in the camp, Sjahrir went through the daily routine in Banda Neira easily and in good spirits.[130] Lily, a Bandanese girl who became very close to Sjahrir, as we shall see, never thought of Sjahrir as a captive, and she never remembered hearing him say anything like "When I'm free...."[131]

"From the few letters which I received," Sjahrir's Dutch friend, Sal Tas, wrote about his correspondence with Sjahrir from that time, "I got the impression that he was not unhappy in Banda."[132] Sjahrir's letters conveyed the same feeling to his Indonesian friends who remained in the internment camp at Boven Digul.[133]

There was also a striking lack of complaint in Sjahrir's letters to Maria. He mentioned his malaria in passing but wrote extensively about himself "living now entirely healthily," sleeping well and doing "regular indoor gymnastics."[134] As far as the news from the outside world was concerned, Sjahrir wrote, he felt "much better" than in Tanah Merah; he was "pleased" with the newspapers he could read now, except that he did "not have much time to read newspapers anyway."[135]

In a letter written after four months in Banda Neira, Sjahrir complained of being, initially, "busy visiting." This, he wrote, "luckily" did not last long, and now he lived "quietly and withdrawn."[136] Another short spasm of suffering was the "wedding season" on the island and the series of invitations he could not refuse. "A bit terrifying," Sjahrir wrote, and: "I have enough of feasts."[137]

---

[128] Iwa Kusumasumantri. "Autobiography," p. 76. Compare Iwa Kusumasumantri, *Sedjarah Revolusi Indonesia*, I: 65, n. 1.

[129] Ibid., p. 73.

[130] Hatta, *Indonesian Patriot*, pp. 191–92.

[131] Interview with Lily Sutantio, Jakarta, April 2, 1982.

[132] Tas, "Souvenirs of Sjahrir," p. 148.

[133] Interviews with Burhanuddin, Jakarta, March 5, 1982, and Murwoto, Jakarta, December 6, 1987. Murwoto says that Sjahrir and Hatta were sending clothes, books, and money back to their friends in Tanah Merah very regularly, often each month.

[134] *IO* October 12, 1936 on a spell of malaria; ibid., August 24, 1936.

[135] Ibid., June 17, 1936.

[136] Ibid., June 1, 1936.

[137] Ibid., June 10, 1937.

Banda Neira
KITLV [DGI] nr. 4871

Sjahrir appears to have worked hard to disentangle himself from evenings at the Javanese doctor's home, where he and Hatta, from the first days after their arrival, regularly played bridge. After a few weeks, also on his own initiative, Sjahrir moved away from the house where he had been living with Hatta. After a few months, eventually, he ceased to attend parties at Iwa Koesoemasoemantri's place, where all the other exiles gathered each week, as they said, to make the isolation more bearable.[138]

---

[138] Ibid., May 31, 1936 and Hatta, *Memoir*, pp. 366–67; Interview with Lily Sutantio, Jakarta, April 2, 1982.

There are some easy explanations for why Sjahrir might have been less depressed than the other exiles. He was younger than the rest. In contrast to Tjipto and Iwa, he did not have to worry daily about a wife and children in exile with him. In contrast to Hatta, who was also a single man, Sjahrir liked to exercise and might thus have been more able physically to enjoy what truly was the island's immense physical beauty.

Just a few years before Sjahrir and Hatta arrived in Banda Neira, W. Somerset Maugham made the island the scene of one of his more charming South Seas novels, *The Narrow Corner*. Banda Neira was an island, in Somerset Maugham's novel, about which sailors talked:

> Used to be a grand place in the old days. Centre of the spice trade and all that. Nutmegs. Never been 'ere meself, but I been told there's marble palaces and I don't know what all.[139]

It was a legend of extravaganza, when "the harbour was full," and planters imported ice for their late-afternoon drinks and granite for their palace-like houses all the way from Holland.

The hero of *The Narrow Corner* comes to Banda Neira after being haunted by its image through all his adult life—its name was that of a fairy-tale island in a book he had read as a child. Then the man sees the island in reality:

> The harbour was far from crowded: there were only two junks, three or four large prahus, a motor-boat, and a derelict schooner. Beyond the town was a hill surmounted by a flagstaff, and from it dangled limply a Dutch flag.... The bungalows on either side of the [main] road had very high roofs, thatched and pointed, and the roofs, jutting out, were supported by pillars, Doric and Corinthian, so as to form a broad verandas. They had an air of opulence, but their whitewash was stained and worn, and the little gardens in front of them were rank with tangled weeds.... The few persons passed, [they] walked quickly as though they were afraid to awaken the echo.[140]

The best way to live on that island, Somerset Maugham wrote, was to live on one's memory. The fort on the hill, was "just a few old grey walls," and yet, "it's like Tristan's castle." The sea was "as wine-dark as the sea on which Odysseus sailed."

> Of course, romance was there, but it was vague, and in your ignorance you could only form pictures as blurred as ill developed snapshots.

As one entered with the novel's heroes the few still inhabited houses of the Dutch planters on the island, there was "the charm of incongruity," which "brought vividly to the mind's eye a demure picture of nineteenth-century Holland."[141]

---

[139] W. Somerset Maugham, *The Narrow Corner* (1932. Harmondsworth: Penguin Books, 1962), p. 91.
[140] Ibid., pp. 91–92.
[141] Ibid., pp. 100, 102, 105, 140.

Sjahrir for the first time saw Banda Neira from the ship which had carried them to New Guinea. And, in a sense, he wrote about the island not unlike Somerset Maugham did:

> The morrow Banda, also famous for its beauty. The area of the bay where we dropped anchor was about fifteen meters deep, but the water was so transparent that you could see clearly everything lying on the bottom of the sea. The sea-bottom was covered with corals. The water of the bay, sheltered by the volcano of Goenoeng Api, was like a mirror.[142]

In his first letter after he returned to Banda Neira from the camp, as he was settling down for a long exile, Sjahrir wrote to Maria: "It is lovely here beyond words."[143]

Some of Sjahrir's evenings were spent on a friend's veranda at the *Herenweg*, "a delightful avenue with grand old cinnamon trees." The men looked across the lawn to the beach beyond, over to the bay with small white houses visible on the other side, and they watched the sunset: hard to resist, Sjahrir wrote, "you are overwhelmed by so much beauty."[144]

In two letters, early in June and at the end of July, 1936, Sjahrir wrote again:

> Here, it is truly a paradise. The nature is stunning, and all agree with you and everything around. There is something of a flower cult here. Most of the Bandanese display grandiose flowers in front of their houses. I myself have already planted a small flower garden, and, as I am writing, there they stand on my desk, orchids from my own plot of land.[145]

> Sometimes I watch the sunset from an old pier. In front of me is a splendid bay. At my feet is the water, limpid, very lightly blue. In the background is Great Banda island, obscure and hilly, and towards the east, the perfect conical silhouette of Goenoeng Api. The stars are white. I have never seen the moon and the stars so magnificent, so great and so clear as here. It feels, sometimes, as if the moon here warms you. On a clear night, you can sit outside and read by the moonshine.[146]

The house Sjahrir moved into with Hatta, after they had spent their first few nights in Iwa's place, was, in Hatta's words, "large indeed."[147] It was one of the former planters' mansions Somerset Maugham wrote about. It was built mainly of stone and had eight rooms. Its central hall, for instance, was fifty square meters; the front veranda was forty meters long, and *achtergalerij*, the "back veranda," in Sjahrir's words, was "almost as large as a tennis court."[148]

It looked like a waste of space, Sjahrir wrote to Maria, but, in fact, it was "a stroke of good luck" to get a house like that. The building was cool, and they paid

---

[142] *IO* February 21, 1935.
[143] Ibid., February 11, 1936.
[144] Ibid., May 21, 1936.
[145] Ibid., June 1, 1936.
[146] Ibid., July 25, 1936.
[147] Hatta, *Memoir*, p. 366.
[148] Ibid,, and *IO* February 26, 1936.

only 12.5 guilders a month as rent. This was less than 10 percent of the allowance they each, as exiles, got from the government. They paid a servant another 6 guilders a month, and their cook got 10 guilders.[149]

Curiously, Sjahrir wrote virtually nothing, bad or good, from Banda Neira about the local Dutch officials. When he wrote about "officials," he meant, as a rule, the two native civil servants, both Javanese: the government doctor, S., and the headmaster of the local government school, M. These were, to Sjahrir, the manifestation of all the "official" (and thus) "bad" qualities he ever wrote about. These were "spineless officials," living by pettiness, narrow-mindedness, and servility. Fortunately—"good for us," Sjahrir wrote—the Dutch authorities took on themselves the unpleasant job of saving Sjahrir from the company of these two men. The Dutch administrator warned the doctor and the teacher not to meet the dangerous exiles too often, and they dutifully complied.[150]

One might expect Iwa Koesoemasoemantri to have been a much more acceptable companion for Sjahrir. Iwa was a Leiden-educated lawyer, a chairman of Perhimpeonan Indonesia during the early 1920s. He had spent some time in Moscow on his way back from Holland, and he was rumored ever afterwards to be in contact with agents of the Communist International or, perhaps, with the mysterious Indonesian ex-Communist and exile, Tan Malaka. Back in the Indies, Iwa settled in Medan, worked as a lawyer, and became a local activist of Sukarno's Partindo. He was arrested in Medan, and exiled in 1929.[151]

Iwa, thus, was a fellow freedom fighter. Besides, he had a very good library in his Banda Neira house, and was constantly getting new books and journals from abroad.[152] Given all this, there were surprisingly very few good words for Iwa in Sjahrir's letters.

Sjahrir stopped attending the regular *zaterdagavondjes*, "Saturday soirées," at Iwa's house after some time because, according to Hatta, on one occasion Iwa's wife humiliated a servant in Sjahrir's presence.[153] Reading Sjahrir's letters, however, there were other reasons. First of all, according to Sjahrir, Iwa found the two Javanese "spineless officials"—meaning the government doctor S. and the government school teacher M.—"fully to his taste." Iwa also, under the stress of exile perhaps, had become dogmatic in his Islam.[154] Finally, in other matters too, Iwa manifested a lack of open-mindedness, "a typical quality," Sjahrir commented, "of our pure nationalists."[155] This was why Sjahrir found the evenings at Iwa's generally "bungled [*verknoeide*]," and why instead he decided to stay "quietly and alone at home."[156]

---

[149] According to Hatta (*Memoir*, p. 369; also *Indonesian Patriot*, p. 183), they got 75 guilders. During the last months of their stay, their allowance was raised to 100 guilders. Tjipto and Iwa, because they were in Banda Neira with their families, got 187.5 and 150 guilders respectively. See *Archief Proc Gen*, no. 262., and Iwa to Tjipto, September 14, 1939 in *Secret Mail Report 1939*, no. 1215.

[150] *IO* June 1, 1936.

[151] Blumberger, *De nationalistische beweging*, pp. 237, 367–68.

[152] Iwa Kusumasumantri. "Autobiography," p. 71.

[153] Hatta, *Memoir*, p. 374.

[154] *IO* May 31, June 1, and September 9, 1936.

[155] Ibid., May 21, 1936.

[156] Ibid., May 31, 1936.

Sjahrir seemed to distance himself deliberately even from his closest political associate, Hatta. As we have mentioned, Sjahrir moved out of the house he and Hatta had originally shared. Still earlier, "after a little exchange of words," he let Hatta attend alone both Iwa's parties and the bridge sessions with the two Javanese civil servants.

How could Hatta bear these people, Sjahrir wondered in a letter to Maria, how could he

> play bridge through the night, as if it was the most normal thing to do, babbling [*babbelend*] about the silliest matters.[157]

The two Javanese were of "the shortsighted, the stupid, the sluggish" officialdom, Sjahrir wrote. Yet, "companionship [*omgang*] like this," seemed to be

> the surest way [*manier*], in which [Hatta] may be tamed. He is almost without resistance against these officials.[158]

Tjipto Mangoenkoesoemo was a man of another generation. He was twenty-four years Sjahrir's senior and had been away from "the world outside" for many years. He himself said repeatedly that politics, to him, was "a closed period."[159] Tjipto, besides, was notorious in Banda Neira for being "the most difficult person for anyone to deal with harmoniously."[160] In the past, he had been considered a "true *kesatria*," true Javanese "noble warrior" of politics. He was the man, indeed, who may have inspired Sukarno's political style as well as Sukarno's Javanese, *wayang* shadow theater rhetoric.[161] But Tjipto never came close to the Javanese *ningrat*, aristocratic mentality as the Pendidikan, for instance, understood it. Tjipto, according to his biographer, "could find no comfort in this traditional culture."[162] And Hatta believed, Tjipto "was against princely rule."[163]

In Banda Neira, Tjipto, moreover, seemed to regain something very important to himself from the initial stages of his political career. In the early 1910s, he had led the Indisch Partij, "Indies Party," a radical movement of "progressive natives and Eurasians." Its aim was an independent Indies as a home for all the races in the archipelago living culturally and harmoniously together.

Now on Banda Neira Tjipto studied mysticism, old Javanese, and old-Javanese epics. He emphasized the *kosmischalverbondenheid*, "cosmic harmony," togetherness of "all religions," namely the companionship of Jesus, Muhammad, and Buddha as the "original, primary and genuine unity of mankind."[164]

---

[157] Ibid., June 1, 1936.

[158] Ibid.

[159] Soejitno Mangoenkoesoemo, "Brief van een Indonesiër," p. 499.

[160] Recollections by Donald in Balfas, *Dr.Tjipto*, p. 123.

[161] Dahm, *Sukarno*, pp. 56, 213.

[162] Balfas, *Dr.Tjipto*, p. 123.

[163] Hatta, *Bung Hatta Antwoordt*, p. 29. Tjipto's symbolism of the Javanese *satria* had been a way to inspire "will power" among the Javanese people. See especially Takashi Shiraishi, *An Age in Motion: Popular Radicalism in Java, 1912–1926* (Ithaca: Cornell University Press, 1990).

[164] Soejitno Mangoenkoesoemo, "Brief van een Indonesiër"; Balfas, *Dr. Tjipto*, p. 124.

Tjipto cut a strange figure on the island. He was said to be unable "to compromise between ideals and reality."[165] He appeared old-fashionedly stubborn. He rejected, for instance, Dutch offers to release him from exile, unless the Dutch authorities admit that they had been wrong in the first place when they had doubted his good intentions.[166] He was "un-disciplined," "Oblomov-like."[167] He liked to welcome guests "in an undershirt and pajama trousers, with his drawers clearly visible." Or he may don "the best piece of clothing he could lay his hands on," the kimono of his Eurasian wife, most likely, "which, being too long, of course, swept the floor wildly while Tjipto talked."[168]

In one of his letters from Banda Neira, Sjahrir described Tjipto's views as *westers-synthetisch*, "Western-synthetic."[169] He referred to Tjipto as the "combative character" or the "spirited fellow,"[170] writing that he liked the old man's unorthodoxy and openmindedness in matters of religion.[171] With special satisfaction, Sjahrir commented upon how Tjipto, "in contrast to Hatta and Iwa," handled the two "spineless" Javanese civil servants in Banda Neira: "always as officials ... so that they always felt awkward with him."[172]

Sjahrir called Tjipto "*Oom*," Dutch for "Uncle." He helped Tjipto "spiritually"—so the old man's relatives strongly believed—because, as they say, Sjahrir was the man in Banda Neira most "congenial" to Tjipto.[173] While he was distancing himself from the other Indonesian intellectuals, fellow exiles, and fellow politicians, Sjahrir frequently came to Tjipto's house. He "moved around the house and he was cheerful and optimistic all the time."[174] Sjahrir borrowed books regularly from Tjipto. Hatta says (and one senses wonder rather than irony here) that the books were mostly *edaran buku* or *trommels*, serialized, cheap, mostly fortnightly published stories of adventure, mystery, and romance.[175]

The Bandanese (Sjahrir liked to use this generic term), the native people of the place, charmed Sjahrir not unlike the sea, the moon, and the flowers. "When compared with the Javanese," Sjahrir wrote about the Bandanese, "they still have a great deal of leeway to make up."[176] They were *achteruitgegaan*, "behind the time;"[177] "man, here, is still decades behind Java and Sumatra."[178] And yet:

---

[165] Van Niel, *The Emergence of the Modern Indonesian Elite*, p. 60.

[166] The Representative of the Cabinet in *Volksraad* to Governor-General, January 6, 1939 in *Secret Mail Report* 1939, no. 31.

[167] Soejitno Mangoenkoesoemo, "Brief van een Indonesiër," p. 501.

[168] Ibid.

[169] *IO* February 21, 1936. Not "thoroughly Westernized" as it is in the translation of Sutan Sjahrir, *Out of Exile*, p. 83.

[170] *IO* February 21, 1936.

[171] Ibid., September 9, 1936.

[172] Ibid., June 1, 1936.

[173] Soejitno Mangoenkoesoemo, "Brief van een Indonesiër," p. 491.

[174] Ibid., and Balfas, *Dr.Tjipto*, p. 126; see also Koch, *Batig Slot*, p. 150.

[175] Hatta, *Memoir*, p. 372.

[176] *IO* March 28, 1937.

[177] Ibid., May 21, 1936.

[178] Ibid., November 2, 1937.

As much as Banda is in arrears, the fact is that the people here have generally a better life than those on Java. The *kampong* [village] inhabitants are here also much more muscular; there are true giants among them, and their women look comely and healthy. People here do not appear to feel so many worries as elsewhere, and they like to be joyful together.[179]

The Bandanese, as Sjahrir described them, were people with a "flower cult" and, also, with a kind of moon cult. "Moon festivals," Sjahrir wrote, were celebrated regularly.[180] And Sjahrir seemed to be eager to identify himself with the cults. He had his "little flower garden," as we have seen, there were orchids on his table as he wrote, and he could read by the moon's light.

The truly original population of Banda Neira, in fact, had been virtually extinguished, during the seventeenth and the eighteenth centuries, as a consequence of brutal policies to enforce the Dutch spice monopoly in the Eastern Archipelago. Afterwards, European planters, Arab and Chinese merchants, immigrants, mostly from Java, and other Indonesian groups from the islands in the north, had populated the place. Banda Neira had an appealing history. Iwa, for instance, included in his exile memoirs from the island passionate lines about the truly original Bandanese, defending their freedom in the distant past, and about the bloody suppression of their struggle.[181]

Sjahrir mentioned this merely in passing.[182] His interest in the Bandanese clearly had a very different focus. What concerned Sjahrir, and what evidently impressed him deeply, was the migrant tradition of the people and the place, or perhaps (one gets a feeling) the looseness of this migrant tradition, the spirit of moving fast, not getting stuck to any definite time and place.

In an early letter from Banda Neira, Sjahrir explained that "Javanese and Boetonese [from Buton, an island south of Sulawesi]" made up the largest part of the local *kampong*, village, population. He quickly passed over this general ethnographical exposé, however, and shifted to what he clearly saw as truly interesting and exemplary:

> It is noteworthy that the Boetonese are coming here in search of a better existence. They land in their own little sailboats, nutshells not even ten meters long, and thus they cross the seass. They remain for a year or more, and then leave again for Boeton with their savings, if they have managed to save anything.
>
> They work here as day laborers. Home-helps, dock-hands, who do the toughest jobs, these are here almost wholly the Boetonese. They are, so to speak, Malays, but even the Malay race is represented by them at its best. They are physically more robust than the Javanese or Sumatrans, and better looking, although often a bit simple minded and less well mannered.[183]

---

[179] Ibid., May 21, 1936.

[180] Ibid., July 25, 1936.

[181] Iwa Kusumasumantri, "Autobiography," p. 73.

[182] For instance, *IO* February 19, 1936.

[183] Ibid., February 19, 1936.

Sjahrir was so intrigued by the remarkable people that he came back to them soon in another long passage. Again, he started with a short general note about the peasants in Banda Neira and then moved quickly, from the sedentary folk to the wanderers:

> One does not hear of misfortunes at sea; they have to be truly good seafarers! . . . They seize in Banda upon anything, be it a job for twenty cents a day, and still they do well and save.[184]

Sjahrir saw the Boetonese voyages as a daring, but, at the same time, calculated, act—sober and rational. This was an all-male, or rather an all-boy, adventure: "all the Boetonese young men here," Sjahrir wrote, "are celibate." However, "most of the money earned is designed to go to families." The whole risky business, in fact, appeared to be performed by the young men to become worthy of marriage.[185]

Iwa Koesoemasoemantri also noticed a kind of migration in Banda Neira, writing in his exile memoirs:

> At present, the situation in Banda Neira is already very saddening. Because the production of the island has declined so much, nobody cares about Banda now, and Banda is becoming a place deserted by its people. As I see it, there is an air around of a dead town. Commerce and trade are finished because too many young people have left for Ambon and Java, in search of a livelihood.
>
> Because business has stopped, and because there is nothing to give to the young generation, the number of youth in Banda Neira who have an education, but no job has become too large. As a consequence, there has been a decline in schools—instead of a Dutch school, as in 1930, we have only a Dutch-native school now.[186]

Sjahrir's description of the same situation, of course, was almost exactly the opposite, in facts and especially in style and spirit:

> There is a surplus of women. Young men are not much to be seen, but, on the other hand, there is a lot of children. Apparently men here are very potent: I know a family with twenty-three children from the same mother.[187]

> Most of our youths now swarm away, overseas. They still frequently come back, with their new experiences and new view of the world, and they also bring new ideas to the people to whom they return. They marry, if they become well-off enough, and take their wives overseas. Thus, the contacts of these islands with the world outside are multiplied, and Banda is also made more quick and intense in its response to what is happening outside.[188]

---

[184] Ibid., October 14, 1936.

[185] Ibid.

[186] Iwa Kusumasumantri, "Autobiography," pp. 73–74. On the migration from Banda as a depressing sign of the island economy, see also, for instance, Hanna, *Kepulauan Banda*, p. 161.

[187] *IO* July 25, 1936.

[188] Ibid., November 2, 1937.

If Sjahrir expressed some worries about migration, these were worries that the movement might slacken.[189]

"The Arab element here is also remarkable," Sjahrir wrote, soon after he arrived in Banda Neira.

> The Arab people have become Bandanese, but some of them still understand Arabic. They even still frequently walk around with a red fez on their heads.[190]

Sjahrir wrote that he was often invited to local weddings, which were performed in a carefully Islamic way, with "all sorts of Arab songs sung," "Arab drums beaten," the Koran recited, "etc." which

> used to be quite a regular event on Sumatra's East Coast in the past, [and which] I remember quite well from the years of my childhood."[191]

Before he broke with Iwa over many matters, Sjahrir regularly attended evening recitations given in Iwa's house by a local highly respected Islamic scholar, one Sjech Abdullah bin Abdurrachman Bahalwan.[192] Sometimes Sjech Bahalwan recited news from the Arab world, at other time stories from "The Thousand and One Nights." Sjahrir wrote to Maria that Sjech Bahalwan was boring, and that he preferred reading Gustav Meyer's biography of Engels, for instance.[193] According to Hatta, however, Sjahrir, in fact, was quite impressed and had even confided to Hatta, after one evening, that, listening to Bahalwan, he felt "as if Hadji Agoes Salim were talking to him again."[194]

Sjahrir saw one difference between himself and Hatta, namely in Hatta's being "a modern version of a self-righteous Islamite."[195] As before, Sjahrir challenged what he called a fanatical and conservative Islam, or the Islam "of the past."[196] If, however, Sjahrir's coolness to Islam had been qualified, hesitant, and curiously ambiguous before, as we have seen from his letter from Boven Digul for instance, it now became even more so.

In quite a number of his letters from Banda Neira, Sjahrir wrote about a family of local *sayids*. *Sayids*, the direct descendants of Prophet Mohammad, he explained, were "usually the most conservative group among Arabs." They "caged" their daughters at home between puberty and marriage, forced their women to wear a veil, and subjected them to numerous other mediaeval restrictions. "It is peculiar," Sjahrir continued, "that, in this regard, the Arabs in Banda Neira are more broadminded than the Indonesians."[197] The girls of the *sayid* family in Banda Neira were

---

[189] Ibid., July 25, 1936.
[190] Ibid., February 19, 1936.
[191] Ibid., October 9, 1936 and June 10, 1937.
[192] Iwa Kusumasumantri, "Sedjarah Revolusi," I: 65, n. 1.
[193] *IO* May 31, 1936.
[194] Hatta, *Memoir*, p. 369.
[195] *IO* September 9, 1936.
[196] Sjahrir in *Poedjangga Baroe*, June 1939, p. 95.
[197] *IO* March 24, 1937.

neither caged nor veiled. They were even permitted to take lessons outside their homes—"something," Sjahrir added, "which would be unthinkable among the Arabs on Java."[198]

In Banda Neira, as far as we know for the first time in his adult life, Sjahrir wrote about himself explicitly as a Moslem:

> [Iwa, Hatta] and I used to walk in public wearing trousers and either bareheaded or in hats, in spite of the fact that *sarong* and *koepia*, "head-cloth," is, here, a kind of requisite dress for Islamites. People do regard us as co-believers, although we go around clothed as *kafir* all the time, even at prayers.... We have not yet had an unpleasant encounter. If we behaved like that in Atjeh, or even in Banten, our lives would be in danger! ... also in Minangkabau, for instance, fifteen years ago, people were manhandled for such an offense, or they were at least boycotted.[199]

The same theme recurred in another of Sjahrir's letters a few months later, with a growing intensity and with some added meaning:

> [Hatta] and I began to appear bareheaded at all Moslem festive occasions, [even] when there were prayers.... First, the people looked very strangely at us, but they did not protest. And, after the religious teachers explained that a head cloth was not considered an essential part of Islamic worship, however new this was to them, they accepted it as an enlargement of wisdom.[200]

The significance of the form of dress during the Moslem prayers, in fact, used to be a crucially important and highly charged theme of Islamic modernism, and namely Minangkabau culture, through the early twentieth century.[201] The formulations Sjahrir used, "enlargement of wisdom," indeed, was as if taken verbatim from that period. Maybe, in the case of Banda Neira Moslems as well as in the case of the wonderful Butonese travelers (were they not "ideal" *perantau*?)—and not unlike when he came to Holland in 1929—"nothing much was strange" to Sjahrir in Banda Neira, his life on the island was "a continuous remembering."[202]

Arabs in Banda, Sjahrir wrote, did not form an exclusive enclave in the island community:

> This is what you truly would find nowhere else in Indonesia. The Arabs in this place do all kinds of jobs. They are not merely in the traditional money-lending and landowning; but in all kinds of professions, working even as

---

[198] Ibid.

[199] Ibid., October 9, 1936.

[200] Ibid., June 10, 1937.

[201] Hatta, for instance, related in his memoirs a well-known story of a famous Minangkabau Islamic leader of the early twentieth century who "showed off his modernist belief by wearing a tie when teaching religion." Hatta, *Indonesian Patriot*, p. 32.

[202] See note 1 of chapter III.

craftsmen like cobblers and tailors, or making a living by repairing bicycles.[203]

Most remarkable, to Sjahrir, was the openness of the Bandanese Moslems to the Bandanese Christians. The Bandanese Christians, Sjahrir wrote, were invited to Moslem weddings and other Islamic festivities.[204] More than that: Christian style and culture were accepted by Moslems to an extent unthinkable, again, anywhere else in the Indies.

This is one of the Moslem weddings in Banda Neira as Sjahrir described it:

> A pair of goats were slaughtered, rice, and, naturally, all sorts of sweets and tea and coffee were served. The feast was also adorned by music, the "brass orchestra" and a jazz-band... both made up of Indonesians from the *kampong*: a local fisherman, a carpenter, a laundry man, and a fish merchant. None of them can read music, but all play the latest hits. These they hear on the gramophone and recently also from the radio.
>
> The bridegroom wore Arabic clothes, but the little bride was in a European dress. They were being congratulated also in a European way.[205]

This Islam, to Sjahrir, was clearly part of a bridge. It was never suggested, in Sjahrir's impressions of Bandanese Islam, that Islam's openness might imply a breaking of Islamic principles—a loosening of an anchor. To Sjahrir, Bandanese Islam was a strict Islam. It was to him a belief genuine and indigenous to the Indies. Bandanese "Arabic customs," Sjahrir wrote, were "typically Malay customs."[206] Bandanese Islam, as Sjahrir saw it, even made Banda Neira into one of the few places in the Indies where "there is still something which has a character, and which is not fully European."[207] Again, we wonder if Bandanese Islam—as the Butonese *perantau*—was not for Sjahrir, first of all, a memory.

To Sjahrir the Europeans in Banda Neira were "so-called Europeans."[208] The situation on the plantations there, he wrote, had worsened in recent years, as a consequence of the world economic depression:

> Yet, the *perkeniers* [planters] here are no sweaters.... Also, the rich are not wholly unlikable people on this island. There are no more true tycoons, here, but quite a few wealthy families, capable of producing a couple of tons and making a monthly profit of four or five hundred guilders for their private use. Also, they live in a simple way, they do not throw their money around, and they do not carry on as a money aristocracy. They have the Bandanese tolerance and friendliness.[209]

---

[203] *IO* February 19, 1936.
[204] Ibid., October 9, 1936.
[205] Ibid., June 10, 1937.
[206] Ibid., October 9, 1936.
[207] Ibid.
[208] Ibid., March 24, 1937.
[209] Ibid., October 14, 1936.

"We had a couple of full-blood Europeans here," Sjahrir wrote in October 1936, "they stand a bit alien to the whole world of the island. But they were not so alien to me, and, after a while, they began to comprehend the *kampong* people here as well. This proves that there are, after all, some meeting points, and apparently more of them here than if one lived somewhere in Central Java, let's say, or in Sibolga among the Bataks, or among the Atjehnese."[210]

Sjahrir, when he came to Banda Neira, lived in the "so-called *kampong blanda*," "dutch village," kind of "European quarter of the town." Among his neighbors, however, as he wrote, there were "almost no *pur sang* Europeans."[211] The inhabitants of the "dutch village" carried names which suggested that they were "descendants of old *perkeniers* or other Dutchmen." "As I can see it," Sjahrir wrote, they were "quiet, genial, and simple people." And they spoke an "uncertain Dutch."[212]

Was there not again a strong quality of "a continuous remembering" in how Sjahrir wanted to see his Bandanese Europeans?

> Thus, you have, for instance, a generally accepted custom here to make visits between two and four o'clock in the afternoon. Everywhere else in the tropics everybody sleeps at that time, if he is not at his workshop and office. Also, whenever they meet a neighbor on the street, they greet him with *"dag"* [Dutch for "hullo"]. In the [native] *kampong*, too, a large number of Dutch words are used, and it is done naturally, without the people even being aware of it.[213]

"Instead of *'roti'* [Malay for "bread"], Sjahrir wrote, here they say *'brôt'* ["brood" is Dutch for "bread"]."[214]

> There is a powerful trend among the people here towards exchange and towards blending things together.... A deep-reaching process of assimilation took place here. Also the Banda Europeans prefer to speak Bandanese, which is Malay, even when they are among themselves, and they live according to customs which are as much old-Dutch as they are Arabic and, after all, predominantly Indonesian.[215]

How far was this image from those of the melting pots of new Indonesian culture, cradles of modern Indonesian man? How much did the memory of Medan during Sjahrir's childhood—one of the most typical of such melting plots and cradles, as we have seen—shape the image? How much did the older "ethical" notion play a role? Where was the place here for Indonesian nationalists—of the Sukarno sort, of the Pendidikan sort?

> Arabs, Europeans, Indonesians, and Chinese here are fairly often related one to the other, because there has been so much mixing of blood among them.

---

[210] Ibid., October 9, 1936.

[211] Ibid., February 26, 1936.

[212] Ibid.

[213] Ibid., May 21, 1936.

[214] Ibid., February 19, 1936.

[215] Ibid., October 9, 1936 and May 21, 1936.

And so you can see it: a consequence of cross-breeding. There is a child here, for instance, whose mother is a daughter of a Chinese and of a Swiss, and whose father is the son of a Menadonese and of a Eurasian, who, again, had her own history of blending in which, in all probability, besides other ancestors, something Arabic might have been found.

This is one of the reasons why the people here are still, in general, fairly tolerant, *except for those of our pure nationalists of the Iwa sort*.[216]

How did the the advance of time mold the image? Apart from the fact that the language in Banda Neira was so filled with Dutch words, Sjahrir wrote,

Malay, here, is pronounced with a good deal of pitch variation, sometimes it sounds almost like the Malay of the Mandailing.[217]

Strange indeed! Out of the dozen possible dialects with which he might have compared it, Sjahrir thought Bandanese was "almost like" Mandailing—the language of the Natal region of West Sumatra, of which in this story we know little except that the woman with the accordion, *Siti* Rabiah, Sjahrir's mother was born there. Bandanese, the language of the island where—as he saw it—races mixed beyond recognition and translation of languages and cultures was a constant norm of life, sounded to Sjahrir "almost like" his mother's tongue.[218]

4. Juffrouw Cressa, Oom Bing, and the Bandanese Children

After living five months in Banda Neira, Sjahrir wrote to Maria, that, besides Tjipto Mangoenkoesoemo, "the spirited fellow," and a few children he had befriended in town (we will talk about them soon), an old Dutch lady, *juffrouw* (miss) Cresa, had become the most notable "diversion [*afleiding*]" that he found on the island.[219]

Miss Malia Mulder, the "*juffrouw* Cresa" of Sjahrir's letters, lived in the "dutch village" in Banda Neira on her pension. She was confined to her chair by an unidentified "nerve illness."[220] Sjahrir wrote that he visited *juffrouw* Cresa "regularly," to listen to music on her gramophone, to read to her (the Bible and a book by his Dutch friend, poet and socialist Jef Last, for example) or just to talk.[221]

As Sjahrir described it, there clearly was nothing about politics in their discourse. Rather, we feel, a son might be talking to his mother. The world outside was largely incomprehensible to the old lady, and as they spoke it might have lost some of its sharpness even for the young man. Their talks, one may perhaps say, hovered above an otherwise rough landscape.

---

[216] Ibid., May 21, 1936, emphasis mine.

[217] Ibid., February 19, 1936.

[218] Des Alwi says he remembers that Sjahrir talked to children most of the time in Bandanese; Hatta, says Des Alwi, practically never talked in Bandanese, using either plain Malay or plain Dutch. Interview with Des Alwi, Jakarta, December 3, 1987.

[219] *IO* July 23, 1936.

[220] Interview with Lily Sutantio, Jakarta, April 2, 1982.

[221] *IO* March 22, 1937 and September 9, 1936; interview with Lily Sutantio, Jakarta, April 2, 1982; see also Lily Gamar Sutantio, dan saudara-saudaranja, "Kenang-kenangan akan jasa-jasa baik Oom Sjahrir, pencinta dan sahabat anak-anak," in *Mengenang Sjahrir*, ed.Anwar, p. 43.

Sjahrir was aware, he wrote, that discussing with *juffrouw* Cresa the "relativity of religions," for instance, might "shake the last fragile pillar on which her soul reposes."[222] Yet, it appears that religion in fact was the main topic of their conversation. Sjahrir's attitude towards religion, indeed, impressed the old Dutch lady immensely and seems to make for many of the bonds between her and the young man.

As if specifics—and actuality—did not matter, Sjahrir read to the old lady from modern and often ultra-modern novels and political pamphlets—from Jef Last's book, for instance. Sjahrir was clearly aware that *juffrouw* Cresa might follow him only in a very peculiar way:

> I do not believe there was much in [what I read] which she comprehended. This is a world of ideas which is distant to her. She perceives matters in her own way, and her understanding of everything is determined by her remoteness. She is ill and chained to her chair, and a long time ago, she stopped reading even newspapers. Even before this, probably, she had never read anything except Banda news and the ladies' pages. She does not know the name of a single leading politician in Europe, not even a Dutch one.[223]

Quite important things, however, and bizarre, too, were happening to Sjahrir exactly in this world-forgetting house of *juffrouw* Cresa. There, he met the local Dutch Calvinist curate, talked to him, again mainly about religion, and the curate seemed—not unlike *juffrouw* Cresa—immensely impressed by the ideas he possibly could not understand. He took Sjahrir for a Christian. Such a good Christian, indeed—so he one day told *juffrouw* Cresa who happily communicated it to Sjahrir—that if the curate ever left Banda Neira, as he planned to do, Sjahrir "could easily take over his place."[224]

It was most probably also at *juffrouw* Cresa's that Sjahrir met Bing Versteeg—*Oom* or "Uncle" Bing, as he was known in Banda Neira—a Dutchman, or perhaps a Eurasian—it did not seem to matter—who was another character in the "dutch village." *Oom* Bing, like *juffrouw* Cresa, was a pensioner, a veteran of the Koninklijke Nederlandsch Indisch Leger Royal Netherlands Indies Army (KNIL). He was often around *juffrouw* Cresa's house; he brought her pension and did various errands for her and others.[225]

It was *Oom* Bing who passed the word around that legal help was available for the Bandanese in cases "involving land, property, trade, debts, etc." Sjahrir, "with his law studies unfinished . . . but with a good enough knowledge of law," was the man supposed to do the job.[226] In contrast to the possible profession of curate, this was slightly more on the real than on the bizarre side. A son of a Medan *hoofddjaksa*, an outcast of the colonial regime, upon the initiative of a colonial army veteran became

---

[222] *IO* September 9, 1936.

[223] Ibid., March 22, 1937.

[224] Ibid., September 9, 1936. Sjahrir described the Dutch curate as "fanatical." But still, he went on meeting him regularly. He explained it in one letter to Maria by the fact that the curate always brought with him his young wife: "a fair Dutch little thing." She reminded Sjahrir of something of the best and most beautiful of what he learned to know in Holland, the freshness, the deliciousness, the fragrance. Ibid.

[225] Sutantio, "Kenang-kenangan," p. 43.

[226] Ibid. Interview with Lily Sutantio, Jakarta, April 2, 1982.

a *pokrol bambu*, "bush attorney," in the "dutch village" of Banda Neira and, perhaps, beyond.[227]

Hatta remembers that during the very first days after they arrived from Boven Digul Sjahrir began to meet Bandanese children.[228] While visiting friends and neighbors or while sitting on the porch of his and Hatta's house, which happened to be close to the local school, he might ask the children, "Do you want to play?" and, sooner or later: "do you want to learn?"[229]

This way, Sjahrir came to know first Tjipto's two foster sons, Louis and Donald, and then quite a number of the local Bandanese kids. The number varied, also, depending upon how much the parents dared to let their children come close to *orang bémbang*, the "exile."[230]

The core of the group consisted of two boys, Does and Des, Des' sister Lily, and their cousin Mimi, all of them between the ages of six and ten and all grandchildren of Baadilla, a man who was a true legend of Banda Neira. Baadilla used to be a rich merchant, but now he was quite poor. He had been a *kaptein Arab*, a Dutch appointed chief of the Arab community in Banda Neira. At the same time, Baadilla was a *Sayid*, and, as Sjahrir did not neglect to note, "honored on Banda, and Arab nobility."[231]

Early in the century, so Banda Neira lore had it, Baadilla presented several Bandanese pearls to the Dutch Queen, and the pearls had been placed in Wilhelmina's Royal Crown; Baadilla was also (like Sjahrir's father) a holder of the Star of the Knight of the Oranje Nassau Order. Just at the time Sjahrir was in Banda Neira, the family was applying to be *gelijkgesteld*, "made alike"—put legally on the same level with Europeans.[232] As Sjahrir saw it, the Baadilla family was *vooruitstrevend*, "progressive."[233] Sjahrir was, clearly, impressed. The girls, he wrote, were "getting a European education, and they even know how to dance in the European way." Imagine, Sjahrir wrote to Maria, "dancing Arab girls!"[234]

---

[227] Ibid. Sjahrir seemed to do the job with a real devotion, and, reportedly, his services years after he had left Banda Neira, were still warmly remembered. Sutantio, "Kenang-kenangan," p. 43. A recent description of the function of a *pokrol bambu* on a Javanese plantation makes it clear how the position was similar, in a different niveau and on a different level, to that of a *djaksa*: "*pokrol bambu* [was] an informal mediator between peasants on the one hand and the local authorities and the plantation on the other. . . . To invoke state authority in peasant protest, someone was always needed not only by peasants but by the authorities, because someone had to play the role representing at once peasant private interest and their subordination to state authority. . . ." Takashi Shiraishi, "Islam and Communism: An Illumination of the People's Movement in Java, 1912–1926" (Ph.D. thesis, Cornell University, 1986), pp. 301–2, 652.

[228] Hatta, *Indonesian Patriot*, p. 191.

[229] Sutantio, "Kenang-kenangan," interview with Lily Sutantio, Jakarta, April 2, 1982.

[230] Ibid.

[231] *IO* March 24, 1937. Actually, the Baadilla family's ties to the Middle East were rather loose. Des Alwi says, as far as memory went, they were from the Moluccas. Interview with Des Alwi, Jakarta, December 3, 1987.

[232] Sutantio, "Kenang-kenangan," p. 41. Des Alwi says that Baadilla was not "*gelijkgesteeld*" but that, because he had been awarded the Oranje Order medal, he had the right to send his offspring to a Dutch school. Interview with Des Alwi, Jakarta, December 3, 1987. Des Alwi also stated that, at the time Sjahrir and Hatta were there, the Baadilla family were quite poor, and that the exiles helped, for instance, to pay for the children's schooling.

[233] *IO* March 24, 1937.

[234] Ibid.

Baadilla's family wanted to provide the children with a good education in Banda Neira first before sending them to a Dutch school outside the island. The exiles were a god-sent chance. The children began to visit Sjahrir's and Hatta's house regularly, in the afternoon, after their classes at the local school.

As the story goes, a vase of flowers was once overturned on Hatta's desk during one of the children's "sessions" with Sjahrir. Some books got wet. Hatta, who was studying in the other room, became angry, and Sjahrir decided that this had gone too far. According to the children as well as to Hatta, this was the real reason why Sjahrir left Hatta's house and moved to a garden pavilion in the Baadilla compound. Said Hatta: "Sjahrir's relations with the Baadilla family got stronger as time passed, they truly were one family."[235]

Much later, in 1966, in his funeral speech over Sjahrir's grave, Hatta recalled, how vastly important to Sjahrir the Baadilla children had been. The children had helped Sjahrir adjust to the new place, Hatta said; they had made him "cheerful again," after an uneasy change from Boven Digul: they had not let him "feel alone," they had been "a remedy for his wounded heart."[236]

According to Sjahrir's Dutch friend, Sal Tas, Sjahrir was "not unhappy" in Banda Neira because

> He could devote himself there to two passions in which he had only begun to indulge in the last years of our acquaintance—playing with children and teaching.[237]

Sal Tas remembered, how, already in the early 1930s, when they were together in Holland, he was "struck" by the way in which Sjahrir could play with children:

> It could not be called relaxation; it was a passion, an act of release. It was as if he, playing with children, vanished in a world without tensions, quarrels and problems.
>
> This revealed to me a new side of Sjahrir, and the few reports that I got from Banda lent strength to that impression. At the bottom of his heart, Sjahrir did not love politics. He engaged in it from a feeling of duty but not from interest. He was not fascinated by that remarkable, turbulent, passionate phenomenon—sometimes noble, often dirty, but utterly human—which we call politics. He had no feeling of vocation. In his youth that was not noticeable; politics and science were discovered by him simultaneously and for a long time went together, and everything was done with the same boyish vitality which was its own reward. But later, when the stakes, the seriousness, and thus the worries began to increase, when his vitality had been sapped by introspection, his internal resistance increased and with it his nostalgia for a child's world. It is dangerous to engage in politics solely from a feeling of duty: no trade can be carried on well without enthusiasm, and the "trade" of politics did not have Sjahrir's.[238]

---

[235] Hatta, *Memoir*, pp. 373–74; also Sutantio, "Kenang-kenangan," pp. 42–43.
[236] The speech is published, for instance, in Leon Salim, ed., *Bung Sjahrir*, pp. 43, 64.
[237] Tas, "Souvenirs of Sjahrir," p. 148.
[238] Ibid.

Sjahrir
(Photo courtesy of Mrs. Maria Duchâteau-Sjahrir)

While they lived in Banda Neira, Sjahrir and Hatta, one source says, helped to unite three separate local soccer clubs—the Club Prins Hendrik, "Club of Prince Hendrik," the Club Koningin Wilhelmina, "Club of Queen Wilhelmina," and the Club Belgica, (Belgica was the old Dutch fortress above the bay)—into one Club Neira.[239] Sjahrir and Hatta also helped organize—and Sjahrir wrote the statutes for—the Persatoean Banda Moeda, or Perbamoe, "Union of Banda Youth," a

> social and educational organization concerned with sports, book-lending, cooperation and help in case of burials, etc.[240]

The two exiles gave books to the youth organization, and they helped it to rent a house, "where youth, coming from outside of Banda, might spend a night." They

---

[239] Sutantio, "Kenang-kenangan," p. 43.
[240] Ibid.

also initiated a plan by the youth organization to establish its own private school; this plan was never realized.[241]

Censorship may be only a partial explanation for the fact that, as far as we know, Sjahrir never mentioned any of this. Whenever, in his letters or other writing from Banda Neira, he touched upon his activities among the Banda Neira youth, it was always about him being with "the children."

Tjipto, the fellow exile with whom Sjahrir became so close, called him the "king of children," saying that when Sjahrir was with the children "he himself became a child again."[242] Hatta, similarly, in an interview in 1980, said that Sjahrir in Banda Neira had seemed to him sometimes "like a naughty boy."[243]

As we have already noticed, Sjahrir wrote to Maria in July 1936 that, besides Tjipto and *juffrouw* Cresa, the children were his only diversion. "The longer I am here," he added about the children, "the more I am about to restrict myself to their company."[244] "They are, here, the best friends I have," Sjahrir wrote after another half year.[245]

Both Hatta and Sjahrir devoted much of their time in Banda Neira to teaching. They prepared correspondence courses for their friends left in Tanah Merah;[246] they taught Tjipto's two foster sons; after some time, three Minangkabau, sent by a friend of Hatta, came from Sumatra, and the two exiles taught them, too. All of this teaching was advanced, well above the MULO, advanced elementary school standard, up to the AMS or the HBS, high school and sometimes even the college level. Hatta taught especially economics and accounting; Sjahrir mainly English, mathematics, and history.[247] Yet, Sjahrir's focus seemed constantly to drift elsewhere: in a letter from Banda Neira, early in 1937, he mentioned Hatta teaching *mensen*, "people," while he himself was teaching *kinderen*, "children."[248]

Sjahrir wrote extensively only about "his" children's—Des' and Does', Lily's and Mimi's—education. He wrote proudly, in February 1937, that he had started "from ABC" and that, after one and a half years of work, his children had advanced as far "as pupils of the fourth grade of elementary school."[249] Besides trivia, Sjarir taught "manners": "They were, at first, rather uncivilized," he wrote to Maria, "but slowly they are improving."[250] "Since I became attracted to them," Sjahrir wrote after another half year, "their little lives have changed. They look now more and more neat and bright."[251]

---

[241] Ibid.

[242] Taufik Abdullah, "Ataukah dialog antara gambaran dan kesan?" in *Muhammad Hatta*, ed. Swasono, p. 542.

[243] Ibid.

[244] *IO* July 23, 1936.

[245] Ibid., February 25, 1937.

[246] Interviews with Burhanuddin and Murwoto, Jakarta, March 5, 1982 and Jakarta, December 6, 1987.

[247] Hatta, *Memoir*, pp. 371, 376, 380.

[248] *IO* February 25, 1937.

[249] Ibid.

[250] Ibid., July 23, 1936.

[251] Ibid., February 25, 1937.

Sjahrir gave the children to read the books he himself had read as a child in Medan—Dutch translations of adventure stories, animal stories, exotic stories, *Till Eulenspiegel, Don Quixote,* Baron von Munchaussen.[252] He wrote to Maria about the children regularly:

> It is with children, after all, that one may experience the purest and most abandoned pleasures.... I feel so fine, as I have not for such a long time.[253]

> The parents of the children are happy and grateful that I have taken pity on their children. If I told them that it is the other way around, that the children, rather, are taking pity on me, they certainly would look at me strangely. And yet, this is how things really are.[254]

Baadilla's grandchildren, and occasionally some other of their friends, visited Sjahrir each day after school. They often also spent weekends with Sjahrir. Afer a year or so, Sjahrir asked and got permission to adopt three of the children—Des, Lily, and Mimi. Soon afterwards, he adopted another Bandanese child, Ali, another cousin of Des and Lily, a boy who at that time was only eight months old![255]

Sjahrir rented a Singer sewing machine and now he worked truly hard to keep his children's clothes in shape. He even made fancy dresses for the girls; he subscribed to fashion journals. He cooked, and his Minangkabau dishes, I was told, were especially memorable. He taught the girls how to care for the baby. The children still called him *"Oom,"* the usual Dutch for "Uncle," but, as they say, Sjahrir became "closer" to them than their actual parents. He was to them, they also say, "both a father and a mother."[256]

Hatta also taught the Baadilla children, for instance, how to swim more stylishly. But, throughout, he remained for the children *Oom Katjamata,* "Uncle Eye-Glasses." Hatta's hectic fighting for the ball during soccer matches was highly popular in Banda Neira, and as he ran fervently his "soft white legs in tennis shoes" rarely failed to make the children, and everybody else, "roar with laughter."

The children remembered later, that Hatta stayed where the water was not too deep and the currents not rough. Sjahrir "with other young boys [*botjah-botjah*]" went, so the children believed, the whole way. Often, Sjahrir swam across the bay to the volcano on the other side, which was quite a feat, even by Bandanese standards:

> Whenever he was not writing letters or articles or reading scholarly books, he invited the children for a trip through the island or to climb Goenoeng Agoeng on the opposite side of the bay. Exiles were forbidden by the authorities to leave the island, but *Oom* [Sjahrir] defied the order, and he often took the children, in his sail boat [*perahu layarnja*] away to have a picnic on Pulau

---

[252] Des Alwi, "Oom kacamata," p. 324; interview with Des Alwi, Jakarta, December 3, 1987, and with Lily Sutantio, Jakarta, April 2, 1982.

[253] *IO* October 12, 1936.

[254] Ibid., October 19, 1936.

[255] Sutantio, "Kenang-kenangan," pp. 41–42; interview with Des Alwi, Jakarta, December 3, 1987, and with Lily Sutantio, Jakarta, April 2, 1982.

[256] Ibid.; see also Hatta, *Indonesian Patriot,* p. 191; Soewarsih Djojopoespito, "De thuiskomst van een oud-strijder," p. 45.

Pisang [Banana Island], or on Pulau Banda Besar, [Great Banda Island]. There, on deserted beaches, he taught us to sing Indonesia Raja [Great Indonesia] a song we sang with great force, because we felt free, and because nobody could hear us.[257]

Sjahrir's letter to Maria, sent in October 1936, told essentially the same story. They, indeed, were "almost like" the magnificent wanderers, the *perantau*, the Butonese—the children and Sjahrir when with them:

At half past four in the morning, I was already on my feet, and at half past five, we were on the sea. We ourselves worked the sails and the rudder. For three hours, we sailed very fast, as we had a favorable wind. We passed over the marine gardens and watched a marvellous sunrise. Later, we landed again, and on the beach we spent the rest of the day, and ate.[258]

In another letter, a week later: "Yesterday, on Sunday, we were, again, out: with twelve children, the whole day on the beach."[259]

Sometimes, Sjahrir wandered along the shore and on the sea without the children, and, on those occasaions it seemed, he got even further:

To the few people I visit now and then, belongs an old fisherman, who lives with his wife and two grandchildren in a little hut on the beach. When I am on the sea, or when I am passing by on my walks, I stop there occasionally. I may sit there quietly, and it is so pleasant to listen to the stories of those dear little old things about their lives at sea and about the islands and the islanders as they see them.[260]

From the old fisherman and his wife, Sjahrir learned about the chronicles of the islands, which were lodged, he was told, in Lonthor,[261] in "the royal center of these islands before Europeans came." The old books had been "kept and guarded, through all those centuries," in a "*kampong* [village or community?] house." The texts were considered holy, and they were "never handed out, [although] great sums of money might be gained if sold." They were recited during festivals, and their words were known to all the Bandanese.[262]

This may be as far as Sjahrir got in Banda Neira and in his journey so far. For "the simple people here," he wrote, "this is the history of their little islands." In these

---

[257] Des Alwi, "Oom kacamata," p. 324 and interview with Des Alwi, Jakarta, December 3, 1988. Sjahrir never mentioned the *Indonesia Raja* lessons as far as I know. There is an interesting comparison with Sukarno, who talked in his autobiography about his exile at the same time in Flores (this was written in 1965): "I taught a group of youngsters 'Indonesia Raja,' our National Anthem. Since this was prohibited, I took the extreme caution of teaching them in a place other than my home. Not that I had anything to lose, but I wanted to protect them. We went on a little picnic. Still somebody reported this grave crime." See Sukarno, *An Autobiography as Told to Cindy Adams*, p. 133.

[258] *IO* October 12, 1936.

[259] Ibid., October 19, 1936.

[260] Ibid., January 25, 1937.

[261] Great Banda is also called Lontor or Lonthor.

[262] *IO* January 25, 1937.

old books, "there is a strongly held confidence in *adat* [customs]." Only according to puritanical thought, can one dismiss these simple beliefs as "superstitions." "Also in this aspect," Sjahrir wrote in the passage about the old fisherman who could be his grandfather, "this island has something unreal about itself, something of a fairy tale."[263]

Years later, after Sjahrir returned to Java, and when he became the prime minister of the independent Indonesian state, a big painting hung on the main wall in the reception room of his private house. It was, I was told by Sjahrir's wife, a painting Sjahrir had asked his friend, a famous Indonesian avant-garde painter, Soedjojono, to do on Banda Neira. The painting—still there—is very dark, and the figures are not too distinct. But it is clear that there, in the center, are the old fisherman, and his wife, both sitting in front of their hut on the beach, and there is Sjahrir, listening.

5. The End of Exile?

As in Cipinang, and as in Tanah Merah, no limits were set on how long Sjahrir and Hatta might be kept in Banda Neira. The exile could last forever. On March 6, 1936, a month after they arrived, Sjahrir asked the local Dutch authorities to allow Maria and her children to join him in Banda Neira.[264] The request was denied, on the grounds that Maria was not Sjahrir's wife. Sjahrir, after this, married Maria by proxy, represented by his brother Sjahsam in a civil court in Haarlem on September 2, 1936.[265]

Fourteen days later, now legally husband and wife, they renewed their request to be reunited. Again, it was rejected, and the official notification reached Sjahrir late in 1937. Then, Maria wrote to the Dutch Queen Wilhelmina herself, asking her to permit Sjahrir to return to Holland in order to "finish his studies." Maria's request was again rejected. She made at least one more request late in 1939, this time again, to travel with her children to Banda Neira; she emphasized that she was willing to pay for the trip herself. There was no answer to this request.[266]

Some time in mid 1938, Alwi, a relative of Sjahrir close to the small circle of Sjahrir's devotees in Java around Soewarsih and Soewarni, translated into Dutch an article which Sjahrir had just published in *Poedjangga Baroe*. The young Indonesians gave the article to the circle's Dutch *guru*, Eddy du Perron. Du Perron was very much impressed, and he immediately arranged for the translation to be published in the Bandung journal of his Dutch friends and literary colleagues, *Kritiek en Opbouw*. In his own long rejoinder, published in two installments by the same journal in June

---

[263] Ibid. On the Lontor festivals and changing memories of the past in Banda see James Siegel and Tsuchiya Kenji, "Invincible Kitsch or As Tourists in the Age of Des Alwi, "*Indonesia* 50 (October 1990), pp. 61–76.

[264] Sjahrir to Resident of Moluccas, March 6, 1936 in *Secret Mail Report* 1937, no. 704. See also communications to the Minister of Colonies (Hague), June 1936 in *Secret Verbaal*, July 8, 1938-U22.

[265] Document no. 705 in *Secret Mail Report* 1937, no. 704; also other correspondence in the same *Mail Report* and *Secret Mail Report* 1937, no. 763.

[266] Minister of Colonies to Governor-General, July 9, 1937, Maria Duchâteau to J. E. Stokvis, Member of Parliament, June 15, 1938 in *Secret Verbaal*, July 8, 1938-U22; Office of the Minister of Colonies to Maria Duchateau, December 20, 1938; Attorney General to Governor-General, November 15, 1939, and Governor-General to Minister of Colonies, November 26, 1939 in *Secret Verbaal*, December 20, 1939-I55. Interview with Maria Duchâteau-Sjahrir, Lorque, February 13, 1988.

and July 1939, du Perron described Sjahrir's text as "in every respect remarkable."[267] Some correspondence ensued between du Perron in Bandung and Sjahrir in Banda Neira. Unfortunately, only a few pages of the exchange, one letter by du Perron to Sjahrir, have survived.[268]

Eddy du Perron, at the moment thirty-nine years old, was a very disturbed man. He reacted more sensitively, perhaps, than anybody else in the colony at the time to the growth of fascism. In contrast to most Indies intellectuals, Dutch or Indonesian—from the time before he came to the Indies in 1936 and when he was a part of the Paris and Amsterdam arts avant-garde—du Perron had some direct and certainly emotionally very charged experience with the European extreme right. Through his stay in the Indies, after 1936, misgivings of his European friends remained with him: it seemed to many that, instead of going so far away "to the East," he should have joined "the real fight" against fascism, namely in Spain.[269]

The growth of fascism affected du Perron in a particular way. It seemed to strengthen his inherent uncertainty, a feeling of being always in the wrong place, forever destined to be *een lastige vreemdeling*, "an annoying foreigner."[270]

Du Perron was unable to settle fully in the Indies and, in spite of all his fervent professions of "universal humanism" and his associations with the Soewarni and Soewarsih circle, he felt his white skin with a growing acuteness. In the only letter to Sjahrir which survived, du Perron wrote that even with his closest Indonesian friends he felt like Drona, the teacher of the Pandawa brothers in the Mahabharata epic: when it came to the final battle, Drona, respected by the Pandawas but belonging by ties of blood to the Kurawas, the Pandawas' worst enemies, was inevitably slain by his pupils.[271]

He felt like a traveler, du Perron also wrote to Sjahrir in the same letter, like "coming home [to the Indies, to his "land of origin"] only to find out that [his] house had been torn down a long time ago." Perhaps, he still might feel "at home" if he could wander back in time, "amidst Indies little boys," amidst the memories of his Indies first years, two or three decades in the past. Of course, du Perron added, such ideas were "irrational," and "pitiful is the intellectual who thinks like that."[272]

Du Perron became increasingly depressed in the Indies. Finally, just a few weeks before the European war started—on another leg of his continual search for where he belonged—he decided to leave for the West again. Someone Indonesian, he wrote

---

[267] E. du Perron, "Notities bij het artikel van Sjahrir," *Kritiek en Opbouw*, June 16, 1939, p. 138.

[268] I am grateful to Hans van Marle for helping me to search for the lost letters. Mr.van Marle went through du Perron's papers in the Letterkundig Museum in The Hague and he also contacted the du Perron family on the matter.

[269] See, for instance, Max Nord, "Du Perron's afscheid van Indonesië," *De Baanbreker*, December 8, 1945. E. du Perron, *Brieven* 7, 8 (Amsterdam: Van Oorschot, 1981, 1984).

[270] This feeling is most thoroughly articulated in du Perron's *Land of Origin (Het land van herkomst*. Amsterdam: Querido, 1935). Also see du Perron quoted in E. M. Beekman, "Dutch Colonial Literature: Romanticism in the Tropics," *Indonesia* 34 (October 1982): 36–37; du Perron to Sjahrir in *Kritiek en Opbouw*, August 16, 1939, p. 95; see also confrontation between du Perron and Zentgraff as commented upon by M. K. (M. Koch) in *Kritiek en Opbouw*, March 1, 1938, pp. 30–31; A. C. (J. H. F. A. de la Court), ibid., April 1, 1938, pp. 58–59. See also Locher Scholten, "Kritiek en Opbouw," p. 227; du Perron on Zentgraff in *Kritiek en Opbouw*, October 1, 1938, pp. 237–39 and du Perron in *Criterium*, 1947, p. 416.

[271] du Perron in *Criterium* 1947, p. 416.

[272] Ibid.

to Sjahrir in exile, someone for whom the Indies was a home beyond any doubt—not Drona—should take over du Perron's aborted mission; someone Indonesian like Sjahrir.[273]

Sjahrir, still, did not publish anything on politics. He, in fact, did not publish a single political article till the end of his exile in Banda Neira, except perhaps the review article on Meyers' biography of Friedrich Engels in Djohan Sjahroezah's journal (it was in part reprinted in 1936 in de Kadt's and Sal Tas' new Amsterdam journal, *De Nieuwe Kern*[274]).

It happened, it seems, as part of Maria's desperate efforts to reunite with Sjahrir that—without Sjahrir's prior knowledge, Maria says—she made a transcript of one of Sjahrir's private letters sent to her from Banda Neira, a summation of Sjahrir's political views at the time, and gave it to the Dutch Ministry of Colonies in The Hague.[275]

Sent from Banda Neira the letter was dated March 25, 1938. It was in particular a response to the growing threat of fascism both in Europe and in the East. Sjahrir elaborated at length, in the text, on what a correct political attitude to the fascist threat, namely in the Indies, might be.

"We are now helpless," Sjahrir wrote, as Japan was poised against the Indies, and Germany against Holland,

> we are more helpless than Holland itself would be without England. We need allies [*bondgenoten*]....
>
> The policy of non-cooperation [with the Dutch] is the purest expression of colonial nationalism.... I have always felt and known that non-cooperation might only be used in our movement as an effective tool of nationalist propaganda, but I could never build my philosophy on it....
>
> A framework [for cooperation] does already exist—that is Indonesia in its present political, economic, and social form....
>
> [What is needed now is], in the first place, a moral turnaround [*omwenteling*] among the Dutch, and, secondly, a change of mentality among the Indonesians -- their liberating themselves from their suspicions, fears, hatred, and inferiority complex.[276]

The aim of the new policy inspired by the threat of fascism, Sjahrir wrote in the letter, should be "an equal reponsibility on both sides, which is a moral as well as a political alikeness [*gelijkwaardigheid*]." Instead of, "You are still not mature enough," the Dutch should tell Indonesians, "Come on, men, let's do things together, show us your brains!" "In practice," Sjahrir wrote,

---

[273] Ibid. On du Perron's conflicts with the Indies Dutch community, see also A. Deprez, *E.du Perron, 1899–1940* (Brussels: Mantaan, 1960), pp. 191ff.

[274] van de Garde (Sjahrir), "Friedrich Engels"; Sjahrir reportedly was very angry about this article because de Kadt appeared to use the text, largely, to prove his own versatility. Furthermore, in a rejoinder, de Kadt portrayed Sjahrir as a rather pathetic defender of "outdated" Marxist doctrines. The affair led to a further cooling of relations between Sjahrir and his former friends in Holland. See also on the affair de Kadt, *Jaren die dubbel telden*, pp. 12–13; Tas, "Souvenirs of Sjahrir," p. 146.

[275] Maria Duchâteau to the Chief of the Office of the Minister of Colonies, April 12, 1939 in *Secret Verbaal*, December 20, 1939-I55; text of the letter is also in *Collection Gobée* no. 97.

[276] Ibid., compare *IO* March 25, 1938.

all the changes in mentality and in administration would have, as their consequence, a speeding up of the so-called ethical policy by which the Indonesian people—let us say for the time being, as many of them as possible, those who are literate and their representatives, the intelligentsia—would be trusted to participate in a responsible co-government [*medebestuur*], and in the responsible co-government's representative bodies.[277]

As far as we know, Dutch authorities gave no response to this letter.

Only sixteen months later, at the end of August 1939—a few days before the outbreak of war in Europe—did Sjahrir appear to be pushed into the political arena again. This time, of all people, it was his fellow exile from Banda Neira, the old irascible Tjipto Mangoenkoesoemo who made the move.

Tjipto himself, evidently, did not have an easy time in overcoming his disgust and involving himself in the hopeless colonial politics again and after so many years. Anyway, in summer 1939, he wrote down his views on the threat of fascism and on possible ways of facing it. He asked the other exiles in Banda Neira to do the same, and he offered to pass on all they wrote together to the authorities.[278]

Sjahrir's first reaction was that it might be "too late" and that the initiative very probably would again be wasted. But he responded, and promptly. In a letter given to Tjipto, and dated August 23, 1939, Sjahrir referred to his letter of March 1938 and wrote further:

> At the moment when the war breaks out in the Pacific, involving Holland and Indonesia, the movement of the population [*de bevolkingsbeweging*] has to cooperate, morally and actively, in the defense of this land.... Towards this aim, [the Dutch authorities] have to immediately transfer a portion of their responsibility to the people's movement [*volksbeweging*]. They must treat the people's movement as a friend and as an ally [*bondgenoot*].[279]

A proper place, Sjahrir wrote, had to be accorded to the Indonesian people in organizing a defense,

> because this is a defense of the Netherlands Indies state [*de Nederlandsindische staat*], which implies also [the state] of the Indonesian people.[280]

Besides, Sjahrir added, the exiled and interned leaders had to be

> given back to the movement, [as] an indication [of] the changed relationship between the government and the people's movement.[281]

Turning to the exiles, Sjahrir wrote in the same letter that they should not observe the war, when it broke out, as if it were some sporting event. Nor should they behave as, for instance, Rooseveltian "benevolent neutrals":

---

[277] Ibid.

[278] See Tjipto's letter explaining the whole action to the head of the local administration H. F. H. Walrabe, September 28, 1939 in *Secret Mail Report* 1939, no. 1215.

[279] Sjahrir to Tjipto, August 23, 1939, ibid.

[280] Ibid.

[281] Ibid.

rather, we should honestly hope that all will not again go awry in that old bureaucratic way, as it, indeed, has been going for over a century. If this time, our trust is not disappointed, we should welcome the new colonial policy with cheers, truly as an act of preservation [*redder*] for our national existence.[282]

Sjahrir took a further initiative after Tjipto started the whole thing. He wrote a letter to Iwa Koesoemasoemantri only a day after he had responded to Tjipto, and he prompted Iwa to join them in writing to the authorities. In this particular letter, Sjahrir—and he might see Iwa's face before him as he wrote—commented bitterly on what he saw as the current state of the Indonesian nationalist movement. Picking out two of the most visible tribunes of this movement at the time, Soetardjo Kartohadikoesoemo and M. Hoesni Thamrin, Sjahrir wrote:

Even the best speeches by Soetardjo and Thamrin can not impress me as anything but a guileless attempt at a sort of refined political blackmailing of the colonial government, using the threat of world war in the Pacific. [Soetardjo and Thamrin] do not believe their own words; they do not build on what the movement has achieved until now. The movement is still unfit.[283]

Tjipto added a note to the letters when ready, stating that "the gentlemen, if given freedom, shall make no abuse of it."[284] The whole file was given to the Dutch administrator in Banda Neira on September 18, 1939.[285] Then it traveled to Batavia, and it reached the high offices of the Governor-General and the Attorney General on October 14.[286] Again, as far as we know, the government did not answer the exiles at all.

In May 1940, German armies invaded Holland, and Queen Wilhelmina with her ministers left for London; now, she, too, was an exile.

There were some changes in the Indies. Amir Sjarifoeddin, a brilliant Batak lawyer, leader of the Indonesian radical nationalist and professedly anti-fascist Gerindo—an author, also, occasionally, of *Kritiek en Opbouw*—was given a responsible job at the colonial Department of Economic Affairs. Hadji Agoes Salim, the Islamic leader and occasionally before 1934, Hatta's and Sjahrir's ally—and also Sjahrir's cousin—began to work for a colonial government publishing firm. The first issue of a "progressive" journal for culture and politics, *Fakkel*, "Torch," appeared in Batavia in November 1940. The new journal was close to *Kritiek en Opbouw* and, according to some, even more open to the Indonesian side.

A few articles appeared in 1940 even in the usually conservative Dutch press, on the *lotsverbondenheid*, "bondage in destiny." Some Dutch officials now proposed that Malay (Indonesian) be extensively taught even in the Indies European schools; they even made a few broadcasts in Malay (Indonesian), appealing—in these difficult

---

[282] Ibid.

[283] Sjahrir to Iwa, August 24, 1939, ibid.

[284] Tjipto to the head of the local administration, Walrabe, September 18, 1939; ibid.

[285] It took so long, probably, because they waited for Iwa to join them. Iwa did not respond to Tjipto until September 14; his letter appears in ibid.

[286] These documents are also in ibid.

times—to "universal," "Islamic," and "knightly [satria]" values.[287] These were acts as flagrant as they were isolated. The appeals were made out of desperation, too late, and by individuals without the proper power. They ended in virtually all cases as blunders.

Escaping from Europe, a number of liberal and radical Dutch intellectuals came to the Indies in late 1939 and in 1940. Among them was Jacques de Kadt—one of Sjahrir's Dutch friends from the time Sjahrir was in Holland in the early 1930s, and later a leader, with Sal Tas, of the Dutch Independent Socialist Party. De Kadt wrote later that he had gotten some back issues of *Kritiek en Opbouw* from Eddy du Perron, who had just returned from the Indies; among them, de Kadt said, was the issue with Sjahrir's article. From Eddy du Perron, de Kadt might also have acquired some Bandung and Batavia addresses—of Soewarsih, Soewarni, and of the Sjahrir-devotees circle.[288]

The circle seemed to be suddenly revitalized.[289] Together with de Kadt, it was behind a campaign, early in 1941, for the release of the political exiles, and, on that occasion, the press mentioned Sjahrir several times.[290] Soewarsih Djojopoespito, in an article published by *Kritiek en Opbouw* in August 1941, demanded "freedom for Hatta, Soekarno, Sjahrir, and Iwa." The exiles' release, Soewarsih wrote—addressing "us" as the Indonesians and the Dutch facing fascism together—would be

> an act of reason, and, first of all, of chivalry, and [a proof] that some struggle instinct still remains in us, that we are willing to face the challenge, and that we would not be helpless, if struck by an unscrupulous enemy.[291]

Yet, the circle fitted the time. It was still no more than a few personal friendships and cultural affinities among a handful of Dutch and Indonesian intellectuals—virtually all of them exclusive and marginal, and, indeed, without any serious experience and even interest in the actual politics. In one of du Perron's self-depreciating puns, it still was a "circle of *K en O*," with the K and the O meaning as much *Kritiek en Opbouw*, "Criticism and Construction," as *Knudde en Onmacht*, "Flop and Impotence."[292]

Eventually, early in 1941, Tjipto and Iwa, with their families, were permitted to leave Banda Neira. For health reasons. Iwa went to Makassar, and Tjipto returned to

---

[287] Abeyasekere, *One Hand Clapping*, pp. 50ff.

[288] de Kadt, *Politieke Herinneringen van een randfiguur*, pp. 139, 196; interview with Beb Vuyk, Loenen, April 16, 1983.

[289] There might have been some other contacts, too. Soegondo might have been in some communication with Tjipto on Banda Neira—there is a report of the men editing a weekly *Pasar Saptu* together in Bogor in the mid-1930s. Anderson, *Java in a Time of Revolution*, p. 444. Soejitno also seems to have been in correspondence with his older brother in Banda Neira. Soegondo, besides, became a teacher at the "Ksatrian Institute," whose director was Douwes Dekker, an old Tjipto companion from the time of the Indische Partij. Ibid.

[290] In *Kritiek en Opbouw*, a demand for the release of interned leaders, namely "Soekarno, Hatta and Sjahrir," appeared in April 1941, and the release was demanded again early in September and on September 24, 1941. See also de Jong, *Het koninkrijk der Nederlanden in de tweede Wereldoorlog*, 11a, p. 611.

[291] Soewarsih Djojopoespito in *Kritiek en Opbouw*, August 2, 1941 quoted in J.H.W. Veenstra, *Diogenes in de Tropen* (Amsterdam: Vrij Nederland, 1947), p. 63.

[292] *Kritiek en Opbouw*, February 16, 1938. Also de Vries, *Culturele aspecten*, pp. 170–72.

Java.²⁹³ The Pendidikan's central executive in Java, about the same time, issued a "manifesto" proclaiming itself on the side of democracy, against fascism, and asked freedom for their exiled leaders.²⁹⁴ Again there was no response, and as far as we know, no information about the efforts in their behalf ever reached Hatta and Sjahrir.

On November 7, 1941, Sjahrir wrote a long letter from Banda Neira to one of his younger brothers, the boy who – till now unmentioned in this story—was in his mid teens and studied at a high school in Batavia.²⁹⁵ Sjahrir addressed his brother and through him his two friends of the same age—Aki and Heda, a son and a daughter of Sjahrir's sister Sjahrizal Djoehana. The letter to the relatives evidently was an answer to the young people's request for advice as to what to do in the disturbingly changing world.

Hardly ever had Sjahrir's feeling of exile appeared so intense as in this letter. "For the whole of the past year," Sjahrir wrote, "I stopped all my correspondence. . . . I did not answer a single letter. . . . I remained silent during this year."

> I feel fine in this place. In a sense, life here is perfect, which means healthy and natural in an exemplary way. . . . The actual state of affairs in Java holds an entirely meagre power of attraction over me. . . . It does me good—as I remain outside [*buiten*] any responsibility—that for so long I have been an exile and have stayed here in Banda. In a sense, I am thankful for this, because I am afraid that things may go wrong.²⁹⁶

He had "no regret"; it was good to be silent, because he understood things in greater depth.²⁹⁷

The letter was advice and confession at the same time. Nietzsche was present in the letter, more, perhaps, than he had ever previously been in Sjahrir's writing. "Nietzsche is culture," Sjahrir wrote to the teenagers, "Nietzsche is art, Nietzsche is a genius."²⁹⁸

The letter, in more than one way, was an invitation. The young people should come to see Sjahrir on the island. "I wish to have you here," Sjahrir wrote to his brother,

> then, I might make it even clearer to you. . . . It may be worthwhile for you to come here when school ends, best of all with Aki and Heda. Then we may talk things over again, and I shall see how I can help.²⁹⁹

As the war was approaching rapidly, Sjahrir gave some advice to the boys even before they might come. To continue their education "outside the colonial sphere" was "out of the question, naturally," Sjahrir wrote, and therefore,

---

²⁹³ Iwa Kusumasumantri, "Sedjarah Revolusi," 1: 65 n. 1.

²⁹⁴ *Overzicht v.d.IMC pers*, 1941, p. 919.

²⁹⁵ The school was Douwes Dekker's "Ksatrian Institute."

²⁹⁶ Sjahrir, "Brief aan een broer (Banda Neira, November 7, 1941) *Criterium* 8/9 (August/September 1947): 476–77.

²⁹⁷ Ibid.

²⁹⁸ Ibid., pp. 474–75.

²⁹⁹ Ibid., pp. 466–67.

I would think it a good idea if you enlisted in the militia and tried to become a reserve officer in the air force, for instance. If I had an opportunity, I too would like to fly. The navy also has a power of attraction for me.[300]

It is clear from Sjahrir's response that his young friends had mentioned the growing popularity of fascism and, in particular, of Hitler among the youth of Java. Sjahrir answered about Hitler:

I hate him with all the strength I am able to exert because I understand that he is the personification of all the forces which work against the advancement and the liberation of man.

I have *Mein Kampf*. The book glitters [*prijkt*] on my bookcase. He has kept himself conscious of everything from the dim past. He knew how, with his *Mein Kampf*, to mobilize and rationalize all the impulses and instincts of the beast in man because he himself possesses all this in the sharpest form. . . . I have been aware, for years, that the power of attraction Hitler has over the youth is so great because he, in a refined way, appeals to the instincts of rowdiness in adolescent little cocks [*djagos*] of boys, because he knows how to exploit, in the most perfect way, the sexual psychology of the pubertal man. He has supplied a theory for the liberation of the repressed sexual complexes of the pubertal man, for contempt for women, and for shyness—a power urge and a dream of power, instead of a feeling of sexual powerlessness, an immorality instead of the eternal doubt and the inward conflict between "can" and "cannot."[301]

"Indonesian youth," Sjahrir wrote,

who in their hearts hate the upright Dutch overlords, [and] who feel that honesty might only bring them closer to the police, look towards Hitler for a consolation of their contorted souls, as towards a remedy which might heal their powerlessness. . . .

In this way, our spiritually deformed youth can, in silence, secretly, after office-hours, and after classes, worship the cock [*djago*] Hitler, forget their own spiritual powerlessness, and gloat over the "dutch" [*blanda*] now being trapped by Hitler.[302]

As the war in the Pacific was about to break out, Banda Neira seemed to have remained one of the last places in the world where life still might have been moving at a healthy—and a healthier—pace. This, at least, is how Sjahrir later described his and Hatta's last months and days in Banda Neira:

---

[300] Ibid., p. 477. For a discussion of the indigenous militia at the time, and on the debate between Parindra and the Pendidikan concerning the matter, see *Overzicht v.d.IMC pers*, 1941, p. 1185. The Pendidikan's attitude was described as *"een 'real politiek'."* The Pendidikan's official attitute towards the militia can be found in "Het hoofdbestuur de Pendidikan standpunt t.a.v. de Inheemsche militie" in *Overzicht v.d.IMC pers*, 1941, p. 1006.

[301] Sjahrir, "Brief aan een broer," pp. 471–72.

[302] Ibid., pp. 472–73.

Our popularity had grown considerably in Banda since the threat of the European war, and it increased further as the situation became more threatening for Indonesia. By the end of [1941], our influence had become so strong on the little island that the civil officials even came to seek our advice on various problems.[303]

"Each evening," Sjahrir wrote about the time, "scores of people came to see me to ask my views on the war."[304]

We naturally tried to calm them, and to point out that on Banda there was little to fear because the people had long been prepared for the possibility that we might be cut off from the rest of the world. We have cassava fields in abundance, and even if our rice imports were completely stopped, there would be no lack of food.[305]

After news of the Japanese attack on Pearl Harbor reached Banda Neira, in December 1941, quoting Sjahrir again,

The Christians formed a crowd in front of the commandant's office. The Moslems gathered in groups around the little square and hundreds of people came to see [Hatta] and me to ask if it were true and what would happen next.... Civil precautions were taken on Banda: an air-raid alarm service, first aid for the wounded, and civil watches were organized. It went as a matter of course that [Hatta] and I were to become part of all this. [Hatta] was made head of the food distribution service and I of the listening post, along with the former sergeant major of the Royal Netherlands Indies Army.[306]

(Was "the former sergeant major of the Royal Netherlands Indies Army" the *juffrouw* Cresa's and Sjahrir's friend *Oom* Bing?)

When the higher and wiser authorities on Ambon were informed of the appointments, they were alarmed. The Banda officials were told they must have lost their heads to put exiles in such responsible positions, and they were immediately instructed to cancel the appointments. On Banda the orders from Ambon were considered bureaucratic and were only partially obeyed. We were no longer to be official chiefs, but instead were asked our "advice" as to how the service must be handled.[307]

An influential nationalist paper in Jakarta, *Pemandangan*, "Viewpoint," on December 8, 1941, the day of Pearl Harbor, demanded again the return of the leaders,

---

[303] Sutan Sjahrir, *Out of Exile*, p. 223.

[304] Ibid.

[305] Ibid., p. 224.

[306] Ibid. It may be noted that at the same time, Tan Malaka, in Singapore and also on the verge of returning from exile, similarly volunteered for "watching out for air raids night and day." Tan Malaka.*Dari pendjara ke pendjara*, 2: 107; translated in Jarvis, ed., *From Jail to Jail*, 2: 113.

[307] Sutan Sjahrir, *Out of Exile*, p. 224.

because "all the people," as the paper wrote, "need truly decent and unselfish leadership."[308] In Jakarta, this was a voice to which nobody seemed to listen. In Banda, at least as Sjahrir saw it, the whole community stood behind them.

As the world went unhearing and irrational, Banda Neira appeared—bizarrely of course—as a tiny island where things still seemed to retain their meaning; or even strengthened the meaning they had had before. Sjahrir wrote about the last hours, that there was

> perceptible growth of a unity among the various population groups: Moslems and Christians, Chinese and Arabs and Indo-Europeans [Eurasians] drew closer to one another, impelled by a common feeling of danger.[309]
>
> In those days, Banda became a close community. We saw and chatted with almost everyone daily. My house became a gathering place for the community "war workers," as well as the center for radio reports. We were no longer treated as exiles by the authorities. They realized that the people came to us in their restiveness and needed advice and leadership. Our relations with the people were closer in these months than ever before.[310]

On January 28, 1942, with the Japanese armies advancing through the Philippines, down through British Malaya, and towards the Indies, the Dutch authorities ordered Hatta and Sjahrir to be transferred to Java.

There might have been a last-minute change in Dutch policy. Some old hands of the Pendidikan later claimed that they had gotten through, at the last moment, to some more pragmatic Dutch officials and made a deal.[311] The decision, however, might have also been made, as some Dutch officials later claimed, on the basis of humanitarian considerations and for the two men's personal safety.[312] Or—and this seems most probable—the Dutch simply might have tried to avoid the Japanese army freeing the exiles and using them as their propaganda tool against the West.

Hatta packed in a hurry his "sixteen chests of books and one trunk of clothes." Sjahrir seems to have spent his last hours in Banda Neira trying to convince the Dutch authorities to give his adopted Bandanese children permission to travel west with him.[313]

On January 31, 1942, the Japanese army invaded Ambon, merely one hour's flight from Banda Neira. Early the next morning, a MLD-Catalina plane, one of the last Dutch bombers escaping from the eastern part of the archipelago, came to pick

---

[308] *Overzicht v.d.IMC pers*, 1941, pp. 171–73.

[309] Sutan Sjahrir, *Out of Exile*, p. 223.

[310] Ibid., p. 225.

[311] This is suggested by Sastra ("Sjahrir untuk Sastra," p. 88). See also Subadio Sastrosatomo, "Masa muda saya: Indonesia 1940–1942" (Vol.I of memoirs, typescript), p. 85, who says that Soebagio and Sastra met with "the representatives of the Governor-General's Adviser for Native affairs" in Java, and that the meeting was connected with the consequent transfer of Sjahrir and Hatta. Also Sastra in interview with Legge; see Legge, *Intellectuals and Nationalism in Indonesia*, p. 40.

[312] Thus it is explained in de Jong, *Het koninkrijk* 11a, p. 983. De Jong believes that Governor-General Tjarda van Starkenborgh acted out of personal consideration for the two men. Ibid.

[313] Hatta, *Memoir*, pp. 380–81.

up Hatta and Sjahrir. "A large flying boat circled over the little place waking the people before it came to rest in the bay," Sjahrir wrote later.[314]

Hatta says they had an hour to board the plane. Sjahrir says they had only fifteen minutes. Three of the Bandanese children were given permission at last to travel with Sjahrir—Mimi, Lily, and Ali (who was three at the time). Of the older boys, Des was to follow later by boat, and Does' parents, in the end, decided against his going.[315]

As the space in the hydroplane was limited, Hatta's sixteen chests of books had to make room for Sjahrir's children. Forty years later and evidently still sad, Hatta wrote: "I was not able to take my books back with me except for a *Bos Atlas* which I managed to put in my leather suitcase. Fortunately it just filled the top of the suitcase."[316] According to Sjahrir:

> All of Banda was on the dock, half awake, half dressed, unwashed and frightened to see us off. The people had acquired such a confidence in us that I felt as if I were committing desertion. I later heard that a half hour after we left, the first Japanese bombs fell on Banda.[317]

---

[314] Sutan Sjahrir, *Out of Exile*, p. 226.

[315] Interview with Des Alwi, Jakarta, December 3, 1988.

[316] Hatta, *Indonesian Patriot*, p. 195; see also Des Alwi, "Oom kacamata," p. 324 and Sutantio, "Kenang-kenangan," p. 45.

[317] Sutan Sjahrir, *Out of Exile*, p. 226.

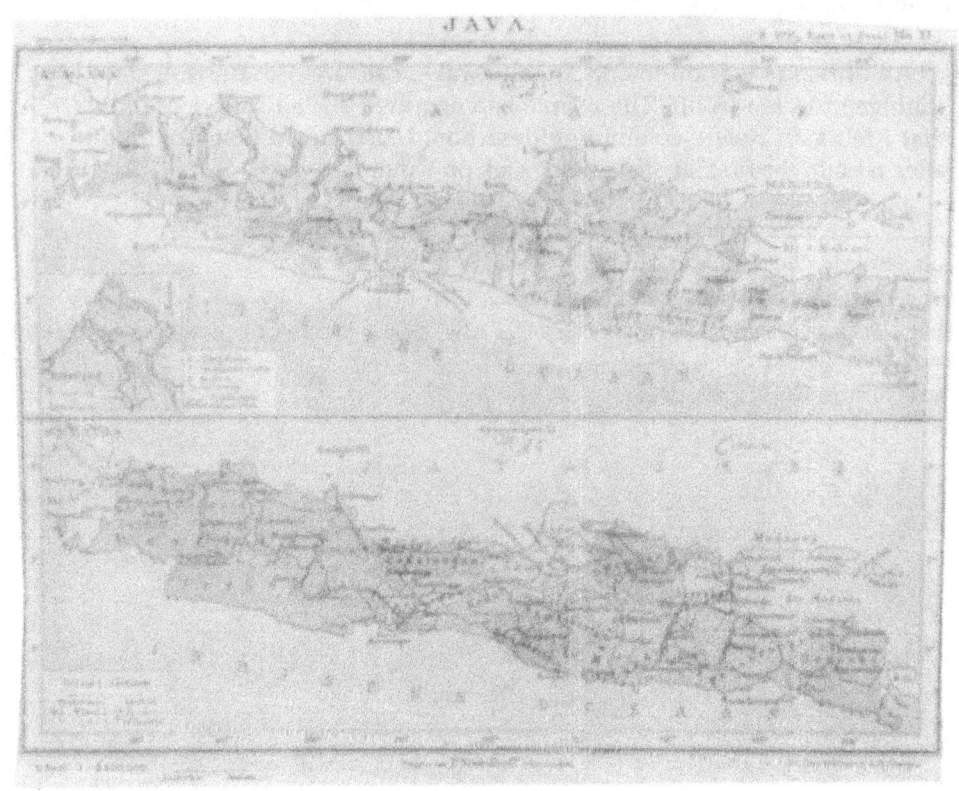

Map of Java
(from the *Bos Atlas*)

7

THE JAPANESE OCCUPATION, 1942–1945

> You are a cadre, and this is like when a ship is sinking—
> each man for himself.
>
> Sjahrir to a Pendidikan activist in 1944[1]

1. SUKABUMI

Sjahrir, Hatta, and the children landed in their hydroplane in Surabaya, East Java, on the same day they left Banda Neira. It soon became clear that the Dutch authorities did not know what exactly to do with them. Sjahrir's later account of the arrival gives a definite feeling of an increasing grotesqueness.

As they landed, and on the way from Surabaya port to the city, according to Sjahrir,

> [Dutch] marine guards looked stern, and when we were in the bus one of them sat next to each of us so that little Ali—small but important—sat with a rugged stern-faced Dutch marine with rifle and bayonet held in front of him. It was so absurd that even the girls were amused.[2]

The events during the next hours moved stage-like; lighting was artificial; the experience was unreal. That same night, in Surabaya, as Sjahrir described it,

> We were turned over to the head police office, and after waiting a few hours, we were brought into a dazzlingly lit room. I noticed that dozens of people came to look at us in turns through a window; evidently informers who would identify us. We had been away from this police state for so long.[3]

Lily, one of the girls adopted by Sjahrir in Banda Neira who was now traveling with him, recalled later the moments of arrival as a series of "errors and misunder-

---
[1] Interview with Tobing, Bandung, January 10, 1988.
[2] Sjahrir, *Out of Exile*, p. 229.
[3] Ibid.

standing."[4] They were put in the city prison, the first night, but next morning, the Dutch authorities decided that this had happened "by mistake," and, without explanation, the group was moved into an *à jour* Dutch hotel in town.[5] They traveled to Batavia by train, under escort, and first class. In Batavia, they lodged again in a very colonial, very Dutch *De Paviljoen* hotel in the center of the city. After about a week in *De Paviljoen* a car took them to Sukabumi, a town in the mountains between Buitenzorg (now Bogor) and Bandung. This was their place to stay. Nobody told them why. Nobody told them how long. And, it seemed, nobody knew.

In Sukabumi, Hatta, Sjahrir, and the children were placed in the police complex, in a vacated duplex, designed originally for police inspectors. There were two rooms and a kitchen for Sjahrir with the children, two rooms and a kitchen for Hatta. They were told that they were "free" to go to town whenever they wanted. They had to register, however, each time they decided to do so. The guard at the gate, however, was very sleepy and generally appeared not to care.[6]

These were the last weeks of Dutch colonial rule. The dynamics of the moment appeared in everything progressively becoming disconnected.

After they arrived in Sukabumi, the two (former?) exiles were told "to report to the local head of the civil administration." When they visited the official, the man seemed at a loss what to tell them. He gave Sjahrir and Hatta each a "special allowance" of one hundred guilders and promised to send a letter of inquiry to Batavia.[7] "During our first days in Sukabumi," Sjahrir wrote later,

> little notice was taken of us ... we got the impression that no one was particularly interested in our lives or safety, so that the removal from Banda remained a riddle.[8]

There had been many rumors, during the same weeks, that certain nationalists, including Hatta and Sjahrir, might be considered for evacuation to Australia; the reason suggested, again, was to keep them away from the Japanese, and from their possibly being used by the Japanese.[9] The person who brought the rumors to Sukabumi was the former Gerindo leader Amir Sjarifoeddin who had since been an official at the colonial Department of Economic Affairs. The man accompanying Amir on that occasion was Soejitno Mangoenkoesoemo—like Amir a lawyer, a younger brother of

---

[4] Sutantio et al., "Kenang-kenangan," in *Mengenang Sjahrir*, ed. Anwar, p. 45; interview with Lily Sutantio, Jakarta, April 2, 1982.

[5] Ibid. and Mohammad Hatta, "Kenang-kenangan masa lampau dengan Sjahrir" in *Mengenang Sjahrir*, ed. Anwar, pp. 38–39.

[6] Ibid. For an earlier photo of the police complex in Sukabumi see, e.g., *Algemeen Verslag van het Onderwijs in Nederlandsch Indië* 29, 70 (Batavia: Landsdrukkerij, 1928).

[7] Sjahrir, *Out of Exile*, p. 230; Hatta, *Indonesian Patriot*, p. 197.

[8] Sjahrir, *Out of Exile*, p. 232.

[9] de Jong, *Het koninkrijk der Nederlanden in de tweede Wereldoorlog* 11 a, pp. 1043–44 ; also L. G. M. Jaquet, *Aflossing van de Wacht: Bestuurlijke en politieke ervaringen in de nadagen van Nederlandsch-Indië* (Rotterdam: Donker, 1978), p. 25, and Hilman Adil, *Australia's Relations with Indonesia, 1945–1962* (Leiden: Hilman Adil, 1973), p. 32. Sjahrir, in his memoir, noted the rumors only in passing. The plan, if it was more than rumor, evidently seemed to him belated and, again, as almost everything else at that time, absurd. Nevertheless, Sjahrir did advise Hatta, in case he were approached, "not to refuse the proposal point-blank." Sjahrir, *Out of Exile*, pp. 235–36.

Tjipto Mangoenkoesoemo, and also a member, through the late 1930s, of the circle of Sjahrir's devotees.

The two men now visited Hatta and Sjahrir in the police school. Sjahrir wrote later about the meeting—and one feels a little disappointment in this—that Soejitno was "enthusiastic" about Amir. Sjahrir, as he makes immediately clear, was not. Amir Sjarifoeddin, according to Sjahrir, was "a gifted orator and was particularly popular among the educated youth." "I knew him," Sjahrir wrote,

> only as a political opponent during a period of conflict between our parties [Hatta's and Sjahrir's Pendidikan and Sukarno's Partindo] before my exile. From my cousin [sic] [Djohan Sjahroezah] and exiles in Digoel who were in prison with him, I heard that he was a well-rounded and idealistic fellow. But from what I myself knew of his political past, I had the impression that stability was not one of his outstanding characteristics.[10]

Amir came with a suggestion that Sjahrir and Hatta take part in a new cooperative scheme between the Indonesian nationalists and the Dutch colonial government. Amir also mentioned a possible evacuation should the Japanese invade Java. To Sjahrir, Amir appeared "overexcited," and, besides, "evidently he did not have much interest in me" (this compared to Amir's keen interest in Hatta), "probably because I had remained so silent."[11] The meeting ended inconclusively, and according to Sjahrir, Amir "did not show up again."[12]

In their first weeks in the police complex, Sjahrir and Hatta were also visited by Sastra, an old activist of the Pendidikan, a "proletarian mentor" of Sjahrir before the police smashed the Pendidikan in 1934. Sastra later described, how he had "sneaked"[13] into the complex, met both men for the first time after eight years, stayed overnight with them in the "prison," and, "after they had talked things over sufficiently [*puas berdiskusi*]," left again through a hole in the fence pointed out to him by Sjahrir.[14]

This must have been the beginning of efforts at Pendidikan revival. Afterwards Sjahrir often left the police school, as he wrote later, "to confer with my coworkers."[15] Hatta also—and as if suggesting that this was coming to be Sjahrir's job rather than his—recalled Sjahrir traveling several times to Bandung, to meet "his friends, like Hamdani and Subagio."[16]

There were more visitors to the Sukabumi police school during these first weeks. Sjahrir mentioned a "well-known writer de Willigen," who, clearly, was Beb Vuyk, a Eurasian woman born in Rotterdam, a writer close to the *Kritiek en Opbouw* circle and to Eddy du Perron personally; a planter's wife besides—her Dutch husband owned an estate on Buru, an island northwest not too far from Banda Neira.[17]

---

[10] Ibid., pp. 234–35.

[11] Ibid., p. 236.

[12] Ibid., p. 239.

[13] This does not fully fit with the same man's claim that he had previously arranged with the Dutch authorities for Sjahrir's and Hatta's transfer from Banda Neira.

[14] Sastra, "Sjahrir untuk Sastra," in *Mengenang Sjahrir*, ed. Anwar, p. 89.

[15] Sjahrir, *Out of Exile*, p. 238.

[16] Hatta, *Indonesian Patriot*, p. 199.

[17] Interview with Beb Vuyk, Loenen, April 16, 1987.

"One week or so before the Japanese landed on Java," Beb Vuyk herself wrote about the event,

> I met [Sjahrir] first, in Soekaboemi, where I lived at the time.... We had common friends, Soejitno Mangoenkoesoemo, the youngest brother of Dr.Tjipto, and du Perron, who was in correspondence with Sjahrir, while he stayed in Java.... Soejitno wrote me that Sjahrir, and also Hatta, were held in the police school complex in Soekaboemi. "Go, and meet him. He has read all of your books, and certainly would be happy to see you."[18]

Beb Vuyk went together with her husband. They let their names be "neatly" registered by the (sleepy?) guard at the gate, and they met Sjahrir:

> We talked about life in Moluccas, about Banda, and about my place in Buru, about the letters he wrote and got from du Perron.... We talked about literature and about the life in the Eastern islands, not a bit about politics. Hatta was also present, but he said little. The whole conversation gave me a feeling of something unreal [onreëel]. Here was a man scaring the Dutch government, and handled by the government as a dangerous rebel, sitting in front of me, talking about Dutch literature. A debate like this might look real if it happened among the literature enthusiasts in Amsterdam. But it was hard to believe that this was truly going on here, in this open prison, or how should I describe the place.[19]

By pure coincidence, Tjipto Mangoenkoesoemo—Hatta's and especially Sjahrir's old friend from Banda Neira—was also living in Sukabumi. In contrast to the uncertain status of Sjahrir and Hatta, Tjipto, legally, was a free man and, after being released from Banda Neira, he moved to Sukabumi in the hope that the mountains might help ease his asthma. As the news spread that Sjahrir, Hatta, and the children had been brought by a police car, Tjipto's sons, Donald and Louis, were sent to fetch them. Then, as was so often the case in Banda Neira, all were asked to stay for lunch, and Hatta remembered: "I was very pleased to taste *Tante* [Aunt] Cip's cooking again, after such a long time."[20]

In these unreal weeks, which clearly were the last weeks of the Dutch rule in the Indies, there was a distinct air of reunions. People from the past, recent and distant, appeared in the flesh. On the other hand—as the Japanese armies closed their grip around the Indies, and as Holland itself was occupied by Germany—Sjahrir's contacts with his wife, Maria, in Holland practically stopped. There were from then on "no mail deliveries from or to Holland," as Sjahrir wrote later laconically.[21] There were only rumors and fragments of news. Maria had heard, she said later, that, after the occupation of Ambon, her husband was brought per aeroplane to Sukabumi.

---

[18] Beb Vuyk, "In memoriam Soetan Sjahrir," *Trouw*, April 16, 1966.

[19] Ibid. For a similar version of events in Indonesian, see Beb Vuyk, "Mengenang Sjahrir" in *Mengenang Sjahrir*, ed. Anwar, pp. 267–68. There "unreal" is rendered as *gandjil*, "odd, queer."

[20] Hatta, *Indonesian Patriot*, p. 197.

[21] Sjahrir, *Out of Exile*, p. 217.

The Japanese Occupation, 1942–1945 213

Japanese Drawings (1)

Then, Maria said, only messages of a few lines could be exchanged via the Red Cross.[22]

As contacts with Maria were cut, however, other women appeared. "First it was Sjahrizal Djoehana, Sjahrir's sister, with her children." Hatta remembered the event:

> They came from Semarang on their way to Tasikmalaja, to stay with a doctor acquaintance of the Djoehana family. The next day my mother arrived from Jakarta [Batavia]. So the house became very crowded. My mother demanded to be given my bedroom for the night, so I slept in the front room on a bench seventy-five centimeters wide. Sjahrir's place was even tighter. Aki [Djoehana's son, Sjahrir's nephew] wished to sleep with Sjahrir, and Ali [a Bandanese adopted son of Sjahrir] was put in the front room. Mrs. Djoehana and Hedda [Djoehana's daughter, Sjahrir's niece] slept in one bed, and Lily with Mimi [Sjahrir's adopted Bandanese daughters] in the second bed in the same room.[23]

Sjahrir added that, besides, one of his younger brothers also arrived and stayed in the place.[24]

On February 14, 1942, the Japanese armies landed in South Sumatra. Within the next fourteen days Java was invaded. On March 8, the Dutch Commander-in-Chief of the Allied forces in the Indies surrendered,[25] and, that day, at midnight, *Radio Bandung* broadcast the Dutch anthem, *Wilhelmus*, for the last time. In a matter of hours the Japanese appeared in Sukabumi and also in the police complex.

"Imagine, how this transaction happened," Sjahrir told Beb Vuyk, when she visited him again, a few days later, and in a new era:

> so many weapons, so much of a stockpile, this and that building. At the end the Dutch police commissar said:
> "—Well, we also have two nationalist leaders, how about that?"
> "—Ah, just let them go," said the Jap.[26]

Hatta, and Sjahrir, with the children and an unidentified number of relatives, were permitted to stay in the police complex until they could find a better place to move into. This was how their exile was supposed to end. They were free.

This was, also, the end of empire. The last Governor-General of the Dutch East Indies, Tjarda van Starkenborgh, who had been seen in the country up till then mostly garbed in an overbearing and ostentatious eighteenth-century-like uniform, appeared, now, in numerous photographs in all the newspapers, in the outfit of a war prisoner.[27]

---

[22] Interview with Maria Duchâteau-Sjahrir, Lorgues, February 13, 1988.

[23] Hatta, *Bung Hatta Antwoordt*, p. 388.

[24] Sjahrir, *Out of Exile*, p. 232.

[25] Kahin, *Nationalism and Revolution*, p. 101.

[26] Beb Vuyk, "Verhaal van een toeschouwer (In memoriam Ida Nasoetion)," *Orientatie* 31 (April 1950), pp. 248–49.

[27] Japanese armies marched through the Javanese towns, through the streets, where huge Pepsidont billboards still hung, left over from the past epoch. It might easily be seen as absurd, bizarre, unreal. Because of his resemblance to the smiling face of the freshly tooth-

Jacques de Kadt, another Dutchman caught in the Indies by the Japanese invasion, remembered the same moments and apparently the same photographs:

> At the time of this relative and uncertain freedom, which preceded my internment in the camp, one day around noon, I saw an Indonesian, dressed in European clothes, approaching my house and stepping up to the front veranda. This was not a normal thing, because the Indonesians, with whom I freely mixed before the Japanese occupation, now avoided any contact with Europeans. The new Indonesians who had positions clothed themselves in a way as Indonesian as possible. The man came closer, and held out his hand to shake mine. He appeared surprised that I did not recognize him instantly, and said he was Sjahrir.[28]

Costumes always, in modern Indies history and in Sjahrir's life, were important—school uniforms, soccer uniforms, the all-white garb of the Koranic school. Costumes marked the passage from one time to another. At this time of apocalyptic change, it seems, Sjahrir kept to his usual clothes as if nothing much had happened.

As he wrote in his memoirs, at the time Sjahrir visited him, De Kadt was in contact with

> a local progressive group which had as its spiritual leader my old friend Marcel Koch, the chief editor of excellent *Kritiek en Opbouw*.[29]

Shortly before Sjahrir came, de Kadt had also been contacted by "an old history teacher from Bandung," who asked him to write a program for an illegal group of his own. The illegal group wanted to "carry on underground action against the Japanese invaders" on the principle that

> the Indies after the war would never be the old Dutch Indies, [and that] Indonesian nationalism [in the new Indies] will play a leading part [*hoofdrol*].[30]

Those were contacts full of memories, of "progressive" Bandung, of du Perron, of the yet earlier "ethical" compassions of some Dutchmen towards the Indonesians. Yet, as the very near future was to show, all these contacts would lead nowhere. The people de Kadt mentioned seemed to surface mainly because the Dutch authorities had done little to prepare a real modern efficient resistance movement for the occupied Indies. All the Dutch or Eurasians who were determined to resist seemed either

---

brushed Dutchman on the advertising billboards, the Governor-General had always been called *"Si Pepsidont,"* "Mr. Pepsidont," by the people. See J. de Kadt, *De Indonesische tragedie: het treurspel der gemiste kansen* (Amsterdam: van Oorschot, 1949), pp. 17–18.

[28] De Kadt, "Sjahrir: Poging tot plaatsbepaling," p. 464. Sjahrir might appear to be acting completely against the current tide. But Tan Malaka, for instance, recorded some stories which point to some movement of compassion among average Indonesians towards the Dutch, who were so suddenly humiliated and reduced to a status lower even than that of the "natives." See especially Tan Malaka, *Dari pendjara ke pendjara* 2: 125; translated in Jarvis, ed., *From Jail to Jail* 2: 133.

[29] De Kadt, "Sjahrir: Poging tot plaatsbepaling," p. 468.

[30] Ibid., pp. 468–69.

to belong definitely to the past or were intellectuals otherwise too much on the fringes of actual politics and power. Indeed, in a few months, if they had not been discovered and executed, they had disappeared, along with the rest of their race, into the Japanese internment camps.

Sjahrir, after the war, apparently referred to the same "old history teacher from Bandung" as de Kadt:

> a certain Professor Fluiter came to see us. I never found out why he came, but he stayed for hours, and while he appeared to have something on his mind, he did not tell us much about it.[31]

This was clearly a feeler put out by the group. De Kadt suggests that it was "on that matter" that Sjahrir came to see him. He says he showed Sjahrir the program he himself had written for the professor's group, a program, which, according to de Kadt, demanded, among other things, "a full dominion status for Indonesians" after the war. Sjahrir, according to de Kadt, "in principle agreed."[32]

This was, we should remember, the time when the Japanese military police beheaded people in the new Indonesia for much less than a conspiracy. Sjahrir was still living with Hatta in the police school in Sukabumi. One day he was returning from one of his increasingly frequent trips to meet his Pendidikan friends in Bandung:

> When I reached the Soekaboemi station, I saw immediately that a Japanese civilian and an Indonesian were watching me.... Instead of going directly home I went into a restaurant opposite the station to see what would happen. Two Japanese then came and sat at a table next to mine. One of them came toward me, made a deep bow, and asked if the other Japanese could speak with me. I agreed. The other Japanese, who was introduced as a high personage, asked me who I was. I gave him a false name, though without any illusion that he would believe me. He then told me all Indonesians should co-operate with the Japanese, and that the Japanese would soon go away and leave the country to the Indonesians to govern themselves. He spoke Japanese and the other fellow translated in high Malay, addressing me with great respect. They also looked with suspicion at a few English books I had brought from Bandoeng.[33]

There is much to say about this passage: Sjahrir carrying clearly visible "a few English books"; his giving a false name, not believing for a moment that it would be taken seriously; most of all, perhaps, the strange process of translation: from Japanese to "high Malay"!

---

[31] Sjahrir, *Out of Exile*, p. 236.

[32] De Kadt, "Sjahrir: Poging tot plaatsbepaling," p. 470. De Kadt added: "however, those who afterwards read the last pages of the *Overpeinzingen* understand that my program went further than his." In Sjahrir's own account of the same affair (de Kadt is "Jacques" in this account, and "Willigen" is Beb Vuyk): "I made contact with progressive Dutch groups, including that of the well-known writer de Willigen and the reformed Dutch politicus Jacques. I had several meetings with these groups in Bandoeng, the result of which was the formulation of a political program of co-operation among all the democratic resistance organizations...." Sjahrir, *Out of Exile*, p. 243.

[33] Ibid., p. 238.

As Sjahrir's story continues, the Japanese let him go, but a few hours later visited him and Hatta in the police complex. Hatta, indeed, and Sjahrir emphasized this repeatedly, seemed to be the person in whom the Japanese were more interested—Hatta was more "real," better known to public, and also he seemed to be more willing to go along. Two days after the Japanese visited them, Sjahrir wrote, Hatta

> received an order to go to Batavia. He left under Japanese escort. No notice was taken of me.
>
> I was left with the three children, and it was not easy for us to find new accommodations. Hence we remained calmly in the police offices, ignoring hints from the police authorities that we would have to leave because we were prisoners of the Dutch, and they didn't want to be mixed up in the matter. Finally we were ordered to leave within twenty-four hours.[34]

The new Japanese rule was based on discipline, clear compartmentalization of life, and especially a brutally sharp delineation between races. Even to wander vaguely off the racial line demanded a great deal of courage. Sjahrir, for reasons which were deeply rooted in him, did it stubbornly, against the reason of the time.

This was one of the most striking things the writer and friend Beb Vuyk remembered about Sjahrir:

> He was often thought to be an Indies Dutchman [*een Indische Nederlander*], this, in spite of the fact that he was actually short in stature, and that his face, definitely, betrayed no European features. It was not something, which would be in his exterior, but it was in his manners, in his pose and in the way he was choosing words.[35]

Sjahrir seemed to flirt with this dangerous role. We may recall, from the first chapter of this book, a legend in Sjahrir's family about "an ancestor with definitely blue eyes." Now, when the bridge between the races was so much in peril, as if the strange family lore—for Sjahrir out of exile—acquired new meaning.

Beb Vuyk—herself Eurasian, and thus biologically and inevitably in-between—returned to this point repeatedly. She told, for instance, how once, during these weeks early in the Japanese occupation, Sjahrir with friends went to visit Tjipto Mangoenkoesoemo. Beb Vuyk, Soejitno, and Sjahrir's Bandanese children took a *deleman*, a horse-driven carriage. Sjahrir followed them, giving a ride on his bicycle to the little son of Beb Vuyk. On reaching Tjipto's house, a little later, Sjahrir told the group how a Japanese guard had appeared unexpectedly in his path, half blocking the road. "It truly was some journey," Sjahrir said then, turning to Beb Vuyk in particular,

> with that blond boy of yours behind me on the bike. When I saw the guard standing there, it came to my mind, how easily I could be arrested for being a European.[36]

---

[34] Ibid., pp. 239–40.

[35] Beb Vuyk, "In memoriam Soetan Sjahrir"; Beb Vuyk, "Mengenang Sjahrir," p. 269.

[36] Ibid.

Soon afterwards, Beb Vuyk remembered, Sjahrir told her a similar story—except this one made it more clear, and this was possibly why it was told, that the keeping off the racial line, the remaining in between, meant to Sjahrir also to keep stiff, aloof, and often lonely.

This had happened to him, Sjahrir said, on a train in which he traveled through ocupied Central Java:

> He sat next to an old Indies lady [*Indische dame*, which is a European or Eurasian woman]. She was on the run, escaping from looting [*rampok*] in Solo, and she had managed to take with her just the clothes she wore. Her husband was in prison, about her sons, both of whom used to be in the [Dutch] army, she did not know whether they were alive or dead. She had not merely lost all of her possessions, but also all her trust in life. She had been very embittered, and, as most Europeans these days, she blamed "natives" for her misery. She bitterly and in detail complained about the scoundrels who had looted and plundered, and then cheered the Japanese as they were marching through the streets.

"How painful this must have been for you," Beb Vuyk told Sjahrir at this moment:

> "Not so bad," Sjahrir answered. "In seventy percent of what she said, I agreed with her. She opened her heart to me completely, she poured out to me all her troubles, she cried frightfully, and it became difficult to calm her down. When she felt a bit better, she asked me, why I was not interned like the other [Eurasians]."

At that moment, Sjahrir said, he tried to answer as well as he could. He told her he "was not in the army," that's why he was left outside the camp. But the old lady persisted; she demanded more and more of "white" solidarity; the train went on. Finally, Sjahrir at a loss what else to do, "pulled out his *pitji*" (a velvet cap, an unambiguously "native" and distinctly Sukarnoist symbol), "and he placed the *pitji* on his knees. After this," so the story ended, "the lady was silent."[37]

Like in Banda Neira, the children, perhaps more than anything else, helped Sjahrir to move loosely through the new disturbing experiences, in the new landscape of politics, and among memories. "Each Saturday or on Sunday evenings," one of Sjahrir's two adopted daughters, Lily, wrote later,

> for *Oom* Sjahrir and us the children, it was a regular program. The whole gang took out bikes and made their way ... to see *Oom* Tjipto. He was very ill, he suffered from asthma; *Tante* Tjip [Tjipto's wife] was still in good health, and she, all the time, kept herself cheerful with a white cockatoo, which she had brought from Banda. From *Oom* Tjipto's house, we often went to the house of *Oom* Soejitno, *Oom* Tjip's younger brother.[38]

There was a negative-like defined topography of these journeys:

---

[37] Ibid.
[38] Sutantio, "Kenang-kenangan," p. 46.

Oom Sjahrir always avoided roads where there were Japanese guards, because, more than anything else, he hated the idea that he would have to bow to the Japanese in respect.[39]

After the police finally forced them out of the "prison" in Sukabumi, Sjahrir with his children seemed to be on the move permanently. From Sukabumi, they went to Semarang, to his sister Djoehana's house; from Semarang to the mountains at Cipanas, above Bogor, where, near the village of Sindanglaya, his sister again had a summer place. They kept moving, even after Sjahrir rented inexpensively, so he wrote, a house in Batavia (now renamed Jakarta) "from a Dutch lady who was soon to be interned."[40]

There was no mother in that family. Sjahrir's sister seemed to be around most of the time. In Semarang, Cipanas, and also in Jakarta (she with her husband also bought a house in Jakarta), Sjahrir with the children could come to eat and to stay whenever they wanted. But as far as money was concerned, a friend of Sjahrir and his relative told me, they got "only pocket money, nothing more."[41]

Sjahrir still did the sewing, for little Ali especially.[42] The girls soon started to work:

> We children were trained to live simply, and to take care of ourselves. We were ordered to learn typing and other skills, to be able to apply for secretarial jobs. *Oom* [Sjahrir] had no income, because he, for some reason, all the time traveled through provinces, away from home. Later we knew that this leaving was connected with an underground movement.[43]

2. Sjahrir's Pemuda

In a few months, the Japanese military police uncovered the illegal circle of progressive Dutchmen in Bandung around "the Bandung history professor Fluiter," and according to de Kadt's account, "several ranking members were slaughtered in a most abominable way."[44] By August 1942, de Kadt had been detained and also most other pure-blooded Dutchmen were locked in the camps.[45] Early in 1943, Beb Vuyk, like other Eurasians, was interned, and for the next three years there was no communication whatsover between her and Sjahrir. Neither did Sjahrir have any contact with de Kadt, nor with any of the Dutchmen and Eurasians he had known before.[46] Only, as Sjahrir wrote later, Eurasian minors "had never been interned by the Japanese."[47]

---

[39] Ibid.

[40] Sjahrir, *Out of Exile*, p. 248; see also ibid., p. 244, Sutantio, "Kenang-kenangan," p. 45. Interview with Sjahrizal Djoehana, Bandung, October 22, 1987. Mrs. Djoehana said that she and her husband had expected Sjahrir and children to tend her orange garden.

[41] Interview with Idham, Jakarta, January 8, 1988. Sutantio, "Kenang-kenangan," p. 46

[42] Interview with Des Alwi, Jakarta, December 3, 1987.

[43] Sutantio, "Kenang-kenangan," p. 46, interview with Lily Sutantio, Jakarta, April 2, 1982.

[44] De Kadt, "Sjahrir: Poging tot plaatsbepaling," p. 470.

[45] De Kadt, *De Indonesische tragedie*, p. 118 n.

[46] Interview with Beb Vuyk, Loenen, April 16, 1983.

[47] Sjahrir, *Out of Exile*, p. 262. Both "enemy" foreigners (Dutch and Allied nationals) and "non-enemy" foreigners (Eurasians and Chinese mainly) had to go, sooner or later, into the camps if

The warm parties at Tjipto's house also soon came to an end. Tjipto's health had rapidly deteriorated, and was not helped by his family moving from the mountains in Sukabumi—too cool for his asthma, they now thought—down to Jakarta.[48] Tjipto died in March 1943. Although Sjahrir did not mention this in his recollections of the time, we know from other sources that it was he, who, it seems, as the only Indonesian political figure of stature, escorted Tjipto's body the whole day-long journey by train, to Salatiga, Tjipto's native Central Java, and then to nearby Ambarawa, where the burial took place.[49]

Another long-standing companion also appeared to be leaving Sjahrir: in contrast to Sjahrir, Hatta decided to cooperate with the Japanese regime. Describing his friend's departure with the Japanese from Sukabumi, as we may recall, Sjahrir wrote that Hatta went "under Japanese escort," making it clear that he was submitting to physical force. It was a time of terror, especially for Indonesians who held higher positions or were better known to the public. As Hatta himself wrote in his memoirs, at the same time and in the town where they lived, in Sukabumi, a Dutch official was shot, and his dead body was exhibited on the town's main crossroad with a sign in Indonesian: "This is what will happen, if you don't obey Japanese orders."[50]

Besides, Hatta, now a man of forty, clearly thought of himself as an elder statesman, or a seasoned fighter, who, in this crucial period of Indonesian history, had an obligation to be involved. He, no doubt, thought of Jakarta as the center of power, whoever held power, and thus as a proper place for him to go.

Some of Hatta's important acquaintances and close friends, especially from the time they were together in Holland during the 1920s, were already cooperating with the Japanese, and, after reaching Jakarta, Hatta immediately met with them.

Hatta's "uncle," Max Etek Ayub of the Djohan Djohor merchant chain, who helped finance Hatta's studies and political career before 1934, waited for him. When Hatta arrived in Jakarta, Max Etek Ayub ordered new clothes and whatever else was needed. The Japanese gave Hatta a room in the prestigious *Hotel des Indes*, until a house could be bought or rented for him. They also provided Hatta with a car as well, as he wrote in his memoirs after the war, "with a special sign in *kanji* [Japanese characters] to be used at night." With the car, Hatta wrote, he got "a driver who was of Minangkabau origin."[51]

A ranking Japanese military officer—a man, who was later crucially important in the Indonesians' attaining their independence—Admiral Tadashi Maeda, described the spring of 1942 as "a frantic atmosphere of welcome [pervading] the entire region of the East Indies."[52] The world of the Indies had changed indeed. Indonesian officials were encouraged to address their Japanese superiors as *saudara tua*, "older brother." Each morning, too, they were obliged to perform the "new *kiblat*," bowing deeply like Moslems do, but in the direction of Tokyo.

---

they were over the age of seventeen. (A. A. Zorab, *De Japanse bezetting van Indonesië en haar volkenrechtelijke zijde* (Leiden: Universitaire Pers, 1954), pp. 63ff)

[48] Balfas, *Dr. Tjipto Mangoenkoesoemo*, pp. 136–37.

[49] Ibid., p. 139; see also Salim, *Limabelas tahun Digul*, p. 508; Des Alwi, "Oom kacamata yang mendidik saya" in *Muhammad Hatta*, ed. Swasono, p. 325.

[50] Hatta, *Indonesian Patriot*, p. 200.

[51] Ibid., pp. 200–201.

[52] Maeda's recollections quoted in Dahm, *Sukarno*, p. 219.

The Christian calender was changed into Japanese: year 1942 became year 2602. Time was also moved two and a half hours forward, to accord with Tokyo time. The use of Dutch, in public, in letters, and on the telephone was forbidden. For some time, alongside Japanese movies, Western pictures were still shown in Indies theaters, and the theaters also kept their prewar names. But each performance now began with a voice chanting: *Sjukur alhamdullilah* . . . "Thanks Be To God, Asia was returned to Asia"; then the audience stood up and the Japanese anthem was played on the gramophone—*Kamigayo*, "The Imperial Age."[53]

According to de Kadt, indeed, during the first weeks "the 'natives' stood in huge crowds whenever the Japanese were marching, and they waved small Japanese flags."[54] In the words of another progressive Dutchman in the Indies at the time, former professor at the law school in Batavia, W. F. Wertheim,

> remarkable was the conduct of many ['native'] civil servants, always loyal to the Government, the pillars of Dutch rule. How easily, now, they bowed to the new masters. They had been yes-men before—they were yes-men now, these antique *prijajis* [aristocratic civil servants], the jewels of feudal society. Their tradition of obedience carried them over towards a new authority.[55]

This was very close to what Sjahrir had written about "fascism" and about the "Eastern spirit" through his exile in Banda Neira. The worst qualities, which Sjahrir so disdained, now, suddenly seemed to come to the surface, and to overwhelm the Indies—the complex of inferiority, the spirit of slaves, and that of servant-like aristocrat-like *ningrat*.

The new times, and the Japanese, called for a man—a son of the place—to give them a face and a voice. The natural choice for this role appeared very soon to be Sukarno—rather than anybody else from the prewar nationalist movement, rather than Hatta, not to mention at all the withdrawn and marginal Sjahrir. Hatta recognized this instantly, and Sjahrir, himself, no doubt knew it perfectly well. As Sjahrir wrote later, and the emphasis is mine, Sukarno "was brought to Java . . . at the request of the nationalists in Java, *supported particularly by [Hatta]*."[56]

Sukarno was picked up from his last place of exile by the Japanese and transported by them to Jakarta early in July 1942. In Hatta's account, immediately after Sukarno arrived in Jakarta he contacted Hatta—via Djohan Djohor's shop—and let Hatta know "that he does not want to speak with anybody before he meets and talks with me."[57] Hatta at that time was already settled in the Japanese Jakarta, and had his own house (on the *Oranje Boelevard*, he wrote). There on the same day, the old adversaries and co-fighters met. Besides Hatta, Sukarno, and Sukarno's confidant and later son-in-law, Asmara Hadi, Sjahrir was present.

There are various accounts of what happened at the meeting. Later recollections of all the three principal participants agree, however, that Sukarno and Hatta were

---

[53] E.g., Mansoer, et al., *Sedjarah Minangkabau*, pp. 211–12.

[54] De Kadt, *Jaren die dubbel telden*, p. 71.

[55] W. F. Wertheim, *Nederland op den Tweesprong: Tragedie van den aan traditie gebonden mensch* (Arnhem: Van Loghum Slaterus, 1946), pp. 17–18.

[56] Sjahrir, *Out of Exile*, p. 245.

[57] Hatta, *Memoir*, p. 412.

Japanese Drawings (2)

encouraged (or permitted) by the meeting to cooperate together and with the Japanese in the interests of the nationalist movement. Sukarno and Hatta, in Sjahrir's words, agreed to

> do everything legally possible to give the nationalist struggle a broader legal scope, and at the same time secretly support the revolutionary resistance.[58]

Sjahrir—and again the recollections of all three, Sukarno, Hatta, and Sjahrir are in agreement—was encouraged (or permitted) by the meeting to work underground, and to organize the "revolutionary resistance."[59]

The Japanese occupation afterwards became very much Sukarno's time. According to one of Sukarno's biographers,

---

[58] Sjahrir, *Out of Exile*, p. 246.

[59] Ibid., p. 248; Hatta, *Indonesian Patriot*, p. 210, Sukarno, *An Autobiography*, p. 173. The formulation in quotations marks is Sjahrir's from *Out of Exile*. Some associates of Sjahrir expressed later their opinion that Sjahrir had written this account in 1947 the way he did in an effort not to compromise either Sukarno or Hatta at a sensitive moment of nationalist struggle. The fact was, according to these people, that Sjahrir, at the meeting with Sukarno in Hatta's house in 1942, and afterwards, did his utmost to keep away, and distant from both collaborating leaders. See de Jong on his interview, in June 1973, with four leading coworkers of Sjahrir from the post-1945 time. de Jong, *Het koninkrijk der Nederlanden in de tweede Wereldoorlog* 11b, p. 273,

The new situation was to prove well suited to his particular talents—much more so indeed than the environment of Dutch empire had been.[60]

According to another of Sukarno's biographers,

> In a spectacular tour through Java that began only a week after his return from Sumatra, he had re-established links with most of the nationalist leaders from former days. Everywhere he was greeted enthusiastically, and the Japanese officials traveling with him could hardly have failed to be impressed by the popularity which now blazed up anew, despite his eight-year absence from Java.[61]

Sjahrir's account written in 1947 looked at the same thing from a slightly different angle. "It appeared," Sjahrir wrote, "that [Sukarno] had been strongly affected by the Japanese successes," and that he "thought the war with Japan would last at least ten years."[62] As far as his own contacts with Sukarno which were supposed to originate from the meeting in Hatta's house, Sjahrir wrote:

> For several months, [Sukarno] kept me fully informed concerning the course of his discussions with the Japanese, and he occasionally came to ask my advice.

But as the occupation and Sukarno's policies developed fully:

> There was no longer any immediate reason for [Sukarno] to see me, and I lost touch with him until just before the proclamation of our independence.[63]

Sukarno became the center of all the Japanese-sponsored nationalist organizations and bodies. Hatta became second in command, second only to Sukarno. At the same time, Hatta was clearly closer to the fringes, more hesitant, less taken by the Japanese successes and thus still closer to Sjahrir. Sjahrir's account of Hatta at that time is of a *qualified* difference between Hatta and Sukarno and *qualified* praise by Sjahrir for what Hatta was doing. Hatta during this time, Sjahrir wrote (emphasis is mine),

> always *regarded himself* as a democrat and a nationalist who had been prevailed upon.... Using this position, *he tried* to do what he could for our cause.... Right up to the present time, *he has always been regarded* as a loyal suppporter of the national cause ... [he] had never made common cause with those Indonesians who went to work for the Japanese because of either material designs or political sympathies.[64]

---

[60] Legge, *Sukarno*, p. 149.
[61] Dahm, *Sukarno*, pp. 234–35.
[62] Sjahrir, *Out of Exile*, p. 245–46.
[63] Ibid., pp. 246–47.
[64] Ibid., p. 242.

While, according to the same account by Sjahrir, Sukarno thought in 1942 that the war with Japan would last "*at least* ten years,"[65] Hatta "gave them ten years," no more, and, in contrast to Sukarno, he clearly anticipated the Japanese defeat.[66] But Sjahrir himself, we read just next to it, gave the Japanese "only three years"![67]

While Sjahrir's view of Sukarno was very clear-cut, his view of Hatta was less so. Sjahrir often formulated his opinion of Hatta in an indirect way. Here, for instance, Sjahrir used Tjipto as an *alter ego*: Hatta's relationship with Tjipto, during Tjipto's last months, Sjahrir wrote, had been "unique." Tjipto

> had only contempt for the nationalists who co-operated with the Japanese. But from the very beginning, although he was disappointed that [Hatta] became a leading figure under the Japanese authority rather than a democratic martyr, he always defended [him], if not politically, then morally. He never spoke harshly of him, not even when I occasionally expressed my dissatisfaction with him.[68]

While Sjahrir emphasized that, after the first weeks of the Japanese occupation, he "lost touch" with Sukarno, he wrote that occasionally he came to see Hatta, "incognito to hear the news," and that he was getting warnings from Hatta on what might be brewing on the Japanese side.[69]

The Bandanese children served to maintain both Sjahrir's contact with Hatta and the contact's ambiguity. Hatta remained an "uncle" to Sjahrir's adopted children. Once at least, for a whole month, when they had no other place to go, the children and Sjahrir with them stayed in the garden pavilion behind Hatta's house.[70] Des, one of Sjahrir's three adopted sons—he did not get on the hydroplane in Banda Neira and got to Java by ship—later wrote:

> As soon as I reached Jakarta, I went directly to meet *Oom* Hatta, and to reunite with my sisters and my brother. Our foster father, *Oom* Sjahrir, was at that time permanently busy with his underground movement against the Japanese, and we could meet very rarely. Thus *Oom* Hatta was the one who sent us to school and who financed our whole education.[71]

In a way, this was a continuation of Sjahrir's exile. Particularly the decision not to cooperate with the Japanese placed Sjahrir into an awkward position. After the Dutch and Eurasians disappeared into the internment camps, while Hatta was mov-

---

[65] This is as quoted from *Out of Exile*, p. 246. Emphasis is mine.

[66] Sjahrir's interview with George Kahin, February 15, 1949.

[67] Ibid. In *Out of Exile*, Sjahrir wrote that at their first meeting in Hatta's house where Sukarno mentioned "ten years," Sjahrir argued "the thesis that the war would be much shorter." (Sjahrir, *Out of Exile*, p. 246)

[68] Ibid., p. 242.

[69] Ibid., p. 244.

[70] Interview with Lily Sutantio, Jakarta, April 2, 1982; Sutantio, "Kenang-kenangan," p. 42. After Tjipto died, Sjahrir took the children quite regularly, to Djoehana's house. There the men played cards and the children ran around. Hatta was there most of the time, and on rare occasions also Sukarno. Ibid., p. 46.

[71] Des Alwi, "Oom kacamata," p. 324.

ing in a different direction, and after Tjipto died, very few men of any political stature and name in Indonesia remained to share this space on the periphery with Sjahrir.

Amir Sjarifoeddin seemed to move not far from Sjahrir. Sjahrir and Amir met again, in the first weeks of the Japanese occupation. According to Sjahrir's later account, Amir talked to him and also to Hatta about possible resistance, and he might even have offered or given them some money—left behind by an agency in the Dutch colonial government—to support the idea. Sjahrir suggests he was little impressed.[72] Amir, Sjahrir wrote, "had let his beard grow but was still easy to recognize." Sjahrir wrote he had even warned his coworkers not to have anything to do with Amir, because to embark on underground action with that unstable man was dangerous.

Amir, very soon indeed, got into serious trouble. Still in 1942, the Japanese police became suspicious of his activity. Hatta, and probably Sukarno, too (Amir was on the political side of Sukarno and Partindo before the war), helped Amir for a while.[73] In Sjahrir's version again, Amir

> was persuaded to give himself up and go to Batavia, on the assurance that if he would work with the Japanese nothing would be done to him.[74]

In spite of all the efforts to the contrary, however, in January 1943 Amir was arrested, and with him more than fifty members of his allegedly anti-Japanese underground mostly in Eastern Java, and especially in Surabaya.

This was the end of any possibility of Sjahrir and Amir working together. In Sjahrir's words:

> We daily heard of arrests, particularly of [Amir's] group and of those of our people who had been in touch with him.[75]

Amir was sentenced to death but was saved as the result of an appeal from Sukarno and Hatta. He remained in prison until the end of the Japanese occupation in 1945.

In retrospect, the arrest of Amir Sjarifoeddin might have been the single most important event in Sjahrir's political life in this period. When Amir left the scene, Sjahrir began to attract a group of young men and young women, who, for years afterwards, were to be called simply "Sjahrir's youth" or "Sjahrir's *pemoeda*," with little or no reference to Amir.

There had been more similarities between Sjahrir and Amir than Sjahrir suggested in his postwar account. Amir wrote for the Dutch "progressive" journal *Kritiek en Opbouw*, to which du Perron, and also the circle of Sjahrir's devotees around Soewarsih Djojopoespito, were very close. Amir had a Dutch education, he in fact spent his high school years in Holland, and he was a graduate of the law school in Batavia.

---

[72] Sjahrir, *Out of Exile*, p. 235-36. This certainly denigrating passage could in part be explained by the fact that it was written by Sjahrir after a later serious estrangement between the two men. Amir might even actually have given some of the money to Sjahrir and also to Hatta. With striking nonchalance, Hatta mentioned later "a couple of thousand guilders for our daily necessities." Hatta, *Indonesian Patriot*, p. 198. Sjahrir did not mention this at all.

[73] Hatta, *Indonesian Patriot*, p. 207.

[74] Sjahrir, *Out of Exile*, p. 241.

[75] Ibid.

Amir, like Sjahrir, wrote and talked culture as much as politics. Amir, also, was as intensively as Sjahrir concerned with colonial education, and student politics in particular. It appears that especially in the two main prewar colonial college-level schools in Batavia, the law school and the medical school, Amir's personal, cultural, and political influence, at the moment when the Dutch rule crashed and the Japanese came, was immense.[76]

The names which later became identified with Sjahrir, and which will be with us often through the rest of this story, surfaced first in student culture or politics during the last years or months of Dutch rule in the same two schools: Hamid Algadri, Subadio Sastrosatomo, Sitti Wahjunah (Poppy) Saleh Mangoendiningrat (later Sjahrir), Hoegeng Iwan Santoso, and Lintong Moelia Sitoroes, were law school students.[77] Soedjatmoko Saleh Mangoendiningrat, a brother of Poppy, Soebianto Djojohadikoesoemo, Daan Jahja, Aboe Bakar Loebis, and Wibowo studied at Batavia Medical School.[78]

These young people—with others who disappeared later or went in other directions—formed a swirl of vaguely felt affinities and personal friendships rather than a solid and easily definable group. At the end of Dutch rule, they might be found in several very different student organizations. Subadio, for instance, was in the oldest, and strongly nationalist Indonesia Moeda, "Young Indonesia,"[79] Sitoroes in the vehemently political Perhimpoenan Peladjar-Peladjar Indonesia or PPPI, "Association of Indonesian Students,"[80] Subadio, Soedjatmoko, Daan Jahja, Hamid Algadri, Soebianto, Iwan Santoso, and Sitoroes in the avowedly non-political (and Latin-labeled) Unitas Studiosorum Indonesiensis or USI;[81] others, like Poppy Saleh, who was also a member of USI, were members of the equally apolitical Indonesische Vrouwen Studenten Vereeniging, IVSV, "Union of Indonesian Studying Women," or even the conservative, more Dutch than Indonesian CORPS.[82]

Both the medical school and the law school were closed when the Japanese came. But the medical school reopened after a year and continued to operate under Japanese supervision and a Japanese name, *Ika-daigaku*. It remained the single platform, and some of the former law school students also transferred there.

Sjahrir wrote later:

> Most educated adults were passive, the only group which showed vitality during Japanese times were students, especially high school students.[83]

---

[76] On Amir Sjarifoeddin before the war see e.g. Wellem, *Amir Sjarifoeddin*, especially pp. 27–126.

[77] E.g., *Orgaan der USI* 2 (January 1940): 4.

[78] Ibid., p. 14; Subadio Sastrosatomo, "Masa muda saya: Indonesia 1940–1942" (typescript), p. 114.

[79] *Orgaan der USI* 2 (January 1941): 13.

[80] Subadio, "Masa muda saya," p. 137; Legge, *Intellectuals and Nationalism*, p. 42; interview with Subadio, Jakarta, October 18, 1987.

[81] "S" in *Poedjangga Baroe* 1936, no. 4 (April 10, 1937); *Orgaan der USI*, 8–9 (January 1935): 176–80, ibid. 2 (January 1940): 44.

[82] Subadio, "Masa muda saya," p. 36; interview with Sudarpo, Jakarta, October 7, 1987; *Orgaan der USI. Lustrum nummer* (1938).

[83] Sjahrir's interview with George Kahin, February 15, 1949.

What Sjahrir might have had in mind, was the fact that high schools, indeed, appeared to be the places where the solidarity among the college students, and Sjahrir's young followers, had originated. Children of the Mangoendiningrat family, for instance, Soedjatmoko, Poppy, and Miriam, together with Zainal Abidin and Moerdianto, who would also become well-known figures in Sjahrir's circle, attended the same HBS high school in Surabaya.[84] Similarly, the common experience in the AMS high school in Yogyakarta was of crucial importance to Subadio, his brother Sudarpo, Aboe Bakar Loebis, Hamid Algadri, Daan Jahja, together with other future Sjahririans like Daan's brother Ibrahim, Listyo, Moeharto, Soemarman, and Rosihan Anwar.[85]

High schools in the Indies made an especially deep impression on their students during the last year or so of the Dutch epoch. As we mentioned, at that time, a number of Dutch intellectuals escaped to the Indies before fascism in Europe. Until the war caught up with them in the Indies, several of these men and women made their living teaching in the Indies high schools. Years later, these Dutch teachers were still remembered by their students with warmness and nostalgia.[86]

The young men and women lived in a way not unlike Sjahrir in Bandung in the 1920s. They socialized in a *clubhuis*, "club" or in a *kroeg*, "tavern," went on *picnics*. The USI student journal wrote, in its May 1940 issue, "a mysterious name echoes through town—'*ballroom*'"; and the Dutch or rather Indies text continued: "*Wij zijn Modern! Soft light and sweet music of nog liever swing en dansen twee aan twee.*"[87]

When jazz was outlawed as the Japanese came, these young people went on dancing in private houses, and they listened to the clandestine radio for "Benny Goodman, Artie Shaw, Cab Calloway, and you name it yourself."[88] They could have found Sjahrir turning the same dials.

For his study of the young people around Sjahrir during the Japanese occupation, John Legge interviewed many of these men and women. Most told him that they did not learn Indonesian till they were in high school, and about a third had not learned Indonesian until they were actually in their early twenties. Soedjatmoko, a Javanese, who spoke perfect Dutch from his childhood, told Legge: "I could follow political speeches in Indonesian but only more or less." This, John Legge commented, had been the case with about four-fifths of them.[89]

When the Japanese came in March 1942, Dutch was outlawed, and, because the Japanese language, of course, took some time to learn, Indonesian became the language of official and public communication. A woman, in her early twenties at the time, and a loyal Sjahrir follower later, told me:

---

[84] Interviews with Soedjatmoko, Sitti Wahjunah, and Paramita Abdurrachman, Jakarta, November 6, 9, and 15, 1987. Zainal Abidin was a member of USI.

[85] Interviews with Sudarpo, Hamid Algadri, Rosihan Anwar, Listyo, A. B. Loebis, Jakarta, between October 1987 and January 1988; also Legge, *Intellectuals and Nationalism*, pp. 174–75. As far as we know, Ibrahim Jahja, Sudarpo, and Parman belonged to USI.

[86] Interview with Hamid Algadri, Soedjatmoko, and Paramita Abdurrachman, Jakarta, November 6 and 9, December 13, 1987.

[87] "We are modern! Soft light and sweet music or better still swing and dance two and two." *Orgaan der USI* 4 (May 1940): 50.

[88] Interview with Listyo, Jakarta, November 27, 1987.

[89] Legge, *Intellectuals and Nationalism*, p. 73.

I had to learn Indonesian suddenly when the Japanese came, and to this day I can not say that I read in it much. But I remember, what pleasure it was to repeat the new words slowly. Even now, sometimes, I say to myself with relish: "senantiasa," "senantiasa," "senantiasa."[90]

Moving largely outside the actual power sphere, being young and jazzy, these young people seemed to pass rather smoothly from one epoch to another. The Dutch and Eurasians in the Indies disappeared; they had to get rid of their properties fast. Several of the then young people shared with me the same recollection: never before, they say, were second-hand bookshops in the Indies so full of good Western books and journals as during the first months of the Japanese occupation, never before were there so many recent editions, so cheap, now, that even "natives" could buy them.[91]

As students, these young men and women belonged to a very exclusive group. Perhaps even more exclusive than Sjahrir's friends in Bandung back in the 1920s. Dutch education programs in the Indies were being progressively reduced from the early 1930s on, as a consequence of the economic depression, and because of the increasingly reactionary colonial policy. No more than 200 young men and women in Jakarta, at the beginning of the Japanese occupation, had graduated from high school and had some college experience.

Being of the elite, there had been as much of daring, as of embarrassment, in stories of their lives during the Japanese occupation, and even, in stories, later, of their underground activity. Aboe Bakar Loebis, for instance, one of the more adventurous of the stream, described himself, on a secret mission performed for Sjahrir as he said. On the train, when a Japanese patrol in search of spies and enemies came dangerously close to him, Aboe Bakar as a last resort took out his student cap and put it on his head. This change of costume enabled him to get through.[92]

Soedjatmoko, another of the group, described the same thing, when he recalled how he, during the occupation, tried to

> stiffen the attitude of his fellow students towards the Japanese ... bolstering their sense of individual independence against the new rulers ... encouraging them, for example, to talk loudly in corridors and elsewhere—about philosophy or literature or other non-political matters—in order to build up their courage.[93]

It was difficult for these young people to escape from being students, and to separate their actions from kinds of classroom happenings. They mostly worked, according to the principal Sjahririan of the postwar period, Subadio Sastrosatomo,

---

[90] Interview with Minarsih (Mien) Wiranatakoesoemah-Sudarpo, Jakarta, October 8, 1987. "Senantiasa" means "always" or "continuously."

[91] Ibid. Also see Takdir Alisjahbana, *Indonesia's Social and Cultural Revolution*, pp. 45ff; Legge, *Intellectuals and Nationalism*, p. 54.

[92] Interview with A. B. Loebis, Jakarta, October 10, 1987; also A. B. Loebis in Legge, *Intellectuals and Nationalism*, p. 59.

[93] Soedjatmoko in Legge, *Intellectuals and Nationalism*, p. 54.

"in the social field." The most important of the jobs at the outset, and the job most memorable throughout, Subadio's memoirs also make clear, was teaching.[94]

Perhaps the most celebrated, and certainly most political and most dangerous, event of this whole period in which Sjahrir's young followers were heavily involved—was a student strike.

The student strike broke out at the medical school, shortly after the school was reopened by the Japanese in 1943. The reason for the strike, according to most accounts, was the humiliation inflicted upon the students by the Japanese teachers slapping the students' faces. The final cause was an order to the students to have their heads shaved in the Japanese fashion. The students went on strike. After a school interrogation, the military police were involved, and the students were repeatedly beaten. Eight of them were expelled including four who were then or later associated with Sjahrir: Soedjatmoko, Sudarpo, Daan Jahja, and Soebianto.[95]

Before Sjahrir appeared from exile and from Sukabumi, two leaders seemed to have been especially important to the young group: Amir Hamzah Siregar and Amir Sjarifoeddin.

Amir Hamzah Siregar was remembered as a "brilliant" student, and then a teaching assistant, at the law school in Batavia during the last years of Dutch rule.[96] He was "brilliant and warm," according to others,[97] an influential figure in the Unitas Studiosorum Indonesiensis and a member of the USI journal editorial board.[98] He also was a recognized poet laureate of the students' circle, writing his poetry in both Dutch and Indonesian. One of the reviews appeared in January 1941:

> How absolutely new, how spontaneous, fresh, strong and individual the vision of Amir Hamzah Siregar is. . . . Amir Hamzah carries us truly towards a new life, towards a *"vie profonde, passionate, lyrique."*[99]

This particular review, written in the USI journal in Dutch, ended with "Indonesian language. Forward!"[100]

"Amir Hamzah Siregar," Subadio remembered, "reprimanded us often for being shallowly, narrowly, and aggressively against the Dutch." Some of the students, also according to Subadio, suspected Amir Hamzah Siregar of being a Dutch government spy.[101]

---

[94] In the house of the Sastrosatomo brothers at Guntur Street 23, for instance, the group organized *Privaat les bahasa Indonesia*, "Private lessons in Indonesian." Subadio, "Masa muda saya," pp. 116, 162.

[95] Margono Djojohadikoesoemo, *Herinneringen uit drie tijdperken: Een geschreven familie-overlevering* (Amsterdam: Nabrink, 1970), pp. 132–33; Sidik Kertapati. *Sekitar Proklamasi 17 Agustus 1945* (Jakarta: Pembaruan, 1964), p. 63; Legge, *Intellectuals and Nationalism*, p. 52. Margono was father of Soebianto.

[96] Interview with Soedjatmoko, Jakarta, November 6, 1987.

[97] Interview with Hamid Algadri, Jakarta, December 13, 1987.

[98] E.g., *Orgaan der USI* 1 (December 1940): 1; ibid. 2 (January 1940): 4.

[99] Ibid. 2 (January 1941): 10. The italicized words are in the original, i.e., in French and in English. The rest is translated from Dutch.

[100] Ibid.

[101] Subadio, "Masa muda saya," p. 58.

Amir Sjarifoeddin, according to most recollections, was even more impressive than Amir Hamzah Siregar. Decades after the war, and decades after Amir Sjarifoeddin himself was dead (and there were very bitter experiences between Sjahrir's and Amir's political groups later, as we will see), when Sjahrir's followers were asked to make a list of the people who had influenced them most positively in the past, Amir still appeared very high on the lists, and frequently at the very top.[102]

It was Soejitno Mangoenkoesoemo who introduced Amir Sjarifoeddin in Sukabumi to Sjahrir. Sjahrir, as we have seen, played down, in an later account, both the meeting and Soetjitno's evident "enthusiasm" for Amir. But there might be something more to the event and to Sjahrir working through it.

Soejitno also knew Amir Hamzah Siregar. In Soejitno's house in Jakarta, and also in the house of another law school graduate, Ali Boediardjo, a small group of young people regularly met through 1941 and 1942—a "study group," Ali Boediardjo called it later. The group studied "assigned literature." Amir Hamzah Siregar appeared occasionally at the meetings, and sometimes, several of the participants, in a smaller group, were taken to another place, to see Amir Sjarifoeddin. Once or twice, such a small group also went to see Sjahrir.[103]

Sitoroes, another of this "study club"—and after the war the general secretary of Sjahrir's party—told me that Amir Hamzah Siregar had been his "mentor" as early as during his first year at the law school, and that it was Amir Hamzah, who introduced him to Amir Sjarifoeddin.[104] Andi Zainal Abidin, also a former member of USI, who later became a known Sjahririan, shared a house at the time with Amir Hamzah Siregar; it was from Amir Hamzah that he had learned about "democracy and fascism," which, as he said, "in due course," he came to see "was what Sjahrir was teaching."[105]

In the case of Sudarpo Sastrosatomo, brother of Subadio, it was again Amir Hamzah Siregar who introduced him to Amir Sjarifoeddin. Amir Hamzah Siregar, Sudarpo remembered, had talked about Sjahrir on these occasions "in a very secretive way."[106] Hamid Algadri, also told me that he was "brought into Amir Sjarifoeddin's circle" by Amir Hamzah Siregar. According to Subadio, Amir Hamzah was also a mentor to Soedjatmoko. Already before the war, Subadio wrote,

---

[102] Interview with Soedjatmoko, Sitoroes, Ali Boediardjo, Jakarta, between October 1987 and January 1988. Besides being a prominent nationalist politician, Amir Sjarifoeddin was also recalled as "brilliant," and again, and more often, as "brilliant and warm." He was a graduate of the Law School, a few years older than Amir Hamzah Siregar, and he was an influential alumnus of the school. Ibid. See also Amir Sjarifoeddin, "Christen Studeren Vereeniging," *Uitzicht*, April 23, 1947, pp. 4ff. Two weeks after Pearl Harbor, on December 22, 1941, Amir introduced a new series of lectures in Batavia Volksuniversiteit, a city evening school or rather a debating society where progressive Indonesians and Dutch mixed. Amir's talk was on the "World after this war." The next lecturer, the next month, was a Dutch writer, and member of the *Kritiek en Opbouw* circle, Dirk de Vries, who talked about du Perron's generation. After Amir and de Vries, Jacques de Kadt was scheduled to lecture, but by that time, the Japanese had already arrived. See *Programma Volksuniversiteit*, 1941-1942, n.p.

[103] Ali Boediardjo, "Sjahrir, manusia yang utuh: apa amanatnya kepada kita?" in *Mengenang Sjahrir*, ed. Anwar, p. 117; interviews with Ali Boediardjo, Sitoroes, Simatupang, Jakarta, between December 1987 and January 1988. Ali Boediardjo mentioned Beatrice's Webb's *Soviet Communism* as one of the books "assigned."

[104] Interview with Sitoroes, Jakarta, December 29, 1987.

[105] Andi Zainal Abidin in Legge, *Intellectuals and Nationalism*, p. 88.

[106] Interview with Sudarpo, Jakarta, October 7, 1987.

Soedjatmoko, as well as Sitoroes, "borrowed books on politics and culture from Amir Hamzah," and it was Amir Hamzah who later introduced Soedjatmoko to Amir Sjarifoeddin.[107] A few weeks later, and also through Amir Hamzah, Soedjatmoko got to meet Sjahrir.[108]

The swirl of personal relations, fleeting meetings, and vague affinities, appeared to acquire a more solid shape toward the end of the first year of the Japanese occupation. This, significantly, was very much facilitated by both Amir Hamzah Siregar and Amir Sjarifoeddin abruptly leaving the scene.

In January 1943, Amir Sjarifoeddin was arrested, as mentioned, and disappeared for the rest of the war, into a Japanese prison. A few months afterwards, the date is not certain, but most probably sometimes in the spring 1943, Amir Hamzah Siregar, after suffering for a long time from tuberculosis, prematurely died. It was, in fact, at Amir Hamzah's funeral, that some of the young people, such as Sudarpo for instance, met Sjahrir face to face for the first time.[109]

3. Network of Power

According to at least one view, the Pendidikan Nasional Indonesia, as Sjahrir found it after his return from exile, was nothing but a *bajangan, sisa,* "a shadow, a remnant."[110]

It was symbolic that, out of all the Pendidikan leaders, it was Sastra who first met Sjahrir and Hatta in Sukabumi. Sastra was the man who, back in 1932 in Bandung witnessed Sjahrir's successful return from Holland and his meteoric rise to the top of the organization. Sastra, also, a former Communist, lived on a small farm near Bandung: if anybody, he was the man Sjahrir might imagine as his link to "the real people," whatever that term might mean.

Sjahrir's next contacts, as we have already noticed, were Hamdani and Soebagio in Bandung. They also had a special meaning for Sjahrir. They were probably his closest personal friends from yet earlier times before he went to Holland, when they were all, first of all, high school students.

In 1935, after Sjahrir and Hatta were arrested, the headquarters of the Pendidikan was moved to east Java, where it remained till 1942.[111] When the Japanese invaded the Indies, as Sastra later put it a little too self-confidently, he "picked up" Soebagio, who was the current chairman of the executive in Surabaya, and "brought him back to Bandung, the place the central executive belonged."[112]

In Bandung, the new, now underground, leadership was put together, and in Bandung it remained through the rest of the Japanese era. Besides Soebagio, Sastra,

---

[107] Subadio, "Masa muda saya," pp. 57, 178.

[108] Interviews with Soedjatmoko, and Hamid Algadri, Jakarta, November 6 and December 13, 1987; also Hamid Algadri, "Pengalaman-pengalaman kecil dengan Bung Kecil," in *Mengenang Sjahrir*, ed. Anwar, p. 123.

[109] Interview with Sudarpo, Jakarta, October 7, 1987.

[110] Sidik Kertapati, *Sekitar Proklamasi*, p. 67. Sidik was a non-Sjahririan or rather anti-Sjahririan youth leader from the time of the Japanese occupation and the Indonesian Revolution.

[111] According to the Pendidikan's own records, its last central executive at the time of the Japanese invasion consisted of Sarbini, Soemadi, and Kartamoehari, under the chairmanship of Soebagio Mangoenrahardja, "Pimpinan Umum Pendidikan Nasional Indonesia, 1932–1945" (Panitia Sejarah PNI, Jakarta May 1980, mimeo), courtesy Leon Salim.

[112] Sastra, "Sjahrir untuk Sastra," p. 88.

and Hamdani, the new executive was made up of two other local Bandung figures, Oesman and Roesni Tjoetjoen. Other members were Anwar Ismoedikarta (of whom we know otherwise nothing); Kartamoehari (who, apart from Soebagio was the only carry-over from the past leadership); and Soemarno who was a Pendidikan activist in the mid-1930s.[113]

From 1942—not unlike in its initial stage in 1932—Pendidikan very much meant Bandung and the region immediately around. Sjahrir wrote later that Pendidikan had been "practically the only organization in existence during the Japanese occupation in Garut, a town about twenty-five miles south of Bandung."[114] Sumedang, another town on the train line a short distance north of Bandung, was also a place where Pendidikan reportedly had a very strong impact.[115] Cirebon, a seaport on the train line from Bandung through Sumedang further north, appeared to be a center of Pendidikan activity during the Japanese occupation, second only to Bandung itself.[116]

There were some signs that Pendidikan activities extended to Tasikmalaya, southeast of Garut, and occasionally as far as Brebes, on the north coast, east of Cirebon. Those seemed, however, to be diminishing echoes of the Pendidikan center in Bandung.[117] Virtually nothing was heard of Pendidikan east of Brebes, at least until the very last months of the occupation, when everything began to change and everybody appeared to awake. Virtually nothing, too, was heard of Pendidikan in the areas outside Java, except, very significantly, for Minangkabau.

In Minangkabau, Pendidikan, appeared to be very much alive throughout the Japanese occupation. While it is very hard to find confirmation in independent sources of Pendidikan activity in Java (sometimes one hears this all was essentially Pendidikan imagination), outsiders had no doubt about its existence in West Sumatra.

The continuity in Minangkabau with the prewar period seemed almost uninterrupted. Leon Salim and Chatib Soeleiman who led Pendidikan from the early 1930s, were still at the head of the organization. There seemed to be no shifting in location

---

[113] Interview with Oesman, Bandung, January 10, 1988. Soemarno was a man, who, we may remember, had, according to Dutch police reports, met with Djohan Sjahroezah in 1936, to discuss reviving the Pendidikan through holding courses, and perhaps shifting Pendidikan's center from east to west Java. See above chapter 6. See especially Police Report to Attorney General, October 20, 1936 in *Secret Mail Report* 193, 6 no. 1057 and *PPO* Batavia, January/February 1936, pp. 13–15.

[114] Sjahrir's interview with George Kahin, February 15, 1949.

[115] Interview with Kartamoehari, Jakarta, January 9, 1988.

[116] In Cirebon namely, Pendidikan was organized by Dr. Soedarsono, who had also been a friend of Sjahrir since the 1920s. Interview with Sitoroes, Jakarta, December 29, 1987. Soegra was another leader in Cirebon—also a schoolmate of Sjahrir from the Bandung AMS; before the war, Soegra had once been the chairman of the Cirebon branch of Pendidikan. Anderson, *Java in a Time of Revolution*, p. 445. Also in the Cirebon Pendidikan leadership, there was a certain Soenarto, a protégé of Soegra, and a Pendidikan activist since at least the mid-1930s. Anton Lucas, "The Bamboo Spear Pierces the Payung: The Revolution Against the Bureacratic Elite in North Central Java in 1945" (Ph.D. thesis: Australian National University, 1980), p. 456. Kartamoehari, from the Bandung central executive, later also moved to Cirebon. Interview with Kartamoehari, Jakarta, January 9, 1988. See also Syahbuddin Mangandaralam, *Apa dan Siapa Sutan Syahrir*, p. 37.

[117] Interview with Apipah, Bandung, January 10, 1988; interview with Oesman, Bandung, January 10, 1988.

of Pendidikan headquarters, as had occurred on Java between the east and west of the island. Padang, Bukittinggi, and Padang Panjang during the whole prewar period and into the Japanese occupation appeared to be the centers and to radiate their influence constantly throughout West Sumatra and as far as Medan.[118] The Minangkabau was a compact center of Pendidikan activity. So compact that it may overshadow the rest of the loose network. It may even put the very existence of a centralized Pendidikan network in question.

As before the war, the politics of Pendidikan as an all-Indies or all-Indonesian organization meant "political" in a very particular sense. The Pendidikan's network remained loose in the extreme, and it is difficult and often impossible to find out where the real center was and what "the center" meant to the organization.

It is a frustrating job to trace either in the documents, or in the memories of participants, any of the Bandung central executive's specific efforts to direct the organization as a whole. The Bandung central executive seemed to restrict its work to Bandung and its immediate environs only. Even there the center's activity appeared to be very limited.

There reportedly was a Pendidikan-controlled trade union, PTTR, at the local Bandung Post and Telegraph Office. This was, according to one of its leaders, a minute organization consisting of a "few people." It also, was not a "strike-designed" union, but "rather a self-supporting collective" essentially used for the "self-education of its members."[119]

Also evidently restricted to Bandung, during the Japanese occupation, were the reportedly Pendidikan-organized Koperasi Rakjat Indonesia or Korindo, "Indonesian People's Cooperatives." Its former leaders again later described Korindo as a union of "consumption cooperatives," which also organized "small banks" for distributing cheap textiles and foodstuffs to members in the suburbs and villages of the wider Bandung, and Bandung-Garut areas.[120]

Both the PTTR and Korindo are remembered by their Pendidikan leaders as essentially "educational" structures. Both organizations, so their cadres believed, were "truly political," because they "prepared the people for freedom."[121] As far as their social composition was concerned, PTTR and Korindo leaders laconically, but consistently, stated when asked that these were "people's" organizations, which in their specification meant: "no *ningrat* [aristocracy] was admitted."[122]

Another categorical and laconic statement one hears from the organizations' leaders is that both PTTR and Korindo were on principle "self-contained," and that they had "no *centrale* [headquarters]."[123] Each of the structures had only a local "board [*pengurus*]," composed of about twenty members, who met in Bandung, and

---

[118] Abu and Suhadi, *Chatib Suleiman*, p. 14; interview with Roestam Anwar, Padang, January 13, 1988; interview with Leon Salim, Jakarta, November 3, 1987.

[119] Interview with Oesman, Bandung, January 10, 1988.

[120] Ibid.

[121] Ibid., and interviews with Kartamoehari, Jakarta, January 9, 1988, and with Tobing, Bandung, January 10, 1988.

[122] The cooperatives, in Kartamoehari's definition, were "non-capitalist, non-soviet, non-individualist, and non-*nigrat*—thus collectivist."

[123] Interview with Oesman, Bandung, January 10, 1988; and interviews with Kartamoehari, Jakarta, January 9, 1988, and with Tobing, Bandung, January 10, 1988.

were expected "to provide literature" for the cooperatives, and for the union: again, as it was specified, "not to direct them."[124]

Pendidikan cooperatives reportedly existed also in Cirebon. They were called Koperasi Rakjat Indonesia, like the Pendidikan cooperatives in Bandung, but they used a different abbreviation—KRI. Kartamoehari, who was involved in the Cirebon KRI leadership at the time, told me that "a great deal" of the village population in the Cirebon area was "touched" by the cooperatives' activities; according to him as many as twenty-nine out of ninety-two districts in the Cirebon region had their own KRI.[125]

Whatever the actual strength of the Cirebon cooperatives—and we will never find out the truth—it is the Pendidikan leaders' perception which interests us most at the moment. The success in Cirebon, according to Pendidikan activists themselves, was caused largely "by the fact that all authority in the area generally had crumbled," and that *lurah*, the last vestige of existing local power "village headmen," "did not mind Pendidikan activities."[126] The cooperatives in Ceribon, also, so one hears, were quite respectable: Soedarsono and Soepardan, two successive top leaders of the Pendidikan cooperatives in Cirebon, were medical doctors, and, at the same time, directors of the main Cirebon hospital.[127]

Even the Japanese authorities, the Pendidikan informants tell us, knew of the existence of the Pendidikan cooperatives in Cirebon. Dr. Soedarsono and another top Pendidikan and KRI leader, Soegra, even accepted seats in the Japanese-sponsored citizen- and advisory bodies.[128] The Japanese "tolerated" the KRI, so the Pendidikan people themselves explained it, because they perceived the cooperatives as playing "a socially positive role." This was naturally only a facade: "the KRI worked for the future."[129]

The "required reading," in Bandung as well as in Cirebon, was still Hatta's *Kearah Indonesia Merdeka*, "Toward Free Indonesia, "Sjahrir's and Soebagio's *150 Tanja Djawab*, "150 Questions and Answers," and whatever old issues of *Daulat Ra'jat*, "People's Sovereignty," the theoretical journal of the Pendidikan from the early 1930s, the cadres could lay their hands on. They tried, unsuccessfully I was told, to find Sjahrir's booklet on trade unions, from the same period.[130]

The classics of the early 1930s by Hatta, Sjahrir, Soebagio, Burhanuddin, Moerad, and others, which were reread and recopied—or merely remembered—held the organization together. According to Oesman, who worked in Bandung's Korindo, and also in Cirebon,

> Soebagio and a few others of us verified and copied the text, and then couriers took the text to the villages, via a cooperatives' local activist. Only local boards, very selective bodies, indeed, got our text. They studied it, and

---

[124] Ibid.

[125] Interview with Kartamoehari, Jakarta, January 9, 1988.

[126] Ibid.

[127] Interview with Oesman, Bandung, January 10, 1988.

[128] Anderson, *Java in a Time of Revolution*, pp. 442, 445. Soedarsono was a member of Putera, Soegra was in Sangikai.

[129] Interview with Oesman, Bandung, January 10, 1988.

[130] Interview with Tobing and with Oesman, Bandung, January 10, 1988.

afterwards, they called a meeting or a course, and there the text was read and interpreted to the regular members.[131]

In West Sumatra Pendidikan also manifested itself prominently through cooperatives. There were many very significant differences, however.

The West Sumatra cooperatives did not seem to exist "because other authority has crumbled down." Sumatran Pendidikan cooperatives appeared rather to be built largely out of the local communities' genuine strength. During the 1930s—as open political work became virtually impossible anywhere in the Indies—people in Minangkabau close to the Pendidikan and some Minangkabau Pendidikan leaders, as we have noticed, had shifted into local predominantly "social and cultural work." Through this, by the end of the Dutch colonial era, they appeared to be installed in some sound, and long-standing Minangkabau commercial ventures—incidentally based, too, on a cooperative basis. Quite powerful and dynamic local economic institutions, like the Persatoean Boemi Poetra, "Indigenous Union," Bank Nasional, "National Bank," or of INKORBA, "Indonesian Indigenous Cooperation," at the moment when the Japanese invaded, were as much a pride of Minangkabau, as a place where the Minangkabau Pendidikan was kept alive.[132]

In contrast to Java, also, the wartime activities of the Minangkabau Pendidikan, were not just "a preparation for the future." The Minangkabau Pendidikan leader Chatib Soeleiman, a man crucial to Pendidikan from the early 1930s, now became one of the most politically powerful figures in the area, well beyond the framework of the Pendidikan. Chatib gained the confidence of the Japanese military governor of West Sumatra. It should be noted, also, that the top Japanese official in the area supported Chatib as part of his respect for "the Minangkabau tradition of dynamism."[133]

Through the Javanese looseness and through the Minangkabau compactness, the Pendidikan all-Indonesian network might appear dis-equilibrated and center-less. After 1942 it was in West Sumatra and not on Java, that the Pendidikan emphasis on *daulat ra'jat*, "people's sovereignty," on modern socialism growing out of the traditional "democratic," self-governing strong indigenous community, *nagari* sounded pure and was applied in a way true to its spirit.

Sjahrir's place in the network of the all-Indonesian Pendidikan was ambiguous. He was not mentioned as a member of the central executive. His extremely loose ties with the movement, indeed, intrigued many of his contemporaries as well as later observers. They led occasionally even to the conclusion that no real Sjahrir movement existed or, at least, no real leadership.

Some of the people who worked under Sjahrir—and who, without reservation, recognized his authority throughout the time—when asked about Sjahrir's leadership, spoke as a rule, of his providing a "compass" or "information." "He kept us aware of the outer world," they might explain; or, "through him, we remained in

---

[131] Interview with Oesman, Bandung, January 10, 1988.

[132] Audrey Kahin, "Struggle for Independence: West Sumatra in the Indonesian National Revolution, 1945–1950" (Ph.D. thesis, Cornell University, 1979), pp. 373–74; Audrey Kahin, "West Sumatra: Outpost of the Republic," in *Regional Dynamics of the Indonesian Revolution*, ed. A. Kahin, pp. 167, 270–72.

[133] Abu and Suhadi, *Chatib Suleiman*, p. 14; interview with Miral Manan and interview with Roestam Anwar, Padang, January 13, 1988;

touch with the current state of affairs"; or "we learned a lot." At this point, automatically, they might add: "such a big brain in so small a body."[134]

Hamdani said that Sjahrir, during the war, "operated as *auctor intellectualis*."[135] Friends and enemies may add almost the same thing with respect to the style of Sjahrir's "brain" leadership. The friends might say: "he fought by teaching the youth."[136] And according to his enemies: "he remained aloof and only taught the youth."[137]

People meeting Sjahrir for the first time during the Japanese occupation, including those who became Sjahrir's ardent admirers, almost unanimously later recalled their first encounter with him as a surprising, often unpleasant, and largely disappointing experience. Ali Boediardjo, a member of the Amir Hamzah Siregar "study group" and later Sjahrir's personal secretary, wrote:

> I first met Sjahrir soon after the Japanese came. I was very disappointed. We, a few of my friends and myself, all of us still very young, were introduced by Soejitno to a man with a short body, who often laughed, who, in fact, was convulsed with laughter.[138]

Abdul Halim, a physician in Jakarta, who was soon also to be considered very close to Sjahrir, recalled:

> As a matter of fact, it is truly difficult to convey the first impression, which Sjahrir made: an intellectual, small body, easily laughing, but, when he talked, he appeared as if people around him did not exist, he looked as if towards a place far away, or at the floor, or at the ceiling. . . . It was very easy to make him laugh, it is true. But, I do not dare to say if he was having fun, then, or if he was making fun of the others.[139]

Soedjatmoko, a student at the Medical School at the time, a foremost follower of Sjahrir and later his brother-in-law, remembered that he had been "disappointed," when he first met Sjahrir. Minarsih (Mien) Wiranatakoesoemah-Sudarpo, another of the young group around Sjahrir, said that Sjahrir, at the first moment, seemed "weird." Subadio, who liked to call Sjahrir his mentor and who spent most of his later life serving Sjahrir's party, remembered how he and a few young friends went to see Sjahrir, for the first time. They wore ties and jackets despite the fact that it was 2 P.M., the hottest hour of the day. Sjahrir received them in shorts and undershirt. He laughed, and told them funny stories, while they had wanted to "talk politics and culture."[140]

---

[134] Interview with Kartamoehari, Jakarta, January 9, 1988; interview with Ali Boediardjo, Jakarta, January 5, 1988; interview with Mien Sudarpo, Jakarta, October 8,1987; see also "X," *Indonesisische politiek*, p. 7.

[135] Interview with Hamdani, Jakarta, October 30, 1987.

[136] Ibrahim Thalib, *Karya dan tjita Sutan Sjahrir* (Jakarta: Photin, 1966), p. 11.

[137] Interview with B. M. Diah, Jakarta, December 8, 1987.

[138] Ali Boediardjo, "Sjahrir, " p. 117.

[139] Abdul Halim, "Sjahrir yang saya kenal," in *Mengenang Sjahrir*, ed. Anwar, p. 114.

[140] Interview with Soedjatmoko, Jakarta, November 6, 1987; with Mien Sudarpo, Jakarta, October 8,1987, and with Subadio, Jakarta, October 18, 1987. Simatupang, another admirer of

Sjahrir, according to Ali Boediardjo again, traveled widely through Java on what he let others know were political missions. Then, he "unexpectedly appeared, returning, so he said, from Tjirebon, Semarang or Surabaja, and told us jokes." Sjahrir's admirers were made acutely aware that he had been constantly meeting other political figures. But, almost as a rule, "he did not tell us one word of what they talked about."[141]

Sjahrir, as a rule it seems, kept his people uncertain about his actual intentions:

> He talked about things outside [hal-hal yang luar], but he never commented on our views of the current situation, and this for us was almost unbearable. He avoided [mengelak] our questions ... when we wanted unambiguous answers.[142]

"He did not propagate a clear ideology, though he had one"; "He was a man who posed more questions than he gave answers"; "He did not wish [the young people] to become reliant on him."[143]

Some of his followers said that Sjahrir "gradually opened himself up" as he came to know them better.[144] But none, as far as I know, could boast a true intimacy developing between him or her, and the leader. "You are a cadre," Sjahrir was remembered as telling one of the Bandung Pendidikan, "and this is like when a ship is sinking—each man for himself."[145]

Even seasoned and, we may assume, the most intimate of Sjahrir's political associates, working in Bandung and thus near where Sjahrir was actually living—men such as Hamdani or Sastra—remembered later that they very rarely met Sjahrir during the occupation. They read his published texts, most of them more than a decade old, and they interpreted these texts for the regular members. But "actual," "immediate," "direct" contact with Sjahrir himself, so they say, was mostly either by messenger, by telephone, or by telegraph. The Pendidikan's tiny PTTR union at the Bandung Post and Telegraph Office becomes more meaningful in this context. After office hours, when the Japanese supervisors left, so I was told, "the air was clear, and we got in touch."[146]

"Those outside the group were sometimes made to feel that they did not belong."[147] From within, however, it appeared as if most of the connections making up Sjahrir's network were indirect to the extreme. A woman, who observed the situation at close range, has told me:

Sjahrir, also remembered his first meeting with him as "strange." But, at the same time, Simatupang, and most of the others indeed, only using different words, expressed the feeling that through their very first meeting with Sjahrir, "a veil was raised." Sudarpo, Subadio's brother, used almost the same term—his first meeting with Sjahrir was "strange," but "it was like bringing things back to their true proportions." Interview with Simatupang, Jakarta, January 4, 1987; and with Sudarpo, Jakarta, October 7, 1987.

[141] Ibid.

[142] Ali Boediardjo, "Sjahrir," p. 117.

[143] Quoted in Legge, *Intellectuals and Nationalism*, p. 59.

[144] E.g., Ali Boediardjo, "Sjahrir," p. 117.

[145] Interview with Tobing, Bandung, January 10, 1988.

[146] Interview with Hamdani, Jakarta, October 30, 1987.

[147] Mohamad Roem was one of the "outsiders" feeling this, quoted in Legge, *Intellectuals and Nationalism*, p. 59.

> Some of those people, who were recognized, from the time of the occupation onwards, as being close to Sjahrir, in fact, throughout the occupation, were merely close to some friends of Sjahrir or to some friends of Sjahrir's friends.[148]

Some of the truly "recognized" Sjahririans from the occupation period, such as Daan Jahja, Tandiono Manu, Soemarman, or Mochtar Loebis, admitted later that they did not meet Sjahrir face-to-face till the end of the war.[149] Some others—Soedjatmoko, Sudarpo, Hamid Algadri, or Simatupang—spent much of their time, during the occupation, for various reasons, outside Jakarta—in Surakarta, Tasikmalaya, Surabaya, or Bandung. They also agreed that they "practically lost" contact with Sjahrir for most of the time, except for one or two visits by him or by his courier.

Sometimes the courier or even Sjahrir himself seemed like hearsay. The courier might reach a "coworker" of Sjahrir, even Sjahrir himself might appear, bringing "information" about the situation, and urging them "to be ready." But it was generally difficult to be quite sure, for instance, Hamdani told me, whether the esteemed visitor did not merely stop by accidentally on his way elsewhere.[150]

Sjahrir wrote later:

> As I look back at the Japanese period, it is clear to what extent everything in the Indonesian community, spiritually as well as materially, was shaken loose from its own moorings.[151]

It is remarkable how much Sjahrir's reference to the loosening of anchors was reflected in his own network, and in his political style—how much the network and, indeed, Sjahrir's power, was based on this tenuous insubstantial quality of anchorlessness.

When talking to a woman admirer who later became his wife, Sjahrir himself touched upon his "awkwardness": *Ik ben eigenlijk verlegen van aard*, "I am shy by nature."[152] Others have described this quality of Sjahrir as arrogance, and this might not wholly contradict what Sjahrir himself said.

During the occupation, as in Banda Neira, Sjahrir clearly knew that shyness, shocks, and revelations, were closely related to power. Describing, for instance, the Japanese "treatment" of Indonesians, he wrote that it

> stimulated a consciousness of self [among the Indonesians], a feeling of self-confidence—partly as a psychological defense against the indignities, but also by virtue of their own work and experience.[153]

Sjahrir, it seems, made his network of power function not rarely by the weirdness, the shyness, and the aloofness. It was not only students and Jakarta intellectuals who

---

[148] Interview with Paramita Abdurrachman, Jakarta, November 9, 1987.

[149] Mochtar Lubis, "Pejuang, pemikir dan peminat," in *Mengenang Sjahrir*, ed. Anwar, p. 200; interview with Mochtar Lubis, October 10, 1987; also Legge, *Intellectuals and Nationalism*, p. 57.

[150] Interview with Hamdani, Jakarta, October 30, 1987.

[151] Sjahrir, *Out of Exile*, p. 248.

[152] Interview with Siti Wahjunah Sjahrir, October 10, 1987.

[153] Sjahrir, *Out of Exile*, p. 249.

were impressed—and controlled, indeed—by Sjahrir in this way. One of the most hardened, most politically experienced, and also brightest of the Pendidikan activists whom I have met, has told me:

> It was so difficult for a man as stupid as me to grasp what Sjahrir was actually thinking about. I wanted to live close to him. I tried passionately to get close to him. I am not saying this to be polite. I felt initiated.[154]

A frequent comment of people in "Sjahrir's movement" was: "He knew people we didn't know,"[155] or "Many friends came to visit him, but we were rarely introduced to them."[156] Sjahrir seemed to succeed in making his politics, at certain crucial moments at least, appear strangely out of place and disturbingly inappropriate. By his own awkwardness, he seemed to succeed in making his "coworkers" feel as if they themselves were awkwardly moving through a political landscape they did not actually know. Thus, Sjahrir seemed to succeed in making his "coworkers" unsettled: thus he kept them on the move.

Sjahrir wrote later that he had established "our working headquarters" in Cipanas. (This was, the reader may recall, near a village above Bogor, where Sjahrir's sister had her summer place, and where Sjahrir, after being forced out of Sukabumi, moved with his children.) Sjahrir goes on—and this is all he has to say about the "headquarters":

> We brought the equipment needed for a radio listening post and throughout the occupation the listening service continued in operation.[157]

Sjahrir's habit of listening to the radio—to the news at least, daily, and often several times a day—a habit already evident in Banda Neira, appeared to fit perfectly into this kind of network and power building.

For Sjahrir's generation, listening to the radio was a modern thing to do. It was an exile habit, too: one might listen in Banda Neira to broadcasts from far away, full of news about the outside world, the Western metropolises. Jazz and other music—we noticed this already—in the East as in the West were important parts of the early radio age.

Listening to the radio in occupied Indonesia, in addition to all this, became also an act of resistance.[158]

For reasons we have yet to talk about, there was virtually no armed resistance against the Japanese in occupied Indonesia, and the Allies, as documents show,

---

[154] Interview with Kartamoehari, Jakarta, January 9, 1988.

[155] Quoted in Legge, *Intellectuals and Nationalism*, p. 58.

[156] Ali Boediardjo, "Sjahrir," p. 118.

[157] Sjahrir, *Out of Exile*, p. 241.

[158] Again, it may be noted, that it was speculated about Tan Malaka, for instance, that he might have had a short wave radio when living incognito in West Java during the occupation. Adam Malik "dismisses such suggestion saying it was far too dangerous to have such an illegal possession. . . ." One of the people Helen Jarvis interviewed, however, "maintains that in late 1945 or early 1946 a certain Adi Sundjojo from the TNI-*Masjarakat* and two other people arrived with a letter for him signed 'TM (Hussein)'. The letter asked (him) to take those people to Hussein's old house to get something . . . they found pieces of gold and a radio receiver hidden in the wall." Jarvis, ed., *From Jail to Jail* 2: 288–89.

accepted the fact as something that could hardly be changed.[159] "Anti-fascist resistance" inside Indonesia, as the Allied directives defined it, actually consisted almost exclusively of listening to the radio. The Allied *Draft Plan for Operations in North Western Areas,* for instance, in 1942 ordered the participants in the resistance movement in Indonesia—whoever the participants might be, through "Phase One," that is until about two months before liberation, to watch for "leaflets raids" and to "establish an organized listening to broadcasts from Allied sources, and spread the news thus obtained."[160]

For Sjahrir, illegal listening to Brisbane might involve additional excitement. In June 1943, the Dutch had evacuated to Australia the remaining 507 internees from Boven Digul.[161] The internees were freed, in a few months, and some of them were employed by the Netherlands Indies Government Information Service or NIGIS. Several of them became, indeed, *trouwste medewerkers,* "the most trusted coworkers," of the NIGIS director, Charles van der Plas, a former Resident of Cirebon and a former associate of the "neo-ethical" journal *Stuw.*[162] They helped to publish in Australia a Malay-English journal *Penjoeloeh-Torch,* and to prepare broadcasts back to Indonesia. Editorials appeared in *Penjoeloeh-Torch*—some with headlines like *Menoedjoe Indonesia Merdeka,* "Toward Free Indonesia"—debating "progress," "democracy," "justice," and "new times."[163] Some former Communists too worked in the group, such as Sardjono, acting in line with the Comintern policy of the united front. Truly prominent among van der Plas' associates in Brisbane, however, were Burhanuddin, Maskoen, Soeka, and Moerad—all of whom, of course, close friends of Sjahrir in Bandung, the Pendidikan, and also Boven Digul.[164]

According to Sjahrir's own account, in the middle of the occupation,

> I also found that in Batavia there were still a few small groups that tried to do such resistance work as they could. A Frenchman and a Ceylonese were involved. The Ceylonese occupied an important position from our point of view; he was a translator of Allied news in the Japanese radio monitor service. We managed to keep in touch with these people...."[165]

---

[159] E.g., van Mook's press conference, Sydney, March 1944, in *Collection van Mook* no. 39.

[160] "Draft Plan for Operation in North Western Areas, December 30, 1942," in *Collection van der Plas* map 6, no. 36; see similarly "Organization of Psychological Warfare in the Pacific Area, July 5, 1943," in *Collection Warners,* no. 419.

[161] Spoor to van der Plas, August 14, 1942 in *MSHS Australia* Hc-23/5; Spoor, *Journal van de reis,* June 18, 1942, ibid. Hc-23/6. See also Rupert Lockwood, *Black Armada* (Sydney: Australian Book Society, 1975).

[162] The term *"trouwste medewerkers"* is used in van der Plas' letter (van der Plas to van Mook, October 14, 1943, in *Collection van der Plas* Map B-8).

[163] E.g., "Menoedjoe Indonesia Merdeka," *Penjoeloeh Torch* March 17, 1944, pp. 12–13; "Demokrasi Marhein," ibid., July 21, 1944, p. 4. See also Mohamad Bondan, *Genderang proklamasi di luar negeri* (Jakarta: Kawal, 1971).

[164] On Burhanuddin, Maskoen, Moerad, and Soeka in *NIGIS* see, e.g., *Penjoeloeh Torch* March 7, 1944; see also 1984, p. 27; see also Murwoto, *Autobiografi selaku perintis Kemerdekaan;* also interview with Burhanuddin, and Moerad. For reasons that will be elaborated upon below, the Pendidikan-Boven Digul group's wartime cooperation with van der Plas is not mentioned in any of the Sjahrir's accounts of the time.

[165] Sjahrir, *Out of Exile,* p. 245.

In all probability, the Frenchman was Charles Damais, a scholar who had settled in Java long before the war and who—based possibly on the fact that Vichy France was an ally of Japan—now belonged to the exceptional few Europeans who were not interned. The Ceylonese certainly was Charles Tambu, a journalist living in Singapore before the war, who was captured there by the Japanese and taken to Jakarta, where he was placed in a Japanese "Radio Camp" on the outskirts of Jakarta. Tambu's task was to monitor Allied broadcasts in English.[166]

Charles Tambu, and another Australian not mentioned by Sjahrir, a certain Rodie, were relatively free to move between the "Radio Camp" and the city. They could also mix with Indonesian employees at the camp and gradually they became especially close to two of them—Oetojo, an announcer at the Japanese Radio foreign service, who already knew Sjahrir at that time, and Mochtar Lubis, a writer for the Japanese radio propaganda section, who, at that time, knew of Sjahrir only indirectly but "already respected him."[167]

The crucial man in this small group, it seems, also goes unmentioned by Sjahrir. He was a Dutchman, Dr. L. F. Jansen. According to Mochtar Lubis' memoirs,

> I was so lucky to meet Dr. Jansen. He used to be the secretary of the Council of the Indies. He was a bachelor, and a very cultured man. He introduced me into the wonders of the Japanese *haiku*. He kept a great library which he left with an Ambonese friend outside the camp, and I helped him get the books into the camp. In exchange, he helped me with my studies of history and economy. He told me which books I might need for continuing studies in school, and he gave the books to me.[168]

Dr. Jansen was a graduate of Batavia Law School—like Amir Sjarifoeddin, Amir Hamzah Siregar, or Djohan Sjahroezah for instance; Dr. Jansen was also a Leiden trained scholar, and a student of the "most ethical" professors, van Vollenhoven and Snouck Hurgronje. In his youth Jansen was "very" leftist, and, in Leiden, he wrote a sympathetic thesis on the "Groundwork of the Soviet State."[169] Late in the 1930s Dr. Jansen also became close to Eddy du Perron; it was he, in fact, who published an obituary for du Perron in Batavia's literary journal *Fakkel* at du Perron's sudden death in 1940.[170]

In the "Radio Camp," Dr. Jansen, because he was a Dutchman, was much less free than the others. Nevertheless, he repeatedly tried to get out, "via a hole in the fence," and "in native attire."[171] During one such effort, a few months before the end of the occupation, he was caught by the Japanese, and spent the rest of the war in jail. The aborted mission was, according to a rather uncertain source, "to contact an

---

[166] *Independent*, January 15, 1946.

[167] Interview with Mochtar Lubis, October 10, 1987. Also L. F. Jansen, *In deze halve gevangenis: Dagboek van Mr. Dr. L. F. Jansen, Batavia/Djakarta 1942–1945* (Franeker: Van Wijnen, 1988), p. 22.

[168] Mochtar Lubis, "Van dingen die ik me nog herinner," *Tirade* 19 (1975): 537–38. Dr. L. F. Jansen is not mentioned in any of Sjahrir's accounts of the time. One reason might be that, after the war, Dr. Jansen was attacked in some circles as a collaborator with the Japanese.

[169] G. J. Knaap, "De Djakarta Overseas Broadcasting Service en Mr. Dr. Leo Jansen," in Jansen, *In deze halve gevangenis*, pp. xix–xxxiv, *passim*.

[170] Jansen, "Na den dood van du Perron," *Fakkel* I, 1 (November 1, 1940): 24–29.

[171] Knaap, "De Djakarta Overseas Broadcasting Service," *passim* and especially, pp. xxivff.

important Indonesian nationalist," Sjahrir's cousin and Djohan Sjahroezah's father-in-law, Hadji Agoes Salim.[172]

If one were to find a single image that might convey most truthfully the elusive nature of Sjahrir's network during the Japanese occupation, the image—apart from that of the wireless immediacy of radio—would be certainly the fast moving and rarely distinct image of Djohan Sjahroezah.

Djohan Sjahroezah worked during the first year of the occupation in Jakarta, part of the time in the office of Mohammad Hatta. In the second year of the occupation he moved to Surabaya, apparently to work for the oil company in nearby Cepu. There, he is reported to have slowly taken over what remained of Amir Sjarifoeddin's resistance movement in Surabaya, when Amir himself was arrested in 1942.[173] At the same time, through his time in Surabaya, Djohan Sjahroezah maintained a connection with the student community in Jakarta, which had originated perhaps in the early 1930s, when he was a founding member, as we noticed, of the radical Perhimpoenan Peladjar-Peladjar Indonesia, PPPI, "Association of Indonesian Students," at the Batavia Law School.[174]

A recent careful study of the period describes Djohan Sjahroezah, in the Japanese time, as "by far the most significant of the active *Pendidikan* members."[175] At the same time, like Sjahrir, Djohan did not hold any official position in the organization, like Sjahrir, he traveled widely through Java. Unlike Sjahrir, he visited West Sumatra twice, and was remembered by the local Pendidikan leaders as probably the single actual contact they had, during the war, with the center and with Java.[176]

Djohan epitomized the qualities of Sjahrir's network. He moved on the brink. He blurred the contours of the movement. One could be almost sure that, when Djohan came to town, he was speaking on Sjahrir's behalf. But the emphasis was on "almost."

Djohan was too strong a personality, with too genuine an experience, for anybody to be absolutely sure that he was, at any moment, merely a messenger. Djohan's activity in Surabaya dealt with workers, and he apparently carried it out with an intensity Sjahrir himself could hardly achieve. Djohan, moving fast, also never lost his contacts with radicals, who were largely outside Sjahrir's network—followers of Tan Malaka, like Adam Malik, Chaerul Saleh, Soekarni, Pandoe Wigoena, or Maroeto Nitimihardjo.

Djohan was thought "purely professional" by those, who knew him well.[177] He was a creature truly and nakedly political, which meant that he was always explicit about actual political power being the aim and principal motivation of his action. He

---

[172] Ibid.

[173] Interview with Sitoroes quoted in Legge, *Intellectuals and Nationalism*, pp. 54–55, 60, 63; Anderson, *Java in a Time of Revolution*, p. 126n. Subadio, "Masa muda saya," p. 175. It may be noted that two decades before, Tan Malaka was active in the same locality, among the oil factory workers at Cepu, being elected, in 1921, a vice-chairman and treasurer of the workers' SPPH union, speaking at mass rallies and working on the editorial board of *Soeara Tambang*, the union's paper. (Jarvis, ed., *From Jail to Jail* 1: 208, n. 39.)

[174] Kahin, *Nationalism and Revolution*, pp. 112–13; interview with Hazil Tanzil, Jakarta, March 2, 1982; Legge, *Intellectuals and Nationalism*, p. 63.

[175] Legge, *Intellectuals and Nationalism*, p. 61, n. 43.

[176] Interview with Miral Manan and interview with Roestam Anwar, Padang, January 13, 1988.

[177] See, e.g., Legge, *Intellectuals and Nationalism*, p. 64.

was perhaps less broadly cultural than Sjahrir, and certainly less "shy" and less aloof. Having Djohan around, having him different, ambiguous, awkward in Sjahrir's network, helped to make that network more itself, more loose, and thus more powerful.

4. NATIONALIST MAINSTREAM

One afternoon, in late 1943 or early 1944, Soedjatmoko, Sudarpo, and Subadio—and perhaps a couple of other young people—after a soccer match, jumped on their bikes and rode to Sukarno's house. Asmara Hadi, who worked as Sukarno's secretary, stopped them at the door, informing them that Sukarno was having his siesta. They should know, they were also told, that the very idea of visiting an older and so distinguished personality as Sukarno, at that time of day, and without an invitation, was highly improper.

Yet they decided to wait. When Sukarno at last came out, the young men, so they remembered it, did three significant things. First, they addressed him in Dutch, which was forbidden. Second, they mentioned "some recent battles and Japanese losses," showing that they had been listening to clandestine radio, which was a crime. Third, they declared that they would "deny their allegiance" to Sukarno.

In the debate which followed, according to their own account, the young men said some more improper things to Sukarno. They accused him of going too far in his cooperation with the Japanese. They compared him with Hitler's Hungarian ally, Admiral Horthy, who was, as they said, "also without a fleet." After this, they "excused themselves [*kami minta diri*],"

> not just to take our leave of him now, from his house, but to leave him, to part ways with him, and to take our own path towards independence.[178]

Sukarno gave his own version of the event later, in his autobiography.

> The medical students had given me much difficulty. Many were Sjahrir's pupils . . . a small band of impatient, dissatisfied young men who nearly succeeded in getting themselves killed. . . ."[179]

By "nearly succeeded in getting themselves killed," Sukarno referred to the student strike at the Medical School. "I gazed into the eyes of my passionate young jurors," Sukarno wrote about the confrontation in his house, and the stare, according to the autobiography, made the young men at the end "speak softly."[180]

Whatever the particulars of the confrontation, the family atmosphere appears to have been essential. The confrontation turned out to be very much an act of disobedience, a kind of a youngsters' revolt.

It was difficult to escape the impression that the students dared to act because they were treated with special care. Sukarno did not fail to point this out. In the same passage, he wrote that it was actually he who saved the students when they got into

---

[178] Interview with Soedjatmoko, Jakarta, November 6, 1987; and with Sudarpo, Jakarta, October 7, 1987; also Subadio, "Masa muda saya," pp. 187–88.

[179] Sukarno, *An Autobiography*, p. 194.

[180] Ibid.

real trouble, after the student strike. Sukarno acted to save the kids, a fact that Sukarno's opponents themselves have never denied.[181]

The attitude of Sjahrir's wartime movement to "real" action is a very peculiar—and also crucial—part of its history. Throughout the occupation, no actual strikes were organized, either by the Pendidikan unions, or by the Korindo and KRI cooperatives. None of the Pendidikan activists, nor the movement as a whole, ever claimed to have attempted any act of actual armed resistance or sabotage against the Japanese. Connections with an armed power in Indonesia—be it hidden weapons, Allied armed forces, Japanese armed forces, or the Japanese-created Indonesian militia after 1943—were either non-existent or indirect in the extreme.

The students in Jakarta most often connected with Sjahrir—Sudarpo, Subadio, Soedjatmoko, Ibrahim Jahja, Simatupang, a Christian Batak, and also, earlier, close to Amir Sjarifoeddin, together with some others—met occasionally in the house of one of their colleagues from medical school, Iwan Santoso. Iwan's father, Raden Soeria Santoso, had been a major in the Royal Netherlands Indies Army (KNIL) before the war and was also a graduate of the Breda military academy in Holland. Raden Santoso began his career in the early 1920s, as a protégé of one of the most prominent of the Dutch proponents of the "ethical" policy, J. H. Abendanon. Now he served as another of the students' mentors.

The meetings with Major Santoso soon developed into another "study club." The students read Leon Blum and Dimitrov, Jan Romein and Petrus Blumberger. They also very ardently studied "doctrines and manuals of the Royal Netherlands Indies Army."[182]

Sjahrir also mentioned Major Santoso in his later recollections of the time:

We managed to keep in touch with . . . an Indonesian major who had been connected with the nationalist movement. The major was closely watched by the Japanese police, but he was still active among the Eurasians, the Ambonese, the former military people, and later also among our students.[183]

In June 1942, the Japanese advance in the Pacific was halted, and there were reports of heavy Japanese losses at Midway. In 1943 news came of the Japanese resistance being broken on Guadalcanal, of the Allies landing on New Guinea and the Solomon Islands. In January 1944, the Marshall Islands were attacked; then the Carolines. In June, Japanese Saipan became the direct target and, in the same month, the Battle of the Philippine Sea began. One would have thought that, as the actual fighting got closer to the Indies, the emphasis on physical struggle and actual action in Sjahrir's movement would also strengthen.

But instead, what seemed to become more pronounced was the movement's detachment in Java from the day-to-day politics of the occupation, and its looseness in itself. Major Santoso, as far as we know—as the war fronts moved towards the islands sometime late in 1943—became very close to Sjahrir's people and to Sjahrir personally. But this closeness occurred—of all possible places—in the Komisi Bahasa

---

[181] Ibid.
[182] Subadio, "Masa muda saya," p. 171; interview with Simatupang, Jakarta, January 4, 1987, and with Sudarpo, Jakarta, October 7, 1987.
[183] Sjahrir, *Out of Exile*, p. 245.

Indonesia, the "Commission for Indonesian Language," an essentially cultural and educational institution, again a sort of "study club."

There is no suggestion from any of the participants that anything but cultural and broadly political "debates" and theoretical "getting ready for the future" was going on in the commission. This institution, with Japanese agreement, was founded in October 1943. Its aim was to systematize Indonesian grammar and vocabulary for more effective use under the new order. Sukarno and Hatta led the commission's directorate, but their control was merely formal.

The executive chief was Soetan Takdir Alisjahbana, a leading spirit in the Indonesian modernist literary journal *Poedjangga Baroe* before the war. (As the reader may remember, this was the journal where Sjahrir, while in exile, published his long essay on culture.) Also in the commission's acting directorate were Dr. Raden Soewandi, former professor of the law school in Batavia, and Dr. Soetomo Tjokronegoro, a professor in the prewar Batavia Medical School. Takdir's personal assistant was Subadio Sastrosatomo, a devoted Sjahrir follower already, while Miriam—a sister of Soedjatmoko and of Poppy Saleh—worked on the commission's staff; Ida Nasoetion was also on the staff, a brilliant young graduate of the HBS high school in Batavia.

Other Sjahrir students such as Daan Jahja, Soebianto, Soeroto Koento, Soedjatmoko, and Sudarpo frequently attended formal and informal debates in the commission. Also Oetojo, an announcer at the Japanese Radio foreign service, friend of Dr. Jansen, Charles Tambu, and Mochtar Lubis of the "Radio Camp," came occasionally.

Several poets and artists took part in the debates and the "intellectual conspiracy" at the commission: people such as Chairil Anwar, a poet and Bohemian, and a distant relative of Sjahrir; Aki Djoehana, Sjahrir's nephew, son of Sjahrizal Djoehana, and also an emerging poet; H. B. Jassin, already a star of the new young Indonesian literary criticism; the painter Soedjojono (who would later paint the portrait of Sjahrir and the old fisherman on the Banda Neira beach) and another painter Basoeki Rebowo.

Soetan Noer Alamsjah, Sjahrir's older brother, worked as an adviser to the commission in legal matters. Major Santoso, reportedly, was a very frequent visitor.

Sjahrir actually came rarely. His influence was indirect—as it was put to me repeatedly, he was "often quoted."[184] Subadio might have been suggesting the same when he wrote that Sjahrir's presence at the commission was that of "a man of culture" rather than of "a man of politics."[185] Sjahrir, also, was not there, when the commission made a blunder, came too close to actual action, and crashed against the rough surface of the occupation regime.

This occurred with the *Manifesto Demokrasi*, "Democratic Manifesto," a document written by Takdir Alisjahbana in October 1944. The aim of the *Manifesto* is not altogether clear, but it was clearly thought to suit well the spirit of the movement. Takdir remembered writing the *Manifesto* "with enthusiasm," even taking three weeks off work in the commission.[186] He consulted mostly a book by "Professor Brailford, chairman of the British Labour Party," so it is remembered. The *Manifesto*, when completed, contained

---

[184] Interview with Takdir Alisjahbana, Jakarta, October 20, 1987; and interview with Subadio, Jakarta, October 18, 1987; Subadio, "Masa muda saya," pp. 154, 190; Lubis, "Pejuang, pemikir," p. 200.

[185] Subadio, "Masa muda saya," p. 154.

[186] Interview with Takdir Alisjahbana, Jakarta, October 20, 1987.

Japanese Drawings (3)

not merely a general vision of a free democratic state, but principles of our struggle ... concerning the development of technology, economy, and art, and especially the problem of education.[187]

This all was condensed into "about ten pages," and the original was copied six times. Of the six copies (none of them, it appears, survived) Takdir kept one and the others were given to Djugito (about whom we do not know much more), Dr. Soetomo, Dr. Soewandi, Subadio, and Major Santoso. The *Manifesto* was discovered in a matters of days, probably during a search of Major Santoso's house, and the Japanese military police considered it dangerous enough for Takdir Alisjahbana, Major Santoso, and Subadio to be arrested. The two older men were soon released, but Subadio remained in jail till April 1945.[188]

This is how Sjahrir himself described his politics during this time:

After a while the Japanese intelligence service naturally found out I had some influence in nationalist circles, particularly among the popular movement and the younger intellectuals. Everyone, however, professed ignorance, and never approached me directly in the first two years. [Hatta and Sukarno] both agreed never to mention me....

Officially I was almost always in the mountains in Tjipanas. The nationalists who were working with the Japanese politically were naturally somewhat unfriendly toward me. The rumor circulated among them that I was not working with [Hatta] because I had suffered a nervous breakdown, or that I was in Tjipanas convalescing from tuberculosis. But since they did not know what I was actually doing, there was not much active belligerence against me.[189]

As we have noted already, Sjahrir wrote how, after a few months of the occupation, he "lost touch" with Sukarno. In the following months, he also wrote, he "turned aside" all attempts by cooperating Indonesians to "draw" him into the circle of occupation politics—thus, into the nationalist mainstream.[190]

As Sjahrir's vocabulary also suggests, however, this was never a clear-cut situation. Sjahrir was never completely out of the picture, never completely away from the mainstream.

He could be seen in Hatta's office, throughout the occupation. It was more than a slight embarrassment to Hatta, one witness said, when Sjahrir—very articulate and not soft-spoken even when someone else was present—commented on what Hatta was doing at the time or what he should be doing.[191]

Sjahrir's children, the girls in particular, occasionally worked on projects, which Hatta had organized and Sjahrir might advise upon. A data-gathering project was mentioned to me, on *romusha*, local labor recruited by the Japanese to help the war

---

[187] Subadio, "Masa muda saya," pp. 185, 196–211. See also Legge, *Intellectuals and Nationalism*, pp. 48, 58.

[188] Ibid.

[189] Sjahrir, *Out of Exile*, pp. 247–48.

[190] Ibid.

[191] Interview with Paramita Abdurrachman, Jakarta, November 9, 1987. Ms. Paramita said, she participated with Sjahrir's two daughters on one of these projects.

effort. The project was clearly bound to question the image portrayed by Japanese propaganda and by Sukarno of the *romusha* as "labor volunteers," rather than modern-time slaves.[192]

It was never difficult for Sjahrir to keep indirect contact with Hatta's office. Soejitno Mangoenkoesoemo, Soekaemi (in 1932 the first chairman of the Pendidikan), and Djohan Sjahroezah before he left for Surabaya, worked at one time or another in Hatta's secretariat; and they were as good friends of Hatta as they were of Sjahrir.[193]

Sjahrir, moving around, talked about, rumored, vaguely influential, appeared to be an increasingly disturbing phenomenon to many in the nationalist mainstream. The mainstream meant cooperating with the occupation regime, to be part of the system. Much of Sjahrir's dynamics, as the war progressed, appeared to be drawn from invitations coming from the various parts of the nationalist mainstream, and his evading these feelers.

On September 7, 1944, a new Japanese premier, Koiso, in a speech to the Japanese Diet, announced that independence might be granted to the former Dutch East Indies "some time in the future." Reflecting, mainly, the advance of the Allied forces on the Pacific front, Japanese policy was becoming more responsive to the Indonesian nationalist mainstream. The Japanese began to grant Sukarno-Hatta greater authority in matters of administration, economy, and native militia. The nationalist mainstream broadened, and to keep moving on the fringes demanded the deftness of a professional wanderer.

Sjahrir wrote about the situation as it began to develop after the "Koiso promise":

Indonesians who had disdained me before sought to reach me, and one of them even asked me, in the name of his Japanese chief, if I would set down on paper my ideas concerning the general situation and what I thought of the future. Naturally I did not accept the proposal.[194]

Wikana was a man of thirty, a member of Amir Sjarifoeddin's Gerindo youth before the war, but not too close to Sjahririans till this moment. In September or October 1944, Wikana visited Sjahrir, and asked him to become a lecturer at a new Japanese-supported Indonesian-nationalist school about to be opened in Jakarta.

The institution Wikana talked about, Asrama Indonesia Merdeka, the "Ashram of Free Indonesia," was designed as a boarding school for patriotic Indonesian men above high school age, but not necessarily high school graduates. Behind the project, and also behind Wikana's offer to Sjahrir, was Achmad Soebardjo, a leader of Perhimpoenan Indonesia in Holland in the 1920s, a friend of Hatta from that time, and also a friend of Iwa Koesoemasoemantri, with whom, as we may recall, Sjahrir had spent a not-too-pleasant six years in Banda Neira. The Japanese Navy liaison office on Java, and the liason office's chief, Rear Admiral Tadashi Maeda, were the most directly involved occupational authorities.

Sjahrir declined Wikana's offer. Then, Soebardjo sent a second invitation. According to Soebardjo's own account,

---

[192] Ibid.

[193] Anderson, *Java in a Time of Revolution*, p. 447; Hatta, *Indonesian Patriot*, p. 205. A. R. Baswedan, "Hatta: Antara Catatan dan kenangan," in *Bung Hatta*, ed. Swasono, p. 473.

[194] Sjahrir, *Out of Exile*, p. 252; see also ibid., p. 247.

First, when I asked him, Sjahrir refused to give the lectures. I succeeded in persuading him only after I said that the youth were very eager to acquire some knowledge of socialism and of the socialist movement generally.[195]

The school was officially opened by Tadashi Maeda, in October or November 1944, at Gunung Sahari, one of the main streets of Jakarta. The first class of thirty students graduated after a six-month course, in spring 1945. A second class of eighty students started in May 1945 and, as the war ended, these students did not have the time to finish the course.[196]

The most prominent figures of the nationalist mainstream were involved in teaching in this school. Sukarno lectured on politics, Dr. Singgih, a lawyer and also a leader of the prewar Partindo, gave lectures on "nationalism from the point of view of culture"; Hatta taught economics. Sanoesi Pane, a poet laureate of the prewar *Poedjangga Baroe*, taught the history of Indonesia, Iwa taught criminal law, Soebardjo international law.

Wikana was the school's "supervisor."[197] Courses were given also by Japanese Navy instructors in karate, judo, and kendo. Sjahrir is remembered as having lectured on "socialism in Asia" or, according to other sources, on the "youth movement."[198]

Some qualities in the "Ashram of Free Indonesia," might have made the school more attractive to Sjahrir than the other nationalist and occupational institutions of the time. The Japanese sponsor of the school, Rear Admiral Tadashi Maeda, as the chief of the Japanese Navy liaison office, was an agent of what, in Java, was a power on the fringe. Java was administered by the Japanese Army.[199] In addition to manifesting and suffering the animosities traditional to the Japanese military establishment, Tadashi Maeda and his staff, according to many reports, exercised a very unorthodox vision of Japanese occupation politics in Java.

Some Indonesians who were in touch with some Maeda staff officers recollected after the war how "surprised" they had been "by the depth of [these officers'] knowledge of Marxism," and, generally, by their thinking in an "extremely progressive manner."[200] It might also not have been merely an accident that both Wikana and Soebardjo were rumored at least to have had earlier leftist or Communist inclinations and connections. Some also said that, throughout the school's short

---

[195] Djoyoadisuryo, *Kesadaran nasional*, p. 256.

[196] Ibid.; also a letter to the author by Mr. Shizuo Saito, a member of the planning section in charge of political affairs in wartime Java (letter, Tokyo, June 29, 1988).

[197] Djoyoadisuryo, *Kesadaran nasional*, pp. 256–58. Written communication by Shigetada Nisjijima to the author (letter, Tokyo, June 28, 1988); also B. M. Diah, *Angkatan Baru '45: Lembaga Perjuangan Pemuda menentang Jepang, mendorong Proklamasi kemerdekaan Indonesia* (Jakarta: Masa Merdeka 1983), pp. xxii–xxiii.

[198] Ibid.

[199] The Japanese Navy was entrusted with administering Eastern Indonesia.

[200] Kahin, *Nationalism and Revolution*, p. 118. Admiral Maeda's principal adviser, Shigetada Nishijima, was possibly more influential among the Indonesians than Maeda himself because of his proficiency in Indonesian and Dutch, and because of his long-standing previous experience in the Dutch Indies. He was known, among the Indonesians, as an ardent socialist before the war, an activist in the Japanese Communist Party indeed, and he liked to tell stories of how he had suffered for his convictions. Information from Takashi Shiraishi.

existence, in one way or another, the "shadow" of the legendary Communist of the past, of Tan Malaka, was "vaguely felt around."[201]

Admiral Maeda himself later insisted that the idea of the "Ashram of Free Indonesia," was a reaction to the disappointment among the Indonesians, when Premier Koiso had promised freedom, and nothing much had happened afterwards. The school was started, Maeda also said, "in an attempt to cultivate really useful men," "men of talent," and all that for "independent Indonesia."[202] Thus, Maeda said,

> I invited almost all the top Indonesian leaders to lecture there on whatever they liked. Even Sjahrir appeared—of course not collaborating with us![203]

Teaching at the "Ashram of Free Indonesia," seemed to be something close to a regular job for Sjahrir. At least one man, close to Sjahrir at the time, believed that Sjahrir was paid for his lectures.[204] According to the recollection of Nishijima, one of Maeda's top aides,

> Sjahrir began to teach regularly at the *Asrama*, and we sent a car each time for his convenience to come to the *Asrama*. But I don't think there had been any strong connection between Sjahrir and students of *Asrama*, [nor] needless to say, any relation between the *Asrama* students and the so-called "Sjahrir's *pemoeda*."[205]

Sjahrir himself, talking about the "Ashram of Free Indonesia" later, emphasized looseness. As George Kahin quoted from one of his interviews with Sjahrir after the war, the teachers at the "Ashram of Free Indonesia,"

> were given complete freedom to say whatever they wished, making open propaganda for Indonesian independence and, according to Sjahrir, even attacking the army-controlled Japanese administration.[206]

Sjahrir agreed to teach at the school, so his explanation seemed to suggest, because the school was loose from the Japanese, and also from the nationalist mainstream. "Sukarno, was always completely aloof from this organization," Sjahrir also told George Kahin, and he illustrated this by insisting that Sukarno "did not trust Soebardjo."[207]

---

[201] Interview with Sitoroes, Jakarta, December 29, 1987. Sitoroes was a man very close to Sjahrir from the occupation on, but, like Djohan Sjahroezah, always maintaining connections also to the stream close to Tan Malaka.

[202] Tadashi Maeda, "On the Eve of Independence of Indonesia 1945," n.p., August 16, 1954 in *Nishijima Collection* P.I.22, p. 7.

[203] Maeda's interview with Anderson in Anderson, *Java in a Time of Revolution*, p. 44.

[204] Interview with Sitoroes, Jakarta, December 29, 1987.

[205] Written communication by Shigetada Nisjijima to the author (letter, Tokyo, June 28, 1988).

[206] Kahin, *Nationalism and Revolution*, p. 116.

[207] Sjahrir's interview with George Kahin, February 26, 1949. Soebardjo, on the other side, later wrote that Sukarno had warned him against letting Sjahrir influence students at the *Asrama* too much in Sjahrir's own direction. Soebardjo Djoyoadisuryo, *Kesadaran nasional*, p. 258.

Sjahrir also emphasized continuity. Again explaining, on another occasion, why, after so long keeping aside, he became involved in the "Ashram of Free Indonesia," he pointed out, in a remarkable combination, his efforts to keep on moving and his pleasure in teaching:

> I realized that my movements were being watched. They had evidently found out that I traveled considerably and had many visitors. In fact, toward the end they tried to restrict my movements.... I realized that it [the invitation to teach at the *Asrama*] was an indirect means of making my travel difficult, and at the same time of keeping an eye on my movement and my ideas....
>
> The courses I gave [at the *Asrama*] concerned nationalism and democratic principles, and I must admit that I derived some pleasure from the results. Quite a few of those who took the courses later became capable fighters for our freedom and our republic.[208]

As the first class of the "Ashram of Free Indonesia" was about to graduate, exactly at the moment of the first American B-29 bombing of Japanese cities, by the way,[209] Sjahrir touched upon occupation politics again. Sjahrir's name now even appeared in the Indonesian newspapers. The name, in fact, made headlines.

The occasion was *zadankai*, a round-table debate organized by a major Jakarta daily, *Asia Raja*, "Great Asia," in the Jakarta Hotel *Miyako*, on March 12, 1945. Several *wakil dari masjarakat*, "representatives of society," were invited and asked "for a few thoughts and commentaries," which "might be used to energize even more the *Gerakan Hidoep Baroe*, 'New Life Movement.'"[210] The "New Life Movement" was the most recent campaign launched by Sukarno's and Hatta's nationalist mainstream, and sponsored by the Japanese. Sjahrir was among those invited.

The invited "representatives of society" were listed in the following order: Messrs. Oto Iskandardinata, Sartono, Soebardjo, and Sjahrir; Mmes. Soenarjo and Maria Ullfah Santoso. An extensive transcript of the round-table was published immediately in three installments on the front pages of *Asia Raja*, on March 15, 17, and 18; other papers also reported the *zadankai*.

Mr. Sartono, of course, was Sukarno's long-standing associate, and the leader of Partindo ten years previously—a man, the reader may recall, who was most fiercely attacked by Sjahrir and Pendidikan during the conflict in the nationalist movement in the early 1930s. Mrs. Soenarjo, through her husband at least, had also been a member of the old Partindo group, and now was also a leader of the Japanese-sponsored women's organization, Fujinkai.

Oto Iskandardinata, was a Sundanese, West Javanese, nationalist leader, now also cooperating with the Japanese. The presence of Soebardjo might again suggest Admiral Maeda in the background. Maria Ullfah was a leader of Fujinkai like Mrs. Soenarjo, but we may remember her also as a Javanese regent's daughter studying in Leiden in the early 1930s, a close friend of Sjahrir, when together in Holland they attended *Volksconcerts*, movies, and political lectures by Jef Last.

---

[208] Sjahrir, *Out of Exile*, pp. 251–52. Regarding these students Sjahrir also said to Kahin: "Actually all became anti-Japanese rather than anti-Western." (Interview February 26, 1949.)

[209] *Asia Raja*, March 12, 2605 (1945), p. 1.

[210] Ibid., March 15, 2605 (1945), p. 1.

Burhanuddin Mohammad Diah, the assistant editor of *Asia Raja*, and a relative of Soebardjo, decades later recalled—and still with traits of irritation—how "elusive" Sjahrir had been, and that it had taken several visits by himself, and then by the chief editor even, before Sjahrir finally consented to come.[211]

The *zadankai*, as recorded, was quite remarkable. The Allied fronts were strangling the Japanese empire. But almost unrestrained optimism appeared to reign at the table. Sartono gave most vehement expression to this, but the feeling appeared to be generally shared, with only light shades of difference.

Sjahrir entered the debate first by remarking that "the new movement" was at risk of "not being accepted by the people." (Sartono had just described the same "movement" as a magnificent accomplishment, and the high tide of the historical Indonesian struggle for freedom.) Sjahrir said he might agree that "a revitalizing power [of the people] is on the rise," but this, he qualified (alluding very clearly to the increasing distress of the common Indonesians under the Japanese), "is because our society failed to fulfill the wishes of the people."[212]

Oto Iskandardinata then spoke with elation about the youth now being "more mature," than they had been ten years ago. Sjahrir, rather coldly, commented on the *pemuda*, "youth," now as a group struggling with "difficulties," and "suffering greatly."[213]

Soebardjo entered the debate praising "the politics of Nippon" in Indonesia to "revive the Eastern spirit [*ketimuran*]." Soebardjo declared that "new life" "began at the moment when the Dutch government broke down." In Sjahrir's comment,

> new life . . . began in Asia a long time ago, at the moment when the Asian nations embarked on adjusting their lives to the spirit of the times.[214]

Education was the next issue. Sartono spoke of a "family, child and youth education," about education as "love [*tjinta*] for the Fatherland," as a "spirit of the East and of Asia," as "respecting [*menghormati*] the Japanese flag and the Indonesian flag, and as singing *Kamigayo* and *Indonesia Raja*." In sum, Sartono said, education was a "spirit of nationalism [*semangat kebangsaan*]." Mrs. Soenarjo advocated education towards a well-ordered family, Oto emphasized "military training," and Maria Ullfah suggested a struggle against analphabetism was most important.[215]

Sjahrir talked on education at greatest length. There was no *tjinta*, "love," in what he said, no *hormat*, "honor," no *ketimuran*, "Eastern spirit," and, indeed, no *semangat kebangsaan*, "spirit of nationalism." Education, as Sjahrir said at the round table, essentially meant

> to renew one's own life first, and then to act as an example, to impel the will power of the people, to sacrifice one's self-interest.

---

[211] Diah, *Angkatan Baru '45*, pp. 59–60; interview with B. M. Diah, Jakarta, December 8, 1987.
[212] *Asia Raja*, March 15, 2605 (1945), p. 1.
[213] Ibid., March 18, 2605 (1945), p. 1.
[214] Ibid., March 15, 2605 (1945), p. 1.
[215] Ibid., March 17, 2605 (1945), p. 1; and March 18, 2605 (1945), p. 1.

Education, Sjahrir told the *zadankai*, meant teaching how to keep a balance between the *materieel*, "material," and *moreel*, "ethical." Each moment, when this balance is renewed, *batin*, "the inner self, the spiritual self, the mind," "is also revived."[216]

The Indonesian youth, those who were to be educated, according to Sjahrir, were "the hope of the nation," "a compass [*pedoman batin*] of how to build a life on an ideal." No movement could live, he continued, "if not based on every one in the movement renewing his own life." All the great historical movements of the past, all earlier great efforts at education, "had been, as a matter of fact, a way to purify the *batin*."[217]

A junior staff member of *Asia Raja* at the time, and later a friend and follower of Sjahrir, recalled Sjahrir's appearance at the *zadankai*:

> Sjahrir did it, basically, in order not to antagonize the Japanese too much. He came, said what he said, and vanished again.[218]

5. Proclamation of Independence

In the days after the *Asia Raja* round-table, and throughout the rest of March, news was coming, through the clandestine radio, and more and more also through the legal media, about the battle of Iwo Jima, about the Allied advance towards Okinawa, and about the end of the war in Europe.

On May 4, 1945, the German armies surrendered in Holland. Besides other things, the full story could now be published in Europe, with some of it filtering through to the Indies—of the Dutch anti-fascist resistance during the war, and of the impressive role played in it by some Indonesians living in Holland. The existence of the wartime underground Contact Commissie, "Liaison Commission," was also made public, which, among other things was to prepare reforms for postwar Dutch rule in the East.

The composition of the "Liaison Commission" was also now announced. The chairman was Professor W. Schermerhorn, a member of the Dutch Social Democratic Labor Party, SDAP, an aerial photography expert with a long-time experience in the prewar Indies. Among other top members of the "Liaison Commission" were Indonesians from the prewar Perhimpoenan Indonesia, such as Setiadjit; and P.J. Schmidt, the former chairman of the "Independent Socialist Party," OSP, even earlier, editor of the journal *De Socialist*, and, thus, a close friend and political associate at that time of Sal Tas, Jacques de Kadt, Jos Riekerk, and also of Sjahrir.

In April 1945, the NIGIS, Netherlands Indies Government Information Service, radio service in Brisbane reported into the still Japanese Indonesia about the historic Conference of the United Nations being opened in San Francisco. The radio also reported that one of the members of the Dutch East Indies delegation was one Burhanuddin, who was, of course, a former internee in Boven Digul, earlier a leader of the Pendidikan, and also a close friend of Sjahrir.

"By mid-July, 1945," Subadio says, "from talks with both Sjahrir and Major Santoso, I concluded that Japan was in a fix."[219] According to Ali Boediardjo,

---

[216] Ibid., March 18, 2605 (1945), p. 1.
[217] Ibid.
[218] Interview with Rosihan Anwar, Jakarta, November 8, 1987.
[219] Subadio Sastrosatomo, *Perjuangan Revolusi* (Jakarta: Sinar Harapan, 1987), p. 11.

> We understood, that Sjahrir was gathering forces and organizing power [*menghimpun tenaga dan menjususn kekuatan*] for a revolution, which—and this we saw clearly—was about to break out. . . .[220]

"Under the leadership of Sjahrir," wrote Sastra, Sjahrir's "proletarian mentor," and an old cadre of the Bandung Pendidikan,

> we were moving underground, accumulating subjective power [*menjusun kekuatan subjektif*], while waiting for the objective situation to develop, and for the psychological moment to come, to seize authority and to get freedom.[221]

Sjahrir's student followers, who had left Jakarta at one or another point during the occupation, still remained in the provinces, often with their families, "reading avidly." They remembered later, as the crucial moment was approaching, the program for the group became: "move fast, move faster." What was desired, a Bandung leader of the Pendidikan explained to me, was "not to tighten organization of the cadres, but speed, initiative of the parts, dynamics."[222]

Initially, from the Cirebon branch, for instance, which was about half a day by rail from Jakarta, someone went each month to see Sjahrir: then they went each week, then "by each train," and, eventually, "two cadres by each train."[223] From Sjahrir, they received, so they later recalled, the latest news about the situation, especially about the situation abroad. This became more exciting with each passing day. They received finally one instruction from Sjahrir, which, in the few dramatic last weeks of the occupation, did not appear to change: *Djangan melawan Djepang! Sambut merdeka!*, "Do not clash with Japan! Answer the call of freedom!"[224]

"To fulfill the needs of the freedom struggle," Sastra wrote later,

> Sjahrir issued a compass [*pedoman*] for comrades in the provinces, which was passed by word of mouth. The directive ran, in short: "Free Indonesia means that the Indonesian people govern their own state and society [and that] the government is capable of protecting peace and order [*keamanan dan ketertiban*] for the well-being of all who inhabit Indonesia. Not merely for the native and original population."[225]

Panitia-Panitia Keamanan Rakjat, "Committees for People's Security," were to be "prepared for," by local Pendidikan branches, but not actually established until the "objective situation" develops and the "psychological moment" comes.[226]

There were also preparations among the Pendidikan for a Komite Nasional, "National Council." While the "Committees for People's Security" were to "watch

---

[220] Ali Boediardjo, "Sjahrir, " p. 118.
[221] Sastra, "Sjahrir untuk Sastra," p. 89.
[222] Interview with Kartamoehari, Jakarta, January 9, 1988.
[223] Interview with Oesman, Bandung, January 10, 1988.
[224] Ibid.; also Kartamoehari used the sentence in almost exactly the same form.
[225] Sastra, "Sjahrir untuk Sastra," pp. 89–90.
[226] Ibid., p. 90.

over the security of the people," and to prove that Free Indonesia had the inner strength to exist, the "National Council" was to be composed of "educated fighters, who, for the sake of Free Indonesia, can talk to the Allies."[227]

Sjahrir's own later account of the last stage of the Japanese occupation, in a way, was very dramatic:

> Under the Japanese, the people had to endure indignities worse than any they had known before.... Want and suffering increased so terribly in the villages that more and more rebellions occurred out of desperation. In the last year of the occupation they were especially widespread.... The situation clearly became more revolutionary as time went on. Everywhere unrest grew.... Tens of thousands filled the prisons. Disturbances and resistance multiplied. Even the Indonesian troops trained by the Japanese as reserve forces began to rebel.[228]

Sjahrir's picture was surprisingly dramatic indeed. There were two rebellions in Peta, the Japanese-sponsored Javanese militia, but both were suppressed quickly, and neither had much of a visible connection to the Allied cause or the anti-fascist movement. Sjahrir's phrase "tens of thousands filled the prisons" could be taken as reflecting reality only if the Dutch and Eurasians in the internment camps were included.

Sjahrir's style was dashing and colorful when portraying the society during the last few weeks of the Japanese period being "shaken loose from their own moorings." When it came to his describing the cooperating nationalists at the same time, however, Sjahrir's language became flat, and his narrative suddenly was reticent:

> During this time the Japanese began to permit Indonesians to assume positions that previously had been reserved for Japanese.... The collaborating nationalists now became hopeful and confident ... that a kind of self-government for Indonesia might be possible even under the Japanese: a Dokurichu, or home rule....[229]
>
> During the last months, when the Japanese army and navy were being forced out of the southwest Pacific, a constitutional convention was called for framing Dokurichu.[230]

Rather than Sukarno-Hatta, and the nationalist mainstream they represented, being openly attacked in Sjahrir's account, they were denied flamboyance. There was nothing in this account by Sjahrir (what one knows from so many, most indeed, other accounts of Sukarno at the time) of Sukarno becoming, towards the end of the war, despite the fact that Japan was losing the war, the unchallenged Great Leader, with hundreds of thousands of Indonesians hanging on his lips.

Sjahrir denied this. When writing about Sukarno's oratory (and, significantly, his oratory on the radio) Sjahrir made it appear hollow:

---

[227] Ibid.
[228] Sjahrir, *Out of Exile*, pp. 249–51.
[229] Ibid., p. 252.
[230] Ibid., pp. 252–53

the air was filled with the palaver of the Japanese propaganda machine. Public radio sets were set up in the remotest villages, and the propaganda squads came with their films and equipment. At first propaganda helped to appease the hungry people. Later it became scorned and hated.[231]

There was an empty space in Sjahrir's account: not a note on a movement so often described by historians of the period, so impressively portrayed by Benedict Anderson especially: no hint of the *jago*,[232] the long-haired young boys, becoming, as the war was nearing its climax, their communities' champions, moving the whole society by the power of their mystical knowledge, of their *ngelmu kedotan*, their "science of invulnerability"; feeding on "utopian voluntarist, and transcendent elements of traditional Javanese thought."[233]

Strikingly there was nothing, in Sjahrir's writing, on the Youth Congress held in the Villa Isola in Bandung in May 1945, an event which established a new nationalist youth federation Angkatan Baroe, "New Generation"—according to a number of other observers, a movement of major importance in the social and political upheaval that was soon to follow.[234]

There are some awkward moments of silence in Sjahrir's later accounts of the last weeks of the occupation. These gaps might result, in part, from Sjahrir's changing perspective as he wrote the accounts. But the awkward memory certainly also reflected actual awkward moments in Sjahrir's moving through July and August 1945, his growing uncertainty as he was finally about to return from his exile (and his self-imposed quasi-exile), to leave the fringes and to enter Indonesian politics unambiguously and fully.

Burhanuddin Muhammad Diah, as we may recall, was the assistant editor of *Asia Raja*, and he became a principal leader of the "New Generation" as it emerged from the Villa Isola in May 1945. Diah recalled later how sometime in mid July 1945, on the verge of the revolution, on one occasion Sjahrir turned to him, "in jest," "laughing in my face":

> This is the earthquake, eh? . . . This is the omen, is it not? This is the time, when shadows would fight, when the wajang performance would truly begin. My dear Burhanuddin, sure, you would like to join the fight.[235]

The mockery (Diah, by the way, was an Acehnese, and the "wajang" Javanese "shadow fighting" jest did not make much sense in his case) might have reflected a growing nervousness in Sjahrir, as events began to suck him in. Sastra from the Pendidikan also recalled an incident in the same month:

> Early in July 1945, I and Sjahrir talked about who should be the right person to step forward as the proclaimer of independence [*proklamator kemerdekaan*].

---

[231] Ibid., p. 250.

[232] It is of some interest to compare Sjahrir mentioning *jago* (*djago*) in his letter from Banda Neira dated November 7, 1941. "*Djago*" in that letter of Sjahrir is a word used for that "cock" Hitler, as reader may recall. See above Chapter 6.

[233] Anderson, *Java in a Time of Revolution*, especially chapter 1.

[234] Ibid., pp. 50–58.

[235] Diah, *Angkatan Baru '45*, pp. 59–60; interview with B. M. Diah, Jakarta, December 8, 1987.

They decided, Sastra wrote, that "the proclaimer" should not be Sjahrir. "He was known among the movement, but not enough among the common people." They also decided on the occasion, Sastra wrote, that—Tan Malaka may be the man![236]

Tan Malaka was a truly curious choice in that context. He had been outside the Indies for more than twenty years. It also seems, from the way Sastra narrated his story, that neither he nor Sjahrir were quite sure where Tan Malaka might be at the moment—if, indeed, he was in the country at all. "There were rumors," Sastra wrote, "that he smuggled himself back into the country, and hid out in Bayah Banten [West Java], under the name Ibrahim."[237]

It appears from Sastra's recollection that this was not merely a fleeting idea,

> Sjahrir sent comrades Itji and Kantaatmaka to contact Tan Malaka. But, alas, they did not find him. [Thus] Sjahrir and myself were compelled to go and look for him, and we met him with help of comrade Marta, a stationmaster at Menes. We asked Tan Malaka, if he was ready to become the Proclaimer, and Tan Malaka, *right away and clearly, said he was not ready.*"[238]

The mission was aborted. Yet, it did not appear, evidently, that Sjahrir might step in as another candidate to be "the proclaimer." Tan Malaka refused to take on the job, Sastra concluded, "and thus, there was no alternative for us, but Sukarno-Hatta."[239]

On July 5, the reconquest of the Philippines had been publicly admitted by the Japanese. Twelve days later, the Supreme War Guidance Council in Tokyo decided that

> the Empire approves independence for the East Indies at the earliest possible moment.... Matters such as national polity, form of government, national name and national jurisdiction of the new independent nation shall be determined on the basis of public opinion,

at the same time,

> vigorous steps shall be taken to prevent obstacles to military operation and war preparedness,

and

> The local execution of these measures shall be entrusted completely to the local [Japanese] military authorities.[240]

Three weeks after this, on the morning of August 9, 1945, Sukarno, Hatta, Radjiman (chairman of a newly established "Investigating Committee for the Preparation

---

[236] Sastra, "Sjahrir untuk Sastra," p. 90.

[237] Ibid.

[238] Ibid. emphasis in the text.

[239] Ibid.

[240] Harry J. Benda, James K. Irikura and Koichi Kishi, eds., *Japanese Military Administration in Indonesia: Selected Documents* (New Haven: Yale University Southeast Asia Studies no. 6., 1965), p. 274.

of Indonesian Independence"), and Sukarno's personal physician Dr. Soeharto, with two Japanese officers, left by military plane for Saigon. There they were to meet Field Marshal Terauchi, the highest Japanese authority in the region, and hear details from him about what was clearly understood to be the almost immediate grant of independence by Japan to Indonesia.

Before the mission left, as Sjahrir recalled later,

> on August 8, I had a talk with Hatta. I proposed that he should press the Japanese for independence. I told him he would be pretty safe.[241]

In an account of the same meeting, in another of his own accounts, Sjahrir appeared to act even more decisively:

> Before they left, I had a long conversation with [Hatta]. I told him I thought it was all over for the Japanese, and that our chance had at last come for a total national effort. I advised him to draw the line between our position and the Japanese as sharply as possible, so that we would be forced into a position of open conflict with them. My point was that the situation be made as revolutionary as possible in order that there would be no division in the nationalist camp between those of the resistance and those who had collaborated.[242]

While Sukarno-Hatta were away in Saigon—and while other figures of the political mainstream passively waited for the two leaders return—events on the fringes of Indonesian politics began to move very fast. Either on August 8 or on the day when the party left for Saigon, Sjahrir wrote,

> The people in our resistance organization were informed that the moment for which we had waited and prepared might arrive within a few days. Communication with all branches accelerated.[243]

On August 10, "at 10 a.m.," poet Chairil Anwar, according to Subadio's account, came to the office of the Soetan Takdir Alisjahbana's "Commission for Indonesian Language,"

> and he brought a message from Sjahrir that the second atomic bomb had been dropped, in Nagasaki, and that Japan had received an ultimatum by the Allies, either to surrender or to expect further atomic attacks to come.[244]

This information, together with an instruction—"when freedom is declared [*dinjatakan*], support [*sokong*] it"—was, again according to Subadio, spread through the city by Sjahrir's young supporters, and it was taken, by the first trains leaving, to

---

[241] Sjahrir in "Wawantjara dengan Tokoh2," a manuscript prepared for *Star Weekly*, dated August 13, 1955; courtesy of Sitti Wahjunah Sjahrir.

[242] Sjahrir, *Out of Exile*, p. 253.

[243] Sjahrir in "Wawantjara dengan Tokoh2."

[244] Subadio, *Perjuangan Revolusi* , pp. 11, 13.

Surakarta and Yogyakarta.[245] "Between August 10 and 14 especially," Subadio wrote,

> there was no peace in our lives. We did not dare to sleep in our homes and were all the time prepared to pick up our towels and toothbrushes and move again.[246]

Sjahrir recalled: "On August 10, I knew definitely that the Japanese would surrender."[247] Still a day later, in Dalat, Vietnam, Sukarno was inaugurated by the Japanese as chairman, and Hatta as vice-chairman, of a new "Committee for the Preparation of Indonesian Independence." On August 12, as they were about to leave Saigon for home, the two leaders were given "final official word from Terauchi" that the proclamation of Indonesian independence was a matter of days.

Sukarno later believed that the date then had been set for August 24.[248] Hatta, as he wrote in his memoirs long after the war was over, was "very thrilled":

> after so many years of struggle to receive this present of Indonesian Independence on that day—August 12 was my birthday.[249]

Sjahrir saw Hatta again on the afternoon of August 14, moments only after the delegation had returned from Saigon. At the same time, Professor Soetomo, formerly of the medical school, and a member of Takdir's "Commission for Indonesian Language," reportedly visited Sukarno and pressed him to move faster.[250] Hatta told Sjahrir what had happened in Saigon, and Sjahrir reacted with an outburst about "a Japanese swindle, because their surrender would be announced at any moment."[251] Now, as Sjahrir later recalled, he became convinced that "the moment to act has arrived, and it was now or never."[252]

According to a Minangkabau writer, and a Pendidikan activist, Ibrahim Thalib,

> as the time of the proclamation of independence approached, during the three days and nights which preceded it, Sjahrir *gelisah*.[253]

The word *gelisah* (or *kegelisahan*) is a word Sjahrir himself would soon make famous, using it to describe the state of Indonesian society in a time of revolution. It reminds us, also, of his formulations in an account written in 1947 about the society "shaken loose from its own moorings." The word *gelisah* means "upset, restless, trembling." No better word could be found, now, for Sjahrir in action.

---

[245] Ibid.

[246] Subadio in "Wawantjara dengan Tokoh2."

[247] George Kahin's interview with Sjahrir, February 15, 1949.

[248] Anderson, *Java in a Time of Revolution*, pp. 63–64; Dahm, *Sukarno*, p. 310.

[249] Hatta, *Indonesian Patriot*, p. 222.

[250] Subadio, *Perjuangan Revolusi*, p. 13.

[251] Sjahrir, *Out of Exile*, p. 253; this account basically agrees with Hatta, *Indonesian Patriot*, pp. 226–27.

[252] Sjahrir in "Wawantjara dengan Tokoh2"; Sjahrir, *Out of Exile*, p. 259.

[253] Thalib, *Karya dan tjita Sutan Sjahrir*, p. 12.

During his meeting with Hatta, on August 14, Sjahrir laid out his plan of what should be done:

> I suggested to [Hatta] that our independence be proclaimed immediately. Everyone would then think that the proclamation was the result of the Saigon discussions. Hence the Indonesian components of the Japanese regime (i.e. the administrative personnel, the police and also a part of the army) would go along with us, and in any case would certainly not oppose the proclamation. At the same time, for those of us in the resistance, the proclamation would be a sign to unleash mass action against the Japanese.[254]

Hatta, according to his own recollections, was "rather startled" by the news he got from Sjahrir about the imminent Japanese surrender.[255] He told Sjahrir, he could do nothing without Sukarno, and left to consult the top leader—or "to persuade" Sukarno, as Sjahrir put it.[256]

As Hatta left to talk with Sukarno, Sjahrir "passed the word":

> I passed the word to our people in the city to prepare for demonstrations and perhaps fighting if the Japanese tried to use force. The sign for the demonstrations was to be the proclamation. We had already drawn up the draft and sent it throughout Java to be printed and distributed on the same day.[257]

Sjahrir never had much confidence in Sukarno, nor in Hatta when Hatta was together with Sukarno. Before leaving for Saigon, as Sjahrir said later, "Hatta promised he would demand complete independence. However he did not. Sukarno discouraged him."[258] Now, Sjahrir was to be proven right again: Hatta returned to say "Sukarno was not convinced that things were really so bad for Japan."[259]

Yet Sjahrir convinced Hatta at least to maintain the pressure. At about midnight, they returned to Sukarno's house together.[260] They talked again, and Sukarno (a little *gelisah* perhaps?) said at the end that, before deciding anything, he had to check with the Japanese authorities the next day.[261] Sjahrir, so he later implied, interpreted this as almost a promise: the Japanese would have to confirm Sjahrir's information, and Sukarno would have to go ahead. Indonesian independence might be proclaimed before the end of that very day, which was August 15:

---

[254] Sjahrir, *Out of Exile*, pp. 253–54. Sjahrir's account was confirmed, in its essential points, by what Hatta himself later wrote about the meeting. Hatta, *Indonesian Patriot*, pp. 226–27.

[255] Ibid.

[256] Sjahrir, *Out of Exile*, p. 254..

[257] Ibid.

[258] Sjahrir's interview with Kahin, February 15, 1949.

[259] Sjahrir, *Out of Exile*, p. 254. Sukarno, at the same time was reported to be telling people not to believe in the rumor about the Japanese capitulation. Abdul Halim, *Di antara hempasan dan benturan: kenang-kenangan dr.Abdul Halim, 1942–1950* (Jakarta: Arsip Nasional, 1981), p. 13.

[260] Hatta, *Indonesian Patriot*, pp. 226–27.

[261] Ibid.

Orders were given as quickly as possible and preparation for the demonstrations was accelerated. Our students were especially active in these preliminaries, as were the fellows who were working at *Domei*, the Japanese press office.[262]

As portrayed in Sjahrir's various accounts, the forces, previously constantly on the fringes—loose, *gelisah*, shaken, trembling, dynamic, and also most sensitive to the world outside—had now begun to close in, around the hesitating "waiting" center. Sjahrir described this graphically, and, indeed, unusually for him, he exaggerated not a little:

On the outskirts of the city we had assembled thousands of the youth, who would move into the city as soon as the proclamation was broadcast by our boys at the radio station.[263]

In the center, there was the radio station—radio was prominent again, and there was the expectation of a voice. Hatta described what happened to him and Sukarno, when, the next day, they went to check with the Japanese. The image Hatta conveys—the sound or rather lack of sound—was very similar to what we have just read by Sjahrir. Hatta (paraphrased by Anderson in this passage)

remarked that the most convincing confirmation of the surrender rumors was the silence and emptiness of the gunseikan's [the head of military administration] office that afternoon.[264]

"There was nobody in the office except a lieutenant," Hatta remembered.[265] It was about 3 p.m. when Sukarno and Hatta eventually found a Japanese, who might either confirm or deny Sjahrir's story. The Japanese was Admiral Maeda. He had just come from listening to the broadcast of the Japanese surrender on the radio:

The voice of His Imperial Majesty the Emperor was broadcast at noon on August 15 from Japan, and it was adversely hampered by atmospheric disturbances. But what His Majesty said could be understood.[266]

To Sukarno and Hatta, Maeda still talked vaguely. There was "no official confirmation yet," he said. Both, Sukarno and Hatta, Anderson wrote, were shaken (*gelisah*?) "shocked and disappointed."[267] Nishijima, the aide who was present at Maeda's side, later recalled himself wondering, as he looked at the two Indonesians: "How miserable and pitiful their fates would be!"[268]

---

[262] Sjahrir, *Out of Exile*, p. 254.

[263] Ibid., p. 255.

[264] Anderson, *Java in a Time of Revolution*, p. 68.

[265] Hatta, *Bung Hatta Antwoordt*, p. 133.

[266] Mohammad Hatta, *Sekitar Proklamasi* (Jakarta: Tintamas, 1969), pp. 27–28.

[267] Anderson, *Java in a Time of Revolution*, p. 69.

[268] Nishijima quoted in ibid.

Maeda urged Sukarno and Hatta to go on with business as usual; "please wait," he said. It was decided to leave things as they were: the "Committee for the Preparation of Indonesian Independence" was to convene as previously planned, the next day, which was August 16, at 10 a.m.[269]

The lack of a voice from the center—and the lack of moving by Sukarno and Hatta—stood out, at that moment, as perhaps the most dramatic feature in Sjahrir's account of the events. Thus Sjahrir wrote about the sunset of the day, August 15, when everything should have happened:

> Five o'clock arrived.... The word had been sent to all of our most important posts in Java that the proclamation would be made after five o'clock that day. In Batavia the demonstration was to be concentrated at the Gambir Park. The radio station and the Kempei [military police] building would be seized. Just before six o'clock, a message came from [Sukarno]. He could not yet issue the proclamation, and he wished a day's postponement!
>
> The situation now became dangerous for us, because the secret police might have discovered everything in the meantime. Moreover, several thousands of people were already concerned.[270]

Sjahrir implied later that he had expected, during these hours, that Sukarno and Hatta, as "the proclaimers," would at the historical moment publicly read his, Sjahrir's text. He, reportedly, had already, on August 14, written his version of the proclamation, which had apparently been clandestinely delivered to friends in the *Domei* press office, and to the radio station, to be published and broadcast as the signal.[271]

Very little is known about Sjahrir's proclamation. According to his own recollection, it was designed "not to isolate pro-Japanese elements," but, nevertheless, "to arouse the people." Also, it was, according to Sjahrir, "anti-Japanese, not anti-Dutch."[272]

> It was typed and about three hundred words long. Its line basically was to describe the suffering of the people under Japanese colonialism and [to proclaim] that the people of Indonesia do not want to become an inventory, which is passed from one colonial hand to another. And finally it stated that, because of this, the Indonesian people want to be released from their bondage and left to order their own life.[273]

---

[269] Hatta qoted in Margono Djojohadikoesoemo, *Herinneringen*, pp. 138–40; also Anderson, *Java in a Time of Revolution*, p. 69.

[270] Sjahrir, *Out of Exile*, p. 255. To George Kahin, in 1949, Sjahrir essentially repeated the story: Sukarno, Sjahrir said, "promised he would proclaim independence [and then] did not keep his promise.... We [were] in a dangerous position. [We] had exposed ourselves to the Japanese by organizing preparations. Sukarno refused to have contact with me. The Japanese began hunting me." Sjahrir's interview with George Kahin, February 15, 1949.

[271] Ibid.; Des Alwi, "Oom kacamata," p. 326; according to Subadio, Sjahrir still was making some changes early on the 15th. Interview with Subadio, Jakarta, October 18, 1987.

[272] Sjahrir's interview with George Kahin, February 15, 1949.

[273] Sjahrir in "Wawantjara dengan Tokoh2."

Sjahrir said, too, that he had later lost his personal copy of the proclamation.[274] No other copy seems to have survived. Almost nobody, it appears, actually saw it. Des Alwi, one of Sjahrir's Bandanese children, who, reportedly, brought Sjahrir's text to the radio station, told me: "sorry, I do not remember what was actually written in it."[275]

One Indonesian, who said he had read Sjahrir's proclamation, on August 15, Dr. Soedarsono, the Pendidikan leader in Cirebon, talked about the document, ten years later, in a press interview. He too did not seem to remember very much about the proclamation's content. What he did recall was that it consisted of words "strange and sweet," such as *"democratic society."*[276] (It is, perhaps, interesting to note that, in the interview, the words "strange and sweet" were in Indonesian—*aneh dan manis*, while *"democratic society"* was in English.)

Subadio remembered that he had come to Sjahrir for instructions on the morning of August 15, and then, with other young men and women, throughout the hot day, on bikes and feet,

> circulated through Jakarta . . . delivering the news, and the plan of action to answer to the call of freedom [*menjambut merdeka*]."[277]

Late in the afternoon, Subadio returned to report back to Sjahrir. By which time Sukarno and Hatta had made it clear, that they would move no faster. Subadio found Sjahrir "as angry as I had ever seen him before." Sjahrir, according to Subadio, "called Sukarno a travestite [*bantji*], and he used a Dutch word for it."[278]

From this time, Subadio's account mentions no further instruction from Sjahrir. He only says that he left Sjahrir's house, met Soebianto, another core member of the group, and together they went to see Hatta. As Hatta described this particular meeting, the two young men "manifested so-called revolutionary views."[279]

Hatta himself at the encounter, so he says, "defended a rational attitude, which was not about to waste power." Hatta also recalled telling the two young men that what they were doing might be compared to the "Hitler putsch" of 1923 in Munich. They told him, in return, that "when the revolution comes," he would not be among those to "be counted on" and that he was "not a revolutionary." Still, according to Subadio, Hatta escorted them "as far as the place, where we had parked our bicycles."[280]

There are reports that one of the copies of Sjahrir's proclamation of independence reached Cirebon, and that Dr. Soedarsono actually read it on August 15, publicly to a meeting of the local population on a city square. There seems to be no independent confirmation of this; the account comes exclusively from Pendidikan circles.[281] Sjahrir himself later mentioned the event very briefly in his recollections.

---

[274] Ibid.

[275] Interview with Des Alwi, Jakarta, December 3, 1987.

[276] Soedarsono in "Wawantjara dengan Tokoh2."

[277] Subadio, *Perjuangan Revolusi*, p. 13.

[278] Ibid.

[279] Hatta, *Indonesian Patriot*, p. 228.

[280] Ibid., p. 229

[281] On the Cirebon affair see Soedarsono in "Wawantjara dengan Tokoh2."

Things went so far in Cirebon, he recalled, because he was not able to stop the people there in time.[282]

It was in those days, Diah remembered that

> the youth began to see Sjahrir as heavy with "a legend," as a sort of an anchor to them, as somebody, who—by a mysterious power—has managed to move things without touching them.[283]

We may recall, Diah was the man mocked by Sjahrir shortly before this, ridiculed for taking history as *"wayang"* theater shadow play.

When they left Hatta, Sjahrir's two young men, Subadio and Soebianto, met Chaerul Saleh, a leader of another youth group, which usually met in a club at Menteng 31—a group sometimes thought to be close to Djohan Sjahroezah, but not under Sjahrir's direct influence. Subadio, Soebianto, and Chaerul Saleh then went together to a larger youth meeting at the building of the prewar *Wilhelmina Instituut* nearby.

The meeting was convened, according to Benedict Anderson, "at the initiative of the Medical Faculty students,"[284] which would mean essentially Sjahrir's young followers. There were representatives of Chaerul Saleh's group present, and also, among others, Wikana, of the "Ashram of Free Indonesia." The meeting decided that a delegation of the young people would immediately go to see Sukarno. Wikana, Soeroto Koento, and Subadio, and maybe some others, made up the delegation.[285]

There are again different accounts of what happened in Sukarno's house that night. By Sukarno's own account, the young people's behavior implied a physical threat.[286] Hatta, who was called later to the house, remembered that the youths asked him and Sukarno to proclaim independence "that very night, and over the radio." Hatta wrote that Sukarno's house was "swarming with young people," and that "the young people were certainly making their demands very loudly."[287] According to Subadio, the older leaders

> whispered for a while and then said if the youth wish to proclaim independence by themselves, they may please themselves and go it alone.[288]

The young people left Sukarno's house, according to most of the participants' accounts, in a state of humiliation and bitterness. They met in a nearby café *Hawaii*, and there, apparently, decided to kidnap Sukarrno-Hatta the same night. The idea of the kidnapping was to bring the two older leaders to a place "free of Japanese interference and of the filth of the Japanese politics."[289]

---

[282] Sjahrir, *Out of Exile*, p. 255.

[283] Diah, *Angkatan Baru '45*, p. 58.

[284] Anderson, *Java in a Time of Revolution*, pp. 70; see also Subadio in "Wawantjara dengan Tokoh2," and Subadio, *Perjuangan Revolusi*, p. 17.

[285] Ibid.

[286] Sukarno, *An Autobiography*, pp. 208–9.

[287] Hatta, *Indonesian Patriot*, p. 229.

[288] Subadio, *Perjuangan Revolusi*, p. 18. According to Malik's record Sukarni (or Wikana perhaps?) exhorted Sukarno as the meeting climaxed, "Hurry up, Brother. Forward!," to which Sukarno, according to the record, responded with "Shut up!" Malik, *Mengabdi Republik* I: 217.

[289] Ibid.

Some of Sjahrir's students were in the kidnappers' group—Subadio certainly, and perhaps Soebianto. But other individuals and groups not influenced by Sjahrir were very much present. Besides Wikana, Chaerul Saleh, and Soekarni, also of Chaerul Saleh's group, a certain Dr. Moewardi became increasingly active; he was the leader of the mostly non-student, Japanese-sponsored, and extremely nationalist youth Barisan Pelopor, "Vanguard Corps."[290] Sukarno, however, according to his later recollections, was convinced that—whatever other forces were behind his and Hatta's kidnapping—Sjahrir was heavily involved. Sjahrir, in the view of Sukarno,

> was the one stirring up the *pemudas*. He was responsible for steaming up the youth against me and for what happened later that night.[291]

Hatta was less certain. In Hatta's view, Sjahrir, after the afternoon of August 15, "distanced himself [*mendjauhkan diri*] from the youth movement of Soekarni and Chaerul Saleh," because, thus Hatta, "he saw that they drifted towards anarchy."[292]

According to Subadio's account, after the meeting at café *Hawaii*, he went to inform Sjahrir. He said he "woke up Sjahrir from his sleep," and Sjahrir, "agreed" with the young people's "efforts to convince Sukarno-Hatta;" but "did not agree" with the kidnapping plan. He "suggested" that Subadio "rather not participate" in the kidnapping.[293]

This is the same ambiguity, one can feel, also, in Sjahrir's own later recollections: "I had no faith in the plan, but I did not oppose it," Sjahrir wrote in one place;[294] and a few lines further on: "I said that that was not necessary, and I guaranteed that the following day I would push the proclamation through."[295]

When some of the youths came to Sjahrir's house still later that night, and told him that the kidnapping was in progress, Sjahrir, again in his own account, advised them to get Sukarno out of town. He recalled that he mentioned a garrison of the Javanese Peta militia at Rengasdengklok, an hour or so from Jakarta. There Sukarno-Hatta, indeed, eventually were taken. "I then stressed," Sjahrir wrote,

> that in any case there must be no trouble or dispute among us. We simply had to ensure that the proclamation would be made rapidly. The same night some of our people from west Java arrived, and the following day those from east Java. We were ready for the grand performance.[296]

It may be that, at this moment, Sjahrir had decided to go with the stream of events, and not to distance himself any more. If it was so, a bitter experience followed, which he would never forget.

---

[290] Anderson, *Java in a Time of Revolution*, pp. 74, 81.

[291] Sukarno, *An Autobiography*, p. 210.

[292] Interview with Hatta in Rachmat Ranuwijaya "Sutan Sjahrir: peranan dan pikiran politiknja dalam tahun 1926–1948" (Ph.D. thesis, University of Indonesia, 1975), p. 123.

[293] Subadio, *Perjuangan Revolusi*, p. 20.

[294] Sjahrir, *Out of Exile*, p. 256.

[295] Ibid.

[296] Ibid.

The kidnappers, with Sukarno, his wife, their infant son, and Hatta, left Sukarno's house for Rengasdengklok, on August 16, at about 4 a.m.[297] At about the same time, an agreement was reached between Chaerul Saleh and the officer second-in-command of the Peta militia garrison in Jakarta, Latief Hendraningrat, to coordinate actions around the city as the proclamation would be set in motion.[298]

Sjahrir remembered later that, late in the afternoon, a day before, he was "still in doubt whether to do it without Soekarno."[299] By the time the kidnappers actually took Sukarno and Hatta away, he wrote:

> We decided to go on with declaration on our own. But we had to insure the Japanese would not use Soekarno against us.[300]

Sjahrir, was getting deeper into action. But at the same time he appeared to be increasingly uncertain. The "whole kidnapping affair," he remembered later, "troubled me," because, among other things,

> it had brought into prominence a clique that had just entered our ranks on the previous night.[301]

> I began to feel that events were taking an unexpected and unfortunate turn for us.... I realized that the game was temporarily spoiled for us. Because of the inexperience of the young guards, the initiative had been taken from our hands.[302]

Probably from Soebardjo and some of his friends among the youth, the Japanese Navy liaison office and Admiral Maeda learned about the kidnapping. In Anderson's description:

> Nishijima was accordingly sent to locate Wikana and succeeded in finding him at the Asrama Indonesia Merdeka. An emotional argument ensued in which Nishijima tried to persuade Wikana to reveal the location of the two leaders [Sukarno and Hatta], promising that if Wikana did so Nishijima and Maeda would cooperate fully in having Indonesian independence declared.[303]

After "a further debate," it was decided that Soebardjo, with a small party of two other Indonesians and a Japanese, would go to Rengasdengklok "and bring the leaders back to town." About 8 p.m., still on August 16, Sukarno and Hatta indeed were

---

[297] W. S. Sanusi, "Perjuangan '45 untuk pembangunan bangsa: Terbentuknja Akademi Militer di Tanggerang (kenangan pribadi)," (August 1975) (Jakarta: *Perpustakaan '45*, an interview project, typescripts in the archives of "Gedung Pemuda"), no. 734, p. 4.

[298] Subadio, *Perjuangan Revolusi*, p. 21.

[299] Sjahrir's interview with Kahin, February 15, 1949.

[300] Ibid.

[301] Sjahrir, *Out of Exile*, p. 257.

[302] Ibid., pp. 257–58.

[303] Anderson, *Java in a Time of Revolution*, p. 76.

brought back to Jakarta. For the rest of the evening, with Maeda, they visited several important Japanese in the town. Then,

> With the assurance that the military authorities would permit a proclamation of independence as long as it was not associated with the Japanese and did not result in disorder, Soekarno, Hatta and Maeda returned to Maeda's house.

In the admiral's study, Sukarno, Hatta, Maeda, Soebardjo, Nishijima, and two other Japanese worked on the actual text of the proclamation.[304]

"Throughout August 16, and till the night," Subadio recalled those same hours,

> I and my friends concentrated all our efforts on building forces to seize power in Jakarta. Through the night, contacts were being established between different headquarters of the youth with a purpose [*guna*] to wait for news that the moment has come. . . . But the news never arrived, and all the youth in the [various] headquarters were shaken [*gelisah*], and one could not predict what the emotions among them might lead to. At about 12 a.m. we got information that action was cancelled for today [*gerakan dibatalkan untuk hari ini*], and we did not know on what basis this happened.[305]

A "delegation," Sjahrir wrote, came to see him again, a few hours apparently after "the action was cancelled," very early on the morning of August 17. They asked Sjahrir to come and "take part" in the meetings still in session at Maeda's house. In Sjahrir's words, "naturally . . . I could not accept."[306]

According to another slightly different account, or perhaps an account about yet another mission to Sjahrir at the same time,

> Word had been sent to Sjahrir of what was afoot. Indeed, a special party had been sent out to look for him—but he was nowhere to be found.[307]

In Sjahrir's recollections of the same morning, it was as if, in the breaking daylight, politics began to appear to him, again, in its usual, and again slightly grotesque, way:

> I still remember it vividly. At three o'clock in the morning, Soekarni, wearing high *laarzen* boots and a *samurai* sword, came to see me in my house in Maluku 19, with a report that our version of the proclamation could not be accepted.[308]

---

[304] Ibid., pp. 80–81.
[305] Subadio, *Perjuangan Revolusi*, p. 21.
[306] Sjahrir, *Out of Exile*, p. 258.
[307] Sidik Kertapati, *Sekitar Proklamasi*, pp. 96–97 quoted in Anderson, *Java in a Time of Revolution*, p. 81.
[308] Sjahrir in "Wawantjara dengan Tokoh2."

As the hour of the proclamation agreed upon in Maeda's house approached, Sukarno, so it was remembered, was "pale and tired-looking."[309] His nervousness seemed to grow, when Hatta, minutes before the official ceremony was to begin, had still failed to appear. "Everybody knows it; I am always so punctual," Hatta commented later on the event, and he might well have said this to Sukarno, when he finally appeared, sharp at five minutes to ten.[310]

At 10 a.m., August 17, 1945, Sukarno read the text of the proclamation of Indonesian independence—as composed in Maeda's place—to the small gathering of people, in front of Sukarno's house. The red-and-white flag was raised on the bamboo pole, and "Great Indonesia" was sung.

Hatta returned to the event several times. In 1952 he wrote:

> The kidnapping of Soekarno-Hatta to Rengasdengklok, and their return back to Jakarta that day, became a historical proof, how bankrupt is a policy exercised without calculation, and based entirely on sentiments.[311]

In his memoirs, another eighteen years later, Hatta essentially repeated what he had said in 1952. Sjahrir and his young followers Hatta wrote,

> were not able to face the revolutionary situation they themselves had created. It was their inner weakness [*dalam batinja*] that they merely reacted to the actuality.... Sjahrir's stand afterwards, when he separated himself from the proclamation ... could not be described as carrying out a revolution, because, in a revolution, it is not permitted to take time out [*waktu terbuang*].[312]

---

[309] Dahm, *Sukarno*, p. 315.

[310] Hatta, *Memoir*, p. 456.

[311] Hatta in *Mimbar Indonesia*, 1952, quoted in Mohamad Roem, *Bunga Rampai dari Sedjarah*, vol. 1 (Jakarta: Bulan Bintang, 1972), p. 123.

[312] Hatta, *Sekitar Proklamasi*, p. 12.

8

THE REVOLUTION, 1945–1949

> It appears that some people in Holland decided, that Sjahrir was an old friend of mine, in spite of the fact that I met him here in Batavia [in 1945] for the first time.... They even say that Logemann is his father.
>
> Van Mook to friends in Holland,
> March 1, 1946.[1]

1. PERDJOEANGAN KITA

On the basis of the proclamation of independence, the new state of the Republic of Indonesia came into being on the territory of the former Dutch East Indies, with Sukarno as president and Hatta as vice-president. Exceptional power was conferred on Sukarno, the president, for the first six months, till a Parliament and a People's Congress could be elected. In ten days, Sukarno with Hatta nominated 135 members of the Komite Nasional Indonesia Pusat, KNIP, "Central Indonesian National Council." Given the fact that this was a revolution, continuity was striking. As during the occupation Sukarno and Hatta remained the top leaders. Virtually all the ministers of the new first state cabinet were the Indonesians who had headed the same departments under the Japanese.

Sjahrir's young followers painted posters and billboards in support of the proclamation by Sukarno and Hatta. They might add some cosmopolitan flavor to the campaign by using, more frequently than other groups, slogans in English. They evidently believed that the age of the Atlantic Charter was coming, and the Atlantic Charter—modern, Western, and non-colonial at the same time—was in English.

Sjahrir's young followers also helped to search for weapons hidden before the war or left around after the capitulation by panicking Japanese soldiers.[2] Hatta gave rather bizarre witness to the activity of Sjahrir's young followers. The "most cunning of the Indonesians," Hatta wrote in his memoirs, were medical students: they electrified poles, during the "war of flags," which had developed between the Indonesians

---

[1] Van Mook to Posthuma and Warsink, March 1, 1946 in *Archief Alg Secr, lste zending*, no. VI-17-17.

[2] Subadio Sastrosatomo, *Perjuangan Revolusi*, p. 29. Strangely, and quite uncharacteristically, Tan Malaka appropriates the idea and installation of the English-language slogans like "The Government of the People, from the People and by the People; Indonesia for Indonesians, Hands off Indonesia," to himself. See Tan Malaka, *Dari pendjara ke pendjara*, 3: 62; translated in Jarvis, ed., *From Jail to Jail*, 3: 98.

and the Japanese, so that the Indonesian flag raised instead of a Japanese flag could not be lowered again by the Japanese.[3]

In spite of reported "splits" and crystallization in the Indonesian radical nationalist youth movement in Jakarta,[4] this was still—through August, September, and a great part of October—a playful, student-like, often bizarre, confusing, and hazy swirl of the young people close to Sjahrir, as well as those of Chaerul Saleh's group or those, for instance, around Adam Malik of the former *Domei* now *Antara* press agency.[5]

Groups which had constituted themselves during the occupation around the wireless radios, still gathered and listened, and spread the news and rumors—except now, as one of them put it, "with greater freedom."[6]

In contrast to Europe liberated from the Nazi occupation, there was no dramatic opening of the prison gates in Indonesia after the war. Amir Sjarifoeddin, in that sense, cut a lonely figure. A man, whom several of Sjahrir's principal young followers had considered their mentor till 1942 when he was jailed, Amir was released from Japanese prison on October 1, 1945, and became the only minister in the first Republican cabinet, who had not cooperated with the Japanese. Amir became the minister of information, and, according to an associate,

> A number of friends from Sjahrir's group soon got in touch with [Amir], and he seemed to feel attracted to their political ideas. . . .[7]

Sjahrir's associates in Pendidikan Nasional Indonesia, after the few unreal days of the proclamation crisis, resumed their usual style of work; except, of course, that they too could now work with greater freedom. Sjahrir's *alter ego* (according to some), Djohan Sjahroezah, got busy, in Jakarta, building trade-unions that would soon become the Sentral Organisasi Buruh Seluruh Indonesia, SOBSI labor federation.[8] Sjahrir's other life-long friends and associates, Soedarsono, Soegra, Hamdani, and Soegondo, traveled through the Jakarta-Cirebon-Bandung area in West Java "to keep the organization alive."[9] A prominent young man among Sjahrir's followers recruited during the war, Subadio Sastrosatomo, left Jakarta for Central and East Java, early in September, so he later recalled, "to check on the existence and shape of the Sjahrir group there."[10]

It is not easy to map the movements of Sjahrir himself. As he recalled it later, during the first weeks after the proclamation, he visited some of his Dutch and Eurasian friends: some of them immediately after they got out of the Japanese camps, others even before. According to Sjahrir:

---

[3] Hatta, *Indonesian Patriot*, p. 247

[4] See Robert B. Cribb, "Jakarta in the Indonesian Revolution, 1945–1949" (Ph.D. thesis, London School of Oriental and African Studies, 1984), pp. 70–72, where in discussing events of August 25 he talks about two splinter groups led by Sudewo and Chaerul Saleh respectively.

[5] E.g., Abdul Halim, "Sjahrir yang saya kenal," in *Mengenang Sjahrir*, ed. Anwar, p. 38.

[6] Ibid., p. 23.

[7] Ali Sastroamijoyo, *Milestones on my Journey*, pp. 104–106. On Amir accepting the position see also Wellem, *Amir Sjarifoeddin*, p. 180.

[8] Interview with Sitoroes, Jakarta, December 29, 1987.

[9] Interview with Hamdani, Jakarta, March 5, 1982; Subadio, *Perjuangan Revolusi*, p. 40

[10] Ibid.

I personally visited several of the internment camps in Java to familiarize myself with the mentality of the Dutch internees, and also to speak with some of my former coworkers who had not yet come out of camp. Those of our friends who had drawn up the program with us for underground work on behalf of democracy and freedom in the early days immediately declared their support of the Republic.[11]

Sjahrir contacted some from the prewar group of Marcel Koch, the Dutch socialist living for years in Bandung, and also some of the *Kritiek en Opbouw* circle, the Dutch prewar "progressive" journal on art, literature, and politics. He saw Beb Vuyk, the Eurasian writer and his prewar friend, while she was still in the camp.[12]

Some time in September 1945, Sjahrir went to Bandung to see Jacques de Kadt, another Dutchman and Sjahrir's friend still from the time when Sjahrir was in Holland as a student in the early 1930s. De Kadt was recently released from an internment camp. Both men talked about the situation and, as de Kadt recalled later, one term Sjahrir used on the occasion was *Indonesisch gekkenhuis*, "Indonesian madhouse." In de Kadt's recollections, Sjahrir also invited him to come to Jakarta and to work with him. They even arranged for a disguise. De Kadt was to travel not as a Dutchman: the hostilities increasing in the area between Bandung and Jakarta, and along the railway, made this already very dangerous. De Kadt would be "J. Catt," a correspondent for "a small British Independent Labour Party."[13]

In the very first days after the proclamation—through Soejitno Mangoenkoesoemo, his devotee from prewar times—Sjahrir also met W. F. Wertheim, a progressive former Batavia Law School professor and also a man, before the war, close to the Unitas Studiosorum Indonesiensis, USI, student organization from which some of Sjahrir's more important young followers originally came.[14]

Sjahrir remained on the fringe. So much so, it appears, that for some especially young Indonesian activists it was very difficult to understand and accept. "We pushed Sjahrir," one of the young leaders, Adam Malik, later recalled.[15] "We forced [actions] on him," another one, Subadio, told me.[16]

Sjahrir's attitude towards the new Indonesian state led by Sukarno and Hatta might also appear ambiguous. "The effect of the proclamation was tremendous," Sjahrir later wrote, "It was as though our people had been electrified."[17] But, at the same time: "The inflamed passion of the people provided another source of anxiety."[18]

---

[11] Sutan Sjahrir, *Out of Exile*, p. 260.

[12] Beb Vuyk, "Mengenang Sjahrir" in *Mengenang Sjahrir*, ed. Anwar, p. 270.

[13] De Kadt, "Sjahrir: Poging tot plaatsbepaling," pp. 470–72; see also de Kadt, *De Indonesische tragedie*, p. 118n.

[14] W. F. Wertheim, *Indonesië van vorstenrijk tot neo-kolonie* (Amsterdam: Boom Meppel, 1978), p. 123; also a letter from Prof. Wertheim to the author (November 27, 1983); see also Subadio, *Perjuangan Revolusi*, p. 78.

[15] Interview with Adam Malik in *Collection Nishijima*, JV40-JV40/1-JV40/2.

[16] Interview with Subadio, Jakarta, March 4, 1982; see also Halim on Sjahrir in October 1945 in Abdul Halim, *Di antara hempasan dan benturan*, p. 31. Also de Kadt, *Jaren die dubbel telden*, p. 145.

[17] Sjahrir, *Out of Exile*, p. 259.

[18] Ibid., p. 264.

To those impatient, or those unwilling, perhaps, to understand the paradox in Sjahrir, this seemed simply to be Sjahrir "distancing himself [*mendjauhkan diri*]": "distancing himself from the first Republican cabinet," as even Subadio, sympathetic to Sjahrir, put it; or, as Adam Malik, much less sympathetic, said, "distancing himself from the bustle [*kesibukan*] of the building of the foundations of this Republic."[19]

It was a time of "government pusillanimity," Benedict Anderson wrote in his book on the revolution, "the period of drift and inertia," and of Sukarno's striking "silence."[20] To the pusillanimous center, Sjahrir's continuous moving on the fringe, as difficult to follow as during the Japanese occupation, worked as an irritant and sometimes as a threat. Ali Sastroamidjojo, a man close to Sukarno, for instance wrote:

> The political tension of that time was caused in particular by the opposition of the young intellectuals under the leadership of Sutan Syahrir.[21]

We only have this from Sjahrir himself, but it seems highly probable: almost immediately after the proclamation, Sjahrir recalled, he was offered and he rejected a seat in Sukarno's first cabinet.[22]

Two days after the proclamation, on August 19, a meeting took place in the club of the medical school in Prapatan 10, attended by both Sukarno and Hatta, and also by Sjahrir. Most of the young people present angrily confronted the "passive" Sukarno and Hatta leadership at the meeting. The atmosphere became so heated that, at the end, the youths locked the older leaders in the room. It was Sjahrir, reportedly, who unlocked the door and let Sukarno and Hatta out.[23]

Three days after this incident, on August 22, some sources say, Sjahrir was offered the chairmanship of the "Central Indonesian National Council," a sort of interim parliament of the new Republic. "Will Sjahrir finally step forward and show his face," Sukarno reportedly agonized at this moment.[24] Sjahrir refused again.

Adam Malik, who later became an outspoken adversary of Sjahrir, wrote about this time:

> Sjahrir's alertness, and the way it contrasted with the feebleness of Soekarno-Hatta, drove the youth again to Sjahrir, even while he still kept himself back.[25]

---

[19] Subadio, *Perjuangan Revolusi*, pp. 53, 43; Adam Malik, *Mengabdi Republik: Angkatan '45*, vol. 2 (Jakarta: Gunung Agung, 1978), pp. 88–89.

[20] Anderson, *Java in a Time of Revolution*, p. 170; see also Anderson's introduction to Sjahrir, *Our Struggle*, pp. 7–8;

[21] Ali Sastroamijoyo, *Milestones on my Journey*, p. 108.

[22] Sjahrir's interview with George Kahin, February 15, 1949.

[23] Hatta, *Sekitar Proklamasi*, pp. 2–3; see also Hatta, *Indonesian Patriot*, pp. 244–45; Sidik Kertapati, *Sekitar Proklamasi 17 Agustus 1945*, p. 125; Sutrisno Kutojo, ed., "Inventarisasi Data Biografi Pahlawan Nasional Sutan Sjahrir," typescript, n.d., Archives Siti Wahjunah Sjahrir.

[24] Malik, *Mengabdi Republik* 2: 57–59; see also Adam Malik, *Riwajat dan Perdjuangan sekitar Proklamasi Kemerdekaan Indonesia 17 Agustus 1945* (Jakarta: Widjajna, 1956), p. 68; Sidik Kertapati, *Sekitar Proklamasi*, p. 126; Subadio, *Perjuangan Revolusi*, pp. 33–34.

[25] Malik, *Mengabdi Republik* 2: 57.

Sjahrir saw the same situation in a slightly different light: In the weeks following the proclamation, he wrote later,

> I traveled through Java. I could see the whole population had begun to fight for independence.... I could not then repudiate the revolution led by Soekarno. I had to face facts....[26]

On September 19, a giant demonstration was convened, of about two hundred thousand people, at Jakarta's central *Gambir* Square. The demonstration appeared to be organized by young activists, many of them the forces and individuals who, five weeks previously, had been responsible for the kidnapping of Sukarno and Hatta. Also this time, according to some reports, the young people escorted the "pale" Sukarno and his ministers; again, this was a young people's effort to activate the center.[27]

Sjahrir's young followers, like Daan Jahja or Soebianto, were sometimes mentioned among the organizers.[28] Not Sjahrir. According to Adam Malik's, and in this case clearly hostile, comment, Sjahrir and a couple of his associates, through the demonstration,

> amidst the surging masses stood on the top of a truck, watching all the happening and criticizing the masses as not quite able to make it.[29]

On September 15, British Rear Admiral Patterson, at the head of the Allied forces, arrived in Jakarta to enact the Japanese surrender and to repatriate the Japanese soldiers and civilians. He was accompanied by Dr. Charles van der Plas, the Dutch delegate with the Allies.

Nobody knew at the moment if the war-criminal trials might involve any of the top Indonesian leaders. Sukarno and Hatta were clearly in danger in this respect. The Allies, no doubt, were looking for "clean" Indonesians. On September 28, 1945, the first meetings between the British military command and the Indonesian representatives took place. Sukarno and Hatta were present. But Sjahrir also sat at the meeting—still without any official position in the government.[30]

Some time around that meeting Sjahrir's ways appear again to turn more decisively towards the center, towards a direct and unambiguous involvement in the politics of the independent state. At that moment, also, and by the same token, the

---

[26] Sjahrir's interview with George Kahin, February 15, 1949.

[27] Again, in a way, the action misfired. Sukarno, brought to face the masses, gave one of his great performances. In a brief speech he told the people they should show their loyalty to the new government by leaving the place in order—and they did.

[28] Djojohadikoesoemo, *Herinneringen*, pp. 146–49; Sidik Kertapati, *Sekitar Proklamasi*, pp. 138–43; Subadio Sastrosatomo, "De Indonesische Revolutie: Sjahrir en Schermerhorn" (notes prepared for a talk in Leiden, ms. 1987), p. 7; Sanusi, "Perjuangan '45 untuk pembangunan bangsa," p. 5; Subadio, *Perjuangan Revolusi*, p. 50.

[29] Malik, *Mengabdi Republik*, 2: 69.

[30] Interview with van der Post quoted in Clifford William Squire, "Britain and the Transfer of Power in Indonesia, 1945–1946" (Ph.D. thesis, School of Oriental and African Studies, n.d), p. 83n. According to the same source, Major Santoso—whom we mentioned as one of the medical students' mentors and an associate of Takdir Alisjahbana's Komisi Bahasa Indonesia—was also present.

process accelerated, which, months and years later, would lead to what may be called Sjahrir's second exile.

On October 7, a petition was sent to President Sukarno, signed by forty members of the "Central Indonesian National Council" (a little less than one-third of the body), demanding changes in the council's status. Rather than merely an "assistant [*pembantu*]" of the president, which was the existing status, the council should become a true legislature of the new state; cabinet ministers should become responsible to the council instead of to the president.

Behind the October 7 petition were reportedly the leaders of the youth group of Chaerul Saleh, namely Soekarni, and also other young leaders such as Adam Malik; several older politicians, who were increasingly dissatisfied with Sukarno's leadership, joined the move. Former students of the prewar Batavia Law School reportedly provided legal expertise to support the argument for change.[31]

On October 16 (against the opposition mainly of Sartono, a life-long ally of Sukarno), Adam Malik became the new chairman of the "Central Indonesian National Council." That same day, while Sukarno was "unavailable," Hatta, as the vice-president, signed a document, *Maklumat X*, "Declaration X," accepting the demands of the petition of October 7.

There was increasingly hectic activity in Jakarta in the hours which followed. In a sense, the situation resembled the days in mid-August, when the young people pedaled around the town on their bicycles and tried to make history move fast.

On October 17, a "Working Committee" was created inside the "Central Indonesian National Council"—a new body with the declared purpose of dealing with the day-to-day matters of the council. As instantly became clear, however, virtually all the political power of the too big and unwieldy council shifted into the new small and efficient "Working Committee." On the same day the "Working Committee" was created, October 17, 1945, Sjahrir—rejecting the offer at least once that day and then accepting—was elected chairman of the new body; Amir Sjarifoeddin, at the same time, became the "Working Committee"'s deputy chairman.[32]

The rest was a logical and almost predictable chain of events. On November 11, as the chairman of the "Working Committee," Sutan Sjahrir was appointed formateur of a new Republican cabinet. The cabinet, in the spirit of the petition of October 7, was to be responsible to the "Central Indonesian National Council," and not to Sukarno, the president. On November 14, 1945, Sutan Sjahrir, at the age of thirty-six, became prime minister.[33]

Perdjoeangan Kita, "Our Struggle," forty-two pages of octavo format, was written by Sjahrir around mid-October 1945, when all these changes were in the making.[34] A

---

[31] Interview with Subadio, Jakarta, October 18, 1987; also Anderson, *Java in a Time of Revolution*, pp. 171-72 and Dahm, *Sukarno*, p. 326; Mrs. Mangoensarkoro, a very Javanese lady (her husband had been active in Komisi Bahasa Indonesia) was prominent among these older politicians.

[32] Interview with Subadio, Jakarta, March 8, 1982; Sidik Kertapati, *Sekitar Proklamasi*, p. 175.

[33] Anderson, *Java in a Time of Revolution*, p. 178. According to some, in this appointment "Hatta helped Sjahrir." Interview with B. M. Diah, Jakarta, December 8, 1987. In another account it was even stated that, "the Working Committee [the venue where Sjahrir became prime minister] was a construction built together by Soetan Sjahrir and Drs. Moh. Hatta." X ambtenaar, "Indonesische Politiek, 1942–1947" (Batavia, October 24–26, 1947) in *Collection van Mook* no.172, p. 25.

[34] Sjahrir, *Our Struggle*, p. 17.

small circle of Sjahrir's friends and political associates saw the manuscript at the end of October, about two weeks before Sjahrir became prime minister.[35] The Ministry of Information (still under the first Sukarno cabinet but with Amir Sjarifoeddin as minister of information) published the booklet on November 10, four days before the inauguration of Sjahrir's cabinet.[36]

"Our Struggle," in an instant and for many years to come, became a fervently disputed issue in the Indonesian political and intellectual debate. With merely one exception, Benedict Anderson wrote in 1972, "Our Struggle" was

> the only attempt made during the post-surrender years to analyze systematically the domestic and international forces affecting Indonesia and to provide a coherent perspective for the future of the independence movement.[37]

For Sal Tas, Sjahrir's Dutch friend from the early 1930s, "Our Struggle" was "perhaps the high point of [Sjahrir's] career."[38] In a later account by Sjahrir himself,

> Under the urging of the action committees to take part in the government, it was necessary to enunciate a definite program in order to make our position clear. I issued a pamphlet setting forth our position in regard to past history and the present struggle, and explaining what we regarded as the stakes and the goal of the revolution. Our position against Japanese influence in the government was sharply emphasized because we wanted our people to play a leading role in the present critical phase of the revolution.[39]

When in the early 1970s, an American scholar, Franklin B. Weinstein, writing a dissertation on the Indonesian elites, interviewed people who had been "Sjahrir's friends," several of them told him that "Sjahrir's way of thinking," late in 1945, was so close to Mao Tse-tung that some people thought the two must have met. Sjahrir's "Our Struggle," they said, was often compared with Mao's "On New Democracy," and even "people in the Communist world accepted 'Our Struggle' as a contribution on the same level as Mao's."[40]

In one of Sjahrir's letters from Banda Neira, indeed, there is this reference to Mao from early 1937:

> the leader of the movement, a genius, now about forty years old, and able to attract the best of China's youth to his cause.[41]

Also, according to a 1946 review of "Our Struggle" written by Djohan Sjahroezah's brother Hazil Tanzil, himself a close associate of Sjahrir,

---

[35] Kahin, *Nationalism and Revolution*, p. 164; Rosihan Anwar, *Kisah-kisah Jakarta setelah Proklamasi* (Jakarta: Pustaka Jaya, 1977), p. 70.

[36] Sjahrir, *Perdjoeangan Kita* (Jakarta: Pertjetakan Repoeblik Indonesia, 1945). I am using the translation by Benedict Anderson in Sjahrir, *Our Struggle*.

[37] Anderson, *Java in a Time of Revolution*, p. 195.

[38] Tas, "Souvenirs of Sjahrir," p. 150

[39] Sjahrir, *Out of Exile*, p. 263

[40] Franklin B. Weinstein, *Indonesian Foreign Policy and the Dilemma of Dependence: From Sukarno to Soeharto* (Ithaca: Cornell University Press, 1976), p. 60.

[41] *IO* January 14, 1937.

when *Perdjoeangan Kita* [Our Struggle] was seen by foreign journalists, they asked the author if he had read Mao's brochure ["On New Democracy"] before. He had analyzed the Indonesian revolution in the same way, and he came to the same conclusion about the problem of a national revolution in the formerly colonized lands, as the President of the Communist Party in Yen An did, when he wrote about the [Chinese] Revolution of 1911, and about the movement as it developed afterwards.[42]

Indeed, the very organization of "Our Struggle"—culminating in chapters X: The Workers, XI: The Peasants, XII: Our Youth, XIII: The Army—points strongly not merely towards Mao but even towards Lenin.

In "Our Struggle," Sjahrir demanded "the mobilization of all conscious revolutionary forces into a disciplined party structure."[43] Sjahrir referred variously to "a revolutionary party,"[44] "a democratic revolutionary party,"[45] or "a revolutionary workers party."[46] Membership of such a party, Sjahrir elaborated on truly Leninist-like model, "need not be large, provided that it form a tightly disciplined army."[47] The image of the army-like-party returned several times.[48] Only such a party, according to "Our Struggle," could be "the core" of "our" Indonesian revolution.[49]

Sjahrir in "Our Struggle," also, sounded very much and undeniably proletarian-like. At great length he dealt with the workers of Indonesia, and the Indonesian workers' role in the coming revolution. According to Sjahrir,

> our workers must ... become the vanguard of the struggle against imperialism in Indonesia, and strengthen the struggle of the international working class against world capitalism.[50]

Among the freedoms enunciated in "Our Struggle" as "the fundamental rights of the [Indonesian] people," "capitalist" freedom—the right to possess as much as money allows—was conspicuously missing.[51] Sjahrir made it very clear that his vision sharply differed from that of "the merely bourgeois-democratic French Revolution": "France and the French Revolution," wrote Sjahrir,

> were the pioneers who cleared the way for the world of capitalism and imperialism, whereas our revolution must be regarded as one of the revolutions contributing to its termination.[52]

---

[42] "H.T." (Hazil Tanzil) "De Partai Sosialis," *Inzicht*, November 13, 1946, p. 1
[43] Sjahrir, *Our Struggle*, p. 30
[44] Ibid., p. 29.
[45] Ibid., pp. 29–30.
[46] Ibid., pp. 35–36.
[47] Ibid., pp. 29–30.
[48] Ibid., pp. 36–37.
[49] Ibid., pp. 29–30.
[50] Ibid., pp. 33–34.
[51] Ibid., p. 29.
[52] Ibid., p. 29.

Throughout "Our Struggle," permeating the Mao-like and the Lenin-like images, appears—as before 1934, as in prison and as in exile—the "Eastern spirit," a notion to be attacked and to be posited against everything good and progressive. The troubles of the new Indonesian state were many, Sjahrir wrote, for instance; they grew,

> in the first place ... because the people in control of the Republican government are men without real character ... [they are] accustomed to kowtow ... many of them still feel morally obliged to the Japanese who "bestowed" on them the opportunity to "prepare" Indonesian Independence.[53]

Slave mentality, feudal mentality, mentality of *ningrat*, still were the qualities defining for Sjahrir the negative contours of life—a propensity "to take orders, to bow down to and to deify [one's] superiors."[54] As so often before, and we hear echoes of the old controversies between Pendididikan and Partindo, between Sjahrir himself and Sukarno, this was to Sjahrir

> a certain kind of nationalism ... a nationalism built on a hierarchical, feudalistic solidarism: in fact on Fascism, the greatest enemy of world progress and of our people.[55]

Given the alleged influence of Mao (or Lenin), there was, in "Our Struggle," curiously little of a catastrophic, or even of a sudden change between historical epochs as they progressively succeed one another. Sjahrir instead posited "foundations" as the essence of his image of historical time and of progress. "Foundations of village society were disrupted," he wrote about the Japanese occupation; and this "caused a steadily rising tension." Because of this, at the moment when Japan collapsed, "the danger of a massive explosion of the accumulated tensions in our society grew still more grave."[56]

"*Kemadjoean*," "progress," to Sjahrir, should not imply the "danger of a massive explosion." Workers, the vanguard, the principal agent of change, should, according to Sjahrir, "strengthen the struggle of the international working class" against "world capitalism." But, back at home, they should struggle against "imperialism" in order to gain "the strongest possible position for themselves." There was much on "class consciousness" and also much on "class solidarity," in "Our Struggle," but— Mao as well as Lenin receded here into oblivion—practically nothing on class struggle.[57]

In fact, for Sjahrir, "the major revolutionary task of the present time" was "systematic prevention of disorder among people."[58] The "masses of the people," Sjahrir argued, had to be "integrated into the structure of government"; this, he wrote, "can easily be accomplished by setting up popular representative councils from the

---

[53] Ibid., p. 27.
[54] Ibid., p. 19.
[55] Ibid., p. 28.
[56] Ibid., pp. 17–18.
[57] Ibid., p. 33.
[58] Ibid., p. 30.

village government up to the highest levels of government." Village government was the "foundation," and the place where "all our ideals for the renewal of our society can begin to be put into practice."[59]

We hear echoes of much earlier views of Sjahrir—and of Hatta, and of *Daulat Ra'jat*: the guild socialism, the *nagari* (Minangkabau) community system, the *asli*, genuine, original (traditional Indonesian) democracy.... Sjahrir also and again specified that what he had in mind, naturally, was a system without *ningrat*, without the aristocracy. The aristocratic civil servants of the past *"for the time being,"* Sjahrir wrote, might be given "positions as advisers or inspectors," "or they can be withdrawn to various departmental offices."[60]

Sjahrir's notion of progress, in "Our Struggle," as before—and maybe more now, as the Indonesian crisis deepened—contained appealing images of a return. "Village government" namely, Sjahrir wrote, must be

> restored to health by the institution of genuine democracy through the utilization of traditional customs—election and village meetings—which will be given the fullest possible authority.[61]

Indeed, as Anderson wrote, "there is no determined outcome [in "Our Struggle"] to the struggle between neo-capitalism and socialism."[62] Indeed, there is an appealing uncertainty in Sjahrir's looking forward; as, perhaps, there often is, when one is very much trying to remember the things future.

Nothing has been quoted more frequently from Sjahrir's booklet than the "sharp and abrasive" language he used in referring to Indonesian wartime collaboration with Japan. Not the "ordinary people who worked for the Japanese simply to earn their daily bread," Sjahrir wrote, but

> those who have worked in the Japanese propaganda organizations, the secret police, and the Japanese fifth column in general ... must be regarded as traitors to our struggle ... as fascists themselves, or as the running-dogs and henchmen of the Japanese fascists, who, it goes without saying, are guilty of betraying the people's struggle and the people's revolution.[63]

Many of those who were now in the leadership of the new state, virtually the whole nationalist mainstream, were hit by Sjahrir's attack on the "running dogs and henchmen" of the Japanese. As it was understood at the time, there were "scarcely

---

[59] Ibid.

[60] Ibid. Emphasis mine.

[61] Ibid., p. 34.

[62] Anderson's introduction to Sjahrir, *Our Struggle*, p. 10.

[63] There is quite a literature on the term. For comments see, e.g., Halim, *Di antara hempasan*, pp. 39–40; Kahin, *Nationalism and Revolution*, p. 166n.; Legge's interview with Ali Boediardjo (1982) in Legge, *Intellectuals and Nationalism*, p. 102; Anderson, *Java in a Time of Revolution*, p.191n.; Y.B. Mangunwijaya, "Dilema Sutan Sjahrir: Antara Pemikir dan Politikus," *Prisma* 6,8 (August 1977): 27n.

concealed references to Soekarno" in those passages of "Our Struggle."[64] Hatta, too, almost certainly, felt himself "to be included."[65]

The proclaimers of independence were targeted: their record in the past, their present mandate and, so it seemed, even the very idea of the state they formed. Sjahrir wrote in "Our Struggle":

> It frequently turns out, that a so-called national victory is, in practice, without meaning for the masses . . . it is for this inner content that we must strive. "The State of the Republic of Indonesia" is only a *name* we give to whatever *content* we intend and hope to provide.[66]

At least some contemporary observers interpreted Sjahrir's statements like a clear message. As one of them wrote,

> Reading the chapter "Struggle for the Content of Freedom" [in "Our Struggle"] one is not contradicted in an impression, indeed is led to it, that this Indonesian Republic is merely a name without a content.[67]

Sjahrir, directing his energy at last towards the center of political power of the independent Indonesian state, resembles at this moment more than ever a Minangkabau *perantau*. Circling for years around his *rumah tunjuk*, a place one may point at as his home, the *perantau*, decides to return. The return should be the climax of his wandering, but the *perantau* knows very well that most probably only old women, children he does not know, vague memories in general, and a half-empty village, would welcome him back.

Sjahrir's harshness towards the nationalist center was more than matched by his harshness towards the Indonesian youth—the group considered to be his foremost ally then and for the future. Maybe, this is not difficult to explain. Sjahrir attacked the same qualities in both cases; there is clear worry felt in "Our Struggle" that, as Sjahrir and his allies entered politics—as they attacked the center—they might be absorbed.

The "present flareup of our young people's enthusiasm," Sjahrir wrote, would not lead them to play their rightful role if their "spirit is not suffused with a real feeling of democracy and social responsibility."[68] "Our youth," Sjahrir wrote,

> were psychologically conditioned [during the occupation] simply to take orders. . . . Although on the surface our youth genuinely loathed the Japanese, many were unconsciously influenced by Japanese propaganda. . . . This psychological influence was manifested most clearly in hatred.[69]

---

[64] Anderson's Introduction to Sjahrir, *Our Struggle*, p. 9; Anderson, *Java in a Time of Revolution*, p. 200.

[65] Interview with M. Roem in Rose, *Indonesia Free*, p.140n. For Hatta being later openly critical of Sjahrir's *Perdjoeangan Kita* see Rose, *Indonesia Free*, p. 221.

[66] Sjahrir, *Our Struggle*, p. 31. Emphasis in the text.

[67] Anonym, "Perdjoeangan Kita van Sjahrir" (1946), in *Archief Proc Gen*, no. 464–3.

[68] Sjahrir, *Our Struggle*, p. 35.

[69] Ibid., p. 19.

Then, Sjahrir continued, Sukarno and Hatta proclaimed the Republic:

> The present psychological condition of our youth is deeply tragic. In spite of their burning enthusiasm, they are full of confusion and indecision because they have no understanding of the potentialities and perspectives of the struggle they are waging.... Many of them simply cling to the slogan Freedom or Death. Wherever they sense that Freedom is still far from certain, and yet they themselves have not faced death, they are seized with doubt and hesitation. The remedy for these doubts is generally sought in constant uninterrupted action.[70]

This was the Sjahrir's image of *pubertus*, adolescence, as conveyed already, for instance, in his Banda Neira letters. This also was his old notion of education as the main political problem and as the main political solution.

The youth were lacking in politics, Sjahrir wrote in "Our Struggle," because they "in their uncertainty were given no education"; they, hopefully, "will learn." The young people "naturally" would be taught "a real understanding and careful calculation of the political realities and potentialities." By learning, the youth will naturally overcome their "moral" and "subconscious" dependence on Japan, their "narrow sentiments"; they will broaden their "skills" from "simply those of the common soldier."[71]

Sjahrir was always a man of the fringes. To use the Minangkabau metaphor once again, he was a *perantau* now about to return. In this context, the notion of the outside world as reflected in "Our Struggle" is very significant. "The end of the Second World War," Sjahrir now wrote in "Our Struggle,"

> has left in existence three military and economic powers which dominate everything else: the United States, England and Soviet Russia.... The political system of the Soviet Union is solidly based on a socialist economy which has successfully survived the appalling ordeal of the last few years, and which does not depend to any significant degree on the general political and economic situation outside Soviet Russia herself.[72]

Sjahrir throughout thought of himself as a socialist, and at the moment of the still-surviving Dmitrov Line, he "naturally" referred to Soviet Russia as a "socialist" state. But, maybe, there is another explanation: to Soviet Russia, Sjahrir could still be ambiguous; in November 1945, Soviet Russia was still distant (and self-contained) enough a force to Indonesia, either to be a help or a threat.

In contrast to Russia, Sjahrir wrote in "Our Struggle,"

> The United States and England... require the entire world as lebensraum for their capitalist and imperialist economies.[73]

They, in another word—to Sjahrir and to Indonesia—were actual:

---

[70] Ibid., p. 21.
[71] Ibid., pp. 23, 19–21, 31–32, 35.
[72] Ibid., p. 23.
[73] Ibid., p. 24.

> Indonesia is geographically situated within the sphere of influence of Anglo-Saxon capitalism and imperialism. Accordingly Indonesia's fate ultimately depends on the fate of Anglo-Saxon capitalism and imperialism.[74]

This was the oppressive force. From that realm, pressure had to be cushioned, thereto ties had to be loosened. The victory against fascism, could not truly be a victory for progress, if it had not in the long term "weakened the capitalist world." It is "by no means clear how capitalism can muster the strength to continue in a healthy existence," Sjahrir wrote—and hoped. Indonesia was "situated within the sphere of influence of Anglo-Saxon capitalism and imperialism." It was the undertone of "Our Struggle" that this might be accepted only as a necessity; one had to live for some more time with the fact.[75]

The threat of Anglo-Saxon "capitalism and imperialism," too close to Indonesia, was conveyed, in "Our Struggle" with a feeling of almost physical discomfort. As Sjahrir saw it,

> the fate of Indonesia, more than that of other nations, is bound up with the international situation and world history. Therefore too we need, more than other nations . . . to eliminate imperialism and capitalism from the world.[76]

To fight against imperialism, for Sjahrir, essentially, was to build a distance: to force political drives and urges of all kinds down to a low key, to create a space in which a weak person could move relatively unoppressed; a space of disinterestedness. According to "Our Struggle,"

> The capitalists judge our struggle by one simple standard—their calculation of profit and loss. If it costs them nothing, they will be neutral. . . . So long as the world we live in is dominated by capital, we are forced to make sure that we do not earn the enmity of capitalism. This involves opening up our country to foreign economic activity as far as possible—always on condition that no damage is done to the welfare of our people. The same is true of the entry of foreigners into our country.[77]

It might appear like accepting a defeat. But to do otherwise, Sjahrir argued, would be "inviting foreign intervention."[78]

Among the various forms of "capitalism and imperialism" in "Our Struggle," as always in Sjahrir's writing, the Dutch form was presented as most immediate, most actual, and most oppressive. It reached, indeed, to the heart of the land and people. It was most threatening because it was most intimate; it was most oppressive because it was almost identical with the qualities of the Indonesians themselves.

In particular, according to "Our Struggle," the Dutch "capitalism and imperialism" was almost identical with the badness of *ningrat*:

---

[74] Ibid.
[75] Ibid., pp. 24–25
[76] Ibid., p. 25.
[77] Ibid., pp. 22, 31.
[78] Ibid., p. 22.

Dutch colonialism clung to every vestige of this feudalism in order to arrest the historical progress of our nation.... Accordingly, in their struggle against foreign domination, our people have from the beginning really been fighting against the bureaucratic feudalism, and ultimately the fascism and autocracy of Dutch colonialism.[79]

For Sjahrir, the world was still made up of concentric circles around Indonesia. The Dutch were closest and most visible, and beyond them there were increasingly more distant powers and forces, shaded more lightly. Fighting against Anglo-Saxon capital, and against its efforts to overwhelm Indonesia, meant to Sjahrir, essentially, preventing "the enormous power of [this] capital being [mobilized] behind the Dutch effort."[80]

The significance and intensity of the passages in "Our Struggle" on Indonesian youth may be better understood in the context of Sjahrir's views of the outside world. Imagining youth, Sjahrir was able to imagine adulthood. And without adulthood, as he made clear he still strongly believed, there was no independence.

Indonesian policy towards the outside world, Sjahrir wrote, should be primarily aimed at gaining "increasing world confidence that we are capable of a disciplined ordering of our state and nation...."[81] The Indonesian struggle for freedom should not disappoint the confidence of positive forces in the outside world; only that confidence could cut through the concentric circles of enemies.

According to Sjahrir writing in "Our Struggle,"

The outside world was initially quite sympathetic to our hope of building a nation of our own. In fact it can be said that at first world opinion was generally on our side, especially the world labor movement.[82]

But very soon, Sjahrir lamented, referring to the increasing hostility and clashes between the Indonesian long-haired youth, the Dutch, the Eurasians, and the former soldiers of the Dutch colonial army as they emerged from the Japanese camps,

The workers [of the world] are disappointed at evidences of fascist cruelty, which is now so notorious throughout the world. It is hard for them to swallow murders of foreigners, let alone murders of Eurasians, Menadonese and Ambonese, who are our fellow countrymen. They will interpret these cruelties as signs of immaturity.... [83]

---

[79] Ibid., p. 26.

[80] Ibid., p. 31.

[81] Ibid., and ibid., pp. 21–22.

[82] Ibid., p. 21.

[83] Ibid., p. 22. Only when these cruelties are overcome, Sjahrir wrote, will the frenzy and the fascist impulses "automatically disappear" with the "flowering of the spirit of democracy and humanity." A "human fellowship" may "envelop the whole world and form it into a single nation of mankind," the "bonds" may "fall off which have blinded us to the barbarousness of our history."Ibid., pp. 31–32.

Sjahrir's mention of "Eurasians, Menadonese and Ambonese" in "Our Struggle," was as significant as his emphasis on "immaturity." At another place in "Our Struggle," he also wrote:

> One of the most important aspects of our struggle is our attitude towards various groups who are more or less isolated from the rest of our citizens: foreigners, Europeans and Asians of mixed descent, Christians, Ambonese, Menadonese, and so forth.[84]

These were the people in-between, and—as Sjahrir was now approaching the center of the Indonesian politics—more and more in-between like Sjahrir himself. The Eurasians, Ambonese, Menadonese (Ambonese being not too far from Banda and the Bandanese), had always been a special part of Sjahrir's memory. Naturally, therefore, Sjahrir considered the behavior of the Indonesians towards these groups to be of special significance. Here he saw, to use his words, "the main impulse behind our actions and behavior."[85] Here, also to him, clearly, was the principal test of Indonesian adulthood.

In these passages memory was working most intensively. Sal Tas, Sjahrir's Dutch socialist friend from the Amsterdam of the early 1930s, remembered that he had been most impressed precisely by those passages in "Our Struggle." He described Sjahrir's thoughts on this issue as "a call for chivalry."[86]

2. Prime Minister

On November 14, 1945, the composition of Sjahrir's cabinet was announced. Besides being prime minister, Sjahrir held the portfolios of foreign affairs and interior. Amir Sjarifoeddin, became the second most important figure in the new cabinet, being the minister of information and public security.

There was no youth activist in the new cabinet. The Indonesian press also immediately noted that, except for Sjahrir and to some extent Amir, virtually all the ministers in the cabinet, had, before the war, been men of quite high standing in the Dutch colonial government service, colonial scholarship, or in both.[87] Over half of Sjahrir's ministers, it was also pointed out, had been educated in Holland. The press targeted in particular such ministers as lawyers Dr. Dr. T.G.S. Moelia, who held the portfolio of education, and Dr. Soewandi, the minister of justice, suggesting that "their 'complete faith in the Dutch Ethical policy' could easily lead the new government astray."[88]

According to Benedict Anderson, besides,

> The presence of four Christians in the eleven-man cabinet heavily overrepresented the small Christian minority of the population ... at a time when all Christians, and especially the formally favored Menadonese and Ambonese

---

[84] Ibid., pp. 31–32.
[85] Ibid., p. 32.
[86] Tas, "Souvenirs of Sjahrir," p. 150.
[87] Anderson, *Java in a Time of Revolution*, p. 196 for the list of ministers and biographical appendix to ibid. for the data.
[88] Quoted in ibid., p. 196.

were regarded with deep suspicion by the pemuda [youth] and much of the public.[89]

"Public reaction" to the cabinet, Sjahrir told a friend a week after the cabinet was inaugurated, was "in part cool and, for the rest, a stark denial."[90]

On November 13, a day before Sjahrir announced his cabinet, Amir, at a meeting in Yogyakarta, initiated a new party of his own—the Partai Sosialis Indonesia or Parsi, the "Indonesian Socialist Party."

Premier Sjahrir

As if Amir was trying quickly to remember something of his own political past before the government was in place, Parsi was made up of his wartime underground mostly from East Java; some of his friends from Gerindo, the prewar nationalist, antifascist, left-wing, and also strongly pro-Sukarno movement;[91] and finally, a

---

[89] Ibid., p. 198.

[90] Abdoelkadir (informed by Sjahrir) to van Mook, November 21, 1945 in *Archief Alg Secr, lste zending*, no. VI-17-17.

[91] Anderson, *Java in a Time of Revolution*, pp. 177–78, 202; Soedjatmoko, "The Role of Political Parties in Indonesia" in *Nationalism and Progress in Free Asia* ed. Philip W. Thayer (Baltimore:

group of men—like Abdulmadjid, Tamzil, and Moewaladi—who had been involved in the anti-Nazi underground in Holland during the war and who might now feel, on that basis, an affinity with Amir.[92]

The young people, students who had been close to Amir before he was arrested in 1942, did not seem to be returning to him in any number.

No member of the prewar Pendidikan became a minister in Sjahrir's cabinet. Five days after the cabinet was inaugurated, however, and less than a week after Amir created his own political party, on November 19, figures familiar from the Pendidikan's history gathered to support Sjahrir, at the *Grand Hotel* in Cirebon.

Present at this gathering were Soebagio, Hamdani, Soemitro Reksodipoetro, and Sastra from the old Bandung Pendidikan; Djohan Sjahroezah, Soegondo Djojopespito, and Soegra; Leon Salim from Sumatra; and, among some others, Kartamoehari and Roesni Tjutjun.[93]

Because the Pendidikan had actually never been disbanded, its last central executive under Soebagio was expected just to pass on its mandate.[94] There was, however, a feeling of the necessity to adjust to a new situation, and to transform the Pendidikan Nasional Indonesia, the "Indonesian National Education," into a regular political party. Most of those present also believed the new situation required a new name. One group, reportedly, "wished" the new Pendidikan's name to be Partai Komunis Indonesia, the "Indonesian Communist Party."[95]

A day or so after the old guard, a delegation sent by Sjahrir arrived from Jakarta—Subadio was on the delegation, together with Soepeno, Sitoroes, and Simatupang—all of them young men Sjahrir had newly recruited to his movement during the Japanese occupation. They came to Cirebon, says Subadio, "to watch in fascination for the first time the meaning of a political party."[96] In a matter of hours, the newcomers from Jakarta were able to catapult themselves into positions of prominence and leadership.

Johns Hopkins Press, 1956), p. 130; Wellem, *Amir Sjarifoeddin*, p. 182. On connections between Gerindo, Amir, and the Partai Sosialis see also Reid, *The Blood of the People*, p. 173.

[92] Documents on that are in *Archief Minog* I A 177–3; and *Archief Alg Secr, lste zending*, no. 2–17.

[93] Leon Salim's letter to the author, November 13, 1986.

[94] Leon Salim, one of the Pendidikan leaders whom Hatta himself had recruited into the organization back in the early 1930s, even wrote about the Cirebon meeting that the Pendidikan's "tenth central executive passed its mandate, in Cirebon, to *Hatta and Sjahrir*." Leon Salim's letter to the author, November 13, 1986. Emphasis mine. According to a later account by Hatta, "I myself as vice-president could not join the party. The people expected that both the President and Vice-President would stand above all parties." Mohammad Hatta, *Pendidikan Nasional Indonesia: A speech presented to a reunion of members of the Pendidikan Nasional Indonesia, ca. 1968* (Brisbane: Griffith Center of Southeast Asia Studies, 1985), p. 3.

[95] Subadio, *Perjuangan Revolusi*, pp. 184–85. A few days before the Cirebon conference in November, Hatta wrote later, another "conference" had been convened in his house in Jakarta, where there was also a debate about the Pendidikan's new name. Hatta wrote that a majority of the participants, including Hatta himself, had decided upon the name Partai Daulat Rakjat Indonesia, "Indonesian Party of Daulat Rakjat"—a clear reference to the ideas of the early 1930s when the movement was started. But afterwards, according to Hatta, "those of our group who had conferred in my house [were] unable to gain enough support, [were] outvoted by others, who concurred with the decision of Sjahrir and Amir Sjarifoeddin to establish a Partai Sosialis." Hatta, *Pendidikan Nasional Indonesia*, p. 3.

[96] Subadio, *Perjuangan Revolusi*, pp. 182–83.

It was finally decided that the name "Pendidikan" should be changed into "Partai Rakjat Sosialis" or "Paras," the "People's Socialist Party." The new party, in a program accepted at the same time, declared its aims were

> to oppose capitalistic, *ningrat* and feudal mentalities; to eliminate autocracy and bureaucratism; to struggle toward a society of *sama rata sama rasa* [equal standing for all] . . . ; to enrich the spirit of the Indonesian people with a democratic outlook, and to urge the government to cooperate with all organizations at home and abroad to overthrow capitalism.[97]

Though we have no clear proof of it, it might have been these young men, eager for actual politics, who made Amir and Sjahrir suppress their divergent memories, and overcome the resistance of their older friends. On December 17, on the basis of a "people's front," "anti-capitalism," and "anti-imperialism," again in Cirebon, Parsi and Paras merged into a single Partai Sosialis, "Socialist Party." Sjahrir, who had stayed away from the Cirebon reunion of the Pendidikan the previous month, now became chairman of the new party. Amir Sjarifoeddin became deputy chairman.[98]

Throughout the weeks before Sjahrir became prime minister, through October and November, additional British troops, and in growing numbers, were arriving in Java and flooding Jakarta. There was, also, increasing distrust in Jakarta regarding Dutch intentions. Some fighting had already started between young Indonesians in revolution and former war detainees returning from the camps, mostly Eurasians and Ambonese, some of whom had put on their old colonial army uniforms.

Initially, the British, charged with the task of repatriating the Japanese and restoring peace—as the British commander in Java put it in late September—were "confident we can put the baby to sleep provided no one outside the house makes a noise."[99] The British Supreme Allied Commander for Southeast Asia, Lord Louis Mountbatten, repeatedly urged the Dutch Lt. Governor-General of the Dutch East Indies (the Dutch believed there still was such a thing), Hubertus J. van Mook, to set a clear time schedule "within which the projected future status of Indonesia would be reached."[100] Van Mook was also urged to open discussions "especially with Soekarno and Hatta."[101]

The Dutch, throughout, responded that Holland was not prepared to go beyond the Dutch Queen's promise made at the beginning of the war—to convene a confer-

---

[97] Anderson, *Java in a Time of Revolution*, p. 203; "H.T." (Hazil Tanzil) "De Partai Sosialis," *Inzicht*, November 13, 1946, p. 1; also *Officiële bescheiden betreffende de Nederlands-Indonesische betrekkingen 1945–1950*. (vols.1–XIV [vols. 1–IX edited by S. L. van der Wal; vols. X ff edited by P. J. Drooglever and M. J. B. Schouten]) (The Hague: Nijhoff, 1971-) (hereafter *Officiële bescheiden*) 2: 563–64.

[98] Sutan Sjahrir, *Indonesian Socialism* (Rangoon: Asian Socialist Publishing House, 1956), p. 33; "H.T." (Hazil Tanzil), *De Partai Sosialis*; Legge, *Intellectuals and Nationalism*, p. 111; Anderson, *Java in a Time of Revolution*, pp. 202 ff; dossier "Soedarsono" in *Archief Proc Gen* no. 5–342; Sutan Sjahrir, "Political Conditions in Indonesia. Written at the beginning of 1948" (March 1948), typescript in *Archives George McT. Kahin*.

[99] Signal for *SAC SEA* (Louis Mountbatten) from *CS5* (Patterson), September 28, 1945, quoted in Squire, "Britain and the Transfer of Power," p. 72.

[100] Mountbatten to van Mook, September 28, 1945 in *Officiële bescheiden*, 1: 190, and summarized in Yong, *H. J. van Mook and Indonesian independence*, p. 50.

[101] Documents in *Archief MSH*, SEAC Fe-6/53 and ibid., SEAC Fe 6/54.

ence on possible dominion status for the Indies in the next ten years.[102] With regard to the negotiations with Sukarno and Hatta, van Mook was not willing to change the instruction issued on October 1, that there was to be "no, repeat no contact with the rebels."[103]

We have noted already how Sjahrir planned to get his Dutch friend de Kadt incognito from Bandung to Jakarta as "J. Catt," a correspondent for "a small British Independent Labour Party." We also recall that Sjahrir's young men and women, during the first days of independence, painted slogans in English, expecting the new era be written in that language. From the earlier part of the book, we may also remember how, in Boven Digul, during the mid-1930s when Sjahrir was in the camp, English was important and charged with hope, as a language in between—modern and yet not Dutch.

The British representatives of the Allies, after August 1945, visibly impatient with the hard-line Dutchmen, became part of the image of hope. The purest expression, however, of the good English-ness, came to Sjahrir, as was usual, from the British fringes.

Two British non-commissioned officers on duty with the Allied forces in Indonesia appeared near Sjahrir just about the time he became prime minister. Tom Atkinson and Peter Humphries were both (as "J. Catt" was supposed to be) connected with the British Independent Labour Party. They, it seems, stood directly behind a new English-language news-sheet, *News from Indonesia*, and indirectly behind the weekly, *Independent*, which appeared in Jakarta on December 7, 1945, and which proudly, though with exaggeration, called itself "the first English paper ever published on Java."[104] *News from Indonesia* and *Independent* were pro-Republic and pro-Sjahrir papers. The *Independent* weekly's editor was Sjahrir's acquaintance from the wartime Japanese "Radio Camp," the Ceylonese journalist working before the war in Singapore, Charles Tambu.[105]

Sjahrir strongly believed that England, seen from the vantage point of Indonesia, was in a way an extension of Holland. "For more than a hundred years now," Sjahrir wrote in "Our Struggle,"

> Dutch power over our country and our people has been a byproduct of the calculations and decisions of British foreign policy. We know that since Britain seized Indonesia from the Dutch at the beginning of the nineteenth century [and then later handed it back], the Dutch have remained in our country not on the basis of their own strength, but by favor of the English, on whose policies they have been wholly dependent.[106]

We do not know how soon Sjahrir became aware of the fact that some other people from his past, moving on the fringes, were working for him in London.

---

[102] Van Mook to Logemann, October 6, 1945, in *Officiële bescheiden*, 1: 286 also quoted in Yong, *H. J. van Mook*, p. 50.

[103] Dahm, *Sukarno*, p. 205.

[104] *Independent*, December 7, 1945, p. 1. See also T. Atkinson, "An Error Corrected," p. 4 (ms. in the *Archives George McT. Kahin*).

[105] Interview with Soedjatmoko, Jakarta, November 6, 1987; van Roijen to Blom and van Bijlandt, May, 13, 1946 in *Officiële bescheiden*, 4: 296–97; also van Bijlandt to Logemann, May 6, 1946, ibid., p. 272, and ibid., p. 406.

[106] Sjahrir, *Our Struggle*, pp. 24–25.

P. J. Schmidt—Sjahrir's old friend from his time in Holland in the early 1930s, the editor of *De Socialist*, the paper which published Sjahrir's first longer articles on Indonesian politics—appeared in London in November 1945. From his correspondence with friends back in Holland, it was clear how hard he was lobbying for Indonesia, and for Sjahrir. Among the people Schmidt contacted, were British trade-unionists, socialist and liberal members of parliament, and statesmen like Attlee, Bevan, and Sir Stafford Cripps.[107]

A significant group of Indonesians, at the same time, were also working for the Republic in London: Soetan Moh. Zainal Zain, a graduate of the prewar Batavia Law School, who had been a student in Leiden in 1939 when war broke out;[108] Soemitro Djojohadikoesoemo, a brother of Soebianto, one of Sjahrir's most fervent young followers in Jakarta during the Japanese occupation; Soemitro was a graduate of the Rotterdam Business School and, like Zainal Zain, he also spent the war in Holland.[109] Burhanuddin also appeared in London—Sjahrir's very old friend from Bandung, from the prewar Pendidikan, and from Boven Digul.[110]

A young Englishman, John Coast, epitomized the "network" in a sense. While in Japanese internment camp in Siam, during the war, he became a passionate admirer of the "classic dance of Indonesia," and had dreamed, through his years in the camp, that some day he might

> bring over a Javanese dancing company to London, to show something of their exotic quality to this surprisingly dance-minded public.[111]

After he got out of the camp and back to England, late in 1945, John Coast met Soetan Zainal Zain in London, and through him a certain Soeripno, a young Dutch-educated Javanese aristocrat, whom Coast came soon to respect deeply as an accomplished dancer. Soeripno was also a member of Perhimpoenan Indonesia. He and Zainal Zain took John Coast to meet Miss Dorothy Woodman, who lived in London on Victoria Street.[112]

"Though she has many typical socialist qualities," Coast recalled later about Miss Woodman, "in very many ways she must be unique." Dorothy Woodman was formed, Coast wrote, by "a deep revolt against a very Christian father, combined with a pure Irishness." She played the "organ and the harp," and on one occasion, Coast wrote, he

---

[107] Schmidt to Schermerhorn, November 7, 1945; the file includes Schmidt's article in *Commonwealth Review*, see *Collection Schermerhorn*, no.4 bundel P. J. Schimdt. Schmidt to Schermerhorn, October 30, 1945, October 11, 1945; Brockway to Schmidt, October 11, 1945, van der Goes and others to Schermerhorn, November 30, 1945 in ibid.

[108] Dossier "Z. Zain" in *Archief Proc Gen*, no. 229; also Schimdt to Schermerhorn, October 7, 1945 in *Collection Schermerhorn* no. 4 bundel P. J. Schmidt.

[109] Djojohadikoesoemo, *Herinneringen*, pp. 4, 102; Van Kleffens to Logemann, February 14, 1946 in *Officiële bescheiden*, 3: 392.

[110] Burhanuddin came to London via the Conference of the United Nations in San Francisco, where he had been sent by van Mook and van der Plas to represent the Dutch Indies. See, e.g., Schmidt to Schermerhorn, September 30, 1945; also Schmidt to Schermerhorn, November 3, 1945 in *Collection Schermerhorn* no. 4 bundel P. J. Schmidt.

[111] John Coast, *Recruit to Revolution: Adventure and Politics in Indonesia* (London: Christophers, 1952), p. 14.

[112] Ibid., pp. 15-19.

watched her solemnly play a record of Benjamin Britten to two Burmese visitors before she even thought of asking them the purpose of their visit or their names.

She was, "for Buddhist reasons," a strict vegetarian:

> her London flat, perched most happily on a house looking straight over Charing Cross Gardens and the river, was hung with scrolls, paintings and embroidered cloth from all over the Orient. Both her flat and her office were open house for every Asiatic student, politician and artist in England.[113]

Journalists, students, artists, and politicians, including some Independent Labour Party members of parliament, spent time in Woodman's house listening to the harp and eating the hostess' "Oriental food." In the house, besides, "bulletins and letters" were typed. Here, John Coast also got his first job: translating Sjahrir's "Our Struggle." "With the aid of Soeripno," Coast wrote,

> this task was completed in time for copies to be handed to all the United Nations delegates when they met [in January 1946] in Westminster Hall."[114]

Dorothy Woodman was well informed, John Coast remembered also, because she had access to "eyewitness accounts of the Indonesian revolution and its leading personalities." The accounts, according to John Coast, came from "two Englishmen in Java with the British Forces, Peter Humphries and Tom Atkinson."[115]

The Dutch were truly irritated by the British connection, and people like Atkinson, Humphries, their *News from Indonesia* or Tambu's *Independent*, were their prime targets. The Dutch in the Indies complained that these papers were being "smuggled .. into the hands of the British troops in order to destroy their morale."[116] Lt. Governor-General van Mook criticized the British command for allowing "a newssheet" to be published in Jakarta and dropped all over Java: van Mook specifically disliked being referred to in the English newspapers without "a proper title," while Sjahrir was systematically described as "prime minister."[117] The Dutch connected the English papers somehow with what they suspected might be British sending radio cars to villages, to recruit "young men of the republican party in order that they may follow certain courses and study in England."[118]

---

[113] Ibid., pp. 18-19.

[114] Ibid., p. 19.

[115] Ibid., p. 20. (Let me add briefly that Coast succeeded in his dream. He brought "a student group of Indonesian dancers" from Holland, with the help of Zain and Dorothy Woodman, through the theatrical people of the West End and by "generous ac(t) of the late Lord Keynes." They performed in Bristol, Cambridge, and London; Ninette de Valois was in the audience, as well as Margot Fonteyn, Frederick Ashton, and Beryl de Zoete, and the prestigious *Stage* magazine described Soeripno "as the greatest compere since the days of Nikita Balieff of the Chauve Souris." Ibid., pp. 22-25.)

[116] *Het Dagblad* quoted in the *Independent*, January 8, 1946.

[117] Van Roijen to van Bijlandt, May 13, 1946 in *Officiële bescheiden* 4: 296–97.

[118] Ibid., p. 297. Also in this document, the *Independent* is mentioned as a threat, and rumors are noted about the British planning to extend the distribution of the paper.

Interestingly enough, the irritation with the *News from Indonesia* or *Independent* and with the British connections in general, seemed sometimes to be most intensive among the more liberal of the Dutch. One wonders why people like van Mook appeared occasionally more pained by the subject than the Dutch ultra-colonials, conservatives, and reactionaries. Perhaps this was because these more open and more progressive members of the Dutch colonial establishment saw the British building a partnership with Sjahrir, which they themselves were willing and felt historically better prepared to build.

Four days before the Sjahrir cabinet was to be inaugurated, Baron F. M. Van Asbeck visited Jakarta. Van Asbeck, among other things, was a former professor at the prewar Batavia Law School, and also a former member of the *Stuw*, "Dam," the "neo-ethical" movement, we recall, made up of "progressive" Dutch officials, journalists, and scholars in the Indies of the early 1930s. Baron Van Asbeck was sent to Jakarta by the new Dutch minister of colonies, J. H. A. Logemann, another prewar Batavia Law School professor, and also a former member of *Stuw*. Lt. Governor-General van Mook—himself an old Indies hand and also a former *Stuw* member—was certainly aware of the mission.

Baron Van Asbeck remained in Jakarta through the Sjahrir inauguration and he met Sjahrir immediately afterwards. Reporting on the meeting, he wrote, among many other things, that Sjahrir appeared "as a candidate taking notes before an examination."[119]

This, no doubt, from the old professor, was a perfectly legitimate and highly positive statement. Van Asbeck met Sjahrir again, and this time they talked at a greater depth about common efforts by reasonable Indonesians and reasonable Dutchmen to work for a better future. This meeting took place in the house of a common acquaintance and also a former law school professor, W. F. Wertheim. Sjahrir, again, impressed his counterparts. As Wertheim later recalled, Sjahrir himself drove his car to the meeting, at the hottest hour of the day.[120]

Sjahrir's becoming prime minister caused a feeling of satisfaction, indeed relief, among this particular group of Dutchmen. This is clearly evident, for instance, from the very first cables Lt. Governor-General van Mook sent to Minister of Colonies Logemann after the Sjahrir inauguration.[121]

The situation appeared quite clear cut. The Dutchmen around van Mook and Logemann—formerly of *Stuw*—appeared impressed by Sjahrir. And they were instantly attacked by, among others, J. W. Meyer Ranneft—a member of the Council of the Indies in 1934, the year when Sjahrir was sent to Boven Digul; or by G. Vonk— the attorney general of the Dutch East Indies also in the 1930s, the man who had signed Sjahrir's order of banishment.[122]

A cartoon appeared, in late 1945, in one of the pro-Mayer-Ranneft and pro-Vonk Dutch journals, depicting a very ugly van Mook (and also van der Plas, another

---

[119] Report by Van Asbeck November 16–30, 1945 in *Officiële bescheiden*, 2: 215. For Wertheim on Van Asbeck see Wertheim, *Indonesië van vorstenrijk tot neo-kolonië*, p. 126; also van Mook to Logemann November 23, 1945 in *Officiële bescheiden*, 2: 154.

[120] Wertheim, *Indonesië van vorstenrijk tot neo-kolonië*, pp. 127–28.

[121] See, e.g., van Mook to Logemann, December 10, 1945 in *Officiële bescheiden*, 2: 329–30.

[122] On Vonk's attack, see J. A. Jonkman, *Nederland en Indonesië beide vrij: Memoires* (Assen: van Gorcum, 1976); see also *Officiële bescheiden*, 4: 508–509,n.; also Gerretson to van Roijen, December 15, 1945 in ibid., 2: 354–57.

member of the *Stuw* and now at van Mook's side), wearing *pici*, the Indonesian national(ist) head-gear. The message of the cartoon was clear: see how some Dutchmen had degraded themselves! The attack was led, in language and in style, as an attack against "neo-ethical" *Stuw*.[123] It was at this moment that van Mook wrote to his friends in Holland:

> It appears that some people in Holland decided that Sjahrir was an old friend of mine, in spite of the fact that I met him here in Batavia for the first time.... They even say that Logemann is his father.[124]

Sal Tas worked, now, in Amsterdam, for a socialist daily *Het Parool*, "The Password"; the paper's correspondent in Jakarta, beginning late in 1945, was Jacques de Kadt.[125] *Het Parool*'s chief editor was Frans Goedhart, an old friend of both Sal Tas and de Kadt and, like Sal Tas and Sjahrir, a former student of law in Leiden.[126]

Het Parool was closely related to another Amsterdam paper, a progressive weekly *De Baanbreker*, "The Pioneer."[127] It was in *De Baanbreker*, in the mid-December, 1945, issue, that a portrait of Sjahrir was published. On the same page, one could read a review of Eddy du Perron's correspondence with Sjahrir in 1938 and, in the same issue also, the first excerpts from some of Sjahrir's letters written in exile and sent to Maria and other friends in Holland.[128]

In December 1945, also, the Amsterdam publishing house *De Bezige Bij*, "The Busy Bee," published a book, *Indonesische Overpeinzingen*, "Indonesian Meditation," signed by "Sjahrazad." This was a more complete edition of Sjahrir's letters from exile, edited by Maria.[129]

A month later, on January 28, 1946, Sjahrir's "Our Struggle" was published in Dutch translation, under the auspices of the Perhimpoean Indonesia, the Indonesian students' association in Holland, and by one of the most prestigious Dutch publishers of the time, *Vrij Nederland* "Free Netherlands." There were 9,000 copies in the

---

[123] I found the cartoon cut out of the newspaper in *Collection Meyer Ranneft* nos. 498, 497, 167 ("J. W. Meyer Ranneft: Over Sjahrir"); Meyer Ranneft to Lord Invershapel April 10, 1946; Meyer Ranneft to Schermerhorn, October 16, 1945); also *Collection Pinke* no. 41.

[124] Van Mook to Posthuma and Warsink, March 1, 1946 in *Archief Alg Secr, lste zending*, no. VI-17-17.

[125] Tas, "Souvenirs of Sjahrir," p. 149.

[126] De Kadt, *Jaren die dubbel telden*, p. 139, M. van der Goes van Naters, *Met en tegen de tijd: Een tocht door de twintigste eeuw* (Amsterdam: Arbeiderspers, 1980), pp. 167–68; interview with Josine W. L. Meijer, The Hague, October 12, 1983. Also Goedhart to Schermerhorn June 24, 1946 in *Collection Schermerhorn*, no. 5: bundel Goedhart.

[127] *De Baanbreker*, besides, had been a kind of an heir of *De Nieuwe Kern*—the newspaper of Sal Tas and de Kadt, where, we may remember, Sjahrir published an important article in 1936. Also, according to de Kadt, du Perron discussed with him and Tas the idea of a weekly like *De Baanbreker* before the war. De Kadt, *Jaren die dubbel telden*, p. 138.

[128] *De Baanbreker*, December 8, 1945; see also ibid., December 15, 1945.

[129] The publisher noted that the book was printed from galley proofs already prepared during the Nazi occupation of Holland and as a title for a celebrated anti-fascist underground series *Het Zwarte Schaap* [The Black Sheep]. Richter F. Roegholt, *De geschiedenis van De Bezige Bij, 1942–1972* (Amsterdam: De Bezige Bij, 1972), pp. 90–93.

first edition;[130] and a second printing of 17,000 copies, an unusually high number for the time, appeared in February.[131]

Still early in 1946, a group calling itself Vereniging Nederland-Indonesië, the "Dutch-Indonesian Association," published a manifesto in support of Indonesia and namely of Sjahrir. The manifesto was signed by liberal and progressive Leiden professors such as J. P. B. de Josselin de Jong and H. Kramer; by representatives of the Indonesian students in Holland from Perhimpoenan Indonesia, T. M. Djaliloeddin, P. Loebis, Setiadjit, and T. M. Joesoef; by socialists from *Het Parool*, Frans Goedhart, J. A. G. Goedhart, and Sal Tas; by L. N. Palar of the Socialist Workers Party; by writer and historian Jan Romein; by former Dutch East Indies Governor-General's Adviser for Native Affairs, Gobée. Among others, the name of W. Lefebvre was also on the manifesto, the former Dutch Resident in Minangkabau, one of the names, we may recall, Sjahrir in his letters from exile quoted to suggest there still might be hope that something good might come out of the Dutch colonial enterprise in the Indies.[132]

Sjahrir, to these people, in various interpretations and formulations, was a reasonable man, a socialist, and a democrat. Shallow, biased, or just compassionate as this vision might be, it became the basis of the slowly emerging and, probably, from the beginning flawed alliance.

Four days after Sjahrir became prime minister, on November 18, 1945, van der Plas—a former *Stuw* member and van Mook's colleague—advised the Dutch government:

> the cabinet of Sjahrir is the last conceivable democratic Indonesian cabinet, the last attempt of democratic elements to get leadership in their hands and keep it.... It is thus necessary to avoid everything which may cause or hasten Sjahrir's fall and do everything, which could, without damaging the Netherlands, strengthen Sjahrir's position.[133]

Sjahrir was believed to be a socialist by his Dutch friends and enemies alike. When Meyer-Ranneft attacked the *Stuw* and "neo-ethical" van Mook and Logemann for supporting Sjahrir, he wrote that they were like "Kerensky, President Ebert, Ramsey MacDonald, Leon Blum."[134] Wertheim, Sal Tas, de Kadt, and many other of Sjahrir's friends and supporters in Holland, spoke of "socialist Soetan Sjahrir."[135] Sjahrir's socialism, more specifically to these people, was most often "educated" and "educational" socialism. Professor Wertheim, for instance, believed that *wetenschappelijke arbeiders*, "learned workers," were Sjahrir's political base.[136]

Sjahrir's politics, in the judgment of van Mook, Wertheim, or van der Plas—however these people might differ in their views of other matters—were "moral." "The groups of Sjahrir play no double game," van Mook wrote to Logemann in De-

---

[130] This is the date in the Perhimpoenan Indonesia's Introduction to the second imprint of Sjahrir's *Perdjoeangan Kita*. See Soetan Sjahrir, *Onze Strijd* (Amsterdam: Vrij Nederland, 1946), p. 7; see also announcement in *Inzicht*, February 16, 1946, p. 4.

[131] Sjahrir, *Onze Strijd*, p. 7.

[132] *Inzicht*, January 26, 1946.

[133] Nota of van der Plas, November 18, 1945 in *Officiële bescheiden*, 2: 115.

[134] Meyer Ranneft to Inverschapel, April 10, 1946 in *Collection Pinke*, no. 41.

[135] Wertheim, *Indonesië van vorstenrijk tot neo-kolonië*, p. 113.

[136] Wertheim, *Nederland op den Tweesprong*, p. 36.

cember 1945.[137] "The group of Sjahrir consists of decent men," one might read in the proceedings of the Dutch Council of Ministers from the same month.[138] Other typical Sjahrir qualities were described as "of a cool mind," beyond "hate" and "sentiments," "rational and sober [*nuchter*]."[139]

Above all things, Sjahrir was classified as cultured. Talking with me after forty years, a Dutch official remembered with what "intensity" and "understanding" Sjahrir talked with him, "amidst the revolution," about philosophy—"imagine, Benedetto Croce!"[140] Aki Djoehana, Sjahrir's nephew, recalled inquiring among Westerners in Jakarta, for his uncle the prime minister, about T.S. Eliot and his latest writings.[141]

Sjahrir himself was soon accepted as a fine writer. The Dutch translation of his writings, from December 1945 and later, was acclaimed as a serious literary contribution.[142] According to one reviewer, the texts were written by a "very talented man, who had studied and learned much"; especially praised was the book's "correct, nice and smooth Dutch."[143] Sjahrir became a prototype of the "intelligent nationalists" (this term is van Mook's),[144] who, as another Dutchman put it at the same time, might be able to

> make the Indonesian people conscious of themselves, and might lead the Indonesians towards the position of equivalence [*gelijkwaardigheid*] with other peoples.[145]

The editor of the socialist *Het Parool* likened Sjahrir, a little prematurely, perhaps, to Egmont![146] A "handbook of a socialist orator" prepared by the Dutch Socialist and Worker's Party for the general elections, in spring 1946, presented Sjahrir as

> through and through a moral politician, sober [*nuchter*], talented, calculating what is possible internally and internationally, an enemy of colonial ties with the Netherlands, and no enemy of the Netherlands.[147]

---

[137] Van Mook to Logemann, December 10, 1945, *Officiële bescheiden*, 2: 330.

[138] Proceedings of council of ministers, Hague, December 21, 1945, ibid., p. 398.

[139] Wertheim, *Indonesië van vorstenrijk tot neo-kolonië*, p. 113; also Nota of van der Plas, November 18, 1945 in *Officiële bescheiden*, 2: 115 *passim*; van Mook to Logemann, November 15, 1945, ibid., 2: 74; J. H. Ritman, "Soetan Sjahrir: Synthese tuschen Oost en West," *Uitzicht* 2, 14/15 (April 9, 1947): 14.

[140] Communication to the author by Mr. Posthuma; The Hague 1987.

[141] Ibid., also interview with M.A.Djoehana, Prague, August 16, 1983.

[142] Paul van 't Veer, "Sjahrir en Schermerhorn," *Holland Maandblad*, 18, 347 (October 1976): 13.

[143] L. de Bourbon, "Indonesische Overpeinzingen" in *Vrij Nederland*, February 23, 1946, p. 107.

[144] Van Mook to Logemann, November 15, 1945 in *Officiële bescheiden*, 2: 74.

[145] K. A. H. Midding, "Indonesische Overpeinzingen van Sjahrazad" in *Uitzicht*, February 5, 1946, p. 3 and February 13, 1946, p. 3.

[146] Pieter 't Hoen (Goedhart), *Terug uit Djokja* (Amsterdam: Het Parool, 1946), p. 59.

[147] *Sprekershandboek PvdA*, 1946, p. 152, quoted in van Tuijl, "Mijn positie is helaas niet erg benijdenswaardig," p. 84.

The metaphor of Sjahrir as a bridge, or sometimes a "link [*schakel*],"[148] was used; "a frail bridge," too.[149] Sjahrir's "hold in the interior was very slim," de Kadt wrote later about Sjahrir's relations especially with Java outside Jakarta.[150] To Wertheim, Sjahrir seemed "very uncertain" also, at the moment when he ascended to power.[151]

In van Mook's view, expressed repeatedly through late 1945 and deep into 1946, Sjahrir during his premiership was "in a state of continual tension." Van Mook connected this with Sjahrir's weak "hold" on the Indonesian side. This was the image of a bridge again. On one occasion, van Mook wrote, for instance,

> After talking with [me] for a few minutes, [Sjahrir] got better, but the prospect of returning to the dangerous community again increased [his] nervousness.[152]

The Bridge

Part of Sjahrir's image for these people, was that his Indonesian "anchor" might fail him completely; as van Mook wrote to Logemann—with a clear apprehension that this would make the bridge sway murderously—Sjahrir might even "pass over to our side."[153]

When Sjahrir became prime minister, in November 1945, and when he announced the members his cabinet, van Mook cabled to The Hague: "they themselves [Sjahrir and his ministers] and not repeat not Soekarno would be responsible for the course of events."[154]

"They are not collaborators like their President Soekarno," Logemann said a fortnight later, meaning the Sjahrir cabinet. "We could never deal with Dr. Soekarno," he added; "We will negotiate with Sjahrir."[155] Sukarno, to the Dutch (this is from van der Plas' communication of November 18), was a "panasiat."[156] "Because of the anti-Western attitudes he openly expressed during the occupation," Logemann wrote to van Mook in early 1946, Sukarno was "a *persona non grata*."[157]

---

[148] R. M. Noto Soeroto, "De Politieke Situatie in Ned. Indië tijdens en na de Japansche Bezetting" in *Collection Meyer Ranneft* , no. 474.

[149] Philip Jessup, *The Birth of Nations* (New York: Columbia University Press, 1974), p. 44 used "frail bridge."

[150] De Kadt, *Jaren die dubbel telden*, p. 153.

[151] Nota of Wertheim, November 21, 1945, in *Officiële bescheiden*, 2: 138.

[152] Van Mook at the 301st meeting of SEAC, December 6, 1945 in *Officiële bescheiden*, 2: 305.

[153] Van Mook to Logemann, May 13, 1946, ibid., 4: 300.

[154] Van Mook to Logemann, November 15, 1946, ibid., 2: 74.

[155] BBC Broadcast, November 28, 1945, ibid., 2: 265.

[156] Nota of van der Plas, November 18, 1945, ibid., 2: 111–21; see also de Kadt, *Jaren die dubbel telden*, p. 151.

[157] Logemann to van Mook, March 5, 1946, in *Officiële bescheiden*, 3: 494.

In contrast to the "cool insight of Sjahrir," a Dutch report from February 1946, for instance, depicted Sukarno as one of the "sentiment-leaders," who were constructing "hate" out of "the Indonesian inferiority complex." Sukarno was seen as leading an "anti-Western revolution out of emotions."[158]

Very early, also, Dutch intelligence reported a revival of "beliefs in the Just Prince" and of Javanese messianism in Central Java.[159] Other Dutch reports at the same time expanded upon "Javanist resistance" against Sjahrir's cabinet, where, as the reports sometimes added, the "two most visible ministers are Messrs. Sjahrir and Amir Sjarifoeddin, thus both Sumatrans."[160]

The old colonial dichotomy reappeared in a new form. The Indonesian Revolution, as Sjahrir emerged, seemed to fit a familiar and very specific topography. As another, highly respected, Dutch expert wrote on January 2, 1946:

> In Central and East Java, compared with Soekarno, Sjahrir's position is not influential.... The situation in this area is not clear, but what is clear is that the status of Soekarno as the president is recognized ... on the strength of him being the symbol of unity and because there is an absence of another power.[161]

Through the early weeks and first four months after the proclamation of independence, Sukarno gave speeches and traveled widely around Jakarta, the seat of the government. From Jakarta, his words were broadcast, explained, and translated throughout Indonesia and to the outside world. As time passed, however, and as the British and Dutch began to arrive in greater numbers, Sukarno's movements were increasingly restricted. Jakarta was the gate into the outside world and thus the place where Dutch and British influence was most strongly felt. Towards the Javanese interior the foreigners' influence weakened.[162]

Four months after the proclamation of independence, on January 4, 1946, the president and vice-president of the Republic, Sukarno and Hatta, together with most of the Republic's top officials and most departments, accepted "the offer from the Sultan of Yogyakarta of his royal domain as an alternative capital."[163] The top officials of the Republic boarded a train in secret and left for the east.

---

[158] "Sjahrir van vroeger" in *Vrij Nederland*, February 9, 1946, p. 42.

[159] Abdoelkadir to van Mook, September 24, 1945, in *Officiële bescheiden*, 1: 157.

[160] Van Asbeck's report on the trip is in ibid., 2: 214ff; see also his nota for Logemann, December 12, 1945, ibid., 2: 344.

[161] Idenburg to Logemann, January 2, 1946 in ibid., 3: 8.

[162] According to Hatta, Sjahrir was only appointed to lead a "temporary parliamentary cabinet ... formed to refute the foreign attacks on Sukarno." To quote Hatta further, Sukarno appointed Sjahrir as prime minister of a parliamentary cabinet, on the understanding that he was delegating his authority in order to overcome some temporary difficulties the government was facing." Hatta, *Indonesian Patriot*, p. 257. "The cabinet under leadership of Sjahrir," Hatta wrote later about this time "gave no shelter to the president and the vice-president, while the twosome [*dwitunggal*, i.e., Sukarno-Hatta] sheltered Sjahrir and his cabinet during his turn in office, and thus made Sjahrir's position as prime minister strong enough." Hatta, *Bung Hatta Antwoordt*, p. 43.

[163] Rose, *Indonesia Free*, p. 132. On how this was arranged see also Rosihan Anwar. *Kisah-kisah Jakarta setelah Proklamasi* (Jakarta: Pustaka Jaya, 1977), p. 41, and Halim, *Di antara hempasan*, pp. 16 and 35.

The tendency of the last four months was suddenly formalized. In Anderson's words::

> It was in Jogjakarta that Sukarno came into his own, after the anxieties and defeats of October and November. He was now in his native Javanese milieu, where his proleptic oratory stirred its deepest resonances, and where none could match him in firing the imagination and devotion of the people ... he was presenting himself to his listeners as the embodiment of Indonesian nationalism, permanent and unchanging, while cabinets might come and go. If, like the cabinet, he called for calm and discipline ... his speeches were always tinged with the messianic imagery that appeals so deeply to the Javanese.[164]

According to one account, Sjahrir was under very strong pressure by "a group, which was in favour of withdrawing the entire government to Central Java."[165] In a later pro-Sukarno account, Sjahrir "rather oddly, did not follow Soekarno and Hatta to Jogja [Yogyakarta]."[166] In view of still another contemporary, one of Sjahrir's friends, Sjahrir remained in Jakarta, because, there, he felt "free."[167]

Sjahrir's offices remained in Jakarta, a few blocks from the headquarters of the British occupational forces, and not far from the offices of van Mook's Dutch East Indies government. Jakarta had always been a city in between, but now it became suddenly much more so. As Sukarno and Hatta moved to the interior, Jakarta—from the metropolis of the Republic and, before, the colony—became a town with a highly uncertain position at the edge of Java.

Only a few days after the capital shifted to Yogyakarta, a representative exhibition of modern Indonesian painting, by Affandi, Patty, Hendra, and others, opened in Jakarta. It was, reportedly, well attended by Indonesians "and also very much by the Dutch living in the city."[168] It was, as soon became clear, the beginning of quite an impressive series of similar art exhibitions and events, during the following year and a half.

On January 19, fifteen days after Sukarno and Hatta left for Central Java, a new weekly appeared in Jakarta, published in Dutch, under the title *Het Inzicht*, "Insight." The people working on the paper were predominantly from Sjahrir's war-time circle—Subadio Sastrosatomo, Aki Djoehana, Soedjatmoko's brother Noegroho, and Ida Nasoetion. In a few weeks, Soedjatmoko became the chief editor, and writers included a Chinese, I Po Gown, a Dutchman, Jaques de Kadt, and a Eurasian, Beb Vuyk.

Het Inzicht wrote on politics and culture. Painters like Affandi, Patty, Hendra, Soedjojono, and Baharoeddin, illustrated the journal. Chairil Anwar, Sitoroes, Noegroho, and Soedjatmoko wrote prose, poetry, political articles, and literary reviews.

---

[164] Anderson, *Java in a Time of Revolution*, pp. 301–2.

[165] Interview with Go Gien Tjwan, Amsterdam, October 5, 1986; also see Cribb, "Jakarta in the Indonesian Revolution," p. 101n.

[166] Ali Sastroamijoyo, *Milestones on My Journey*, p. 119.

[167] Interview with Sitoroes, Jakarta, December 29, 1987.

[168] Interview with Burhanuddin, Jakarta, March 5, 1982; also Burhanuddin, "Sjahrir yang saya kenal" in *Mengenang Sjahrir*, ed. Anwar, p. 68. Also "Tentoonstelling van Indonesische schilderijen en tekenkunst," in *Inzicht*, January 19, 1946.

Het Inzicht came to speak for a much broader cultural stream which came to represent the new city mood. *Berita Indonesia*, another new Jakarta journal, in which Aboe Bakar Loebis of Sjahrir's group worked, wrote on February 5, 1946:

> Japanese flattery has exaggerated the importance of semangat [spirit, passion, sentiment] beyond all limits, and has derided and aroused hatred for akal [reason], as though akal were simply a Western invention—an invention of the imperialists and capitalists, which has had an evil influence among our people, both old and young.[169]

What this group valued highly was, as *Het Inzicht* wrote, a voice:

> Grim and unsettling in self-reproach and in analysis, daring in breaking the language, flattening and disturbing. . . .[170]

These people declared they abhorred everything "exotic."[171] Theirs, they wrote, was "revolution," "poetry," "music," "Marx, Nietzsche and Freud," "vitalism," "dynamism," and "dissonance."[172] As a sympathetic Dutch observer put it in a slightly different way, what they were being moved by, was a "*Démasqué of Beauty.*"[173]

Roeslan Abdoelgani, who in late 1945 was one of the young men quite close to Sjahrir, wrote about this time:

> We began also to discover the "excitement" of possessing the hundreds of cars we have taken over from the Japanese. They were instrumental in speeding up our movement. It was really a dynamism of an unprecedented nature. . . . We felt as if we were on the race track.[174]

These people—dandy-like and jazzy as much as they were disturbed and uncertain—listened to Artie Rich and Benny Goodman as they had done before the war and, on underground radios, during the Japanese occupation. Now, of course, they did it with a greater freedom.

A contemporary remembered later that none of the towns in the territory of the Indonesian Republic

> could approach Jakarta's importance as a center of Indonesian as opposed to Javanese culture, and so the establishment of a consciously Republican cultural community in Jakarta was an important part of keeping the Republic

---

[169] *Berita Indonesia*, February 5, 1946 quoted in Anderson, *Java in a Time of Revolution*, p. 310.

[170] *Inzicht* quoted in *Oriëntatie*, December 20, 1947, p. 11.

[171] Ibid.

[172] Takdir Alisjahbana in ibid.

[173] W. A. Braasem, "Doorbraak uit oude bedding," *Oriëntatie* 44 (January/June 1952): 451.

[174] Ruslan Abdulgani, *Nationalism, Revolution and Guided Democracy: Four Lectures* (Clayton: Monash University, 1973), p. 22.

panIndonesian and avoiding the risks of Javanization inherent in fighting the revolution from Jogjakarta.[175]

Poet Sitor Sitoemorang seems to be saying something similar:

> The essence of the "Generation of 1945" art stood in no kind of relation to the past. Boroboedoer had, by now, absolutely nothing to say.[176]

In a review of the January 1946 art exhibition, *Het Inzicht* wrote, clearly in order to show how much it opposed "narrow tradition" and "local definiteness":

> The only painting with an Indonesian, precisely Javanese atmosphere, is that of Baharoeddin—a son of Sumatra.[177]

Het Inzicht closely observed cultural life in Holland. It printed extensive reviews of publications from the Amsterdam publishing houses like *De Bezige Bij* or *Vrij Nederland*. Sal Tas' new book, for instance, was lavishly praised in the journal.[178] Eddy du Perron and his generation of Dutch poets and writers were remembered frequently and always with a respect bordering on reverence.[179]

Articles from such Dutch journals as *De Nieuw Nederland*, "The New Netherlands," *De Baanbreker*, or *De Brug-Djembatan*, "The Bridge," were frequently reprinted in *Het Inzicht*, sometimes, indeed, not even distinguished from *Het Inzicht*'s own editorials.[180] In the introductory article to its first issue entitled "What do we want," *Het Inzicht* represented itself as "a manifestation" that *samenwerking*, "cooperation," between Indonesia and Holland, in all fields, "is possible."[181]

The group got its first martyr. Soebianto, a medical student during the war and a loyal follower of Sjahrir, died in one of the outbursts of violence near Jakarta. A notebook, in which the young man transcribed his favorite poetry, was found in his pocket. Soebianto's friends selected a Dutch poem by Henriette Roland Holst, *Tante Jet* of Sjahrir's generation, we may recall, and Rosihan Anwar, one of the group, translated four lines out of it into Indonesian. These were cut in stone on Soebianto's grave.[182]

---

[175] A. K. Abbas interview in Cribb, "Jakarta in the Indonesian Revolution," p. 125n.

[176] Sitoemorang quoted in Braasem, "Doorbraak uit oude bedding," p. 452. Ida Nasoetion wrote, in *Inzicht*, against "the 'unwordly Javanism' of purely speculative character," which, according to her had been "in essence motionless, standing in an involuntary isolation from currents and turbulences beyond its boundaries, a second bloom of Hinduism, and thus, inherently decadent..., powerless against the vigorous bourgeois Islam..., knottily hierarchical..., absolutely alien to humanism. "I.N." (Ida Nasoetion) in *Inzicht*, August 17, 1946. Also de Vries, *Culturele aspecten in de verhouding Nederland-Indonesië*, pp. 86–87.

[177] "Tentoonstelling van Indonesische schilderijen en tekenkunst" in *Inzicht*, January 19, 1946.

[178] *Inzicht*, I,27 (July 20, 1946): 4; also interview with Beb Vuyk, Loenen, April 16, 1983.

[179] Ibid.

[180] *Inzicht*, January 26, February 23, March 19, 1946.

[181] Ibid., January 19, 1946.

[182] Djojohadikoesoemo, *Herinneringen*, p. 164.

Het Inzicht wrote about "universal character,"[183] and a "universal *fluidum*."[184] The youth of *Het Inzicht* professed a belief that it was their "task" to "connect" the "small milieu," in which they lived, with the "great milieu," which was "the world".[185] Ida Nasoetion, she was also soon to die in the revolution, wrote about the Dutch in Indonesia as about *bannelingen*, "exiles"—people torn from their true homelands, and shaken to their core by what Ida described, using a charged word of the colonial Indies, as *tropenkolder*, "the tropical frenzy."[186] It was natural that *Het Inzicht* devoted strikingly prominent space to debates about, and to writing by, the people in between: the Dutch in Indonesia, minorities, and especially Eurasians.[187]

These were not the other youth—the *jago*, "cocks" with long hair, bamboo spears, and knives, in the Javanese small towns and in the interior. The youth of *Het Inzicht* also fought for Indonesian freedom, but they were different. They could never, as the other youth, enforce a ban on the use of Dutch in the Republic's post and telegraph service, or, for instance, as was done by a *jago* in December 1945, to broadcast over Radio Bandung: "The voice of Holland is in our ears like the roaring of a toothless lion."[188]

These young people remained with Sjahrir. Sjahrir, in an effort to ease growing tension and to facilitate negotiation with the British and the Dutch, on November 19, only days after he came into office, ordered the armed forces of his Republic out of Jakarta. When Sukarno and Hatta were leaving Jakarta six weeks later, indeed, they were following their armies.

"Did it mean that we, who had not followed, were less spirited?" Rosihan Anwar asked for all those who remained in Jakarta and with Sjahrir:

> Apparently not. Yet, I occasionally felt deserted staying in Jakarta. Because a great number of friends had already moved to Jogja: Oesmar Ismail, Cornel Simandjoentak, Surio Soemarto, Djayakusuma and others and others. Chairil Anwar still stayed in Jakarta, but we met rarely.[189]

One of Rosihan Anwar's poems of the time, he later recalled, was dedicated to *Gunung Arjuna*, a mountain named after the most popular Javanese *wayang* hero:

> You, even in your loneliness, are eternal,
> my loneliness just comes and goes.[190]

Trains ran regularly between Jakarta and Yogyakarta, and the trip took about fifteen hours. Sjahrir often traveled by train, to get his instructions from the president and the vice-president, and to inform Sukarno and Hatta about his dealing with the Dutch and British.

---

[183] *Inzicht*, January 19 and August 17, 1946; also de Vries, *Culturele aspecten*, pp. 86–87.

[184] *Inzicht*, January 19, 1946.

[185] Ibid.

[186] Ida Nasoetion in *Inzicht*, September 25, 1946, p. 3.

[187] E.g., *Inzicht*, April 6 and 27, May 4 and 18, 1946.

[188] G. W. Overdijkink, *Het Indonesische probleem: De feiten 1946* (The Hague: Nijhoff, 1946), p. 110; *Radio Bandeong*, December 22, 1945, quoted ibid.

[189] Anwar, *Kisah-kisah Jakarta setelah Proklamasi*, pp. 114–15.

[190] Ibid.

It is not merely a metaphor, to say that the mood, style, culture, and politics of Jakarta traveled with Sjahrir on the train. As a rule, Sjahrir went on what was called *Keretaapi Loear Biasa*, *KLB*, the "Special Train":

> two special cars attached to the daily Jogjakarta local.... The prime minister's [Sjahrir's] party occupied a sleeping car; the press traveled in one half of a chair car, with twelve plush seats and six folding tables among them. Those elegant carriages were air conditioned.... The air conditioning did not work.... The rest of the train was covered with Indonesians like bundles of grapes, and the long string of cars was slowly and wearily towed by an old engine which burned.[191]

If there were foreign visitors to Java at that time, they almost certainly traveled on the train: Martha Gellhorn, for instance, who Indonesians knew "had been once a wife of American writer Ernest Hemingway";[192] Han Suyin, a Malay-Chinese novelist; John Floria, of *Time Magazine*;[193] a number of Dutch journalists....[194] Some Indonesians traveling on the Special Train had been on political business. Some of Sjahrir's closest future followers met him, for the first time, on the train.

The world of Java in a time of revolution was moving beyond the carriage windows. Javanese peasants worked in the fields; the Javanese fields were "brilliant green" as Martha Gellhorn did not forget to note. *Romusha*, the forced labor from the Japanese period, were "lying and squatting" on the stations' platforms, "dressed in gunny sacks and looking like skeletons of Dachau."[195] "In the train on the return trip," Martha Gellhorn wrote,

> Johnny, an Indonesian poet, came and perched on the arm of my chair like a very young, very thin bird. One of the greatest charms of the Indonesians is the place they give a boy like Johnny; they know he is good for nothing except to write poetry once in a while but everyone loves him and even respects him, and he is supported by his friends, since he owns nothing and does not bother to earn money.[196]

"Johnny" was Chairil Anwar, I was told.[197] Frans Goedhart of the Amsterdam socialist *Het Parool*, who traveled on the Special Train at about the same time, remembered another of Sjahrir's young followers—Rosihan Anwar. "Rosian," as he is called in Goedhart's story, "a journalist, politician, writer, actor," sang in the train a popular song of the time about "the girls of Jogja who are desolated because soldiers of the Republic seem to prefer young Eurasian girls, still held in the camp not far from town." Goedhart wrote:

---

[191] Martha Gellhorn, "Java Journey," *Saturday Evening Post*, June 1, 1946

[192] Rosihan Anwar, *Kisah-kisah Jakarta menjelang Clash ke-1* (Jakarta: Pustaka Jaya, 1979), pp. 19–20.

[193] Ibid.; also Anwar, *Kisah-kisah Jakarta setelah Proklamasi*, p. 97.

[194] Interview with Rosihan Anwar, Jakarta, November 8, 1987.

[195] Gellhorn, "Java Journey."

[196] Ibid.

[197] Interview with Rosihan Anwar, Jakarta, November 8, 1987.

half of the train comes to our part of the carriage: officials from the ministries, nurses of the Red Cross, journalist and secretaries of the ministers—there would be a [true] revolution in Jogja, Rosian sings, the girls would kidnap the President, if he will not send the fair skinned sirens back to the Dutch; and the president is in trouble because the Eurasian girls never want to go back to the Dutch. "Never back! Never back!" sings the whole of the train's half.[198]

Sjahrir moved very much with these young people. Drawings and paintings by Affandi and Baharoeddin still hang in the house where he lived. The art exhibitions of 1946 were widely referred to as "inspired" or even "done" by Sjahrir.[199] Chairil Anwar, who was already becoming a legend for the whole revolutionary "Generation of 1945," was widely seen as Sjahrir's protégé. And Chairil Anwar himself "was talking everywhere, and always with a pride, about his '*oom*'[uncle] who had stimulated him, also in his poetry."[200]

Wat een lieveling is onze premier, "What a darling is our prime minister," a woman spectator was overheard to comment at one of Sjahrir's public appearances in Jakarta during these late months of 1945.[201] Sjahrir now played tennis almost daily, "to lose weight;" he appeared on the tennis court "in immaculate white," and he is remembered arguing over every "foul ball."[202] He could also be seen on the Jakarta streets,

> bareheaded, in a sports shirt . . . himself behind the wheel—not of the shaky little Ford as during the first few weeks, but in a decent black automobile.[203]

It was at this time, possibly in this "decent black automobile," on official business, and with the Indonesian flag displayed on the front of the car, that Sjahrir was stopped by a group of soldiers in Dutch colonial army uniforms—the Ambonese. The soldiers were clearly looking for trouble, and, in spite of the protests from Sjahrir's entourage that this was the prime minister's party, the Ambonese ordered Sjahrir and the others to the wall. Dr. Halim, who was in this group with Sjahrir, recalled later:

> I raised my hands as fast and as high as I could, because it would not be the first time the *NICA* [Netherlands Indies Civil Administration] soldiers opened fire. . . . But Sjahrir, instead, put his hands leisurely in the pockets of his trousers. He calmly looked into the Amboneses' blank faces and just before the soldiers might shoot, he asked them '*What time is it?*' [in English!].

---

[198] 't Hoen (Goedhart), *Terug uit Djokja*, p. 6.

[199] Burhanuddin, "Sjahrir," p. 68; Lubis, "Pejuang, pemikir dan peminat," in *Mengenang Sjahrir*, ed. Anwar, pp. 203–4.

[200] Jassin in *Mimbar Indonesia* 3, 20 (May 14, 1949), quoted in H. B. Jassin, *Kesusasteraan Indonesia Modern dalam kritik dan esai* (Jakarta: Gunang Agung, 1962), p. 87.

[201] Suwarsih Djojopuspito. "Yang tak dapat kulupakan: Pengalaman seorang ibu (perintis) pada masa kemerdekaan (1945–1949)," (Jakarta: Perpustakaan '45, an interview project, typescripts in the archives of "Gedung Pemuda," n.d.), no. 117, p. 4.

[202] Halim, "Sjahrir," p. 114.

[203] J. de Kadt, "Soetan Sjahrir: Indonesia's Prime Minister," *The Voice of Free Indonesia* 3 (December 1945), p. 4.

With a bayonet, now, pressed into his chest, Sjahrir slowly pulled his hand out of the pocket. In it he held a huge ancient clock. He checked the time and then he put the clock back. . . .
I wonder, what made Sjahrir play this mad game, play with his life. I do not know. Till this day, I do not understand it. [And this was not an exceptional case. Once Sjahrir was hit by a colonial army soldier.] Next time I saw him, his left eye was red and yellow, and his face was scratched. The crazy little man [*gila si ketjil*], they almost killed him."[204]

Perhaps, remembering what Sjahrir wrote in "Our Struggle" about the Eurasians, the Medanose, the Ambonese, "our fellow countrymen," and what he wrote earlier to Maria about the Bandanese saying *brôt* instead of *roti*, one may understand the madness.

3. TAN MALAKA

Revolution is as good a time for a metaphor as any. Another "train" rushed through Java, besides Sjahrir's Special Train:

> Just look at this machine! How hard it works! The smoke of its breath is puffing out! I feel the heat of its sweat. Listen to its whistle warning: Step aside! Step aside! I'm running! Don't get in my way! How many thousands of kilos of goods am I carrying as I speed on my way! How many hundreds of souls ride behind me! Men, women, girls, boys, children and babies! Step aside, step aside, I cry again. Your danger is my shame! I am responsible for your safety, I must keep to my promise. One minute late destroys my reputation. My brother, the machinist, is directly responsible. James Watt was my grandfather's name. Fast, sure and safe is my slogan. Perfection is my future!

This was Tan Malaka's train, of *Madilog*, "Materialism, Dialectics, Logic," a text written by Tan Malaka during the Japanese occupation—a train carrying all the people towards what Tan Malaka believed would be a Free and Socialist Indonesia of the perfect future.[205]

There were differences between Sjahrir and Tan Malaka—in their political culture, their style and rhythm. But there was a strong resemblance, especially in both men keeping to the margins, and gaining a similar quality of power from this. They both also were Minangkabau.

Tan Malaka, Anderson wrote, was "both a stranger and a legend" to Indonesia after 1945.[206] According to Tan Malaka himself, writing when all his actual life in politics was in fact over, "it is not yet the time to reveal in detail the role played by

---

[204] This is a story told by Halim in Halim, "Sjahrir," p.101–2, 104, and in a slightly different version in Halim, *Di antara hempasan*, pp. 34–35. Also there is a reminiscence by Mohammad Natsir concerning this incident in the collection of Siti Wahjunah Sjahrir; Dutch and British correspondence on the incident is in *Officiële bescheiden*, 3, for example pp. 101–3.

[205] Tan Malaka, *Madilog* (Jakarta: Widjaja, 1951), p. 396; see also Mrázek, "Tan Malaka," p. 34.

[206] Anderson, *Java in a Time of Revolution*, p. 277; also interview with Paramita Abdurrachman, Jakarta, November 9, 1987.

Tan Malaka

PARI [Party of the Indonesian Republic] from its founding in July 1927 until now (July 1947)."[207]

We have mentioned the Dutch colonial police's constant suspicion that Tan Malaka's movement had connections with the Pendidikan during the early 1930s; that Sjahrir's close ally Djohan Sjahroezah was Tan Malaka's follower and, perhaps, agent. Tan Malaka's shadow, late in the Japanese era, was "felt," we recall, around the "Ashram of Free Indonesia," where Sjahrir also taught. There is the weird story, quoted in the chapter above, of Sjahrir's old associate, Sastra, and Sjahrir himself, looking for Tan Malaka, in mid-1945, and suggesting that he, and not Sukarno and Hatta, might be the "Proclaimer."

According to the official history of Sjahrir's party, published later,

> The Proclamation of Independence on August 17, 1945, and the ensuing national revolution was prepared by the radical left wing of the nationalist movement. Among them were also active cells of the illegal Communist Party and of the *Partai Republik* [Pari] of Tan Malaka. The leadership of this

---

[207] Tan Malaka, *Dari pendjara ke pendjara*, 1: 152; translated in Jarvis, ed., *From Jail to Jail*, 1: 142.

revolution in the beginning, therefore came also into the hands of these leftist radicals, which included many pronounced socialists and Marxists.[208]

Tan Malaka reportedly spent the dramatic days of the proclamation crisis in mid-August 1945, in a pavilion at the house of Achmad Soebardjo, whom he knew from Holland in the early 1920s.[209] Tan Malaka's whereabouts might be known to a few of the revolutionary young activists; he might attend some political meetings during the crisis, but, like Sjahrir, he was not present when Sukarno and Hatta proclaimed the Republic on August 17.

Like Sjahrir, Tan Malaka watched the first days of the revolution from the sidelines. He witnessed the huge demonstration in Jakarta on September 19, clearly with as strong feelings of disrespect for Sukarno as Sjahrir felt. Tan Malaka later wrote that Sukarno spoke on the occasion

> not to make [a speech] putting forwards demands and unleashing the spirit of struggle, promising to continue mass action of the people, by the people, and for the people ... but to request the masses to "have faith" and "obey" and to order them to go home.[210]

Like Sjahrir, at least according to Hatta, Tan Malaka was offered a seat in Sukarno's first Republican cabinet and, like Sjahrir, Tan Malaka refused.[211]

Some time in September 1945, at the time of increasing uncertainty about war-criminals trials and about the Allies' intentions in general, Sukarno signed what became known as the *Soerat Warisan*, "Testament": if Sukarno and Hatta "become powerless [*tidak berdaja lagi*]," "leadership of this revolution" would pass to a directorate of four—to Iwa Koesoemasoemantri (representing Islam), to Wongsonegoro (for civil servants), and to Tan Malaka and Sjahrir.[212]

Both men, Tan Malaka and Sjahrir, moved around, during the first six weeks after the proclamation, both kept distant and both were "sensed around." They also seemed to be well aware of each other. Tan Malaka later recalled a "shadow cabinet [*Kabinet Bajangan*]" of the Revolution, which was, he said, "composed of Soekarno, Hatta, Soebardjo, Sjahrir and myself."[213] According to Sjahrir, in an interview with George Kahin three years later,

> Soekarno, Hatta, Soebardjo, Tan Malaka, Iwa and myself [were made] unofficial leaders of the first stage of revolution.[214]

---

[208] Sjahrir, *Indonesian Socialism*, p. 32.

[209] Anderson, *Java in a Time of Revolution*, pp. 276-77; interview with Paramita Abdurrachman, Jakarta, November 9, 1987.

[210] Tan Malaka, *Dari pendjara ke pendjara*, 3: 63; translated in Jarvis, ed., *From Jail to Jail*, 3: 100.

[211] Interview with Hatta in 1960, in Anderson, *Java in a Time of Revolution*, p. 278.

[212] Kahin, *Nationalism and Revolution*, pp. 148-50; Subadio, *Perjuangan Revolusi*, p. 94; Ahmad Subardjo Djoyoadisuryo, *Kesadaran nasional*, p. 364; Anderson, *Java in a Time of Revolution*, p. 279n; Interview with Adam Malik in Collection Nishijima, JV40-JV40/1-JV40/2, p. 13; Hatta in Rose, *Indonesia Free*, pp. 126n, 139n. For a version of the Testament see M. Jamin, *Proklamasi dan konstitusi Republik Indonesia* (Jakarta: Djambatan, 1951), pp. 32-33.

[213] Tan Malaka, *Dari pendjara ke pendjara*, 3: 64; translated in Jarvis, ed., *From Jail to Jail*, 3: 102.

[214] Sjahrir's interview with George Kahin, February 15, 1949. In the same interview, Sjahrir described the "leadership—Soekarno, Hatta, Tan Malaka, Soebardjo and I."

On October 1, feeling increasingly oppressed in Jakarta, as he later wrote, Tan Malaka left the city for nearby Bogor.[215] Sjahrir, in the following days, moved towards the premiership. The paths of both men seemed to diverge. In fact, however, Tan Malaka merely decided to maintain his distance a little longer.[216]

In Bogor, early in October, a group of young rising stars of metropolitan politics coming from Jakarta visited Tan Malaka. Soekarni and Adam Malik, two men who already before the war were rumored to be close to Tan Malaka, led the group. Sjahrir, who was just a few days from accepting the chairmanship of the "Working Committee" of the "Central Indonesian National Council," came with them.[217]

According to Sjahrir's later account of the event, Tan Malaka suggested on that occasion that he, Tan Malaka,

> be President and Sjahrir be prime minister with portfolios of defense, economic affairs, home and foreign affairs. Sjahrir would practically be dictator and he [Tan Malaka] only nominal head.[218]

Others agree and remembered Sjahrir, instead of giving a clear answer, suggesting that Tan Malaka travel through Java and check on Sukarno's power: "If you are only ten percent as popular as Sukarno, we would consider making you the President."[219] This was a curious statement. Whatever its implications, however,[220] Tan Malaka and Sjahrir "agreed to meet again."[221]

They met, in fact, merely a week or so later, certainly still in the first part of October. Once more it was Sjahrir who traveled to see Tan Malaka. Tan Malaka was an "older man," this was explained to me,

> and Sjahrir very much respected Tan Malaka; he called him exclusively *Engku*, a most respectful way of address by a Minangkabau.[222]

---

[215] Tan Malaka, *Dari pendjara ke pendjara*, 3: 67 ; translated in Jarvis, ed., *From Jail to Jail*, 3: 105–6.

[216] Helen Jarvis notes on the basis of the interviews she had with some people who were close to Tan Malaka in Jakarta during the fall of 1945: "The legacy of his twenty-year exile hung like a shadow over Tan Malaka's personality. While he retained the ability to make political judgments and to project the way forward, in the latter stage of his life he was hindered by a reluctance to act or to take center stage. He hesitated, held back, waited for confirmation of his views. Time and again he missed the moment for action completely. Suspicion of and lack of confidence in his supporters proved his undoing on more than one occasion." Jarvis, ed., *From Jail to Jail*, 1: lxii.)

[217] Malik, *Riwajat dan Perdjuangan*, p. 83; see also Malik, *Mengabdi Republik*, 2: 73–74.

[218] Kahin's interview with Sjahrir, February 15, 1949.

[219] Anwar, *Kisah-kisah Jakarta menjelang Clash ke-1*, pp. 24–25; slightly different in Subadio, *Perjuangan Revolusi*, p. 95; also interview with A. B. Loebis, Jakarta, October 10, 1987.

[220] According to some of the participants, this amounted to a "flat refusal" by Sjahrir of Tan Malaka's offer. This is the interpretation of Dr. Soedarsono, who according to some accounts was also present at the meeting. George Kahin's interview with Soedarsono, December 31, 1954. The interview was graciously made available to me by Professor Kahin.

[221] Tan Malaka, *Dari pendjara ke pendjara* 3: 67; translated in Jarvis, ed., *From Jail to Jail*, 3: 107.

[222] Interview with Paramita Abdurrachman, Jakarta, November 9, 1987.

This second meeting took place in Serang, a town about eighty kilometers west of Jakarta. In addition to Sjahrir, in Tan Malaka's account,

> among those, who came were Kusniani [?], Djohan Sjahroezah, Dr. Soedarsono(former Mantri), Soekarni, Maroeto, Adam Malik, Pandoe Wigoena, Djalil, Soegra, Karta Moehari and others.[223]

According to Sjahrir and another pro-Sjahrir account, Tan Malaka had, indeed, made the trip through Java and now told the visitors that he had "found Sjahrir right and Soekarno necessary."[224] According to Tan Malaka's own recollection of the meeting, however,

> the young visitors asked if I would not mind becoming a chairman of a Socialist Party, *Partai Sosialis*, to be formed soon in Yogyakarta.

Tan Malaka recalled that he declined the offer, and, instead, "advised" Sjahrir and the other "young people" to work to strengthen "revolutionary leadership" inside the government. Besides, Tan Malaka recalled Sjahrir's striking silence during this particular meeting. "When one of the pemuda [youth] asked Soetan Sjahrir," Tan Malaka wrote,

> if he was going to Yogyakarta to set up this party, he gave no reply. In fact he did not speak a single word that night.[225]

There is still another account of the Serang meeting, by Adam Malik. There, Tan Malaka's voice sounds strong. And this is how, on the basis of future events, we believe it in fact might have happened: "I can still hear Tan Malaka telling Sjahrir," Malik recalled:

> "Let the two of us together build the fighting power and defend the proclaimed Republic; I would travel around [*berkeliling*] in Java and other areas, and you, comrade Sjahrir, would strengthen the ranks in capital Jakarta to be ready against all possibilities."[226]

The clashes between the Indonesian revolutionary youths, the Dutch, and soon also the British forces, grew into allout fighting and, by early November 1945, into a major and bloody battle for the East Java port and city of Surabaya. Sjahrir, who at this moment was assuming the post of prime minister, desperately tried to prevent the fighting from destroying the chances of an agreement with the Allies and the Dutch.

Tan Malaka's memoirs written two years later told his own story of the same time:

---

[223] Tan Malaka, *Dari pendjara ke pendjara*, 3:68; translated in Jarvis, ed., *From Jail to Jail*, 3: 107.

[224] Kahin's interview with Soedarsono, December 31, 1954. Sjahrir's interview with George Kahin, February 15, 1949.

[225] Tan Malaka, *Dari pendjara ke pendjara*, 3: 68; translated in Jarvis, ed., *From Jail to Jail*, 3: 106–107; see also ibid., 3: 141; translated in Jarvis, ed., *From Jail to Jail*, 3: 208.

[226] Adam Malik, "Sambutan untuk peringatan hari lahir 70 tahun almarhum Bung Sjahrir" in *Mengenang Sjahrir*, ed. Anwar, p. 4.

In Djokja [Yogyakarta], early in November, I have heard *Radio Rebellion Soerabaja* broadcast that "Tan Malaka is in Soerabaja as the leader of the revolt." At that time I did not know yet that there was a False Tan Malaka and I rejoiced to hear that I was having many children fighting at this moment in Soerabaja. In a hurry I got ready to leave for the center of the fighting, to Soerabaja.[227]

Tan Malaka reached Surabaya just at the moment when the battle climaxed. He got into the very middle of the fighting, to the headquarters of the Surabaya freedom fighters, and there he stayed, "day after day, amidst the boomings of mortar shrapnels and bombs, writing a few brochures." "Just an hour," before the headquarters were abandoned by the young revolutionary fighters leaving the city, as the battle was being lost, Tan Malaka went, too:

First I tried to remain at the city outskirts. But because it was becoming clear that the youth would leave the city of Soerabaja, I just continued on my journey ... to Malang, to think which fast steps should be made now.[228]

The "few brochures" Tan Malaka said he had written amidst the bombardment, were *Moeslihat*, "Strategy," *Politik*, "Policy," and *Rentjana-Ekonomi*, "Economic Plan."[229]

"I feel happy to live, because, for a week already, I am allowed to witness the fighting in Soerabaja," we read on the first page of Tan Malaka's *Politik*.[230] Further on, however, it becomes clear that this is a portrayal of doubts and reservations as much as of happiness. Tan Malaka, indeed, especially in *Politik* and *Moeslihat*, wrote a story of "shortcomings" as much as of a "heroic battle." "Feeling," strikingly, constantly, and painfully, is contrasted in the brochures with "the rules of the struggle's ideology and organization."[231] Tan Malaka himself, "amidst the fighting," appears essentially as a "witness."

In Surabaya, Tan Malaka defined the "struggle" as first political and economic, and only then as military.[232] He warned against "senseless sacrifice."[233] *Paréwa* is a traditional Minangkabau version of *jago*, the fighting cock. According to Tan Malaka,

paréwas with their underlying spirit of rebellion must be brought under healthy leadership and supervision. If not, they would act on their own, and perhaps will harm our struggle.[234]

---

[227] Tan Malaka, *Dari pendjara ke pendjara*, 3: 68; translated in Jarvis, ed., *From Jail to Jail*, 3: 107. According to one source, Tan Malaka traveled to Surabaya with Djohan Sjahroezah; see *Dokumentasi Pemuda: sekitar Proklamasi Indonesia Merdeka* (Yogyakarta: Badan Penerangan Pusat SBPI, 1948), pp. 60–61.

[228] Tan Malaka, *Dari pendjara ke pendjara* 3: 69; translated in Jarvis, ed., *From Jail to Jail*, 3: 107.

[229] Tan Malaka, *Politik* (Yogyakarta: Badan Oesaha Penerbitan Nasional Indonesia, 1945), p. 1.

[230] Ibid.

[231] Ibid.

[232] Tan Malaka, *Moeslihat* (Bukit Tinggi: Nusantara, 1945), pp. 15–16 and *passim*.

[233] Tan Malaka, *Politik*, p. 21.

[234] Tan Malaka, *Moeslihat* (this passage is quoted in Anderson, *Java in a Time of Revolution*, p. 287).

Watching the Surabaya fighters, Tan Malaka saw "discipline" as "our weakest point."[235] The most powerful "weapon," a fighter might ever possess, Tan Malaka wrote, was "consciousness and integrity [*kejakinan dan konsekwensi*]."[236]

One's "will and wishes," we read in *Politik*, are "not absolute, but are relative."[237] Freedom, to Tan Malaka, was relative, too; and "only when one is aware of the relativity of one's freedom, is one rational [*masoek di akal, berakal*]."[238]

Radio Rebellion Soerabaja introduced its broadcasts, during the fighting in Surabaya, with the cry "*Allahuakbar!*" and "*Sa'abiloellah!*"[239] Tan Malaka, as the fighting went on, warned that beliefs in the "charms of Islamic leaders [*djimats kijajis*], and in invulnerability through magic," must not be permitted to become a part of "our struggle."[240] Tan Malaka demanded that the fighting youth "harness holiness with reins we made ourselves."[241] He wished the youth in revolution to "be level-headed and practical."[242]

A niece of Soebardjo, who met Tan Malaka first in Jakarta in 1945, was impressed by him as a man "quick, brilliant, sharp to the bones, open, completely Western." The woman also remembered him, through August 1945, as he stayed in her uncle's garden house, "playing on his violin for long hours."[243]

"We must show them a big stick," Tan Malaka wrote in *Moeslihat* about the Western powers resisting the Indonesian revolution.[244] However, he qualified the big stick as being merely a part of *diplomasi berdjoeang*, a "fighting diplomacy."[245]

The aim of the Indonesian struggle to Tan Malaka was *100% Merdeka*, "100% Independence" or "100% Freedom." But the "100% Freedom," as any freedom in Tan Malaka's system of beliefs of course, was a relative freedom. People might ask, Tan Malaka wrote in Surabaya, whether 100% Freedom meant "that no foreign goods and capital and things of foreign origin would be admitted into Indonesia?" After a long exposé on how "machines" and "scientists" were inevitable, this was Tan Malaka's answer:

> Foreign goods are admitted, and they shall be admitted without interruption, and, I hope, until Doomsday! . . . Moreover, even foreign capital would be invested here to create things we still are not able to make ourselves, of course, lest they endanger our own industriousness, welfare, and freedom.[246]

---

[235] Tan Malaka, *Moeslihat, passim*; also Tan Malaka, *Politik*, p. 22.

[236] Tan Malaka, *Moeslihat*, p. 15.

[237] Tan Malaka, *Politik*, p. 30.

[238] Ibid.

[239] On the atmosphere of the holy war see Anderson, *Java in a Time of Revolution*, pp. 156–57.

[240] Tan Malaka, *Moeslihat, passim*.

[241] Ibid., p. 2 and *passim*.

[242] Ibid.

[243] Interview with Paramita Abdurrachman, Jakarta, November 9, 1987.

[244] Tan Malaka, *Moeslihat*, p. 2 and *passim*.

[245] Ibid., p.16; see also ibid., p.61. Tan Malaka, *Politik*, pp. 24, 28.

[246] Tan Malaka, *Politik*, p. 28. See also Tan Malaka, *Dari pendjara ke pendjara* 3: 98; translated in Jarvis, ed., *From Jail to Jail*, 3: 151–52.

Tan Malaka wrote about *paréwa*. He did this in Surabaya, a city teeming with *jago*, the "fighting cocks" par excellence, and he used the Minangkabau term, which made practically no sense in the East Javanese milieu.

Tan Malaka's Surabaya brochures, *Moeslihat* and *Politik*, were built on five voices—an intellectual, an official, a businessman, a peasant, and a worker. These five voices spoke for the society in revolution. But, like the *paréwa*, they were strangely out of tune with the place. They had Javanese names, but highly curious Javanese names to say the least. They were clearly Javanese appellations invented by a stranger: positive or negative, revolutionary or reformist, Tan Malaka's actors bore names, which to a Javanese, as one reader put it, sounded sardonic and often derogatory.[247]

Not unlike Sjahrir's, Tan Malaka's source of memory, and, perhaps, his actual center of gravity, appeared to remain elsewhere. In *Moeslihat*, for instance, he defined, what 100% Freedom or 100% Independence truly meant to him: "people's self-respect [*kehormatan atas diri sendiri*]"[248] and "sovereignty of the people [*kedaulatan rakjat*]."[249] It must not mean "sovereignty of the lords," Tan Malaka emphasized and added: "and where, in Indonesia, has the sovereignty of the lords been as restricted as in Sumatra... and especially in Minangkabau?"[250]

In *Politik*, Tan Malaka wrote that, to be capable of progress, the Indonesian people should follow "lights" like Charles Louis Montesquieu or Jean Jacques Rousseau. However, and this was the conclusion of his chapter on "State and Sovereignty,"

> Indonesia does not have just to run abroad. Indonesia possesses its own "voice of the people." At the glorious time of Minangkabau...
> People were ruled by their Leaders
> Leaders were ruled by Agreement
> Agreement was ruled by debate and decency.

This was, wrote Tan Malaka, "the people's sovereignty in the Minangkabau style, [*Kedaulatan Rakjat Minangkabau*]."[251]

The meaning of Sjahrir's Special Train lay in the train's moving between Yogyakarta and Jakarta, on the fringe, between the Republic and the outside world. Sjahrir's Special Train was fastest when it was most jazzy. It was truly meaningful, when it was between the stops, at neither of its destinations. The meaning of Sjahrir's train was in the train's passing.

Tan Malaka's train was hard-working and it pushed uphill. This train stopped at each station, to unload the goods and the people. Everybody was invited on board. There was no in-between. Tan Malaka was much more explicit than Sjahrir about the final destination of his journey, and about the aim of his struggle.

Tan Malaka was only a little more than ten years older than Sjahrir. But there was the watershed of 1908 between them—the anti-tax rebellion in Sumatra and the fundamental changes in Minangkabau consciousness as we have described them in the first chapter of this book. The respective milieux in which the two men grew up

---

[247] Anderson, *Java in a Time of Revolution*, p. 284.
[248] Tan Malaka, *Moeslihat*, p. 16.
[249] Tan Malaka, *Politik*, pp. 8–9.
[250] Ibid., p. 8.
[251] Ibid., p. 12.

were similar and different at the same time. Tan Malaka's memory of Minangkabau was not broken, as Sjahrir's was, by the "ethical" translation.

Tan Malaka had left for Holland in 1913, as a teenager, and, with the exception of a short period between 1922 and 1924, he stayed abroad for three decades. He was exposed to Western cultures at an earlier age and for much longer periods of time than Sjahrir. But, throughout, he lived his experience, consciously, clearly, and unambiguously, as a proud Minangkabau's experience of *rantau*. Tan Malaka was much less uncertain than Sjahrir in looking back, and rested more confidently on his foundations, which he believed natural, native, and wholesome.

Tan Malaka's bridges did not tremble so much as Sjahrir's did. Tan Malaka was not so much torn between things Western and things Indonesian, when the revolution started. In Surabaya, he wrote, almost exactly like Sjahrir:

> Our diplomacy, by all force, has to make the outside world [*doenia lain*] aware that we want, and can behave as a free state."[252]

But Tan Malaka also wrote what Sjahrir would hardly be able to write:

> A recognition of the Indonesian Republic by another state is not a condition for the existence of the Indonesian Republic. That recognition is incidental, something outside the question of the Indonesian People's right to be free.
>
> To get, to build, and to exercise freedom, is not a matter between Indonesian People and another state, but it is a matter of the Indonesian People itself.[253]

Tan Malaka predicted, during the Japanese occupation, that the Indonesian Revolution would start in, and spread from, the valley of the river Solo, which flows from the slopes of Mount Lawu near Surakarta, north and then east to Gresik on the seacoast of Java, just a few miles from Surabaya. Tan Malaka was consistent in his vision: the same Solo-Valley scenario, he had already suggested in his brochure *Naar de Republiek*, "Towards the Republic" in 1924.[254]

In the Solo Valley, Tan Malaka saw the crucial center of the Indonesian economic power and of the Indonesian working class. He was aware, naturally, that this had also been the center of traditional Javanese culture and the most powerful Javanese political tradition. Tan Malaka's train was rather old-fashioned, heavier, and more straightforward than Sjahrir's. Tan Malaka's structure of experience propelled the man more directly, to the heartland, to the center, headlong against the fortress. Tan Malaka had to be aware of this, and, possibly because of it, he waited longer.

There was a curious silence in the Jakarta press about Tan Malaka throughout the three and a half months after the proclamation. As much of the press was controlled by Sjahrir, or by young people like Adam Malik, one explanation might be that some agreement between Sjahrir and Tan Malaka, indeed, was reached in October in Serang, and that the agreement, by early December 1945 at least, still worked.

---

[252] Tan Malaka, *Moeslihat*, p. 16. Note Tan Malaka's use of *"doenia lain"* for the outside world. Sjahrir would never have done that.

[253] Tan Malaka, *Politik*, p. 31; similarly in Tan Malaka's *Moeslihat*, pp. 15–16.

[254] Tan Malaka explicitly referred to the 1924 concept in talking about his postwar actions; see Tan Malaka, *Dari pendjara ke pendjara*, 3: 65; translated in Jarvis, ed., *From Jail to Jail*, 3: 103. Also Tan Malaka, *Dari pendjara ke pendjara*, 3: 113; translated in Jarvis, ed., *From Jail to Jail*, 3: 120.

Indeed, in words Adam Malik remembered from the Serang meeting, Sjahrir in early December, as prime minister, might still have been "strengthening the ranks in capital Jakarta," while Tan Malaka, in terms of the same meeting, might still be "traveling around." According to Benedict Anderson,

> It seems plausible to assume that the press silence, which was not broken until December, was the result of a general respect in Djakarta circles for Tan Malaka's wish to remain in the background until the time seemed ripe for him to emerge.[255]

By late December 1945, four and a half months after Sukarno and Hatta proclaimed independence, and more than two months after Sjahrir stepped into the limelight, Tan Malaka "emerged." On December 31, a Yogyakarta journal, *Kedaoelatan Rakjat*, announced that *Politik* written by Tan Malaka in Surabaya was about to be published—a book, the paper added, "as big as Sjahrir's 'Our Struggle.'"[256]

About the same time, a brochure by another Minangkabau writer and politician, Muhammad Jamin, was announced in Jakarta under the title *Tan Malacca: Bapak Repoeblik Indonesia*, "Tan Malaka: Father of the Indonesian Republic."[257] Tan Malaka was introduced. On January 3, 1946, at a large rally, announced as a "people's congress" and organized by a group of young leaders around Soekarni, in Purwokerto, in Central Java, and not far fom the Solo Valley, Tan Malaka appeared before the Indonesian public for the first time after twenty-one years.[258]

Tan Malaka spoke in Purwokerto about spirit of the youth, and about reason. Senseless fighting "must stop," he said, and the uncontrolled spread of fighting "must stop." He spoke also about "confiscation and control of industry and plantations," about "people's government," and about the "people's army."

In Purwokerto, Tan Malaka declared a "Minimum Program" for the revolution: negotiations should be conditional upon foreign troops leaving Indonesia, and must be based on 100% Freedom; unity was categorically necessary, and there should be leadership able to inspire the people in their struggle. It was a program radical to the utmost, but at the same time a "temporary measure" that should be taken "only to face the enemy if the enemy persists in dealing with us in a military way." To this enemy Tan Malaka turned during his speech, switching from Indonesian curiously into German: *Bis hier, meine Herren, und nicht weiter*, "Up to this point, Gentlemen, and no further."[259]

---

[255] Anderson, *Java in a Time of Revolution*, p. 283. Adam Malik is more explicit, and connects the silence around Tan Malaka directly to the agreement between Tan Malaka and Sjahrir reached in Bogor and Serang. Malik, *Riwajat dan perdjuangan*, p. 83.

[256] *Kedjaulatan Rakjat*, December 22, 1945, quoted in Anderson, *Java in a Time of Revolution*, p. 289n.

[257] Muhammad Jamin, *Tan Malacca, Bapak Republik Indonesia: Riwajat politik seorang pengadjar revolusioner jang berfikir, berdjoeang dan menderita membentoek negara Repoeblik Indonesia* (Jakarta: Berita Indonesia, 1946).

[258] Malik, *Mengabdi Republik*, 2:74; Anderson, *Java in a Time of Revolution*, p. 289.

[259] Tan Malaka's speech, January 5, 1946, is in Jamin, *Tan Malacca*, pp. 11–13; also Anderson, *Java in a Time of Revolution*, p. 290; most completely in *The Voice of Free Indonesia* 4 (January 1946): 7–9.

Persatoean Perdjoeangan, the "Fighting Front," was established, on January 15, 1946, around Tan Malaka and his "Minimum Program." Practically every personage and group of the Republic joined in. The old man emerged after decades of legendary absence and he became the flame of the revolution. Beyond that, however, it was not very clear what the political content of the "Fighting Front" and Tan Malaka's world view actually were. Soon comments began to appear, on Tan Malaka's Indonesian being, in fact, old-fashioned (and he, of course, did not know Javanese at all), and on Tan Malaka's speeches being in fact lecture-like and, indeed, boring.

Tan Malaka's *Politik*, as we noticed, had been announced as a book "as big" as Sjahrir's. Muhammad Jamin published his "Tan Malaka: Father of the Indonesian Republic" in *Berita Indonesia*, where Sjahrir's influence was also strong. Subadio, a follower of Sjahrir, wrote later:

> I saw the efforts of the people's congress, which took place in Purwokerto, as efforts to put Tan Malaka into the limelight [*menonggolkan Tan Malaka*], and to shake [*menggeser*] the position of Soekarno. I did not see the congress as opposition against the cabinet of Sjahrir.... The emergence of Tan Malaka, and his coming up with the *Minimum Program* at the Purwokerto people's congress, had, indeed, been an effort ... to continue the spirit of the *Testament* [where Sjahrir together with Tan Malaka were mentioned as Sukarno's and Hatta's successors].[260]

Benedict Anderson suggested that Tan Malaka, if he had built a powerful political organization to support him, might have played a role in the Indonesian revolution comparable to that of Ho Chi Minh in Vietnam.[261] According to Anderson, also, the only other attempt in the post-surrender years, besides Sjahrir's "Our Struggle," to analyze systematically and to give a coherent perspective to the Revolution were the writings and speeches by Tan Malaka.[262] It is impossible to say what might have happened, if these two extraordinary men, during late 1945 and early 1946, had been able to work together.

Adam Malik dated the beginning of "separation" of Tan Malaka from Sjahrir at the "time of Purwokerto," which is at the begining of January.[263] Amir Sjarifoeddin wrote later that Tan Malaka and his group were not "wholly in agreement" with Sjahrir's cabinet policies "already in January."[264] According to Sjahrir himself, "animosity" and "bitterness" arose between his and Tan Malaka's camps "two months" after the cabinet was formed, thus again in mid-January.[265]

One thing was striking. Both men, Sjahrir and Tan Malaka, appeared to play a passive role in the separation. "Others," neither Sjahrir nor Tan Malaka, appeared to be the principal actors.

---

[260] Subadio, *Perjuangan Revolusi*, pp. 213, 216. Tan Malaka's Purwokerto speech was also reprinted by *The Voice of Free Indonesia*, a thoroughly pro-Sjahrir Jakarta English language paper, without any visible qualm by the editors whatsoever. *The Voice of Free Indonesia*, loc. cit.

[261] Anderson, *Java in a Time of Revolution*, p. 408n.

[262] Ibid., pp. 195, 284 *passim*.

[263] Malik, "Sambutan untuk peringatan," p. 4.

[264] July 3rd Affair trial proceedings in *Archief Proc Gen*, no. 577, p. 4.

[265] Sjahrir's interview with George Kahin, April 19, 1949.

According to Subadio's memoirs:

> It was Abdoelmadjid who was sent as a representative of the Socialist Party [of Amir and Sjahrir] to the people's congress at Purwokerto. He reported back about the congress to other party leaders—Amir Sjarifoeddin, Tan Ling Djie and myself.... He explained the events as a true Marxist-Stalinist, and in terms of the Comintern and Dimitrov line. Thus, he described Tan Malaka as a Trotskyist, which is a renegade, an opponent, and an enemy.... Amir Sjarifoeddin, as a member of cabinet believed that the congress was an effort to begin an opposition, and thus it was not difficult for him to accept the ideological explanation which Abdoelmadjid, and also Tan Ling Djie, gave.[266]

I asked L. N. Sitoroes, a political companion of Sjahrir, and also a man who was known at the time for his liking of Tan Malaka, if Sjahrir and Tan Malaka could ever have made it to the top and led the Republic together. "No way," Sitoroes answered, "it could not be done. Not in the Indonesia of the time. At least one of them would have to be a Javanese."[267]

It seems that Tan Malaka and Sjahrir were increasingly being used. It also seems that they both failed at the same historical moment, for the same reason and, perhaps, by the same design. The scene of the failure of both of them was the center, the fortress—Yogyakarta, the Javanese interior, the place where Sukarno, as we noted above, "came into his own."

On February 6, 1946, in Yogyakarta, the executive of the Masjumi, the Islamic and strongly nationalist republican political party, making public its loss of patience with compromises with the West, declared its non-confidence in Sjahrir's cabinet. The Indonesian National Party—close to Sukarno, resembling strongly the prewar Partindo and also led by Sartono, Sukarno's lifelong ally, and Sjahrir's life-long rival—immediately followed suit.

On February 17, Sukarno, in Yogyakarta, decided to speak out. Reading his speech later, one can not but be impressed by how much and how well Sukarno used Tan Malaka's rhetoric and Tan Malaka's flame; and how he was able, at the same time, to display truly paternal benevolence when speaking about Sjahrir:

---

[266] Subadio, *Perjuangan Revolusi*, pp. 240, 212. Mr. Raden Mas Abdoelmadjid Djojoadiningrat, in particular, was singled out. Back in 1931, as the reader may recall from Chapter 3 above, Abdoelmadjid had been one of the Indonesian students who had forced Hatta and Sjahrir out of Perhimpoenan Indonesia. At that time, he was allied with those who accused Hatta and Sjahrir of disrespect for Sukarno. (Sjahrir and Hatta, in their turn, pointed at Abdoelmadjid's high aristocratic origin, and defined him as a typical Javanese *ningrat*.) By mid-December 1945, as a part of their efforts to build bridges to pro-Western Indonesians, the Dutch administration repatriated a group of Indonesians, mostly of leftist, some of Communist, orientation, all with brilliant records in the wartime anti-fascist resistance in Holland. Abdoelmadjid was one of these. A few days after the group arrived from Holland, still in mid-December, Abdoelmadjid joined Sjahrir's and Amir's new Socialist Party, becoming a member both of the party's Political Section and Secretariat. Anderson, *Java in a Time of Revolution*, p. 204. See on biodata of Abdoelmadjid for example, ibid., pp. 411-12. Tan Malaka clearly reciprocated Abdoelmadjid's feelings. On his attitude toward Abdoelmadjid and the "group of five" or "gang of five" (Abdoelmadjid, Setiadjit, Tamzil, Moewaladi, Maruto Daroesman) see, for example, Tan Malaka, *Dari pendjara ke pendjara* 3: 81, 117, 121; translated in Jarvis, ed., *From Jail to Jail*, 3: 128-129, 173, 178.

[267] Interview with Sitoroes, Jakarta, December 29, 1987.

> Be confident that our prime minster will not swerve in his determination to maintain the demand for 100 per cent independence [100% Freedom]. But if it should ever turn out that Sjahrir is not maintaining the demand for 100% independence [100% Freedom] that all of you, my brothers, want, then I have the right to dismiss him.[268]

On February 23, Sjahrir, traveling hastily from Jakarta on the Special Train to Yogyakarta, sent Sukarno a secret letter of resignation.[269] This still might have been, and it probably was, just a tactical step. On February 26, according to Tan Malaka, Sjahrir also demanded to see him. "I hurried to Yogyakarta to meet him on February 26, 1946," wrote Tan Malaka, "However the meeting never took place."[270]

On the same day, February 26, in Surakarta, a Javanese princely town an hour's drive from Yogyakarta, and in the Solo Valley, a plenary meeting of the "Central Indonesian National Council," took place. The delegates did not know about the letter of resignation which Sjahrir had sent three days earlier, and to which Sukarno had not yet responded. The meeting started with Sjahrir reporting "what he had attained through his conferences with the Dutch and the British till now." Then Sukarno took the rostrum.[271]

Sukarno began by handing Sjahrir a big file of "about 250 telegrams from local leaders." Then turning to the audience, Sukarno spoke out:

> All these telegrams demand exactly the same—"100% Freedom," and that a war against the Dutch be declared. Further, all these men and women ask that the conferences [with the foreigners in Jakarta] be stopped. One has been conferring for four months already and nothing is achieved.... The Dutch made me duck. Each subsequent day they come one more step in my direction. Because they were not in a state to play an open game, they called in the British. My boys are depicted as war criminals by them, and so am I.[272]

After Sukarno, Tan Malaka was given the platform. This probably was the crucial speech in the old man's life. During "a heated exchange of words," a report says, Tan Malaka urged Sjahrir "not to drift too much to the Dutch side."[273] Sjahrir then asked Sukarno to permit his cabinet to be expanded. This Sukarno waved away by saying that this should be decided by the plenum.[274]

At the next session of the "Central Indonesian National Council," held two days later, on February 28, many further telegrams from Sukarno's file were read—so many, indeed, that it took the whole session, and any further decision on the fate of Sjahrir's cabinet had to be delayed till March 2.

On March 2, more telegrams were read, and then Sukarno gave another speech:

---

[268] Translated in Anderson, *Java in a Time of Revolution*, p. 313.

[269] Ibid, p. 306.

[270] Tan Malaka, *Dari pendjara ke pendjara* 3: 80; translated in Jarvis, ed., *From Jail to Jail*, 3: 126.

[271] A "very confidential" reports on the Surakarta conference, February 25–27, 1946, in Spoor to van Mook, *Collection van Mook* no. 144.

[272] Ibid.

[273] Ibid.

[274] Ibid.

We are in war, the Indonesian Republican Army must be strengthened. Its strength shall be brought up to 1,000,000 men. . . . A course is already embarked upon to develop an "Indonesian atom bomb" filled with nitrogen. . . . No Dutchman shall be admitted into our offices and into our public enterprise. Eurasians may be appointed only when this is especially approved by the President.[275]

Now, it was no more Tan Malaka's but Sukarno's flame. It was also announced that "Soekarno would not go to Jakarta, and would not negotiate with the Dutch."[276] This also was the moment when Sjahrir resigned—as he said later—"because I could not get enough cooperation from the top leadership."[277]

Some people believed that with Sjahrir defeated, Tan Malaka might be offered Sjahrir's job.[278] According to Hatta, however, he and Sukarno now decided to block Tan Malaka's road to power.[279]

The weakened Sjahrir was used. Hatta announced a new cabinet on the very day of Sjahrir's resignation. Sjahrir again was its premier, but, without Sjahrir being able to resist, a few new people entered his cabinet, representing the Masjumi and the Indonesian National Party.[280] Significantly, Sjahrir called the program of his second cabinet "Soekarno's 'five points'."[281] Tan Malaka, in his own way, spoke about the same thing. He criticized the second Sjahrir cabinet, but, as Anderson commented,

> It is very noticeable that in his critique Tan Malaka makes almost no mention of Sjahrir but constantly refers to the "Soekarno-Hatta government," in effect attributing the program to those two men.[282]

On March 17, 1946, two weeks after the crisis, Tan Malaka, together with some of his followers, Abikoesno, Jamin, and Soekarni, was arrested in Surakarta. "I did not know," Tan Malaka wrote in 1948, two years later, and when still in prison, "I did not understand who did it, why, and on what official authority."[283]

It appears again that "others," neither Sjahrir nor Tan Malaka, were the main actors. Of course, Sjahrir was prime minister at the time of the arrest. Amir Sjarifoeddin, the minister of defense—his signature was on the warrant—later claimed that he

---

[275] Ibid.

[276] Ibid.

[277] Kahin's interview with Sjahrir, April, 19, 1949.

[278] E.g., commander of AMACOB to van Mook, March 7, 1946, in *Officiële bescheiden*, 3: 523.

[279] Hatta, *Indonesian Patriot*, p. 259.

[280] This was still only a small step, an initial entry. Sjahrir's Socialist Party still had a majority in the cabinet. The Masjumi representatives were still mostly men not antipathetic to Sjahrir, and the Indonesian National Party was represented by a single and not very influential representative.

[281] Anderson, *Java in a Time of Revolution*, pp. 317–18.

[282] Ibid., p. 317, n. 16. See also Tan Malaka, *Dari pendjara ke pendjara*, 3: 68–93; translated in Jarvis, ed., *From Jail to Jail*, 3: 133–45. In an evident contrast to his view of Sjahrir, Tan Malaka could occasionally be vitriolic against Sukarno and also appeared almost constantly irritated by Hatta. See, e.g., Tan Malaka, *Dari pendjara ke pendjara*, 2: 144–45, 171–72; translated in Jarvis, ed., *From Jail to Jail*, 2: 153–54, 184.

[283] Tan Malaka, *Dari pendjara ke pendjara*, 3: 120; translated in Jarvis, ed., *From Jail to Jail*, 3: 177.

acted on a written order from Sjahrir. No such written order, however, was ever seen by a third person. Adam Malik, who later spent some time in prison with Tan Malaka, and who had no reason to shelter Sjahrir from responsibility, wrote that Tan Malaka was arrested "on orders of the minister of defense Amir Sjarifoeddin."[284]

Tan Malaka was jailed, and Sjahrir, at the same time, was pushed further to the margin. The dynamics of the months following the Surakarta crisis were the increasing nationalism in the center and the increasing hopelessness in negotiations with the foreigners. Sjahrir, the gravely weakened prime minister, was the man who was seen talking to the other side. This was the image of the bridge as it stood now. The principal Dutch negotiator, van Mook, wrote to his colleague Logemann in The Hague, in mid-March:

> He [Sjahrir], with the kind of luggage he carries, now can not pass, either onto our side, or towards the [Indonesian] extremists of the day.[285]

The weeks after the Surakarta crisis were spent by Sjahrir preparing what he believed might be a critically important conference of Indonesian and Dutch delegations. The conference met at Hoge Veluwe in Holland, in April and May 1946, and it ended in complete failure.[286] A break of contacts, silence and frustration followed. It was not until June 17, 1946 that Sjahrir sent a secret letter to van Mook, suggesting that serious negotiations might perhaps begin again.

There was nothing à priori explosive in this particular letter of Sjahrir. There was a vague acceptance of van Mook's idea of a transitional period before full independence be given to Indonesia; there was also a still vaguer note of a possible acceptance by the Indonesian Republic of a federated Indonesia—the former Dutch East Indies divided into several independent states, of which the Republic might be only the most significant part. As a possible basis for a compromise, this had been discussed in secret many times previously, and all the major political figures in the Republic knew about it well.[287]

The very next day, however, after Sjahrir sent his letter secretly to van Mook, the letter was leaked to the press by a newspaper in Holland.[288] On June 24, van Mook cabled to The Hague:

---

[284] Malik, *Mengabdi Republik*, 2: 168. On Tan Malaka's view of Amir and of Sjahrir see Tan Malaka, *Dari pendjara ke pendjara*, 3: 79; translated in Jarvis, ed., *From Jail to Jail*, 3: 125. Amir's name, and below it that of Soedarsono, Sjahrir's minister of the interior, was on the first official report of the arrest—not Sjahrir's name. *Antara*, March 22 and 30, 1946 quoted in Anderson, *Java in a Time of Revolution*, p. 327.

[285] Van Mook to Logemann, March 15, 1946 in *Officiële bescheiden*, 3: 579.

[286] Records of the negotiations in Hoge Veluwe, April 14, 1946 in *Officiële bescheiden*, 4: 120ff; see also British diplomatic correspondence from Singapore to Foreign Office on May 19, 1946 quoted in Squire, "Britain and the Transfer of Power," p. 219; and van Roijen to the Dutch ambassador in London, May 23, 1946 in *Officiële bescheiden*, 4: 328. For more detail see Idrus Nasir Djajadiningrat, *The Beginnings of the Indonesian-Dutch Negotiations and the Hoge Veluwe Talks* (Ithaca: Cornell Modern Indonesia Project, 1958).

[287] Anderson, *Java in a Time of Revolution*, p. 381; C. Smit, *De liquidatie van een imperium: Nederland en Indonesië, 1945–1962* (Amsterdam: De Arbeiderspers, 1962), p. 37.

[288] *Trouw*, June 18, 1946; for Dutch complaints about that see Logemann to van Mook, June 22, 1946 in *Officiële bescheiden*, 4: 512.

> According to dependable sources, the counterproposals [i.e., Sjahrir's letter] had not been approved by Soekarno and when he saw them, he got angry. It is not clear, which course the anger might take.[289]

At the same time, an Indonesian newspaper demanded that the rumors be explained about Sjahrir being willing to accept de facto recognition of the Republic limited to Java and Sumatra.[290]

On June 27, in a radio-broadcast speech, celebrating the Prophet Muhammad's Ascension to Heaven,

> Vice-President Hatta explained the content of the counterproposals before a huge crowd in the main square of Jogjakarta, in the presence of Sukarno and most of the top political leaders.[291]

Hatta, in the speech, expressed his support for Sjahrir. But, as one analysis has it,

> the wide publicity, which Hatta gave to the letter, has led to a coup against Sjahrir and to Sjahrir's kidnapping on the same evening.[292]

On June 27, in the evening, Sjahrir, as a "traitor, who sold out his fatherland,"[293] was kidnapped in Surakarta, where he had stopped on a political tour through Java. Sjahrir was brought to Paras, a town nearby, into the empty summer palace of a Surakarta prince, and he was kept there, under the guard of the local battalion commander.[294]

A little more than twenty-four hours later, Sukarno spoke on Yogyakarta radio. He announced that

> In connection with internal developments which endanger the security of the state and our struggle for independence, I, the President of the Republic of Indonesia, with the agreement of the cabinet in its session of June 28, 1946, have assumed all government powers for the time being.[295]

Two days later, on the evening of June 30, Sukarno was on the radio again. In what sounded like an emotional speech "more in sorrow, than in anger," Sukarno reminded his nation that "Lenin himself had warned against radicalism as an infantile disorder," that

---

[289] Van Mook to Logemann, June 24, 1946 in ibid., 4: 518.

[290] *Kedaulatan Rakjat*, June 25 and June 26, 1946, quoted in Anderson, *Java in a Time of Revolution*, p. 381.

[291] Ibid., p. 381.

[292] J. T. M. Bank, *Katholieken en de Indonesische Revolutie* (Baarn: Ambo, 1983), p. 187.

[293] Statement by Gen. Soedarsono during the trial on the July 3rd Affair, in *Archief Proc Gen*, no. 577, p. 5. Jamin stated that Sjahrir and Amir "committed diplomatic treason," ibid., p. 2. For the documentation of Sjahrir's kidnapping, see dossier "Ontvoering Sjahrir" in *Archief Proc Gen*, no. 340.

[294] Anderson, *Java in a Time of Revolution*, p. 385; Wertheim, *Indonesië van vorstenrijk tot neokolonie*, p. 199 (the local commander is mentioned by Wertheim as "*overste* Soeharto"; ibid.).

[295] *Merdeka*, June 29, 1946 quoted in Anderson, *Java in a Time of Revolution*, p. 387.

slogans of popular sovereignty [*kedaulatan rakjat*] had been recklessly abused to turn "our children" against the government,

and that some of the idealistic youth "had fallen into the trap." Sukarno demanded Sjahrir's release.[296]

Immediately, indeed, Sjahrir was released and flown back to Jakarta.[297] His movements now, physically and flagrantly so, appeared to be possible merely thanks to Sukarno.

Tan Malaka remained in prison after his mid-March arrest. Still, the conspiracy was immediately tied to Tan Malaka and soon described as the "Tan Malaka Coup."[298]

This was the July 3, 1946 affair, which Benedict Anderson describes as the end of the Revolution. Sjahrir's kidnappers were arrested, but somehow, they instantly left their prison and in an extremely bizarre fashion, however decimated their ranks, they boarded a few trucks and decided to demonstrate their power. They rode to see Sukarno in the palace in Yogyakarta, and on arriving there and presenting their demands for a fundamental change of government, were instantly arrested again.[299]

Sjahrir, on the same day, "under heavy escort," also arrived to Yogyakarta.[300] He reached the palace after all was over. As he later recalled, he came just in time to see the key rebels and kidnappers being arrested and taken away.[301]

Many aspects of the July 3 affair still remain unclear today. Why, for instance, were the rebels and kidnappers of Sjahrir dealt with so leniently? Adam Malik, close to the conspirators but not taking a direct part in the events of July 3, wondered later:

---

[296] Ibid., p. 390.

[297] Hong Lee Oey, *War and Diplomacy in Indonesia, 1945–1950* (Townsville: James Cook University Press, 1981), p. 92; Anderson, *Java in a Time of Revolution*, p. 391.

[298] The kidnapping was apparently done by radicals, some of whom had been connected with Tan Malaka before March 1946, but who were not in any apparent contact with him at the time of the event. Anderson, *Java in a Time of Revolution*, pp. 399, 404. Tan Malaka, *Dari pendjara ke pendjara*, 3: 140–42; translated in Jarvis, ed., *From Jail to Jail*, 3: 206–10. See also Malik, *Mengabdi Republik*, 2: 202.

[299] In spite the coup being described as Tan Malaka's doing, "Tan Malaka himself, throughout, had been rarely mentioned." Dossier "Achtergrond' ontvoering Sjahrir" in *Archief Proc Gen*, no. 262. Also in his first account of the affair, on the very day it happened, Sjahrir mentioned Tan Malaka only in passing. Sjahrir in *The Voice of Free Indonesia*, July 17, 1946, p. 3. The language of the rebels' proclamations issued on July 3, was "in sharp contrast" to Tan Malaka's previous ideas and programs. He possibly did not even know what was going on. See Anderson, *Java in a Time of Revolution*, p. 399. In the cabinet list the rebels asked Sukarno to accept on July 3, Tan Malaka was among the ministers, but only as minister of prosperity. Tan Malaka, *Dari pendjara ke pendjara*, 3: 138; translated in Jarvis, ed., *From Jail to Jail*, 3: 203–4. Everything indicates that Tan Malaka, always "the wandering revolutionary," "always the outsider," had finally became "a powerless scapegoat," and a man who was "expendable." Anderson, *Java in a Time of Revolution*, pp. 404-5. On Tan Malaka's name being deleted from the list of the accused in the July 3 Affair, see Tan Malaka, *Dari pendjara ke pendjara*, 3: 1; translated in Jarvis, ed., *From Jail to Jail*, 3: 4. This seems close to Sjahrir's own perception, at least in retrospect. Sjahrir told George Kahin in 1949 about the principal conspirators on July 3, 1946: "Yamin was pro-Tan Malaka only as a means of getting power, Soebardjo even more so ... Iwa was not pro-Tan Malaka." Sjahrir's interview with George Kahin, April 19, 1949.

[300] Anderson, *Java in a Time of Revolution*, p. 402n.

[301] Sjahrir in *The Voice of Free Indonesia*, July 17, 1946, p. 3.

"No capital punishment, not even ten years."[302] Within two years, indeed, all of the conspirators were free, and quoting Adam Malik again

> time had given [to many of these men] still another chance to play a significant role in Indonesian history and under Sukarno.[303]

Why had Sjahrir's kidnappers embarked on the strangely theatrical business of challenging Sukarno without any significant military force being mobilized behind them? Why was Mohammad Jamin, one of the key participants in the rebellion, already in the palace before the others arrived?[304] How much truth was there in the rumors that the conspirators, while still in prison, and before their action,

> received occasional visits from such persons as Sukarno, Hatta and [the chief commander of the Republican army] Soedirman (the purpose of which are not at all clear).[305]

For what reason did a long-time, intimate political associate of Tan Malaka, Djamaloeddin Tamin, insist later that the whole kidnapping and coup affair was *een schijnvertoning*, "a put-up job"?[306]

On July 3, once "the coup" was over, at a meeting of the representatives from the government, political parties, struggle organizations, and the army—Sukarno and General Soedirman are said to have been the decisive men there—it was agreed that

> the Sjahrir cabinet would not be revived and that for the time being Sukarno would continue to head the government, assisted by the State Defense Council.[307]

The State Defense Council's composition was agreed upon at the same meeting. It included Sukarno, Amir Sjarifoeddin,[308] and General Soedirman at the top of the list, besides seven other members. Sjahrir's name "was notably missing" from the list.[309]

---

[302] Malik, *Mengabdi Republik* 2: 171.

[303] Ibid.

[304] Ibid., pp.170–71.

[305] In Anderson, *Java in a Time of Revolution*, p. 384n. See also what Sjahrir later told George Kahin: "Soekarno certainly knew about the kidnapping beforehand. Soedirman knew about the whole business beforehand.... Soekiman [of Masjumi and close to both Hatta and Soebardjo] informed Soekarno in advance that the insurrection would take place. Soekiman was closely in contact with Soebardjo, Iwa and Jamin." Sjahrir's interview with George Kahin, April 19, 1949.

[306] Djamaluddin Tamin to "Mr. Healey" (of "Queensland Traders and Labour Council, Canberra," sent from Malang, May 11, 1947), in dossier "Bondan-Slamet cs" in *Archief Proc Gen*, no. 8-771.

[307] Anderson, *Java in a Time of Revolution*, p. 402.

[308] In a cable sent to Holland on the eve of the crisis, van Mook mentioned that "Soekarno's position has recently been strengthened by the influence of Amir Sjarifoeddin." The two men, van Mook suggested, Sukarno and Amir, were getting closer, because both of them were uneasy about Sjahrir's going too far in the negotiations with the Dutch. See van Mook to Logemann, June 19, 1946 in *Officiële bescheiden*, 4: 484. Hatta, years later, talked about some of his experiences during the July 3 affair. He had got his first information that something was going on, he said, from a man who came from Amir Sjarifoeddin. And Hatta continued: "I went

Not unlike Tan Malaka, and at the same moment, Sjahrir crashed against the center, and lost. In an account, three years later, in a text almost as rambling as the events were, Sjahrir described what happened. The only two steady names, the only two constant points, around which the account and the events as Sjahrir saw them, appeared to circle, were first, Solo (Surakarta, the center, the center also, remember Tan Malaka, of the Solo Valley) and second, Sukarno:

> I felt that *Solo* was the real center of all the disturbances.... I planned to clean up *Solo*.... It was the headquarters of Tan Malaka, *Barisan Banteng* and the armed troops of the *Masjumi*.... The *Barisan Banteng* had been trained by the Japanese as *pelopors* [shock troops] and their headquarters was in Solo. During the Japanese period Soekarno was their commander; therefore they were loyal to Soekarno. Their leadership remained after the Republic in the hands of admirers of Soekarno. Moewardi was chief of *Barisan Banteng*. Soediro, their deputy chief was close to Tan Malaka but also a nephew of Soekarno and married to his sister. After [my] kidnapping the *Barisan Banteng* was successful in getting Soediro appointed as *resident* of *Solo*. Except for the small group backing Tan Malaka the main opposition group was on their side [not outwardly], backing Soekarno against me....
>
> When I was kidnapped ... Soekarno tried to ease the situation ... first by compromising with Soedirman. Gave the latter the authority to clear up the situation in *Solo*. This meant that the *Pesindo* [armed corps of Socialist Party at that time still loyal to Sjahrir] was forced out and the old *Solo* group brought back.... I had to acknowledge complete failure in *Solo*."[310]

Why, indeed, had Sjahrir been released from captivity at all? Because of Sukarno's timely and impressive, truly paternal radio speech, because of Sukarno's

---

immediately to the President's office. There I met Abdul Majid Joyodiningrat again for the first time since my student days in Holland. He intercepted me to say that it appeared as if the Tan Malaka group was going to undertake a 'coup d'etat.' He and his friends hoped that I would act forcefully and liquidate these enemies from within. I said that I would certainly act forcefully." Hatta, *Indonesian Patriot*, p. 261. Amir Sjarifoeddin appeared to be on Sjahrir's mind, also, during the affair. At a news conference immediately afterwards, Sjahrir, strangely enough, did not refer to widespread rumors that the conspirators had tried to kidnap not just him, but Amir as well. Sjahrir did not even mention Amir. Rather, he took quite a long time to talk about a series of "misunderstandings," which occurred between him and Amir during the affair. There were "reports," for instance, Sjahrir said at the press conference, which stated that he had been "kidnapped for a second time." This happened, explained Sjahrir, when, after he was released from the first kidnapping, he was waiting for a plane to take him to Jakarta. But, as "it was later found out," Sjahrir explained, "Dr. Amir Sjarifoeddin had sent a special train with guards to fetch me....The guards had a written order to bring me to Jogjakarta." Which they did. According to the editorial comment, at the press conference "The whole affair...was blamed by P. M. Sjahrir on Dr. Amir Sjarifoeddin, who had not given timely notice, and Dr. Amir Sjarifoeddin blamed him for the same reason." Sjahrir in *The Voice of Free Indonesia*, July 17, 1946, p. 3. See also Wellem, *Amir Sjarifoeddin*, pp. 198–99. Sjahrir seemed to know, and wanted others to know, that Amir was very much on Sukarno's side. At the same news conference, and the emphasis is mine, "P.M. Sjahrir also stated that it ought to be kept in mind that the submission of all executive power to the President, after and in connection with his abduction, took place upon the proposal of the other members of the cabinet, *especially Dr. Amir Sjarifoeddin*." Ibid., p. 2.

[309] Anderson, *Java in a Time of Revolution*, p. 402; compare with p. 386n.

[310] Sjahrir's interview with George Kahin, April 19, 1949.

voice demanding that the kidnappers behave in a mature way? Whatever the doubts about the July 3, 1946 affair, nobody among contemporaries, even among Sjahrir's followers, seemed to doubt this.

Poppy Saleh, later Sjahrir's wife and at the time of the affair his ardent supporter and secretary, added another detail, which, I believe, exemplifies as well as the others, how Sjahrir had truly been defeated by the center. Mrs. Sjahrir told me:

> Sukarno made his call on the kidnappers to release Sjahrir, after consulting his Javanese sorcerer [*dukun*] at the Yogyakarta palace. Javanese sorcerers kept their guard over Sjahrir, you know.[311]

4. Road to Linggadjati

In a radio speech celebrating the first anniversary of the Revolution, on August 17, 1946, six weeks after the July 3 affair, Sjahrir talked as much about his own feelings as about the politics and the mood of the nation:

> In the year that is now behind us, we have shared so many new and strange experiences, individually as well as collectively, that it appears as if we have become new humans and a new people.
>
> Many of us have lived like in a dream, often in a beautiful dream, sometimes in a nightmare.... Energy was released, and it took us by surprise, as we had not suspected that anything like that existed inside of ourselves.... An intensive self-confidence has arisen, and an almost unrestrained belief in actual power.... Sentiment provided the propelling force, and there was little time to reflect and think.[312]

For more than a month Sukarno retained the broad powers he assumed during the July 3 affair. On August 14, 1946, Sjahrir was asked again to form a cabinet.[313] On October 2, he became prime minister for the third consecutive time.[314] "Internally," Sjahrir commented later,

> my position was weakened in the third cabinet as opposed to the second and first. I had to compromise in the third cabinet with the Indonesian National Party and Masjumi ... [I] had to take in people like Gani and Maramis via Soekarno with whom I had to consult in forming the cabinet.[315]

The State Defense Council, created in the midst of the July 3 affair, during Sjahrir's absence, remained a powerful body parallel to the cabinet and deciding the day-to-day national, especially military policy. Sjahrir stood very much outside this body. According to Ali Sastroamidjojo, who was the council's secretary,

---

[311] Interview with Siti Wahjunah Sjahrir, Jakarta, January 11, 1988.

[312] Sjahrir's radio speech in *Inzicht*, August 17, 1946, p. 3.

[313] *The Voice of Free Indonesia*, August 23, 1946, p. 1.

[314] Kahin, *Nationalism and Revolution*, pp. 194–95.

[315] Sjahrir's interview with George Kahin, April 19, 1949.

> In the opinion of the minister of defense [Amir Sjarifoeddin] a situation could be better dealt with if sovereignty was in the hands of a single authority rather than being divided among a number of ministries or between the government and the Working Committee of the [Central Indonesian National Council], which functioned as a body representing the people. I put it to Amir Sjarifoeddin that such a single authority could be made to work if it was given to the president. . . . Amir agreed with me.[316]

According to Ali again,

> Fearing that the State Defense Council would destroy the legislative power of the Working committee of the [Central Indonesian National Council], Sjahrir was opposed to its establishment.[317]

After October 1946, Sjahrir, as prime minister, became formally also the State Defense Council's chairman. Yet, according to Ali, Sjahrir "never attended [the council's] meetings."[318] "Usually," Ali wrote,

> it was the minister of defense [Amir], with the help of the council secretariat [led by Ali], who framed . . . regulations [and who] in practice . . . carried out the work of the State Defense Council.[319]

The State Defense Council, besides, was responsible not to Sjahrir as prime minister, but to Sukarno as president.[320]

In retrospect, people around Sjahrir dated his split with Amir Sjarifoeddin and the division, or redivision, of the Socialist Party between the factions of Sjahrir and Amir to some time after February and before June 1947.[321] According to one later statement from circles around Sjahrir,

> Since March 1947, it had become clear that in the circles of the central executive of the Socialist Party, fundamental differences of opinion existed regarding the way in which the national revolution should be safeguarded and continued.[322]

Of the four socialist members of Sjahrir's third cabinet, only Dr. Soedarsono, old friend of Sjahrir and leader of the prewar Pendidikan, could be counted upon as being safely on Sjahrir's side. The position of Wijono, the new vice-minister of the

---

[316] Ali Sastroamijoyo, *Milestones on my Journey*, p. 123. On the Council see also Wellem, *Amir Sjarifoeddin*, p. 194.
[317] Ali Sastroamijoyo, *Milestones on my Journey*, p. 124.
[318] Ibid.
[319] Ibid.
[320] This was noted, e.g., in the proceedings of the council of ministers, Hague, July 29, 1946, in *Officiële bescheiden*, 4: 104–106.
[321] Interviews with Subadio, Jakarta, March 4, 1982, and with Soedjatmoko, Jakarta, November 6, 1987.
[322] "Manifesto PSI, February 1948" reprinted in "Partai Sosialis Indonesia" in *Sedjarah Singkat Kepartaian di Indonesia*, pp. 168–72; also in Sjahrir, *Indonesian Socialism*, p. 40.

interior, was uncertain.[323] The remaining two socialist cabinet members were clearly and increasingly on Amir's side—Abdoelmadjid, and another newcomer from Holland, Setiadjit Soegondo.[324]

L. N. Palar, an Indonesian expert of the Dutch "Labor Party," (PvdA, formerly SDAP), came to report on Java in the spring of 1947. According to what Palar saw, Sjahrir was

> still [*nog steeds*] the leader . . . but he stands under powerful [*geweldige*] pressure exerted from the interior, and also by his own party."[325]

There was a familiar topography to the split. As one contemporary put it, "Sjahrir guided our diplomacy in Jakarta and Amir guided the building of our armed forces in Jogjakarta."[326] In the words of another witness, who used the image of the "Special Train,"

> on the train between Jogjakarta and Djakarta one could sense that, at a certain point, we passed out of the sphere of influence of the Defense Ministry

---

[323] Wijono had been reportedly close to Amir after the war but in February 1948 he joined Sjahrir's party; see Anderson, *Java in a Time of Revolution*, p. 204n.

[324] The reader may recall that Setiadjit, back in 1931, had cooperated with Abdoelmadjid in expelling Hatta and Sjahrir from the Perhimpoenan Indonesia. He too had been active in the anti-fascist resistance during the war in Holland and had represented Perhimpoenan Indonesia in the underground Dutch "Contact Commissie" led by Professor Schermerhorn; see, e.g., P. J. Schmidt, *Buitenlandsche politiek van Nederland* (Leiden: Sijthoff, 1945), pp. 68–69. Setiadjit remained in Holland later than Abdoelmadjid. He became part of the Indonesian delegation at the aborted Dutch-Indonesian Hoge Veluwe talks, in April and May 1946, and he returned to Java immediately afterwards. On Setiadjit, and Daroesman with Saroso, joining the Indonesian delegation in Hoge Veluwe see the records of the April 24, 1946 session, in *Officiële bescheiden*, 4: 163; also ibid., p. 129. It seems that Setiadjit renewed his friendship with Abdoelmadjid easily, and that he also soon became close to Amir. He did not enter the Socialist Party as Abdoelmadjid did, but instead became one of the top leaders of another, small socialist party, Partai Buruh Indonesia, the "Indonesian Labor Party." As late as October 1946, Sjahrir expressed his high respect for Setiadjit as a labor leader. "De Politieke visies van Soetan Sjahrir" (1947) *Collection Koets* no. 327, p. 2; also "N.N." De naaste toekomst van Indonesië," October 25, 1946, in *Collection Meyer Ranneft* no. 486. Reportedly Sjahrir tried, at the same time, to bring about a fusion between his and Setiadjit's parties. Ibid. Setiadjit, however, very soon appeared to gravitate away from Sjahrir. Also in October 1946, as Sjahrir's third cabinet was being announced, Setiadjit confided in private that, it was "Soekarno himself" who was pushing him forward. Setiadjit to Schermerhorn, October 20, 1946, in W. Schermerhorn, *Het dagboek van Schermerhorn. Geheim verslag van prof.dr.ir.W.Schermerhorn als voorzitter der commissie-generaal voor Nederlands-Indië. 20 september 1946–7 october 1947*, 2 vols. (Groningen: Wolters-Noordhoff, 1970), October 20, 1946 (1: 54). Rumors circulated, through early 1947, that Setiadjit, a high aristocrat by blood and behavior, was gaining a growing influence over Sukarno. "At the time," Abu Hanifah, for instance, wrote, "it was very difficult to approach Soekarno. If one wanted to talk to him, one had to ask for an appointment through Setiadjit."Abu Hanifah, *Tales of a Revolution*, p. 272; Setiadjit served as the vice-minister of communication in the 3rd Sjahrir cabinet. Professor Anderson believes this particular story is highly improbable; Setiadjit was quite new from Holland, and besides, Anderson says, Sukarno was known to be highly accessible. Letter from Benedict Anderson, October 1990.

[325] Palar to *PvdA* Council, March 15, 1947, in van Tuijl, *Mijn positie*, p. 97.

[326] Quoted in Cribb, "Jakarta in the Indonesian Revolution," p. 90.

in Jogjakarta [which was Amir Sjarifoeddin] and entered that of the [Sjahrir's] Foreign Ministry in Jakarta.[327]

Sjahrir had to resist increasing "suggestions" from Indonesian politicians and from the public to move also the remaining government offices and personnel, including himself, to the center, to Yogyakarta. Most of the offices and symbols of power by early 1947 had already departed. There were Sukarno and Hatta safely settled in the interior, and increasingly so, now also Amir Sjarifoeddin. Virtually all significant meetings were held in Central and East Java, and Sjahrir appeared at them always as a visitor, sometimes as a man coming from abroad, and not rarely as a species from another world.

Inevitably, he made blunders. During an important speech to the plenum of the "Central Indonesian National Council," in February 1947, which took place in Malang, a town deep in East Java,[328] Sjahrir attacked the *ningrat*, aristocratic traits of the Republic's bureaucracy. The Republican officials present, predominantly Javanese and very many of them of some noble blood naturally, took this as an insensitive attack against the civil corps of the Republic.[329] In the same speech, Sjahrir declared that the soldiers of the revolution must be "tools" of the cabinet, and—as if to make sure that all the *jago* present, all the "fighting cocks" amidst the revolution, understood him well—he translated what he meant into Dutch: they should be, he said, *machtswerktuig*.[330]

One of the deputies present at this Malang session of the legislature recorded his feelings:

> I just could not understand why Prime Minister Sjahrir at this KNIP plenum acted the way he did. Even at the [prewar colonial] semi-parliament Volksraad, the opinion of each member was accepted by the government of the "Dutch Indies" in a *parlementair* style, through *gemachtigde* [assignee] or his deputy (usually a head of a Department) on the basis of mutual respect, and there were truly debates, arguments were exchanged, and much of the time was spent on this. But Sjahrir, whom I had regarded as a convinced and loyal adherent of the system of parliamentary democracy, answered questions from the deputies in an abrupt way, there was not much of any argument. This is what confused me. Was he so sure that he would prevail? Did he think it wise, not to work in an *openbare* [open] way, thus not to answer questions at length?[331]

---

[327] T. B. Simatupang, *Report from Banaran: Experiences during the People's War* (Ithaca: Cornell Modern Indonesia Project, 1976), p. 80.

[328] Typescript of the draft of the Sjahrir's speech to the KNIP in Malang is in the *Archives Siti Wahjunah Sjahrir*.

[329] Sjahrir called the Republic's officials with *ningrat* traits "a difficult problem..., a heritage of colonial times [which] must vanish, [and] we should work to that aim fast... lest they gain time to defend themselves." Ibid., p. 1.

[330] Ibid., pp. 4–6.

[331] I. J. Kasimo, "Bung Kecil dalam pandangan saya" in *Mengenang Sjahrir*, ed. Anwar, p. 172.

Sjahrir on the Radio

At this plenum in Malang, the "Central Indonesian National Council" was enlarged, from the original 200, to 514 members.[332] The main beneficiaries of the enlargement were, in particular the Partai Komunis Indonesia, the "Indonesian Communist Party," newly revived under one of its prewar leaders Alimin, and Setiadjit's new Partai Buruh Indonesia, "Indonesian Labor Party"; the representation of Alimin's party grew from two seats to thirty-five, and that of Setiadjit's party from six deputies to thirty five.[333] According to a historian,

> Sjahrir's position had been considerably weakened by the new appointments... for those had favoured the labour and the communist parties, which were politically much closer to Sjarifoeddin than to Sjahrir.[334]

Het Inzicht, "Insight," continued to be published in Jakarta, and the original pro-Sjahrir group remained on the board. Ida Nasoetion now headed the journal, and Sudarpo served as her deputy.[335] A new weekly appeared in Jakarta early in 1947, *Siasat*, "Tactics." The idea behind it came from other key members of the same

---

[332] X ambtenaar, "Indonesische Politiek," p. 26. This expansion might initially have been Sjahrir's idea, but it was carried out now by presidential decree, after Vice-President Hatta pushed it through. Kahin, *Nationalism and Revolution*, pp. 200–203. Hatta, *Indonesian Patriot*, p. 265. X ambtenaar, "Indonesische Politiek," p. 26.

[333] Kahin, *Nationalism and Revolution*, pp. 200–201, 204–5; also Ali Sastroamijoyo, *Milestones on my Journey*, p. 170.

[334] Cribb, "Jakarta in the Indonesian Revolution," p. 196.

[335] *Inzicht*, January 1, 1947.

group—Soedjatmoko, Rosihan Anwar, and Aboe Bakar Loebis. Rosihan Anwar recalled later that Sjahrir expressed "a strong interest."[336]

Siasat was a big success in the city, expanding its sales, reportedly, from 3,000 to 12,000 copies in four months.[337] Its cultural magazine, *Gelanggang*, "Arena," became a well respected forum for Jakarta's artists and intellectuals. Poets and novelists Sitor Sitoemorang, Mochtar Loebis, and Riwai Apin, with painter Ramalan, were on the *Gelanggang* board. Chairil Anwar was also very much involved.[338]

Painters like Affandi, Hendra, Soedarso, Soedjojono, and Mochtar Apin, went on organizing regular art exhibits. New paintings and illustrations by Salim, Sjahrir's prewar friend who still lived in France, were reviewed in Jakarta and highly praised.[339]

In May 1947, an Indonesian edition of Sjahrir's letters from prison and exile was published—a translation by H.B. Jassin of the Dutch *Indonesische Overpeinzingen*. The book had a cover designed by Baharoeddin.[340]

"Internally my position was weaker," Sjahrir said in a later interview, talking about the months following the July 3, affair.[341] The word "internally" was emphasized by Sjahrir:

> Though my position was internally weaker, I felt I had to accept the post of prime minister [in August 1946] if a settlement with the Dutch was to be reached."[342]

Indeed, frequently now, even by his political associates, and offhandedly, Sjahrir was called, "foreign minister Sjahrir."[343]

The next phase of the Indonesian-Dutch negotiations, after the July 3 affair and the pause that followed, opened in early October 1946. The Dutch Government now appointed a special "Commission General" to lead the negotiations. The chairman of the Commission was Professor Willem Schermerhorn, a member of the Dutch Labor Party—PvdA, and, earlier, a leader of the anti-Nazi underground. During the war, Schermerhorn also served as chairman of the "Liaison Commission," a consultative body deliberating possible reforms for the Indies.

Clearly, Schermerhorn was a figure who would very probably be sympathetic to Sjahrir. At the same time, Schermerhorn's very emergence on the scene exemplified diminishing hopes. He came to Indonesia as a recently defunct Dutch prime minister, a man whose power was in decline; he and his party had just lost the elections in the previous May.

Immediately upon his arrival in Indonesia, in late July 1946, and before he ever met Sjahrir, Schermerhorn noted in a letter to a friend his "extraordinary interest" in

---

[336] Rosihan Anwar, *Kisah-kisah Jakarta menjelang Clash ke-1*, p. 73 ; also ibid., pp. 121–22 and interview with Soedjatmoko, Jakarta, November 6, 1987.

[337] Anwar. *Kisah-kisah Jakarta menjelang Clash ke-1*, p. 128.

[338] Ibid., pp. 124–25, 128.

[339] *Inzicht*, August 15, 1946, a review of Salim's illustrations of *Baba Tahir XI*.

[340] Sutan Sjahrir, *Renungan Indonesia* (trans. H. B. Jassin) (Jakarta: Poestaka Rakjat, 1947), p. 3.

[341] Sjahrir's interview with George Kahin, April 19, 1949.

[342] Ibid.

[343] E.g., "Partai Sosialis" a report on the Partai Sosialis Congress in Ceribon, July 31–August 3, 1946, in *The Voice of Free Indonesia*, August 23, 1946, p. 14.

Sjahrir; also he wrote about a "great trust" he had in Sjahrir's "character and qualities."[344] A day before Schermerhorn and Sjahrir saw each other for the first time, the Dutchman wrote in his diary:

> How remarkable that beforehand I had imagined relatively little in my thoughts. Whether this was a sort of mental laziness I do not rarely find in myself, or a firm trust that I would at the moment react correctly to the other personality I do not know.[345]

This was a kind of *déjà vu* feeling, a kind of remembering: maybe, somehow like Sjahrir's when coming to Holland in 1929. Schermerhorn also was pleased by a report he got that Sjahrir "appears uniquely flattered by the fact that such especially big 'uncles' [*Hooge 'ooms'*] were sent over."[346]

Sjahrir and Schermerhorn met on October 2, 1946, under mediation by a distinguished British diplomat, Lord Killearn. "Sjahrir is fond of laughing and drank quite a few glasses of wine," Schermerhorn wrote into his diary the same evening:

> At half past three Killearn left us. The talk switched immediately into Dutch.... In a personal exchange, I gave him, first, a look at political developments in Holland, and especially of the *PvdA* [Schermerhorn's Dutch Labor Party]. I reminded him that we both are in a way socialists and that, thus, if we, who are congenial in spirit [*geestverwanten*], can not solve the problem between Indonesia and Holland, probably nobody can, at least the way we think it should be solved.[347]

On October 7, the first plenary meeting of the new round of negotiations took place with Sjahrir and Schermerhorn at the head of the delegations. Introductory speeches dealt with the need for Indonesian-Dutch relations to "mature"; the speakers urged that one should resist "passion" and work in a spirit of "progress," "decency," and "humanity.[348]

"Sjahrir is a nice little fellow with an intelligent head," the secretary of Schermerhorn noted in his diary.[349] It was also Lord Killearn's impressions that Sjahrir liked Schermerhorn, the Dutchman's "professorial" manners and "turn of mind" notwithstanding.[350]

Schermerhorn appeared to enjoy his debates with Sjahrir increasingly. "It was remarkable," he noted after a meeting on October 16,

---

[344] Schermerhorn to Goedhart, July 22, 1946; Goedhart to Schermerhorn, August 9, 1946 in *Collection Schermerhorn* no.5. bundel Goedhart.

[345] Schermerhorn, *Het dagboek*, October 2, 1946 (1: 18–19).

[346] Dutch ambassador to London reporting to the minister of foreign affairs in The Hague, August 21, 1946 in *Officiële bescheiden*, 5: 245.

[347] Schermerhorn, *Het dagboek*, October 2, 1946 (1: 19–20.)

[348] Records of the 1st meeting in *Officiële bescheiden* 5: 502–12. The meeting was held in the former Maeda's house, where the Independence Proclamation of August 17, 1945. had been decided upon. As far as I know the possible symbolism of this was never mentioned.

[349] P. Sanders, "Dagboek alleen voor Ida, 1946–1947," typescript in *Collection Sanders* no. 1, October 2, 1946 (1: 19–20.)

[350] Killearn to Foreign Office, October 24, 1946 (marked "top secret," and "not to the Dutch") in *Officiële bescheiden*, 5: 626–27.

how, in this talk, Sumatra came on the table. Sjahrir believes that the republic, in overcoming all the difficulties that lay ahead, would proceed more easily in Sumatra than in Java. He remarked on a Sumatran being far soberer [*veel nuchteerder*], than a Javanese. This means that [the Sumatran] is better equipped for rational deliberation and less vulnerable to anguish [*angst*] and suspicion. He is capable of constructive thinking. Sjahrir also summed this up in quite a remarkable way: Sumatra would never bring forward a Soetomo and certainly not a Soekarno. I asked him, naturally, if he was not overrating a bit his native land, but he stated with emphasis that this was the truth.[351]

It might be continuuous remembering as well as a feeling of being marginal which helped both men to get closer to each other. There had been a constant and occasionally violent campaign in Holland against "soft-boiled" Schermerhorn, and Schermerhorn met opposition even inside his own "Commission General." Equally, dissent against "pro-Dutch" Sjahrir, and also within his own delegation, was strong and increasing.[352]

Schermerhorn might at times be snubbed by other Dutchmen even in the conference room. When, on the other side, dissenting Indonesians appeared, the negotiations might at any moment turn into a farce. General Soedirman, namely, representing the Indonesian Republic's military, might choose to talk in "deliberately bad Dutch" at the conference table, or alternately, "say nothing but '*baik*' or '*tidak baik*'," "well" or "no good," in Indonesian.[353]

Schermerhorn noted about an early meeting with Sjahrir:

> It was very important what Sjahrir told me—if he does not succeed in bringing forth these agreements, it would mean he would have to quit. I answered shortly that vis-à-vis Holland [I was] in the same position.[354]

The presence of Sukarno loomed incessantly over Sjahrir and over the negotiations. Sjahrir was given general permission to reopen the negotiation in September. He was prepared to start the conferences already on September 27, 1946, and he waited in Jakarta for the final word from the president. But the final word did not come. Schermerhorn was waiting. Lord Killearn, also waiting, cabled angrily to London:

> It is after all well over the odds, that an ex-Prime Minister of Holland and a representative of His Majesty's Government are kept harping around because Mohammed sticks to his mountain fastness.[355]

---

[351] Schermerhorn, *Het dagboek*, October 16, 1946 (1: 51–52).

[352] As Sjahrir put it, the delegation was composed of "*socialisten*" (himself, Amir, Soedarsono), Masjumi (Roem), and the "Indonesian National Party" (Soesanto). See ibid., October 20, 1946 (1: 20–21, 25).

[353] Spoor in records of the session of the council of military advisers to the government, Hague, January 21, 1947 on an October session in Batavia, in *Officiële bescheiden*, 7: 119; see also on "soldaten" in Sanders, "Dagboek alleen voor Ida," October 11, 1946 (1: 19).

[354] Schermerhorn, *Het dagboek*, October 7, 1946 (1: 93)

[355] Killearn to Foreign Office, September 27, 1946, in Hong Lee Oey, *War and Diplomacy*, p. 96.

Throughout the negotiations, Sjahrir warned both Dutch and Indonesian delegations against what he defined as the

> danger that we underrate the strength of the psychological factors ... trying to change too fast the present antithetic situation into a synthesis[356]

Schermerhorn understood these remarks instantly, as referring to *binnenland*, "the interior": Yogyakarta, where Sukarno was residing, was "clearly the antithetic."[357]

At a meeting on October 30, according to Lord Killearn, Sjahrir "did refer to losing the psychological effect of getting the agreement through really quickly."[358] The inevitability that the delegations should meet Sukarno and Hatta gradually became one of the main themes at the conferences.[359] On November 5, 1946, Sjahrir visited Lord Killearn and, as Killearn reported to London on the same day,

> [Sjahrir] said, he and his colleagues were proceeding to Jogjakarta either tomorrow, Thursday, or the day after. But he had little hope of persuading Soekarno or Hatta. He referred to Schermerhorn's spontaneous suggestion that he and possibly one other member of the Commission General should go to see Soekarno.[360]

The next morning, on this "spontaneous suggestion," it was decided that both Sjahrir and Schermerhorn, and indeed their entire delegations, and also Lord Killearn, go. As Lord Killearn put it, they all "should visit the interior."[361]

On November 10, not exactly in the interior but well on the way to it, in Linggadjati, a mountain resort four hour's drive east of Jakarta, the foreigners and Sjahrir met Sukarno and Hatta. In Schermerhorn's words, even in Linggadjati, Sukarno "remained largely passive."[362] Yet, the perspective changed. Lord Killearn cabled to the Foreign Office, for instance, that Sukarno

> blandly assured me that all reports of divergence between Sjahrir and Soekarno were untrue. He and Sjahrir "were one."[363]

Traveling from Jakarta to Linggadjati, Sjahrir and the foreigners moved into a very different climate. "Sjahrir told me a remarkable story," Schermerhorn wrote in his diary three days after their arrival in Linggadjati:

---

[356] Minutes of the second Dutch-Indonesian meeting on October 24, 1946 in *Officiële bescheiden*, 5: 631.

[357] *Commissie Generaal* to Jonkman, October 24, 1946, in *Officiële bescheiden*, 5: 636–37; Schermerhorn, *Het dagboek*, October 26, 1946 (1: 64).

[358] Killearn to Foreign Office, October 30, 1946, in *Officiële bescheiden*, 6: 19; see also the minutes of the 4th Dutch-Indonesian meeting, November 4, 1946, ibid., 6: 119.

[359] Killearn to Foreign Office, November 4, 1946, in ibid., 6: 120. Also see minutes of the 23rd session of the Commissie Generaal, November 5, 1946, ibid., 6: 121.

[360] Killearn to Foreign Office, November 4, 1946, in ibid., 6: 143.

[361] Ibid.

[362] Schermerhorn, *Het dagboek*, November 7, 1946 (1: 92).

[363] Killearn to Foreign Office, November 10, 1946, in Hong Lee Oey, *War and Diplomacy*, pp.106–7.

There is great excitement in this place, about the fact that the talks have moved here. According to a legend [Schermerhorn's editor noted that this was the "*Djojobojo* legend"], a miraculous gathering would once take place at the foot of Tjerimai, a volcano we look at from our windows. [Sjahrir said that he] got a large number of telegrams and telephone calls, which call attention to that. . . .[364]

On November 13, Sukarno invited the Dutch delegation to dinner. Sjahrir did not attend, "however I made sure to ask him to," Schermerhorn recalled.[365] Sjahrir excused himself, telling Schermerhorn that he was "*kaput*" and had a "racking headache."[366] "He did not suspect," Schermerhorn's secretary wrote later about Sjahrir, "what a curious meeting this would be."[367]

According to a cable Lord Killearn sent to London that day,

Sjahrir did not repeat did not accompany [Schermerhorn] saying he was tired and arranged that Sjarifoeddin and Gani should go with them.[368]

(This is a curious detail—in light of the growing tension between Sjahrir and Amir Sjarifoeddin, and also in light of Sjahrir's remark, quoted above, on Gani, of the Indonesian National Party, being forced onto Sjahrir and into Sjahrir's third cabinet by Sukarno. While Lord Killearn was not quite sure "whether Sjarifoeddin and Gani were actually present or in the next room,"[369] Schermerhorn was positive that the two men sat between Sukarno and Hatta; in fact, he called what happened at the dinner, "a communique with Soekarno, Hatta, Gani, and Sjarifoeddin."[370])

A general, vague, hotly disputed and repeatedly rejected framework for a possible Dutch-Indonesian agreement had been around since late 1945: a sort of federation; the Republic possibly limited to Java and Sumatra; the rest of the former Dutch East Indies made up of independent Indonesian states loosely related to Holland. As the dinner on November 13 progressed, after some small talk, and after some "small points" were gone over, Sukarno, suddenly, gave a little speech in such a "positive way" that the painful, frustrating negotiations Sjahrir had labored through hopelessly for months, were brought to a preliminary agreement almost as dessert was brought to table. The draft of what became known as the *Linggadjati Agreement* had been born![371]

Sjahrir in the meantime, ate some snacks with Wright, an assistant of Killearn, and with Sanders, Schermerhorn's secretary. In the words of Sanders' diary, throughout the evening,

---

[364] Schermerhorn, *Het dagboek*, November 13, 1946 (1: 113).

[365] Ibid.

[366] Ibid., p. 115.

[367] Sanders, "Dagboek alleen voor Ida," November 21/24, 1946 (1: 38).

[368] Killearn to Foreign Office, November 12, 1946, in *Archief Alg Secr, lste zending*, no. 3–29; see also Sanders, "Dagboek alleen voor Ida" (1: 38).

[369] Killearn to Foreign Office, November 13, 1946, in Hong Lee Oey, *War and Diplomacy*, pp. 106–107.

[370] Schermerhorn, *Het dagboek*, November 13, 1946 (1: 116–17).

[371] Sanders, "Dagboek alleen voor Ida" (1: 38) Killearn to Foreign Office, November 13, 1946, on briefing by Wright.

> Sjahrir was in the bleakest of moods, talking about how we were further away from an agreement than ever ... and that the Republic, as the things looked now, has achieved nothing. . . .[372]

Killearn, who also did not attend the dinner with Sukarno, joined Wright, Sanders, and Sjahrir, just when Sjahrir was telling the others that, now, the only thing he wanted was "to throw the towel in."[373] Wrote Killearn:

> At this moment, the Commission General arrived and handed across the table to Sjahrir the communique which had already been issued without consulting him, and told us the rest of what had passed. They suggested holding a plenary meeting tonight so that they could [be] tomorrow on their way to Holland.
> Sjahrir was completely taken aback but agreed to a plenary meeting.[374]

In Sanders' version, "Sjahrir looked barren, but said nothing."[375] In the version by Schermerhorn, "it struck him immobile, and he made a face as if he actually did not understand much."[376]

At the plenary session which followed immediately, in Killearn's recollection, "Sjahrir said little," "looked blacker and blacker,"[377] and when he stood up to give the speech that was expected of him on such a happy occasion, he said, he was in "rather a queer position," but, of course, he was

> willing to accept Professor Schermerhorn's statement and to hope that the optimism which the Dutch delegation now have, after the talk with Mr. Soekarno, has strong foundation.[378]

Both delegations returned to Jakarta, and Sukarno with Hatta went back to the interior. Two days later, on November 15, in Sjahrir's house in Jakarta, the initialling of the Linggadjati agreement was officially performed.

Sjahrir did the last checking of the Dutch text, while van Mook went through the text in Indonesian.[379] According to Sanders, Schermerhorn's secretary, who was also present,

> Sjahrir's house was full of truly good Indonesian paintings. They were worth finding a quiet time to look at. There were quite a number of Abdullah's, who is now increasingly in demand in Holland. . . . A portrait of Soekarno's

---

[372] Sanders, "Dagboek alleen voor Ida."
[373] Killearn to Foreign Office, November 13, 1946.
[374] Ibid.
[375] Sanders, "Dagboek alleen voor Ida."
[376] Schermerhorn, *Het dagboek,* November 13, 1946 (1: 117).
[377] Killearn to Foreign Office, November 13, 1946.
[378] Sjahrir's speech, November 12, 1946, in *Officiële bescheiden,* 6: 288n.
[379] Ibid., 6: 261.

wife hung in the hall and it can also be seen on the pictures taken during the initialling.[380]

Sjahrir said, in his short speech at the ceremony, that the Linggadjati agreement was not a "magic key."[381]

It was Sukarno—like the portrait of his wife above the scene—who appeared as the real power making the agreement possible. It was Sjahrir who was the actual personage identified with the draft, and who was to be made responsible if things went wrong. Sukarno might say later—and he did:

> Linggadjati was a shower of ice water on the fire of revolution. Sjahrir, then Prime Minister, was its architect, not I.[382]

5. THE END OF SJAHRIR'S CABINET

It still took many moments of a "subdued mood" or "near fatalism," threats to resign, fits of hopelessness, travels to the centers either in Yogyakarta or in The Hague, "last chances," and even an ultimatum, before the intialled Linggadjati agreement finally was signed.

On March 24, 1947, Sjahrir arrived in Jakarta by the Special Train from Yogyakarta, where he had received final permission from Sukarno and Hatta to sign. The next day, on March 25, Sjahrir, Schermerhorn, and van Mook signed the Linggadjati agreement under the larger-than-life portrait of the Dutch Queen.

That same evening, van Mook held a reception in the Governor-General's palace in Jakarta. As described by Sanders, Schermerhorn's secretary:

> No less than seven hundred men and women gathered at the Palace. The Indonesian toilettes of the women offered a lively sight. A general feeling of relief prevailed. Many old acquaintances and friends [from the Dutch and Indonesian side] saw each other again.... In town, fifteen thousand food-parcels were distributed among the population. Indonesian mayor Soewirjo and our deputy mayor Bogaerdt, as was the old custom, scattered new coins among the crowds. At 8 p.m., there was a great fireworks display and at 9 p.m., a cold buffet.[383]

Selamatan, ritual communal meals traditional in Java, were held in some villages.[384] Djohan Djohor, the well-known Minangkabau shop in Jakarta, renamed one of its branches *Toko Linggadjati*, "Linggadjati Store."

Amidst the celebrations, Sjahrir was seen attending a concert by the *Röntgen Quartet* from Holland. Poppy Saleh, his secretary and Soedjatmoko's sister, sat on his right, the Sultan of Pontianak, representative of the future state of Kalimantan

---

[380] Sanders, "Dagboek alleen voor Ida," p. 32.

[381] *Het Dagblad*, November 20, 1946.

[382] Sukarno, *An Autobiography*, p. 238.

[383] Sanders, "Dagboek alleen voor Ida," March 27, 1947 (1: 93).

[384] Charles Wolf Jr., *The Indonesian Story: The Birth, Growth and Structure of the Indonesian Republic* (New York: Day, 1948), p. 105.

The Linggadjati Signing Ceremony

(Borneo), sat on his left. According to Schermerhorn, who was also there, Sjahrir appeared to enjoy the music.[385]

In the few days following the celebrations, Sjahrir was about to leave Indonesia on a mission abroad. It was to be his first trip out of country since he went to Holland in 1929. The destination was India.

The trip had been a long time in the making. India, in Sjahrir's vision, was as much an extension of Britain as Britain was an extension of Holland. India had also been an actual presence in the Indonesian Revolution from its beginning.

British troops were largely composed of soldiers from British India. India, also, was the emerging Asian entity in the power vacuum left after the defeat of Japan. Already in April 1946, Sjahrir made a sensational offer to ship 500,000 tons of Javanese rice to India to help relieve the Indian famine. Sjahrir's trusted friend, Dr. Soedarsono, was put in charge of the project, and the bulk of the rice was to go through the town and port of Cirebon where the Pendidikan traditionally was strong.[386]

---

[385] Schermerhorn, *Het dagboek*, March 29, 1947 (1: 400).

[386] A. Sofyan, "Perjuangan '45 untuk pembangunan bangsa: Perjalanan penulis selama bertugas di Sumatra sebagain wakil pemerintahan (th. '45, th '46, th '48)," (September 12, 1975) *Perpustakaan '45, Archives "Gedung Pemuda,"* no. 86, pp. 18–19. Sofyan was a participant at the

The Dutch were naturally enraged, especially by Sjahrir's acting in foreign affairs without their previous agreement.[387] But even some among the Indonesian Republic's officials were uncertain and not a few of them "shocked."[388] There was not enough food even for the Javanese, these Indonesians argued; some even thought Sjahrir's deal "equivalent to shooting a freedom fighter."[389] An anonymous writer, usually sympathetic to Sjahrir, considered the offer of rice to India, "from the point of view of the interior, a blunder."[390]

The British reacted "ambiguously"; both Lord Killearn and Lord Mountbatten argued that this was a complex situation involving Sjahrir and Nehru, leaders of the movements for independence.[391] But the Dutch knew better. Once again they felt deserted by their allies:

> About Sjahrir's rice offer, and how it is to be handled, the British do talk to us abruptly, and one feels, what is behind this—even one rice shipment to India would be most welcome, even though the British know damned well that this is, first, economically irresponsible, and, second, very difficult practically to realize.[392]

Clearly, this was another effort by Sjahrir to break the bad Dutch-ness, and to reach towards the broader world. As the Indonesians around Sjahrir saw it, the British were "evidently happy" about the rice deal, and eager to get Indian merchandise to Java in exchange.[393] According to some of the Indonesians, even, the Linggadjati agreement

> was an achievement with maximum pressure from the British on the Dutch, due to Sjahrir's move to offer surplus rice to India via the British navy through the blockade by the Dutch.[394]

The formal purpose of Sjahrir's trip to India in March 1947 was Indonesian participation at the Asian Relations Conference convened, on Jawaharlal Nehru's initiative, in New Delhi.[395] For the Dutch this was another form of the "rice business."

The Dutch government tried hard to prevent this appearing as Sjahrir breaking again out of their embrace. Van Mook even offered him a special KLM plane for the trip.[396] The Dutch cabinet in The Hague declared itself to be "ready to invite Mr.

---

negotiations; see also Mohamad Roem, *Bunga Rampai Dari Sedjarah*, vol. 3 (Jakarta: Bulan-Bintang, 1983), p. 282.

[387] See, e.g., Cabinet of van Mook to Logemann April 15, 1946, *Officiële bescheiden*, 4: 136.

[388] Roem, *Bunga Rampai* 3: 282.

[389] Quoted in Cribb, "Jakarta in the Indonesian Revolution," p. 157.

[390] X ambtenaar, "Indonesische Politiek," p. 24.

[391] Proceedings of 45th meeting at Supreme Allied Command, May 25, 1946 in *Officiële bescheiden*, 4: 338–39.

[392] Van Bijlandt to van Roijen, May 27, 1946 in ibid., 4: 363.

[393] Roem, *Bunga Rampai*, 3: 282.

[394] Abdulgani, *Nationalism*, p. 31.

[395] For the plans for the conference and reaction in Jakarta see *Inzicht*, June 1, 1946, p. 1.

[396] Commissie Generaal to Jonkman March 15, 1947 in *Officiële bescheiden* 7: 778; van Mook to Sjahrir, March 28, 1947 ibid., 8: 55.

Sjahrir, as an extension of his India trip, to visit our country."[397] The Dutch consul in Singapore was instructed:

> in case Sjahrir passes through, welcome him at the airport, without going to a grand scale entertainment offer him your house to stay overnight, or at least invite him for a meal to smooth his way and to avoid his being monopolized by local Indonesians and Englishmen.[398]

There was a disturbing possibility for the Dutch that Sjahrir might travel to India "on a British plane."[399]

On March 31, according to Schermerhorn's secretary who went with him to the airport, Sjahrir left for India "in the best of moods."[400] He traveled on the private plane of a Bengali businessman and a friend of Nehru, Biju Patnaik, whom he befriended during the rice negotiations.[401] Ali Boediardjo, one of the young men who became Sjahrir's loyal followers during the Japanese occupation, and Poppy Saleh, went with Sjahrir as his secretaries. Soedjatmoko was also on the plane, going to report on the conference for the Sjahrir group's weekly, *Siasat*.[402]

In New Delhi, Nehru himself welcomed Sjahrir at the airport.[403] According to various reports, in the following days, Sjahrir became "an extraordinarily popular figure in New Delhi," an *"enfant chéri"* of the Asian conference,[404] a "little bombshell of the Pacific," and even an "atom bomb of Asia."[405] Nehru offered Sjahrir his own house to stay in, and Sjahrir was also received by Lord Mountbatten.

Nehru's Asian conference agreed to establish a permanent "Asian Relations Organization," and hold a "Second Asian Relations Conference" in 1949 in China. The "Southeast Asian Section" was to prepare its special convention in April 1948; India, Indonesia, Burma, Siam (Thailand), Malaya, and possibly the Philippines were to be the participants.[406]

Hadji Agoes Salim, Sjahrir's cousin and Djohan Sjahroezah's father-in-law, was the official chairman of the Indonesian delegation. After the conference ended, Salim did not return to Indonesia but traveled to the Middle East, where in Cairo he started a Republican office. By early June 1947, Egypt, Syria, and Iran, on the initiative of the

---

[397] Minutes of the Dutch cabinet council, March 15, 1947, ibid., 7: 781.

[398] Foreign minister to consul in Singapore. March 20, 1947 in "Inlichtingen Sjahrir" in *Archief Buiten. Zaken* V.R.III-910.

[399] H. N. Boon, "Dagelyksche notities vanaf 11 December 1946 tot einde 1947,"*Collection of Boon* no. 99. see also Boon to the Dutch minister of foreign affairs, March 13, 1947 in *Officiële bescheiden*, 7: 768.

[400] Sanders, "Dagboek alleen voor Ida," March 31, 1947, p. 96.

[401] See B. Patnaik, "Mengenang Dr. Mohammad Hatta," in *Bung Hatta*, ed. Swasono, pp. 358–61.

[402] Interview with Siti Wahjunah Sjahrir, Jakarta, January 11, 1988.

[403] Hanifah, *Tales of a Revolution*, p. 235.

[404] Schermerhorn, *Het dagboek*, April 13, 1947 (1: 436), interview with Siti Wahjunah Sjahrir, Jakarta, January 11, 1988; minutes of the meeting of the council of ministers, Hague, May 29, 1947, *Officiële bescheiden*, 9: 83.

[405] Soeripno, "Appel van Asiatische volken," *Opbouw-Pembinaan*, June 7, 1947, p. 6; C. H. Ch. de Wilde in ibid., June 21, 1947, p. 7.

[406] "Asian Relations Conference Proceedings" in NEFIS report no. 545 (January 26, 1948); *Archief Alg Secr, lste zending*, no. V-17; Anwar, *Kisah-kisah Jakarta menjelang Clash ke-1*, p. 178.

office, had recognized the Indonesian Republic *de facto* and, at the same time, a pact of friendship and a commercial treaty were signed between Egypt and the Republic. Early in July 1947, Salim's mission signed similar treaties with Syria and a high-level visit by an Iraq delegation to Yogyakarta was at the same time also agreed upon.[407]

Sjahrir himself, on his way back from New Delhi, stopped in Rangoon, where he talked with the top Burmese national leaders including Aung San. Via Bangkok, Sjahrir went back to Singapore,[408] and there he probably met leaders of the United Malay Nationalist Organization.

All this appeared to be an immense success. A triumphant journey. Breaking a blockade indeed. Watching Sjahrir, however, the impression was different.

Sjahrir actually arrived too late in New Delhi to work seriously at the conference. As one source has it, Sjahrir came just in time to address the closing session.[409] Many in the Indonesian delegation in New Delhi, moreover, were not people of Sjahrir's choice. Hadji Agoes Salim was almost an exception, having a distinguished position in New Delhi and being, perhaps, on Sjahrir's side. Abu Hanifah, a senior and very active member of the delegation, was a leader of the Masjumi and not too friendly to Sjahrir. Ali Sastroamidjojo, of the Indonesian National Party, another influential member of the delegation, as we recall, was a figure increasingly close to Amir Sjarifoeddin, and even more so to Sukarno. There were some figures on the delegation that might have suggested closeness to Sjahrir; but the truly "Sjahririan" names—Hamdani, Zainal Zain, or Soebandrio—belonged to the wives of Sjahrir's followers and not to the cadres themselves.[410]

Soeripno appeared, arriving from London—the former Leiden student, accomplished dancer, translator of Sjahrir's "Our Struggle" into English and associate of John Coast and Dorothy Woodman. But Soeripno was also increasingly becoming a part of the Abdoelmadjid and Setiadjit circle, and thus, again, close to Amir Sjarifoeddin rather than to Sjahrir.[411] When the "Asian Relations Organization" was established as a follow-up to the New Delhi conference, its "Provisional General Council" was led by Nehru; Abu Hanifah became the permanent Indonesian representative, and Soeripno became the Indonesian representation's secretary.[412]

In a long private talk after his return from abroad, Sjahrir told Schermerhorn that he "*strictly speaking* had a very high opinion of Nehru."[413] Sjahrir also said that, in

---

[407] Dutch Embassy in Cairo to The Hague, May 29, 1947 in *Officiële bescheiden*, 9: 88. C. Van Dijk, "The Muslim Contribution to the Indonesian Revolution," in *The Indonesian Revolution: Papers of the Conference held in Utrecht, 17–20 June 1986*, ed. J. van Goor (Utrecht: Utrechtse Historische Cahiers, 1986), p. 159. Wolf, *The Indonesian Story*, p. 113. Ide Gde Agung Anak Agung, '*Renville*' als kernpunt in de Nederlands-Indonesische onderhandelingen (Alphen: Sijthoff, 1980), p. 51.

[408] Hanifah, *Tales of a Revolution*, pp. 243-44; Schermerhorn, *Het dagboek*, April 13, 1947 (1: 438ff); Coast, *Recruit to Revolution*, pp. 41-42.

[409] Hanifah, *Tales of a Revolution*, p. 235.

[410] Suzanna Hamdani, Yetti Zainal Zain, Tien Subandrio. Hazil Tanzil, Djohan Sjahroezah's brother, was with Sjahrir in New Delhi, but he was never an influential political figure. Ali Sastroamijoyo, *Milestones on my Journey*, p. 134, described the delegation as dominated by the "Socialist Party."

[411] Hazil Tanzil, ed., *Seratus Tahun Haji Agus Salim*, p. 159; Anwar, *Kisah-kisah Jakarta menjelang Clash ke-1*, p. 177; interview with Go Gien Tjwan, Amsterdam, October 5, 1986.

[412] Anwar, *Kisah-kisah Jakarta menjelang Clash ke-1*, p. 178.

[413] Schermerhorn, *Het dagboek*, April 13, 1947 (1: 436). Emphasis mine.

spite of the fact that he stayed in Nehru's house, "he had relatively little opportunity to talk to Nehru in greater depth. Only on the last day, one hour."[414] Indian politicians in general, Sjahrir told Schermerhorn,

> follow very much in the steps of the British-India princes, and they live in palaces. Nehru himself might be to all appearances simple, but his surroundings are anything but that.... Three servants jumped up as [Sjahrir] entered Nehru's house, the first to untie his shoelace, the second to take Sjahrir's jacket off, the third one, apparently, to set his chair right.[415]

Rather than a spirit of modern and socialist leadership, Sjahrir appeared to find in Nehru's India a reflection of what he so disliked as qualities of the *ningrat*, the Eastern aristocratic spirit. Sjahrir met Gandhi during the conference and told Schermerhorn about him:

> Gandhi plays a very special role; by all the present events he is enormously strengthened in his belief in the power of defenselessness [*weerloosheid*]. Gandhi also stressed [to Sjahrir] with greatest conviction his opinion that Europe as well as America would go down in ruins, and that out of British India salvation of the world would have to come.[416]

Schermerhorn added: "Sjahrir, naturally, shrugged his shoulders at this."[417]

Sjahrir found mass politics in India, the Gandhi appeal, and the Nehru appeal derived from it, based on "messianic beliefs," and on charms:

> When there were twenty thousand people slain, in Bihar, Gandhi let himself be invited to make an end to the upheaval, in the firm belief of his invulnerability à la Gandhi.[418]

It was not even two years after the Japanese defeat in Asia, and,

> through Gandhi, ideas of nationalism live in India side by side with pan-asiatic sentiments [and] emulations of Asia for Asians.[419]

On his way back from India, Sjahrir found Burma "much too simple," "dominated by Buddhism," her nationalist leaders "neglecting practical matters," and the country as a whole "*miserabel.*"[420] Siam, to Sjahrir, was a Buddhist country—this Sjahrir stressed again—and

---

[414] Ibid.
[415] Ibid.
[416] Ibid., p. 437.
[417] Ibid.
[418] Ibid.
[419] Ibid.
[420] Ibid. Schermerhorn thought this special comment on Burma and Buddhism a "proof," as he put it, of Sjahrir's "religious" bias, and "intellectual haughtiness."

an especially good country to visit for many of [Sjahrir's] associates, as a learning exercise—a decaying and through and through corrupt country. His men could see there to what level a country might descend in a relatively short time.[421]

Sjahrir also told Schermerhorn that he was "stormed by British-India Moslems of various kinds."[422] As Sjahrir saw this,

The problems of the Moslem League [in India] are the same as those of the Masjumi [in Indonesia], namely its Islam does not allow any modernist broadening [of the Islamic creed], and, thus, a great part of the intellectuals are estranged from such an Islamic movement.

Jinnah, the Indian Moslem League leader, to Sjahrir, was "a Macchiavellian."[423]

In contrast, Singapore seemed a hopeful place. Leaving Indonesia for India, Sjahrir took with him Oetojo, a young associate from the "Radio Camp" during the Japanese occupation. Oetojo got off the plane in Singapore, with a task from Sjahrir to establish an "Information Bureau" for the Republic in the British colony.[424] John Coast arrived from London at the same time, and the two young men set out immediately to work together.[425]

Singapore seemed the best place to break through the Dutch encroachment. On his way back from India, Sjahrir met in Singapore with the British mediator of the Linggadjati agreement, Lord Killearn. According to an alarming report by Dutch intelligence in Singapore,

During [Sjahrir's] stay in Singapore, in April, 1947, talks were held between Soetan Sjahrir and Lord Killearn with regard to working out a blueprint of an economic treaty between London and Jogjakarta, by which the republican government would give concessions [to Britain] completely circumventing [*uitschakeling*] the interests of Holland.[426]

British power, however, was rapidly declining. Decimated by war, Britain was looking for the first opportunity to disengage herself from all non-essential obligations; and Indonesia was certainly one of these. Five months before Sjahrir met with Mountbatten in New Delhi and with Killearn in Singapore, the British government,

---

[421] Ibid., p. 438.

[422] Ibid., p. 436.

[423] Ibid., p. 437. Sjahrir appeared very cool to the successes of Indonesian diplomatic missions starting from New Delhi to the other Islamic countries in the Middle East. There is, on the record, a letter by Hadji Agoes Salim, the chief inspirer of the mission, in which he complained from Cairo, on June 17, that Sjahrir had not yet answered his last letter of three weeks previously. Letter by Hadji Agoes Salim to his wife in Yogyakarta, June 17. 1947 in Hazil Tanzil, ed., *Seratus Tahun Haji Agus Salim*, pp. 469–70.

[424] Dossier "Oetojo" in *Archief Proc Gen*, no. 3–331

[425] Ibid. Dossier "Republic's foreign relations" in *Archief Alg Secr, Iste zending*, no. III 29–22; Coast, *Recruit to Revolution*, pp. 40–42.

[426] Headquarter NEFIS Singapore to Beel, December 31, 1948 in *Archief Proc Gen*, no. 231.

in December 1946, ordered its troops to leave Java.[427] The Allied Southeast Asia Command, led by Mountbatten, was dissolved. Killearn's mission ended. A few British remained in the area trying, as a Dutch observer put it, "to play little Killearns [*Killearntjes*]."[428]

Dashing into the broader world, beyond the bad Dutch-ness, moved Sjahrir into an empty space. He was disappointed in Nehru—a man supposedly of a progressive British imperial experiment, a politician, British-trained and supposedly modern and socialist. Looking for an affinity, Sjahrir found in Nehru—as well as in Gandhi, in the Indian Moslems, and in the Burmese and Siamese nationalists—the "Eastern" and "Hindu" qualities which he so disdained at home. In spite of the Dutch, Sjahrir wandered far and met sympathetic, understanding, and liberal British in New Delhi and in Singapore. But this appeared to have been accomplished months if not a whole era too late.

Meeting with his wife Maria in New Delhi, after fifteen years of forced separation, might be a part of the same experience. According to a story told by Abu Hanifah, who arrived in New Delhi before Sjahrir,

> Soetan Sjahrir . . . arrived in New Delhi a few days before the closing session. . . . He was met at the airport by our Delegation, Pandit Nehru, his daughter Indira Gandhi and also Sjahrir's Dutch wife Mies du Chateau [*sic*], who had come from Holland intending to surprise him. . . . We were a little embarrassed, not knowing how Sjahrir would react to this big surprise. When the plane arrived and the door of the plane opened, Sjahrir came out smiling as usual. Pandit Nehru and I had Mrs. Sjahrir between us and we let her go alone to meet her husband. The meeting was not as warm as expected. Sjahrir embraced her fleetingly and gave her a peck on both cheeks. The young people who expected something else were disappointed. A member of my Delegation whispered to me that a charming young Indonesian lady was now his favorite. She was with him on the plane. We all felt the situation was a little awkward. Without too many formalities Sjahrir was put into Nehru's car and back we went to the city.[429]

According to Maria Duchâteau herself, she found her husband "changed," but attributed this to his "becoming a statesman." Sjahrir told her, so Maria remembered, to wait until the situation cleared a little before she joined him in Java, to which she responded that she had waited too long already. Maria recalled her stay in New Delhi as an experience "unpleasant," "very difficult," and "full of tensions," but not that of an open clash—not a foregone conclusion.[430]

Poppy Saleh, apparently the "charming young Indonesian lady" on the plane, said later that things went quite well between her and Maria; she also remembered

---

[427] Sjahrir's speech at the airport to departing British units was clearly emotional: "You were pinched between loyalty to an ally in war and the recognition of the legitimate aspiration of a people . . . we learned to appreciate and to admire you." Quoted in *Economist*, December 7, 1946, p. 902; a copy also in *Collection Meyer Ranneft* no. 496.

[428] Sanders, "Dagboek alleen voor Ida," February 27, 1947 (1: 66).

[429] Hanifah, *Tales of a Revolution*, p. 235; see also press clippings in Boon to The Hague, April 19, 1947 especially Bouwer, "Mevrouw Sjahrir and Charles Tambu," in *Archief Alg Secr, lste zending*, no. V-17; also Leon Salim, ed., *Bung Sjahrir*, p. 14.

[430] Interview with Maria Duchâteau Sjahrir, Lorgues, February 13, 1988.

Maria complaining to her about being the wife of a rebel. Poppy felt that relations between Sjahrir and Maria were cool, but she too could hear no harsh sound.[431]

There is no account by Sjahrir on record about the meeting, except perhaps an allusion, when Sjahrir told Schermerhorn, after he came back from the trip, how he

> found it typical ... that all the Dutch officials, he had met on the way, had been married to non-Dutch women.[432]

Sjahrir still lived surrounded by modern Indonesian paintings "betraying very good taste."[433] He was still seen as often with writers and painters as with politicians. He still played tennis, but, however he tried, he gained weight anyway.[434]

The guest book for the wedding of Sudarpo Sastrosatomo in Jakarta in March 1947, shows that Sjahrir was present with his Bandanese children and with Aki Djoehana, his nephew, the poet. Also attending were friends of Sudarpo and his new wife from among Sjahrir's young followers during the occupation; a certain Omar Dhani; friends from the Dutch intellectual and journalist community; also Major Santoso, one of the mentors of the same young people during the war, a veteran of the prewar Dutch colonial army, and now again, as a major in the Dutch army, on the opposite side.[435]

A month after Linggadjati was signed, the pro-Sjahrir *Het Inzicht* Jakarta magazine declared that it was going out of existence. Another Jakarta journal, the paper of the Dutch information service, *Het Uitzicht*, "The Outlook," published a similar statement and at the same time *Het Uitzicht* also ceased to exist. This, as both papers stated explicitly, was done by mutual agreement, and in order to open the way for a new Dutch-Indonesian "independent weekly" which might more effectively serve as a bridge.

The new journal appeared on June 7, 1947, under the Dutch-Indonesian title *Opbouw-Pembinaan*, "Construction." The *Opbouw-Pembinaan* editorial board was led by a "progressive" Dutch Professor R. F. Beerling, by Aki Djoehana, and by Ida Nasoetion. On the front page of the first issue there was a greeting to the new magazine from Sjahrir and Schermerhorn.[436]

Articles, essays, and poetry appeared in the following weeks in *Opbouw-Pembinaan* by Professor Resink (we mentioned him as a man vaguely connected with Sjahrir's network during the war), Professor Wertheim, Marcel Koch, Tien Soebandrio, and Soetan Takdir Alisjahbana among others; there were illustrations by Baharoeddin. The first issue's editorial, Marcel Koch's and Eddy du Perron's Dutch Indies

---

[431] Interview with Siti Wahjunah Sjahrir, Jakarta, November 15, 1987.

[432] Schermerhorn, *Het dagboek*, April 13, 1947 (1: 439).

[433] Boon, "Dagelyksche notities," January 21, 1947, p. 17.

[434] Sanders, "Dagboek alleen voor Ida," February 19, 1947 (1: 66). On enlightening pictures of Sjahrir playing tennis see *Uitzicht*, November 27, 1946; the pictures were published on the same page as the announcement and the draft text of the Linggadjati agreement.

[435] I am grateful to Mrs. Minarsih Wiranatakoesoema Sudarpo for letting me see the guest book and other family documents.

[436] *Opbouw-Pembinaan*, June 7, 1947; interview with M. A. Djoehana, Prague, August 16, 1983.

prewar "progressive" journal, *Kritiek en Opbouw*, was mentioned as a major inspiration for the new magazine.[437]

Throughout the same months, as the British presence weakened, the Dutch right wing became visibly bolder. The Dutch Catholic journal *Linie*, "Line," now wrote that Sjahrir had not been sent to Boven Digul in 1935 "without some kind of trial," that there naturally were some reasons for him being punished and that, as *Linie* put it, "he himself knows it very well."[438]

The Dutch military were also increasingly outspoken in their opposition, namely to continuing reliance on Sjahrir. Vice-Admiral A. S. Pinke, second only to the top-ranking Dutch naval officer in the East, believed that Lt. Governor-General van Mook had a dangerously strong pro-Sjahrir bias.[439] General S.H.Spoor, the top ranking Dutch army officer in the Indies, argued that Sjahrir was no longer a man to rely upon because he was powerless:

> in Soekarno-Sjahrir relations, Sjahrir retreats continually, and with growing speed to the background. Almost no basis whatsoever remains on which he can base his power.[440]

The chief of the Dutch navy, Admiral Helfrich, wrote in March 1947 from The Hague to Vice-Admiral Pinke:

> When [General] Spoor was here, we had numerous talks with the people in the government and he assured me positively that "it is now in the open," and that a military action would take place. That did not happen.... We made an "agreement" [Linggadjati agreement], which is no agreement.... I ask myself in earnest, how much longer we still have to play this little game.[441]

As the months passed, the negotiations dragged on, the interior resisted compromises, and the British were leaving, the confidence of the "pro-Sjahrir" Dutchmen also perceptibly waned. One of the first, van der Plas, had already written to van Mook before the Linggadjati was initialed:

> The point is that Sjahrir, now, is merely a manager for Soekarno, and that talking to Sjahrir gives nothing which talking to Soekarno would not.[442]

A confidential memorandum prepared for van Mook, in mid-1947, still noted that Sjahrir was among the four men who made up the Republic's top leadership; Sukarno, Hatta, Sjahrir, and Setiadjit were the four. But, the memorandum already

---

[437] "Waar wij staan," *Opbouw-Pembinaan*, June 7, 1947, p. 2. See similarly Goedhart to Schermerhorn October 21, 1947 in *Collection Schermerhorn* no. 5. bundel Goedhart.

[438] *Linie*, November 15, 1946 in *Collection Meyer Ranneft* no. 167.

[439] E.g., A. S. Pinke, "Memoires van de Commandant zeemacht Nederlands-Indië," typescript in *Collection Pinke* no. 43, and Pinke to the council of military advisors to the government in The Hague, March 11, 1947 in *Officiële bescheiden*, 7: 741–43.

[440] Minutes of the council of ministers, Hague, August 5, 1946 in *Officiële bescheiden*, 5: 177.

[441] Helfrich to Pinke , March 30, 1947. *Collection Pinke* no. 19; also Pinke, "Memoires," p. 102.

[442] Memorandum by van der Plas, July 18, 1946 in *Collection van Mook* no. 147.

qualified this: Sukarno was by far the most powerful of the four, and to look to him would be "of the greatest value in the future."[443]

In May 1947, in another report written for van Mook by a highly respected and liberal Dutch expert, Yogyakarta appeared as "the center of the Republic," and the symbol of the "unity" of Republican forces. The essence of Yogyakarta's power rested on "a typical Java-Hindu syncretism." The powerful figures in this center of power, according to this report, were, first, President Sukarno, second, the Sultan of Yogyakarta, Hamengku Buwono ("a Javanese prince of high style," as the report noted), and, third, Ki Hadjar Dewantoro, the "old Javanese nationalist" and principal spokesman for Javanese cultural and Java-centrist nationalism since before the war.[444]

According to the same report, "Sumatrans" in Yogyakarta, were "practical," "less inward," and playing "a significant role" by working against the dominant and "total" "Eastern inefficiency." The report listed the prominent examples of the practical and significant "Sumatrans"—Hatta, Amir Sjarifoeddin, and Gani. The name of Sjahrir was missing.[445]

Even among the Dutchmen who in late 1945 strongly believed in Sjahrir, the conviction grew that

> Soekarno counts his followers in hundreds of thousands, among the younger generation especially. Sjahrir's influence is limited to a small superstratum of intellectuals.[446]

Even the liberal, progressive, and socialist Dutch were weakening in their belief at the same time in the long-standing principle of cooperation: conviction that Indonesians were "able to mature." In the words of one of them, in May 1947,

> Even in progressive circles, there are grave doubts, now, about the capabilities of the Indonesian leaders to put their house together.[447]

The Dutchmen who still remained on Sjahrir's side were becoming defensive. Professor de la Court, for instance, formerly of the law school in Batavia, and believing in the Linggadjati agreement as in a progressive act in the spirit of the prewar *Stuw*, felt in May 1947 that he had to argue that the agreement was not in fact a Communist plot.[448]

A cartoon appeared in *Opbouw-Pembinaan*, in early June 1947, depicting an extremely shaky-looking bridge, with "LINGGADJATI" painted in big letters across it. Sjahrir and van Mook are seen standing at opposite ends of the bridge. Rather than looking towards each other, their eyes are fixed behind their shoulders. There, on

---

[443] Nota from van Mook in *Collection Koets*, 249–32.

[444] Memorandum by Idenburg, "Indrukken omtrent Djokja" May 31, 1947 in *Officiële bescheiden*, 9: 110–35. On Ki Hadjar Dewantoro see especially Kenji Tsuchiya, *Democracy and Leadership: The Rise of the Taman Siswa Movement in Indonesia*. (Honolulu: University of Hawaii Press, 1987).

[445] "Indrukken omtrent Djokja."

[446] Minutes of the council of ministers, September 23, 1946 in ibid., 5: 382.

[447] Minutes of the council of ministers, May 28, 1947, in ibid., 9: 64.

[448] Koch, "H. J. van Mook," *De Nieuwe Stem* 12 (1958), p. 298.

Sjahrir's end of the bridge, a long-haired Indonesian *jago* youth gesticulates wildly with a *samurai* sword; a dinner-jacketed Dutchman shakes his fist from where van Mook's anchor is supposed to be.[449]

In mid-May 1947, Schermerhorn still vehemently argued that, "if Sjahrir's cabinet does not hold ... the Republic probably will go down in chaos."[450] Yet, even this believer in Sjahrir wavered visibly. By mid-May, Schermerhorn was already listening to some suggestions that "Soekarno, actually, is the most moderate among all Indonesians."[451] On May 14, 1947, Schermerhorn noted in his diary that some people from the Masjumi, the Islamic nationalist party, visited him from Yogyakarta with a report that "in their circles" there was "a fear that Sjahrir's cabinet was drifting towards the left," and perhaps to communism.[452] Hatta, perhaps through some emissaries from Yogyakarta, appeared now also to warn Schermerhorn that he "concentrated too one-sidedly on Sjahrir." According to Hatta's own recollections, he told Schermerhorn that Sjahrir was

> an extraordinarily competent man ... but lacked broader political support ... his followers were a thin layer of intellectuals, [and he] did not go on to broaden his base in spite of Hatta repeatedly urging him to do so.[453]

Dutch friends of Sjahrir, were getting uneasy about where the real power rested, and where they might therefore direct their sympathy. According to a socialist, Frans Goedhart of *Het Parool*, a friend of Sal Tas and de Kadt, reporting from Java,

> Hatta and Sjarifoeddin stand closest to, and behind the President. ... To my taste, Sjahrir is a well developed, very intelligent and artistic man, dependable and an integrated personality, but he must be reproved for being sometimes too philosophical, contemplative and not vigorous enough. Apart from that, he faces impossible problems.[454]

Old names still lingered, but it was questionable what real power, if any, they could exude. Some Indonesians from Sjahrir's inner circle of young people asked Goedhart to send books from Holland. The list of the books, Goedhart was asked for and sent, is instructive. Besides a few mysteries and "Practical Dentistry" (these directly arranging for the books were the Soebandrios, both of them doctors),

> Boeke ... Sal Tas, Huizinga ... de la Court, P. J. Schmidt, Jef Last, Wertheim, Koestler, du Perron ... Stokvis, de Kadt, Leon Blum, Jan. Romein, Sjahrazad. ... .[455]

---

[449] *Opbouw-Pembinaan*, June 7, 1947, p. 3.

[450] Schermerhorn in minutes of the Commissie Generaal meeting, May 15, 1947 in *Officiële bescheiden*, 8: 699.

[451] D. J. Baluseck of *Algemeen Handelsblad* in Schermerhorn, *Het dagboek*, May 17, 1947 (2: 545).

[452] Ibid., May 14, 1947 (2: 534).

[453] Hatta to Jaquet in the 1970s on his conversations with Schermerhorn in 1947, in Jaquet, *Aflossing van de Wacht*, pp. 223–24.

[454] Goedhart to Schermerhorn August 9, 1946 in *Collection Schermerhorn* no. 5. bundel Goedhart; compare also 't Hoen (Goedhart), *Terug uit Djokja*, pp. 12ff, 46.

[455] Letters in dossier "Boediardjo" in *Archief Alg Secr, lste zending*, no. XXI-6.

In Yogyakarta, the Indonesian nationalist forces either opposing the Linggadjati agreement outright or warning Sjahrir not to make one step further, got together in a coalition fittingly called *Benteng Republic*, "Fortress of the Republic."[456]

On May 27, 1947, a Dutch ultimatum was sent to the Indonesian government in Yogyakarta, demanding just that further step. The Republic was asked to accept Dutch authority in Indonesia through the interim period and until sovereignty was finally transferred. The Republic's answer dated June 8 was interpreted by the Dutch as "totally negative." The previous day, the journal-bridge in Jakarta, *Opbouw-Pembinaan*, published a large front-page photograph of Sjahrir and Schermerhorn. They were sitting at one table smiling broadly. The journal's caption under the photograph was: "Will they still smile after a little while?"[457]

On June 18, 1947, amidst growing tensions the British consul-general in Jakarta invited Sjahrir for what one Dutchman described as "a sort of fatherly talk."[458] Perhaps also on British prompting,[459] Sjahrir made a radio speech the next day declaring that

> everyone, who still respects himself, and is a civilized and cultured man, has the duty to stand up against a catastrophic war.[460]

On June 20, Sjahrir wrote a letter to Schermerhorn and to the Dutch delegation (an explanatory memorandum by Sjahrir followed, on June 23) in which he agreed to take the further step the Dutch were asking for: He agreed to recognize, during the interim period, the special position of the representative of the Dutch Crown in governing Indonesia, including the Republic. Sjahrir also accepted that a new mixed Dutch-Indonesian body be created, which would, during the interim period, direct Indonesian foreign relations.[461]

Schermerhorn's secretary described Sjahrir's radio speech on June 19, as a "courageous act."[462] Schermerhorn himself thought, after the speech and after Sjahrir's letter of June 20, that the chances of the catastrophic war Sjahrir warned against, dropped "from eighty to forty percent."[463]

H. N. Boon, a Dutch official in van Mook's cabinet, writing in his diary also on June 20, found it "remarkable" that Sjahrir's radio speech of the previous day "was not reported in Yogyakarta." Boon added: "it remains to be seen what will actually happen."[464] On the same day, Schermerhorn heard from a "well informed" source

---

[456] Kahin, *Nationalism and Revolution*, p. 199.

[457] *Opbouw-Pembinaan*, June 7, 1947, p. 1

[458] Dutch Ambassador to London to the minister of foreign affairs, Hague, June 17, 1947 in *Officiële bescheiden*, 9: 390.

[459] On the talks, see a cable from Schuurman to the minister of foreign affairs, Hague, June 19, 1947 in ibid., p. 416. On Sjahrir's speech as being related to the meeting see e.g. Anak Agung, *'Renville'*, p. 45.

[460] Speech in *Officiële bescheiden*, 9: 422–24.

[461] Wolf, *The Indonesian Story*, p. 122.

[462] Sanders, "Dagboek alleen voor Ida," June 21 1947 (1: 131).

[463] Schermerhorn, *Het dagboek*, June 21, 1947 (2: 652).

[464] Boon, "Dagelyksche notities," June 20, 1947, p. 94.

that Sjahrir had written the critical letter on "delegation stationery," but that he disclosed it to "no other member of the delegation."[465]

According to George Kahin's account, based on later interviews with Sjahrir,

> Before making his counterproposals of June 20, 1947, [Sjahrir] had secured the concurrence of those members of his cabinet then in Jakarta.[466]

According to Kahin, after Sjahrir made the radio speech and wrote the critical letter, he decided to send an emissary "to Jogjakarta to explain to the rest of the cabinet why the concessions had been made."[467]

The best explanation of what followed seems to be that Sjahrir was tired.

Of all the people available, Sjahrir decided that Abdoelmadjid would go to Yogyakarta to speak for him and for the compromise. Dr. Halim, close to Sjahrir at the time, recalled later that he had tried to dissuade Sjahrir from sending Abdoelmadjid. Dr.Halim also wrote about the "strangeness" of the Sjahrir's decision:

> I do not believe that Sjahrir, as I knew him, did not know where Abdoelmadjid stood at that moment, and if so, the problem is why Sjahrir chose him and not for instance Subadio, Soepeno or myself, who were normally entrusted with various kinds of missions. Again and again, till the present time, I try to answer this question, and I can not.[468]

On June 23, Sjahrir spent an evening with H. N. Boon. Boon noted in his diary under that day:

> Debating about art, scarcely a word about politics, [Sjahrir talked] about his time in Holland, about his love for Amsterdam [and] differences between the Dutchmen in Holland and Dutchmen in the Indies.[469]

On the same day, Frans Goedhart came to Jakarta hastily, and brought an urgent letter from the Dutch Labor Party,

> to make Sjahrir aware, as quickly and as plainly as possible, of the difficulties we have here in Holland and ... to appeal to him strongly to reach a fast, peaceful and viable solution.[470]

---

[465] Schermerhorn, *Het dagboek*, June 23, 1947 (2: 665).

[466] Kahin, *Nationalism and Revolution*, p. 207.

[467] Ibid.

[468] Halim, *Di antara hempasan*, pp. 108–9. Subadio, when asked, "tended to remember" that Sjahrir at that time still trusted Abdoelmadjid or, at least, that he saw Abdoelmadjid as the figure most capable of winning the left wing in Yogyakarta over to the concessions. Subadio "tended to disagree" with Dr. Halim when Dr. Halim suggested "that Sjahrir might have welcomed his [own] departure from government, if he, actually, did not help to bring it about." Ibid. and interview with Subadio in Legge, *Intellectuals and Nationalism*, p. 119.

[469] Boon, "Dagelyksche notities," June 23, 1947, p. 95.

[470] Goedhart to Schermerhorn June 13, 1947 in *Collection Schermerhorn* no. 5 bundel Goedhart.

At the same time, Admiral Helfrich debated with Vice-Admiral Pinke, opining that the Dutch ultimatum to the Republic the previous May might have not been a wise step, as it might "forestall the moment of surprise in an eventual military action."[471]

Sjahrir left for Yogyakarta, on June 25, to face the cabinet, his party, the opposition, and Sukarno. At the moment of his departure, he was already aware of at least one important piece of news from the center. Abdoelmadjid, as George Kahin described it:

> upon arriving [in Yogyakarta], both before the cabinet and before a meeting of the *Sajap Kiri*, Left Wing [coalition of which Sjahrir's, Amir's, and Abdoelmadjid's Socialist Party was a core member], strongly opposed the concessions and attacked Sjahrir for having made them. When Sjarifoeddin arrived the next day [from Jakarta], he found that several of the top leaders of the *Sajap Kiri*, including Tan Ling Djie and Wikana, had lined up with Aboelmadjid and finally agreed to follow them in condemnation of Sjahrir's concessions.[472]

On June 25 also, Sukiman of the Masjumi was reported by Associated Press as suggesting that it was "very possible" that his party would attempt "to oust Sjahrir."[473] Sjahrir spoke to the leaders of the Left Wing in Yogyakarta on June 26. As the speech was described by an otherwise very pro-Sjahrir observer, Sjahrir

> actually shared practically nothing with [the meeting] about the causes of all the difficulties; he did not tell them about the international pressure, as if he only with an effort kept himself to the text he read, he behaved as a lecturer, and as if the politicians in front of him were a student auditorium.[474]

On June 27, Sjahrir handed in his resignation. The same day, a formal note by Sukarno from Yogyakarta informed the Dutch authorities that

> because Sjahrir's cabinet resigned in the face of events, thus because of the present critical situation, we Soekarno, President of the Republic of Indonesia, from today, June 27, 1947, will exercise the power of Government.[475]

6. ADVISER TO THE PRESIDENT

On June 28, 1947, at the moment of deepest crisis between the Dutch Kingdom and the Indonesian Republic, the United States issued an aide memoire strongly supportive of a compromise and, thus, implicitly, of Indonesian concessions. The news of the note, allegedly, had already reached Yogyakarta on June 27, but not soon enough to give Sjahrir's cabinet another chance before its resignation.

---

[471] Helfrich to Pinke, June 25, 1947 in *Officiële bescheiden*, 9: 464–65.

[472] Kahin, *Nationalism and Revolution*, pp. 207–8.

[473] Associated Press from Yogyakarta, June 25, 1947 quoted in Wolf, *The Indonesian Story*, p. 123.

[474] X ambtenaar, "Indonesische Politiek," p. 31.

[475] Nota by Sukarno to the Dutch government, June 27, 1947 in *Officiële bescheiden*, 9: 482.

This was the moment when the United States, after months of ambiguity and after leaving the initiative largely in British hands, entered the scene. Already on June 28, the day the US aide memoire arrived, Sukarno wrote to van Mook informing him that he, in fact, agreed with the Republic's concessions to Holland as formulated in Sjahrir's letter of June 23. "Within nineteen hours of Sjahrir's resignation," an American observer wrote later, the Left Wing coalition, which had helped to bring about Sjahrir's fall, "reversed itself and announced that it would support his policies...."[476]

On July 5, *Opbouw-Pembinaan* published a cartoon picturing a small boat, a barrel rather, precariously keeping afloat on what clearly was a very rough sea. Sjahrir had just been thrown out of the "boat"; only his head was visible above the waves as he clutched at the side. Van Mook, Schermerhorn, and one other member of his commission, Amir Sjarifoeddin and two other members of Sjahrir's (former) delegation were crowded inside. None of them looked very safe either. The caption read: "The darkest hour is always just before the dawn." Indeed, above the horizon, and above the scene, the sun was rising with a big sign of a US dollar on it.[477]

On July 3, a new Indonesian cabinet was announced. The Indonesian National Party got key positions, with Sukarno clearly behind the party's appointees.[478] Amir Sjarifoeddin became the new prime minister—according to insiders because Sukarno and Hatta needed him for further negotiations with the Dutch.[479] Sjahrir, a former prime minister, was appointed by Sukarno "adviser to the president," and, as a part of his new function, was expected to reside most of the time in the Yogyakarta presidential palace.[480]

Schermerhorn initially was disturbed by Sjahrir's Indonesian socialist friends turning against Sjahrir.[481] But he soon let himself be consoled. On the same day that Sjahrir resigned, Schermerhorn had an "extremely pleasant" talk with Setiadjit, a leader of the socialists—a man, as Schermerhorn happily noted in his diary on that day, "who knows Holland wonderfully, and who knows the world and looks at things in an utmost rational manner."[482] Three days later Schermerhorn wrote: "My only hope is that Setiadjit's influence will work."[483]

---

[476] Wolf, *The Indonesian Story*, p. 123. Wolf was US deputy consul in Jakarta till shortly before the events. See also Kahin, *Nationalism and Revolution*, p. 208 and Robert J. McMahon, *Colonialism and Cold War: The United States and the Struggle for Indonesian Independence, 1945–1949* (Ithaca: Cornell University Press, 1981), pp. 163–66. The documents are in Foreign Relations of the United States: Marshall to Foote, June 26, 1947 (*FRUS* 1947, 6: 959–60); Marshall to Baruch, June 26, 1947 (ibid., pp. 960–61).

[477] *Opbouw-Pembinaan*, July 5, 1947.

[478] A. K. Gani became deputy prime minister and minister of economic affairs, Ali Sastroamidjojo became minister of education, Maramis minister of finance, and Susanto minister of justice.

[479] Ali Sastroamijoyo, *Milestones on my Journey*, p. 138.

[480] "Riwajat Hidup Soetan Sjahrir," p. 2; in *Archives Siti Wahjunah Sjahrir*; M. L. Tobing, *Perdjuangan Politik Bangsa Indonesia: Linggadjati* (Jakarta: Gunung Agung, 1986), p. 79; "X," *Indonesische politiek*, p. 31. Wolf, *The Indonesian Story*, p. 124 says "Special Adviser to the Government."

[481] Schermerhorn, *Het dagboek*, June 27, 1947 (2: 673).

[482] Ibid., June 27, 1947 (2: 674–75).

[483] Ibid., July 1, 1947 (2: 704).

Another five days later, Setiadjit told Schermerhorn about Sjahrir's "contempt for the masses."[484] In Schermerhorn's diary entry for July 10, a fortnight after the Sjahrir cabinet's fall, Setiadjit was already compared with Sjahrir in the following way:

> the former is less philosophical and in a significant measure more matter-of-fact [zakelijker] in his disposition, and thus, from our point of view, of much greater potential for making the governing work.[485]

But all this—the shallow affections, the vague memories, the sudden desertions—seemed, by July 1947, to matter no more. As Schermerhorn talked with Setiadjit, Dutch intelligence graded Schermerhorn's role as "according to the latest impressions, to all effects, finished."[486] In spite of Schermerhorn's desperate appeals—and in spite of the fact that the new Indonesian cabinet was willing to retreat even further than Sjahrir did—Schermerhorn's and Sjahrir's blueprint for the future was abandoned.

Holland decided to use force. On July 20, 1947, Dutch Prime Minister Beel,

> ordered the Dutch army to launch an all-out attack designed to crush the Republic. The next morning Dutch armored columns with powerful air support fanned out inland from their seaport bases in Java and Sumatra.[487]

Yogyakarta was spared the immediate and direct attack; the Dutch were mindful of international opinion in that case, and they also did not dare strike so deeply into the interior. Jakarta, on the other hand, the exposed place in between, was among the first targets.

On July 22, on the second day of the military action, Dutch soldiers broke into Sjahrir's private residence in Jakarta and arrested a group of Indonesians who happened to have gathered in the house. Most of these were people intimately involved in the previous negotiations, Sjahrir's associates and friends. Given the fact that this was a Dutch-Indonesian war, the Indonesian prisoners were asked weird questions, indeed, during the interrogations:

> 1. Had you ever had a contact with [Schermerhorn's] Commission General?
> 2. If so, how frequently? 3. What did you talk about on those occasions?

Sudarpo, who was among those arrested (we mentioned Sjahrir attending his wedding a few weeks previously), appeared to be particularly "arrogant" during the interrogation; this young ardent follower of Sjahrir perhaps expected that Sjahrir and Schermerhorn might still be able to intervene.[488]

---

[484] Minutes of the 75th meeting of the Commissie Generaal, July 6, 1947 in *Officiële bescheiden*, 9: 595.

[485] Schermerhorn, *Het dagboek*, July 10, 1947 (2: 752).

[486] Dutch consul general in Singapore to the minister of foreign affairs in The Hague, July 9, 1947 in *Officiële bescheiden*, 9: 635–36.

[487] Kahin, *Nationalism and Revolution*, p. 212.

[488] The records of the interrogations are in *Archief Alg Secr, lste zending*, no. III-29-31; also Schermerhorn, *Het dagboek*, August 22, 1947 (2: 783) (Schermerhorn protested but to no avail); also interview with Sudarpo, Jakarta, October 7, 1987. Among others arrested in Sjahrir's

Early in the afternoon of that same day, July 22, Sjahrir arrived by plane in Singapore. The local press reported that he came "with one piece of luggage" and with two of his Bandanese children—Ali aged eight, and Mimi aged eighteen. Sjahrir looked tired; he had also just suffered from an attack of malaria (an illness he brought from Boven Digul).[489] He spoke to newsmen at the airport, and described how he had found out that the Dutch were attacking:

> At seven o'clock on Monday morning [July 21], I was in Jogjakarta. I looked up and saw a number of fighter planes overhead. At first I thought they were Indonesian planes, but then I realized that they were so modern and so fast that they could only be Dutch.[490]

Dutch military intelligence first believed that Sjahrir had left Yogyakarta "in a personal plane of Lord Killearn," and this was, perhaps, why "no Dutch fighters intercepted the Dakota."[491] In fact, Sjahrir used, as the previous March when he went to India, the plane of Biju Patnaik, his Bengali friend who happened to be in Yogyakarta at the time of the attack.[492]

When asked, at the Singapore airport, about his future plans, Sjahrir said that they were

> not definitive and depend entirely on instructions from Indonesia. I expect that they may call me back at any moment. . . .[493]

Already the next day, however, July 23, on two-hours' notice according to one report,[494] and, reportedly canceling an appointment to see Malay nationalist leaders in Penang and in Kuala Lumpur, Sjahrir left Singapore. Now, he traveled to India, on a British commercial plane, but still as a guest of Patnaik.[495]

During a fifty-minute press conference upon his arrival in New Delhi, Sjahrir, "speaking with emotion," said "he had been sent by the President Dr. Soekarno on a mission to make the world stop the colonial war in Indonesia." He came to India first

---

house were Gani, Tamzil, Ali Boediardjo, Darmasetiawan, Joesoef Jahja, and Mohammad Natsir.

[489] *Straits Times*, July 23, 1947, *Nieuwsgier*, July 23, 1947 in *Archief Proc Gen*, no. 262. According to Tobing, *Perdjuangan Politik Bangsa Indonesia: Linggadjati*, p. 138, Tambu and Soedjatmoko were on the plane, too.

[490] *Straits Times*, July 23, 1947.

[491] Spoor in minutes of a meeting of his staff July 24, 1947 in *Officiële bescheiden*, 10: 40.

[492] Ibid.; also Wirjawan,"Bila gelap telah mendatang," *Siasat*, December 23, 1951, p. 11. In Singapore, Sjahrir immediately contacted Oetojo, and also Soebandrio, another of his young followers from wartime, who had just returned from a trip to Amsterdam. Dutch intelligence report from Singapore to consul general Singapore in dossier "Sjahrir" in *Archief Proc Gen*, no. 3–262; also dossier "Soebandrio" ibid., no. 259.

[493] *Straits Times*, July 23, 1947. According to "Riwajat Hidup Soetan Sjahrir," "surat peringatan Pemerintah Republik Indonesia," dated July 22, 1947 stated "Duta Besar Keliling dengan tugas mewakili R.I. dalam urusan2 dan penundjuk dengan semua negara2 dan pemerintah2 asing."

[494] *Statesman*, July 25, 1947.

[495] Dutch intelligence report from Singapore to consul general, Singapore, in dossier "Sjahrir" in *Archief Proc Gen*, no. 3–262.

"because it is a friendly country [and] Pandit Nehru is a friend of mine."[496] Asked how long the Republic might hold on,

> Dr. Shariar [sic] said that in Java where the Dutch forces had mechanized units and a large air force, a decision could be made within a matter of weeks, but extensive guerrilla war would be carried on in the hinterland ... which would be for a very long time.... In Sumatra, he thought, the Dutch would not have any success. In fact Indonesian troops held the initiative there.[497]

Sjahrir also told the newsmen that, besides Nehru, "he hoped to see Mr. Jinnah and would possibly see Lord Killearn who is now in New Delhi."[498]

As Sjahrir wrote in a letter to Nehru the previous May, and as he repeated now, in case of a military attack by the Dutch against the Indonesian Republic, "the big powers [were expected] to make a joint move to intermediate"; "America and Britain [should] endeavor to make Holland see through the unreasonableness of its action."[499] "If this should not happen," then it should be Nehru's turn "to bring the matter up to the Security Council of the United Nations Organization."[500] This was the belief that the broader world would act.

As Sjahrir arrived in New Delhi, however, no mediating action by the big powers was in sight. Nehru himself, a day after the Dutch invasion, gave a very strong speech: "The spirit of the new Asia will not tolerate such things," he said among other things.[501] But—as the Dutch ambassador in New Delhi happily reported—Nehru also delayed a straightforward move "for two days and then still for a day ... at the request of England."[502]

With hesitation, after a week of waiting, and also after Australia, another British ally, had agreed to join him, on July 30, Nehru officially requested that the case of the Dutch military action in Indonesia be placed on the agenda of the UN Security Council. Sjahrir was again on the way.[503]

On August 5, as the journal *Frères Mousulmans* in Cairo, Egypt, reported:

> An American plane landed at the Farouk Airport, and Dr. Soutin Shahir [sic] stepped out, wearing a sport suit and without a hat.... He exchanged greetings with El Hag Aghoes [Hadji Agoes Salim?], and was saluted by a

---

[496] *Statesman*, July 25, 1947.

[497] Ibid.

[498] Ibid.

[499] Sjahrir, July 27, 1947, quoted in *Nieuwsgier*, July 28, 1947.

[500] Ibid.

[501] *New York Times*, July 25, 1947, quoted in McMahon, *Colonialism*, p. 172.

[502] Report by Dutch ambassador in New Delhi to the ministry of foreign affairs in The Hague, August 1, 1947 and August 5, 1947 on a private talk with "Indian diplomats" in *Officiële bescheiden*, 10: 169 and 245. According to the same source, "Sjahrir, indeed, is a great personal friend of Nehru and Nehru has a great sympathy for Indonesia, yet Sjahrir is no official personality. British India, moreover, had recognized the Republic merely *de facto*, which does not imply any diplomatic representation...." Ibid.

[503] Wolf, *The Indonesian Story*, p. 137.

group of Indonesian youth chanting "Dikka" [*Merdeka*] "freedom," and raising their right hands.[504]

From the very few reports we have, Sjahrir did not appear comfortable in Cairo. He seemed to move around largely guided by Hadji Agoes Salim and Soetan Nazir Pamoentjak, both of whom were older men, well respected Moslems, and very much at ease in the Islamic center. Sjahrir did not seem to know anybody in Cairo.

On his arrival Sjahrir announced that he would remain in Egypt "only as long as strictly necessary."[505] He met with the chief of King Farouk's cabinet,[506] and gave an interview to another local paper, *Al Misri*, where he was quoted—or misquoted?—as saying that both Britain and the United States, were responsible for what was going on in Indonesia, because they supported the Dutch.[507] The day after he arrived, on August 6, taking Hadji Agoes Salim with him, and again aboard an American plane, Sjahrir left for New York.

In Holland, J. A. Jonkman, the new Dutch minister for the overseas territories, and also formerly a member of *Stuw*, at a cabinet meeting,

> declared himself worried over a new debate in the Security Council, especially as Sjahrir was coming to take part.[508]

Schermerhorn offered to go to New York, and to put his weight behind the negotiations. The Dutch Labor Party supported the idea; the Dutch cabinet, however, rejected the offer.[509] Dr. van Kleffens, the Dutch delegate to the United Nations, persuaded the cabinet that it was "naive" to expect that Schermerhorn could still influence anybody.[510]

Sjahrir arrived in New York on Friday, August 8, at 10 p.m., and, as van Kleffens' office—almost cheerfully—reported,

> was welcomed by two British Indians, one Egyptian and a group of circa forty whites, negroes and Indonesians belonging to the Indonesian League [an association of solidarity with Indonesia]. There was only one photographer present and a few reporters, but no interview was given, so that [Sjahrir's] arrival was reported by a few lines on the last page of the Times and Herald Tribune. Till now, no headlines, no photos, no publicity of any import.[511]

---

[504] *Freres Mousulmans*, August 6, 1947, in "Inlichtingen Sjahrir," *Archief Proc Gen*, no. 3–262.
[505] Ibid.
[506] Ibid.
[507] *Al Misri*, August 6, 1947 in *Officiële bescheiden*, 10: 285n.
[508] Minutes of the council of ministers, Hague, August 4, 1947 in *Officiële bescheiden* 10: 231–32.
[509] Bank, *Katholieken*, p. 336; Schermerhorn, *Het dagboek*, August 10, 1947 (2: 811–14).
[510] Telephone conversation between van Kleffens and minister of foreign affairs in The Hague, August 6, 1947 in *Officiële bescheiden*, 10: 269.
[511] Snouck Hurgronje from New York to the minister of foreign affairs in ibid., 10: 325.

Van Kleffens also reported "no success" at Sjahrir's first press conference on the following day, August 9.[512] Sjahrir himself, recalling the events later, readily agreed: "The atmosphere in the United States," he wrote, "was very unfavorable to Indonesia, when we came."[513]

Sjahrir clearly did not feel comfortable in New York as well. The first news conference made no headlines. Sjahrir talked about the Dutch "assault," and about "flame-throwers." This was a "real war," he said, and "baser than the Japanese invasion of Java in 1942." At the same time, Sjahrir stated that he still believed in the Linggadjati agreement as a possible basis for a solution.[514] He seemed to speak to the audience which was not there.

Sjahrir's hesitation towards a pronouncedly United States solution soon became striking. He acknowledged the offer of "good offices," that had just been announced by the United States, but he emphasized that he thought of this only as "an accessory [onderdeel] to an action, which should be taken by the United Nations." To solve the conflict, Sjahrir said, "it would be much better" if other states acted, and he named Australia and India.[515]

On August 12, in spite of van Kleffens' protests, Sjahrir was officially allowed to participate in the UN Security Council debate, and two days later, on August 14, he addressed the Council. Sjahrir spoke in English, and talked about "fair play and justice." He suggested that an "authoritative commission" be appointed by the UN Security Council as an arbiter between the Dutch and the Republic. He demanded the withdrawal of Dutch troops behind the line of October 14, 1946: this was the line between the Dutch and Republican forces as agreed upon in Linggadjati.[516]

It might have been a typical speech by the Sjahrir of old. Except for the highly discordant, and disturbingly new way in which he built the speech around the image of "a thousand years" of Indonesian history, namely of

> the Empire of Madjapahit, which embraced all the islands of Southeast Asia and expanded from Papua to Madagascar.[517]

This was something that Sjahrir had always previously considered and disdained as a typical notion of the "Eastern spirit." "The rapid expansion of Western people," Sjahrir also said, "led to the decline and fall of my people...."[518] These seemed to be clear echoes of Yogyakarta, "Fortress of the Republic," the Javanese interior, Sukarno, the center around which Sjahrir moved with increasing uncertainty.

---

[512] Van Kleffens to the minister of foreign affairs in The Hague, August 10, 1947 in "Inlichtingen Sjahrir" in *Archief Buiten. Zaken* V.R.III–910.

[513] Sjahrir in Salam Solichin, *Hadji Agus Salim: Hidup dan Perdjuangannja* (Jakarta: Djajamuri, 1961), p. 22.

[514] *New York Times*, August 9, 1947, and also as reported in *Nieuwsgier*, August 11, 1947; also Wolf, *The Indonesian Story*, p. 139.

[515] Ibid.

[516] Tape of Sjahrir's speech was graciously given to me by Siti Wahjunah Sjahrir. Text of the speech is in Security Council Official Record, 2nd year, 184th meeting, August 14, 1947, pp. 2002–2003; also in "Indonesië in de V.R. app. IX" in *Archief Buiten. Zaken*, and in *Officiële bescheiden* 10: 432–33n.

[517] Ibid.

[518] Ibid. For an interesting Dutch "neo-ethical" reaction on Sjahrir's "Madjapahit" remarks see an undated memo in "Inlichtingen Sjahrir" in *Archief Buiten. Zaken* V.R.III-910.

The *New York Herald Tribune* presented Sjahrir's speech as "one of the most moving statements heard here at Lake Success."[519] Dr. van Kleffens considered the speech most biased.[520]

On the day following this second speech, Sjahrir met a Dutch friend from his time in Holland in 1929, P. J. Schmidt, who had lobbied for Sjahrir, as we recall, in London, late in 1945, and who was now working at the United Nations. Hadji Agoes Salim was present at the meeting; he knew Schmidt also from that time eighteen years previously. They talked several hours, and Schmidt immediately reported to a few friends in Holland on the meeting: how pleased he had been still to find some "trust" by Sjahrir in Schmidt himself, in Schermerhorn, and in the spirit of the Linggadjati agreement. As Schmidt interpreted what Sjahrir had told him, Sjahrir still believed that a socialist and reasonable Holland, rather than Australia, India, England, France, or the United States, might play a positive role in the Indonesian future.[521]

This was the old tension between the good and bad among the Dutch, between the Dutch monopoly and the broader world. Sjahrir gave another speech at the Security Council on August 19. This speech was described by van Kleffens as "very weak." Its theme was a plea to the world community not to leave Indonesia with the Dutch alone in the dark.[522]

The morning after the second speech, accompanied by Hadji Agoes Salim, and also Charles Tambu—an old associate from the Japanese "Radio Camp," who had now joined the Republican delegation—Sjahrir traveled to Washington. As the Dutch Embassy got the information,

> It was a surprise for Mr. Penfield [deputy chief of the Southeast Asia section at the State Department] that it was not Sjahrir who was the spokesman of the group. The talking was done by Messrs. Salim and Tamboe, while Mr. Sjahrir, according to my source, kept sitting silent through the visit.[523]

Sjahrir later again confirmed this. He recalled that on the occasion

> a representative of the State Department . . . was far from being sweet to us, it was only the capacity of Hadji Agoes Salim to warm everybody, which kept the talking going.[524]

---

[519] *New York Herald Tribune*, August 15, 1947, quoted in Wolf, *The Indonesian Story*, p. 94n.

[520] Van Kleffens to the minister of foreign affairs, August 8 and 14, 1947 in *Officiële bescheiden*, 10: 411 and 510–11.

[521] Schmidt to van der Goes, August 16, 1947 in *Collection Schermerhorn* no. 35 bundel Schmidt.

[522] Security Council Official Record, 2nd year, 187th meeting, August 19, 1947, p. 2075; also in "Indonesië in V.R. app. IX, p. 104" in *Archief Buiten. Zaken* V.R. III-919; van Kleffens to the minister of foreign affairs, August 20, 1947 in *Officiële bescheiden*, 10: 521; van Kleffens to the minister of foreign affairs, Hague, September 3, 1947 ibid., 3: 910.

[523] Dutch ambassador to Washington to to the minister of foreign affairs, August 21, 1947 in "Indonesië in V.R. IV-911" in *Archief Buiten. Zaken* . Minutes of the meeting are in *FRUS (1947)*, 6: 1037–38. The same day the delegation met with officials of the European division at the State Department; Sjahrir was again reported as "silent throughout the visit." van Kleffens to the minister of foreign affairs, August 21, 1947, in "Indonesië in V.R. IV-911" in *Archief Buiten. Zaken*.

[524] Sjahrir in Solichin, *Hadji Agus Salim*, p. 23.

The Americans were impatient. According to their own account, the State Department officials told Sjahrir and his associates during the meeting

> that through the offer of good offices by the United States, a step was taken in the [right] direction, yet the Republic did nothing but react negatively. The gentlemen were made to understand that now the Republic was expected to do something for the solution of the difficulties in the [Security] Council and with other [powers].[525]

On August 27, the UN Security Council, as suggested by the United States, proposed to the Dutch Kingdom and to the Republic of Indonesia that they should accept a commission of good offices to assist in the settlement of their dispute. The United States was to be "the key member" when the commission was constituted.[526] Sjahrir spoke of his immediate reaction to a reporter for the *Nieuwe Rotterdamsche Courant*:

> We submit to the decision of the Council, yet, we can not see how there may be objective reporting, and we expect little from the commission's inquiry. We shall cooperate loyally with the commission, but we do not expect that much may come out of it.[527]

On September 18, the Security Council announced formation of the commission, called the Committee of Good Offices, a body made up of the United States, Belgium—suggested by Holland, and Australia—suggested by the Republic.[528]

This was a new international backdrop against which Indonesia was to view its internal affairs. Sjahrir appeared restless. As if he found it difficult to accept that now the center of gravity in the broader world rested in New York, and increasingly with the United States. In spite of the fact that the business of his delegation in New York was still far from finished, Sjahrir, on September 20, left Lake Success for London.

The press reported that Sjahrir was going to London as a guest of India's High Commissioner in England, V. K. Krishna Menon, and "in order to see firsthand how the British government solved its colonial problem."[529] Sjahrir on his arrival was welcomed by Soebandrio, his young follower from war time, who had now come from Singapore to become the Indonesian Republic's representative in Britain. At their first meeting, Sjahrir told Soebandrio that "New York had been a disappointment," and that he, Sjahrir, actually, had not accomplished anything.[530]

---

[525] This is what the Americans present told their Dutch counterparts in Washington in private. See Dutch ambassador to Washington to the minister of foreign affairs in The Hague, August 21, 1947. The US memo of the meeting—conveying the same atmosphere, except in more polished words, is in *FRUS* (1947), 6: 1037–38.

[526] A. M. Taylor, *Indonesian Independence and the United Nations* (Ithaca: Cornell University Press, 1960), pp. 54-57.

[527] *Nieuwe Rotterdamsche Courant* quoted by *APN*, September 2, 1947, also in *Nieuwsgier*, September 2, 1947.

[528] Taylor, *Indonesian Independence*, p. 55.

[529] *Nieuwsgier*, September 22, 1947.

[530] Dutch ambassador to United Kingdom to the minister of foreign affairs, September 23, 1947 on a direct communication from Soebandrio in *Officiële bescheiden*, 11: 155.

Within a week, a meeting was arranged for Sjahrir with the British foreign minister, Ernest Bevin. The two met, on September 26, but just for fifteen minutes. Sjahrir told the press afterwards, that Britain did not agree with the Dutch resorting to war in Indonesia. Bevin, in his turn, informed the Dutch ambassador in London privately that Sjahrir might still be interested in a negotiated settlement on the basis of the Linggadjati agreement.[531]

It was explained that Sjahrir's wish not to antagonize the British government and the British political mainstream meant that he

> during his London visit carefully evaded any contacts with Labour Party leftists which might be seen "compromising." He did not, for example, attend a conference organized by the Union of Democratic Control, where he knew he would be warmly welcomed, and which discussed Indonesia.[532]

The Union of Democratic Control, of course, was the body to which Dorothy Woodman and her circle belonged, which had translated and distributed his "Our Struggle" in 1945, and where the core and hope of his support in the broader world, in 1945 and 1946, seemed to rest.

Sjahrir was invited to talk on the BBC: but not on a domestic station, merely on the Far Eastern Service.[533] During the first days of the Dutch attack, a few weeks before, there had been regular and compassionate front-page reports on Indonesia in the London papers. There was almost no reporting, now, when Sjahrir was in town. In the words of a Dutch reporter,

> one could hardly describe Claridge's Hotel, where the Indonesian mission stays, as a focus of journalistic activity. There were a few interviews with Sjahrir, when he came, but afterwards the newspapers took no notice of him.[534]

P. J. Koets, a highly respected Dutch expert on Indonesia, and a man close to the members of the prewar *Stuw*, was sent for by the foreign ministry in The Hague, as soon as news came of Sjahrir's arrival in London. Koets had to leave on a minute's notice, crossing the English Channel by the night-boat, despite his protests that he hated night-boats.[535] Three weeks later, on October 15, Koets reported from London:

> neither Sjahrir nor anybody from his circle, has yet made an attempt at an official contact. I have met him several times, as well as old Salim and

---

[531] Dutch ambassador to United Kingdom to the minister of foreign affairs, September 27, 1947 "Inlichtingen Sjahrir" in *Archief Buiten. Zaken* V.R.III-910.

[532] *Suraisia Daily Special Cable*, October 20, 1947 quoted by the Dutch ambassador to Canberra to the minister of foreign affairs, October 28, 1947 in "Ambassade Parijs," *Archief Buiten. Zaken.* file GAA4A, blok I 1945–1951, doos 2.

[533] A transcript of the speech, which was sent by Sjahrir to the Dutch embassy two days in advance, is in "Inlichtingen Sjahrir" in *Archief Proc Gen*, no. 262.

[534] *Het Vrije Volk*, December 1, 1947 in ibid.

[535] Correspondence on Sjahrir between the Dutch minister of foreign affairs and his political advisers, September 19 and 22, 1947 in *Officiële bescheiden*, 11: 146–48, and "Inlichtingen Sjahrir" in *Archief Buiten. Zaken* V.R.III-910

Soebandrio, as we accidentally came upon each other in the hotel, but such encounters were always limited to a few friendly and personal remarks.[536]

Late in September, Krishna Menon, perhaps at Nehru's instigation, appeared willing to go to Holland to mediate; the effort failed because the Dutch, it seems, were not able to find out if Sjahrir was or was not behind the Indian's initiative.[537] In October, Buchman's Moral Re-Armament offered to arrange for the Dutch and the Indonesians to meet, and suggested Caux sur Montreaux as a meeting place. There were some hectic preparations, but in the end Sjahrir excused himself because he was "not in very good health."[538]

Soebandrio was led to believe, initially, that Sjahrir's visit to Britain would last "for a few days."[539] Then, nothing much appeared to be happening, but the visit was being steadily extended.

A file of men traveled to London from Holland in the days after Sjahrir arrived—truly a procession of figures, who in a more or less distant past, in a more or less significant way, had touched upon Sjahrir's political and private life. Logemann, Wertheim, de la Court, Gobée, de Kadt, Goedhart, Sal Tas, and van Randwijk (a journalist close to Goedhart's and Sal Tas' circle), came to London, late in September, ostensibly to attend a conference of the Institute of Pacific Relations.[540] If it was an effort at a reunion, it was a failed effort.

Most of these men, did not meet Sjahrir in London at all. Some, like van Randwijk, attempted a kind of diplomacy, but failed and felt afterwards that they were not taken seriously enough by either Sjahrir or The Hague.[541] Sal Tas was one of the few who actually saw Sjahrir:

> Almost twenty years separated us from our youthful memories, which were buried under exile, war, and civil strife. We shared the painful consciousness of having grown older, together with the question: what had remained of our old friendship?
>
> He came into the room at Claridge's with a bound. The tension which had been growing in me was released with the stupid remark: "You've gotten fat!" He grimaced, but after some hesitation and a few awkward gestures, contact was established again. I found him greatly changed. Because he had become stouter ... his face had become fuller; it had lost the concentrated beauty which had once made me think of a classical carving. His features had become rougher. He spoke faster, more decisively, and with the certainty of someone who is accustomed to take decisions and bear heavy

---

[536] Koets to van Mook. October 15, 1947 in *Officiële bescheiden*, 11: 307.

[537] Dutch ambassador in London to the minister of foreign affairs, September 14 and 25, 1947, in *Officiële bescheiden*, 11: 305 and in "Inlichtingen Sjahrir" in *Archief Buiten. Zaken* V.R.III-910.

[538] Note s from the council of ministers (October 13, 1947) on the meeting of minister Neher and Mr. Sjahrir in *Officiële bescheiden*, 11: 287–88.

[539] Soebandrio to Luns, September 12, 1947 in "Inlichtingen Sjahrir" in *Archief Buiten. Zaken* V.R.III-910.

[540] Minister of foreign affairs to the Dutch ambassador to the United Kingdom, September 19, 1947 in "Inlichtingen Sjahrir" in *Archief Buiten. Zaken* V.R.III-910. Koets to van Mook, October 15, 1947 in *Officiële bescheiden*, 11: 308.

[541] Gerard Mulder and Paul Koedijk, *H.M.van Randwijk: Een biografie* (Amsterdam: Nijgh en Van Ditmar, 1988), pp. 601–3.

responsibilities. . . . For the first time I found in his manner a quality which he had never shown as a young man: impatience. He was undoubtedly overworked—or rather overburdened—at that time, weighed down by responsibilities, tensions, and justified fears. But that does not completely explain the hardness with which he now dealt with his surroundings.

It was the first time that I met Subandrio, who functioned as Sjahrir's personal secretary. He was treated as an office boy in my presence.[542]

Sjahrir left London on October 18, after a month in the city, and, to all appearances, without having accomplished anything. From London, he went to Paris. The most remarkable aspect of this part of the trip seemed to be the fact that Sjahrir bypassed Holland on his way.

Sjahrir had exchanged some letters from London with the director general of UNESCO in Paris, Julien Huxley. Huxley wrote to Sjahrir in London that he would gladly meet him. But two days before Sjahrir arrived, Huxley left on a trip to Mexico.[543] Already before Sjahrir's departure from London, it was clear that French Foreign Minister Georges Bidault would not meet with him—only the minister's secretary, perhaps, or the chief of the ministry's East Asia section; and this merely on "a strictly unofficial basis."[544]

After he arrived in Paris, Sjahrir himself gave as the reason for the visit to "have a rest after London," and "no politics."[545] He was closely watched by the Dutch through the few days he spent in Paris, and the Dutch agents reported that he stayed in The Hotel Royal Manceau, with Krishna Menon at the same place, that he was being shown around Paris by one Salim, a painter, and that he spent his evenings and nights either in Salim's company "(movies a. *Films d'amour* b. *Silence est d'or!!* c. *Boîte de nuit Espagnole Miraega* d. *Palais Challot*; restaurants a. *Monte Carlo*, avenue de Wagram b. *Lion Chung*, 5 rue Molière)," or with some ladies ("Mme.Nadine Bartier, 8 rue Anabele de la Forge 16c") or with some journalists ("Mr. Gomperts of *Het Parool*").[546]

A day after Sjahrir left Paris, *l'Humanité*, the Communist daily, published, what it said was its interview with Sjahrir, misspelling Sjahrir's name as "Sutan Chahrir." Under the headlines "Faced By Imperialist Offensive I Believe Peoples Will Be Victorious," the interview attacked primarily Wall Street: "It is for Wall Street," Sjahrir was alleged to have said, "that the Dutch colonialists are fighting their war."[547]

In Paris, Sjahrir also met Jef Last, the poet socialist he listened to in Holland two decades before, and whose book he read with *juffrouw* Cresa in Banda Neira. Jef Last worked in Paris as a correspondent for the Brussels socialist paper, *Volksgazet*, and for this paper, he interviewed Sjahrir. "I am very serious about the idea," Jef Last reported Sjahrir as saying,

---

[542] Tas, "Souvenirs of Sjahrir," p. 151.

[543] Dutch ambassador in Paris to the minister of foreign affairs, October 16 and November 12–13, 1947 in "Ambassade Parijs," *Archief Buiten. Zaken.* file GAA4A, blok I 1945–1951, doos 2.

[544] Dutch ambassador in Paris to the minister of foreign affairs, October 16, 1947, in ibid.

[545] Dutch ambassador in Paris to the minister of foreign affairs, October 22, 1947 in ibid.; also Mulder and Koedijk, *H.M.van Randwijk*, p. 602.

[546] Ibid; also interview with Salim, Paris, February 2, 1988.

[547] *l'Humanité*, October 30, 1947.

that a kind of "Linggadjati agreement," not between two governments, but between two socialist parties, may be presented to the socialist labor movement of the whole world.[548]

Indonesia, Sjahrir was also quoted as saying in this interview, was at war with Holland, but not with the majority of the Dutch people, and certainly not with the Dutch socialists:

> If men like Schermerhorn, whose honesty I still highly respect, would [step] into the place of the diehards of the present ... if such change comes in Dutch politics, then my government perhaps may permit me again to travel to Holland—and nothing would be dearer to me than to feel again the bondage of friendships, which I have always thought so precious.[549]

Jef Last noted the respect of progressive peoples of the world for the Indonesian government in Yogyakarta defending the country against the Dutch aggression. He asked Sjahrir about the present strength of the Republic, in particular about Sukarno and Hatta in Yogyakarta. Sjahrir was reported as answering that the situation was similar to that during the Japanese occupation:

> we have fallen back upon a primitive stage of social system where men, to all effect, live exclusively on rice. Rice, and thank god for this, is what we do not lack. Therefore, our people refuse to go again to work on plantations and in factories—they feel a Dutch colonial trap in this. This is why our guerrilla army is so large in numbers. [This is the trend now] "Back to *sawahs*, to the ricefields.[550]

On October 29, 1947, *Radio Jogjakarta* announced that Sjahrir was leaving Paris, and traveling "east."[551] Sjahrir left Paris on October 29, indeed. But, his return was very slow.

After a direct flight he arrived in Cairo, and, in spite of an epidemic of cholera in the city, he remained there for two weeks. Saudi Arabia, Yemen, and Afghanistan by that time already recognized the Republic—leaving Jordan and Iraq as the only countries in the Islamic world which had not yet done so.[552] Yet, this evidently was an achievement of Hadji Agoes Salim and Soetan Nazir Pamoentjak, rather than of Sjahrir. From Sjahrir's point of view, even, these achievements by others might contrast unpleasantly with what he himself was able to achieve in the West.

This time in Egypt, Sjahrir met with the king once, and with the prime minister twice. As during his earlier visit, however, publicity was limited. He gave an interview in Cairo to the Dutch *Vrije Volk*, "Free People," which seems never to have been published. Much of Sjahrir's time in the city was apparently spent in efforts to mend

---

[548] *Volksgazet*, November 6, 1947. A transcript of the interview is also in "Ambassade Parijs," *Archief Buiten. Zaken.* file GAA4A, blok I 1945–1951, doos 2.

[549] Ibid.

[550] Ibid.

[551] *Nieuwsgier*, October 29, 1947.

[552] Van Dijk, "The Muslim Contribution," p. 159.

Sjahrir Leaving by Air
L. ro R.: Amir Sjarifoeddin, Mohammad Hatta, Sjahrir, Hadji Agoes Salim

a split in the local Indonesian community: a task for which Sjahrir, not being a strict Moslem, was only moderately qualified.[553]

On November 13, Sjahrir left Cairo. He stopped briefly in Pakistan, where, reportedly, and without success, he tried to convince Jinnah to recognize the Indonesian Republic *de jure*.[554] On November 16, he arrived again in India.

Sjahrir stayed in New Delhi, "with his children," first in Lord Mountbatten's house, and after ten days, again in Nehru's house. He also reportedly tried to convince Nehru to recognize the Indonesian Republic *de jure*, and, as in the case of Pakistan, he did not succeed.[555]

He was invited to speak at the Indian Council for World Affairs, giving his lecture in the same building, where the Asian Relations Conference had been held seven months before. Now, Sjahrir said:

> The world seems to force us to make a choice between the existing antagonistic powers: between the American bloc and the Soviet Russian bloc. But we rightly refuse to be forced. We are seeking international

---

[553] Dutch Ambassador in Cairo to the minister of foreign affairs, October 30, November 3, 7, 12 and 13, in "Ambassade Parijs," *Archief Buiten. Zaken.* file GAA4A, blok I 1945–1951, doos 2.

[554] Ibid. in dossier "Sjahrir" *Archief Proc Gen*, no. 3–262.

[555] Ibid. Also "Ambassade Parijs," *Archief Buiten. Zaken.* file GAA4A, blok I 1945–1951, doos 2.

coexistence, which is in harmony with our internal life and we don't wish to be captured in systems that do not fit us and certainly not into systems that are hostile to our cause.[556]

The speech was given in a prestigious Indian institute, in a building located in the middle of the city. Besides the general public, the diplomatic corps was also invited. But, only the representatives of the Australian and Canadian embassies attended in addition to a Dutch attaché. According to the Dutch attaché's report, Sjahrir spoke to a half-empty hall. He apparently felt that, under the circumstances, a thirty-five minute speech was enough.[557]

On December 3, 1947, Lord Killearn, several Australian officials, and a small crowd of Indonesians, welcomed Sjahrir at the Singapore airport, where the trip had begun about four months before. In an eyewitness report:

> At Sjahrir's arrival at the airport many of the Indonesians present were disappointed by his "cool" behavior. Sjahrir did not say a word at the airport and above all, he did not use the "Merdeka" greeting when getting out of the plane. [He] has tried to conceal it, but it was noticeable how spent he was spiritually as well as physically. . . . His smile was forced.[558]

There was quite a debate in the Singapore press as to whether Sjahrir would return to Yogyakarta. His hesitation was evident.[559] Sjahrir decided: not yet. He went to Australia, by-passing Java, on December 9. In Canberra he met with the Australian prime minister and thanked him for his action in the United Nations. But he also played the warmness down by stating publicly that neither the Australian press nor

---

[556] Quoted from Sutan Sjahrir, "Speech by Sjahrir for the Asian Relations Organization, New Delhi, November 25, 1947," typescript in *Archives Siti Wahjunah Sjahrir*. It is interesting to compare this with another document of the same time. On December 16, 1947, Soedjatmoko wrote from New York to Subadio, Sjahrir's political associate working in Yogyakarta. Written in English, the letter essentially dealt with what Soedjatmoko thought was "the present trend in American internal politics, red-baiting, extensive fear of communism which has mounted to outright hysteria and its accompanying reaction against all liberal groups. . . . Wall Street never relaxed its hold on the State Department at any time in the history of this country and as a matter of fact, both Wall Street and the militarists have succeeeded in extending their power over the State Department in the years since Roosevelt's death, to an extent never before achieved." Debates in the Security Council made it clear, according to Soedjatmoko's letter, that US policy was driven by a wish to keep Holland as a US ally in Europe. It was true that some American business circles were interested in Asia. But, Soedjatmoko warned, in dealing with them, in "any political move we make we should avoid very carefully any possibility of our being dragged into the middle of the American-Soviet conflict." The solution Soedjatmoko offered was "cooperative action among the Southeast Asian countries . . . a construction, [which] would enable us, first, to coordinate our action towards the achievement of our political freedom, second, provide the possibility for a global policy keeping ourselves out of the growing American-Soviet antagonism." Soedjatmoko to Subadio, December 16, 1947 in *Collection Beel* no. 19.

[557] Reports by the Dutch press attaché on the meeting, October 28, 1947 in "Inlichtingen Sjahrir" in *Archief Buiten. Zaken* V.R.III-910. There is also the text of the speech almost identical with that quoted above.

[558] Dutch consul general in Singapore to the minister of foreign affairs, December 3 and 8, 1947, in "Inlichtingen Sjahrir" in *Archief Buiten. Zaken* V.R.III-910. Also Dutch intelligence report from Singapore no. 633, December 8, 1947. Dossier "Sjahrir" *Archief Proc Gen*, no. 3-262.

[559] *Singapore Free Press*, December 8, 1947, a copy of the paper is in Dossier "Sjahrir," ibid.

the Australian public could be described as exactly "championing our cause."[560] Bypassing Java again, he returned to Singapore on December 23.

He now let it be known privately that he did not intend to return to Indonesia in the near future, and that he wanted "to work for the Republic abroad."[561] On December 29, it was reported that

> Sjahrir does not show he has any plans to go back to Indonesia, and [among Indonesians] rumors spread that he wishes to buy a house in Singapore.[562]

In another report, dated January 8, 1948, with Sjahrir still in Singapore:

> Indonesians in Singapore, generally speaking, are frustrated by Sjahrir. Not just because he is pessimistic in his own circle about the current chances of the Republic, but also because of the fact that Sjahrir, as he now for some time has lived among them as an average citizen, retains little of his reputation as a great leader.
>
> The man they have, now, in their midst, is quite different from the great man they had known.... This Sjahrir is a tired and disappointed man, not outshining in any way other Indonesian politicians. Now the veil of his greatness has fallen down, and criticism is unleashed: "Why does he always take his foster daughter Mimi with him? Who pays for the study trips and the living costs of his other foster children abroad? He is married to a Dutch woman, [thus] he is not, heart and soul, truly an Islamite! Why did he accomplish so little?"[563]

7. Madiun

Many observers had been surprised when, attacking the Republic in July 1947, the Dutch did not capture the heart of the state. This had been widely expected, and Sjahrir's departure on his world tour was sometimes described as "escape from Yogyakarta." To the chagrin of many among the Dutch, especially the military, Yogyakarta was not attacked either in July 1947 or in the months that followed. Such an attack, the Dutch prime minister explained early in August, would only make the Republic shift its resistance towards Sumatra and abroad.[564] Yogyakarta continued to function as the Republic's capital. The Javanese interior remained the center.

Connections between Sjahrir, on the world tour, and the center were extremely loose. There was the bitterness between Sjahrir and Amir, who was widely seen as deserting Sjahrir to become the new prime minister. Sjahrir's relationship to Sukarno and Hatta remained ambiguous.

In New Delhi, after he "escaped from Yogyakarta," Sjahrir told the press, we recall, that he had been "sent by the President." In New York, he was permitted to par-

---

[560] *Reuter*, December 25, 1947 and *Indonesian News Service*, December 24, 1947, in ibid.

[561] Director of the cabinet of van Mook to Commissie Generaal, December 23, 1947, ibid.

[562] Dutch consul general to the intelligence centre (Alg.Inlicht.Dienst) in Batavia, December 29, 1947 ibid.; also the consul general's "General Report," January 2, 1948, ibid.

[563] Report by consul general to Singapore, January 8, 1947, ibid.

[564] Minutes of the council of ministers, August 13, 1947 in *Officiële bescheiden*, 10: 382.

ticipate in the debate at the Security Council "pursuant a letter by President Soekarno."[565] The Dutch intercepted some messages from Sjahrir asking Yogyakarta for its "opinion" on various matters of his mission.[566] Nehru reserved part of Bombay's radio station for the Republic, to allow radio connections between the center and its representatives abroad.[567] But, by and large, van Mook seemed to be right, in August 1947, in believing that "Sjahrir and the Republican government knew about each other from reading newspaper reports."[568]

There were complaints in Yogyakarta that Sjahrir sometimes did not even let the center know where he was at any moment.[569] In mid-August, Hadji Agoes Salim, and, in another account of the same event, Sjahrir, too, while in New York, were requested by telegram to return to Yogyakarta; they disobeyed, checking—for three weeks!—whether or not the telegram was a fake.[570]

The US consul general on his visit to Yogyakarta in mid-August "inquired many times re status powers and duties" of both Sjahrir and Salim. The answer when it came was, in "Soekarno's exact words, 'Sjahrir is not accredited to anyone but is merely advocate of the Indonesian cause.'" The prime minister, Amir Sjarifoeddin, then let the American see the original of the instruction Sjahrir allegedly received in July 1947. By this instruction Sjahrir was empowered to "advocate our cause wherever possible to anybody who listens." As the American read the document, there was "no power [to] make arrangements or reach decisions."[571]

It was even beginning to appear like exile again. A special Indonesian issue of a prestigious Amsterdam journal *Criterium* appeared in 1947, and it caused a small literary sensation in Holland. The volume was edited by Tien Soebandrio and poet Moeljono; among the authors, all writing in or translated into Dutch, was Sjahrir (his letter from Banda Neira to a younger brother), Chairil Anwar, Moeljono, Rivai Apin, Soejitno Mangoenkoesoemo, Aki Djoehana, Beb Vuyk, and Ida Nasoetion; illustrations and layout were by painter Salim.[572]

Some of Sjahrir's followers still worked in the center. The *Christian Science Monitor* published a long article, early in October 1947, entitled *"Java Revolutionary: Portrait of a Press Chief."* It described the reporter's meeting with the ardent Sjahririan, Sudarpo, and with Sudarpo's wife Mien in Yogyakarta:

> Except for his deep brown skin and Asiatic features you might reasonably expect to find him as an instructor on an American campus. His pretty

---

[565] Van Kleffens to the minister of foreign affairs, August 18, 1947 in ibid., 10: 508.

[566] Sjahrir to Yogyakarta via Gani to the ministry of foreign affairs, October 8, 1947, ibid., 11: 269n.

[567] Interview with Idham, who represented the Republic in Pakistan, Jakarta, January 8, 1988.

[568] Van Mook to Jonkman, August 11, 1947 in *Officiële bescheiden*, 10: 331.

[569] Latuhary in minutes of the meeting of the Indonesian delegation, ibid., 12: 440.

[570] Schmidt to van der Goes, August 16, 1947 in *Collection Schermerhorn* no. 4 bundel Schmidt; Tobing, *Perdjuangan Politik Bangsa Indonesia: Linggadjati*, p. 190; Tobing dates this to October.

[571] US consul general to Batavia to the State Department in Washington, August 12, 1947 in *FRUS 1947* 6: 1022–23; similarly see van Mook to Jonkman, August 12, 1947, in *Officiële bescheiden*, 10: 362 on the US consul general informing van Mook about the matter.

[572] *Criterium*, August 1947; also Veenstra, "Schrijvende Indonesiërs," in *Oriëntatie*, November 22, 1947; D. de Vries, "Twee vaderlanden," *Oriëntatie* 5 (February 1948), p. 30; interview with M. A. Djoehana, Prague, August 16, 1983.

young wife, Mien, might pour at faculty teas. Darpo and Mien could talk intelligently in fluent English about Hemingway, Mozart, Ingrid Bergman or the Marshall Plan.[573]

The *Monitor*'s reporter suggested to Sudarpo that there perhaps might have been too much anti-Dutch propaganda by the Republic:

> Darpo admits it. But it comes from Jogjakarta, which is the boss. "The trouble with the boys down there is that they've no opportunity to contact the world, to get the feel of things."[574]

Sometimes it seemed as if everyone close to Sjahrir was moving abroad. Charles Tambu, we recall, and soon also Soedjatmoko, left Java, to accompany Sjahrir to New York; the two men remained in the US to staff the Republic's mission, even after Sjahrir left. Oetojo, and also Ali Algadri—a brother of Hamid Algadri and another of the young people close to Sjahrir from the early months of the Revolution—now worked in Singapore.[575] Dr. Soedarsono, the prewar Pendidikan leader and ever since a close associate of Sjahrir, became the chief of the Republic's mission in New Delhi, and from there he controlled the Indonesian offices in Rangoon, Bangkok, and also in Islamabad; in Pakistan, Idham, another of Sjahrir's followers and one of his relatives, was in charge.[576]

The looseness between Sjahrir and the center often appeared to be simply a problem of money. The Republic's missions were certainly inadequately funded from Yogyakarta; Sjahrir's men abroad often felt that they were getting "nihil." Some complained that facing foreigners and trying to work on their limited budgets, they were often "embarrassed."[577] At the same time, nationalist pride was demanded of them. As Soebandrio, for instance, wrote from London to Soedarsono in New Delhi on December 9, 1947,

> I am getting advice over and over, from the official side, and from the unofficial side, too, to depend on the strength of the Republic and not on help from the outside world, including the United Nations. It is admitted that this

---

[573] *Christian Science Monitor*, October 10, 1947. the copy is also in *Collection Meyer Ranneft* no. 496.

[574] Ibid.

[575] "Proces verbaal van verhoor van de ex-President Directeur der Staatsbank van de Indonesische Republiek Heer Margono Djojohadikoesoemo, in zake buitenlandsche actie en opium transacties der 'Republiek,' Djokjakarta 30 Maart 1948" in dossier "Margono Djojohadikoesoemo" *Archief Proc Gen*, no. 3-311, p. 10.

[576] Palar to Jonkman quoted in a communication from the Dutch ministry of foreign affairs to van Kleffens, August 14, 1947 in *Officiële bescheiden*, 10: 411–12, interview with A. B. Loebis, Jakarta, October 10, 1987, and interview with Idham, Jakarta, January 8, 1988; Soedarsono was mentioned by *Criterium*, August 1947 as "currently the charge d'affaires in New Delhi."

[577] Tobing, *Perdjuangan Politik Bangsa Indonesia: Linggadjati*, p. 60; interview with Soedjatmoko, Jakarta, November 6, 1987; interview with Idham, Jakarta, January 8, 1988; and interview with Sudarpo, Jakarta, October 7, 1987.

is tragic and unfair, but the world as it now exists is not yet made for fairness and honesty.[578]

Whenever he dealt with Yogyakarta from abroad, Sjahrir had now to work through A.K.Gani, who was Amir's deputy prime minister, minister of economic affairs, and acting minister of foreign affairs; Gani was assisted in foreign affair by Tamzil—one of the people who had accompanied Abdoelmadjid from Holland in 1945, and who since then had been a close ally of Abdoelmadjid, Setiadjit, and also Amir. All the Republic's missions abroad, and also Sjahrir personally, were dependent on Maramis, who was the new minister of finance. We may recall how Sjahrir had complained a short time before this about Gani and Maramis being forced upon his cabinet by Sukarno.[579]

Beneath the looseness between Sjahrir and Yogyakarta was clearly a deepening difference in policy. When the US consul general visited Yogyakarta, on August 12, 1947, besides finding out how vague Sjahrir's credentials were, he reported to Washington:

> After several hours with Soekarno and cabinet, he [Sukarno] asked member of staff if [he] could talk with me alone. We then went to another room and locked all doors. He then said, "I have been talking all day with American ConGen. Now I wish as younger man to talk as to my father. We are in terrible situation, having appealed to Security Council and adopted Australia's offer good offices. How can we get out and save our face?"[580]

Through another cable, on the same day, went additional information from the consul general:

---

[578] Soebandrio to Soedarsono, December 9, 1947 in *Collection Beel* no. 19.

[579] See above; Sjahrir's interview with George Kahin, April 19, 1949. Crucially important for funding the Republic's missions abroad was the "Banking and Trade Coy," a company in which Gani was heavily involved, and which was controlled by Margono Djojohadikoesoemo, a protégé of Vice-President Hatta, with Saroso, Margono's son in law, and Soemitro, Margono's son. On the "Banking and Trade Coy" see e.g. Margono Djojohadikoesoemo to Amir Sjarifoeddin, October 15, 1947 in dossier "Margono Djojohadikoesoemo" *Archief Proc Gen*, no. 3-311; memo by Saroso for the cabinet, October 14, 1947, ibid., no. 267; Dutch intelligence reports from Singapore no. 612 and 21, November 19, 1947 and January 17, 1948, ibid. Also X ambtenaar, "Indonesische Politiek," pp. 28–29; Dutch police report from Batavia, January 24, 1948 in *Collection Beel* no. 19. John Coast, who moved from Singapore and worked in the Republic's office in Bangkok, described the situation: "The Board which now headed our [i.e., Republic's] overseas political administration, seemed to work on an ill-balanced see-saw principle, while we tried to keep the Bangkok office as neatly balanced as possible. At one end of the plank, as we had foreseen, there was the acting Foreign Minister, Maramis, backed by Saroso, with the trump of Matty Fox and his finance up his sleeve. He offered to pay the Bangkok monthly budget; and we of course professed to accept. On the other end of the same plank sat Oetojo and Soedarsono and Zain, the first two like us [i.e., Coast and Zain], Sjahrir supporters, with certain vague funds in Singapore and Penang." Coast, *Recruit to Revolution*, p. 250. As for the "vague funds in Singapore," Minangkabau-based companies might have provided a substantial part of them.

[580] US consul general in Batavia to the State Department, August 12, 1947, FRUS 1947 6: 1024.

During secret conversation Soekarno openly stated preference for US offer good offices but said did not know how to get out of present situation—appeal to Security Council and acceptance of Australia's offer good offices.[581]

While Sjahrir was so strikingly uncertain and clearly hesitant to accept the growing US involvement in Indonesia, Sukarno and Yogyakarta seemed to be pushing vehemently and effectively toward this very American solution. Sjahrir, evidently, still thought in terms of his broader world—the good Dutch, Britain as the extension of the good Dutch, British dominions as a further projection of this. While Sjahrir traveled around—touching upon London, Paris, Cairo, New Delhi, Singapore, Canberra, feeling increasingly disconnected with everything at home and abroad—another solution was being worked out between Yogyakarta and The Hague: a compromise and possibly a new agreement under the auspices of the United Nations, as suggested, initiated, pushed ahead, and overseen by the United States.

On October 8, 1947, a delegation of the Republic of Indonesia was appointed for a new round of negotiations. Amir Sjarifoeddin, the prime minister, was the chairman; Iskaq Tjokroadisoerjo, a long-time associate of Sukarno, was the secretary; Ali Sastroamidjojo, Hadji Agoes Salim, Tjoa Sek Ien (to represent the Chinese minority), Dr. Djoeanda, and Sjahrir, in this order, were listed as the delegation's members.[582] Sjahrir, reportedly, had requested that Ali Boediardjo and Sudarpo also be appointed, but this "was rejected by Jogjakarta."[583] According to another report from Yogyakarta, it had not even been easy to get Sjahrir on the delegation.[584]

The conference of Dutch and Indonesian delegations under UN supervision was expected to start in December 1947. On December 8, The *Singapore Free Press*, reporting on Sjahrir's trip from Singapore to Australia, wrote:

> He had delayed his departure for Australia because it was thought his presence might be required at the U.N. "good offices" commission talks which begin today on board of the US freighter Renville in neutral waters off Java.
>
> Official Indonesian source in Singapore stated that Mr. Sharir [sic] was originally included in the Indonesian delegation. However uncertainty regarding the date of the talks and of Mr. Sharir's itinerary made it necessary to reorganize the delegation. It is unlikely, it was said, that further changes will be made in order to include the former premier.[585]

Sjahrir, indeed, was still outside the country, when the talks on the USS *Renville* got on track. He still remained away as the negotiations began clearly to move towards a new agreement. P. J. Schmidt, still in New York, on December 23, 1947,

---

[581] Ibid., p. 1025.

[582] There were, besides, fifteen advisers, not mentioned by name, *Aneta-Antara*, October 8, 1947. On Sjahrir's predictions about the delegation see Sjahrir to Joekes and Logeman, September 29, 1947 in "Inlichtingen Sjahrir" in *Archief Buiten. Zaken* V.R.III-910. Tobing, *Perdjuangan Politik Bangsa Indonesia: Linggadjati*, pp. 186–87 lists M. Roem as a member and Sjahrir as an adviser.

[583] See Political report on the period October 24 to 31, 1947 in *Officiële bescheiden*, 11: 483–84.

[584] Letter to Saroso from his wife, October 9, 1947 in *Archief Proc Gen*, no. 267.

[585] *Singapore Free Press*, December 8, 1947 in "Inlichtingen Sjahrir" in *Archief Buiten. Zaken* V.R.III-910.

wrote to Schermerhorn about this matter: "Sjahrir appears yet another step further away from the leadership."[586]

In the second week of January 1948, the Renville negotiations already appeared to be entering their final stage. Sjahrir, at last, arrived by plane from Singapore to Jakarta, on January 9, and, on January 13, on USS *Renville* he attended what was to be one of the conference's last sessions. According to the official record, Sjahrir remained silent throughout.[587]

On January 19, the Renville agreement was signed. The Republic's territory, for the interim period till a final solution was reached, was to be even more restricted than by the Linggadjati agreement: only Central Java, and the western extremity of the island—Bantam, were left to the Republic. A plebiscite was to be organized deciding the future of the territories newly acquired by the Dutch through the military action. No notice was taken of the Republic's demands that its right to exercise fully its own foreign relations, during the interim period, be respected. This was a painful concession by the Republic. Yet, the Republic was not destroyed as had been the initial Dutch aim. The Dutch prime minister explained why the agreement was signed: the Dutch, he said, could not afford to "antagonize America."[588]

In a sense, this was a repetition of what had happened during and after the Linggadjati negotiations. As through the Linggadjati agreement, through the Renville agreement Sukarno and Hatta gained as symbols of Indonesian independence and unity. Yogyakarta survived; the heart of the Republic kept beating. This again was the center's gain. As after the Linggadjati agreement, also, another personage away from the center was identified with the agreement—then Prime Minister Sjahrir, now Prime Minister Amir—who was to be held directly responsible if anything went wrong or looked wrong.

Amir's downfall, indeed, came even faster than Sjahrir's six months earlier. Instantly, Amir was accused—again by the Masjumi especially and then by the Indonesian National Party—of going too far to meet the foreigners. Merely four days after the Renville agreement was signed, on January 23, 1948, Amir Sjarifoeddin and his whole cabinet resigned. A new cabinet was formed and its composition announced on January 29. Hatta while keeping his office of vice-president, became the prime minister.[589]

There seemed to be less of an escape for Amir, now, than for Sjahrir after the Linggadjati agreement; and there was more humiliation. A few days after Amir resigned, in early February, Hatta took Amir with other Republican dignitaries on a tour through the provinces. Amir was expected to explain the Renville agreement. At a mass rally in Bukittinggi, West Sumatra, in Hatta's birthplace and at what evidently was arranged as the most important stop of the tour, Hatta spoke about the perseverance of the Republic, and his speech was very warmly received. Then Amir took the stage, and as Hatta described it later,

---

[586] Schmidt to Schermerhorn, December 23, 1947 in *Collection Schermerhorn* no. 35 bundel Schmidt.

[587] For the United Nations commission minutes of the meetings see McMahon, *Colonialism*, p. 204, n. 100. Dutch report dated January 17, 1948 is in *Archief Proc Gen*, no. 267.

[588] Statement by prime minister Drees during a meeting with van Mook, Spoor, and others, December 31, 1947 in *Officiële bescheiden*, 12: 361.

[589] Kahin, *Nationalism and Revolution*, p. 232.

He seemed so confused as if he hardly knew what to say. He felt that the people of Bukittinggi were not happy with him especially in the light of the agreement with the Dutch. When he relinquished the podium hardly anyone applauded.[590]

According to another participant in the same event, the "face of Amir Sjarifoeddin looked like that of a lost man."[591]

Sjahrir was also invited to this Bukittinggi rally; he came from Singapore, and gave a speech. According to Leon Salim—an old cadre of the prewar Pendidikan and still a member of Sjahrir's party—Sjahrir also "looked tired and rarely smiled."[592] In the words of another witness, it was "as if there was something 'frozen' in Sjahrir's face," and when his turn came to address the rally, "he merely raised his hand in the *Merdeka* salute and stepped back."[593] Hatta wrote later laconically about Sjahrir, too: "his speech was short."[594]

Then these two men embarked on essentially the same paths they had traveled before. Amir, immediately returned from Bukittinggi to Yogyakarta with Hatta and the rest of the Republican party. Sjahrir remained a little longer, till February 27. Then, Lord Killearn, on his way from Ceylon, took Sjahrir on his plane and they flew back again to Singapore.[595]

Sjahrir was still rumored as a possible member, "among others," of a newly planned Indonesian-Dutch Executive Council, a body supposed to supervise Indonesian-Dutch relations in the interim period after the Renville agreement, and before sovereignty was transferred to Indonesia.[596] There were also reports, late in January, that he might still become a member of Hatta's new cabinet.[597] Neither possibility materialized, however, and Sjahrir remained in Singapore.[598] It was not until April 16, 1948, that he finally arrived in Jakarta, still leaving his secretary, Poppy Saleh, and his Bandanese children behind.[599]

---

[590] Hatta, *Indonesian Patriot*, p. 277.

[591] Hamka, *Kenang-kenangan Hidup*, p. 380.

[592] Salim, ed., *Bung Sjahrir*, p. 36.

[593] Hamka, *Kenang-kenangan Hidup*.

[594] Hatta, *Indonesian Patriot*, p. 277.

[595] Dutch consul general in Singapore to the minister of foreign affairs, March 12, 1948 in dossier "Sjahrir," *Archief Proc Gen*, no. 3-262; also police report from Singapore for second half February 1948, ibid. Also Sjahrir as interviewed by Singapore press, March 1, 1948, ibid.

[596] Dutch intelligence report from Singapore no. 21, January 17, 1948 in *Archief Proc Gen*, no. 267.

[597] Van Mook to Jonkman January 27. 1948 in *Officiële bescheiden*, 12: 640.

[598] Throughout January, Sjahrir was preparing, so it was suggested, for a mission—which also never occurred—to China. Correspondence between the ministry of foreign affairs in The Hague and the Dutch embassy in Chungking-Nanking relevant to Sjahrir's planned trip, is in files dated January 3, 21, and 29, "Ambassade Chungking-Nanking," *Archief Buiten. Zaken*, w34 1948 doos 52; also *Archief Alg Secr, 2de zending*, no. 1030; also consul general in Singapore to The Hague January 15, 1948 in "Ambassade Parijs," *Archief Buiten. Zaken*. file GAA4A, blok I 1945–1951, doos 2.

[599] Ibid. Also Neher memo, May 9, 1948 in *Archief Alg Secr, 2de zending*, no. 1082. Sjahrir arrived in Singapore from Bukittinggi on February 28. He suggested he would merely stop in Singapore for a "a week" or "ten days," "to handle some private affairs... before departing for Jogjakarta for talks with the Republican government." *Dagblad*, March 11, 1948 in dossier "Sjahrir," *Archief Proc Gen*, no. 3-262. According to other reports, in a few days Sjahrir would

"For a long time, since Renville," wrote Hatta, "Sjahrir had not wanted to be included in delegations negotiating with the Dutch."[600] Mohammad Natsir, an Islamic politician of the Masjumi, but friendly and politically close to Sjahrir, recalled:

> he seemed to withdraw from government, as if he were an onlooker. When I asked him to play a more significant role in government, Sjahrir's reply was: "Do it yourself!"[601]

On February 12—or, according to another account, the day before—"about ten men" met in Yogyakarta, in the house of the mother of two of Sjahrir's followers, Subadio and Sudarpo Sastrosatomo. According to Dr. Halim, who was also present at the meeting, Subadio, Soepeno, Djohan Sjahroezah, Soegondo Djojopoespito, and Tedjasoekmana were the principal participants. As the discussion got under way, Dr. Halim recalled,

> A problem arose, what about Sjahrir who, at the time was in Bukittinggi? Should we not wait till we hear from him, before we proclaim the birth of a new party, as he is expected to become its chairman? . . . I have to admit that I took a very active part in the discussion, arguing that it was not necessary to wait for news from Soetan Sjahrir.
>
> Djohan Sjahroezah, who was a man with a very gentle temperament, wondered what would happen if Sjahrir did not agree with this step we were taking? To this I responded that I was confident that Sjahrir would agree and that also, we would present Sjahrir with a *fait accompli* [*mangafait akomplikan Sjahrir*].
>
> As far as I remember, several of those present, among them Subadio, supported my view and thus the *Partai Sosialis Indonesia*, PSI, "Indonesian Socialist Party," was born in Kliteran, Yogyakarta, with its chairman being in Bukittinggi at the time.[602]

In this way, or a similar one, the Socialist Party of Sjahrir and Amir—as it had been established amidst the revolution in December 1945, and as it lasted through the time of increasing tensions and animosity between its two leaders—eventually broke apart. Sjahrir's group, the men who met in the Sastrosatomo house in Kliteran, declared its secession on February 12, 1948. Amir's group kept the party's old name.

Practically all the followers of the prewar Pendidikan, and most of the young people who came close to Sjahrir during the Japanese occupation, now joined Sjahrir's new Socialist Party of Indonesia. Amir and his Socialist Party kept a large part of the members of the prewar Gerindo, and also most of the left-wing socialists and Communists who had returned from Holland after the war.

---

return to Yogyakarta to serve as Hatta's adviser on foreign policy matters; he had just come to pick up the children. Ibid., also Neher to Beel and Jonkman, February 2, 1948, in *Officiële bescheiden*, 12: 684. One week later, Sjahrir was still in Singapore, and, reportedly, "not willing to go to Jogjakarta until he was assured of getting a position of some power there." Police report from Singapore for first half of March 1948 in *Archief of Proc. Gen.* no. 3-262.

[600] Hatta, *Bung Hatta Antwoordt*, p. 35 quoted in Rose, *Indonesia Free*, p. 157.

[601] Interview with Natsir in 1983 in Rose, *Indonesia Free*, p. 185n.

[602] Halim, "Sjahrir," p. 110.

Ali Sastroamidjojo (we may recall he worked as a bridge between Amir Sjarifoeddin and Sukarno during the whole previous period) described what happened during the next half a year basically in terms of Amir's moral destruction:

> Amir Sjarifoeddin's attitude, which had been such a friendly one to me from the time of the *Partai Nasional Indonesia, Partindo* and *Gerindo*, changed completely. He became hostile and did not want to talk to me. His wife, who was a very close friend of my wife, often came to our house in Jogjakarta, complaining about the complete change in her husband's behavior. He was often angry with her and had even threatened to beat her. This was very strange, because all the time my wife and I had known him, Amir had always given us the impression of being a loving family man."[603]

On August 1, 1948, Soeripno returned to Yogyakarta from a mission for the Republic abroad. He brought with him certain Muso Manowar, a man who was part of the prewar executive of the Indonesian Communist Party, a leader of the failed Communist uprisings in 1926 and 1927, who had lived in exile in Moscow since. In a matter of days, joined quickly by many, Abdoelmadjid and Setiadjid among them, Muso rose to the leadership of Amir Sjarifoeddin's wing of the Indonesian socialist movement.

On September 1, 1948, Amir—clearly losing the ground under his feet rather than gaining by Muso's arrival—declared that he "had been in fact a member of the Indonesian Communist Party" for many years and since before the war; he also "said that the *Gerindo*, which he had led before the war, in reality was nothing else but the Indonesian Communist Party."[604]

By mid-September 1948, tensions between the left front, led by Muso with Amir, and the government of Sukarno-Hatta, had grown into armed clashes. On September 18, a few pro-Muso units seized the telephone exchange and other strategic points in the provincial town of Madiun, in East Java.

Sukarno acted instantly; he went on the radio and declared that the nation was threatened by a Communist coup. Sukarno asked the people to make a choice between Muso versus himself and Hatta. Muso—either because he had been abroad so long and knew so little about the situation, or out of despair—accepted the challenge, and called on the people to rise against the "Japanese quislings" Sukarno and Hatta.

The people did not rise and, after a few days of military action, the main body of the pro-Muso forces retreated to the mountains. On September 30, government troops retook the town of Madiun, and on October 31 Muso himself was killed. Amir Sjarifoeddin became an outcast. He was hunted down, and arrested finally, together with Soeripno, at the end of November.[605]

---

[603] Ali Sastroamijoyo, *Milestones on my Journey*, p. 162; on the change in Amir see also Simatupang, *Report from Banaran*, pp. 78-79.

[604] *Nieuwsgier*, September 1, 1948.

[605] Amir Sjarifoeddin and with him Soeripno were captured on November 29. When the Dutch attacked the Republic three weeks later for the second time, the military governor of Surakarta, Gatot Subroto, ordered Amir and other leaders of the left imprisoned with him to be shot. They were executed on December 19, 1948. Wellem, *Amir Sjarifoeddin*, pp. 163, 244, 246-47.

Sjahrir's "Political Guidelines," written at the moment of the split between Sjahrir's and Amir's factions, in February 1948, contained little to support the argument that the split had occurred simply because Amir had inclined towards the Soviets and towards the Soviet way of communism. Rather, the split was explained by another statement from Sjahrir on the importance of maintaining a distance, in general and in principle. As far as world affairs were concerned, according to Sjahrir,

> America became the center of world international capital, the center of the power of capitalism. In this it is opposed by socialism in the Soviet Union and Eastern Europe, which still stands upright in spite of the damage and loss it suffered through the great war.... The international capital of England (however much it also suffered) is still strong enough to survive and to recover in new forms.... All the efforts of the movement for independence and democracy in Asia ... must be made into an autonomous factor ... free from influence of the capitalism of the United States and also from the politics of the Soviet bloc.[606]

In an interview given two days after the split, Sjahrir objected to a reporter trying to put into his mouth terms such as "Russian totalitarian socialism" and "American democratic capitalism." As Sjahrir said, "to use them would mean to stand on the side of one of the parties."[607]

In another text by Sjahrir, written for members of his new party in March 1948, "Political Conditions in Indonesia," Amir's alleged or real turn towards communism was again not the most prominent issue. Sjahrir rather emphasized that in Amir's movement, there was a lack of organization and lack of understanding of the real nature of socialism.[608] As Sjahrir saw it, there were in Indonesia at the time "only one or two labor leaders, who knew anything of socialism." In Amir's movement, and generally in the Indonesian "Communist" movement,

> There is hardly any connection with Marxism and Leninism which is based on the interpretation of political realities and on an analysis through a dialectic materialistic approach....[609]

---

[606] It is contained in "Manifesto PSI, February 1948" reprinted in "Partai Sosialis Indonesia" in *Sedjarah Singkat di Kepartaian di Indonesia*, pp. 168–72; also in Sjahrir, *Indonesian Socialism*, pp. 40f, from where the translation is taken. Some from Sjahrir's circle might see Amir's tragedy, at least in part, as a result of his overdue dependence on the United States. Simatupang, for instance, who was a friend of both Amir and Sjahrir, related to me how he, years later, told Frank Graham, the US representative at the Renville meetings: "You left Amir up in the air; it was your doing what happened to him"; at which Frank Graham, according to Simatupang, had acknowledged some guilty feelings and that his tactics had failed. Interview with Simatupang, Jakarta, January 4, 1987. The point of Amir Sjarifoeddin believing strongly in US help at the time is also stressed by Amir's recent Indonesian biography. In particular, Amir's speech to the people and government of America of July 6, 1947, thus immediately after Amir formed his government, is quoted to this effect. See Wellem, *Amir Sjarifoeddin*, p. 200.

[607] *Sikap Kita*, February 14, 1948.

[608] Sjahrir, "Political Conditions," p. 14.

[609] Ibid., p. 22.

Amir Sjarifoeddin, Sjahrir wrote in the same text "has not a high level of political understanding, particularly as regards socialism and true marxism."[610] The Communist Party in Indonesia, also,

> is not a party of the calibre of the communist parties in other countries where membership is invariably comprised of convinced socialists who are consistent and orthodox in applying Marxist theory and who have an understanding of genuine dialectic materialism.... The Indonesian Communist Party has no real Marxist policy, it has not yet even achieved a socialist policy.[611]

What was truly wrong with Amir, according to Sjahrir, was that he was not able to keep a distance from the "big powers" outside Indonesia—this meant the United States as well as the Soviet Union, and from the mainstream nationalism inside Indonesia. The latter Sjahrir now defined as "nationalism of *gotong rojong* [mutual help]."

What Amir's "socialists" were proclaiming as their truth, according to Sjahrir, was a "sterile demagogy," and a "nationalist demagoguery."[612] What this movement presented as their "idea of Socialism," wrote Sjahrir,

> would accordingly be more correct to assess ... as a spirit of patriotism, anti-imperialism, and attachment to gotong-rojong.[613]

Gotong-rojong was a traditional Javanese concept, and increasingly in vogue, in 1948, as a concept of the new national unity. The Pendidikan before the war, we recall, rather carefully avoided *gotong-rojong*, and used instead a Malay or Sumatran term and concept of *sama rata, sama rasa*, which they also frequently translated as "democracy" or "equality." As to the Pendidikan in the early 1930s, to Sjahrir now, it seemed, *gotong royong* meant a concept of unity under Sukarno.

Sjahrir, in "Political Conditions in Indonesia," made it clear how important, and adverse, he considered the concept of *gotong royong* to be. It was to him, clearly, the crux of the ideology of the contemporary political fortress of the Republic, of the nationalist mainstream; "Communists" to him were, or were on the verge of becoming, part of the *gotong rojong* mainstream:

> all from the Masjumi to the group calling itself the Communist Party [are] putting forward an anti-imperialist and anti-capitalist stand and advocating adherence to the practice of gotong rojong.[614]
>
> The doctrines propagated by Soekarno are really no more than ultra-nationalism and what is termed socialism by the disciples of Soekarno is no more than anti-imperialism and attachment to gotong rojong.[615]

---

[610] Ibid., p. 21.
[611] Ibid., p. 27.
[612] Ibid., pp. 9, 11ff.
[613] Ibid., p. 28.
[614] Ibid., p. 5.
[615] Ibid., p. 21.

As if to make it absolutely clear that he was writing also about Amir, and about the split, Sjahrir described Amir on the same page of this text as "ex-*Gerindo*," and he elaborated on this: "those from the *Gerindo* [have] the characteristics of the pupils of Soekarno."[616]

Through the months after the split with Amir, Sjahrir and Sjahrir's associates warned repeatedly that it was "not yet" time for a deliberate sharpening of class struggle in Indonesia, and that "policies of class struggle should be consciously avoided."[617] Rather than social-democratic moderation against Communist radicalism, this seemed much more to be a restating of Sjahrir's old credo again: to keep a distance from the fortress, from the center, from *gotong rojong*. As it was formulated in the *Manifesto* of Sjahrir's new party in February 1948: "the danger of a clash of groups and ranks should be evaded [*mendjauhkan*]."[618]

Nationalism, Sjahrir wrote in late summer 1948, as the tensions in the internal politics of the Republic grew, was "rooted in irrational regions of the soul." At the same time, however, Sjahrir accepted that nationalism still dominated this world, and to think otherwise would be "utopia or illusion."[619]

> If the socialists attempted to impose their leadership on the Republic at the present stage, the result would be division and disruption in the struggle, or alternatively a moderation of socialist strategy to a point corresponding to the strategy of the nationalists and democrats.... Such action would also subsequently commit the socialists to a preparedness to join in a campaign against the Communists such as that now being waged in India and Burma.... The PSI [Sjahrir's Socialist Party of Indonesia], not only in the desire to align with the international left-wing stand, but also on the basis of its own analysis of the political situation in Indonesia, has proposed that Indonesian socialists should be leaving responsibility of government to the nationalists and democrats, avoid any obligation to compromise.... In the immediate future the nationalists and democrats in the Republic, with the leadership of Soekarno and Hatta will for the time being, maintain a controlling position in the state....[620]

Sjahrir warned against a "sharp struggle," a "real showdown." This, according to Sjahrir, "could only lead to a defeat [of the socialists] and a consolidation of the power of the nationalists and democrats." Speaking of decisive action, in the same breath Sjahrir spoke of danger. If one let himself be provoked into action, Sjahrir prophesied," he would be "devoured."[621]

---

[616] Ibid., pp. 21, 20. Also when explaining the split in the Socialist Party to George Kahin, in an interview a few weeks later, in July 1948, Sjahrir said the split went as far back as before the war, when he and Amir had been "in different parties"—"Amir with a succession of short-lived parties in which Soekarno was usually a leading member." Sjahrir interview with George Kahin, July 27, 1948.

[617] "Manifesto PSI, February 1948" and Sjahrir, "Political Conditions," pp. 2–5, 14, 17.

[618] "Manifesto PSI, February 1948."

[619] Ibid.

[620] Sjahrir, "Political Conditions," pp. 32, 34.

[621] Ibid., p. 34, Sjahrir in *Aneta* reprinted by *Nieuwsgier*, June 11, 1948; see also Sjahrir, *Indonesian Socialism*, p. 40.

At the moment of its formation, Sjahrir's group declared its support for Hatta's cabinet. In fact, however, it let only one of its members, Soepeno, sit in the cabinet, and then only as a minister without portfolio.[622] This was the strategy for the party as Sjahrir stated it very clearly in his guidelines of March:

> accepting no position of governmental responsibility in this present phase of retreat and decline, concentrating [the party's] energies on the building of the movement and the strengthening of the struggle for a future revolutionary phase. In this way it is hoped that the socialists would be recognized by the masses as not being responsible for the future compromises which must inevitably take place in this present period of retreat. . . .[623]

Sjahrir, as noted, returned to Java from Singapore on April 16. He spent a few days in Jakarta, putting his house in order after more than eight months abroad, and then moved to Yogyakarta. He accepted a suggestion that he reside, as he was still an "adviser to the president," in Sukarno's palace in Yogyakarta. Sjahrir was somewhat idle in the months which followed. One is also reminded of one of his letters from exile, when he said he tried to be superficial to evade brooding.

John Coast, who arrived in Indonesia from Singapore and Bangkok also late in 1948, described how he went to visit Sjahrir in Yogyakarta, to meet him, actually, for the first time face to face:

> At the far end of Malioboro [street], a low white wall guarded by TNI [Indonesian National Army] sentries flanked the grounds of Soekarno's residence. It was a fair-sized white marble building approached up an arch shaped drive, ornamented with ancient Buddhistic monuments from Central Java's pre-Moslem era. Our car drove past a guard room, round to the palace's right flank, and there as [our guide] knocked on the two white swing doors of a high-ceilinged room, I prepared to meet the man who had so long had my remote admiration and sympathy.[624]

John Coast came, so he said, in the hope of finding, in revolutionary Java, what Dorothy Woodman suggested, might be "a state of utter youth and complete freedom." After a few weeks of working for the Republic in Yogyakarta, Coast found, "there was something bizarre in my partisanship."[625] The exoticism and the image of the Asian revolution, as conceived in London, did not work. But did not Sjahrir feel at least in part like this? John Coast, experiencing the Revolution in Yogyakarta, was "saddened" by what he described as the style of the revolutionary youth. Young men sitting in "steaming offices wearing a suit with collar and tie," young women in

> very short skirts, which showed for the first time the unfortunate broadness of the Javanese female knees . . . costumes, which had the effect of making

---

[622] "PSI van Soetan Sjahrir" Recomba Report West Java in *Archief Proc Gen*, no. 5-526. See also Sjahrir, *Indonesian Socialism*, pp. 40, 44.

[623] Sjahrir, "Political Conditions," pp. 32–34.

[624] Coast, *Recruit to Revolution*, p. 89.

[625] Ibid., p. 98.

this already youthful looking people appear as overgrown children on the Dutch model.[626]

Abu Hanifah of the Masjumi and, we recall, never an ally of Sjahrir, remembered that he at this time saw Sjahrir often. Sjahrir was, Abu Hanifah wrote, "only an adviser of the President":

> I still kept visiting Sjahrir in his rooms at the palace, and had lunch with him.... We had many things in common. He was well read, was interested in culture, literature, and his theories about Marxism were interesting because he tried to adjust them to the Indonesian way of life. I was pessimistic about the practicability of his theories, but our debates always ended in friendly joking and gossiping about other leaders.[627]

Sjahrir was also being gossiped about. Through the mid and later part of 1948, people talked, and there were even some newspaper reports, about Sjahrir's alleged romance with Siti Nurul, princess of the royal palace in Surakarta.[628] At the same time, on August 12, 1948, Sjahrir divorced Maria.[629]

Early in June 1948, Hatta planned to reform his cabinet. Sjahrir let it be publicly known that he and his party "would accept no seat."[630] Both he and the PSI, Sjahrir added, would have "no dealings" with the national program newly accepted by Hatta's cabinet. According to what Sjahrir told reporters on that occasion,

> It is part of the principles of the party that unity of the Republic has to be respected before anything else. The PSI cares about this so much that it has offered no proposal of its own for the new program, that it has kept itself absent from the committees preparing the program, and that it is little interested in taking or not taking part in the new cabinet.[631]

This was "shocking," wrote a Jakarta paper, which was usually critical of Yogyakarta politics, but sympathetic to Sjahrir. After printing the above quoted remarks of Sjahrir, the paper commented:

> We knew that in the narrow-minded sphere of Jogjakarta politics, under the pressure of circumstances, some disintegration was going on. That this would go so far, that a political party would sacrifice its whole program rather than cause a friction with its opponent, is heard of rarely in the

---

[626] Ibid., p. 96.

[627] Abu Hanifah, *Tales of a Revolution*, p. 298.

[628] Interviews in Jakarta 1987–1988, also *Merdeka*, December 4, 1948 in dossier "Sjahrir" in *Archief Proc Gen*, no. 3-262.

[629] On September 1, in Greenwich, New York, Maria married again—to Sjahrir's younger brother Sjahsam. See for documents, Dutch ambassador in Belgium to the ministry of foreign affairs, November 26, 1948 in *Archief Alg Secr, lste zending*, no. VI-17-17; there also are documents filed with the ministry of justice, February 15, 1949, ibid.

[630] *Nieuwsgier*, June 11, 1948.

[631] Ibid.

history of democracy. For such an enfeebling [*ontkrachting*] of a political life one can use only one term—"decomposition [*ontbinding*]."[632]

Ali Boediardjo—who knew both Sjahrir and Amir well—described the two men's political differences in terms of temperament. Amir Sjarifoeddin, Ali said, was prone to live more in the middle of crowds, had a "weakness for them," believed he might act to draw politicians and the people into a warm companionship. Sjahrir, on the other hand, Ali said, was more "a realist."[633]

Sjahrir and his followers, describing their split with Amir, used such words for their move as "seceded," "withdrew," or "loosened [our]selves."[634] In his March 1948 guidelines, Sjahrir wrote that, as his new party was initiated by "the former members of *Pendidikan*," once it had loosened itself from Amir, it could again be true to its cadre tradition.[635] In June 1948, Sjahrir repeated this:

> We do not strive for a [mass] broadening of our party, because this would inevitably cause a sharpening of a party struggle.[636]

As in the 1930s, during the Japanese occupation and in the early Revolution, Sjahrir assumed that detachment from actual politics would maintain purity and power. Amir had every reason to be biased, at the moment of the split, but he, actually, had been referring to the same thing: "only intellectuals joined Sjahrir, I have the masses."[637]

Some people watching Sjahrir and the PSI from a short distance, during mid and late 1948, even though sympathetic to Sjahrir, were perturbed. John Coast, sitting in Yogyakarta, and working for Sjahrir, certainly felt this way:

> Just at this time the Socialist Party of Sjahrir and Sjarifoeddin also split. Sjahrir, nominally the special adviser of the President, henceforth retired to his private eyrie, where only the independently minded and a few faithful adherents followed him, while Sjarifoeddin [took] the bulk of the Socialists with him."[638]

Another observer at the time called Sjahrir "a politician on vacation," and used for Sjahrir's movement—for the first time, as far as we know—the term "clique."[639]

---

[632] Ibid.

[633] Schermerhorn, *Het dagboek*, July 8, 1947 (2: 740).

[634] Sjahrir, *Indonesian Socialism*, p. 40; Halim, "Sjahrir," p. 110.

[635] Sjahrir, "Political Conditions," pp. 22, 20.

[636] *Nieuwsgier*, June 11, 1948.

[637] Amir interviewed in Yogyakarta, February 20, 1948 quoted in Arnold Brackman, *Indonesian Communism: A History* (New York: Praeger, 1963), p. 71. Of forty-seven members of the original Socialist Party executive, twenty-three joined the PSI, twenty remained with Amir, and four left altogether. Of the thirty-five original Socialist Party members of the KNIP, eighteen went with Sjahrir, sixteen with Amir, and two left. No official party membership report on the split was published until the early 1950s; see "Laporan Organisasi Partai. I Kongres PSI" in *Suara Sosialis* 4, 2 (April 1952).

[638] Coast, *Recruit to Revolution*, p. 61.

[639] Anoniem, "Sjahrir: De Politicus 'Met Vakantie'," July 17, 1948, *Archief Alg Secr, Iste zending*, No. XXXI-3.

8. The End of Revolution

When the fighting around Madiun erupted, Sjahrir might have felt justified in his warnings: "devoured," indeed, was a term that well described Amir's defeat.

Sjahrir talked about the Madiun affair to George Kahin on September 30, 1948, as the fighting was still in progress. In that interview, Sjahrir did not talk about Amir as about a danger to the established order. Rather, he emphasized Amir's inability to resist being tempted: Sjahrir said that Amir had "unstable political and philosophical and religious moorings"; he repeated a story about Dutch pastor Schepper converting Amir to Christianity when Amir was in the Dutch prison before the war; he described also how Amir "panicked" when Muso came to Java.

Amir Sjarifoeddin, according to Sjahrir,

> has long been a convinced Socialist, but he was undoubtedly pushed into the self-assumed role of a Communist by the dictates of expediency and general political opportunism.[640]

As Sjahrir put it in another interview at the same time, Amir Sjarifoeddin, as he joined Muso, and as the Madiun affair evolved, was *opgegaan*, "wrapped up in, lost in it."[641]

Those who "devoured" Amir, who "wrapped him in," Sjahrir argued, might call themselves Communists, but "with the exception of Moeso," and "probably" Soeripno and Tan Ling Djie, they were "political opportunists as well as being primarily nationalists."[642] "They," Sjahrir said, for instance, in November 1948,

> were able to exploit the feudalistic heritage of the people building a powerful party organized along totalitarian lines. The Communist leaders themselves exemplified the effects of the heritage on leaders. Most of them came from feudal families and are of high feudal position. Ingrained in them is a paternalistic authoritarianism paralleled by the attitude as old feudal leaders towards their subjects.[643]

There were the most varied explanations as to why and how the Madiun affair had occurred. A dominant thesis at the time was of a Moscow-inspired coup d'état. There was an almost equally influential thesis of the "Trotskyite provocation," a thesis inspired by the fact that Tan Malaka, "the Trotskyite," was released from prison by presidential amnesty just days before the Madiun affair, and that he indeed actively campaigned against Muso.[644] There were other more or less wild rumors of other alleged designs and conspiracies.[645]

---

[640] Sjahrir's interview with George Kahin, September 30, 1948.

[641] Sjahrir to Associated Press quoted in *Nieuwsgier*, September 2, 1948.

[642] Sjahrir's interviews with George Kahin, September 30, and November 21, 1948.

[643] Sjahrir's interview with George Kahin, November 21, 1948. The fact that Sjahrir rejected the term "Russian totalitarian socialism" strongly suggests that he evidently, still at this time, connected totalitarianism predominantly with the (Indonesian) feudal heritage.

[644] Sukarno's announcement, on August 17, 1948, thus just a few days before the conflict broke out, that he would pardon Tan Malaka and his followers still in prison, was widely discussed. The strong animosity between some people around Amir and some people around Tan Malaka was well known. The group was released, indeed, on September 16, only hours before the affair began. In March 1948, for instance, Hatta reportedly expressed his hope that

Sjahrir naturally tried to make sense of the Madiun affair in terms of his structure of experience. Thus, the topography of the Madiun affair as he presented it, was very familiar. In an interview he gave a day after Muso had called on the people to rise, Sjahrir said:

> in a few days, it will become clear how the situation will develop . . . there is a possibility of a complete civil war . . . in which case the regions east of Madioen would be cut off from the central government.[646]

Sjahrir located the causes of the affair clearly and squarely in central Java, and specifically Yogyakarta. When asked, on September 21, 1948, about the causes of the Madiun affair, Sjahrir answered:

---

the Indonesian Communists would not join in the new Soviet aggressive campaign in the Cold War, and the reason he gave for the hope was existence of "the group of Jamin-Tan Malaka, which is popular for instance in the circles of former Perhimpoenan Peladjar-Peladjar Indonesia (PPPI) and in Padang." Dutch police report from Batavia, March 7–13, 1948 stating as its source a personal communication from Hatta. In *Archief Proc Gen*, no. 3-297. (PPPI, of course, before the war was a group with which Djohan Sjahroezah was also connected.) On the amnesty see *Aneta*, August 28, 1948 in the dossier on the July 3 Affair, *Archief Proc Gen*, no. 1-33 and Malik, *Mengabdi Republik* 2: 201–2.

[645] There were rumors of Sjahrir's followers "infiltrating the Indonesian Communist Party before the Madiun affair" with encouragement of British Secret Intelligence. *NEFIS* file in *Archief Proc Gen*, no. 661 also the Dutch Central Military Intelligence Report (CMID), October 18, 1948 in *Archief Alg Secr, lste zending*, no. XIV-5-81; also secret report by "X" in *Archief Proc Gen*, no. 231. Similarly, a conspiracy was rumored between Sjahrir and the Communists in Java, and also in West Sumatra and Singapore. Report by the Dutch consul general in Singapore, October 9, 1948 in *Archief Alg Secr, lste zending*, no. VII- 5-7. Other rumors, contradicting these, suggested a conspiracy, between followers of Sjahrir and Tan Malaka in Java (Secret report by "X" in *Arch Proc Gen*, 231), West Sumatra (Lorgion to van Mook August 23, 1948 in dossier "Hatta" *Archief Proc Gen*, 3-297), and in Holland (Secret report by "X" in *Archief Proc Gen*, no. 231, allegedly on the basis of talks with Soemitro Djojohadikoesoemo in November 9, 1948; also Nugroho, a brother of Soedjatmoko and Poppy Saleh, and the "left wing of the PvdA socialists" were named as the contacts). One report by Dutch intelligence in Bandung, "via an informant, who is very pro-Sjahrir oriented," stated that it was Hatta who let Madiun happen, "at the instigation of American agent A. J. Campbell." Dutch special inteligence report from Bandung, June 15, 1949 in *Archief Alg Secr, 2de zending*, no. 17-365-8. On the US attitude to the Madiun affair see, e.g., McMahon, *Colonialism*, pp. 243ff. McMahon writes a.o.: "Cochran met with Hatta on September 10 [there is evidently a typographical error in the book, and it should be September 19, i.e., after "Madiun" broke out] and . . . informed the prime minister [Hatta] that, although he regretted the Madiun revolt, 'crisis gives Republican Government opportunity [to] show its determination [to] suppress Communism." McMahon, *Colonialism*, p. 243.

[646] *Aneta*, September 21, 1948, also in *Archief Proc Gen*, no. 340. According to a detailed study of the Madiun affair by a historian of the Indonesian military, "The autonomous character of the East Javanese armies and their brand of radical populism . . . local sentiments . . . collective cultivation of spiritual powers (*kesaktean*) and the duty (*dharma*) to defend the local community against external threat . . . the ideological preference of the (East) Java army leaders for the maximum amount of communist participation in the struggle for independence . . . strongly contrasted with the narrow brand of rational orthodoxy by the reformers in Yogyakarta. . . ." David Charles Anderson, "Military Politics in East Java," pp. 310–16.

> One of the prominent causes of the enmity between the respective groups, sure, was the rationalization plan of Hatta [for the Indonesian army], which, for that matter, had been prepared by Sjarifoeddin.[647]

Sjahrir interpreted the Madiun affair as a conflict with its dynamics locked inside the political center in Yogyakarta—the center of which Hatta was a representative and from which Amir was not strong enough to detach himself.

Sjahrir was not in Yogyakarta during the Madiun affair. On September 21, during the critical moment of the affair, he told a reporter in Jakarta, "that already for a week he had planned to travel to Jogjakarta, but plane defects delayed the trip."[648] The leaders of Sjahrir's party who were physically present in the center took pains to make it clear that politically they were distant. During the hours when Sukarno, Hatta, Amir, and Muso were engaged in the fatal battle, the *Aneta* press agency reported that

> leaders of Sjahrir's socialist party present in Jogjakarta published a declaration ... regretting that the relation between political parties and between the Indonesian Communist Party and the Republican government developed in an inimical way.... The declaration expressed a hope that the government would behave in a democratic manner and ... a belief that action by government would be exclusively directed against rebellions and not against a political ideology.... If the Madiun affair indeed is what it is pictured by the government to be, then it is in its form revolutionary, but in its essence reactionary and counter- revolutionary.[649]

Efforts to keep aloof from the Madiun affair, or to evade the confrontation, became easier as the geographical distance from Yogyakarta grew. Audrey Kahin wrote on Minangkabau:

> On September 22, a meeting of all socialist and communist party leaders, together with those from the Masjumi and *Partai Nasional Indonesia*, expressed their loyalty to the government and agreed to avoid disturbances that would destroy unity.... As a result, the West Sumatra government did not ban the Communist Party and few communists were in fact arrested [and those for only] a couple of days.[650]

Still further off, in Singapore, on October 8, 1948, Dutch intelligence reported on the attitude towards the Madiun affair by the local Indonesia "Information Bureau"—a body, we recall, which was almost completely in the hands of Sjahrir's people. The "Information Bureau" in Singapore, according to the report,

---

[647] *Aneta*, September 21, 1948.
[648] Ibid.
[649] The declaration can be found ibid.
[650] Audrey Kahin, "Struggle for Independence," p. 269.

did not choose sides sharply when the communist rebellion broke out, and did not stand unequivocally for the Soekarno-Hatta government.[651]

Given the fact that Sjahrir might have felt proven correct by the Madiun affair, and that the one who was defeated there was Amir, whose previous relationship to Sjahrir was so bitter, there was very little sense of victory among Sjahrir's followers. Late in December 1948, according to a confidential report from "a pro-Sjahrir source,"

> the PSI, in [its attitude to Madiun], follows a more or less "balance of power" policy. Sjahrir disapproved of the Communist rebellion, yet he laments equally the reprisals, which the government has now embarked upon, and he is afraid of too great an influence of the rightist parties as a result of the red-baiting drive.[652]

In Sjahrir's words, from early October 1948, after the Amir fiasco in Madiun, "a sharply anti-left tide has arisen, also among the moderate parties of the center." It was not just Communists, Sjahrir said, but also "we," who were "persecuted."[653]

In November 1948, Sjahrir further elaborated on the same theme:

> The elimination of the Communist Party, does not eliminate the threat of totalitarianism [rooted in Indonesia's] feudalistic heritage.

On the contrary. After the Madiun affair, as Sjahrir put it on the same occasion, Indonesian politics was overwhelmed by "mass parties with uneducated followings led by leaders who themselves decide all party policy," parties with members who "are accustomed to look up to leaders for orders."[654]

Already in July 1947, as he watched the fall of Sjahrir's cabinet and Amir become prime minister, the Dutch head of government at a session of his cabinet noted a gradual and steady decline in the independent power of the figures in Indonesian politics who might still be willing and able to build a bridge: as the Dutch prime minister put it, "the decent and constructive elements in the Republic, first Sjahrir, then Sjarifoeddin."[655] Now, after the Madiun affair, this comment appeared almost prophetic.

With the "well disposed" Indonesians gone, dissidents in Dutch colonial politics, figures like Schermerhorn, also lost their influence and often resigned. Others less on

---

[651] Dutch consul general in Singapore to the attorney general in Batavia, October 9, 1948 in *Archief Alg Secr, lste zending*, no. VII-5-7.

[652] Central Military Intelligence Report (CMID), December 27, 1948 based upon information by "X" in *Archief Alg Secr, lste zending*, no. XIV-5-81.

[653] Sjahrir to *Aneta*, October 3, 1948 in dossier "Sjahrir," *Archief Proc Gen*, no. 3-262. According to the later PSI official history, as a consequence of the Madiun affair, "all forms of socialism, including the one that the PSI stood for were discredited in the Republic . . . the prestige which [socialism] had in the beginning of the revolution had dissipated. . . . It was not till two years after the establishment of the party [i.e. till 1950] that an executive council meeting could be held. . . . And it was only after the transfer of Sovereignty [i.e., after December 1949] that the party could find the opportunity and the time to think about its organizational consolidation and expansion." Sjahrir, *Indonesian Socialism*, p. 45.

[654] Sjahrir's interview with George Kahin, November 21, 1948.

[655] Notes on the meeting of the council of ministers, July 17, 1947 in *Officiële bescheiden*, 9: 715.

the fringe, like van Mook prominently, frustrated in their efforts to realize their liberal or socialist *Stuw* and "neo-ethical" concepts, let themselves be absorbed into their own mainstream, pulled by their own center. In 1948, Holland was changing as fast as the Indonesian Republic, and in a curiously similar way.

This encouraged a simple black-white power-balance vision of Dutch-Indonesian relations, and it led, logically, to another attempt at a military solution. The Dutch government held back for more than two months from the time of the Madiun affair, letting Sukarno and Hatta deal with Muso and Amir, with the extreme left, and with much of the moderate left as well, and then the Dutch struck again.[656] On December 19, the second Dutch military action was launched.

This time, the center of the Republic, Yogyakarta, was to be the primary target. Sjahrir, at the time, was in the city. This time he did not escape as he had during the Dutch first military action more than a year previously. Much of his power to move on the fringe, to keep a distance, and to translate that distance into power, seemed to be spent. This time, he did not even seem to try very hard.

T. B. Simatupang—Sjahrir's young follower from the time of the occupation, and now a high-ranking Republican military officer stationed in Yogyakarta—recalled later how, on December 19, early in the morning, he heard the news of the Dutch attack, and how he hurried to the presidential palace. In the left wing of the palace, "in front of the bedrooms reserved for guests," Simatupang ran into Sjahrir. Sukarno was "apparently still in his room"; Simatupang and Sjahrir "had a chance to eat some fried rice and drink a cup of coffee undisturbed ('Who knows when we will get another chance to eat today')." They waited for Sukarno to join them, and then together they waited for the Dutch.[657]

The previous November, in planning for this contingency, the Republic instructed its minister of economy, Sjafroeddin Prawiranegara, to move to Bukittinggi, West Sumatra, and, should Sukarno and Hatta become incapacitated, "to form an emergency government to take over temporary functions of the central government."[658] This was now done, and Sjafroeddin established his government "somewhere" in West Sumatra.

Some people had also expected that in case of a Dutch military attack, Sukarno with Sjahrir would escape on a plane to India, and Hatta, on the same plane, to Sumatra, perhaps to join Sjafroeddin.[659] The Dutch, however, were able to turn back the plane which Jawaharlal Nehru indeed had sent from India for that purpose.

Still on the morning of December 19, some Republican officials present in the presidential palace, especially soldiers, were making a last minute case for the top leaders before the Dutch came to move away from the palace and into the mountains to lead the armed resistance. Both Sukarno and Hatta rejected the idea, Hatta

---

[656] In November 1948, a new round of negotiations on what was to be the finalization of the Renville agreement of the previous January started. Already on December 11, the negotiations had broken down again, over the persisting issue of how much authority in Indonesia the Dutch and the Republic would have during the interim period before sovereignty was transferred.

[657] Simatupang, *Report from Banaran*, p. 20.

[658] Kahin, *Nationalism and Revolution*, p. 392. The quote above is from Anak Agung, 'Renville', pp. 209–10; also Hatta, *Indonesian Patriot*, p. 295.

[659] Simatupang to Lia Boediardjo, December 12, 1948 and Warsink to Schermerhorn, December 12, 1948 in Collection Schermerhorn no. 5 bundel Oost Indonesië; also personal communication from Professor Kahin.

Sjahrir under Arrest
Left to right: Soeryadarma, Sjahrir, Kusnan

explained later, partly because too large a force would be necessary to guard the leaders.[660] According to Soegondo Djojopoespito, always close to Sjahrir, and also present in the palace at the time, Sjahrir sided with Sukarno and Hatta on this issue.[661]

For Sjahrir this might be now more than ever a vacuous center. The power appeared to be with Sjafroeddin in Sumatra, or in the mountains; certainly somewhere else. Soegondo described how the Dutch commander entered the palace:

> we all from the Palace were led to the local post office [for identification], and then back to the Palace together with the commander of the Dutch army. We talked for a while on the front porch, a picture was taken and we became prisoners in the Palace with Dutch soldiers as our guards.[662]

---

[660] Hatta estimated "one battalion of soldiers" would be necessary. Hatta, *Indonesian Patriot*, p. 295.
[661] Suwarsih Djojopuspito, *Yang tak dapat kulupakan*, p. 20.
[662] Quoted in ibid.

They were kept for the next four days in the palace under guard. On the fourth day, Hatta recalled, he was informed

> that Soekarno, myself, Sjahrir, Hadji Agoes Salim, [and other leaders] Mr. Asaat, Mr. Gafar Pringgodigdo and Soerjadarma were to be be moved to another place, though I was not told where.[663]

They were taken by a Dutch bomber from Yogyakarta to Pangkal Pinang on the island of Bangka, off Sumatra's east coast. From there, Hatta with Asaat, Pringgodigdo, and Suryadarma were moved into *Hotel Menumbing* in the island mountain resort near the town of Muntok. Sukarno, Hadji Agoes Salim, and Sjahrir were taken to Brastagi in North Sumatra, and a few days later, on January 1, 1949, further east to Prapat on the shore of Lake Toba.[664]

Sjahrir was again close to Medan, where he had spent his early years. From Medan the most beautiful way, as Willem Brandt wrote in his nostalgic book about the prewar "Land of Deli,"

> leads toward the pleasure-grounds of Brastagi or Prapat with their glittering bungalows, hotels *de luxe*, golf courses, *maneges* and guided tours to the mountains.[665]

The bungalow where the prisoners were put in Prapat belonged to the East Sumatra *wali negara*, the top "native" official under the Dutch, who offered it for that purpose.[666] It was very probably furnished with turn-of-the-century rattan rocking chairs, oriental curiosities on small tables, a lot of standing lamps, and perhaps faded photographs of prewar horse races. It was, to Sjahrir, a familiar landscape.

December 28, 1948, a week after the Republican leaders were put in prison, the Dutch military district head wrote to the Dutch attorney general in Jakarta:

> Messrs. Soekarno and Hadji Agoes Salim asked me for permission to write a letter to their families. You will find (as included) that those are completely neutral letters.
> From Mr. Sjahrir came no such request, and, also, when he was offered this possibility, he said he would not use it.[667]

---

[663] Hatta, *Memoir*, pp. 542ff.

[664] Report on the interned Republican "prominents"—as they were called by the Dutch—by KNI Intelligence section is in *Archief Alg Secr, lste zending*, no. IX-2-1; another report, by the Dutch army, January 22, 1949 is in ibid., IX-2-1; IV-2.

[665] Willem Brandt, *De aarde van Deli* (The Hague: van Hoeve, 1948) quoted in review by de Vries in *Oriëntatie*, April 1949, p. 58.

[666] The Dutch army report, January 22, 1949 in *Archief Alg Secr, lste zending*, no. IX-2-1;. IV-2; also a cable from the army command in Batavia to the local military commander in Medan, December 21, 1948, ibid.

[667] Local administrator, North Sumatra, to the Attorney General, Batavia, December 28, 1948 in dossier "Correspondentie met geïnterneerde leiders" in *Archief Proc Gen*, no. 1-41-2. On the censorhip applied see Attorney General to the Dutch representative at the State of East Sumatra in ibid., 1-61.

In a sense, this was like another soft colonial prison for "the academically formed" natives. In the words of the Dutch internal report on the place, dated December 30,

> The security is strict, the behavior of the officers is model. Food [for prisoners] is from the officers' mess, and religious objections [to diet] are respected.[668]

Also,

> Mr. Sjahrir requested a weekly edition of the *Nieuwe Rotterdamsche Courant*, Hadji Agoes Salim an English dictionary, and Mr. Soekarno wished some more items of clothing.[669]

In the Dutch archives in The Hague, there is a letter in Sjahrir's handwriting, dated December 31, 1948, and addressed to the prison commanding officer in Prapat, Major Geelkerken:

> Dear Major Geelkerken:
> Your friendly urbanity and the correct and cultured [*beschaafde*] behavior of your officers and men, has made our enforced stay at Brastagi, given the circumstances, not an unpleasant experience [*herinnering*].
> Would you be so nice as to convey my compliments to the above-mentioned officers and men?
> I wish you a happy new year and all the best.
> Once more with friendly thanks
> Sjahrir.[670]

A similar letter was written, at the same time, also by Hadji Agoes Salim and by Sukarno.[671]

On January 9 and again on January 11, a Dutch government representative visited the prisoners and offered them a more relaxed prison regimen if they promised not to use it for political activity. As the Dutch official reported it, all—Sukarno, Sjahrir, and Hadji Agoes Salim—assured him orally of this. Then the Dutch official asked the prisoners "which family members they might like to see." Hadji Agoes Salim wanted "1. wife, 2. an eight-year old son, 3. both his daughters, age twenty-seven and twenty." Sukarno wished to be joined by

---

[668] The Dutch representative at the State of East Sumatra to the Attorney General, December 30, 1948. Ibid.

[669] Ibid.

[670] Original of the letter is in *Archief Alg Secr, lste zending*, no. IX-2; a copy and some comments are, e.g., in *Collection Spoor* no. 87.

[671] More exactly, there is a letter written in Sukarno's hand and signed by Sukarno, Hadji Agoes Salim and Sjahrir. Ibid. There is no letter in the file, however, written individually either by Sukarno or by Hadji Agoes Salim.

1. wife, 2. son, 3. daughter, 4. mother-in-law (if she is prepared to come), 5. Kemala, the maid, 6./7. Amin, his *boy*, and Amin's mother, if they are willing to come, all of them living in Jogjakarta.

Sjahrir

has asked for his two fosterchildren, if they are inclined to come: 1. Lily age twenty-two, 2. Ali age ten, both living in Jawaweg 61, Batavia.[672]

Never before had Sjahrir lived so close to Sukarno as now. Sjahrir and Sukarno, and Hadji Agoes Salim, were locked in a three-bedroom house. Colorful stories about their being together seemed to come especially from the gossip-loving Hadji Agoes Salim. Sjahrir was said to be constantly irritated by Sukarno, by Sukarno's asking the Dutch guards "for Arrow shirts and gabardin coats," by trifles.[673] Sukarno himself two decades later seemed to remember his stay with Sjahrir vividly: "He told the Dutch I didn't mind exile because I had seven mirrors in my room."[674] According to Sukarno, too, Sjahrir had called him in Brastagi and Prapat, "a plain, bloody, old fool."[675]

Abu Hanifah liked stories of this kind no less than Hadji Agoes Salim. He heard, he wrote, that Sjahrir called Sukarno "'stupid', 'idiot', 'coward', and other ugly names."[676] Others reported that they also called themselves "Your Excellency President," and "Mr. Prime Minister."[677] Once, it is said, Sjahrir, infuriated by Sukarno singing at the top of his voice in the bath, shouted (in Dutch) *houd je mond*!, "shut up!" The song, the gossip specified, was "a sweet melody by famous Johann Strauss 'One Day When We Were Young'," and Sukarno sang it in English.[678]

The Dutch second military action against the Republic was a blunder from the beginning. Yogyakarta, precisely because it had been attacked, and Sukarno and Hatta, precisely because they were arrested, became more powerful symbols than before. For the world, Sukarno and Hatta now meant the Republic. The logical consequence was that they had to be returned to Yogyakarta.

It was initially the Dutch plan to keep the Indonesian leaders' place of internment "as secret as possible."[679] Already on January 16, 1949, however, barely a month after the Dutch launched their military action, a United Nations representative visited Hatta in his prison at Menumbing and inquired about the possibility of resuming negotiations.

Hatta was reluctant. As he wrote later, he informed the visitor that

---

[672] The Dutch representative at the State of East Sumatra to the Attorney General in Batavia, January 11, 1949 in *Archïef Proc Gen*, no. I-61.

[673] Mohamad Roem, "Bung Kecil yang berbuat besar" in *Mengenang Sjahrir*, ed. Rosihan Anwar, p. 159 says he did not get the story from Salim (who was his father-in-law and who was living in one house with Roem often afterwards).

[674] Sukarno, *An Autobiography*, p. 259.

[675] Ibid., p. 258.

[676] Abu Hanifah, *Tales of a Revolution*, pp. 309–10.

[677] Subadio Sastrosatomo in *Bisnis Indonesia*, August 18, 1987.

[678] Roem, "Bung Kecil," p. 159.

[679] Cable from Batavia to the Resident of Medan December 23, 1949 in *Archief Alg Secr, lste zending*, no. IX-2;

neither I nor Soekarno had any authority any longer because on December 19, 1948 we had transferred leadership of the state to Mr. Sjafroeddin Prawiranegara in West Sumatra.

To this, as Hatta wrote, the UN diplomat had responded that:

> the world at large and in particular the UN recognized only Sukarno-Hatta as leaders of the Republic of Indonesia.[680]

Next day, two Dutch emissaries visited Hatta, with an invitation for him to come to Jakarta "to exchange views informally" with Dutch Prime Minister Drees, who had just arrived from Holland. Hatta again refused to make the move, arguing this time that, if he were to travel to Jakarta, it would appear as a capitulation by the Republic.[681] If Prime Minister Drees wanted to talk to him, he might come to see him in Bangka. This was the fortress strategy.

The Dutch had argued, Hatta recalled further,

> that Prime Minister Drees was getting on in years and it would be very difficult for him to come over from Jakarta. But I stuck to my position.[682]

The same day, however, that Hatta rejected the offer by the Dutch emissaries, a Dutch "top priority" cable was sent from Jakarta to The Hague, reporting that "Sjahrir declared himself ready to talk with Drees."[683] The next day, on January 18, 1949, Sjahrir, indeed, arrived in Jakarta. For the next year, many would marvel about what strategy this was a part of.

Hatta, in his memoirs, wrote that he discussed the matter with other Indonesian leaders at Menumbing as soon as they heard the news, and that he repeated on that occasion what he had said to the Dutch a short while previously: he would "refuse to go."[684] Sukarno, as usual, was much more outspokenly anti-Sjahrir in his memoirs, but, in this particular case, at least, his version is not very different from what Hatta wrote:

> In January, after we had been in Prapat a couple of weeks, the Prime Minister of the Netherlands, Dr. Drees, asked to speak to Sjahrir instead of Sukarno "because Sjahrir is more pro-Dutch."
>
> Sjahrir jumped at the opportunity to go to Djakarta and be the big man of the Republic. "I am dead against this move," I warned. "Again it is negotiating from the standpoint of a prisoner."

---

[680] Hatta, *Indonesian Patriot*, p. 299; also report by Resident on Bangka and Billiton, January 24, 1949 in *Archief Alg Secr, lste zending*, no. IX-2.

[681] Correspondence between the Representative of the Queen in Batavia and the Dutch resident in Bangka, January 16, 1949, and Beel to Jonkman, January 17, 1949, in ibid.; note on the cable reads *"antwoord Hatta nog wachtende."* On the visit of Hatta by the Dutch emissaries see Gieben, "Kort verslag," January 17, 1949, in ibid.

[682] Hatta, *Indonesian Patriot*, p. 301.

[683] Beel to the prime minister, January 17, 1949 in *Archief Alg Secr, lste zending*, no. IX-2.

[684] Hatta, *Indonesian Patriot*, p. 301.

We were sitting in the small living room onto which our three bedrooms opened. "I will only go," he swore, "to report back to you what is really in the minds of those Dutchmen. In one week I shall return and we shall discuss everything that happened."

The agreed-upon week went by. He did not come back. He never came back. He never reported. He went to Djakarta, had a talk with the Dutch Prime Minister, showed his willingness to cooperate and ended up a free man.[685]

The crucial question is, what it meant for Sjahrir, in December 1948, to "end up a free man"?

On January 19, the day after his arrival in Jakarta, Sjahrir met representatives of the non-Republican areas of the planned Indonesian federation, namely Sultan Hamid II of Kalimantan and Anak Agung of Bali.[686] That same day, Sjahrir talked to the Dutch Prime Minister Drees, and, according to Associated Press, "considered [Drees'] plans of a national agreement acceptable for Indonesia."[687] Still on the same day, Sjahrir, back in his Jakarta house, gave a news interview, in which he said that his "visit to Batavia" was carried out "with knowledge and agreement of president Soekarno."

Was this to be a repetition of Sjahrir's mission of 1947? In the news interview on January 19, Sjahrir explained that it was

> more possible for him to accept premier Drees' invitation, because he [Sjahrir] does not have any official function and, thus, is in no form restrained.[688]

On January 22, 1949, another conference of Asian nations was convened on the initiative of Jawaharlal Nehru in New Delhi, and it demanded that

> the members of the government of the Republic of Indonesia be released and that the government be returned to Jogjakarta.[689]

Six days later, a resolution by the Security Council of the United Nations demanded an immediate cease-fire, "withdrawal of the Dutch forces" behind their lines before hostilities, "free elections," a fixed date for "transfer of sovereignty" to Indonesia, and a "new UN Commission" with "greater powers." Also, the "Republican government was to be restored in Jogjakarta."[690] Nowhere in this was Sjahrir mentioned as a significant agent.

---

[685] Sukarno, *An Autobiography*, p. 259.

[686] *Aneta*, January 19, 1949 in *Archief Alg Secr, lste zending*, no. IX-2.

[687] Associated Press, January 19, 1949 in ibid. Report on the Drees' trip by Drees himself is in *Collection Romme* no. 25; see also W. Drees, *Zestig jaar levenservaring* (Amsterdam: De Arbeiders, 1962), p. 146 and Roem, *Bunga Rampai*, 3: 239.

[688] *Aneta* and *Pedoman*, January 19, 1949.

[689] Ali Sastroamijoyo, *Milestones on my Journey*, p. 187. Compare *Siasat*, March 13, 1949.

[690] Security Council Official Record, 4th year, 406th meeting, January 28, 1949, pp. 18–19. see also McMahon, *Colonialism*, pp. 272ff and De Beus, *Morgen bij het aanbreken van de dag*, p. 187; compare Drees, *Zestig jaar*, p. 246.

Sukarno was right. Sjahrir did not return to Prapat. He stayed in Jakarta for weeks and then for months. He again lived in his house on Jawaweg 61, with the Bandanese children and he went around with those of his friends who were not abroad.

Strikingly, after the flurry of the few first meetings, nothing happened between Sjahrir and the Dutch. In another interview, after months of no visible result on his part, and no visible action, Sjahrir was asked, in essence, who he was—in what capacity was he in Jakarta, how did he feel?

> As a private citizen? Or as a representative of a government, which still exists, although, at present it is physically powerless?

Sjahrir answered in what was partly a statement of ambiguity, partly a statement in the past tense:

> Since the time I came back to Indonesia, in April of last year, I merely had the function of an adviser, that is to say, I was an adviser to the president and to the Republican delegation [to negotiate with Holland]—a sort of a track-over [overbaantje]. I was never again appointed a representative of the Republican government, and I can not thus feel like one.[691]

Pro-Sjahrir journals were still published in Jakarta, and art exhibitions were still being organized by people near Sjahrir. Soedjatmoko, a man close to Sjahrir during the war and since, debated with Professor Soepomo a "meeting of East and West"; what was *kuno*, "ancient or old-fashioned" and what was *riil*, "real"; if *nasionalisme*, "nationalism," was an absolute concept or merely a transitory stage to a "new culture."[692]

Siasat still published reviews of Sal Tas' writings.[693] *Siasat*, also, in March 1949, announced that the English edition of Sjahrir's prison and exile letters with a short autobiography covering the subsequent years up to 1947, "Out of Exile," had been published in New York and selected as a Book of the Month.[694]

Sjahrir still talked about possible "cooperation" with Holland, about "mutual understanding" and about "trust," although, as he said, "for the present time, alas, this does not look like an actual possibility."[695] He still spoke of *pendidikan*, "education," as an essential part of politics; still, talking politics and power struggle, he in fact talked "psychology," "subconscious fear," "self-consciousness," and spiritual "equilibrium." The tendency of today, he said, was, alas, "towards politics of power and violence [*macht- en geweld-politiek*]."[696]

Some groups near Sjahrir worked as if not much had changed since the Japanese occupation or even since the Pendidikan time of the 1930s. The Komisi Kebudajaan, "Cultural Commission," for instance, a body of which we know very little otherwise, was made up of familiar names—Soetan Takdir Alisjahbana, Maria Ullfah, Soewan-

---

[691] Interview with Sjahrir in *Kritiek en Opbouw*, July 1, 1949, p. 1.
[692] *Gema*, May 1949, pp. 217–24.
[693] R. A. (Rivai Apin) in *Siasat*, June 12, 1949.
[694] Ibid., March 6 and 27, 1949.
[695] *Kritiek en Opbouw*, July 1, 1949, p. 1
[696] Ibid.

di, and also Sjahrir. It dealt with "the problem of language," and, in June 1949, issued a special manifesto proposing that

> Indonesian should be introduced [in the schools of future independent Indonesia] as the official medium of instruction, while Dutch should be taught as a study subject.[697]

Stories and rumors abounded—as during the Japanese occupation, and during the Pendidikan time—about what Sjahrir was actually doing.

A Front Nasional Indonesia, "National Indonesian Front," was reportedly established sometime late in 1948 by Ali Boediardjo, Sjahrir's follower from the time of the occupation, and afterwards Sjahrir's personal secretary; the Front reportedly became a kind of a secret network of Sjahrir's power. The Front, as the rumor-mill had it,

> spread over the whole archipelago—among other places in Tebing Tinggi, Medan, and Palembang, on Sumatra; Menado, Makassar, and Samarinda in East Indonesia; and Malang, Banjoemas and Poerwokerto on Java.[698]

Sjahrir's followers were still posted abroad. Before the Dutch attacked, in December 1948, an instruction was sent to New Delhi from Yogyakarta, "to Soedarsono and his people," that in case the agencies of the Republic were incapacitated at home, "to form in India a government of the Republic of Indonesia in exile."[699] The instruction was never revoked as far as was known. And neither was it ever implemented; it merely was rumored about, and it added to the weirdness of the real or alleged "Sjahrir networks"; thus, it further inflamed the rumors.

On December 21, 1948, as the Dutch attacked the Republic, Tan Malaka re-emerged, and, in a speech from a local radio station in Kediri, East Java, he called upon the nation to rise up against invaders in a guerrilla war.[700] "Information" followed that Tan Malaka was, in fact, organizing his resistance on the basis of the Sukarno "Testament" from 1945; thus, together with Sjahrir.[701] Sjahrir, for his part, was reported "inconspicuously" working towards "an open clash" to regain leadership of the Republic, and "in cooperation with Tan Malaka."[702] Whatever the truth—and no real action ever came out of this—the rumors carried little power.

Early in March 1949, just as it was becoming clear that the Dutch military action had failed, and that Sukarno and Hatta might be soon re-invested in the center of the Republic in Yogyakarta, or in nearby Surakarta, perhaps, the following piece on Central Java appeared in *Siasat*:

---

[697] Intelligence report by the Dutch general staff, no. 81, June 30, 1949 in *Archief Alg Secr, 2de zending*, no. 17-365-8.

[698] "Politieke Groeperingen in Indonesië. 1948" *Collectie Koets*, no. 622.

[699] "Ali Boediardjo," *Siasat*, April 17, 1949; Anak Agung, "Renville," pp. 209–10; telegram quoted in Tobing, *Perdjuangan Politik Bangsa Indonesia*, p. 204. Also *Aneta*, December 22, 1948 in dossier "Republikeinse fondsen in buitenland" in *Archief Proc Gen*, no. 1-96.

[700] Dahm, *History of Indonesia*, p. 138.

[701] Intelligence report by the Dutch general staff, West Java, May 17, 1949 in *Archief Alg Secr, lste zending*, no. X-28-10.

[702] R. S. Soerjaprawira to Director of the cabinet HVK, secret, July 1, 1949 in ibid. VI-17-17.

Optimism that the Republic would return is heavy. We only wonder, if it would not be a return to an empty town. Not only did people spill out of Surakarta, also many animals, and many backpacks and briefcases disappeared ... and buffaloes, thousands of buffaloes."[703]

Ten days later, *Siasat* wrote about Yogyakarta. The passive resistance against the Dutch in Yogyakarta had been so effective, *Siasat* wrote, because

no peasant [*Pak tani*] would move his hoe without an order by *Dorodjatun*, His Highness [the Sultan]. No civil servant would move his pen without permission from Him the Sultan....[704]

It was perfectly natural, the disrespectful, sometimes bitter, sometimes funny, sometimes cynical, sometimes desperate, and clearly pro-Sjahrir *Siasat* wrote, on April 24, that Sukarno and Hatta wanted to return to Yogyakarta. His Highness the Sultan of Yogyakarta had promised "four million rupiah" to the Republic if it re-establish its capital in his princely realm. *Siasat* described how the people were already working hard to divide the money; "Democracy Brother!" the journal concluded and added a poem:

Our *djago* [cocks] remain steady
Eyes shining, medals pinned on
For the moment they do not think of victory
They think of return
In Jogjakarta there is a tranquility
And the real fight for them
At a round table
Jogjakarta is large enough for all of them.

Now, there is something to defend
In Jogjakarta the game would be decided.

Sultan, let's pray, would help.
The first alms are here already
Four million in cash....[705]

In an April 3 editorial, *Siasat* referred to Sukarno and Hatta as merely "the men in Bangka," and as "several leaders in prison." They, *Siasat* wrote, were eager to "play politics" instead of

contacting Sjafroeddin [his emergency government in Sumatra] and his people, although these hold a valid mandate to govern.[706]

---

[703] *Siasat*, March 3, 1949.
[704] Ibid., March 13, 1949.
[705] Ibid., April 24, 1949.
[706] Ibid., April 3, 1949, editorial.

On April 24, *Siasat*'s editorial disputed if "anybody" had the right to take the "legal mandate" away from the "Sjafroedin government";[707] in the same issue, *Siasat* opined that it was "misguided to put the top priority on Sukarno and Hatta being returned to Yogyakarta";[708] in its May 1 editorial, *Siasat* questioned if a possible Dutch willingness to clear "a five-mile area around Yogyakarta" for the return of Sukarno and Hatta might ever be called a great victory for the Republic, as "some" suggested.[709]

In two sudden flashes of tragedy, two men who had given the Indonesian revolution—and Sjahrir's life of past years—much of their dynamics and meaning, reappeared and disappeared forever. After the Dutch attacked in December, allegedly because he was a security threat to the Republic in grave danger, Amir Sjarifoeddin was executed by Republican authorities in Ngalihan prison in Surakarta. Four months later, in April 1949, near Blitar in East Java, it seems on the order of a local Republican military commander, as an incorrigible rebel and as a threat to peace, Tan Malaka was shot to death.[710]

Not Sjahrir, but Prof. Soepomo and Dr. Darmasetiawan, became the working link between the outside world, the Dutch, and the Republic, as the negotiations got on track again. Both Soepomo and Darmasetiawan were close to Sjahrir at one time or another during the Japanese occupation and in the early revolution. Now, however, they were chosen by Sukarno and Hatta.[711] Hatta in particular, with visible

---

[707] Ibid., April 24, editorial.

[708] Ibid.

[709] Ibid., May 1, 1949.

[710] The reason allegedly given was that Tan Malaka had not respected the cease-fire as declared by the UN Security Council on January 28. On the date of Tan Malaka's death, see, for example, Jarvis' Introduction to *From Jail to Jail*, 1: cxxiii. On the death of Amir, see above n. 605.

[711] It had always been Hatta, rather than Sjahrir, who was considered the champion of the non-Javanese areas in the future independent Indonesia. In Sumatra, it was Hatta again, and not Sjahrir—always more vague about being a Sumatran and a Moslem—who was the big and popular figure; at that time, according to various contemporary sources, Hatta was seen even by peasants in distant villages, of West Sumatra especially, as *"mamak,* the uncle" of the people, or as *"radja Islam,* Islamic king." Hamka, *Kenang-kenangan Hidup,* p. 362. According to Ali Sastroamidjojo, while still in Bangka, Hatta "was in general looked on as a strong man with the authority to overcome any difficulties that might arise." Ali Sastroamijoyo, *Milestones on my Journey,* p. 200. In contrast to Sjahrir, Hatta never let himself appear detached from the center, and he seemed to attract much power precisely because of this. Those Indonesian leaders representing the non-Republic regions of a future federation, who met Sjahrir after his return from Prapat, on January 19, the following day went to see Hatta on Bangka. Jonkman to Sassen, February 2, 1949 and an exchange between Batavia and the Dutch Resident and commandant in Bangka, January 20, 21, and 24 in *Archief Alg Secr, Iste zending,* no. IX-2. When, afterwards, they talked about two centers of power they were moving between, they referred to them them as "Holland and Bangka." Dutch military intelligence report, April 6, 1949 in *Archief Proc Gen,* no. 9-791. Sjahrir himself visited Hatta on Bangka a few days after he went to Jakarta from Prapat. He talked to Hatta, but nothing is known about their discussion. See *Archief Alg Secr, Iste zending,* no. IX-2. More is known about the visit by Sudarpo, who clearly came to Bangka as Sjahrir's envoy a few weeks later, in early April. By that time Sukarno had also been moved to Bangka, and Hatta and Sukarno lived together there. Sudarpo, reportedly, tried to advise Sukarno-Hatta to take the Sjafroeddin emergency government in Sumatra more seriously. As Sudarpo himself summed up the result of his visit to Sukarno-Hatta, "they did not listen." Sudarpo to Dutch diplomats in New Delhi, report dated May 30, 1949 in *Archief Alg Secr, Iste zending,* no. IX-28-40; see also Intelligence report by the Dutch general staff which

satisfaction recorded that, while the Dutch top negotiator had the title of *Hogevertegenwoordiger van den Kroon,* "High Representative of the Crown,"

> people gave Dr. Darmasetiawan the title H.V.H., *Hogevertegenwoordiger van Hatta,* High Representative of Hatta.[712]

When the Indonesian delegation was appointed to lead the negotiations, in March 1949, Sjahrir was left out. From their place of internment, Sukarno and Hatta decided that Mohamad Roem would be the chairman. Sjahrir was not even an ordinary member of the six-man team; he was merely listed, in small print, as one of the delegation's six advisers.[713]

The Australian representative on the UN mediation team, Thomas K. Critchley, had visited Hatta on Bangka shortly before this. In discussing the matter with Hatta, he learned that

> Hatta related better to and was more comfortable with Roem than he would have been with Sjahrir [even while] Sjahrir would also have been a valuable adviser and negotiator.[714]

According to Mohamad Roem, Hatta did not make Sjahrir the head of the delegation because

---

based its information on a "very Sjahrir oriented informant, "Republikeinse visie" in *Archief Alg Secr, lste zending,* no. 9-385; also Roem, "Bung Kecil," p. 157.

[712] Hatta, *Indonesian Patriot,* p. 281.

[713] Besides the chairman and vice-chairman, the members were: Leimena, Djuanda, Soepomo, Latoehary; advisers were Sjahrir, Laoh, Natsir, Darmasetiawan, Soemarto, D. A. Koesoemaatmodja. See Ali Sastroamijoyo. *Milestones on my Journey,* p. 191. When the letter of appointment came, signed by Sukarno, Sjahrir was said to have torn it to pieces asking the man who brought it: "Who is it this Soekarno? Why should he appoint me? The one who should appoint me is Syafrudin!" Sukarno, of course, had promptly been informed and, as Hatta put it, "felt it to be a humiliation directed at him personally." Roem, "Bung Kecil," pp. 140–41; Hatta, *Bung Hatta Antwoordt,* pp. 188–89; the translations are those by Rose. *Indonesia Free,* pp. 167, 157. According to Ali Sastroamidjojo, who became vice-chairman of the delegation, "Sjahrir's argument, the accusation that we 'ignored' the emergency government [was] weak [and] could be refuted this way: It was a fact that at that time the international world, in particular the U.N. bodies such as the Security Council and the U.N. Commission for Indonesia, always communicated with us on Bangka, especially Soekarno and Hatta, ever since our detention there. They never communicated with the emergency government in Sumatra. So the conclusion could be drawn that the government of the Republic of Indonesia as mentioned by the January 28, 1949, Security Council resolution referred to us in Bangka. Ali Sastroamijoyo, *Milestones on my Journey,* p. 188. Sjahrir remained aloof. According to Ali Sastroamidjojo, every time the Republican delegation met, Roem officially invited Sjahrir to attend but he never put in an appearance. Ibid. On Sjahrir, also, being notoriously "almost never" present at the talks, see report by Soerjaprawira, July 1, 1949 in *Archief Alg Secr, lste zending,* no. VI-17-17. According to another report, "Mr. Mohammad Roem ignored Sjahrir's advice and based his policy completely on that from Prof. Soepomo." Director of Central Military Intelligence (CMID) to the Attorney General, April 17, 1949 in *Archief Proc Gen,* no. 262.

[714] Critchley interviewed in Rose, *Indonesia Free,* p. 157.

Since Renville, Sjahrir did not want to sit on any delegation.... And why did he not want to? Because his views were different from those of both Hatta and [me].[715]

Three weeks after his return from Prapat, Sjahrir talked in Jakarta with George Kahin. On this occasion, one of his themes was Sukarno. "Essentially," Sjahrir told Kahin, Sukarno was

a real Javanese—Believes in Buddhist-Hinduistic heaven ... is superstitious, believes in Hinduistic magic and superstitions and that is the secret of his success; he uses the language of people and they are convinced he has the same beliefs as they. No other leader can approach the people's mentality as well as Soekarno. This is the primary basis of his leadership. He can talk to people, arouse their inspiration—and convince them that he can help them.

Not as ideological leader. He never says to people you must do this and that and this must be policy. He knows what people want.

This Republic would never be realized so quickly but for Soekarno. At one stage the Republic meant Soekarno. He must be in the limelight—he can't stand daylight.[716]

When the Dutch attacked, Sukarno went neither to India, nor to the mountains. Sukarno remained in the palace and was arrested as he waited for the Dutch to come. Sukarno let himself to be taken to Prapat and then to Bangka; he insisted that the only possible next move for him would be to return to Yogyakarta and to the palace. Staying immobile, Sukarno kept to himself.

Many of the Republic's military officers felt very bitter towards Sukarno, because in December 1949 he did not join the guerrilla forces. Some of them were said to have "never forgiven Soekarno" for his "surrender" in the palace.[717] Most, however, as time passed, began to see Sukarno again as the symbol of the forces standing upright, as a man speaking the unambiguous language of the nation, as the personification of the new identity of Indonesia in struggle, or, at least, of the Indonesian fortress keeping to itself.

After early February 1949, the leaders in Bangka[718] were permitted more freedom within a restricted area of few miles around their place of internment. They could now talk to the people if the gatherings were kept small. In a report by the Dutch Resident in Bangka, Sukarno used the new freedom for organizing *straattoneeltjes*, "little street theaters," for the local population.[719] Another Dutch report from Bangka, of March 31, 1949, summarized Sukarno's speech on one such occasion:

---

[715] Roem, "Bung Kecil," p. 155.

[716] Sjahrir's interview with George Kahin, February 15, 1949.

[717] Ulf Sundhaussen, *The Road to Power: Indonesian Military Politics, 1945–1967* (Kuala Lumpur: Oxford University Press, 1982), p. 228.

[718] Sukarno had meanwhile been moved also to Bangka where he stayed together with Hatta and the others.

[719] Resident Bangka Billiton to the Attorney General, February 7, 1949 in *Archief Alg Secr, lste zending*, no. IX-2.

With the greetings of *Assalam alaikum* and Freedom!
. . . First war between the East and the West was lost by the East; this was the war between Persia and the Roman empire. The second . . . war between the East and the West, the recent war between Japan and the Allies, was lost by the East again. But, till this day, the West does not think it has eaten enough fruits of victories. Now, the West is heading towards a third war. Now, it is time for the Indonesian people to triumph.[720]

Sukarno had been moved out of Yogyakarta. Yet, the Javanese interior did not lose its magic as the powerful fortress, the Republic's sole and legitimate center.

Sukarno—and through his *straattoneeltjes* among other things—kept himself part of the place. Sukarno's myth still existed in 1949, and it grew stronger. There were other myths, besides, keeping the center meaningful. The myth surrounding the Sultan of Yogyakarta Hamengku Buwono, became most significant—the Sultan never did allow the Dutch into his princely palace in Yogyakarta, after December 1948; he declared himself and his high authority to be on the side of the Republic. There was another myth, almost as powerful as the Sultan's, and equally connected with the Javanese tradition, with the mood of the interior, with the Republic, and with Sukarno—the myth of the Republic's first soldier, *Panglima Besar*, the "Great Commander," General Soedirman.

General Soedirman was now in his early thirties. He was suffering from a fatal illness of the lungs, but, in spite of this, he left for the mountains when the Dutch attacked. Since then he had led the resistance. He was often so weak that he had to be carried through the jungle on a stretcher. His headquarters moved from place to place, but always deep in the Javanese interior—most often at Dekso, Central Java, close to the Hindu-Buddhist temples of Mendut and Borobudur. From the early days of the Revolution, from the late days of the Japanese occupation, indeed, Soedirman appealed to many by a powerful mixture of Japanese-inspired soldier's professionalism and Javanese-inspired mysticism and belief in invulnerability. Now that kind of power was at its apex.

Now, also, and increasingly, Soedirman even attracted people like Colonel Simatupang—a Sumatran, a Christian, and always before considered a disciple of Sjahrir.[721] Ali Boediardjo, another follower of Sjahrir since the Japanese occupation (but, besides, a very Javanese aristocrat)—not unlike Simatupang after late 1948 a very influential figure in the Republican military establishment—now also came equally under the strong spell of Soedirman.[722]

It seemed natural to Simatupang, when Soedirman, in 1949, gave him the order:

---

[720] Dutch police report from Pangkal Pinang to the police headquarters in Bangka, March 31, 1949 in ibid.

[721] See especially Simatupang, *Report from Banaran*, pp. 83, 151–53; Sundhaussen, *The Road to Power*, p. 32.

[722] E.g., Simatupang to Lia Boediardjo, December 12, 1949; Warink to Schermerhorn December 14, 1949; Coast, *Recruit to Revolution*, p. 152; "Riwajat Hidup Soetan Sjahrir," n.d., n.p. typescript in *Archives Siti Wahjunah Sjahrir*. As *Siasat* also put it in April 1949, Ali Boediardjo "since Madiun, [has become] more and more the right hand of Hatta." "Ali Boediardjo" in *Siasat*, April 17, 1949.

> It is my desire that you, too, *hold firmly to the stand* expounded in yr own letter that everything should be *discussed in Jogjakarta and not in Djakarta*.[723]

The Javanese interior did not lose its power, and neither did the character of its power change. It expanded. New alliances were built, and Sjahrir was being left out.

Almost nothing was heard about Schermerhorn. Van Mook, however he tried to conform with the Dutch military and hard-liners, was losing his position, and was almost in disgrace. New people—less affected by the prewar Indies liberal socialist or "neo-ethical" notions—formulated Dutch policy towards Indonesia. The new world order also was taking a more definite shape, and the United States, in Indonesia as abroad, became the decisive force.

In mid-February 1949, T. B. Simatupang had noted in his guerrilla diary:

> Speculation suggests that . . . [the new American representative on the UN committee for Indonesia] Cochran will go to Bangka to meet President Sukarno . . . and Vice-President Hatta. [This does] not conflict with our objectives and interests. However, dangers do exist of which we should take cognizance. . . . If the political settlement leaves us too dependent on the United States, then we may be branded as American "puppets."[724]

Two weeks later, Simatupang returned to the topic:

> For Cochran, clearly, the Republic means Sukarno and Hatta. . . . Nothing indicates that Cochran intends to contact the [Sjafroeddin] Emergency Government of the Republic of Indonesia. . . .[725]

Merle Cochran was a diplomat very different from his American predecessor in the UN commission in Indonesia, Professsor Frank Graham. Merle Cochran, in particular, was much less "impeded" than Frank Graham by "liberal," and "anti-colonialist" ideas of the past era. With a growing US interest behind him, Merle Cochran became a tough, prominent and occasionally decisive figure in the Dutch-Indonesian politics of 1949.[726]

"On April 22, 1949," Hatta wrote in his memoirs,

> I received a note from Mr. Cochran urging me to come to Jakarta to discuss with Dutch delegate Van Royen the boundaries of the Yogya territory to be handed over to the Republic. On 24 April 1949 I left for Jakarta and the following day I discussed the question of the return of the Republican Government to Yogya with Van Royen.[727]

---

[723] Simatupang, *Report from Banaran*, p. 107. (Emphasis in the text.)

[724] Simatupang, February 14, 1949, in ibid., p. 60.

[725] Simatupang, February 22, 1949, in ibid., p. 62.

[726] Professor Graham was accused of something short of un-American activities—because of calling the Dutch "totalitarian" and referring, allegedly, to the Republic as the "forces of freedom." See Dr. Harry D. Gideonse, President Brooklyn College (Address before the Chicago Council of Foreign Relations, February 2, 1949, p. 7).

[727] Hatta, *Indonesian Patriot*, p. 303.

On May 7, 1949, a Dutch-Indonesian agreement was signed by J. H. Van Roijen and Mohamad Roem. The Dutch agreed to withdraw their forces from an area around Yogyakarta. The Republic agreed in exchange to be satisfied with only one-third of the seats in the representative assembly of the future federal Indonesia.

Fighting was to be stopped on all fronts. Republican leaders were to be released, and final discussions were to be held about the transfer of sovereignty—the Round Table Conference in The Hague—later in the year. In George Kahin's words,

> It was generally believed among educated Republicans that the Roem-Van Royen Agreement had been engineered through strong American pressure on the Republican leaders.[728]

A week after the Roem-Van Roijen agreement was signed, on May 15, *Siasat* published a cartoon depicting a confused stranger somewhere on Java asking a rickshaw driver: "Is this Restaurant *Roem-Cochran-Cola*?"[729]

Both Sjahrir and his PSI explicitly opposed the Roem-Van Roijen agreement.[730] According to a voice from mid-June 1949, reportedly of "a very pro-Sjahrir informant,"

> The orientation of the State Department appears to be directed at feudal circles, with the people in Washington fixing themselves upon a political induction of feudal-inclined organizations like the "Indonesian National Party" or Masjumi, whose leaders often are outwardly Western-oriented, yet inwardly remain chained to conservative-psychological impulses and urges.[731]

According to the same report, Sjahrir himself regarded the current American policy as "most highly unreliable." He was said to be particularly worried about one consequence of US policy:

> a possible feudal revival via the sultan of Yogyakarta, the "Indonesian National Party" and Masjumi, as a result of which all the prospects of modernization of the Indonesian society might be destroyed. . . .[732]

On May 22, 1949, *Siasat* dismissed as gossip and "wishful thinking" reports that Sjafroeddin's emergency government in West Sumatra might have already returned its mandate to Sukarno and Hatta or to the Sultan.[733] On May 29, another *Siasat* cartoon showed Sjafroeddin beaten over the head with a big hammer, on which was written "For the Sake of Unity."[734]

---

[728] Kahin, *Nationalism and Revolution*, p. 426; see also McMahon, *Colonialism*, pp. 295–96.

[729] *Siasat*, May 15, 1949.

[730] Ali Sastroamijoyo, *Milestones on my Journey*, p. 194.

[731] "Republikeinse visie," June 17, 1949, *Archief Alg Secr, 2de zending*, no. 17-365-68.

[732] Ibid.

[733] *Siasat*, May 22, 1949, editorial.

[734] Ibid. May 29, 1949. On June 19, *Siasat* published among its "Letters from our readers," an inquiry from one Comrade Rasidi: "Did *Siasat*, judging from the way it is now writing, lose its confidence in the leadership of Sukarno-Hatta?" Maybe, *Siasat* itself invented the letter, in order to make an opening for it to answer. *Siasat* responded to "Comrade Rasidi" in a way,

On June 5, *Siasat* explained why Sukarno and Hatta moved so slowly, why they acted so "hesitantly," why their policy was so "improvised." They were "afraid [*takut*]," *Siasat* wrote, because if they should truly get moving, the people [*rakjat*] might find out that these two men were, in fact, marching "in a yoke [*binnen het gareel*]."[735]

In mid-1949, rumors still had some life in Jakarta that Sjahrir might act in opposition against Sukarno and Hatta, and that he might ally in this with Sjafroeddin's emergency government in Sumatra. This government, the same reports suggested, was still at that time considered by Sjahrir the sole legal authority in the Republic.[736] Then even the rumors died away. Two missions were sent by Hatta to Sjafroeddin. In early July (reportedly after some hesitation) Sjafroeddin agreed to move back to Yogyakarta after the Republic was restored there, and to return his mandate to Sukarno and Hatta.[737]

The restoration of the Republic in Yogyakarta, was agreed by Roem and Van Roijen in May, and the date of the return of the top leaders was set for July 6, 1949. Simatupang was in the welcoming party at the Yogyakarta airport:

> I saw for myself how enthusiastically the people welcomed them all along the road and at the Palace. Who can deny that the *Dwitunggal* [the twosome, Sukarno and Hatta] was a powerful factor, having an almost "magic" nature, during our revolution?[738]

The Sultan of Yogyakarta, Hamengku Buwono, led the procession, wearing the uniform of a Republican general. Behind him rode General Soedirman, referred to, on that occasion, by a most elevated ancient Javanese title reserved for the commander of the kingdom—*Gusti Tentara*.

On July 13, as agreed, Sjafroeddin Prawiranegara arrived and returned his mandate to Sukarno and Hatta. Yogyakarta became the Republic's capital again. According to a historian,

> The passions of warfare notwithstanding, the transfer was effected smoothly. It was a major feat of personal negotiation for the Republic's Coordinator of Security, Sultan Hamengku Buwono.[739]

In a cartoon, published shortly before Sukarno and Hatta returned to Yogyakarta, *Siasat* presented the chairmen of the Dutch and Indonesian delegations, Van Roijen and Roem, with President Sukarno, driving a car up a tortuous and very steep

---

which perfectly summed up their attitude and their language over the previous months: "We have never," *Siasat* answered, "said so categorically." Ibid. June 19, 1949.

[735] *Siasat*, June 5, 1949, editorial.

[736] Intelligence report by the Dutch general staff, West Java May 21, 1949 in *Archief Alg Secr, lste zending*, no. IX-28-10; also military intelligence report, Batavia no. 77, May 3, 1949 *Archief Alg Secr, 2de zending*, no. 17-365-8.

[737] Hatta, *Indonesian Patriot*, p. 305; Intelligence report by the Dutch general staff no. 79 in *Archief Alg Secr, 2de zending*, no. 17-365-8. Halim, *Di antara hempasan*, p. 95.

[738] Simatupang, *Report from Banaran*, p. 144.

[739] Herbert Feith, *The Decline of Constitutional Democracy in Indonesia* (Ithaca: Cornell University Press, 1962), p. 54.

road. Sjahrir, in the *Siasat* cartoon, sat on a fence, watching—whistling to himself, it seemed. The caption read, in English: "It's a Long-Long Way to The Hague."[740]

Some expected that Sjahrir might still be offered a government position.[741] According to Hatta, Sjahrir was offered the post of an adviser to the delegation to the final Dutch-Indonesian Round Table Conference in The Hague. Sjahrir "refused."[742]

Sjahrir was now very rarely heard of. Early in September, *Keng Po*, a Jakarta daily, described him as

> being still of the opinion that the political conduct of the Republican government vis-a-vis the Round Table Conference is not correct, that its advance towards The Hague is overhasty at a time when so many problems are not yet solved.[743]

"There are some intellectuals," *Siasat* wrote at roughly the same time,

> who say that they have stopped reading our weekly, because the only thing we can do is "criticize, criticize, and criticize."[744]

Early in August, an anonymous memo informed Meyer-Ranneft in The Hague that the Republican government, by now, was being "scrupulously rid of the persons belonging to the *Stuw* group, like [for instance] Sjahrir."[745]

To celebrate the approaching transfer of sovereignty, the government in Yogyakarta issued a commemorative set of postage stamps portraying the leaders: Sukarno, with George Washington in the background, for one rupiah; Hatta, with Lincoln, for forty cents; Maramis, with Hamilton, for twenty cents; Hadji Agoes Salim, and Benjamin Franklin, for seventeen and a half cents. As a comment put it, "poor Sjahrir came out as the cheapest—he is at three and a half cents including Jefferson."[746]

The Round Table Conference opened in The Hague, on August 23, 1949. Hatta led the Indonesian delegation, and he was assisted by Mohamad Roem. At or near the conference were some of the men and women one has learned to associate with Sjahrir. But they did not seem to matter very much.

Poppy Saleh was in Holland at the time. She had remained in Singapore when Sjahrir left for Java in 1948, and from there in late 1949 she traveled to Holland:

> we told ourselves we should keep distant for a year or two, myself and Sjahrir, to find out if we are good enough to each other for marriage.

---

[740] *Siasat*, June 5, 1949.

[741] *De Vrije Amsterdammer*, September 1949, p. 28 in *Collection van Kempen* no. 7.

[742] Rose, *Indonesia Free*, pp. 158–59. Also *Lukisan Mingguan* no. 35, 1949; copy in *Archief Alg Secr, lste zending*, no. XXI-12.

[743] *Keng Po*, September 9, 1949 in "Info on S.S." *Collection Meyer Ranneft* no. 497; also a "confidential" anonymous report dated September 16, 1949," ibid.

[744] *Siasat*, July 24, 1949.

[745] Anonymous memo August 9, 1949, *Collection Meyer Ranneft* no. 597.

[746] E.J.Mulden in *Elsevier Weekblad*, September 3, 1949 in *Collection Meyer Ranneft* no. 167.

Five Stamps (Sukarno, Hatta, Maramis, Hadji Agoes Salim, Sjahrir)
(Collection Post, Telegraph, Telephone Museum, The Hague)

Poppy Saleh did not attend the conference in any capacity, she only moved through the social circles in between the meetings. She also did some lecturing, and on one of these occasions, at a women's club, she met Maria Duchâteau; we know nothing more about their encounter. For the next year, Poppy Saleh enrolled in the University of Leiden to study law.[747]

Two of Sjahrir's Bandanese foster children were near the conference. Des Alwi appeared one day, surprising "Uncle" Hatta, so Des Alwi recalled, and making Hatta angry: "What are you doing here? You have nothing better to do than hang around like that?" Hatta gave Des Alwi fifty guilders anyway, as a month allowance, but "Mimi got one hundred," as Des Alwi remembered.[748] Mimi, the younger of Sjahrir's two foster daughters, worked at the conference. John Coast, who was also in The Hague, and on Hatta's staff, remembered later that he had to translate into English some text by Hatta, at the conference, "that had first been attempted and bewitched by Mimi Sjahrir."[749]

Among some others, Daan Jahja, of the medical school during the Japanese occupation, and one of Sjahrir's young followers at that time, now worked on the conference's military commission. But there are no records of any communication between Daan Jahja in The Hague and Sjahrir in Jakarta. Hamid Algadri, another of Sjahrir's young followers in the recent past, worked on the law commission; he recalled that, indeed, he was sent to The Hague by Sjahrir, to write reports. He did this, and he also repeatedly asked Sjahrir to come. Sjahrir did not, and Hamid Algadri, three decades later, still strongly felt that it had been a grave mistake.[750]

Painter Salim, a friend of Sjahrir from the prewar years, also appeared. He had left Holland in 1947, in part as a protest against the first Dutch military action in Indonesia. Now, Salim visited Holland from Paris, where he lived most of the time, to exhibit some of his paintings and thus to contribute to "the days of victory." An Indonesian art historian heard from Salim later how unpleasant in fact this had been:

> The exhibition was opened on October 8, by Charles Roelofsz at the gallery De Boer in Amsterdam.... Mohammad Hatta, the chairman of the delegation, sent his apologies for not being present and wished Salim success. The official in charge of cultural affairs [in the Indonesian delegation] did not come till the last day of the exhibition, and then he criticized Salim's work as "too Western," evidently because he did not see the landscapes with rice fields, which he thought representative of the Indonesian identity. The Dutch papers referred to Salim as an Indonesian painter and his work they described as Oriental.[751]

---

[747] Interview with Siti Wahjunah Sjahrir, Jakarta, January 11, 1988; "Riwajat Hidup Soetan Sjahrir."

[748] Interview with Des Alwi, Jakarta, December 3, 1987.

[749] Coast, *Recruit to Revolution*, p. 268.

[750] Interview with Hamid Algadri, Jakarta, December 13, 1987.

[751] Yazir Marzuki, *Pelukis Salim*, p. 55; also Hazil Tanzil, "Pelukis Salim: Barat atau Timur," *Indonesia* II,4 (1951): 16; interview with Salim, Paris, February 2, 1988.

Under pressure the Republican delegation accepted that the huge sum of 4,300 million guilders be paid by the future Indonesian state as a debt to Holland.[752] Other painful concessions were agreed to by the Indonesians in the fields of economic, administrative, and military affairs. The future Indonesian state was to have a federal structure, with the Republic of Indonesia territorially restricted only to parts of Java and Sumatra. The Indonesians also capitulated to the Dutch demand that West New Guinea should be recognized as an area in dispute, and thus remain, for the time being, a Dutch possession.

On November 2, 1949, the Round Table Conference ended. December 27, 1949, was agreed upon as the date on which sovereignty would be formally transferred. *Siasat* welcomed the outcome, on November 6, by depicting Hatta hurrying back home carrying a pitiful bundle over a shoulder. There was a big hole moreover, in the sack, and a package labeled "Irian," the Indonesian name for New Guinea, was seen falling out through the hole. The *Siasat* caption read: "You have dropped something, Comrade!"[753]

Two years after all this happened, Sjahrir told John Coast "that Hatta had achieved more than he [Sjahrir] had believed" was possible. Yet, Sjahrir added, it became clear, at the moment of the agreement, "that it would now be impossible to carry out a Socialist economic policy or a really free foreign policy."[754]

This was the moment that might be described as the end of the Indonesian Revolution. On December 15, 1949, a plenary session of the provisional parliament of the "United States of Indonesia" ratified The Hague Agreement by 236 votes against 62, with 31 abstentions. In the words of a historian,

> Opposition votes were cast by members of the two communist parties and of various smaller organizations related to one of these. The [Sjahrir's] Indonesian Socialist Party and its sympathizers accounted for most of the abstentions.[755]

Hatta, recalling the events later, seemed even to forget to mention the "nays" cast by the Communists. He remembered with bitterness the vote of December 15, as "opposition by Sjahrir and his party."[756]

The formal transfer of sovereignty, on December 27, 1949, was carried out simultaneously in The Hague, Jakarta, and Yogyakarta. In The Hague,

> Hatta made a brief speech in which he expressed his hopes for the future of Indonesia. Queen Juliana then shook his hand, while a carillon of palace

---

[752] Especially Soemitro Djojohadikoesoemo, close to Hatta through his father Margono, but increasingly close to the PSI and Sjahrir, too, was reported as working against accepting such a large debt. See, e.g., *Siasat*, October 11, 1949, Rose, *Indonesia Free*, p. 160; Roem, *Bunga Rampai Dari Sedjarah*, 2: 67.

[753] *Siasat*, November 6, 1949.

[754] Coast, *Recruit to Revolution*, p. 293.

[755] Feith, *The Decline*, p. 56.

[756] Hatta, *Indonesian Patriot*, p. 309.

bells rang out the *Wilhelmus*, the Dutch anthem, followed by *Indonesia Raja*.[757]

In Jakarta, Sultan Hamengku Buwono received the charter of sovereignty in the name of the United States of Indonesia; in Yogyakarta, Sukarno received it, for the Republic.[758]

It was decided, that, now, when the world recognized the new state, the capital might move back to Jakarta. On December 28, 1949—not in the Special Train, but in "his newly painted red-and-white Dakota plane"—Sukarno arrived from the interior.[759] He spoke briefly, on his arrival, to a triumphant welcome:

> For four years, four times three hundred and sixty five days, I have been away from Jakarta. It feels like forty years. I salute all. Officers and soldiers. Civil servants. Comrades rikshaw drivers and comrades vegetable men. The lowest officials. Nobody should be forgotten. I thank you all.[760]

It is not easy to find Sjahrir among the prominent figures at the celebrations. Among about twenty photographs printed in the official *Lukisan Revolusi*, "Pictures of the Revolution," there is only one picture of him: among the foreign guests.[761]

---

[757] Rose, *Indonesia Free*, p. 162. We read in McMahon: "although a note on the program requested the participants and witnesses to the ceremony not to sing, the sound of voices soon filled the hall." McMahon, *Colonialism*, p. 10.

[758] Feith, *The Decline*, p. 57.

[759] McMahon, *Colonialism*, p. 10.

[760] From the caption under the picture of Sukarno addressing the people, in *Lukisan Revolusi Indonesia: Indonesia, 1945–1950* (Jakarta: Kementerian Penerangan Republik Indonesia, n.d.).

[761] Ibid. The caption under the picture is "*Utusan-Utusan Luar Negeri jang turut hadir.*" Sjahrir is not mentioned, though he is quite visible and smiling broadly.

9

THE FIFTIES, 1950–1959

> One bright spot in all this is that our country people have not yet been greatly disturbed by all the problems at the government level. [There is] the regenerating strength of the Indonesian people.... The people in the *desa* or village produce their own food and do not have so many needs from the outside world. The *desa* has shown in the past that it can survive without money. In our national existence then, it goes to make up a vast area where the tendency toward stability and order is at its greatest.
>
> Sjahrir in Atlantic, June 1956.[1]

1. THE FLUIDITY OF POWER

In the first cabinet of the United States of Indonesia, USI, inaugurated in December 1949 by Vice-President Hatta, who was also the prime minister, Sjahrir's party, the Socialist Party of Indonesia, PSI, held no seat. However, according to Herbert Feith's classic on the period, "a number of the members of this cabinet were regarded as being among its [PSI] sympathizers."[2] In the first cabinet of the Republic of Indonesia, inaugurated at the same time, a member state of the USI federation, according again to Feith,

> three [PSI] members held portfolios, and a number of other ministers, including [the premier] Dr. Halim himself, were PSI sympathizers.[3]

In about a year after the Round Table Conference, the federal structure of independent Indonesia crumbled, and a unitary republic was declared in the whole area of the former Dutch East Indies except for the western part of New Guinea or Irian Barat. In the first cabinet of the unitary and all-Indonesian Republic, in a cabinet which came to office in September 1950 and was led by Mohammad Natsir of the Islamic party, Masjumi, according to Feith,

---

[1] Sutan Sjahrir, "Problems the Country Faces," *Atlantic* 107, 6 (June 1956): 120.
[2] Feith, *The Decline of Constitutional Democracy*, p. 129
[3] Ibid.

the PSI obtained great influence. The party obtained one important portfolio in its own name, in that Dr. Sumitro Djojohadikusumo . . . moved into the Trade and Industry post. But more important was the fact that all of the five nonparty members of the cabinet had PSI sympathies in one or another degree.[4]

In the Sukiman cabinet that followed in April 1951, there was continuity in some government policies, namely continued pursuit of Soemitro's economic plan. But, according to Feith, Sjahrir's "Socialist Party was in no way included." Other groups rather grew to prominence—some friends of Sukarno from the prewar Indonesian National Party, a small cluster around Soebardjo—people largely involved on the antigovernment and anti-Sjahrir side in the July 3 affair in 1946—and an orthodox wing of Islamic politics in the Nahdatul Ulama party; Sukiman's faction prevailed in the Masjumi, at the expense of the "religious socialists," men like Natsir, Roem, or Sjafroeddin Prawiranagara, who were known as often being close to the PSI and Sjahrir.[5]

The Wilopo cabinet, which came next, in April 1952, according to Feith,

> encountered a number of difficulties as it became clear that he [Wilopo] selected men on the basis of a policy approach like that of Sjahrir and Natsir. . . . The important posts [were] given to Roem, Sumitro, and Sultan Hamengku Buwono."[6]

The following cabinet of Ali Sastroamidjojo, which took office in July 1953, was described, by Feith, as

> an inversion of the Natsir cabinet situation. The PNI [Indonesian National Party], with its four major portfolios, dominated the new cabinet. The Masjumi was excluded for the first time in the post-revolutionary period, along with the PSI . . . the cabinet may be regarded as marking the return to power of the groups which Sjahrir and Hatta had displaced from top positions in the latter part of 1945. . . .[7]

Herbert Feith characterized the whole period between 1949 and 1956 as that of the "decline of constitutional democracy." He argued, throughout his book, that

> the Indonesian leaders [did] commit themselves to a Western type constitutional democracy [largely because] there was no other system of legitimacy symbols and constitutional arrangements on which consensus could have been achieved in the political elite at the time.[8]

The dynamics of the period, according to Feith, were essentially of loosening and weakening the predominance of what he termed "administrators" as against "soli-

---

[4] Ibid., p. 151
[5] Ibid., pp. 211, 180–82.
[6] Ibid., pp. 228, 230.
[7] Ibid., pp. 339, 342.
[8] Ibid., pp. 43-44.

darity makers." Feith wrote of the "fluidity of power relations" through the 1950s,[9] a fluidity, which—however paradoxical it might sound—grew with the growing prominence of the "solidity makers," and with the growing role of government in all aspects of Indonesian life.[10]

Clifford Geertz has called Indonesia as it developed out of the Revolution

> a state *manqué*, a country which unable to find a political form appropriate to the temper of its people, stumbles on apprehensively from one institutional contrivance to the next.[11]

Ruth McVey reflecting on the looseness of the political system, and especially on its failure to inspire deeper social change, wrote about the Indonesian leaders:

> they have looked to filling the gap between elite and masses through education and economic growth, arguing that as the populace becomes ready for constructive participation it will be allowed a greater voice in the running of its affairs.

"Again," McVey added, "the argument is similar to that of colonial reform."[12]

---

[9] Ibid., p. 311.
[10] Ibid., pp. 105, 106.
[11] Clifford Geertz, "The Politics of Meaning," in *Culture and Politics in Indonesia*, ed. Holt et al., p. 323.
[12] Ruth T. McVey, "Local Voices, Central Power" in *Southeast Asia Transitions: Approaches through Social History*, ed. Ruth T. McVey (New Haven: Yale University Press, 1978), p. 22.

The prewar *Koningsplein*, "Royal Square," the huge plaza in the middle of Jakarta, was, now, *Médan Merdeka*, "Freedom Square." The palace on the plaza's north side, of white marble and with tall pillars, formerly the seat of the Dutch Governor-General, was now the Presidential Palace. A large white bungalow across the square, recently the office of the commandant of the Dutch army, was now the residence of Vice-President Hatta. The former building of the *Volksraad*, the colonial semi-parliament, also a pillared palace in an adjoining street, served now as the Republican Ministry of Foreign Affairs. Next to it, in the seat of the former Council of the Indies, the cabinet of the Republic now held its sessions.

The new state was expected, to "divorce" from Holland. John Coast, who returned for a visit in the early 1950s, described how the agreement of the Round Table Conference of 1949 was implemented, which guaranteed former colonial government servants employment in Indonesia for two more years, at least, after sovereignty was transferred:

> Most comic of all was the so-called Ministry of Information in Jakarta. Though [Indonesians were formally the bosses], the Ministry was simply the old R.V.D.—the Dutch Government Information Service ... these same people would be expected to help make *free* Indonesian internal and foreign propaganda for two years. Everywhere in the Ministry there were Dutchmen and Eurasians; the few Republic Indonesians were lonely, half-amused and half-furious.[13]

Herbert Feith wrote also of "different 'cognitive maps'" of the new Republic— two streams, essentially, which he defined as "the Javanese aristocratic culture," principally in East and Central Java, and the "Islamic-entrepreneurial culture," mainly outside this area, in Sumatra principally, and in other Outer Islands. The divisions on the map, according to Feith, were "latent in 1949," as the nation was more united in its struggle against the common enemy, "but the rapid expansion of mass communications of subsequent years was likely to make them much less so."[14] The Indonesian National Party, in Feith's words, "was in fact the principal organization representing the 'Javanese-aristocratic political culture.'" The Masjumi, especially its "progressive" wing represented by Natsir, "was the principal representative of the 'Islamic-entrepreneurial political culture.'"[15]

Besides, Feith wrote, "in the atmosphere of political drama and excitement produced by the unitarian movement," as the experiment with constitutional democracy was failing, and as the "solidarity makers" were becoming increasingly prominent, "Soekarno began to re-emerge."[16]

---

[13] Coast, *Recruit to Revolution*, p. 294. Emphasis by Coast.

[14] Feith, *The Decline*, pp. 600, 30, 32.

[15] Ibid., pp. 139, 137.

[16] Ibid., p. 77. The position of Hatta was ambiguous. He was still playing very much the part of the center, the role of the vice-president. Sometimes, as Hatta's moves towards the mid-1950s became more independent of Sukarno, they were too easily perceived as moves towards Sjahrir. Hatta still clearly and often very strongly disagreed with his prewar friend and colleague. He especially shrugged at what he saw as Sjahrir's continuous shedding of responsibility first for the revolution and now for the new state. There were some bitter encounters; however very few of them surfaced at the time. As noted, shortly before sovereignty was transferred, late in 1949, the PSI opposed a constitutional clause which was to give the vice-

It is striking how often Herbert Feith in his book used the term "sympathizers" in describing the power of the PSI and Sjahrir after 1950; how often, also, in the same connection, words like "alleged" have been used by other authors. Some of the most prominent Sjahrir "sympathizers," such as Ali Boediardjo or Dr. Halim, were in fact men of very divided loyalties; what did it truly mean, these complex and largely independent personalities, or Sultan Hamengku Buwono, for instance, being "allegedly" close to Sjahrir? The language in which the 1950s are conveyed makes one wonder again: what was the meaning of the looseness; and what was the real nature of Sjahrir's power.

There was, as noted, rarely a PSI member in the cabinet during the 1950s. Those few who became ministers behaved with a striking and uncommon independence. Soemitro Djojohadikusumo, the most powerful "Sjahririan" ever in a Republican cabinet after 1949, was also the most flagrant case of the looseness of the political, as well as personal, ties both to the PSI and to Sjahrir.

To the Hatta cabinet and to the subsequent cabinet of Natsir, the PSI behaved with detachment, and the distance grew with each successive administration. The PSI's campaign against corruption in government gained in intensity through the first half of the 1950s, and it added to an increasingly pervasive public image of the PSI: not as an ethical and pure party necessarily, but certainly as the party keeping itself, for whatever reason, aloof from the open and actual working of the state.

Not in the least pro-Soviet, the PSI opposed the cabinet's pro-US drive in 1951, to participate in the San Francisco conference on the peace-treaty with Japan. Not in the least pro-Communist, the PSI distanced itself, in the same year, from the police raids ordered by Sukiman's cabinet against the left trade-unions; the PSI made a point of declaring, on this occasion, that it considered the raids part of the Indonesian cabinet's excessive willingness to succumb to US world dominance.[17]

As the Wilopo cabinet came to power, in 1952, with fewer Sjahrir "sympathizers" and "alleged" Sjahrir allies in its ranks, the PSI did not go into opposition—it lengthened its distance. When the next prime minister, Ali Sastroamidjojo, in 1953, announced the composition of his cabinet, pro-PSI papers reacted "with expressions of shock and contempt": when it came to a motion in the parliament to give the Ali cabinet an "opportunity to work," the PSI deputies did not vote against—they abstained.[18]

One is reminded of the emphasis by the prewar Pendidikan and personally by Sjahrir on *akal*, "mind, brains, intellect," as the true essence of power. One is also reminded of the prewar image, and self-image especially, of the Pendidikan as an organization broader, or higher, than ordinary political parties—a matrix for educating cadres, whatever the cadres' particular politics or even party affiliation.

Some observers, indeed, wrote also about the PSI of the early 1950s, as about a "brains'-trust" of the independent Indonesian state and politics. According to John

---

president, in case of an emergency, broad powers to govern by decree. Years later, Hatta still complained about this. This behavior by Sjahrir's party, Hatta believed, weakened him substantially after 1950—and weakened him very much also in his capacity to balance Sukarno. Rose, *Indonesia Free*, pp. 173–74; interview with Subadio Sastrosatomo, Jakarta, March 4, 1982.

[17] See PSI official statement, November 28, 1951, in *Suara Sosialis* 3, 11 (October 1951).

[18] Feith, *The Decline*, pp. 343–44.

Legge, "Sjahrir's socialist Party was important for its intellectual influence on the elite...."[19] In Feith's words, Sjahrir's party

> was a party of "administrators." ... Its greatest source of strength was its position in the higher echelons of the bureaucracy. Its influence at the level of departmental and divisional heads in the capital was second only to that of the PNI. Within the top leadership of the army it could count on more sympathy than any other party.... One further source of PSI influence was the brains-trust function which the party fulfilled within the political elite generally ... outside the party itself, both in the bureaucracy and army and within leadership groups of several of the other parties, in particular the Masjumi and to a lesser extent the PNI.[20]

At the same time, not unlike before 1949, and, indeed, not unlike before the war when the Dutch were trying to explain to themselves the "strangeness" of the Pendidikan, another image of the PSI gained wide currency—that of a party which under the surface of apparent disinterest in and detachment from open and actual politics, worked as a compact group "silently" and "underground."

Very few political parties, groups, or individuals inspired so many rumors, during the early 1950s, as the PSI and Sjahrir. The rumors might range from rather innocent Jakarta gossip, such as that, in September 1950,

> Natsir, when composing his cabinet, consulted more with Subadio Sastrosatomo from the party of Soetan Sjahrir than with Jusuf Wibisono [from his own party],[21]

to very serious allegations like the *sub rosa* and anti-government influence of Sjahrir and his party among the Republic's military officers corps. When, indeed, there was the first attempt at a military coup in Indonesia, the so-called "October 17, 1952 Affair," and as the attempt quickly failed, Sjahrir and the PSI, almost automatically and clearly with gross exaggeration, were rumored as the principal force behind the affair.[22]

---

[19] Legge, *Sukarno*, p. 244.

[20] Feith, *The Decline*, pp. 129–31.

[21] Adam Malik, *Mengabdi Republik*, 2: 184.

[22] I have written about the affair in more detail in Rudolf Mrázek, *The United States and the Indonesian Military, 1945–1965: A Study of an Intervention*, vol. 1 (Prague: Academia, 1978), pp. 79–113. What was curious about this conspiratorial image, was the fact that the PSI seemed not to be especially eager to resist the charges—not as eager, at least, as one might logically expect. The accusation of their complicity in the October 17 Affair appeared occasionally even as if some in the PSI were using it to imply that there was some activity at least by the party. The author had the impression that whenever he started to talk in his interviews about the October 17 Affair, former PSI leaders and "pro-PSI officers" became suddenly secretive, although the point was never pressed too strongly and although the affair, at that time, was already a matter of the very distant past, with few evident implications for the present. Sukarno, who never hesitated to assault Sjahrir and the PSI, defined the attempted coup of October 17, 1952, in retrospect as a moment "where the army came in"; it was Nasution, Sukarno wrote, who was "in charge of this attempted 'half a coup'." Neither Sjahrir, the PSI, nor "PSI officers," were mentioned by Sukarno in the passage. Sukarno, *An Autobiography*, pp. 266–67. For Nasution's dismissal of rumors and charges of the PSI or Sjahrir having an extensive influence in the army and on the October 17, 1952 Affair see, e.g., A. H. Nasution,

There still might be, in the early 1950s, differing views about how influential Sjahrir in fact was. In 1950, John Coast, on a visit in Indonesia, still believed that

> In this newly sovereign Indonesia, Soekarno, Hatta and Sjahrir remained as the big three, with the Sultan of Jogja instead of Sjarifoeddin as the fourth.[23]

A Jakarta newspaper poll of mid-1951, however, seemed to reflect Sjahrir's position much more realistically: Sjahrir, in the poll, scored eighth among Indonesian political figures, not merely below Sukarno and Hatta, but also trailing the Sultan of Yogyakarta Hamengku Buwono, Mohamad Roem, Soekiman, Natsir, and Hadji Agoes Salim.[24]

It was not easy for any observer to define the ideology of Sjahrir and the PSI at the time. According to Herbert Feith, the PSI's policies after 1949, contained "less of Marxism than of Fabianism."[25] According to a more recent study by Fritjof Tichelman, the PSI economic platform expressed "no clear idea," and this could be explained by the fact that

> there were no economic forces among the PSI elite which if the circumstances had been favorable could have provided a starting point for economic development.[26]

The PSI's "social base" the author added, "was primarily among neo-*priyayi* bureaucracy."[27]

The term "neo-*priyayi*" in postrevolutionary Indonesia referred to the officialdom of the new state; the "neo-*priyayi*" strata was most often identified with the "Javanese-aristocratic stream." The term "neo-*priyayi*, in fact, was not far from being a current modification of the term which Sjahrir and the Pendidikan had used, before the war and through the 1940s, to describe the old-fashioned, the reactionary, the inward-looking, the "Eastern," in culture, administration, and politics—the *ningrat*.

What Fritjof Tichelman suggested, was not that the PSI had become strong through the neo-*priyayi* and among the neo-*priyayi*. Rather, according to Tichelman,

---

Memenuhi Panggilan Tugas III: Masa Pancaroba (Jakarta: Gunung Agung, 1983), p. 157. Herbert Feith was present in Jakarta at the time. He also did not appear to have much faith in the charges of a PSI conspiracy. He described the forces of the "coup" as an extremely loose alliance without a clear leader. In Feith's description of how the affair proceeded, it is also clear how it differed from Sjahrir's style of behavior: the coup alliance, for instance, was built on a "Djojobojo prophesy revival," and on a vague promise that, were the coup successful, a "prince of the ancient land of Java" would become the leader. The actual show of force, on October 17, according to Feith, appeared to have been decided upon and organized by younger officers, zealots of very mixed, if any, political background. The decision to train cannons on the Presidential palace in Jakarta, the climax of the affair, in Feith's words, appeared "to have been taken by a single battalion commander." Feith, *The Decline*, pp. 253–54, 262–64.

[23] Coast, *Recruit to Revolution*, p. 291.

[24] *Abadi*, June 25, 1951, quoted in St. Rais Alamsjah, *10 orang besar Indonesia*, p. 10.

[25] Feith, *The Decline*, p. 130.

[26] Tichelman, *The Social Evolution of Indonesia*, pp. 218, 220. Dr. Tichelman works at the International Institute for Social History, a body affiliated with the Socialist International.

[27] Ibid., p. 220.

if the PSI still wanted to broaden its support in any significant way, it did not have, by the early 1950s, much of an alternative left apart from courting the neo-*priyayi* group and, thus, the "Javanese-aristocratic stream."

In such an attempt, naturally, Sjahrir and the PSI—in the context of all their previous experience and policies—could hardly be expected to be very active and to succeed. Other individuals and groups were better equipped and more willing to appeal to the neo-*priyayi* and "Javanese-aristocratic" sense of governing. Sukarno, as might have been expected, became the most prominent individual in that way. The Indonesian National Party became the most prominent group: from after 1945 this party was thought to be the most representative of the Republic's officialdom and also, as Feith wrote,

> much more successful in arousing the enthusiasm of its adherents while avoiding the impression of being extremist. In part this was because its [the PNI] ideology built as it was on Hindu-Javanese religious foundations, had a diffuse, syncretistic, and all-enveloping character.

This very constellation, wrote Feith, left the PSI standing as "extremist, alien and inimical to the shared central core of nationalist attitudes."[28]

Between February 4 and 5, 1950, a conference of the PSI central executive, the first since the party's split with Amir Sjarifoeddin two years previously, took place in Yogyakarta. According to the PSI journal *Suara Sosialis*, "Socialist Voice," one aim of the conference was "to move the party back into the field of politics and organization."[29]

At the conference, in the words of the party's official history, "it turned out that the PSI numbered only a few thousand members."[30] Nevertheless, as the communique of the conference worded it, "the PSI cannot see the time ripe for defining strictly its attitude."[31] The PSI leadership decided that the party was to continue "to work as a close organization, membership of which was not easily to be obtained. . . ."[32] Also in the foreseeable future, "The organization was to be built up as 'a cadre party.'" Only after at least two years could "the party . . . be opened up."[33]

The conference also decided to move PSI headquarters from Yogyakarta to Jakarta. The party secretariat was housed in the center of the city, first in *Molenvliet Barat* no.188, and then in quite imposing offices, not far from the Presidential Palace, at the western side of *Médan Merdeka*.[34]

Two trimester PSI "top-cadre" courses were opened in Jakarta for thirty-six people from Java, Sumatra, Madura, and Sulawesi in February and May 1950;[35] a six-week "top-cadre" course took place in Jakarta for twenty-seven people from Java,

---

[28] Feith, *The Decline*, pp. 358–59.

[29] *Suara Sosialis* 2, 1 (August 1950).

[30] Sutan Sjahrir, *Indonesian Socialism*, p. 47.

[31] *Pedoman*, February 7, 1950.

[32] Sjahrir, *Indonesian Socialism*, pp. 47–48.

[33] Ibid.

[34] *Pedoman*, March 6, 1950; L. M. Sitoroes, "Laporan Organisasi dari Pebruari 1950 sampai 12 Pebruari 1952," *Suara Sosialis* 4, 2 (April 1952), p. 11.

[35] *Suara Sosialis* 2, 1 (August 1950).

Sumatra, Kalimantan, and Sulawesi, between March and May 1951.[36] Regional conferences of the PSI met in North Sumatra, in November 1951, and in West Kalimantan, in the same month.[37] Yet, still by the end of June 1951, one and a half years after the first PSI central executive conference, *Suara Sosialis* denied reports, "originating from Bandung," that the second all-party conference might materialize any time soon.[38]

There was continuous debate inside the PSI as to how long the party should remain "closed," and when it should "open up."[39] It took no less than four years after the party was established, till February 1952 indeed, before the PSI leadership finally decided to hold the party's First Congress.

At the time, there were 3,049 full members in the party, and about 14,480 candidate members.[40] The Islamic Masjumi, at the same time, claimed six million members; the Indonesian Communist Party, however much it had been crippled by the Madiun affair in 1948, already had a membership estimated at "slightly less than 100,000."[41] A proposal was prepared for the PSI's First Congress, to adopt a collective membership for the party in order, it was argued, to broaden its mass base: "Although in principle there was no objection to it," according to the PSI history, the proposal was "put aside" as "premature."[42]

During the congress and afterwards, some people inside the PSI suggested that it might be useful to "recruit local leaders," and, with their help, broaden the PSI base. To some extent, this was done;[43] when the Second Congress of the PSI convened, in June 1955, PSI membership had grown to 50,000. However, the Indonesian Communist Party at that time already claimed ten times as many; the Indonesian National Party, in 1955, had already a membership of several millions.[44]

Much of this might be explained by the PSI's traumatic experience in the split of February 1948, and by the damage done to the whole Indonesian left in the aftermath of the Madiun affair. As late as mid-February, 1951, the PSI leadership considered it necessary to respond by a special "declaration" to "numerous inquiries" from the party branches—to assure the branches that the PSI still existed in the form as established at the moment of the split with Amir in February 1948, and that it

> was not changed in the process by which [Amir Sjarifoeddin's] Socialist Party was dissolved and absorbed into the Communist Party.[45]

---

[36] Sitoroes, "Laporan Organisasi," pp. 11, 13.

[37] Ibid., also *Suara Sosialis* 2, 5 (December 1950).

[38] Ibid., 3, 9 (July 15, 1951).

[39] For instance, see editorial in ibid.

[40] Feith, *The Decline*, p. 130n; see also Sjahrir, *Indonesian Socialism*, p. 45;

[41] Sjahrir, *Indonesian Socialism*, pp. 50–51.

[42] Ibid., p. 49; "Instruksi Pimpinan Umum no. 6. Konperensi 2 Karya se-Daerah, 1950," quoted in Sitoroes, "Laporan Organisasi," p. 4.

[43] Kahin's interview with Sjahrir, Jakarta, December 9, 1954.

[44] Sjahrir, *Indonesian Socialism*, pp. 52–53, Jone Bos "Tien jaar democratisch-socialisme in de Republiek Indonesië 1945–1955" (Ph.D. thesis, University of Amsterdam 1979), p. 64.

[45] *Suara Sosialis* 3, 7 (February 1951). As late as April 1952, according to the report to the PSI Congress, "a great part of the comrades in the regions have not enough courage to cut their

Whatever the PSI wanted to do—if it tried to heal the trauma, if it tried to keep true to the prewar traditions of the Pendidikan, or if it merely reflected the personal moods of its leaders—furthering a distance and blurring the edges were the characteristic features of the process. In the "Principles" of the PSI, published early in 1948, under "article 1," "class struggle" was still included, albeit only as a concept for the future. By early 1952, "class struggle" had disappeared from the PSI platform. The term "socialist society," cited before as the principal aim of the PSI, was modified, in 1952, into "socialist society based on democracy."[46] Marxism, was still recognized, "but as a guide, not as a dogma."[47]

At a time when each Indonesian political party was fervently trying to create mass organizations as a vehicle for its political power, the "mass organizations" of the PSI—the Gerakan Pemuda Sosialis, GPS, "Socialist Movement of Youth"; the Gerakan Mahasiswa Sosialis, GMS, "Socialist Movement of Students"; the Gerakan Wanita Sosialis, GWS, "Socialist Movement of Women"; and the Gerakan Tani Nasional, GTN, "National Movement of Peasants"—were essentially clubs and almost "purely" educational institutions. Their character was designed again to create an image, and a self-image, of the PSI as a party with perspective, detached from the messy and increasingly dirty day-to-day politics of Indonesia. Even some PSI members, however, voiced doubts, whether this was not rather a sign of the party's unwillingness or impotency to act in politics at all.[48]

The 1950s were a time, when it was increasingly difficult for anybody in Indonesia to escape Sukarno. The president's face was everywhere; even the hero of the *Palmboom-Margarine*® advertisement, which appeared regularly in most of the newspapers, seemed to have Sukarno's features.[49] Journals like *Siasat* were still published in Jakarta, and, as in 1949, they still appeared to question Sukarno's political leadership. But often the criticism was too veiled; sometimes, now, it was difficult to say if a particular piece was a weak joke or hesitant praise. Was it an irony, for instance, when *Siasat*, in September 1951, published a big photograph of Sukarno, with a commercial-like kid on his lap, with commercial-like girls around, and with a caption: "Sjahrir says: 'Sukarno likes to be photographed'—Next week: another photo of Sukarno, this time in front of Javanese mountains"?[50]

In spite of the considerable amount of space devoted to the issues of party discipline and organization in the PSI daily press and theoretical journals, PSI veterans,

---

ties and to make their choice. A number of other (PSI) branches still hesitate as they do not truly know how indeed to understand the problem of the (February 1948) split." Ibid., 4, 2 (April 15, 1952).

[46] Ibid.

[47] Ibid., 3, 10 (August 15, 1951), ibid., 3, 11 (October 15, 1951), and ibid., 3, 12 (November 15, 1951).

[48] T. A. Moerad, for instance, an associate of Sjahrir from the time of the prewar Pendidikan, and now in the PSI leadership, made a rare appearance in 1953, at a discussion organized by Soetan Takdir Alisjahbana, where Sjahrir was also present: "In the past, when we were amidst our people, in the villages, we felt safe and tranquil. But now, when we visit villages, as if we were dropped in a jungle, it scares us and it makes us hesitant as we walk." Murad in *Symposion tentang kesulitan-kesulitan zaman peralihan sekarang* (Jakarta: Balai Pustaka, 1953), pp. 59–60.

[49] Even Moerad, on the occasion just mentioned, said—or was it sarcasm?—"Our people like technology, radio on their village commons; when they can hear Sukarno's voice, they work harder." Ibid.

[50] *Siasat*, September 23, 1951, p. 6.

when asked later, found it rather difficult to recollect how guidelines from the center were actually implemented. The old-timers tend to explain, instead, how the feeling of being a body-special kept them together: "What tied us together? Was there any party discipline? Sure: intellectual discipline."[51]

There seemed to be not much regularity in party meetings, not even in the center. There seemed to be no written invitations; not many systematic records seemed to be kept, not many files stored. Once, in an interview with a former PSI cadre, the "Rotary Club" came up as a possible comparison with how the party might have worked: the comparison seemed to work surprisingly well.

The PSI rank and file seemed to be organized first of all by attending courses, and by distributing PSI journals such as *Suara Sosialis* and *Sikap*, "Attitude." The older members might believe that this was like the situation when they had distributed the journal *Daulat Ra'jat*, twenty years ago for the Pendidikan; or like when they had moved in a loose swirl around Sjahrir during the Japanese occupation. Subadio, who became the PSI representative in Parliament in the early 1950s, when later asked about this style, explained: "We demanded that our members, our cadres, be prepared, which is get educated, and wait for when a power vacuum appears."[52]

These, however, were not the 1930s nor the 1940s. In postrevolutionary Indonesia, the actual Indonesian state existed. The politics of struggle materialized: the freedom fighters handled actual ministries, funds, cars, secretaries, ambassadorships, foreign trips. To build a political identity on detachment might easily result either in isolation or in loss of principles. Followers of Sjahrir might draw sharp and brilliant caricatures of the mainstream politicians and of Sukarno. But this could easily backfire. Sal Tas, the old prewar Dutch friend of Sjahrir, visited Indonesia in the mid-1950s and wrote later about what he described as the "rationalistic hygiene" of the PSI:

> With Sjahrir's followers, who possessed neither his originality of character nor his modesty, this attitude became exaggerated into a caricature of arrogance, typical for an elite grown sterile.[53]

There remained, by and large, familiar faces around Sjahrir throughout this period. There were not many defectors. One of them should be mentioned for future reference: Soebandrio, Indonesian ambassador to London after February 1950, began to drift away from Sjahrir at this time.[54]

Among the forty-three members of the PSI executive in 1952, many of Sjahrir's important friends and associates from the past might be encountered:

---

[51] These statements repeated through most of the interviews with the PSI (ex) members.

[52] Interview with Subadio, Jakarta, October 18, 1987.

[53] Tas, "Souvenirs of Sjahrir," pp. 153–54. This may be too harsh an image marked by nostalgia for Sjahrir as remembered, or invented, from the 1920s and from the young Amsterdam times; but to some extent it might be a part of the Sjahririans' self-image, too. The otherwise striking fact was that it was these Sjahririans, who reprinted the passage from Tas in the memorial volume for Sjahrir in 1980. See H. Rosihan Anwar, ed., *Mengenang Sjahrir*, pp. 215–32.

[54] *Pedoman*, February 25, 1950.

1. Djohan Sjahroezah, 2. Subadio . . . 4. Soemitro, 5. Moerad . . . 10. Sastra, 11. Hamdani . . . 22. Soegra . . . 24. Soebagio . . . 29. Leon Salim . . . 31. Ibrahim Jahja . . . 34. Riekerk, 35. Soewarni Pringgodigdo . . . 37. Soekaemi. . . .[55]

Others, not listed as members of the PSI executive, moved nearby. Charles Tambu, for instance, served the Republic in the Philippines, and still was believed to be loyal to Sjahrir;[56] Soedjatmoko went to study at Harvard, in the early 1950s, but was recalled to work at the Indonesian embassy in London.[57]

Djohan Sjahroezah, Moerad, Idham, Hamid Algadri, and Hazil Tanzil, were on the editorial staff of the PSI journal, *Sikap*; Ibrahim Jahja was the *Sikap* board's secretary. Mochtar Lubis was in charge of the Jakarta influential, "independent" but pro-Sjahrir daily, *Indonesia Raja*, "Great Indonesia." Mochtar also became close to Sjahrir personally. With him Sjahrir realized one of his dreams, it seems—he took an aviation course, and attempted a flight even from Jakarta to Bandung; friends recall that Sjahrir lost his way but landed safely.

Some "progressive Dutchmen" remained at a short distance from Sjahrir. Dirk de Vries and Rob Niewenhuys worked on the board of the Jakarta Dutch-language fortnightly, *Oriëntatie*; both men had been close to *Kritiek en Opbouw* before the war. Jan Boon, a Eurasian, also near du Perron's circle before the war, wrote now under his pseudonyms, Vincent Mahieu or Tjalie Robinson, in *Oriëntatie* and elsewhere; he was described in one of the *Oriëntatie*'s editorials as the author who was keeping alive an important tradition of "a sort of 'Creole literature' in Indonesia"; Tjalie Robinson himself defined the style as *creoolse surrealism*, "Creole surrealism."[58]

In *Oriëntatie*, poems by J. E. Tatengkeng were also published. We recall Tatengkeng's polemic with Sjahrir in 1939. Now Tatengkeng became a member of Sjahrir's PSI. Something very significant from the past echoed faintly. Tatengkeng's poems in *Oriëntatie* were translated into Dutch by W. Lefebvre—a man cited by Sjahrir in his letters from Banda Neira as a positive example of Dutch "ethical policy"— and the poems were dedicated to Jef Last![59]

Another journal, similar to *Oriëntatie* but in Indonesian, a fortnightly *Konfrontasi*, "Confrontation," appeared in Jakarta at this time. Soetan Takdir Alisjahbana was in charge of the journal. He was assisted among others by Beb Vuyk, Sjahrir's Eurasian friend from before the war, and by Djohan Sjahroezah's brother, Hazil Tanzil.[60]

There were still debates going on about "the East" and "the West." In a public debate, in 1953, where Sjahrir was also present, some participants complained that the PSI discussants, as usual, were too sharp in accusing others of having too much of "Eastern mentality," and "reactionary Javanism." One of the accused declared, turning to T.A.Moerad, an old associate of Sjahrir, and now a leading member of the PSI, "If I am not mistaken, comrade Moerad believes that I still live in the world of Madjapahit."[61] Another man, reprimanded by Soetan Takdir Alisjahbana for

---

[55] *Suara Sosialis* 4, 2 (April 1952): 19.

[56] *Pedoman*, February 10, 1950.

[57] Interview with Soedjatmoko, Jakarta, November 6, 1987.

[58] *Oriëntatie* 36 (September 1950): 2.

[59] *Oriëntatie* 44 (January/June 1952): 457.

[60] Altogether about 35 numbers of *Konfrontasi* were published in the six years between 1954 and 1960.

[61] Dr. Ismail in *Symposion tentang kesulitan*, p. 72.

criticizing Sjahrir as too pro-Western, defended himself vehemently against the accusation:

> Comrade Takdir says that I have accused comrade Sjahrir of thinking too much in a Western way. No... I should say that I myself lean towards Western culture, I myself want the Western cultural standard to become the standard of ourselves.[62]

Siasat liked to present Sukarno as "the wajang enthusiast," and as a man, who "does not like Picasso."[63] Every *Siasat* reader was supposed to understand what was meant by this.[64] Salim, the painter, Sjahrir's prewar friend, was now lauded by the people around *Siasat*, *Oriëntatie*, and *Konfrontasi* as "one of the greatest painters of our nation."[65] Salim's ways were "Picasso's ways"—"modern." But Salim still lived in France, and made it increasingly clear that he did not intend to return to Indonesia, except "perhaps to visit, for some time, Jakarta, Jogjakarta, the island of Banda, or the land of Toradja."[66]

Sjahrir opened an exhibition of Salim's painting in Jakarta, in 1951, with a speech in Indonesian. It was not a big success:

> Yet, the people applauded at the end. Perhaps because it was Sjahrir, perhaps because the speech was over, perhaps because it was short. All three explanations may be correct, but not that people applauded because they enjoyed the speech: the majority of the audience were Dutch and they understood Dutch only.[67]

The expression "dead end," in Indonesian *djalan buntu*, was now often used in the circles around Sjahrir. We may recall that back in 1931, twenty years before, young Sjahrir had been careful to use the (Dutch) expression *dood punt*, "standstill," instead of "dead end." Then, what seemed to be most important was to imply that dynamism, the movement, might be renewed in future.[68]

When Sjahrir's friend Mochtar Lubis published his big novel on the 1950s, *Sendja Djakarta*, "Twilight in Jakarta," he used a motto from Arthur Koestler. The motto in a sense dealt with the notion of "dead end," too; and there was no standstill. It had the theme of a perfect executioner. The man condemned was about to die smoothly, without feeling, indeed without even being aware that he already was dead:

> When this man began to ascend the steps of the scaffold Wang Lun's sword flashed with such lightning speed across his neck that the man's head re-

---

[62] Ibid., p. 74.

[63] *Siasat*, September 18, 1951, p. 21.

[64] The "*wajang [wayang]*," the shadow play often dramatizing themes from Hindu epics, of course, was the epitome for everything "Javanese," "traditional," and "Eastern."

[65] Trisno Sumardjo, "Salim diantara Kita," *Zenith* 1, 6 (1951): 330.

[66] Sitor Situmorang, "Salim," *Zenith* 1,1 (1951): 15–16; Yazir Marzuki, *Pelukis Salim*, p. 55; Hazil Tanzil, "Pelukis Salim: Barat atau Timur," pp. 17–19.

[67] Ida Anwar (pseud.), *Cultureel Nieuws* 16 (January 1951), p. 174; reprinted from *Zenith* (Jakarta) of June 1950.

[68] For instance, Takdir Alisjahbana introducing Sjahrir at *Symposion tentang kesulitan*, pp. 9–10.

mained where it had been before, and he continued to walk up the steps without knowing what had happened. When he reached the top of the scaffold, the man addressed Wang Lun as follows. "Oh cruel Wang Lun, why do you prolong my agony of waiting when you dealt with the others with such merciful and amiable speed?" A serene smile appeared on [the executioner's] features; then he said with exquisite courtesy to the waiting man: "Just kindly nod, please."[69]

Jakarta culture seemed to be still in place, but it moved with an increasingly evident stiffness. "Western" movies were again shown—in 1950, for instance, *Under the Red Robe* at the *Astoria*, *Pirates of Monterey* at the *Rex*, and *The Thief of Baghdad* at the *Thalia*.[70] *High Noon* was "a tune very popular" in Mochtar Lubis' novel. A hero of the novel also listened to Schubert ("Death and the Maiden," of course); the story's villain at one moment became so pleased that

> he pulled his wife off the bed and made her dance with him turning around the room to the tune of *The Blue Danube* waltz he was singing at the top of his voice.[71]

The notion of "the West" was always vacillating in Indonesia between two poles: between being a disturbing, exciting, and inspiring culture, and being an empty farce. Now, in the world of Mochtar Lubis' novel—and perhaps not too far from Sjahrir's—it progressed clearly towards the farcical sphere.

In August 1950, in a panel discussion on the current state of Indonesian art and culture organized by *Siasat*, Rosihan Anwar, a young follower of Sjahrir, a poet and a journalist, said that "In poetry, except for a few epigones of Chairil Anwar, one can see little that is new"; what remained, Rosihan Anwar added, was merely "virtuosity of language." According to Idrus, another young author of the revolutionary "Generation of 1945," the situation in prose-writing was no better; besides, "Idrus declared that for the time being he himself would not write anything." Modern Indonesian drama, according to the same *Siasat* panel, also "offers a sorry spectacle." There were two terms used repeatedly through the debate, a sort of variation on the theme of "dead end"—"impasse" and, even more often, "weariness."[72]

Chairil Anwar had died fifteen months before this, on April 28, 1949, and his funeral in Jakarta, where Sjahrir was also present, was seen by many as the end of the generation. One poem, found in Chairil Anwar's last notebook, was later often quoted by those who survived him:

> Let's
> Leave here
> Just as we planned, just
> As we agreed
> Once

---

[69] Mochtar Lubis, *Twilight in Djakarta*; translated by Claire Holt (New York: Vanguard Press, 1963), p. 13.
[70] *Pedoman*, May 1950.
[71] Lubis, *Twilight in Djakarta*, p. 205.
[72] *Siasat*, August 20, 1950.

> And one by one
> Give up everything
> In this most progressive of worlds
>
> Before we go
> Let's strip the waving trees
> Let's shave off women's long waving hair
>
> But don't cut down desire.[73]

J. E. Tatengkeng, newly a cadre in Sjahrir's PSI, still wrote poetry. This particular little poem by him became quite famous in Indonesia at the time. It had a title *Penumpang Klas I.*, "Traveller First Class":

> Before I was thirty
> I was never more than a deck passenger.
> Thanks to the efforts of my friends
> And the transfer of sovereignty
> I'm now a traveller first class.
>
> I'm one of the army
> Of inspection officials
> Wandering
> From island to island
> Building up the country.
>
> Every evening I play bridge in the salon
> And drink my beer
> And rage at the waiter.
>
> I've never written a report.
>
> I disembark
> And give half a rupiah
> For the workers on the First of May.[74]

Beb Vuyk visited Banda Neira in 1950. She wrote a serialized travelogue for the PSI's paper *Pedoman*, "Compass." "There is not much passion in the people here," Beb Vuyk wrote from the place where Sjahrir had spent seven years of his exile,

> no national consciousness, no spirit to carry on social struggles; they accept [slogans of] colonialism, [regionalism], Indonesian Republic, without their feelings being touched....

---

[73] Chairil Anwar translated by Burton Raffael. See Burton Raffael, ed., *Anthology of Modern Indonesian Poetry* (Berkeley: University of California Press, 1964), p. 52.

[74] Ibid., p. 48.

Beb Vuyk, while on Banda Neira, also visited one of the increasingly frequent nationalist ceremonies of the new state: "*Indonesia Raja*," she wrote, "was sung by the youth ... [it jittered] in uncertain voices of school children; adults did not join in."[75]

2. ORACLE OF DELPHI

Sjahrir continued living in his house in Jakarta, *Javaweg* 61, the street was now renamed *H.O.S. Tjokroaminoto*, with his adopted Bandanese children. For some time, his youngest brother also lived there with him.

It seems that Sjahrir's personal library had changed little when I saw it in the 1980s. There were not too many shelves, but the books were visibly frequently used—the collected works of Dutch poet Hendrik Marsman, a contemporary and a friend of du Perron, several volumes by *Tante* Henriëtte Roland Holst, several other anthologies of Dutch poetry of the twentieth century, novels by Beb Vuyk, a Dutch encyclopaedia, a couple of reference books and booklets on socialism in Italy, Britain, and generally in Europe; books in Dutch, English, and German; quite a number of English paperbacks, novels, and mysteries; books mostly published in the late 1940s and early 1950s.[76]

In the first half of the 1950s Sjahrir traveled once to the West. Between April and October 1951, he visited Egypt, then via Italy he went to Paris, London, Amsterdam, Scandinavia, Poland, Yugoslavia, and through Singapore back home. One of the reasons for the trip was to meet Poppy Saleh, after two years of separation. "I went to Europe, in 1949, Leiden first," Poppy Saleh recalled,

> to study law; then to London to the London School of Economics. When I was in London, a letter came from Sjahrir proposing marriage. I let my brother, Soedjatmoko, know, he was in New York at the time, and asked him to come to be present at the wedding.[77]

The wedding had originally been planned to take place in a mosque in London. For some reason, finally, Cairo was decided upon. On May 26, 1951, the rector of *al Azhar* university officiated at the marriage. The ceremony was performed in a purely Moslem way. The bride says she was not admitted to the ceremony, and only after everything was over was she allowed to come in from the back and the couple exchanged rings. "To have some proof that I am married," Sjahrir then said to her, and "I've bought you for ten piastres"; jokingly so, Mrs. Sjahrir says, but "otherwise he took everything very seriously."[78]

From Cairo, the newlywed couple, and also Mimi, the younger of Sjahrir's Bandanese adopted daughters, went to Italy. They honeymooned in Capri, Venice, Florence, then went to Paris and Amsterdam. The trip, in Mrs. Sjahrir's recollection, was paid for by a certain Mr. Dreher, a Dutch friend of Sjahrir, but she did not remember from where Sjahrir had known him.[79] There was a short notice about the trip published in *Siasat*, in late June 1951. Above a caption "*Honeymoon*," there is a

---

[75] Beb Vuyk, "Banda Tiada Bertjita-tjita," *Pedoman*, October 18, 1950.

[76] Visit to Sjahrir's house, graciously permitted by Siti Wahjunah Sjahrir.

[77] Interview with Siti Wahjunah Sjahrir, October 17, 1987.

[78] Ibid., March 1982. Report on the wedding and a photo from a reception at the Indonesian Embassy in *Siasat*, June 17, 1951.

[79] Interview with Siti Wahjunah Sjahrir, Jakarta, November 15, 1987.

photograph of the two of them, in a motorboat "traveling around Venice"—Poppy is smiling at Sjahrir, Sjahrir is wearing a checked sports jacket, with, as far as the black-and-white photo allows one to judge, a rather loud tie.[80] Sjahrir was forty-one at the time.

From Amsterdam, Sjahrir continued on his trip through Europe—to study European socialism, and to talk to some European socialist leaders. We will return to the trip later. Poppy and Mimi, returned together to Indonesia.

As it happened, the two women traveled on *Willem Doos*, the same ship as Maria, Sjahrir's former wife. Maria had meanwhile married again, and again into Sjahrir's family. She and Sjahrir's younger brother Sjahsam had become close, and had lived together from the time Sjahrir sent Sjahsam to Holland, back in the early 1930s. By now, Sjahsam was a very successful businessman, and was sending Maria to look for a house in Jakarta. Sjahsam and Maria's little son were also on the ship, and Poppy recalled:

> Maria Duchâteau traveled a different way than we did. She had *de luxe* class, and she and the boy had a *de luxe* deck for themselves. But to us, she was very nice.[81]

Since January 1950, Sjahrir had held no official state position. He was not seen very often at PSI functions either. This, at least, is the impression one gets from the party newpapers and, also, from the later histories of the party.[82] He did attend the top-level party conference, in early February 1950. Afterwards, however, and till almost ten months later, there was virtually no mention of him, not even in the PSI press. In November 1950, Sjahrir was reported again, as visiting a conference of the PSI's North Sumatra branch in Medan.[83] Again, more than two months passed before he appeared in the news again, this time, between February 25 and 28, as touring the Kalimantan PSI branches in Balikpapan, Bandjermasin, and Barabai "to explain attitudes and policies of the party and observe the organization"; from Kalimantan, between March 3 and 10, 1951, Sjahrir went to Sulawesi and visited PSI branches in Makassar, Singkong, Pare Pare, and Makale.[84]

While Sjahrir was in Europe, between April and October 1951, Djohan Sjahroezah was in charge of the PSI. In fact, the decision about the date of the First Party Congress was made while Sjahrir was absent.[85] Shortly after Sjahrir came back in October 1951, he attended a PSI regional conference in Western Kalimantan.[86] Then again, there was practically no mention of him until the First PSI Congress convened, in Bandung, in February 1952.

At the same time, and as if by the same token, Sjahrir's position in the PSI became extraordinary. Rarely in the news, and rarely, evidently, in the day-to-day politics of the party, yet Sjahrir, in a sense, became the party. The PSI principles and

---

[80] *Siasat*, June 24, 1951, p. 4.
[81] Interview with Siti Wahjunah Sjahrir, Jakarta, November 15, 1987.
[82] "Riwajat Hidup Soetan Sjahrir," n.d., n.p. typescript in the *Archives Siti Wahjunah Sjahrir*.
[83] *Pedoman*, November 28, 1950.
[84] *Suara Sosialis* 3, 7 (February 1951).
[85] Sitoroes, "Laporan Organisasi," p. 13.
[86] Ibid.

the party structure also manifested this clearly. In February 1950, the PSI central executive conference decided,

> to deactivate [men-non-actievkan] the Party Council [the central executive], and to give a full mandate [mandaat penuh] to lead the Party, at the moment [which was till the first congress], to the General Leader [Pemimpin Umum].[87]

At the same meeting, Sjahrir, who, of course, was the "General Leader," had been "authorized" for the whole next period till the first congress, among other things, to

> appoint commissaries in areas which are considered of [special] importance for the activities of the party... appoint a successor to himself and to empower him to act for him if necessary; organize cadre and training courses at the highest level.[88]

As this "transitory" period ended, when the First PSI Congress convened in Bandung, in February 1952, a "proposal to adopt [a system of] collective leadership" was, after a short debate, "put aside." "It was argued that although in principle there was no objection to it, such action would be premature."[89]

According to Mochtar Lubis, the best time to talk to Sjahrir, was early in the morning:

> Usually he ate *pecal* [vegetable salad in peanut oil] for his breakfast, and if one could arrange the time so as to come to Sjahrir's house just when the *pecal* vendor passed by, certainly he would be offered a *pecal* portion, too. Then one might share in *pecal* and one might share in talk.[90]

L. M. Sitoroes, who was a core member of the PSI central executive through the first half of the 1950s, recalled that "during those years, Sjahrir became a sort of guru for the party."[91]

Memoirs suggest that a special and often an uneasy feeling increased at this time: especially when during the debates, where Sjahrir was present, it came to politics. Even such old friends of Sjahrir as Soegondo Djojopoespito or Djohan Sjahroezah, or Mohammad Natsir, who remained outside the PSI but was Sjahrir's neighbor and a frequent visitor, remembered that, increasingly, it was difficult exactly to follow the ways in which Sjahrir was explaining things. Some of the inner circle began to call Sjahrir *orakel van Delphi*, "oracle of Delphi."[92] Listyo, a party leader from Bandung, and later a cadre of the PSI in Jakarta, told me during an

---

[87] Sitoroes, "Laporan Organisasi," p. 11.

[88] Sjahrir, *Indonesian Socialism*, p. 46.

[89] Ibid., p. 49. See, e.g., *Suara Sosialis* 4, 2 (April 1952), calling Sjahrir "Pimpinan Umum," which, in the years following, became quite a norm. Even Herbert Feith occasionally wrote of Sjahrir of the 1950s as "Sjahrir-PSI."

[90] Mochtar Lubis, "Pejuang, pemikir dan peminat," *Mengenang Sjahrir*, ed. Anwar, p. 209.

[91] Interview with Sitoroes, Jakarta, December 29, 1987.

[92] Abdul Halim, "Sjahrir yang saya kenal," in *Mengenang Sjahrir*, ed. Anwar, pp. 114–15.

interview: "Perhaps only Sitoroes understood him every time." When I asked Sitoroes about this, he protested: "No, certainly not every time."[93]

There is agreement among those who believed they were close to Sjahrir that some time around 1950, he began to fast during the Moslem holy month of Ramadan. But nobody seemed to interpret this as a radical change, or a sudden rediscovery on the part of Sjahrir of the ancestral religion, or cultural roots.[94]

Sjahrir visited Minangkabau a few times after 1949. With his new wife, in the early 1950s, he traveled to Kota Gedang, and they also visited Medan. Again, at least as others saw it, there was not much feeling of a return home. "We went to Kota Gedang, and to his family home, which still stands there." Mrs. Sjahrir told me:

> But the key was with a relative in Bukittinggi, thus we just looked inside, at what we could see through the windows. The place was not cleaned, it was empty, and decaying.[95]

Sjahrir, now, seemed to live quietly. It is difficult to uncover any tension in his life. Maria, his former wife and now his sister-in-law, had bought a house for herself and Sjahsam near where Sjahrir and Poppy lived, in fact on the same street and on the same block. The families occasionally visited each other. "It was Maria," Poppy recalled,

> who suggested the way in which we then remodelled our house; she advised us, for instance, to remake the garage into a place for the Bandanese children.[96]

Old friends, like Soewarni Pringgodigdo still, in the early 1950s, found it possible to compare Sjahrir with Eddy du Perron. But the accent changed. As du Perron, Soewarni wrote in 1952, Sjahrir remained "an individualist possessing his own texture and style, capable of living in solitude in the world of his intellect."[97] Greater inwardness seemed to be accompanied by a growing softness. Detachment, always a characteristic feature of Sjahrir, as some of his old friends became afraid, was taking on too much the form of *tolerantie*, "tolerance." The "tolerance," as Soewarni noted, was being "misused as weakness by those friends, who do not truly know Sjahrir's soul."[98]

Sal Tas described Sjahrir, as he saw him in Jakarta in 1955, seven years after their last meeting in London:

> He had lost much of his impatience, and the hardness had been replaced by a calmer decisiveness. But in losing his tenseness, he had lost a good part of

---

[93] Interviews with Listyo, Jakarta, November 27, 1987, and with Sitoroes, Jakarta, December 29, 1987.

[94] Interviews with Apipah, Hamid Algadri, Subadio (Bandung and Jakarta, November, December 1987 and January 1988).

[95] Interview with Siti Wahjunah Sjahrir, Jakarta, November 15, 1987.

[96] Ibid.

[97] Soewarni Pringgodigdo, "Du Perron dan Pengaruhnja," p. 33.

[98] Ibid.

his dynamism. In his appearance, his speech, his argument, he had come to a reflectiveness that sometimes bordered on a lack of interest.[99]

In 1951, W. Lefebvre, wrote a review of a new edition of Sjahrir's letters from exile. He noted "a faint air of melancholy about this idealistic story."[100] One wonders if this Dutch "sympathizer" of Sjahrir from prewar times, was not reflecting on Sjahrir's "melancholy" and "idealism" of the early 1950s, rather than on Sjahrir's texts from the past.

In 1953, Sjahrir wrote to George Kahin: "I suppose, you know that I was an enthusiastic letter writer when I was in exile but since then I've been a poor one."[101] It seems that in his loss of enthusiasm for letter writing, a deeper loss was reflected. What Harry Benda described as the "quiet intensity" of Sjahrir's exile letters,[102] now, in Sjahrir's writing of the early 1950s, rather resembled a whisper one has difficulty in hearing. Most of the values and concepts, familiar from reading his prewar texts, were still there, in the early 1950s—most of the building blocks were recognizable. But something of the architecture seemed to be gone.

"Sjahrir," Sal Tas wrote, reflecting on his visit to Indonesia and discussions with Sjahrir in 1955, "could never completely free himself from the traditional concepts of socialism."[103] Sjahrir's texts on socialism written in the first half of the 1950s, indeed, closely resembled—in their notions, metaphors, and words—what Sjahrir had written before the war. Only now, what Sjahrir wrote—on the proletariat, social revolution, on his role in all this—appealed to a reader almost as comfortable reading.

In a text, for instance, in 1953, Sjahrir wrote about Marx and Engels, who, as he declared, were his constant companions:

> In fact neither Marx nor Engels could see what would happen in the century ahead. They did not want to become astrologers, they wanted to provide a basis for a scientific understanding of man's social development, a basis for a scientific understanding which is nothing else but an experience and reality.[104]

What Marx and Engels did was the opposite of "philosophizing in a speculative way";[105] Marxism, to Sjahrir, still was "a model" of "critical thinking," "a test" of whether one is capable of being "aware of reality";[106] Marxism, in the Sjahrir of the early 1950s, still inspired "calculation and healthy reason [*perhitungan dan akal sehat*],"[107] "progress of awareness [*kemadjuan kesadaran*]," "level of rationality" as

---

[99] Tas, "Souvenirs of Sjahrir," p. 152.

[100] W. le Fèbre, "Taman Siswa en de nationalistie van het onderwijs in Indonesië," *Oriëntatie* 43 (October–December, 1951), p. 371.

[101] Sjahrir's letter to George Kahin, Jakarta, October 2, 1953.

[102] Harry Benda's introduction to Dahm; Dahm. *Sukarno*, p. vi.

[103] Tas, "Souvenirs of Sjahrir," p. 152.

[104] Sjahrir, "Teori Marx," *Suara Sosialis* 6 (1953).

[105] Ibid.

[106] Sjahrir, "Pengaruh sistim demokrasi," in Sjahrir, *Sosialisme dan Marxisme: Suatu kritik terhadap Marxisme* (Jakarta: Djambatan, 1967), p. 34.

[107] Sjahrir, "Pandangan kaum sosialis kerakjatan [1953–1954]" in *Sosialisme dan Marxisme*, p. 62.

against "a multiplication of terms and words, which are empty and false."[108] Marxism, to Sjahrir, was still the best way of practicing *akal*, "reason," and retaining confidence in *kemadjuan*, "progress"; what Marxism opposed still was essentially *kuno dan feodal*, "outdated and feudal," *prae-rationeel*, "pre-rational," and *bodoh*, "ignorant";[109] still, "education, above any other function that may come to one's mind," was the truest Marxist method of change.[110]

It appeared as merely a shift in emphasis, a hard-to-define change in how the notions, metaphors, and words were being arranged. The ethical or "ethical and spiritual" approach appeared to be stronger in Sjahrir, now, than it was twenty years before. When Sjahrir was asked, in 1953, for instance, to give a "sociological lecture on contemporary Indonesian problems," he gave a talk about what he himself described as, "psychology," but what more appropriately would have been called ethics.[111] "The problem of development," Sjahrir said on another occasion,

> is fundamentally a problem of development of our nation's soul, a problem of the creation of a good and strong character.[112]

What Sjahrir, now, was most truly worried about, were "spiritual attitudes," and "disintegration of character." "Education," to Sjahrir, more than before, was "character education." If character education procceeds in a correct way, "maturity" will follow.[113] Sjahrir's speech to the PSI's First Congress in Bandung ended with something which would hardly be imaginable, say, at a Pendidikan meeting of the 1930s: *Demikianlah! Merdeka Sempurna*, "So be it! Pure Freedom."[114] It was Sjahrir, reportedly, who in 1950 wrote into the PSI program: "The progress and development of all the potentialities of each human being towards goodness and beauty."[115]

As before throughout his life, Sjahrir presented "good" Islam as a force opposed to *kaum ningrat*, "the aristocrats," to *kaum feodal*, "the feudalists," and to *kaum kolonialisme*, "the colonialists." However, not unlike in his current attitude to Marxism, there was a feeling that a good creed is a jewel—something one can safely believe in and sustain just by taking proper care that the creed does not change. More than before, Sjahrir now defined Islam as a *pusaka*, "heirloom."[116]

---

[108] Sjahrir, "Soal kerakjatan," *Sikap* 3, 12 (December 27, 1950), p. 1; also Sjahrir at *Symposion tentang kesulitan*, pp. 37–38.

[109] Ibid., p. 19–20, 36–37.

[110] E.g., Sjahrir, "Sosialisme di negeri kita," *Suara Sosialis* 6, 2 (February 1954), p. 6.

[111] Sjahrir at *Symposion tentang kesulitan*, esp. pp. 16–17.

[112] Sjahrir, "Pembangunan ekonomi negara kita," 1953, published later in Sutan Sjahrir. *Sosialisme, Indonesia, Pembangunan: Kumpulan Tulisan* (Jakarta: Lembaga Penunjang Pembangunan Nasional, 1982), p. 242.

[113] Ibid., p. 237, 239; see also Sjahrir, "The National Program" in Sjahrir, *Indonesian Socialism*, p. 22.

[114] Sjahrir, "Pidato pembukaan pada kongres ke-1 PSI di Bandung" (February 12, 1952), *Suara Sosialis* 4,2 (April 1952) (typescript with long-hand corrections, p. 10; *Archives Siti Wahjunah Sjahrir*).

[115] Sjahrir, "Principles of the Socialist Party" in Sjahrir, *Indonesian Socialism*, pp. 13–14.

[116] Sjahrir at *Symposion tentang kesulitan*, pp. 31–32.

Nafsu, "uncontrolled passion and lust," was still, for Sjahrir, equal to non-awareness, non-reason, and non-morality.[117] He still occasionally used *ilham*, "divine inspiration, brainstorm," as a term to describe revolutionary enthusiasm.[118] But again, and by a slight shift in style, all these references to unbridled sensuality appeared less irritating, less provocative, and thus less inspiring. There were fewer doubts, less excitement, fewer qualifications, fewer explanations of explanations. Sjahrir now, found it easy, meaning nothing special, to address his party's First Congress in Bandung with Koranic *Silaturrachmani*, "I came in good will."[119] He now evidently found it easy to define "pragmatism" by using the most charged words of Islam and describing with them something like a very careful and ordinary journey: "between possible and impossible, forbidden [*haram*] and allowed [*halal*], beautiful and rotten."[120]

Sjahrir still wrote extensively about "the will to change and the will to progress."[121] He still wrote that a feeling for change was "the key" to Marxism;[122] he still wrote against "stiffness," and against "*Nirwana*";[123] also against viewing the world as "absolute [*mutlak*]" and "mysterious [*gaib*]."[124] The notion of "power" was still very much a part of Sjahrir's texts, as was the related notion of power as "a belief in oneself,"[125] as a "reason,"[126] as "the power to think and the power of soul."[127] Sjahrir still wrote extensively about *vitalitas*, "vitality" as a "joy."[128] But while he, in prison and exile before the war and the Revolution, wrestled so much with Nietzsche, the "subconscious" and the "dark" regions in himself, now he wrote increasingly and almost exclusively, about a "cleanliness of the body," "a cleanliness of the soul," a cleanliness of the people, about "the health of the people" and "hygiene."[129]

What Sjahrir wrote in one of his letters from Banda Neira comes to mind: how he tried to keep *oppervlakkig*, "superficial," against the threat of the subconscious, in an effort, as he put it, to escape "brooding." Now, in 1953 for instance, Sjahrir wrote something, which, on its face, looked very similar:

> In a way, I loosen my views and my commentaries, which means, also, I deliberately avoid ways that may give rise to sentiments [*perasaan*] or emotions [*emotie*]. Because of this, also, my explanations [often] do not have

---

[117] E.g., Sjahrir, "Ramalan krisis ekonomi tidak terjadi" published later in Sjahrir, *Sosialisme dan Marxisme*, p. 51.

[118] E.g., Sjahrir at *Symposion tentang kesulitan*, p. 20; these were his concluding remarks.

[119] Sjahrir, "Pidato pembukaan pada kongres ke-1 PSI di Bandung," p. 3.

[120] Sjahrir at *Symposion tentang kesulitan*, p. 20; or, in another version, "between rotten and good, desirable [*wadjib*] and *haram*, between rotten and beautiful." Sjahrir, "Pidato pembukaan pada kongres ke-1 PSI di Bandung," p. 3.

[121] For instance Sjahrir, "Teori Marx, "*Suara Sosialis* 6 (1953).

[122] Ibid.

[123] Sjahrir, "Soal kerakjatan," p. 1.

[124] Ibid.

[125] See, e.g., Sjahrir's interview with a Moroccan journalist quoted in Chalid I. F. M. Salim. *Limabelas tahun Digul*, p. 527.

[126] Sjahrir at *Symposion tentang kesulitan*, p. 21.

[127] Sjahrir, "Teori Marx," *Suara Sosialis* 6 (1953).

[128] Sjahrir, "Pembangunan ekonomi," in *Sosialisme, Indonesia, Pembangunan*, p. 240.

[129] Ibid., p. 237–38; Sjahrir at *Symposion tentang kesulitan*, pp. 36–37.

the quality of politics, and are prone to put aside, as much as possible, matters which have the quality of actual politics [*politik jang aktuil*].[130]

"Loosening," now, seemed to be the crucial word: loosening, instead of dynamizing the surface; loosening instead of building trembling bridges over the depths of oneself. Now, to Sjahrir, the source of trouble seemed to be not the inner tensions, and not the dark forces inside himself and inside his movement. The source of trouble, now, seemed to be located outside: amidst the enemy, on the other side, among the opponents of the PSI; these were *kasar*, "rough and unclean," and *tidak sopan*, "bad mannered."[131]

Sjahrir still wrote and talked extensively about Indonesian youth. Hope, he wrote, could never come from those who "are old in spirit and weak in soul." The true "sons and daughters of our nation," still to him, were those "full of confidence and joy," "sincere and pure."[132] Hope could not come, Sjahrir wrote, from those who "cut their desire"; which clearly was a referrence to Chairil Anwar's poem-epitaph for the 1945 Generation.[133] Again, however, there was the different accent. There was no *pubertus*, for instance, in Sjahrir's texts of the early 1950s; there was in particular very little of the uncertainties of the anxious youth with the uncertainties of an anxious Sjahrir. In Sjahrir's writing, youth, now, figured simply as pure, and simply as an ideal. As if he had left youth behind and matured alone, matured lonely, and thus got old.

Ningrat, the "aristocratic," the quality of "the East," still, was to Sjahrir the essential manifestation of everything wrong, old-fashioned, and reactionary in Indonesia. However, Sjahrir's image of *ningrat*, appeared now less as a static center squeezed by a dynamic margin, and more like fragments of culture scattered through the society, and thus omnipresent, and thus, so it sometimes seemed, invincible. According to the Principles of the PSI, written in the early 1950s, largely by Sjahrir,

> In general, Asian society has never really emancipated itself from the feudal and agrarian type of society, at least not before the twentieth century....
>
> Feudalism in our country as an economic system has already broken down because of its impotence and cannot be revived again. Its remnants, however, are still to be found in the agricultural field and in the mentality of a part of the people.[134]

Among Indonesian intellectuals, according to another of Sjahrir's texts of the same time, "nine of every ten come from *ningrat* and bureaucratic circles."[135] And, Sjahrir added, "Everything I said about the intellectuals, is also true about the leaders of our society."[136]

---

[130] Ibid., p. 78, during a question period.

[131] Sjahrir, "Pemimpin dan Pemuda, "1952, n.p., typescript in the *Archives Siti Wahjunah Sjahrir.*

[132] Sjahrir, "Pembangunan ekonomi," in *Sosialisme, Indonesia, Pembangunan,* pp. 240, 242.

[133] Ibid. For Chairil Anwar's poem see above pp. 415–16.

[134] Sjahrir, "Principles of the Socialist Party," p. 4. Ibid., p. 10; also Sjahrir at *Symposion tentang kesulitan,* pp. 28–29, 78.

[135] Ibid., pp. 19–20, 25–27.

[136] Ibid., p. 77.

In an article "Our Society: Feudal and Parasitic," also in the early 1950s, Sjahrir described "our elite of feudal origin, and of feudal attitudes," as being, "only intent on show and exhibition."[137] "Government in our country," wrote Sjahrir, "village headmen [*lurah*], district heads [*wedana*], provincial heads [*bupati*], state officials," the state itself, live by the *ningrat*-motivated "parasitism... waste," and "big splendor."[138]

The "consumer spirit," in turn, produced excessive government support to imports, a "fortress policy," which, Sjahrir wrote, favored *pemuka Jawa*, "the Javanese promoters," and worked against *kaum pedagang Indonesia*, "the Indonesian traders." The "consumer regions" were preferred by the central government over the "non-consumer regions," described by Sjahrir as "areas throughout Indonesia and especially on the islands outside Java."[139]

Instead, Sjahrir wrote, the state should be merely "a model" and, "whenever possible, it should be decentralized."[140] The state should guarantee progress "not merely [for] one group and one class"; it should be "a common affair," based on *mufakat*, "mutual agreement."[141] The state should work by "community control," *bedrijfsdemokratie*, "industrial democracy," and *kedaulatan rakjat*, "sovereignty of the people."[142]

This all seemed almost word for word like what Sjahrir had already written in the Pendidikan manifestoes in the 1930s and consistently afterwards. There were proletarians, in Sjahrir's vision of the 1950s, as there had been twenty years before. But the proletarians, of Sjahrir now, were no longer the half-suppressed, tiny, almost grotesque, and by the same token the most exciting and most unsettling concept of the 1930s. Instead, the proletarians of Sjahrir in the 1950s have grown in numbers, become amorphous and, so it sometimes appeared, almost flabby. When talking about the Indonesian social structure, in 1953, Sjahrir did not seem to be able to find much more to say about the proletarians than that "workers and the unemployed [became] the largest part of our nation living in towns."[143] What was rather on his mind, it seemed, when it came to *element mobil*, "the mobile element" and *potentie revolutie*, "the potential of revolution," was the growing migration on Java, from the villages into the cities: the Javanese peasants overflowing their communities, and

---

[137] Sjahrir,"Pembangunan ekonomi," in *Sosialisme, Indonesia, Pembangunan*, pp. 261–64.

[138] Ibid., pp. 260, 250.

[139] Ibid., pp. 245–46.

[140] Sjahrir, "Perajaan Mei Dulu dan Sekarang," *Suara Sosialis* IV, 3–4 (June 1952), p. 5. See also Sjahrir, "Pembangunan ekonomi," in *Sosialisme, Indonesia, Pembangunan*, p. 271, and Sjahrir, "Principles of the Socialist party," p. 17.

[141] "Sosialisme kita bersifat kemanusiaan umum dan tidak ditundjukan hanja untuk satu golongan proletar atau golongan buru," (Sjahrir, "Perkembangan Socialisme di negeri kita sedjak berdirinja PSI," 1953, later published in Sjahrir, *Sosialisme, Indonesia, Pembangunan*, p. 79. See also similarly Sjahrir, "Peranan Negara di-Negara2 jang Baru Merdeka," later reprinted in Sjahrir, *Sosialisme dan Marxisme*, pp. 42–47; Sjahrir, "Pidato pembukaan pada kongres ke-1 PSI di Bandung," p. 10. Also "Kita hendak bekerdja atas dasar kemerdekaan djiwa orang atas dasar *sukarela, mufakat dan kerdjasama*." Sjahrir, "Kerakjatan," in *Sosialisme, Indonesia, Pembangunan*, p. 271. See also Sjahrir, "Principles of the Socialist party," pp. 7 and 13.

[142] Sjahrir, "Pengaruh Sistim demokrasi," in *Sosialisme dan Marxisme*, p. 32; Sjahrir, *Sosialisme dan Pimpinan. Tjeramah dalam peringatan Dies Natalis Gerakan Sosialis di Bandung tgl. 16 Oktober 1957* (Jakarta: Secretariat PSI, 1957), p. 4.

[143] Sjahrir at *Symposion tentang kesulitan*, pp. 34–35.

flooding the towns. How much remained of the notion of the static center and dynamic margin? Indonesian towns, Sjahrir was saying now, "are the centers of skill and progress... a dynamic part of our society"; but, as the migration grew, these towns "do not differ much from big villages."[144]

Before the war Sjahrir had also often written about migration. Then, it was essentially a movement into a more open space, in search of broader perspectives. Then, this was the notion of *rantau*. Now, one question seemed to recur in Sjahrir's mind—would not, through the growing migration, the conservative qualities of the "Eastern" village, and the negative qualities of Java and *ningrat*, overflow the island, and flood the whole archipelago?[145]

Sjahrir still, in the early 1950s, warned against the *ningrat*-like "nationalistic," "anti-foreign," and "racial attitudes."[146] He still made a parallel between the Indonesians' behavior towards the Eurasian community in the country and the nation's progress toward adulthood;[147] as before, being anti-foreign and racist, to Sjahrir, was being pre-modern.[148]

The causes of revolution, and thus of progress, Sjahrir still appeared to believe, were universal. It was in all probability he, who wrote into the PSI program in 1952:

> We are convinced that the socialism as we envisage it cannot be established within the boundaries of a single country.... The lives of all mankind now are very closely related.[149]

The Indonesian Revolution had happened, Sjahrir said in 1952,

> not only because of the will of our people... but mainly because the colonialist opponent did not change in accordance with the changes in the world in general....[150]

There seemed to be the same milestones and highlights in Sjahrir's image of history, in the 1950s as in the 1930s: "classical Europe" preceded the "Renaissance"; a part of the process was "also the culture of Islam."[151] Indonesian history and universal history were still seen by Sjahrir as essentially unilinear:

> our towns are still at the stage of the European towns of the Middle Ages... they have not yet become *werkplaats* [workshops] or the centers of factories.... The Indonesian language we are using today, does not help us [yet] to express ourselves.... Generally it still is difficult to use this language as an abstract language.... For the time being, we can often solve this problem only by using some of the Western languages, which already are on that

---

[144] Ibid., pp. 80, and *passim*.

[145] *Symposion tentang kesulitan*, pp. 254–55.

[146] Ibid., p. 25.

[147] Ibid.

[148] Ibid., pp. 26–27; Sjahrir, "Pembangunan ekonomi," in *Sosialisme, Indonesia, Pembangunan*, p. 247.

[149] Sjahrir, "The National Program," p. 24.

[150] Sjahrir, "Pidato pembukaan pada kongres ke-1 PSI di Bandung," p. 3.

[151] Sjahrir at *Symposion tentang kesulitan*, p. 17.

level.... If we truly want social progress [*kemadjuan*], we have to think the Einstein-way and Pasteur-way ... not like a man in the interior of Irian.[152]

It looked almost exactly like Sjahrir's "Our Struggle" of 1945, when he wrote, in 1953: "it is the view of us, the [Indonesian] Socialists that we have to hope for changes in [global] capitalism."[153] The waiting period, now, in 1953, as in his "Our Struggle," in 1945, was not very clearly defined. However, the very idea of waiting seemed, now, strikingly less oppressive and less threatening. In contrast to himself in "Our Struggle," Sjahrir wrote, now, extensively and with great involvement, about what he described as "structural changes"—to him the true contents of the waiting period, things which were already and safely in process, global capitalism changing in a flagrantly un-catastrophic, almost tension-less way.

Describing the Cold War, Sjahrir wrote little in terms of a confrontation between the American and Soviet systems. Rather, he explained,

> development of the world, which is called the capitalist world [would] steadily progress through a broadening of its concepts, through a strengthening of its awareness, through producing more goods according to the needs of the society and for general welfare, [towards] a world, which is better structured, and which carries on while practicing calculation and healthy reasoning [*akal sehat*].[154]

Loosening, again, appeared to be the key word: the "capitalist system," according to Sjahrir, would become "very weak";[155] tensions such as "class struggle" would "not grow steadily sharper, but on the contrary, would grow hazy";[156] the capitalists would become *anemis*, "anaemic."[157]

Keeping distant from both the United States and the Soviet Union was still very much part of Sjahrir's texts, in the early 1950s, as in 1945. In an article "Theory of Crisis," in 1953, Sjahrir praised those who

> managed to untie themselves from the necessity of US assistance ... without becoming a prey of the colonialism of Russia.[158]

Both systems still were to be evaded. The United States, to Sjahrir, remained the "imperialist-capitalist" power.[159] To "keep out of the ranks of Moscow," to Sjahrir, equalled "thinking and acting broadly and being above things."[160]

---

[152] Ibid., pp. 22–24, 34., 76–77.

[153] Sjahrir,"Pandangan kaum sosialis kerakjatan," in *Sosialisme dan Marxisme*, p. 61.

[154] Ibid., p. 62.

[155] Sjahrir, "Sosialisme di Eropa Barat," *Suara Sosialis*, 14 (January 1953).

[156] Sjahrir, "Masjarakat berkembang," in *Sosialisme dan Marxisme*, p. 20.

[157] Bujung Saleh interpreting Sjahrir at *Symposion tentang kesulitan*, p. 55.

[158] Sjahrir, "Teori krisis," p. 57

[159] E.g., Sjahrir on Brackman in Sutan Sjahrir, "Tinjauan Buku" (variously dated, Madiun 1962–1963, Jakarta, 1963–1964, part I,II and III) III (1963), p. 31; in *Archives Siti Wahjunah Sjahrir*. These Sjahrir texts from prison were graciously provided to me by Siti Wahjunah Sjahrir.

[160] Sjahrir, "1 Mei 1951," *Suara Sosialis* 3, 8 (May 1951), p. 1.

Thus, what was in-between, was praised as before. However, much of what had been very meaningful during the 1930s and 1940s, became much less so, now. "Just remember," Sjahrir wrote in 1952,

> that Prime Minister Drees and the Labor party [*Partij van de Arbeid*] bear responsibility for the colonial war launched during the Dutch Second Military Action.

"Western socialism," Sjahrir still appeared to believe, should not be dismissed. Social democracy, Sjahrir wrote, should not be criticized, because it had chosen "parliamentarism, peaceful ways, and compromises." The state of the world has fundamentally changed, Sjahrir argued. Western socialism should be praised, because it was "well ordered" and "planned."[161]

There was another word Sjahrir now used frequently, especially when he defended Western socialism—*menyesuaikan*, which may be translated as "to adjust," "to adapt," or "to reconcile." Only occasionally now, in Sjahrir's writing of the early 1950s, were there sharp moments of remembering the past, short flashbacks to the prewar period, when, as he once put it remarkably, "socialism was still radical and revolutionary."[162]

Instead of the tiny, almost grotesque, fast moving, marginal groups and individuals—the Western "independent socialists" of the 1920s, 1930s, and 1940s—a more solid construct was being built in the Sjahrir of the early 1950s—almost a comforting image of the global revolution as a massive social-democratic enterprise.

The welfare states of Western and Northern Europe became perhaps Sjahrir's main theme during this period. The "welfare states," he wrote with an almost unqualified respect, "work consciously and according to a plan." They embodied a "socialist" experiment, yet, at the same time, they represented "the most advanced and the most mature" segment *inside* the capitalist world.[163] They were "neither coercive nor oppressive." They "are seen as a property of the people"; they "forward the consciousness, the skills and the authority of their workers." They

> defend a position not merely of the one group in power, but they serve the whole society, they safeguard the welfare of the whole coutry, the well-being, the progress and the health of everybody."[164]

They "aim at abolishing the difference in quality of life between proprietors, the wealthy, and the workers."[165]

Perhaps the most strikig feature of this new vision of Sjahrir was, how much it allowed to pass through the trappings of the actual international power constellation at the time. Looking at the actual world this way, one did not need to feel too obliged to say much about the Soviet Union and the United States. Both states just, for what-

---

[161] Sjahrir, "Teori krisis," in *Sosialisme dan Marxisme*, pp. 51–54.

[162] Sjahrir, "Sosialisme di negeri kita," in *Suara Sosialis* 6, 2 (February 1954), p. 5.

[163] Sjahrir, "Teori krisis," in *Sosialisme dan Marxisme* pp. 51–52; Sjahrir, "Sosialisme di Eropa Barat," *Suara Sosialis* 3, 12 (November 15, 1951); see also Sjahrir, "Perubahan kedudukan hak milik,"in *Sosialisme dan Marxisme*, pp. 22, 25.

[164] Ibid., pp. 26, 27.

[165] Ibid.

ever reason, had not made it—had not *yet* made it—into the community of welfare-states. They, hopefully, would do so; one day. Not much more, about the two powers, was said by Sjahrir.

Britain, so immensely important for Sjahrir during the 1940s—and, of course, not wholly negligible in the actual world of the 1950s—was also almost completely missing from the picture. Sjahrir listed Britain a few times among the welfare states. On these occasions, however, the list of these states was exceptionally long, and Britain appeared very low on it, among insignificant and merely vaguely potential welfare states, not rarely below Switzerland.

France, with its important colonial past and also the scene of a crucial postwar socialist experiment, was also almost unmentioned by Sjahrir. Italy was cited, but only as an example of a failure—a failure, as Sjahrir wrote, of "the Italian communist party and Nenni's socialist party" to disentangle Italy from the United States and the Soviet Union.[166]

Yugoslavia was, through the early 1950s, a critical theme for the world in motion—and for the world in between "capitalism" and "socialism." For Sjahrir, however, Yugoslavia seemed to be simply a poor place close to failure. Sjahrir visited Yugoslavia on his European tour, late in 1951. He came from Amsterdam through London and brought a message for the Yugoslavian leaders from the British left-wing Labour party leader, Konni Zilliacus. Sjahrir spoke to Milovan Djilas, and to Marshal Tito, and there seemed to be nothing that impressed him. In his private travel diary, Sjahrir noted that Tito and Djilas accepted weapons from the United States, and that they also accepted "the *U.S.I.S.*" Sjahrir ridiculed Tito's protestations of his independence from Moscow: "how is it, that [Tito] managed to live in Russia for so long, and did not see the wrongs, he is now so much talking about?"[167] For Sjahrir, the top Yugoslav leader was "like our own Big Brother [*Bung Besar kita*] . . . like Sukarno."[168]

Now, Sjahrir also wrote little on China and on the Chinese revolution—strikingly little, given his earlier respect for Mao Tse-tung, and given the role China, now, played in the actual world and the debate about socialism. Djilas and Tito, in fact, suggested to Sjahrir that China was "something like Yugoslavia."[169] China was mentioned in a few scattered places in Sjahrir's writings of the early 1950s, and always ambiguously. At one time, he related it to the socialist family stretching from the Scandinavian welfare states, through Russia, to the East.[170] Another time, China, in effect, was just another capitalist, or potentially capitalist power: "after Mao Tse-tung had established himself," Sjahrir wrote for instance on the Chinese Revolution as it affected Indonesia after 1949, "more Chinese capital was invested in our country."[171]

Scandinavian countries, almost as a rule, were at the top of the list. India was hardly mentioned at all. Holland surfaced once or twice among (potential) socialist welfare states—close to Britain in importance, and near Switzerland.

---

[166] "Italia 1951," typescript of Sjahrir's diary, n.p. in *Archives Siti Wahjunah Sjahrir*.

[167] "Yugoslavia 1951," ibid.

[168] Ibid.

[169] Ibid.

[170] Sjahrir, "1 Mei 1951," p. 1.

[171] Sjahrir at *Symposion tentang kesulitan*, p. 24.

The meaning of all this seemed essentially to be to ensure that incongruous things could be placed safely side by side. Language, as always, reflected the change very well. When Sjahrir wrote in the early 1950s about the welfare states, for instance, one might expect him to use technical terms from either "progressive national" Indonesian language or "modern Western" English. Yet, virtually all the relevant welfare-state technical terms Sjahrir used in his Indonesian writing were—in Dutch. Retirement policies were *ouderdomspensioen*, accident insurance was *ongevallenverzekering*, industrial democracy was *bedrijfsdemokratie*, white-collar workers were *hoeden-proletariaat*. One particular detail was especially telling. In sharp contrast with the 1920s, 1930s, and 1940s, there were rarely brackets—little visible effort at translation.[172]

3. General Elections

For the most varied and often contradictory reasons, no major political force in Indonesia disputed the fact that general parliamentary elections should be held. Throughout almost the first five years, the legislature of the independent Republic was an interim one, and the constitution as enacted in 1950 was provisional. The turmoil of Indonesian life—political, cultural, public, as well as private—throughout the first half of the 1950s, in a sense, was the turmoil of a prolonged election campaign. There was a constant fight over the date of the elections, and, after the date was finally set for September 29, 1955, wild rumors circulated that it still might be changed.

Sjahrir defined his movement as "parliamentary socialism,"[173] and he defined "a progressive state" as "a democratic system with general elections and a government based on the will of voting citizens."[174] By this, he made the upcoming general elections an inseparable part of his and his party's policy and image. The PSI Program in 1952 declared:

> For Socialism to become the principle which will shape the course of the Indonesian Republic, the Socialist Party must win the support of the people in elections to all the representative bodies....[175]

At the same time, however, the "opening up" of Sjahrir's party remained an extremely hesitant process. As the day of elections approached, pressure naturally grew on the PSI to move "closer to the masses." There were some, indeed, among the PSI leaders, who were believed to advocate this cause vehemently—namely Sitoroes, who was the PSI's general secretary at the time. But even Sitoroes emphasized in retrospect, how uncertain he had been at the time, lest he, through the electioneering, involve his party too deeply with "cheap politics" and "demagogy."[176]

Sjahrir talked to George Kahin at the end of 1954, at a time when elections were only a few months ahead. Sjahrir told Kahin that now the PSI would concentrate on

---

[172] Sjahrir, "Perubahan kedudukan hak milik," in *Sosialisme dan Marxisme*, pp. 21, 22. Sjahrir "translated" the term *hoeden proletariaat*; but not as simply "white-collar workers" or rather "worker's aristocracy" but as *"proletariaat bertopi."* ibid.

[173] Sjahrir, " Sosialisme di Eropa Barat," *Suara Sosialis* 12 (November 1952).

[174] Sjahrir, "Pengaruh sistim demokrasi [1953–1954]" in *Sosialisme dan Marxisme*, p. 27.

[175] Sjahrir, "The National Program," p. 23.

[176] Interview with Sitoroes, Jakarta, December 29, 1987.

"recruiting local leaders," because these had roots in the regions, and, implicitly, among the masses.[177] However, it is difficult to find anything showing that this was actually done.

A photograph appeared in the PSI journal *Suara Sosialis*, early in April 1955, of Sjahrir "surveying" the electioneering symbols of the PSI:

> a five-point star in a wreath of rice for central Sumatra, a sailboat and a five-point star for Central and South Sulawesi, an image of Ganesha with a five-point star for the Lesser Sundas, a bundle of rice and a five-point star for West Java and the Moluccas, a five-point star with an Atjehnese house and a *kris* dagger for North Sumatra, a five-point star and a *mandau* sword for East Kalimantan.[178]

Sjahrir is not on record as saying anything, on that occasion, about the meaning of the symbols. What, indeed, could he say?

Early in June 1955, the PSI held its Second Congress, merely weeks before election day. The congress, convened in Jakarta, was clearly expected to become the climax of the PSI election campaign. After it was over, Sjahrir wrote a long article on its results for *Suara Sosialis*:

> The congress succeeded well ... it is proper to say, *alhamdulillah*. "Well done," as Englishmen would say. [Some friends gave money] to make it possible for the PSI to celebrate [*berhari raja*]. There were banquets. ... Our party and its activities in the capital are now better known, and recognized by many members, who had previously thought that their party was in shambles, slackening in its daring and energy or having no daring and energy at all.[179]

The delegates, Sjahrir continued, enjoyed being in Jakarta, the party had been generous in arranging places for all of them to stay, the PSI transport services had functioned well.

This took up the larger part of the article. Then, suddenly, as if running out of steam, Sjahrir ended on a subdued note. There were "some uncertainties about the political outcome [*hasil*]" of the congress, Sjahrir wrote:

> It is not surprising that there are some among our friends who hesitate to give a clear answer, when asked: "Does the outcome of our Second Congress justify the money it has cost?"

There, indeed, wrote Sjahrir, was quite widespread feeling that the congress "did not settle issues," that it was "rushed," that it was more successful in its "propaganda outward" than "in acting towards its own members." How much better things would have been, Sjahrir concluded, if the delegates had come to the congress truly prepared, and not merely "to visit the Congress as if going on an excursion, as if just celebrating."[180] The word used at the optimistic beginning of Sjahrir's article,

---

[177] Kahin's interview with Sjahrir, Jakarta, December 9, 1954.
[178] *Suara Sosialis* 3, 4 (April 1955).
[179] Sjahrir, "Kongres kita jang ke-II," *Suara Sosialis* 7,7–8 (July 1955), pp. 1, 5.
[180] Ibid.

"*berhari raja*," "to celebrate," returned as the article ended, to express the political exercise's futility and frivolousness.[181]

A photo was later published from the opening session of the PSI's Second Congress. Sukarno, president of the Republic and the most distinguished guest, is shown sitting in the front line of seats, in the limelight, and he is smiling broadly. Sjahrir sits at Sukarno's side.[182] Another photo appeared in *Sikap*, also from the congress. The caption of this photograph read: "Comrade Sjahrir 'pushed' by his friends around the city in a pedicab." In the picture, Sjahrir—now he is in the limelight—is shown sitting in a brightly painted and richly decorated trishaw, surrounded by a large, and rather curious crowd, delegates perhaps. Sjahrir's face shows how awkward he feels about the scene, and—you feel he feels—that he is behaving like a fool.[183]

As the elections approached, even to some sympathetic observers occasionally, Sjahrir manifested a behavior bordering on laxness or on snobbery. Sal Tas saw Sjahrir shortly before the elections. "He told me," Tas wrote later,

> that a leader of the *Nahdatul Ulama* had come to him to ask if he would not place a few intellectuals from his group at the disposal of the NU, which had practically no cadre. It was a possibility, for acquiring influence.... "But I couldn't help him; my people find it much too boring to deal with people of that level," Sjahrir added cheerfully.[184]

It still remains an open question, and witnesses widely disagree, as to how much Sjahrir was truly apprehensive about the election results—how much he was bothered by the strength of the PSI's rivals, and how much he tried to cultivate the PSI's potential allies.

In an interview, in December 1954, Sjahrir opined that the Communist Party of Indonesia, together with the PSI, made up "the two most highly organized parties" of current Indonesian politics.[185] At the same time, however, Sjahrir added that the Communist Party lacked support of local leaders "with substantial roots," that D. N. Aidit and M. H. Lukman, the top Communist leaders, were not wholly in control of the politburo, and that, besides, they had been members of the party for "only" seven years.[186]

So much for the potentially most serious competitor for votes: the Indonesian Communist Party, like the PSI, was professedly left-wing, Marxist, and the party of the working masses. As for potential friends, Sjahrir's attitude to his closest prewar associate Mohammad Hatta was most illustrative.

In spite of a growing general awareness that Hatta was becoming more independent of Sukarno with each year, little attention was paid to the man in Sjahrir's articles, speeches, and, to all appearance, in his mind. Personal coolness between Sjahrir and Hatta seemed to last. According to Hatta's biographer Mavis Rose, for instance,

---

[181] Ibid

[182] *Suara Sosialis* 10, 1 (February 1958).

[183] *Sikap* 8, 21–22 (July 4, 1955).

[184] Tas, "Souvenirs of Sjahrir," p. 153.

[185] Kahin's interview with Sjahrir, Jakarta, December 9, 1954.

[186] Ibid.

Stamps with Sukarno
(Collection Post, Telegraph, Telephone Museum, The Hague)

Having spent the major part of 1951 overseas, Sjahrir sought out Hatta on his return to Indonesia. "Sjahrir felt rebuffed by Hatta," recalled Subadio, "because he showed more interest in National Sports Week than in listening to what Sjahrir had to tell him." This may have been Hatta's way of reminding Sjahrir that it was the PSI that had assisted in relegating him [in 1950] to the role of an impotent vice-president, whose main function was to officiate at occasions such as National Sports Week.[187]

Sjahrir either could not, did not want, or was not interested to see Hatta's potential. In a December 1954 interview, he presented Hatta as a man of lost opportunities, and of the past that would not return. According to the interview,

> some of the major problems confronting Indonesia today are a result of the lack of leadership displayed by Hatta in 1950. [Sjahrir] blames Hatta for not harnessing his government to the revolutionary ardor and altruistic outlook which still existed at the end of 1949. He notes that a major reason for the disillusionment and cynicism which is so prevalent today stems from the fact that most of the people who sacrificed most during the revolution were forgotten by Hatta's government.[188]

In contrast to Hatta, Sukarno was very much present in whatever Sjahrir wrote, said, and probably thought, as the elections approached. Whoever were Sjahrir's friends, and whoever were his enemies, Sukarno was the center, and Sjahrir appeared to view the coming elections in terms of Sukarno's centrality:

> because of his fear of a possible victory by the Islamic parties and particularly the *Masjumi*, [Sukarno] is willing to work with the Communist Party of Indonesia ... but also a Soekiman [i.e., Masjumi]-Soekarno alliance is possible and more dangerous than the Soekarno-Communist.[189]

This was, in Sjahrir's vision, a vaporous center—Sukarno acted out of fear, alliances were made at the dead end of politics. This was the center, nevertheless, which Sjahrir believed would decide which way the elections would go. If Sjahrir was optimistic about the elections, his was a particular kind of a "negative" optimism. One should read carefully, for instance, what George Kahin recorded after his interview with Sjahrir at the end of 1954:

> In general, [Sjahrir] seems rather optimistic concerning the ability of the PSI to make a reasonable showing in the election; [he did not believe much], as many people did, [in] the possibility of the Indonesian National Party and the [Javanese aristocratic] *Parindra*, Party of Greater Indonesia winning strength as a result of *wedanas* [district heads], and *lurahs* [village heads], and

---

[187] Rose, *Indonesia Free*, p. 176, citing an interview with Subadio in 1982. The issue here was the PSI not supporting in the parliament the clause in the Indonesian Constitution giving the vice-president extensive powers under certain circumstances of political crises. See above, n. 16.

[188] Kahin's interview with Sjahrir, Jakarta, December 9, 1954.

[189] Ibid.

bupatis, [the provincial heads], being from those parties.... As an example he mentioned that some of the districts and *bupati* areas which are nominally Indonesian National Party... regularly read [the PSI] *Pedoman*. [Sjahrir is also optimistic because] the vote amongst the peasant population is going to be much smaller than many people expect... primarily because of general apathy.[190]

Elections were held on September 29, 1955, as planned, and, by early October, the results became known. The PSI got less than eight-hundred thousand votes—about 2 percent of the votes cast. Eight and a half million people voted for the Indonesian National Party, slightly less than eight million for the Masjumi, seven million for the Nahdatul Ulama, a little more than six million for the Communist Party. Even the second-rank parties, like the Islamic PSII or the Christian Parkindo and Partai Katolik, got more votes than the PSI. The PSI, till then considered a major Indonesian political party, got merely five seats in the new 257-seat parliament.[191]

Whatever Sjahrir's expectations, the peasants did vote. In Herbert Feith' words,

> The villager was told two simple things about elections, that they were part of independence and that they would make independence better....
>
> His understanding was not perception of a cause-effect relationship; it was perception and acknowledgement of a moral (and in most cases also religious) duty.[192]

More significantly, the Javanese masses voted. The victorious parties won, because they won on Java. The Indonesian National Party obtained 85.97 percent of its vote on Java, Nahdatul Ulama 85.6 percent, and the Communist Party 88.6 percent.[193]

According to Leon Salim—the old Minangkabau cadre of the PSI and Pendidikan—Sjahrir, when leading his party into elections, "forgot about the power of emotions... slogans... monuments [and] theatrical stage."[194] Salim might say "mass politics" instead. According to T. B. Simatupang, another long-time and devoted ally of Sjahrir, "After the PSI failed in 1955, the political role of Sjahrir came to an end."[195] In the words of Mochtar Lubis,

> The failure of the PSI in general elections, closed the door for Sjahrir, once and forever, to return to high office in the government.[196]

---

[190] Ibid.

[191] Feith, *The Decline*, p. 434; Bos, *Tien jaar democratisch-socialisme*, p. 80.

[192] Feith, *The Decline*, p. 431.

[193] Ibid., p. 436.

[194] Salim, ed., *Bung Sjahrir*, p. 37.

[195] T. B. Simatupang, "Apa arti Sutan Sjahrir bagi kita sekarang ini?" in *Mengenang Sjahrir*, ed. Anwar, p. 187.

[196] Lubis, "Pejuang, pemikir dan peminat," p. 202.

Subadio, as usual more optimistic than the others, estimated, in July 1956, that it would take "twenty to thirty years" before the PSI could again play the role of a major political party.[197]

The PSI suffered a crushing defeat—a crushing defeat in mass politics that is. In a long editorial, entitled "General Elections," published in January 1956, Sjahrir explained:

> the Common People [*Rakjat Banjak*] did not vote, recently, on the basis of their consciousness and their affection for the spirit of nationalism, democracy and revolution, or on the basis of some other noble and high motives, but because they have followed leaders, and those, whom they respected in their everyday life ... neither the heroes, nor the youth of the revolution, but Islamic scholars [*kijaji*], instructors in learning the Koran by rote [*guru mengadui*], village headmen [*lurah*] and overseers [*mandoor*]....
>
> The elections reflected the soul and the views of the people as clearly as a photograph.... Now, it is clearly evident that our people are influenced merely by what immediately surrounds them in their everyday life—by religion [*Agama*], customs [*Adat*], local government etc.... The influence of religion seems to be strongest, and most widespread, especially on Java, [as well as] the influence of devoted submission [*ketaatan tunduk*] or of a fear of an official authority such as the village headman, sub-district head [*tjamat*], *wedana*, *bupati* etc.—in other words, [the people] have the soul of a serf [*kawula*] facing his king [*ratu*] or lord [*gusti*]; [also] the deception and demagogy to which the people are subjected, are strong especially on Java.
>
> General elections made it clear that the influence, which made the people vote the way they did, is the influence felt every day, the influence of the Islamic scholars, the influence of the village headmen or of a feared or respected cock [*djago*]....[198]

Sjahrir, thus, did not challenge the validity of the elections results. General elections, he even wrote in the same article,

> have a great historical significance for our nation.... Things had been stated before as assumptions or as probabilities, and this is, now, over. The picture of the spiritual state of our people and of our nation, the state and the level of political knowledge and consciousness, has been provided by these general elections, and could be accepted, in the future, as the foundation of our social and national thinking. It does [no more] need, to be taken as an assumption or a speculative opinion.[199]

Essentially in the same way Sjahrir wrote, at the same time, for the *Atlantic Monthly*, an article published in English, and aimed at the outside world:

> The country's first general elections were held a few months ago, and the seriousness with which they were taken indicated that the people will be

---

[197] Kahin's interview with Subadio, Jakarta, July 15, 1956.
[198] Sjahrir, "Pemilihan Umum untuk Konstituante," *Sikap* 8, 40 (December 5, 1955), p. 1.
[199] Ibid.

able to assume a share—if only a small one—in responsibility for the course of affairs. Up to now it has been only the intelligentsia, the politicians, at best the literates, who have been responsible. With their lack of knowledge and experience, the politicians may lead the new Indonesian state into a deadlock; nevertheless one is certainly justified in believing that the people as a whole will muster the strength to help the country find its way.[200]

Sjahrir made it clear that he acknowledged that "responsibility for the course of affairs," through elections, had been shifted from "intelligentsia," "politicians," and "literates," to "the people." This Sjahrir accepted—demonstratively almost—although he knew how "small" the people's share might be, and although he knew that the "responsibility," was being shifted primarily from those who were defeated in the elections—prominently including the PSI and himself. Might one not hear, in what Sjahrir now was saying, a sigh of relief?

In December 1955, a second round of elections were held in Indonesia, this time for a new Constituent Assembly. These elections confirmed that the September results were not an accident. The same parties scored largely the same results.[201]

As the new cabinet was inaugurated, led by Ali Sastroamidjojo and based on the September 1955 elections results, there was a widespread hope that, by now, the Indonesian state might pass beyond its interim period, towards true stability and healthy politics. It soon became clear, however, that, while the political parties defeated in the elections had lost a mandate to act, the parties which won the elections could not even agree on a working coalition. The elections appeared, soon, as a ritual of a wholly different kind: "mass politics," began to drift in the direction of extra-party, and extra-parliamentary forces—most significantly in the direction of the military and Sukarno.

In March 1957, Ali Sastroamidjojo's cabinet fell, largely under the pressure from the Indonesian army. Instantly, Sukarno announced that he, "listening to the demands of the people," had decided to remake Indonesia according to his own concept.

An outsider, curious as to why Sukarno's self-confidence had risen so spectacularly around 1956, might surprisingly often get a standard pair of answers at the time. First, he might be told that Sukarno had married a new wife, Hartini.[202] Second, he might be reminded that, in 1956, the Republic abrogated the Dutch-Indonesian Union, agreed to in The Hague in 1949—the last formal bond, in the mid-1950s, between Indonesia and the former colonial power.

To many observers, the years 1956 and 1957 marked a fundamental watershed in postrevolutionary Indonesian history—the final break with what still remained of Dutch influence, bad or good. According to one author, for instance,

> Dutch, the original second language of Indonesia ... was replaced in the role by English during the "second wave" of anti-Durch sentiments in the mid-

---

[200] Sjahrir, "Problems the Country Faces," p. 121.

[201] Feith, *The Decline*, pp. 448-49.

[202] The marriage was considered as important as that to Inggit Garnasih a quarter of a century previously; it was Inggit, who earlier supported Sukarno, and who, according to many, was very much behind his meteoric rise in the late 1920s. The importance of both marriages is noted also for example, in Legge, *Sukarno*, p. 14.

1950s. Although English was not advocated as a second language for political reasons, Dutch definitely was dropped for political reasons.[203]

In December 1957, the Indonesian government (and mainly the military profited from this) seized most of the remaining Dutch property in the archipelago. A massive exodus of the Dutch and the Eurasians from Indonesia, accelerating through the early and mid-1950s, culminated dramatically at the same time, late in 1957. Pictures of overcrowded ships leaving Indonesian ports symbolize this period as well as anything. This was sometimes described as a passage "back to Holland"; in spite of the fact that many, if not most, of the Dutch and the Eurasians leaving had spent their whole life in the Indies, and that their families had lived in the Indies often for generations.[204]

Herbert Feith described the "second wave," which gave Sukarno new prominence, as a significant change in the nation's politics as well as its self-image:

> The leaders of the earlier cabinets had tended to see Indonesia as a young country with formidable internal problems to solve, a country which had to prove itself before the world—and by this they meant the Western world and India. Those who led the later cabinets saw Indonesia more as a leader of the Asian renascence, a country which had no need to keep up with the standards that others set for themselves and thus no need to follow Western political models . . . ; the "negative" symbols were, "free fight liberalism," "Dutch thinking," "individualism," "cosmopolitism." . . .[205]

Clifford Geertz, who did his research in Indonesia at this time, recalled later a "great crescendo of slogans, movements, monuments, and demonstrations . . . designed to make the nation-state seem indigenous."[206] Ruslan Abdulgani, who was close to Sjahrir during the 1940s, and who became Sukarno's main ideologue by the 1950s, presented Sukarno's new *konsepsi*, "concept," as a step up, from "political" to "socio-economic" revolution. At the same time, according to Abdulgani, this was an effort to weaken the growing "class dissension."[207] It was the sheer power of Sukarno's all-absorbing personality, and the philosophy of the syncretic center, that were from now on to move Indonesia beyond its crisis. The twin-like related terms used by Sukarno to label his solution: "guided democracy" and "Indonesian socialism," were as contradictory or syncretic—depending which way one looked at them—as the *konsepsi* itself.

Bob Vuyk left Indonesia, with some of the last remaining Dutch and Eurasians, in 1958. She retired afterwards into a small village of Loenen, near Leiden. Later, she wrote about her departure laconically:

---

[203] S. A. Douglas, *Political Socialization and Student Activism in Indonesia* (Urbana: University of Illinois Press, 1970), p. 83.

[204] *Pedoman*, December 7, 1950 gives the number of "Indo-Belanda" who had already left at 90,000 to 120,000.

[205] Feith, *The Decline*, pp. 576–77.

[206] Geertz, "The Politics of Meaning," p. 326.

[207] Abdulgani, *Nationalism, Revolution and Guided Democracy*, p. 37.

> When we were leaving in the hectic hurry for Europe, [Sjahrir] seemed not to be in Jakarta, and it was not given that we might say a few words of farewell.[208]

Salim, the painter and Sjahrir's friend from the 1920s, finally visited Indonesia in 1956. His trip was in part paid for by Sjahsam, Sjahrir's brother and Maria's husband; there is no record, however, of the painter meeting with Sjahrir. Salim did some outdoor painting on Java: Tegal on the coast, particularly, "reminded him of Sèta," the place in southern France where he now lived. Salim stayed a few weeks in Indonesia, and then returned to France, because, as he said on his departure, he still expected to live and work for some years.[209]

Sjahrir still published articles in the PSI journals; some of them he signed *Realpolitiker*. One of his favorite themes, now, was that a "gifted orator," or a "propagandist," however talented they might be, in "real politics" could be no more than *kadet*, "midshipmen."[210]

Sjahrir still was the General Leader of the PSI. In this capacity, he issued an "Organizational Directive No.1," on January 6, 1956, directing that the party "should come nearer to the people, and open itself to the people as much as possible."[211] There, however, were internal difficulties that seemed to absorb the PSI almost completely. One clear sign was that no issue of the PSI monthly, *Suara Sosialis*, appeared between July 25, 1955—the last number before the elections—and January 1956.[212]

Some of the PSI insiders later recalled that some bitterness developed in the party executive as a result of the defeat in the elections. According to most of these recollections, however, the bitterness was directed rather narrowly against Djohan Sjahroezah, who became the party's general secretary during the Second Congress, and who was, thus, blamed as the man "responsible for the election defeat." At the second conference of the Party executive, held in late March and early April 1956, for a moment even Sjahrir's position appeared to be in danger, and Soemitro Djojohadikoesoemo, so the rumors go, was the man favored by the dissenters.[213]

---

[208] Beb Vuyk, "Mengenang Sjahrir" in *Mengenang Sjahrir*, ed. Anwar, p. 271.

[209] Interview with Salim, Paris, February 2, 1988; Marzuki, *Pelukis Salim*, pp. 55, 57.

[210] Sjahrir, "Pemilihan Umum untuk Konstituante," p. 1.

[211] *Suara Sosialis* 10, 1–2 (February–March 1958), p. 27.

[212] Ibid.

[213] Elections for the politburo, according to the party constitution, were on the program. To the surprise of many, including Sjahrir, two-thirds of the votes cast for the post of General Leader reportedly went not to Sjahrir, but to Soemitro. Feith described this as an "attempt by Soemitro to challenge the leadership of Sjahrir." Feith, *The Decline*, p. 479. Also interview with Sitoroes, Jakarta, December 29, 1987. On the congress see *Suara Sosialis* 8, 3 (March/April/May 1956), pp. 8ff. It appears, however, that the party apparatus was able to handle the crisis. According to one account, the voting was repeated in a more serious and better prepared manner, and Sjahrir won. Almost ten years later, Sjahrir commented on the affair. After reading Feith's account, he noted in his diary: "First I did not understand what he meant. Then I remembered that, indeed, there had been a little commotion (*kegontjangan sedikit*), among the party leadership, about if Soemitro was to be admitted into the politburo or not, as a consequence of which, he got one more vote than myself, which is all the votes of the [party] branches." Sjahrir's comments on Herbert Feith' book in Sutan Sjahrir, "Buku-buku cacatan harian" (variously dated, Madiun, 1962–1963), March 26, 1963; in *Archives Siti Wahjunah Sjahrir*.

It is not easy to say how much Sjahrir changed. In his texts after 1955, "socialism" was still cited as the most important "guide," "teaching," and "view of life."[214] *Akal*, "mind, brains, intellect," to Sjahrir, was still the summation of all the positive values he knew: the organization of economy, welfare, democracy, the party, practically everything was still connected to "reason."[215] "Matter-of-factness"—Sjahrir still used *zakelijkheid*, the Dutch term—appeared in his texts as frequently as before. A word which suggested some change seemed to be *objektivisme*, "objectivism." It appeared now overused; sometimes, as if *objektivisme* was to supply a all-explaining notion and an ultimate solution.[216]

Sjahrir still wrote about *kemajuan*, "progress"; this still to him was, essentially, the process of maturing. Socialism, Sjahrir wrote, would become the "adulthood of mankind."[217] The aim of socialism, also, was still *moril*, "moral"; Dutch words were still used by Sjahrir to qualify morals—*moraliteit* and *ethiek*.[218]

Ethical, to Sjahrir, more than before it seemed, meant an endeavor compassionate and noble. In 1957 he wrote, for instance:

> There is a most widespread lack of justice and lack of sense of responsibility among our intelligentsia, among the prosperous and the powerful towards the common folk—a lack of human feeling towards the common folk that still lives in poverty and ignorance.... Common justice must be equalled with the happiness and loftiness [*kemuliaan*] of our whole nation.[219]

Progress, more than before, it seemed, appeared to Sjahrir as a process of man being progressively relieved of tensions:

> The new life, we hope in, and we dream about, does differ from the present life, in which there still are anxieties and confusions. Certainly, in what we hope, is balance and harmony in the new life.[220]

And about the same time Sjahrir wrote: "We, the socialists, in a very definite sense, are professional dreamers [*tukang mimpi*]."[221]

As it became evident, after the elections in 1955, that the PSI would not get a single seat in the new cabinet, "the press of the excluded PSI," according to Herbert Feith, "was critical, but not severely so."[222] When Sukarno, a short time later, asked all the Indonesian political parties to support his new *konsepsi*, "only the Masjumi

---

[214] Sjahrir, "Sosialisme," *Bunga Rampai Sosialisme Kerakjatan* (Jakarta: Dewan Pimpinan Pusat Gerakan Mahasiswa Sosialis, 1957), pp. 21, 9.

[215] See especially Sjahrir, *Sosialisme dan Pimpinan; tjeramah dalam peringatan Dies Natalis Gerakan Mahasiswa Sosialis di Bandung, tgl.16 Oktober 1957* (Jakarta: Sekretariat Dewan Partai, 1957); also in *Sikap* X, 35; XI, 36 and 38 (November 7, 14, and 28, 1957), pp. 4, 16, 18, 19; Sjahrir, "Pedoman kehidupan bangsa," in *Sosialisme, Indonesia, Pembangunan*, p. 128.

[216] Ibid., pp. 129–31.

[217] Sjahrir, "Sosialisme dan Pimpinan," in *Sosialisme, Indonesia, Pembangunan*, p. 110.

[218] Sjahrir, "Sosialisme," *Bunga Rampai Sosialisme Kerakjatan*, pp. 9, 16.

[219] Sjahrir, "Pedoman kehidupan," in *Sosialisme, Indonesia, Pembangunan*, pp. 126-27.

[220] Ibid., pp. 121-22.

[221] Sjahrir, "Sosialisme sekarang," part V, *Sikap* 5 (February 6, 1957).

[222] Feith, *The Decline*, p. 470.

and the Catholic Party gave him directly negative answers"; the PSI's response, again, according to Feith, was "vague, ambiguous, noncommittal."[223]

On March 1, 1957, a group of top leaders from major political parties visited the chief public prosecutor in Jakarta to complain about the political intimidation they were being exposed to because of their opposition to Sukarno's *konsepsi*. There were leaders of the Masjumi, the PSII, the Catholic Party, and even of the Nahdatul Ulama in the group—but not one PSI representative.[224] When Sukarno speeded up the transformation towards his "guided democracy" and "Indonesian socialism," during the following months, Feith made a list of politicians who in 1957 spoke against: Sjahrir was not on the list.[225]

One of the younger men close to Sjahrir from the time of the early revolution told me later about this time:

> We were furious. Sometimes we were quite willing to kill Sukarno. . . . And Sjahrir, at such a moment, was able to tell us: "It is not an easy job he has"!

Lack of knowledge, or, perhaps, a desire not to know all the details, appeared with growing frequency in Sjahrir's texts, and sometimes, it made up a major part of Sjahrir's explanations of what happened and how he reacted. In his private diary, five or so years later, Sjahrir wrote, how, on reading studies on the period, several times he was *agak terkedjut*, "rather startled," to find that this or that important document concerning the PSI or his person had escaped him at the time.[226]

Arnold Brackman explained Sjahrir's behavior after 1955 in purely balance-of-power terms. Sjahrir, wrote Brackman, "foresaw the destruction of democracy but [was] powerless to prevent it; only Natsir, who had a mass organization [Masjumi], was in a position to resist."[227]

I believe the reasons were deeper. Sjahrir envisioned the topography of Indonesian politics and culture essentially the same way he had done five or twenty years ago. The center, to him, was a pool of all the anti-values, as he wrote in 1957, "an escape from anxieties towards mystical [*mistik*], shaman [*dukun*], Islamic scholars [*kijaji*], towards stories like the Djojobojo prophecy";[228] the center was, to him, a realm of *nafsu*, "unbridled passion," "a sort of *overcompensatie*," of *pikiran emosioneel*, "emotional thinking"; and again, a world of *mistik*, "the mystical Javanese way."[229]

Sukarno and his concept of "guided democracy" and "Indonesian socialism," no doubt, were seen by Sjahrir as part, the embodiment, of the center. "Leadership and guidance are presented as a remedy against anxieties"—Sjahrir wrote, in 1957, about the new regime—as a charm, as a key for the weak, who waited for their soul to be helped by something or somebody from above.[230] "Guided democracy, in its form,"

---

[223] Ibid., p. 544.

[224] Ibid.

[225] Ibid., pp. 603, 603n.

[226] This in reference to the Five-Year Plan (1955–1960); while Subadio, Sjahrir wrote, had known about it, he, Sjahrir had learned of it only in prison. See Sjahrir's comments on Paauw's "Financing" in Sjahrir, "Buku-buku cacatan harian," September 18, 1962.

[227] Arnold C. Brackman, *Indonesian Communism: A History* (New York: Praeger, 1963), p. 264.

[228] Sjahrir, "Pedoman kehidupan bangsa," in *Sosialisme, Indonesia, Pembangunan*, p. 125.

[229] Ibid., pp. 123, 129–30.

[230] Sjahrir, "Sosialisme dan Pemimpin," in *Sosialisme, Indonesia, Pembangunan*, p. 95.

Sjahrir wrote in the same text, "can be traced back to the fundamentally hierarchical and oligarchical structures, [and it can be traced forward, to] a new feudalism."[231]

Sjahrir saw the center as sharply as before. Except that, now, he seemed to respect it more. He seemed to be slowing down in his movement around the center and off the center. As he himself slowed down, all marginal or fringe forces threatening to explode or merely irritating the center, appeared increasingly outside Sjahrir's limits of understanding and tolerance.

In 1956, the main complaint by the PSI executive, and thus by Sjahrir, about the cabinet in power, was that it might bring about instability.[232] Questioning a picture which Herbert Feith had drawn of him as the champion of "constitutional democracy," Sjahrir wrote later in his diary:

> I myself learned many big lessons from the general elections, so that later ...
> I agreed that we should move back to the Constitution of 1945, in which certainly the position of the Executive is pushed forward and takes on a quality of leadership that rather surpasses that of the day-to-day powers of Parliament, [but] which also gives the Executive enough space and time to work. As is the case with the US Constitution, the [Indonesian] Constitution of 1945 is succinct enough to be perfected later in accordance with further experiences. . . . It appears that Feith did not think about this, as his book bears a title "The Decline of Constitutional Democracy in Indonesia."[233]

An important thing to recall, of course, is that Sjahrir, back in late 1945, had come to power exactly through challenging and then initiating the change of the "Constitution of 1945," pushing back the executive and Sukarno, at the expense of the day-to-day powers of the Parliament.

Soedjatmoko, Sjahrir's follower from the time of the occupation, defined Indonesian politics after the 1955 elections as a "diffusion of power." Voices "can only be felt rather than explicitly heard," Soedjatmoko wrote; and even "serious political crises" merely emphasize the "slowness and comparative uneventfulness" of the time.[234]

Soedjatmoko probably expressed well what Sjahrir himself came to believe. From Sjahrir's perspective, there certainly appeared to be a diminishing number of alternatives to the power of the center, and namely of Sukarno. Perceiving things to be diffuse, as Soedjatmoko suggested, might help, in this situation, at least to blur a vision which would otherwise be too depressing. "Guided democracy" and "Indonesian socialism" were already commonly being described as a triangle of variously powerful and mutually inimical centers—Sukarno, the Communists, and the army. Sjahrir's perception was different. Sjahrir appeared to blur the differences among all the three "centers" into an essentially loose and amorphous whole.

---

[231] Ibid., pp. 108–109.

[232] "Partai Sosialis Indonesia, resolution of the party conference, March 30 to April 2, 1956. Info Asian socialist conference. File PvdA, September 11, 1956" in *Collection Schermerhorn* no. 4.

[233] Sjahrir's comments on Feith in Sjahrir, "Buku-buku cacatan harian," March 26, 1963. (Compare his writing on the same subject in October 1957 in Sjahrir, *Sosialisme dan Pimpinan*, p. 15.)

[234] Soedjatmoko, "The Role of Political Parties in Indonesia" in *Nationalism and Progress in Free Asia*, ed. Philip W. Thayer (Baltimore: Johns Hopkins Press, 1956), pp. 134–36.

Sjahrir talked, now, about the army often in the same breath as about what might easily be defined as *ningrat*—the blurred notion as he occasionally painted it was that of "civil service, army and police."[235] If the military were left to act, Sjahrir wrote, it might lead "towards an aristocratic or military dictatorship."[236]

The Communist threat, to Sjahrir, seemed to work in the same register. Lines between the military, the Communists, and *ningrat*, were made hazy. Sjahrir warned that if any one of the forces moved, it would result in a "trend towards an aristocratic or military dictatorship or, on the other side, towards a dictatorship of the Bolshevik style."[237]

Rather than the old dichotomy of "dynamic" versus "static," a new duality of "order" versus "chaos" appeared to dominate Sjahrir's writings. Both, the military and the Communists, acted dangerously as far as they might become disruptive of the established order.[238]

What was the order? Those, Sjahrir wrote in his article for the *Atlantic Monthly* in 1956, who wanted to disrupt Indonesia, believed that "the Indonesian existence as a nation will end in a complete fiasco." However, Sjahrir explained in a passage about "the regenerating strength of the Indonesian people,"—a passage which, a few years earlier, he himself might have described as a piece of Sukarnoist and Javanist conservativism:

> One bright spot in all this is that our country people have not yet been greatly disturbed by all the problems at the government level.. . . . The people in the *desa* or village produce their own food and do not have so many needs from the outside world. The *desa* has shown in the past that it can survive without money. In our national existence then, it goes to make up a vast area where the tendency toward stability and order is at its greatest. Only in the regions where there are rebels and guerrillas operating is the *desa* in turmoil. Provided the areas of turbulence do not expand, the order and stability of the *desa* will prove the factor able to prevent the complete national chaos. . . .[239]

4. CIVIL WAR

Clifford Geertz, in a study published in 1963, wrote about Indonesia:

> the new nation has become an almost classic case of integrative failure. With every step toward modernity has come increased regional discontent; with each increase in regional discontent has come a new revelation of political incapacity; and with each revelation of political incapacity has come a loss of

---

[235] Sjahrir, "Problems the Country Faces," p. 24.

[236] Sjahrir, *Sosialisme dan Pimpinan*, p. 15.

[237] Sjahrir, "Problems the Country Faces," p. 25; Sjahrir, "Masa depan sosialisme kerakjatan," *Sikap* 10,7 (February 20, 1957), *passim*; Sjahrir, *Bunga Rampai Sosialisme Kerakjatan, passim*; Sjahrir, *Indonesian Socialism*, pp. 40, 44, 49, 52, 65; Sjahrir, "Sosialisme sekarang," part I–III, *Sikap* 1–3 (January 9, 16, and 23, 1957).

[238] Sjahrir, "Sosialisme sekarang," part IV, *Sikap* 4 (January 30, 1957).

[239] Sjahrir, "Problems the Country Faces," pp. 120-21.

political nerve and a more desperate resort to an unstable amalgam of military coercion and ideological revivalism.[240]

Ruslan Abdulgani described essentially the same development as "new symptoms":

> increase of population without adequate increase of food production ... increase in number of graduates from high schools and universities without new jobs, [and] increase of financial, economic and political power in the centralized capital of Jakarta without a fair distribution to the provinces.[241]

The government's "heavy reliance on the politically exposed *pamong-pradja* corps"—the officialdom of the Republic and very much the heirs of the prewar *ningrat* officials—was seen by Herbert Feith as "a major reason why little was done about regional autonomy."[242] Moreover, the number of appointments of Javanese *pamong-pradja* as high officials, Feith wrote, grew, and a feeling grew with it, in the areas outside Java, that this was part of "efforts to 'Javanize' Indonesian culture."[243] In consequence, the year 1956

> saw the birth of new ethnically based organizations among the Sundanese, the Lampongese, the Minangkabaus, the Achehnese, the people of East Sumatra;

all of them had their headquarters in Jakarta, and together they infused the atmosphere of tension between the center and the provinces into the politics of the capital.[244]

The division penetrated all the bodies of the state. Describing the principal cleavage in the Indonesian army in 1956, Feith wrote:

> Significantly, the cleavage tended to parallel two lines of conflict. ... On the one hand, it paralleled the conflict between Djakarta and the islands outside Java. ... On the other hand, it approximated the cleavage which was created by the rise and open voicing of feeling against the ethnic Javanese.[245]

On July 20, 1956, Mohammad Hatta, the Sumatran in the top leadership of the state, submitted his resignation as vice-president, and in December of that year Hatte left office. He talked of "chaos" and of the national revolution not being "dammed up at the appropriate time."[246] Much of the next year, according to his biographer, Hatta spent

---

[240] Clifford Geertz, "Primordial Sentiments and Civil Policies in the New States" in his *Old Societies and New States* (Chicago: Free Press, 1963), p. 131.

[241] Abdulgani, *Nationalism*, p. 36.

[242] Feith, *The Decline*, p. 567.

[243] Ibid., p. 286.

[244] Ibid., pp. 491–92.

[245] Ibid., p. 502.

[246] Mohammad Hatta, *Past and Future* (Ithaca: Cornell Modern Indonesia Project, 1960), p. 15. (This is a translation of the speech delivered by Mohammad Hatta at Yogyakarta on November 27, 1956.)

touring Sumatra, where he received an enthusiastic welcome as if he were a returning hero responding to his people's call. He emphasized that his intent was not to incite rebellion but to prevent it. The Sumatrans assured him that they wanted to remain part of Indonesia but were not prepared to accept the type of government being practiced in Jakarta. Anti-Java feeling was running high.[247]

Regional restlessness, supported often by local army commanders, was as old as the Republic. Through 1956, however, the restlessness grew rapidly. In the same month, in which Hatta left office, December 1956, the Dewan Banteng, the "Wild Buffalo Council," a solidarity body of soldiers with a history reaching back to the time of the Revolution of the 1940s, declared itself the governing authority in West Sumatra. Hatta visited Sumatra soon afterwards:

> In his press statements Hatta denied that the regional rebellion was a Minangkabau affair. "In my estimation [he said] the movement which emerged on December 1956 was not an ethnic but a regional movement, which demands improvement and development in an area which so far has been neglected."[248]

Regional or ethnic, the movement spread from Sumatra to Sulawesi and to several other eastern islands of the country. Through 1957, there was not a month when an additional "scandal in the provinces" or "another act of regional disobedience" was not reported in the Jakarta press.

During the last weeks of 1957, several prominent leaders of the parties opposing Sukarno's *konsepsi*, namely the Masjumi's Mohammad Natsir, Sjafroeddin Prawiranegara, and Burhanuddin Harahap, left Jakarta, explaining their move by citing growing pressure and political intimidation in the capital. In a matter of days, these political leaders reappeared in Sumatra, and, more or less clearly, on the rebels' side.

Soemitro Djojohadikoesoemo, one of the top leaders of Sjahrir's PSI, had left Jakarta earlier, already in May 1957. As it was reported, Soemitro's motivation at the time was to evade an interrogation in process in Jakarta on his alleged corruption.[249] At the turn of 1957 and 1958, however, Soemitro's exile acquired a new meaning. Soemitro, who now lived in Singapore, became the most conspicuous of the "defectors from supporters of the central government." While the other "defectors," former premiers Natsir and Burhanuddin, or Sjafroeddin Prawiranegara, the chief of the emergency government in 1949, were widely respected men with their dedication to public affairs generally acknowledged, Soemitro, was rather rumored and believed to like working behind the scenes, to be very rich, and thus, implicitly, conspiratorial and egoistical.

---

[247] Rose, *Indonesia Free*, p. 190.

[248] Yet Hatta's biographer adds: "There was an unmistakable tone of ethnic pride as Hatta wrote about the achievements of the Banteng Council and the Minangkabau people." Ibid.

[249] Feith, *The Decline*, p. 585. It was alleged that Soemitro misused his government position, serving at the same time as the chairman of the PSI election committee, and that he, for his party, misappropriated some state money. See Mochtar Lubis, *Cacatan Subversif* (Jakarta: Sinar Harapan, 1980), pp. 67–68 (entry for June 1, 1957).

The Jakarta press by early 1958 nicknamed Soemitro *miljoener kerakjatan*, "millionaire of the people's power" (mocking the PSI's *kerakjatan*, of course), and the *PSI-er Sumatra*, "the PSI man in Sumatra."[250] Soemitro's defection, the PSI, and Sjahrir, were now talked about in one breath.[251]

On February 10, 1958, an ultimatum was sent to the central government by the Dewan Perdjuangan, the "Struggle Council" based in Sumatra, a body related to the "Wild Buffalo Council" mentioned above. The ultimatum demanded that brakes be put on implementation of Sukarno's *konsepsi*, and that the dual leadership of Sukarno-Hatta be restored. On February 16, after the government did not respond, the "Struggle Council" declared that a new government was being established in Bukittinggi, West Sumatra. The prime minister of the new Pemerintah Revolusioner Republik Indonesia, PRRI, "Revolutionary Government of the Indonesian Republic," was Sjafroeddin Prawiranegara of the Masjumi. Among the other ministers were local army commander Colonel Simbolon, former premier and Masjumi leader Burhanuddin Harahap, and also Soemitro.[252] The regional movement in Sulawesi, under Perdjuangan Semesta, Permesta or "Common Struggle," declared itself to be in full agreement with the PRRI leaders and joined the rebellion.[253]

Over the following days, Sukarno began to confer with representatives of major political parties, and also with Hatta. The talks were reportedly to explore the possibility of a peaceful solution.[254] Amidst the talks, however, and some suggest that both Sukarno and Hatta might have been caught by surprise, the planes of the Indonesian armed forces attacked towns and bases in Sumatra and Sulawesi under PRRI-Permesta control.

During the first week of March, the Indonesian armed forces loyal to the central government landed at Bengkalis, on the east coast of Sumatra, and on March 12, the PRRI base and town of Pekanbaru in East Sumatra was occupied.[255] On April 17, central government forces landed in West Sumatra. The city of Padang, on the coast, was taken instantly, and, on May 4, 1958, Bukittinggi fell. Resistance lasted longer in Sulawesi, especially because the distance from Java was greater and actions against the uprising required much more complicated logistics. With the fall of Bukittinggi,

---

[250] Quoted in *Pedoman*, January 17, 1958.

[251] On January 24, 1958, the Indonesian government asked the British authorities, "for Dr. Soemitro Djojohadikoesoemo, who is, at present, in Singapore, to be returned to the Indonesian government." *Pedoman*, January 25, 1958. Five days later, on January 29, the Indonesian minister of information asked about the threat by Sumatran rebels to declare a separate government, answered in Javanese: *Takon bae karo Soemitro*, "This is a voice of Soemitro." *Pedoman*, January 30, 1958.

[252] List of the PRRI ministers see, e.g., in Justus M. van der Kroef, "Disunited Indonesia," *Far Eastern Survey* 27, 4 & 5 (April and May, 1958), p. 63.

[253] Barbara S. Harvey, *Permesta: Half a Rebellion*. (Ithaca: Cornell Modern Indonesia Project, 1977).

[254] *Pedoman*, February 20, 1958.

[255] One of the reasons for this hurried action, apparently, was an effort by the army chief, A.H. Nasution, to preempt a possible move by the US 7th Fleet. Indeed, some elements of the force, at the time, were already in Singapore, and might intervene, in case of a prolonged conflict, in what many in the United States saw simply as a struggle against Sukarno and communism.

however, the threat by the PRRI-Permesta to the central government, to Sukarno, and to "guided democracy," ceased to be a crucial factor of the national politics.[256]

The strength of the center suddenly increased. The loyal segment of the army in a matter of weeks acquired a large set of new responsibilities. The "state of war and siege," which had already been declared as the regional unrest began to grow, in 1956, remained in force, and new emergency laws gave the army additional administrative powers.

Newspapers and journals were the first to feel the army's newly strengthened role. According to Feith, "Communist-sympathizing publications" became a target, in spite the generally acknowledged fact that the Indonesian Communist Party supported the central government against the rebels. The other prominent target of the army became the press "supporting the Masjumi and PSI."[257] In fact, Feith wrote, the army repression "hit the Masjumi and PSI-sympathizing press hardest, with the Communist-sympathizing press dealt occasional blows."[258]

On September 5, 1958, Nasution, at the head of the army, banned branches of the Masjumi, the Catholic Parkindo, and the PSI, in the areas where the rebellion had occurred. This was a prelude to August 1960, when a "Commission for Retooling," under Nasution's chairmanship again, issued a decree banning the Masjumi and the PSI. The reason given was the involvement of the parties in the rebellion and/or their failure to condemn the rebellion.

In 1960, the Parliament which had emerged out of the general elections in 1955 was dissolved, and a new legislature was convened by presidential decree. The "Constitution of 1945"—which had governed Indonesia after September 1945 until effectively abolished by Sjahrir's "constitutional coup" in November— was renewed. The extensive presidential, and thus Sukarno's, powers, were renewed by this Constitution. In April 1961, a further decree dissolved all political parties except a privileged ten—including the Indonesian National Party, the Nahdatul Ulama, and the Indonesian Communist Party—parties which had demonstrated sufficient willingness to support the new system and the president.

"I had the clear impression," Ruslan Abdulgani later wrote

> that all the ten political parties considered President Soekarno more or less as their symbolic Chairman; while the President himself conceived his position as a kind of collective Chairman of all the Political Parties.[259]

Sukarno himself spoke of "colored party coats," by which he meant: "all the colors [are] bleachable."[260]

There was a very little resistance. In spring 1960, shortly before the reform of the party system, fifteen members of Parliament from various political parties formed a *Liga Demokrasi*, "Democratic League,"

---

[256] Lt. Col. Rudy Pirngadie, *The "P.R.R.I. Affair" (as seen in the light of the history of the Armed Forces)* (Jakarta: Nusantara, 1958). See also Audrey R. and George McT. Kahin, *Provoking a Civil War: The Eisenhower Administration's Indonesia Crusade* (forthcoming).

[257] Feith, *The Decline*, p. 590.

[258] Ibid., p. 593.

[259] Abdulgani, *Nationalism*, p. 56.

[260] Ibid., p. 55.

to establish democratic life in Indonesia in the fields of politics, economics and socialism, [opposing] all fascism, totalitarianism, imperialism, feudalism and bureaucracy.[261]

According to Ruslan Abdulgani again, "some army circles" gave "covert support" to the "Democratic League"; according to Arnold Brackman, the army "looked the other way."[262] Hatta, in the words of his biographer,

> although fully supportive of the league's intentions, was skeptical about its effectiveness. He saw weaknesses in its structure in that it was "built by parties who participate in the [new] *Gotong-royong* parliament."[263]

Some army officers, especially from military intelligence, almost certainly were involved. Some members of the PSI reportedly also participated, primarily as advisers. Whoever was involved, however, took part in an exercise in futility. The "Democratic League" merely succeeded in demonstrating the new strength of Sukarno and the system. According to Brackman's rather dramatic conclusion, "The League was shortlived. The sharks swam after the little fish."[264]

Sjahrir was a good target. His opponents connected him easily to Soemitro and the few others "of the PSI," who had openly joined the rebellion. What Sjahrir himself actually had done, was apparently not very important. It was rather difficult, indeed, to find out what he actually did. It was not easy to find either what his attitude and his party's platform had truly been through the crucial time. Re-reading statements by Sjahrir and his party of that period, echoes of the 1920s, and of the Pendidikan, and of the Revolution of the 1940s occasionally resound. At other times, however, and most often, in fact, the statements sound strikingly uncertain, and erratic under the pressure of events. Frequently there is a silence.

Regionalism was the critical issue. Through the mid-1950s, as through the decades before, Sjahrir and his party presented it as something which, if permitted to grow distinct and explicit, would gravely harm Indonesian unity.[265] According to Sjahrir through the mid-1950s, any highlighting of regionalism was undesirable. As always, Sjahrir warned against "particularist cultures."[266] In the twelve-point program of the PSI from early 1956, only a single point and a single paragraph in another point might be construed as raising the regional issue: point 11 stated that "instituting elections in regions and regional autonomy have to strengthen people's power"; point 10d expressed a concern over the "development of production especially in the areas outside Java."[267]

As late as April 1957—four months after the Wild Buffalo Council's regionalist *pronunciamento* in West Sumatra—Sjahrir offered the following statement on regionalism:

---

[261] *Pikiran Rakjat*, June 7, 1960, quoted in Rose, *Indonesia Free*, p. 198.

[262] Abdulgani, *Nationalism*, pp. 48–49; Brackman, *Indonesian Communism*, p. 275.

[263] Rose, *Indonesia Free*, p. 198.

[264] Brackman, *Indonesian Communism*, p. 278.

[265] "Badan Aksi Sosialis (PSI)" in *Sikap* 8, 40 (December 5, 1957), p. 7.

[266] Sjahrir, "Pemilihan Umum untuk Konstituante," p. 4.

[267] "Partai Sosialis Indonesia, resolution of the party conference, March 30 to April 2, 1956. Info Asian socialist conference. File PvdA, September 11, 1956" in *Collection Schermerhorn* no. 4.

As if our nation, after attaining the most perfect and pure integration through its fight for freedom and nationhood, experiences a disintegration again.... Our nation now acts as if it has lost its compass and anchor ... it drifts in search of self-assurance towards ancient customs [adat istiadat jang lama], and towards unities of ethnic groups and tribes.[268]

Now, of course, Indonesian unity was largely identified with "guided democracy" and Sukarno—a Javanese Sukarno without a Sumatran Hatta. In 1956, Feith wrote,

The Masjumi and PSI press in Djakarta gave full play to the development of ethnic and regional protest and was charged by the papers of the PNI [Indonesian National Party] and PKI [Indonesian Communist Party] with stirring up anti-Javanese feeling.[269]

Sjahrir and the central executive of the PSI were under growing pressure from actual everyday events. Pressure grew from their own regional branches. In September 1957, for instance, the PSI branch of Central Sumatra, the area including the Minangkabau, issued the following declaration:

The PSI of Central Sumatra, in its policy and party organization, shall always follow the path which agrees with the perspectives of a development of this region; support given to the regional movement led by the "Wild Buffalo Council" is nothing but a contribution to this—to a development of the society of this region.[270]

Of course, the statement added:

The PSI Central Sumatra accepts and submits to whatever correction might seem proper to the party's General Leader [Sjahrir].[271]

In particular Soemitro's escape from Jakarta and then his joining the rebels pushed the PSI and Sjahrir personally very uncomfortably into the spotlight. In addition to Soemitro, the Indonesian ambassador to Rome, Mr. St. Mohd. Rasjid, appeared in the headlines as "another man of the PSI choosing the rebel side"; this despite the fact that Rasjid's connection with the PSI had always been very loose and that he himself emphasized that he was joining the PRRI not because he was "a PSI-man," but because he was a Minangkabau.[272] Des Alwi, one of Sjahrir's Bandanese children, always a very independent man, joined the PRRI, and became the rebels' "official spokesman abroad, mainly in Singapore, Manila and Hong Kong."[273]

---

[268] Sjahrir, "Pedoman kehidupan bangsa," in *Sosialisme, Indonesia, Pembangunan*, pp. 124, 126.

[269] Feith, *The Decline*, pp. 492–93.

[270] "Keterangan Koordinator Umum PSI Sumatra Tengah Taher Samad kepada *PIA*," in *Suara Sosialis* 9, 9 (September 1957).

[271] Ibid.

[272] Ambassador Jones to the State Department, incoming telegram no. 900 US Embassy Jakarta, September 9, 1958.

[273] Hanna, *Kepulauan Banda*, p. 144; also *Pedoman*, March 1, 1958, p. 1.

Whatever the connections, accusing fingers pointing at Des Alwi, again logically pointed also at Sjahrir. Soemitro, Rasjid, and Des Alwi were, in fact, the only three prominent figures associated with the PSI and Sjahrir, who directly and openly joined the uprisings. Yet, it became almost impossible to argue that Sjahrir was not involved.[274]

Sjahrir's wife told me about the time in the fall of 1957 in Jakarta:

> Sjahrir became very depressed, and he was feeling, as he told me, with each coming day increasingly "as if in an empty space." Natsir was still here, he lived just across the street. But there was a guard in front of his house, and many other people had already left. Still I remember how unusually angry Sjahrir became whenever someone suggested that he should go, too.[275]

Gloom certainly was reflected in the January 1958 issue of the PSI journal *Sikap*. There was a "Happy New Year!" greeting on the cover. The editorial, however,

---

[274] Soemitro's "defection" marked the true beginning of Sjahrir and the PSI being implicated. As already mentioned, Soemitro did in fact leave Jakarta in May 1957, not to join the rebels but rather to escape an investigation of alleged corruption. Also the case of corruption was never cleared up. "Soemitro did it for the party," Djohan Sjahroezah is reported by other PSI friends to have said, at the time, "if he is corrupted, so am I." Interview with Subadio, Jakarta, October 18, 1987. Sjahrir, according to close associates at the time, "disliked the idea" of Soemitro escaping before the trial interrogation started. But, according to the same sources, he had told Soemitro in his usual style, "you decide for yourself." Soemitro went into hiding in a friend's house in Tanah Abang [a quarter of Jakarta], then when he found out it was difficult to leave Java, Sjahrir helped him out. Ibid. Afterwards, Soemitro reappeared in various places in Sumatra and in Singapore, and began to move very fast in his self-imposed exile. During the months following his escape, messengers traveled almost incessantly, it seems, from the PSI executive and from Sjahrir, to dissuade Soemitro, so they say, from getting involved in the regional protest. There is some reason to believe this. Even if the PSI had wanted a representative with the PRRI government, Soemitro would not have made a very effective one. He was vulnerable because of the corruption rumors; he was unpopular, and inside the PSI itself he was well-known for being difficult to control. According to Sitoroes, one of the messengers sent by Sjahrir to Soemitro, he went to demand Soemitro's promise not to get too close to the regionalist politics; even in this, he says, he failed. Interview with Sitoroes, Jakarta, December 29, 1987. Djohan Sjahroezah went to see Soemitro twice—late in August 1957 and again early in 1958. He, reportedly, got a promise from the PSI regional leaders in Sumatra that they would keep quiet and distant if it came to an armed rebellion; but, like Sitoroes, Djohan was unable to convince Soemitro. Interview with Rosihan Anwar, Jakarta, November 8, 1987. Sudarpo traveled to Sumatra, so he says, with a personal message and "suggestion" from Sjahrir to Soemitro: that he "teach at Padang University but not join a rebel government." According to a comment by a PSI figure who saw it from a slight distance: "Soemitro did not listen, and got us all in trouble." Sjahrir himself told George Kahin, in January 1961: "Soemitro intentionally avoided PSI emissaries sent to Minangkabau. Thus it is inferred he both knew the party's opposition and he was already committed." Sjahrir's interview with George Kahin, Jakarta, January 1961. Djuir Mohammad, another high functionary in the PSI, was sent by Sjahrir to talk to Soemitro, at the moment the rebellion had already started. Djuir was captured by a rebel army unit, and was interned for some weeks in a PRRI internment camp. Salim, ed., *Bung Sjahrir*, p. 38. It is worth noting, perhaps, that Sjahrir's people stuck to their story even after 1966, when it would have occasionally been advantageous to claim involvement in the PRRI and against the "guided democracy."

[275] Interview with Siti Wahjunah Sjahrir, Jakarta, January 11, 1988.

signed by *Sindo*, which almost certainly was Sjahrir, carried a headline, "The Year 1958: Without Hope."[276]

As events gained speed, the behavior of the PSI, and of Sjahrir in particular, more than anything else seemed to grow wavering, and erratic. On January 2, 1958, for instance, an interview "given by Sjahrir a few days earlier" to the Calcutta *Statesman*, was "reprinted," by the Jakarta *Pedoman*, a paper very close to the PSI. Under the headline "Civil War If Communists Seize Power While President Is Abroad" Sjahrir was quoted as saying that the PSI was a party aware more than others of the threat by the Communists "who are already strong on Java"; Sjahrir was quoted describing Sukarno as a leader, who "thinks that the Communists would not stand up against him."[277] The next day, *Pedoman* published a denial: "No interview was given. Those were only answers given to hypothetical questions during a general discussion."[278]

This made headlines anyway. The minister of information at an instant news conference in Jakarta responded to the Sjahrir interview. "With a smile" he told the newsmen that Sjahrir appeared to be suggesting that the Indonesian Communists were about "to burn down *Reichstag*"; there is nothing new under the sun, the minister added.[279] *Harian Rakjat*, the the Communist Party daily, took the lead, and the next day it published a cartoon with the caption: "Sjahrir As Hitler."[280]

At the same time, when every mistake counted, Sjahrir was reported, again, to have sent a letter to the British prime minister Macmillan, who was on a state visit to India. The contents of the letter, as reported, were similar to Sjahrir's *Statesman* interview. The letter was never published in full; it was never disavowed; nor was it defended by Sjahrir. There is no reaction on record either by Macmillan or by Nehru. No new opening, evidently, was accomplished towards possible allies abroad. Rather, it made Sjahrir look even more "cosmopolitan" and conspiratorial, and thus an even better target.[281]

Only a few days later, and as the crisis in Indonesia climaxed, on February 4, Subadio Sastrosatomo, in the name of the PSI, and in a speech published on the front page of *Pedoman*, declared:

> The PSI admires the struggle in the regions. To create a "new central government of the Indonesian Republic" would be a catastrophe. [But], because we are confronted with the breakdown of the nation, the PSI wants [the present government] to step down.[282]

In the same issue, the paper (seen, we may remember, as strongly pro-PSI) announced: "Sjahrir Invited to Speak at Mass Rally in Padang." As if to make it clear what kind of a rally this would be, the paper added that "certainly" Natsir and

---

[276] *Sikap* 10, 1 (January 4, 1958).

[277] *Statesman*, January 2, 1958; *Pedoman*, January 2, 1958.

[278] *Pedoman*, January 3, 1958.

[279] Ibid.

[280] *Harian Rakjat*, January 3, 1958.

[281] *Pedoman*, January 17, 1958. For Macmillan's visit to India see ibid., January 15, 1958.

[282] Ibid., February 5, 1958.

Sjafroeddin Prawiranegara, among others, would be present. Erratic indeed: on the very same page, another news item was printed:

> The Secretary of the PSI . . . does not know about the invitation . . . it appears that neither a letter nor an oral invitation have yet arrived.[283]

The Padang rally took place and prominent rebel leaders gave the key speeches. Sjahrir remained in Jakarta.[284]

On February 12, on the tenth anniversary of the split in the Socialist Party, and also two days after the Sumatra ultimatum to the central government had been issued, and three days before the rebel government was proclaimed, Sjahrir, still in Jakarta, gave a big and well publicized speech:

> Today, on February 12, 1958, we have to admit that in all the efforts—conceived and defended with so many sacrifices—to use the Indonesian Republic as a means to change the fate of our people, its poverty and suffering, no result and no progress is visible.[285]

Sjahrir talked about the "privation of the people," which "is greatest on the island of Java." He warned against a "new Madiun" and against imperialism, which might use the crisis as it had after the "first Madiun." Sjahrir drew a telling parallel between the current PRRI and the "Madiun uprising after which the Dutch military action followed" in 1948.[286]

Sjahrir was mainly worried, so he said in the same speech, about the destruction of "the feeling of solidarity and humanity," and the fact that "distrust and animosity prevail." His main theme was a feeling of encirclement and disorder—an encirclement by disorder:

> The danger of dissension turns up everywhere. Dissensions in the state, and also dissension in the society threaten on all sides; we are surrounded by them.[287]

A few hours before the separate government on Sumatra was proclaimed and civil war started, the PSI secretariat issued a statement describing the rebels' ultimatum to the central government as "harmful to the search for a solution to overcome the present situation." "On the other side," the PSI statement added, the central government in Jakarta went too far—"cutting communications with Central Sumatra for instance, and thus aggravating the tensions still further."[288]

Everyone, the PSI secretariat stated, had to restrain their *nafsu*, "uncontrolled passion and lust."

---

[283] Ibid.
[284] Ibid., February 10, 1958.
[285] Sjahrir in ibid., February 12, 1958.
[286] Ibid.
[287] Ibid.
[288] Statement was reprinted in *Suara Sosialis* 11,2 (February/March 1958), p. 5.

The only way to avoid a breakup of the nation and to preserve the integrity of the state is a return of Sukarno-Hatta to the leadership of the state.[289]

Beneath the text, without a comment, a three-year old, well-known photo of Sjahrir and Sukarno was republished. Both men were sitting at the opening of the PSI second congress in Bandung: Sukarno still smiling broadly in the center; Sjahrir again flagrantly out of focus, at Sukarno's side.[290]

From that moment—the time when the PRRI was declared, the opening of the civil war, and in fact for more than three months afterwards—virtually nothing was heard from Sjahrir. Little of substance, also, came from the PSI. As the civil war broke out, in the words of Daniel Lev's study of the period,

> The PSI leadership dissociated itself from the PRRI as contrasted with the Masjumi, but did not take measures against Soemitro Djojohadikoesoemo as was demanded.[291]

It was not until mid or late May 1958—with the PRRI to all effects already defeated—that Sjahrir spoke out again. He wrote a long position paper exclusively for his PSI colleagues—something he had already done once, after his group and Amir Sjarifoeddin split, in March 1948.

In the paper, Sjahrir seemed most concerned with the notion of violence. An assassination attempt against Sukarno, he wrote, which had taken place late in 1957, opened up a sequence of events leading to the uprisings. "Throwing a grenade at Sukarno," according to Sjahrir, "enabled Sukarno to invalidate what had been achieved up till then."[292] Throughout the paper, Sjahrir used extensively such words as "sickness" or being "tired of." "Sickness caused by the PRRI uprisings," Sjahrir wrote, could never be "healed," say, by "the military being victorious over the PRRI." Sjahrir wrote how tired he was of "uprisings coming and going, in this country, one after another, and without an end." No real leadership, "different and better," "can ever be born" out of these uprisings. They "burn uselessly."[293]

Violence equaled *nafsu*. The regionalist movements turning violent were a sign to Sjahrir that

> the youth of our country certainly too easily contract [*dihinggapi*] sentiments and emotions of regionalism, their souls are too vulnerable to the inflammation by the sentiments of regionalism, one's own ethnic group, the forces endangering Indonesian unity and public life.[294]

Four months later, in September 1958, talking to an American diplomat, Sjahrir referred to regionalism and to the PRRI-Permesta as to "tribal affair":

---

[289] Ibid.

[290] Ibid.

[291] Daniel S. Lev, *Transition to Guided Democracy: Indonesian Politics, 1957-1959* (Ithaca: Cornell Modern Indonesia Project, 1966), p. 135.

[292] Sjahrir, "Peninjauan dan Pernilaian," 1958, later published in Sjahrir, *Sosialisme, Indonesia, Pembangunan*, p. 147.

[293] Ibid., pp. 150ff.

[294] Ibid., pp. 151–52.

> He said [that] generally all political parties in rebel areas with [the] exception of the Indonesian Communist Party, supported [the] rebel government. In other words, he explains, they placed their loyalty to their "tribal groups" above their duty to their party.... He said much to his surprise, PSI leaders in Central Sumatra had obeyed his orders and not joined [the] rebels.[295]

There still were echoes in Sjahrir, of his old notion of the dynamic margin and the static center. In the paper of May 1958, Sjahrir still talked about "sources for increasing welfare and development through modern means on islands outside Java," while "on the island of Java sources of a new life have yet to be found."[296] He found some justification for the illegal trade and by-passing Jakarta as it had developed between the "outer islands" and abroad, because the central government "neglected" the needs of those areas.[297] But the dynamics of the margin had changed its character. It now appeared, in Sjahrir's writings, as "an anarchistic drift in most parts of Indonesia." Rather than dynamizing the center, the margin appeared to work, in Sjahrir's current vision, as "a drive at loosening from the corruption and dilapidation of the center."[298]

Sjahrir's writing reflected a mood of an outflowing of power. "Parliamentary democracy," Sjahrir wrote,

> is bankrupt, it is depraved by groups of *nouveaux riches*, who have led national and religious parties during the past eight years.[299]

And a few pages further on:

> The image of politics in our country may be simplified into that of the collapsing of the political system, as it has existed from after 1950, and of political parties, which had neglected the interests of the nation, of breaking national unity into pieces, of inflaming nationalist emotions, a flame fed mainly by an antagonism against the ethnic group on Java and against the center, the government on Java.[300]

Sjahrir's theme was that of a tide receding. Every segment of Indonesian politics seemed to be affected. The Indonesian military, increasingly seen by experts and most of his contemporaries as the power of the future, were to Sjahrir a part of the spreading weakness. The high point of the army's postwar history, Sjahrir believed, came in 1954. At that moment the army, as he put it, stood nearest to "overcoming sentiments"; at that moment "the largest body of "the officers [with distinction] from the time of the struggle for sovereignty" came together, and almost succeeded in

---

[295] Ambassador Jones to State Department, telegram no. 900, September 9, 1958.

[296] Sjahrir, "Peninjauan dan Pernilaian," in *Sosialisme, Indonesia, Pembangunan*, p. 136.

[297] Ibid., pp. 139, 148–49.

[298] On talks with Sjahrir see Ambassador Jones to State Department, telegram no. 1170, October 3, 1958.

[299] Sjahrir, "Peninjauan dan Pernilaian," in *Sosialisme, Indonesia, Pembangunan*, p. 145.

[300] Ibid., p. 154.

formulating a new and modern philosophy of their own. After this, came a decline.[301]

Once or twice, in what Sjahrir was now writing about the military, some hope was expressed—in "educated youth and officers not yet corrupted and with souls not yet depraved."[302] The very way, however, in which Sjahrir presented the hope, positioned these "not yet corrupted," and "not yet depraved" officers as an atypical segment; the "not yet" temporality subdued the hope further.

After the PRRI-Permesta, the Indonesian military became for Sjahrir increasingly a part of the "anarchistic drift" in contemporary Indonesia. As they moved into non-military spheres, they were, he wrote, "inexperienced at administration, and ignorant at economics." They were becoming, in the process, increasingly corrupt, and, because of the corruption it was increasingly difficult to control them, especially at the local level.[303] As the military were taking over, Sjahrir appeared to believe, "army officers are deriving more ill-gotten gains than their civilian predecesors."[304]

At the time when the military, and the army in particular, were becoming the major political and economic force of the new Indonesia, Sjahrir demanded that his party "concentrate fully on cutting the role of the armed forces," down to a "symbolic level." He wanted to limit the military's role in internal affairs to a strictly limited "policing role." In the field of external defense, Sjahrir proposed "creation of a militia open to each citizen."[305]

"The fundamental tasks of the state," he wrote in 1958,

> the development of welfare and happiness, could certainly not be attained through establishing a military junta. . . . From what we can see now, we may say for sure that the military are not capable of solving fundamental problems of this country and this nation.[306]

"The military tend towards militarism and fascism," Sjahrir wrote at the same time; "the military of Nasution, in fact, harbor a militaristic and fascist ideal."[307]

---

[301] Ibid., p. 158. Indeed, according to Ulf Sundhaussen, a historian of the army, after the PRRI-Permesta rebellion, a distance grew between the PSI and the army officers classified as "pro-PSI": "Those officers, whose ties to the PSI had always been overestimated, came to disagree strongly with the PSI leadership over how to evaluate the political situation." Sundhaussen, *The Road to Power*, pp. 100–101. The core of the disagreement, thus Sundhaussen, was that the officers concentrated on the strengthening of the role of the army, while the PSI leadership did not. Ibid. After the PRRI and Permesta rebellion, some of the "pro-PSI officers" were relieved of their command. They remained, however, very—perhaps equally—influential in the military establishment, through their new positions, especially in army training institutions, the "think-tanks" of the army. Ibid.

[302] Sjahrir, "Peninjauan dan Pernilaian," in *Sosialisme, Indonesia, Pembangunan*, pp. 145, 154–55.

[303] Ambassador Jones to the State Department, telegram no. 1170, October 3, 1958.

[304] Ibid., telegram no. 900, September 9, 1958. To this the American noted, in his report to the State Department on the meeting, that Sjahrir's view of army corruption was, according to Jones' view, too gloomy, and that, in view of other sources at the diplomat's disposal, the situation was not so bad.

[305] Sjahrir, "Peninjauan dan Pernilaian," in *Sosialisme, Indonesia, Pembangunan*, p. 166.

[306] Ibid., pp. 194, 192.

[307] Ibid., p. 143.

The US ambassador to Indonesia, Howard P. Jones, met with Sjahrir early in October 1958, and was very surprised by the way in which Sjahrir talked about the Indonesian Communist Party. The Communist Party, Jones wrote, "he believes presently weaker," "definitely losing ground ... throughout Indonesia." The Indonesian Communists, Sjahrir also told the American diplomat, were "afraid" to exploit the situation, they were driven by "fear," their leaders were "seeking [to] avoid [an] open clash."[308]

At the time when to so many respected observers at home and abroad Indonesia was a country, where—after the failure of the anti-Communist rebellion—the Communists were well and dangerously on the march, Sjahrir's words sounded strange. The Communists have no "material power," he told George Kahin in an interview, early in 1961. The Soviets, according to Sjahrir, were interested in the Indonesian military, rather than in the Indonesian Communist Party. Whenever the Indonesian army acted against the Communist Party, Sjahrir argued, the Communist Party's reaction "has been mild, not militant," and, again, driven by "fear" and "hesitancy."[309]

There were echoes, again, of Sjahrir as we recall him from the 1930s. The Communists, now as during the colonial period, were "a false group and imposters," and all their strength was derived from an outside power.[310] The Indonesian Communists were not "real revolutionaries." Now, however, in contrast to the 1930s, it was not altogether clear if Sjahrir really knew who the "real revolutionaries" were. One can not help hearing Sukarno, as one reads this: as if indeed, even in Sjahrir's arguing, now, all the colors were "bleachable."

To Sjahrir after 1958, Indonesia appeared as a "Sukarno-led" country, a country with "Sukarno's ideology," a "Sukarno-type" country.[311] "Without Sukarno," Sjahrir said in 1959,

> the Javanese would be without effective leadership (unless some central figure such as perhaps the Sultan would emerge around whom they could rally). Without such a central charismatic leader many [people in] the Indonesian National Party and possibly much of Nahdatul Ulama would look to the Indonesian Communist Party for leadership.[312]

Sjahrir, now, appeared hardly able to perceive Indonesia but through Java and Sukarno; virtually all the basic Indonesian qualities were measured by Java and Sukarno:

> In the present situation it is difficult to describe the nationalist and religious parties on Java as a balance against the totalitarian power which is assem-

---

[308] Ambassador Jones to the State Department, telegram no. 1170, October 3, 1958.

[309] Sjahrir's interview with George Kahin, Jakarta, January 1961.

[310] Sjahrir, "Peninjauan dan Pernilaian," in *Sosialisme, Indonesia, Pembangunan*, pp. 143–44, 184–86.

[311] Sjahrir's interview with George Kahin, Jakarta, January 1961.

[312] Sjahrir's interview with George Kahin, Jakarta, February/March 1959.

bled under the leadership of Sukarno. Because of this, it is difficult to think of a possibility of political change on Java through a parliamentary way.[313]

The major political parties of the system, such as the Indonesian National Party or the Nahdadul Ulama were, to Sjahrir, Sukarno's "children."[314] As always Sjahrir remained critical of Sukarno. Now, however, more than ever before, he appeared to believe that Sukarno truly functioned as "a *dalang*, a master in the shadow puppet theater, in the middle of his performance."[315] He even used Sukarno's vocabulary for it.

Sjahrir still saw Sukarno as the static and passive center. "Sukarno is getting nowhere with guided democracy."[316] Sukarno, Sjahrir still believed, was unable to establish "an effective non-Communist radical left."[317] "Sukarno's major political concern," Sjahrir wrote, "is defensive."[318] Exactly because of this, however, the country belonged and would for a foreseeable future belong to Sukarno. Indonesia heading nowhere was an extension of Sukarno heading nowhere. Different colors were bleachable indeed, into the one color of Sukarno.

It was not exactly that, in Sjahrir's vision, the future became gloomy. Rather, his vision of progress became another few shades more opaque—or bleached perhaps. Sjahrir wrote in 1958:

> Only if our society returns to its belief that our state and nation truly aim at welfare and justice, only then will the soul of the people and of the nation again be tranquil and the spirit of obedience to the leaders of the state be restored.[319]

The words like *tentram*, "tranquil," and *kepatuhan*, "obedience," had occasionally appeared before in Sjahrir's writing and speaking, most often as the essence of negative qualities. Now, however, they seemed to be wholly positive and crucial.

---

[313] Sjahrir, "Peninjauan dan Pernilaian," in *Sosialisme, Indonesia, Pembangunan*, pp. 144–45.
[314] Ibid.
[315] Ibid.
[316] Ambassador Jones to the State Department, telegram no. 1170, October 3, 1958.
[317] Sjahrir's interview with George Kahin, Jakarta, January 1961.
[318] Ibid.
[319] Sjahrir, "Peninjauan dan Pernilaian," in *Sosialisme, Indonesia, Pembangunan*, p. 150.

10

THE DEATH

> An old teakwood easy chair was ceremoniously brought into the house by the youth of the "1966 Generation," the easy chair Sjahrir used to sit in, in prison, during afternoons, to read and to listen to the radio.
>
> Leon Salim on Sjahrir's funeral in 1966[1]

1. PRISON

Els Postel-Coster has written on prewar Minangkabau novels:

> In a few cases, there is a happy ending, but usually before the end of the book the young people, and a good many others too, have died from sorrow, fighting or illness.[2]

There was very little feeling of death in Sjahrir's texts before the 1940s, and virtually nothing afterwards. Sjahrir's thinking was "positive." Poppy Sjahrir told me that her husband did not talk of dying until his very last months.[3]

Death, as the 1950s moved into the 1960s, was making its appearance in an opposite corner. "Secret information" leaked, late in October 1961—and it was reprocessed and reproduced by the Jakarta rumor mill—on the grave state of the president's health: Sukarno had "a non-functioning left kidney," which "might be dead and might turn cancerous or cause uremia." The doctors urged an operation "within three months." But Sukarno instead, it was said, consulted his *dukun*, "medicine man":

> He believes that if his body is cut, and a part of it removed, his authority and his inner strength [*kewibawaan dan kesaktian*] would disappear.[4]

Sukarno still proclaimed "guided democracy" and his *konsepsi* to be the "rediscovery of the revolution." At the same time, in Ruslan Abdulgani's words, he

---

[1] Leon Salim, ed., *Bung Sjahrir*, p. 50.
[2] Els Postel Coster, "The Indonesian Novel" in *Text and Context*, ed. Jain, p. 137.
[3] Interview with Siti Wahjunah Sjahrir, Jakarta, November 15, 1987.
[4] Rosihan Anwar, *Sebelum Prahara: Pergelakan Politik Indonesia, 1961–1965* (Jakarta: Sinar Harapan, 1981), pp. 114–15.

still believed in himself, now, at the head of the system "as a rediscovery of the young Sukarno of the 1926–1933 period."[5]

The vocabulary grew "youthfully" explicit, indeed. Sukarno, now, used a term *cucungkuk*, "cockroach" to label his opponents: a Sundanese term used for police informers when Sukarno and Sjahrir were young. Sukarno warned against "the Dutchified groups, reformist groups, conservative groups, chameleon, and cockroach groups."[6] Everyone knew that these words often, and perhaps most often, referred to the PSI and Sjahrir.

Both were, after the PRRI and its failure, very easy targets. Des Alwi, deeply, directly, and flagrantly involved in the rebellions, and still "at large," was easy to report on as Sjahrir's son who was jazzing it up in a highlife style in Kuala Lumpur, Singapore, or Manila. Soemitro, still in exile as well—however greatly distrusted he might be even among many of his former PSI friends, however loose his contacts might be with his former party and with Sjahrir—remained also readily available whenever Sjahrir was to be compromised with the "rebel connection."

After more than a decade, stories were now suddenly being "discovered" about Sjahrir's "true activity" during the great period of revolution; sensational articles were published, with "jolly" photographs from Singapore in the 1940s, for instance, with Sjahrir shown "plotting with a 'three-star gang of pretty women [*berkomplot dengan Gerombolan Bintang Tiga-wanita aju*].'"[7]

Sjahrir's friends, who still remembered Pendidikan or Boven Digul of the 1930s, old friends like Moerad, Hamdani, or Moerwoto, were aging fast. In most cases they

> did not make it in their material lives, their financial situation was often precarious, not rarely they lived outside the fashionable quarters of Jakarta and were practically unknown beyond their immediate neighborhoods.

Moerad, for instance, told me how, in those days of the late 1950s and the early 1960s, he often looked in the mirror, and asked himself "What have we done? What remains?"[8]

Even some close friends and colleagues of Sjahrir from a more recent period appeared to have been increasingly left behind. Charles Tambu, for instance, who had published the *Times of Indonesia* during the 1950s, found his paper banned after the PRRI/Permesta, and himself writing letters to his more fortunate friends asking for support: "There is not a cent in the house." Naturally, these people often saw their personal situation as a commentary on the general state of Indonesian affairs. In Charles Tambu's words,

> the situation and the climate in our country will not improve in the foreseeable future. The authoritative regime will go on for at least another generation. "We are a lost generation."[9]

---

[5] Abdulgani, *Nationalism, Revolution and Guided Democracy*, p. 52.

[6] Ibid., p. 4.

[7] *Belodo* 1, 44 (March 8, 1959); *Sikap* 12, 7 and 9 (March 21, 1959), p. 5; and (April 14), 1959, p. 4.

[8] Interview with Moerad, Jakarta, January 5, 1988.

[9] Quoted in Anwar, *Sebelum Prahara*, pp. 13–14.

Even Sjahrir's better-off friends, men and women usually able to find their way through changing times, were now touched and restrained in much that they did. Whatever their position or wealth might be, they became, and had to behave like, leaders of a banned party. Mochtar Lubis wrote later:

> I was put under house arrest not long after the resistance of the PRRI against the Sukarno regime had been broken; but still I could often see Sjahrir, because he came to play tennis several times a week at a court which was next to my house. When he passed by, while I was working in the garden amidst my orchids, Sjahrir always nodded and looked at me with his broad smile. But we could talk no more.[10]

Leon Salim recalled the late 1950s and the early 1960s as a time when Sjahrir was "still free." Sjahrir, Salim wrote, might regularly be seen on a Jakarta street "in his B 61 car from the Republican era"; by "Republican era," in a strange twist of postcolonial Indonesian language, Salim referred to the Revolution of the 1940s. Sometimes, Salim wrote, Sjahrir pleasure-cruised in the car around the town with his little son.[11] Sjahrir now, indeed, had a family of his own. No more a marriage by proxy, lovemaking by correspondence, and adopted children. His son, Bujung, and his daughter, Upik, were born in the late 1950s; and everybody knew, Poppy was a most devoted wife, and Sjahrir a most happy father.

Sjahrir traveled very rarely after 1958 and during the early 1960s. Almost never, in fact; and very occasionally did he even go outside Java. One of these very rare trips, his trip to Bali, proved to be fateful.

The former *raja*, "king," of Gianyar was to be cremated according to Balinese custom, on August 18, 1961, in a huge ceremony. Anak Agung, the *raja*'s son—also an important political figure in postcolonial Indonesia, and a man through the 1950s associated with the PSI— invited a number of his friends. Sjahrir, Hatta, Roem, Sultan Hamid of Pontianak,

---

[10] M. Lubis, "Pejuang, pemikir dan peminat," in *Mengenang Sjahrir*, ed. Anwar, p. 212.
[11] Salim, ed., *Bung Sjahrir*, p. 44.

and Subadio attended, together, of course, with tens of thousands of other guests and spectators.

Nobody, except those immediately involved, will probably ever know what, if anything, happened in Gianyar besides the cremation and social talk. In a matter of days, however, Soebandrio—as we recall a former associate of Sjahrir and at one time his personal assistant and now increasingly important in Sukarno's system and chief of the Badan Pusat Intelidjen, "Central Intelligence Organization"—received a confidential report that a conspiracy had taken place in Bali and that subversive actions against the state were being discussed. Sukarno got the report instantly and ordered an investigation.[12]

Anak Agung, still more than two decades after this happened, and when the heat was clearly out, categorically denied to me that there was any conspiracy. He made a *faux pas*, he said, when he initially invited only his friends and allies, and not Sukarno. He realized this after a while, and sent an additional invitation to the president. But Sukarno, so Anak Agung believed, was already offended, and declined to come. Then, according to Anak Agung, Sukarno became suspicious.[13]

Hamid Algadri, also attended the Balinese *raja*'s funeral. Mrs. Sjahrir could not go, and he took her place at the last moment. He shared a room with Sjahrir, and as he said, he was with Sjahrir most of the time. Also he, in an interview in 1987, emphatically denied any intimation of conspiracy. Not even much of a political discussion took place, he said; not much happened other than the ordinary harmless chatting and complaining. "Why of all places in Bali," Hamid Algadri argued, "why on an occasion as exposed as that, when all of the 'conspirators' lived all the time close to each other, and saw each other, in Jakarta, anyway?"[14]

No charges were brought against Anak Agung and the others during the four months following the Balinese funeral. Instead, there arose another tide of rumors: about Sukarno's health very significantly; and, at the same time, about Indonesian military intelligence agents uncovering a secret document on an illegal organization, of which nothing else seemed to be known except its bizarre name, more bizarre even, a Dutch name: *Nederlandse Indische Guerrilla Organisatie*, the "Guerrilla Organization for the Netherlands Indies."[15]

Sukarno spoke with increasing vehemence about the unfinished revolution. On December 16, 1961, he ordered a mass mobilization to liberate Irian Barat (Dutch West New Guinea), the last part of the former Indies still denied to the Republic.

---

[12] Anwar, *Sebelum Prahara*, p. 90 (August 25, 1961). There is a mention of Sukarno and Soebandrio discussing the funeral, in Nasution's memoirs. Sukarno, Nasution says, forbade all the cabinet ministers who got an invitation to the funeral, from accepting. A. H. Nasution. *Memenuhi Panggilan Tugas 5: Kenangan Masa Orde Lama* (Jakarta: Gunung Agung, 1985), p. 395.

[13] Interview with Anak Agung, Wassenaar October 15, 1986.

[14] Interview with Hamid Algadri, Jakarta, December 13, 1987. Another participant, M. Roem, mentions the funeral very briefly in Mohamad Roem,"Bung Kecil yang berbuat besar" in *Mengenang Sjahrir*, ed. Anwar, p. 144.

[15] Anwar, *Sebelum Prahara*, pp. 126–27, 168; Rosihan Anwar, ed, *Perdjalanan terachir Pahlawan Nasional Sutan Sjahrir* (Jakarta: Pembangunan, 1966), pp. 45–46. Nasution writes that Chief of the Army General Staff Yani obtained the information on the NIGO. Nasution suggests as a possible source of the information, via the president, Ahmad Soebardjo, who, according to Nasution, provided "a 'secret document' containing names of the NIGO members." Nasution, *Memenuhi Panggilan Tugas*, 5: 390, 395.

On January 7, 1962, while Sukarno was on a speaking tour in Makassar, Sulawesi, for "the upcoming" final stage of the Irian Barat campaign, a hand grenade was thrown at the president's cavalcade. The grenade fell 150 meters behind the last car, killing three people, one child and two adults; twenty-eight onlookers were injured, none of the casualties belonging to Sukarno's entourage.

A week later, on January 15, two Dutch nationals were arrested. It was rumored that something pointed towards the "Bali connection." Sukarno ordered further investigation. This time, in addition to Soebandrio's agency, military intelligence and the military police were involved. Another organization began to be rumored about, with a name even more bizarre—Verenigde Ondergrondse Corps, "United Underground Corps"; the "corps" initials, VOC, suggestive, of course, of Verenigde Oostindische Compagnie, "United East Indies Company."[16] Was this the climax of our story? It was as if *komedie stambul*, so much fun in Sumatra in the 1920s, was now being replayed, but dead seriously.

Many, especially among Sjahrir's friends, later presented Soebandrio as the principal villain behind what then happened to Sjahrir. Sal Tas, who watched this from Holland, suggested that Soebandrio took personal revenge for the humiliations he had suffered from Sjahrir when on his staff in London in the late 1940s.[17] Soebandrio himself, when asked by Sjahrir's friends while all this was still in the making, argued that Nasution had been a more active player in the matter than he was.[18] Virtually everybody, of course, felt that Sukarno was looming in the background.

The warrant for Sjahrir being put in prison, it appeared later, was issued by the Peperti, the Supreme War Command, of which Sukarno was the head. The document was apparently signed by Soebandrio, as minister of foreign affairs, and Nasution, as minister of defense.[19] Nasution was heard a few days after the warrant was issued, saying that he was "*fait accompli*-ed" in the affair.[20] Nasution also told Soedjatmoko—and later repeated in his memoirs—that

> actually Sukarno was behind giving him, Nasution, a warrant, with names not filled in the document, and he asked Nasution to sign the paper as it was.[21]

On January 16, 1962, at four o'clock in the morning, Sjahrir was arrested in his house at *Tjokroaminoto* 61. At the same hour, also Anak Agung, Subadio, and Sultan Hamid

---

[16] Ibid., pp. 390–91; Anwar, *Sebelum Prahara*, pp. 139, 158; Rosihan Anwar says a "friend" has it from Prime Minister Djuanda (p. 155). See also Anwar, ed., *Perdjalanan terachir*, p. 46.

[17] Tas, "Souvenirs of Sjahrir," p. 151; for more on this subject, see above, chapter 8.

[18] Anwar, *Sebelum Prahara*, p. 158.

[19] Interview with Subadio, 1982, quoted in Rose, *Indonesia Free*, pp. 199–200. See also Mohammad Hatta and Anak Agung, *Surat-menjurat Hatta dan Anak Agung* (Jakarta: Sinar Harapan, 1987), p. 13.

[20] Rosihan Anwar says an "officer"; Anwar, *Sebelum Prahara*, p. 158.

[21] Interview with Subadio, Jakarta, October 18, 1987. This is confirmed by Nasution's own published record. Nasution writes about "*surat penahan blanko untuk saya teken*, a blank warrant for me to sign." "What names would be filled in," Nasution writes further, "was to depend on the result of the investigation. Thus, on January 16, arrests began of what soon became clear were Sutan Sjahrir and the others." Nasution, *Memenuhi Panggilan Tugas*, 5: 391.

were arrested, as were several leaders of the banned Masjumi—Prawoto Mangkusasmit, Yunan Nasution, Kijaji Isa Anshary, and Mohamad Roem.[22]

"This means living by the law of revolution," Sukarno said, in explaining two years later what he had done,

> smash your enemies. Kill or be killed. Jail or be jailed.
> I can understand when malcontents try to kill me. I also, therefore, understand I must retaliate and try to get them. A while back Sjahrir hatched a plot to overthrow me and grasp the government. Sjahrir is now in prison. I bear no malice. I am aware this is a two-sided terrible game in which I'm involved. The game of survival.[23]

At the end of January, after two weeks of interrogation, it was rumored, indeed, that some compromising documents had been found—against the Masjumi and in the house of Prawoto. But there was nothing, either in that rumor or elsewhere, against Sjahrir or the former PSI. Soebandrio's intelligence, so the gossip went in Jakarta, felt "embarrassed [*merasa malu*]," and would keep the prisoners locked up, if only in order not to lose face. Sukarno "reportedly" "washed his hands of Sjahrir's case"; according to another "report," Sukarno promised to look into the case (*Ik zal zien wat ik eraan kan doen*, "I'll see what I can do"). Everybody in Jakarta seemed to know that it "may still take a long time before Sjahrir is released." Another "piece of information" was leaked, and it floated around: Sjahrir and the others were, in fact, "not interned but only isolated."[24]

There is, on record, that Soebandrio was once asked publicly about the fate of Sjahrir and of the others in prison, and that he answered: "They have no place in our society."[25] However, neither Soebandrio nor anybody else responsible and powerful at the time, seemed to be asked very often about Sjahrir's fate and the fate of the other prisoners.

There was, indeed, depressingly muted reaction abroad. As became almost a tradition in postcolonial Indonesian history, *Radio Nederland* in Hilversum was later believed to have broadcast the news about the arrests before they actually happened. Even in the Netherlands itself, however, after all these years, Sjahrir seemed to be not much more than a name from a distant past remembered with some difficulty. Dr. W. Drees, who had been prime minister in 1948, and who had negotiated with Sjahrir at the time, recalled:

> The other day we read that two leaders of the Indonesian federation, Anak Agung and Sultan Hamid, who evidently a long time ago had already been pushed off, were put in a Jakarta prison, and with them Mohamad Roem, who was an important figure in the Republican delegation, and Sjahrir, who earnestly tried to reach an agreement with the Netherlands.[26]

---

[22] Salim, ed., *Bung Sjahrir*, pp. 42, 73, where the list appears.//
[23] Sukarno, *An Autobiography*, p. 271.//
[24] Anwar, *Sebelum Prahara*, pp. 169, 192, 194 (March 25, 1962).//
[25] Brackman, *Indonesian Communism*, p. 306.//
[26] Drees, *Zestig jaar levenservaring*, p. 250.

An American diplomat in Jakarta privately told Rosihan Anwar, five days after Sjahrir was arrested that the United States "thought the issue of West Irian more important than the internal implications of the Sjahrir affair."[27] At the same time, also, an "Asian diplomat" talked with Rosihan Anwar about Sjahrir:

> The diplomat said that at the beginning of the revolution the name known abroad was that of Sjahrir rather than a name of any other Indonesian leader. The Asian leaders then identified Indonesia with Sjahrir.... Together with Nehru, Sjahrir was the famous man of Asia.... "I do not understand it," the Asian diplomat said, "What has happened to Sjahrir? Could the problems between him and Sukarno possibly make him vanish like this? As if he just was letting himself withdraw towards the edge or evaporate in the air. Why did he let himself wither away? And now, he is arrested. Why? I don't understand."[28]

In Indonesia, only a few people, mostly the exclusive Jakarta political circles and intimate friends, knew, however vaguely, what was going on. As Rosihan Anwar wrote in his diary, "the public did not really notice."[29]

Hamid Algadri recalled that within a day or two after the arrests, Mohammad Hatta—who had been at Gianyar, but was not put in prison—began to draft a personal letter to Sukarno.[30] According to Hatta himself, the letter complained about the imprisonment having been carried out in a "colonial style," and being "non-rational [*tidak masuk akal*]."[31] On or about January 22, Hatta sent the letter, and it was, it seems, the most that could be done. In the words of Rosihan Anwar's diary,

> Hatta right-away entered hospital for a medical check-up; it can be said, perhaps, that Hatta is suffering a diplomatic illness.[32]

On March 6, more than two months later, Rosihan Anwar's diary mentioned Hatta's letter again. The letter, we read in the diary, had "no effect whatsoever."[33] After another month, in April, Hatta himself was quoted as saying that, as far as Sjahrir was concerned, "something must be done, but now we are absorbed by the West Irian problem."[34]

There was reportedly some reaction to the arrests among a few army officers. But the only result of this movement of solidarity with the prisoners seemed to be a rather pathetic and half-hearted act of destroying the weakest pawn in the game: a

---

[27] Anwar, *Sebelum Prahara*, p. 165.

[28] Ibid., p. 206.

[29] Ibid., p. 189 (March 19, 1962).

[30] Interview with Hamid Algadri, Jakarta, December 13, 1987. There were rumors at the same time that Hatta had also been arrested. See, e.g., Mochtar Lubis, *Cacatan Subversif* (March 2, 1965, January 28, 1962), p. 196.

[31] Ibid., Anwar, *Sebelum Prahara*, p. 159 (January 19, 1962); also Hatta's speech at Sjahrir's grave quoted in Anwar, ed., *Perdjalanan terachir*, p. 26.

[32] Anwar, *Sebelum Prahara*, p. 169 (January 22, 1962).

[33] Ibid., p. 183 (March 6, 1962).

[34] Ibid., p. 203 (April 12, 1962).

certain Manoppo was arrested on army initiative, as "the informer who helped to put Sjahrir in jail."[35]

According to Ulf Sundhaussen, rumors appeared throughout the early 1960s of

> PSI-underground, men who had been active in various attempts, such as the May 1963 riots in West Java, to discredit the Sukarno government, PSI politicians around Soedjatmoko and Subadio who had quietly tried to influence [general] Jani and his headquarters group, and intellectuals who had attempted to keep the leading universities in Jakarta and Bandung as free as possible from Sukarnoist and communist influence, [of] the PSI-leaning officers or veterans who, like Daan Jahja and Suwarto, had excellent relations with Jani and constantly had argued against the Indonesian Communist Party, *konfrontasi* [Sukarno's policy against West Irian and later Malaysia] and the President.[36]

Sukarno seemed to believe he knew perfectly well what was going on:

> The recent riots of May 10 in Bandung, which had an anti-Chinese character, were caused by a counter-revolutionary action by former members of the PSI, Masjumi, PRRI, and by subversion from abroad.[37]

After the Bandung unrest of May 1963, Hamdani, Sjahrir's very old friend from the 1920s and later, was arrested "in connection with the conspiracy," together with some Mahdi from the Bandung *Pharmacy Abadi*, about whom we otherwise know nothing.[38] There were no trials whatsoever.

On the morning of his arrest, January 16, 1962, Sjahrir and the other six detainees were taken to the dormitories of the Military Police at Hayam Wuruk Street in Central Jakarta. From there, Sjahrir, Roem, and Prawoto, were moved to the city quarter of Kebayoran Baru, South Jakarta, into a house on Daha Street. The rest of the prisoners—Yunan Nasution, Isa Anshari, Anak Agung, and Subadio—were kept at Hayam Wuruk Street a few days longer, and then they were taken to another location in Jakarta not far away, at Indramayu Street 14.[39]

For about three months, Sjahrir, Roem, and Prawoto lived in the house on *Daha* street. "For two months," Mohamad Roem recalled, "families were not permitted to visit and our location was kept secret."[40] (Except, a few days after they were moved there, Sjahrir was taken to his house at *Tjokroaminoto* 61 for a few hours, to witness the search of his personal papers; a military policeman was on guard, yet Sjahrir was able to whisper to his wife that they were "in Kebayoran."[41]) According to Roem again, "families could send food, clothing, books, and other things we needed." The

---

[35] Gatot Subroto was named as the officer involved in this. Ibid.

[36] Sundhaussen, *Road to Power*, p. 228.

[37] Quoted in Anwar, *Sebelum Prahara*, p. 367 (May 27, 1963).

[38] Interview with Hamdani, Jakarta, October 20, 1987.

[39] Roem, *Bunga Rampai Dari Sedjarah*, 1:163; *Kompas*, April 14, 1966 quoted in Anwar, ed., *Perdjalanan terachir*, p. 21; Anwar, *Sebelum Prahara*, pp. 153–54, 170, 189; interview with Subadio, Jakarta, March 14, 1982. Hatta and Agung, *Surat-menjurat*, p. 13.

[40] Mohamad Roem, "Memoirs," n.d., p. 21; typescript in the *Archives Siti Wahjunah Sjahrir*.

[41] Anwar, *Sebelum Prahara*, pp. 168–69.

first family visits to the prisoners were permitted in March. Each visit could last half an hour, and for it the prisoners were moved to the headquarters of the Supreme Military Administrator in Central Jakarta.[42]

Each of the three prisoners at the *Daha* street had a room to himself. The house used to be the private residence of the director of the Goodyear Company branch in Indonesia. "We were lucky," Roem wrote in his memoirs,

> to be detained in a house which had a swimming pool. Prawoto and I swam and bathed each morning and each afternoon. Sjahrir did not swim, but he often sat at the edge of the pool and chatted with Prawoto and me, while we were swimming.[43]

Rosihan Anwar, who kept in contact with both Soedjatmoko, Sjahrir's brother-in-law, and Poppy, Sjahrir's wife, wrote on *Daha* street in his diary:

> As far as Sjahrir is concerned, so I have heard, he suffers from his detention much more than while he was exiled by the colonial Dutch government to Boven Digoel. In Digoel, he experienced many difficulties, such as bad food, for instance, while now, at Daha Street he is being taken care of as well as possible. But what he feels now is a spiritual torment, because in Digoel, he was still a bachelor, while now he has a wife and children, and thoughts of separation from the family disturbs him greatly.[44]

One day, Mohamad Roem wrote, he wandered into Sjahrir's room without knocking on the door. He was taken aback momentarily by the sight of what was supposed to be Sjahrir's working corner:

> Photographs, as if on an exhibit, all over the desk, surrounding the open book Sjahrir was reading. A photo of Mrs. Sjahrir, of five-year old Bujung, of three-year old Upik, of them together and them in various combinations.[45]

Another day, Roem also by chance wandered again without a warning into Sjahrir's room. This time Roem saw "the exhibition enlarged": pictures of the Bandanese children had been added, "a photograph of Lily, of her husband, of her children, and a snapshot of Ali."[46]

Three months after their arrest, Sjahrir, Prawoto, and Roem, and also Subadio, Anak Agung, and Sultan Hamid from the other location, were moved across Java to Madiun, and placed in the local Wilis Street military prison.[47] "Not too bad," Anak Agung told me later,

> this used to be a women's prison, and it had been emptied to make room for just the six of us. There was a considerate jailer, reading was accessible; after

---

[42] Roem, "Memoirs," p. 23; see also Salim, ed., *Bung Sjahrir*, p. 43.
[43] Roem, "Memoirs," p. 23; see also Roem, *Bunga Rampai Dari Sedjarah*, 1: 165.
[44] Anwar, *Sebelum Prahara*, p. 189.
[45] Roem, "Memoirs," p. 22; see also Roem, *Bunga Rampai Dari Sedjarah*, 1: 163, 169.
[46] Ibid.
[47] *Kompas*, April 14, 1966 quoted in Anwar, ed., *Perdjalanan terachir*, p. 21.

the first eight weeks of isolation, visits were permitted once a month. There was not much control: our womenfolk might easily smuggle a letter or two in their skirts or blouses.[48]

Sjahrir and Sultan Hamid each got a room to himself. These were quite large rooms; fifteen women prisoners had lived in each of them before. Anak Agung together with Subadio were assigned another large cell, and Roem stayed in yet another room with Prawoto.[49]

"During the first two months," Roem remembered, "there was still tight security."[50] After that, the prisoners could play tennis, and also a public swimming pool nearby was reserved for them a few hours a week. The men did some calisthenics together, and Sultan Hamid was put in charge of it: "Max, you are a former officer of the K.N.I.L. [Royal Netherlands Indies Army], would you lead us in the exercise each morning?" Roem remembered one of them suggesting. The Sultan agreed and, indeed, did the job

> enthusiastically, behaving increasingly like a military instructor, so that, at the end, we could not take it any more.[51]

They also played badminton in the hall between their cells and, "when friends in the outside learned about this, there was never a scarcity of balls, rackets and nets in our prison."[52] The prisoners, too, played bridge and scrabble in the evening, and in this Sjahrir did not take part. He played tennis, however; and he swam—as Roem remembered,

> in his own style, floating on the surface of the water with a minimal movement by his hands and legs, for an hour and more. This was, he said, as he had learned it while in exile, at Banda Neira, when he swam in the sea.[53]

Sjahrir had "two places of work" in his prison cell. From 8 to 11.30 A.M., he did "heavy reading" at a desk in his cell's corner at the window; during the rest of the day, when he stayed inside, he "debated and did light reading," mostly in an easy

---

[48] Interview with Anak Agung, Wassenaar October 15, 1986. See also Anak Agung's introduction to Hatta and Agung, *Surat-menjurat*, pp. 16–17.

[49] Roem, "Memoirs," p. 23; also Roem, *Bunga Rampai Dari Sedjarah*, 1:165.

[50] Roem, "Bung Kecil yang berbuat besar," p. 143. Mochtar Lubis, who became prisoner in Madiun shortly after Sjahrir left, described a clearly more relaxed situation: "The prison of Madiun was cleaner [than the Jakarta prison Lubis had just come from]. Small but neat [*Kecil, tapi rapi.*] Service differed greatly from the military prison in Jakarta: morning, fresh milk and bread; midday, *nasi mie, goreng ayam, sambal, gulai, sayur, pisang*; evening, the same. A friend told me that all the medications are guaranteed. The behavior of the guards was correct and friendly [*korek dan ramah*].... There were iron bars in the windows and on the doors. But there were curtains and the door was not always locked. The canteen was large. Several cells were empty. We have helpers [*pembantu-pembantu*] to sweep the floors of our rooms, to wash dishes and to do our laundry. They were OH [*orang hukuman*] prisoners borrowed from the large prison. Guards were from the military police." Lubis, *Catatan*, January 25, 1963, pp. 219–20.

[51] Roem, "Memoirs," pp. 143–44.

[52] Ibid., p. 145.

[53] Ibid.

chair, which stood in the middle of the room.[54] He "did his own sewing," a skill, which, according to Roem's impression, "did not grow out of necessity." Sjahrir liked to instruct the prison cook—how to use a minimal amount of oil, for instance—something, he said, he had also learned at Banda Neira, when he was a *chef* in his own house.[55]

Sjahrir, like the others, was permitted to write to his wife. He asked Poppy for books, which she brought to Madiun, mostly from his own library at the house at *Tjokroaminoto* 61. Sjahrir worked hard in prison, so at least was his wife's impression.[56] He wrote, what his co-prisoners believed at the time, to be "a sort of a diary." Occasionally, he read to the others from what he had written the day before—something, we recall, he had done in Boven Digul, too, reading to his friends letters to be sent to Maria.[57]

Soedjatmoko, as a relative, could visit Sjahrir more easily than others, and he reported, late in May 1962, that "Sjahrir and his friends could follow events on the outside by reading newspapers and listening to the radio."[58] Roem, too, recalled Sjahrir's listening to the radio:

> Three minutes before six, Sjahrir was already in my and Prawoto's room for a collective listening to the news from the whole world, beginning with the *Radio Republik Indonesia* broadcast.... Throughout the time we were together in prison, Sjahrir listened to the radio most regularly of all of us; never before, indeed, had I met a man who would follow the events and the progress in the world via radio in the way Sjahrir did.
>
> Like the *imam* in a mosque checks on the sun five times a day so that he would not miss any of his daily prayers, so Sjahrir looked at his watch many times a day so that he did not miss a single one of the many broadcasts in all the languages he knew.[59]

Once, at a dinner, when Sultan Hamid attempted to make a joke about Minangkabau men being weak "because they live in a matriarchy," Sjahrir left the table, and it took a few days of intensive diplomacy by the others, and the Sultan's public apology, before Sjahrir resumed taking his meals with the group.[60] This, however, seems to be the only open conflict reported by any of the men living together in the Madiun prison. On one occasion, when a friend visiting the prison seemed to get the impression that Sjahrir might be brooding, he was quickly and vehemently set aright by

---

[54] Roem, *Bunga Rampai Dari Sedjarah*, 1: 166; Anwar, *Sebelum Prahara*, p. 214.

[55] Roem, "Memoirs," p. 27.

[56] Interview with Siti Wahjunah Sjahrir, Jakarta, March 15, 1982.

[57] Interview with Anak Agung, Wassenaar, October 15, 1986, on Sjahrir "sibuk belajar ilmu ekonomi." See also Anwar, *Sebelum Prahara*, p. 214.

[58] Anwar, *Sebelum Prahara*, p. 225.

[59] Roem, "Memoirs," p. 24; interview with Subadio, Jakarta, March 14, 1982.

[60] Roem felt it important enough to describe this extensively and to compare it to what had happened between Sjahrir and Sukarno in Prapat (Roem,"Bung Kecil," pp. 145–46). There might also have been political tension reflected in this particular incident—Sultan Hamid had been involved, in 1951, with some Dutch officers of the former colonial army, in a plot against the Republic, which all of the others represented at the time.

Sjahrir and by all the other prisoners: the reason was merely an attack of flu. "Tell the friends outside it is not true that I can not stand the prison," Sjahrir also said.[61]

Idham, Sjahrir's relative and political friend from the distant and more recent past, told me about his visit to Sjahrir in the Madiun prison at this time:

> I had expected complaints, but there were absolutely none at all. Sjahrir was in a very good mood throughout the several hours of my stay.[62]

Rosihan Anwar, who went to visit Sjahrir and Subadio some time in October 1962, also reported back that he found Sjahrir in good shape, complaining only about the fact that he could not follow the developments outside the prison in greater detail.[63]

But Sjahrir's "exhibition of photographs" had been noticed again. Subadio recalled how Sjahrir had told him in Madiun: "If I had known, that I would go to prison again, I would not have married in 1951."[64] In Madiun, Sjahrir was seen kissing the pictures of his family "one after the other"; "I have seen it with my own eyes," Subadio said.[65]

One day in mid-November 1962, a report reached Jakarta that Sjahrir in Madiun was not well. Poppy Sjahrir with her brother Soedjatmoko and Dr. Supandi, the family doctor, traveled to Madiun in a hurry, and managed to see Sjahrir on November 18. It was found out that Sjahrir was suffering from high blood pressure (diastole 150, systole 245). His state might not have been as bad as it was, so the family thought, if the official in charge of the prisoners' health, *mantri juru*, had ordered Sjahrir to go more easy on his tennis and swimming. There was no resident doctor in the prison, and the visitations from the local hospital were clearly not frequent enough. After some effort, permission was given by the top state authorities for Sjahrir to be moved to Jakarta, where it might be easier to get good medical care.[66]

By train and under escort, Sjahrir arrived in Jakarta on November 23, 1962. To the friends and family who gathered at the Gambir railway station, he looked tired, but, so they say, he managed to smile and wave, before being taken away by a waiting police car. For the following eight months he stayed in the Central Army Hospital in *Kwini* street.[67]

Security there appeared more relaxed. T. B. Simatupang, a long-time admirer of Sjahrir, visited the hospital for a medical check one day during this time, and took his little son with him. While he was being examined, Simatupang recalled later, the boy wandered around, and was found, after some search, at the bedside of a nice patient, both of them chatting and having great fun. The man was Sjahrir.[68]

---

[61] "*Katakan kepada kawan2 diluar bahwa tidak benar saja tidak bestand terhadap gevangenschap.*" Anwar, *Sebelum Prahara*, p. 228.

[62] Interview with Idham, Jakarta, January 8, 1988.

[63] Anwar, *Sebelum Prahara*, p. 261.

[64] Interview with Subadio, Jakarta, March 14, 1982.

[65] Ibid.

[66] Anwar, *Sebelum Prahara*, pp. 273, 281; Siti Wahjunah Sjahrir, "Bung Hatta: Beberapa Catatan," in *Bung Hatta*, ed. Swasono, p. 480.

[67] Anwar, *Sebelum Prahara*, p. 286.

[68] T. B. Simatupang, "Apa arti Sutan Sjahrir bagi kita sekarang ini?" in *Mengenang Sjahrir*, ed. Anwar, pp. 192–93.

During the *Lebaran* celebrations, at the end of the Moslem fasting month, in February 1963, Sjahrir was allowed to spend two days in his house. Guests could come and see him, and some did; however there was a police guard stationed at the gate throughout the holiday.[69]

Mrs. Sjahrir and other relatives and friends could visit Sjahrir more frequently now that he was in the Jakarta hospital. Lily, one of Sjahrir's Bandanese children living in Jakarta, visited him quite regularly. Djohan Sjahroezah, too, saw him in the hospital.[70] Sometimes, Djohan and Lily, so Lily recalls, took this or that PSI friend with them.[71]

Hatta suffered a stroke in mid-1963, and Sjahrir, from the hospital, decided to ask the authorities for permission to visit him, "because Hatta is acutely ill, and we do not know what may happen tomorrow." While Mrs. Sjahrir was trying to get the permission, however, Hatta got better. On hearing this, during one of his wife's subsequent visits, Sjahrir told Poppy that "the crisis is over," and that she could withdraw the request.[72]

After mid-1963, it was decided that Sjahrir was well enough to be moved from the hospital back to an ordinary prison. On the intervention, probably of Maria Ullfah—Sjahrir's old friend from as far back as the 1920s and now the wife of Subadio—Sjahrir was permitted not to return to Madiun but to remain closer to his family, in Jakarta, in a prison on *Keagungan* street.[73]

As in Madiun, there were only medical officers at this prison and doctors visited only occasionally. Sjahrir's health was worsening. Idham visited Sjahrir at the *Keagungan* street prison in 1964:

> You needed permission, but then you could speak with Sjahrir without anybody else being present, and for as long as you might wish. He could give instructions, he could organize. He might, but he did not. They left the prison so open, because they knew that they no longer had anything to be afraid of.[74]

Sjahrir had suffered two milder strokes, the family says, while he was at *Keagungan* street, in 1963 and 1964. The third stroke, much stronger, came three days after he was moved to yet another prison, the military jail at *Budi Utomo* street, also in Jakarta. There, Sjahrir met again with two of the men who had been arrested at the

---

[69] Anwar, *Sebelum Prahara*, p. 337 (Feb. 28, 1962).

[70] Interview with Lily Sutianto, Jakarta, April 2, 1982.

[71] For Ibrahim Thalib's visit see Ibrahim Thalib, *Karya dan tjita Sutan Sjahrir*, pp. 21–22.

[72] Siti Wahjunah Sjahrir, "Bung Hatta," p. 481. Some tension between people connected with Sjahrir's circle and Hatta is evident from the exchange of letters between Anak Agung in prison and Hatta. Hatta was quite explicit, so the letters show, in agreeing with Anak Agung's criticism, and ridicule occasionally, of the Sjahririans' hope "to be called by Sukarno any moment"; more on this below. Besides, there is a mention, in one of Anak Agung's letters, of Soedjatmoko telling his friends that Hatta, in effect, did not disagree with Sukarno's dissolving several political parties, thus, implicitly, including the PSI . For Anak Agung's letter and Hatta's denial see Anak Agung to Hatta, June 30, 1964 and Hatta to Anak Agung, July 21, 1964, in Hatta and Agung, *Surat-menjurat*, pp. 65–75.

[73] Lubis, *Cacatan Subversif*, March 2, 1965, January 2 and 17, 1964, pp. 274 and 279. Anwar, ed., *Perdjalanan terachir*, p. 22.

[74] Interview with Idham, Jakarta, January 8, 1988.

same time as he, Yunan Nasution and Sultan Hamid, and also with two imprisoned military leaders of the 1958 PRRI-Permesta rebellion, Simbolon and Sumual. Sultan Hamid recounted the story of what happened on the fourth day of Sjahrir's stay at *Budi Utomo* prison:

> The month of fasting, year 1965, January 14, military prison Budi Utomo in Jakarta. Almost all the political prisoners of the Islamic faith had already finished their midnight prayers. I was playing scrabble with Simbolon, Sumual, and Sukarto. Suddenly, an officer reported that *Pak* [Father] Soetan Sjahrir collapsed in his room and could not get up. The officer ordered me to go quickly, and without thinking twice I ran towards the place followed by the other friends.
>
> Sjahrir had already got back into his easy chair by the time we reached the room. When asked and then checked on, it became clear that his left leg could not move.[75]

A brain tumor was suspected as Sjahrir had for some time also complained about his eyes. A surgical probe was administered, after the collapse at Budi Utomo, but something went wrong, and Sjahrir's right arm and his right leg, now, became paralyzed. The doctors made another attempt; this time sensitivity returned to Sjahrir's arm and leg, but other areas of the brain had apparently been damaged in the process. Sjahrir lost the capacity to write and, in a few weeks, to speak.[76]

Hamid Algadri became very close to Sjahrir during these last months. (It was explained to me several times by other Sjahrir friends that this happened because Hamid Algadri was of Arab descent, and a grandson of a *kaptein Arab*, "not unlike the Bandanese children.") Hamid Algadri now visited Sjahrir in prison frequently. "I used the opportunity," he wrote later,

> for trying to teach Sjahrir to write again, so that he might communicate at least a little. I started with teaching him to write his name. He appeared to be very happy about what I did with him, he tried with a great eagerness and diligence, but with no result at all. Seeing all the eagerness, I was very much afraid that he would lose hope, and that the frustration would add to his suffering. Not so, apparently. Each time he failed and saw my face getting sad, he hugged me and laughed loudly [*tertawa terkèkèk-kèkèk*], as if he wanted to say: "It's not your fault, Mid, it is me who is stupid!"[77]

---

[75] Sultan Hamid's untitled reminiscences(typescript), pp. 28–29; in *Archives Siti Wahjunah Sjahrir*; see also Yunan M. Nasution, *Kenang-kenangan dibelakang terali besi di zaman rezim orla* (Jakarta: Bulan-Bintang, 1967), p. 62; Sutrisno Kutojo, ed., "Inventarisasi Data Biografi Pahlawan Nasional Sutan Sjahrir," p. 2.

[76] Interview with Siti Wahjunah Sjahrir, Jakarta, November 15, 1987; *Kompas*, April 14, 1966 quoted in Anwar, ed., *Perdjalanan terachir*, p. 22. Mochtar Lubis writes that, according to the information he got in prison, Sjahrir "*tak dapat bicara dan tak kenal keluarganya*, can not talk and can not recognize his family." Lubis, *Cacatan Subversif*, p. 343.

[77] Hamid Algadri, "Pengalaman-pengalaman kecil dengan Bung Kecil," in *Mengenang Sjahrir*, ed. Anwar, p. 126; also interview with Hamid Algadri, Jakarta, December 13, 1987.

2. Last Writings

There was a certain youthfulness about what Sjahrir wrote during his last years—something like a fresh beginning about his texts from prisons and the hospital after 1962, and before he was paralyzed. Sjahrir seemed, also, more than during the 1950s, to take pleasure in reading. He opened his books with eagerness: "I do not know yet what is in this book," he noted more than once in the prison diary he kept.[78] He often read, now, so he said, as one might meet old friends.

In Madiun prison, on May 6, 1962, Sjahrir wrote on the first page of his new notebook:

> Together with this notebook, which I shall use for recording my days, they sent me from the outside two volumes of collected works by Marx and Engels, as I had requested; also a book by Ralph Linton on anthropology and a book by Karl Wittfogel on Oriental Despotism.
>
> First, I look at the writing of Marx and Engels. Clearly, the articles in those two volumes are written by a pen which twenty or thirty years ago powerfully influenced my thinking, my feeling, my views and, because of that, the direction my life has taken. It is as if I am meeting again with very dear friends from the past [*sahabat-sahabat karib lama*], but being aware, at the same time, that the world had changed and my views, too. I know that reading these texts again will cause a great reckoning with an old love [*tjinta lama*], a new reckoning with the influences in my life which belong to the past, but maybe, also to this very moment. I am sure that much good awaits me as I am about to encounter this again. I have postponed this reading in order to postpone the reckoning, because I felt sure that this would become a very personal [*persoonlijk*] matter to me.[79]

There were few "newcomers" admitted into the Pantheon of "classical writers," Sjahrir had built through his life. Merely, the notion of "classical," as Sjahrir had learned it from the 1920s on, had become transparent again—an island of warmth—and the past perhaps—amidst the flow of otherwise aimless actual time.

In his diary, in Madiun prison, in October 1962, for instance, Sjahrir compared a volume of Max Weber's sociological essays with a book on the same themes by a contemporary, W. F. Ogburn:

> The character of this book is very different from that of Ogburn. Weber is a kind of scholar of the 19th century, a universal man of letters [*pudjangga universil*] like Goethe, Nietzsche, or others, who lived only to read and write down their extraordinary explanations of the world, that is, men who possessed an unusual capacity to learn and to remember from the time when they were children. In the 20th century one perhaps would not meet men like that, because the specialization in scholarship has advanced so much that it is impossible to follow all the directions. What is impressive is that

---

[78] For Sjahrir's comments on Galbraith see "Development and perspective," in Sjahrir, "Buku-buku cacatan harian" (variously dated, Madiun, 1962–1963), July 31, 1962, pp. 28–29; in *Archives Siti Wahjunah Sjahrir*.

[79] Opening page of Sjahrir, "Buku-buku cacatan harian" (May 6, 1962), n.p.

much of what Max Weber wrote is still true for today, and that it is, thus, the essential and fundamental [*pokok dan dasar*] truth.

I am very much attracted to this writing. As if it had been written for the time we are now living in, although it was written around 1920. The style is truly appealing, in spite of the fact that it is a translation. I decided to read all the writing by Max Weber in the original. In spite of the fact that the style of his writing is that of classical German, [growing out of] Latin or Greek, with very long sentences, I find it even more interesting than, for instance, the writing of Marx, even more spirited, even more lively.

And, a few lines below: "My impression of Weber is that he is a genius, like Shakespeare and Goethe," and "I think, he also belongs to the classics [*ia pun termasuk klasik*]."[80]

As one might expect rather in the texts of a very young man, Sjahrir's reading of his masters was strongly and often wholly personal; reading them, therefore, came always close to an almost emotional defense of them against the others. J. A. Schumpeter, an Austrian economist of the early twentieth century, for example, appeared "provocative" to Sjahrir, when he dared to move himself too close to Marx or when he even tried to behave "as if he was Marx's superior."[81] Walter Rostow, similarly, who has structured his Stages of Economic Growth "so as to challenge Marx's and Engels' Communist Manifesto," "did not even," according to Sjahrir, "attempt a duel."[82]

Marx and Engels, as Sjahrir read them now—more even than when he had read them as a very young man—were first of all fascinating human beings:

> From Marx's writing it is clear that most earnestly of all, he was a hero to the working class. Thus, it is easier for us to explain all his shortcomings and weaknesses as a sociologist and an economist. Because Marx and Engels, both of them, were first of all heroes, who sided with the workers, and were not men who would mainly devote their lives to science.... Their political articles are more interesting than their theoretical writings, because it is in the former, where there is the sincerity of their souls and their energy.[83]

Sjahrir read Marx in prison eagerly: "mainly [Marx's texts] from before 1840, but also from the time afterwards."[84] This meant, of course, that Sjahrir read "mainly" Marx from the time the master reached the age of twenty-two! Sjahrir's particular liking for Engels, a preference that was already visible in the very young Sjahrir, was revived now with great force. Sjahrir became truly angry, for instance, reading Schumpeter's classifying Engels as "far below Marx's level." Such a view, Sjahrir wrote, was "cynical." Sjahrir was equally "disturbed" by Engels himself sometimes assuming the position of an inferior towards Marx. "On the reverse," Sjahrir wrote, Engels was "more sensitive"; it was, indeed, only after Marx died, that the writing of

---

[80] Sjahrir's comments on Max Weber's "Sociological Essays" in ibid., October 4 and 5, 1962, vol. 1, p. 276.

[81] Sjahrir's comments on Schumpeter's "Kapitalism" in ibid., July 3 to 6, 1962, vol. 2, p. 58.

[82] Sjahrir on W. W. Rostow's *The Stages of Economic Growth* in ibid., August 22, 1962, n.p.

[83] Sjahrir's comments on Marx and Engels' "Collected Works" in ibid., 1962, vol. 5, p. 13.

[84] Sjahrir, "Buku-buku cacatan harian," n.d., p. 109.

Engels, "in spirit and in letter, began to express truly strongly the author's personality;" only then, indeed, the personality's "subtle shades of meaning surfaced."[85]

The time of the 1920s, sometimes described as the "time before 1933," returned to Sjahrir's prison texts again and again.

On June 24, 1962, Sjahrir wrote that he had received from the outside a book by Mills and Montgomery on the American labor movement. The book had, Sjahrir wrote, "almost 600 pages, but I was able to finish the book in less than a week." Sjahrir then went on commenting upon how "surprised" he had been,

> to become aware again that, from the beginning of the 20th century and till 1933, Marx's critique of the capitalist society was not merely correct in its essence, but—still thirty years ago—real and viable.[86]

Also in prison, Sjahrir wrote a very long entry on "The Middle of the Journey" by Lionel Trilling, a novel about the American Left of the early 1930s. Sjahrir clearly identified himself—or his youthful self rather—with the heroes of the novel,

> the intellectuals, who, driven by a passion for progress, often, and generally at that time, accepted Marxism and Communism.... Idealism, which at that time took on a form of politics, meant almost the same as leaning towards or standing on the side of Marxism and Communism, as all the great and pure ideals of life and society seemed to become full-fledged only if understood as the ideals of progress and Communism....
>
> To read a book of this kind, at the present time, in the situation I am now, does cheer me up, and does truly provide a consolation.[87]

Trilling's novel was a personal gift, so Sjahrir also noted, from a journalist Harold Isaacs, who himself had belonged to the generation of the book and to the prewar Left. Isaacs had visited Indonesia late in 1945, and it was probably then that he gave the book to Sjahrir.[88]

Many of the volumes Sjahrir read in prison, if not most, had some story behind them even before Sjahrir opened them. Books were brought to him according to the list which he himself had made in prison and from memory; generally, his wife says, these were books he recalled as standing for years on the shelves of his own library at home.[89]

Sjahrir now appeared to read many books, which, even among the intellectual and political elite of Jakarta of those days, might be called outdated. He read Ogburn's "Handbook of Sociology," as we saw, which, as Sjahrir himself noted, "was

---

[85] Sjahrir's comments on Marx and Engels' "Collected Works" in ibid., 1962, vol. 5, pp. 14, 18–19.

[86] Sjahrir's comments on Mills' and Montgomery's "Labor Progress" in ibid., June 24, 1962, p. 37.

[87] Sjahrir's comments on Lionel Trilling's "The Middle of the Journey" in ibid., June 28, 1963, vol. 8, p. 75.

[88] On Isaacs' visit see Hanna Papanek, "Note on Soedjatmoko's Recollections of a Historical Moment: Sjahrir's Reaction to Ho Chi Minh's 1945 Call for a Free People Federation," *Indonesia* 49 (April 1990): 141–44.

[89] Interview with Siti Wahjunah Sjahrir, Jakarta, October 10, 1987.

written in the mid or late 1940s."[90] He read Gunnar Myrdal, a fashionable author of the time; but he read Myrdal's book "from 1953 or 1954"—ten years old by that time.[91] Dobb's study "On Economic Theory and Socialism," as Sjahrir also noted, "was published twenty years ago."[92] A book by Rosa Luxemburg that Sjahrir studied in prison was, so he said, "printed in gothic characters."[93] At least in one place in his diaries, Sjahrir addressed the fact explicitly: the more he read, he said, the less he regretted that he was spending his time on "largely obsolete" books.[94]

Repeatedly and with evident pleasure, Sjahrir recalled the time—a decade or two in the past, the time of the Trilling novel, too—when he had read this or that book, met this or that author for the first time. It was as if a circle was being closed. This was a book, he wrote before beginning to read Karl Wittfogel in Madiun, the first volume of which he had read a quarter century ago: "wanting from that time on to read the second volume very much."[95] Commenting on yet another book, Sjahrir wrote: "I have read a large part of this already, as I had been preparing courses on the topic."[96] This had to be the time of *Daulat Ra'jat*, before 1933. In another entry before opening a book he requested: "most of this is reprinted from a volume I had in my library in Banda Neira."[97]

With hesitation, even some among Sjahrir's very close friends and long-time admirers, discussing Sjahrir's late years and his writings from prison in particular, talk about an intellectual decline. His analyses, they sometimes say, were hazy, his interest wandered, his language was flat. This was most saddening, they might add, when the writing was compared with what Sjahrir produced during the 1930s, and the 1940s.

Nuchterheid and *zakelijkheid*, "soberness" and "matter-of-factness," were still the values appearing regularly in what Sjahrir wrote—now as two decades previously. As before, Marx and Engels were the most glamorous champions, and the exemplary manifestations of these high values. Marx and Engels, Sjahrir wrote in the Madiun prison,

> said that all knowledge, including the exact sciences, possessed only a temporary certitude, which had to change or weaken with growing experience. . . . Thus also, much of what had been put forward by [Marx and Engels] as certitude, and as an explanation based on reality, that is on exact scientific thinking, has, at present, to be regarded that way.[98]

---

[90] Sjahrir on Ogburn's "Handbook of Society," in Sjahrir, "Buku-buku cacatan harian," September 27, 1962, n.p.

[91] Ibid., September 13–17, 1962, vol. 1, p. 232.

[92] Sjahrir on Dobb's "Political Economy and Capitalism" in ibid., June 18–21, 1962, vol. 2, p. 62.

[93] Ibid., 1962, vol. 5, p. 24.

[94] Sjahrir on Ogburn, ibid., September 27, 1962.

[95] Sjahrir on Wittfogel's "Oriental Despotism" ibid., 1962, vol. 5, n.p.

[96] Sjahrir on "Das Kapital I," ibid., 1962, vol. 5, p. 21.

[97] Sjahrir on Weber's "Sociological Essays," ibid., vol. 1, p. 276.

[98] Ibid., 1962, vol. 5, p. 17.

Sjahrir still believed in *nuchter* and *zakelijk*, sober and matter-of-fact. But now, often, this sounded less as keeping alert to change, and more as becoming resigned to the stream of life, to the notion that one has to flow with one's experience.

Experiences, now, often appeared to assume rather a gray coloring. This was, for instance, how Sjahrir reflected upon himself and others who were involved in the Revolution after 1945:

> as if being merely pushed forward, with a feeling that it was not certain what would happen to one tomorrow ... this was what I had experienced myself during our Revolution. ... Each man, who lives through and amidst the revolution, seems to forget its lesson ... we know it from reading histories of the Greek states, the Old Testament, the Gospel, the Koran ... and always the reaction, which we have seen so many times in the history of mankind, and always the same result.[99]

"Objectivism," it seemed, assumed now, in Sjahrir's late writing, a status of almost the absolute. Sjahrir praised a historian, Hugh Trevor-Roper, because he "does not take sides." He commended another author he had read at the time,

> because he can so easily detach himself from the society he studies ... is so aloof towards what he is talking about ... does not feel himself to be called upon to convince anybody. ...[100]

At the same time, Sjahrir became deeply disappointed in E. H. Carr, because he "suggested that a historian is free to be consciously subjective." By this, E. H. Carr lost his appeal to Sjahrir—so completely, in fact, that Sjahrir decided not to read Carr's study on the Russian Revolution; however he had already placed it on his list of required reading.[101]

There was still the old familiar unwillingness in Sjahrir to see the world "too abstract," too "clean," too "logical," as "purely a theory [*reintheorie*]."[102] But, Sjahrir wrote in Madiun:

> It is startling, how the very fundamentals of physics can only be ascertained through mathematics and through theories like those of Einstein, Max Planck and Bohr, which, indeed, almost 99 percent of the time depend on capabilities and power of thinking, so that they represent philosophies and speculations which so easily come close to mysticism. There is not much of close connection with our experience and with our five senses. ... It is frightening, also, to realize that certainty of this [world] exists only if confirmed by other sciences, but that it disappears when we make an effort to inspect it by connecting our action and the power of our thinking with the world and its actual state. It is clear that, basically and at its roots, all our certainty is measured and proved right or wrong by exact sciences, by our

---

[99] Sjahrir on Trotsky's "Tentang Revolusi 1917," in ibid., 1962, vol. 5, n.p.

[100] Sjahrir on Trevor Roper and E. H. Carr in ibid., vol. 2, p. 49; on C. H. E. Kinalberger (?), ibid., August 7 and 9, 1962, n.p.

[101] Sjahrir on Trevor Roper and Carr, ibid., vol. 2, p. 49.

[102] Sjahrir on Dobb, Schumpeter, and Luxemburg in ibid., vol. 2, pp. 62, 58,

belief that whatever we do or think, although we cannot explain it out of ourselves, might be correct and useful.... We have to decide upon the laws of the universe and upon the laws of our little world, which can not be seen and checked with our five senses, but only with mathematics, while mathematics also might become a vehicle driving us towards the world of phantoms [*alam kechajalan*], being an abstract power of mankind, a science of symbols—remember just algebra, integral and differential calculus—in short [again] something which becomes mysticism very easily.[103]

And yet:

I am very much attracted by books ... on the exact sciences' views of progress, of life and of the limitations of progress and life, views, which are not based merely on dialectical materialism; I am attracted by books about quantum theory, the theory of relativity, the hypothesis of the finite and the infinite world and universe.[104]

Sjahrir still weighed what he had read on ethical scales. The authors he commented upon negatively were most often also "cynical" and did not distinguish between "just [*adil*]" and "unjust."[105] Authors, on the other hand, whom Sjahrir believed to be of high quality intellectually, were also, regularly, "far from being cynical," and explained history by "honesty" and/or "responsibility."[106]

In an entry into his diary in prison, on June 3, 1963, Sjahrir wrote:

My memories and my thoughts turn and fly home, to my children, whom I wish to be more happy in a future, and better than me. I hope they will grow into *edel* human beings, which means honest, straight, lovingly disposed to all other human beings, and not proud of rank or distinctions. Certainly I hope that their brains will also be sharp, sharper and better trained than mine, but what I have said above can be best summarized with this most important word *edel*.[107]

Edel, is a Dutch word usually translated as "noble" or "generous," and, as far as we know, it had never been used by Sjahrir in such a context before. *Edel* evokes a sense very close to *adel*, "nobility." Remembering Sjahrir, one would have much rather expected the use of the dynamic, irritant, powerful, action-laden, as much intellectual as ethical, and, indeed, anti-*adel* Indonesian word *akal*.

Education, as before, was referred to very frequently. Sjahrir was familiar with some of the books he had in prison because he had used them "in political courses years ago."[108] Some other books he passed over, as he thought them not useful,

---

[103] Sjahrir on Weyler's "Philosophy of Mathematics and Natural Science" (?), ibid., September 22, 24, and 25, 1962, p. 254.

[104] Sjahrir's comments on Wetter's "Dialectical Materialism" ibid., 1962, vol. 5, pp. 75–76.

[105] Sjahrir on Schumpeter, "Buku-buku catatan harian," vol. 2, p. 58.

[106] Sjahrir on Weber, ibid., vol. 1, p. 276; see also ibid; 1962, vol. 5, pp. 58–59.

[107] Ibid., June 3, 1963.

[108] Sjahrir on "Das Kapital I," ibid., vol. 5, p. 21.

"which means that [they] can not be used as teaching material."[109] It was the old notion of the classroom permeating whatever Sjahrir wrote and thought about. But the 1930s dynamic notion of "social pedagogics" and "political pedagogics," education being instantly translated into power, education equaling power—has become, in Sjahrir's late writings, increasingly difficult to discerrn.

Often, now, Sjahrir gave the impression of a student toiling with too difficult an assignment. Strikingly many "a sort of an introduction" and "handbooks" figured on the list of readings Sjahrir asked to be sent to him in prison. In October 1962, for instance, he began to read "Mathematics Made Simple":

> If I am not mistaken, this book belongs to Ali [the youngest of Sjahrir's Bandanese children]. At the beginning, there is a test for the pupils. It is an easy test, evidently, and I finished it, 100 percent correct, in half an hour. At the end, there is another test, of which I succeeded in answering only at 60 percent.... It appears, that what I have learned in the Mulo [elementary] school, I can still remember, but what had been taught at the A.M.S. [intermediary], including stereometry and trigonometry, has become already very dim....[110]

Five months before reading "Mathematics Made Simple," Sjahrir went through Weyler's "Philosophy of Mathematics and Natural Science." "Not easy," he commented on this, "I would have to come back to it after I first do mathematics and physics."[111] On the margin of a text by Marx Sjahrir wrote at the same time: "very abstract and too long."[112] On yet another Marx text, he scribbled: "I must read this again, and all through, however boring it is."[113]

Sjahrir, through his books, lived in the past, perhaps more than ever. But his memory appeared, now, as if built largely, and carefully perhaps, out of not-too-disturbing and even not-too-exciting particles. Forgetting seemed to be accepted calmly. In August 1963, Sjahrir wrote on his home in Sumatra and on the places where he lived as a boy:

> It has not been possible to retain many recollections of Medan from the time I lived there, especially not after I visited it again in the 1950s. In a greater part, my image of the city is already completely wrong. Already, everything has changed, especially the Palace Road, the Mantri Street, and the back yard of the house, where I spent my childhood.... Thinking of the time more than thirty years back, this Medan has already become to me an Alien Town [Kota Asing]. The same, in part, is true about Bandung.[114]

This, again, suggested a closing circle. Past and future became one in being remembered vaguely; or in being calmly forgotten. Sjahrir kept his youthful "friendship" with Marx and Engels. And he did not doubt that

---

[109] Ibid., p. 23.
[110] Sjahrir on "Mathematics Made Simple" in ibid., 1962, vol. 10, p. 10.
[111] Sjahrir on Weyler, ibid., vol. 1, p. 276.
[112] Sjahrir on "Das Kapital I," ibid., vol. 5, p. 21.
[113] Ibid.
[114] Sjahrir "Tentang Negara Inggris," in ibid., August 31, 1963.

in this world, still called capitalist, it is no longer possible to imagine proletarian action of an international character;[115]

and also:

for me, now, it is very clear that the world revolution, as Marx and Engels dreamed about it in their Communist Manifesto, will never happen.[116]

Sjahrir read in prison a magazine article about current developments in the Soviet Union. The Soviet youths' calling for change reminded him of the young *Bohème* of Western Europe, the *Quartier Latin, Pango,* and Greenwich Village.[117] But, strikingly, he did not make a connection to himself and to his *Bohème* of the 1920s—to the painter Salim, politician Sal Tas, writer du Perron. What Sjahrir added, at this place, when one might expect a sharp flash of personal memory, was merely an "objective" statement that the Soviet youths essentially wanted a return to the bourgeois style of life, and to the bourgeois times of the past.[118]

Sjahrir still wrote not unlike a Marxist, viewing history as a linear development; the "progress of the society of man ... started in classical Greece," then came the "feudal stage." Yet then came: "and finally capitalism."[119] The "paradise on earth," he wrote, "did not happen."[120]

Thinking of progress did not give much pleasure:

A great part of mankind during the last hundred years was ignorant of modern medicine, penicillin, streptomycin, child-care, and so forth, and, in spite of that, mankind multiplied three times during those 100 years!!! Truly frightening.[121]

Or:

It is rather discouraging [*agak mengetjilkan hati*] to realize that, in her industrialization, Russia, in 1914, was already much more advanced [*madju*], than we are today.[122]

Healthy social and political system implied "caring about equilibrium [*kesetimbangan*] and about certainty of life [*kepastian hidup*]":

---

[115] Sjahrir on "Ten Years After Stalin (from 'Problems of Communism')" in ibid., 1962, vol. 5, p. 56.

[116] Ibid., p. 58.

[117] Sjahrir on "The New Russian Literature" ibid., 1962, vol. 5, pp. 80–82; on "Khruschev dan kebudajaan" ibid.

[118] Ibid., also ibid., 1962, vol. 5, pp. 29–30; 1963, vol. 1, n.p.

[119] Ibid. 1962, vol. 5, p. 6.

[120] Ibid., June 28, 1963, p. 75.

[121] Sjahrir on Ralph Linton's "Seizure of Revolution"(?), ibid., 1962, vol. 5, pp. 10–11.

[122] Sjahrir on M. H. Dobb's "Soviet Economical Developments since 1917," ibid., September 10, 1962; and Sjahrir, "Tinjauan Buku" (variously dated, Madiun 1962–1963, Jakarta, 1963–1964, parts 1, 2, and 3) 2: 53; in *Archives Siti Wahjunah Sjahrir*.

Equilibrium, it is what is desired ... certainty, it is what is searched for ... equilibrium or order [*orde*] ... which will be very long-lasting [*agak kekal*] and steady [*stabiel*].[123]

Kegelisahan, "tremblingness," the word, which had so characterized Sjahrir in the past—his dynamism, alertness, power—became amost wholly a negative label. To Sjahrir, now, the equation seemed to be: the more "tremblingness" grows in a society (*kegelisahan bertambah terus*), the more the milieu for our work becomes dilapidated (*pun terus bertambah buruk*).[124] Now, more than anything else, "tremblingness" meant "confusion [*rasa kurang pasti dan gelisah*]." If the youth in Indonesia "began to tremble [*gelisah*]," so, to Sjahrir, "obstacles" grew ominous, and "risks," too [*risiko dan halangan*].[125]

While on his short *Lebaran* parole, in February 1963, Sjahrir reportedly told a friend that "there has to be some possibility for a patriotic group to emerge inside the Army."[126] A few months later, back in prison, Sjahrir wrote somewhat similarly, in a paper to be distributed among the former PSI leaders:

> ... among educated circles, both civilian and military, there still are people with ideals, who mean well, and who are not cynical. They may gather and try to change the present structure of our state power from the inside. An effort like that has to get full support in all fields, especially in the field of education....[127]

On yet another occasion, at about the same time, Sjahrir was reported to suggest "supporting the position of Nasution."[128]

They were, however, extremely rare occasions on which Sjahrir at this stage of his life was still mentioning "possible action." There are strong suggestions, moreover, that these attempts at suggesting actions might have been done less on Sjahrir's own initiative and more as concessions to his more eager friends.

Rosihan Anwar wrote in his diary in April 1962, while Sjahrir was in prison, about a meeting he had just had with two friends, long-time admirers and followers of Sjahrir—Daan Jahja and Wibowo. Both of the men, in fact, had belonged to Sjahrir's wartime medical-school student circle; Daan Jahja, besides, had throughout the postcolonial history of Indonesia been one of the most often-mentioned "PSI officers" in the Indonesian army. According to Rosihan Anwar,

> we talked with Daan and Wibowo about Sjahrir. Daan is of the opinion that Sjahrir is not the right man to lead the Indonesian Socialist Party ... the party now is scattered in all directions [*bertjerai-tjerai*], has no common aim and ideal; its sinking still deeper can be prevented only if a new leadership

---

[123] Sjahrir on H. Finer in Sjahrir, "Buku-buku cacatan harian," July 16 to August 16, 1962, n.p.

[124] Sjahrir, "Keadaan dan Tugas" later published in Sjahrir, *Sosialisme, Indonesia, Pembangunan*, pp. 196–97.

[125] Ibid., pp. 211, 204.

[126] Anwar, *Sebelum Prahara*, p. 337.

[127] Sjahrir, "Keadaan dan Tugas," in *Sosialisme, Indonesia, Pembangunan*, p. 209.

[128] Sjahrir to Soedjatmoko as communicated by Soedjatmoko to Anwar; Anwar, *Sebelum Prahara*, pp. 356–57 (April 5, 1963).

emerges with a spirit not like that of Sjahrir, but with a spirit of action, capable of organizing efficiently and effectively.

"I for myself," Rosihan Anwar commented,

> did not oppose this view of Daan, however I do not think that he is entirely right. I believe that in this problem we face two elements—one of power and the other of morality.[129]

There is no indication that Sjahrir changed his previous, strongly, and at times emphatically, negative attitude towards the Indonesian armed forces. There might have existed a "patriotic group" inside the armed forces, Sjahrir wrote in the paper just mentioned, "however, the armed forces as a whole have been made into a privileged child [*dianakemaskan*] by the state." There might have been some "positive tendencies" inside the armed forces, Sjahrir was occasionally willing to admit, "however, [these were] not even as strong as outside the armed forces."[130]

Indonesian military officers, according to Sjahrir, were living even better than the civil servants did, and they were thus, implicitly, even more open to corruption.[131] "The Army, and especially its leadership," Sjahrir wrote early in 1963, "behaves as a traveler, who has lost his compass."[132] And, in another text from the same time:

> The banished parties, like Masjumi and our PSI, can not challenge the established power, and they are particularly weak when compared to the armed forces, which till now position themselves as the protégés of this country.[133]

The Indonesian armed forces "and especially the army," according to the same Sjahrir text, have greatly profited from the policies of Sukarno's government "since 1957." They have made themselves into "the first priority" of the Sukarno state; "they imagine themselves as the force, which safeguards and empowers the state in the name of President Sukarno."[134] They, together with Sukarno, "have benefited from the breakdown of party politics," and they "behave as if their symbol and essence was President Sukarno."[135]

There did not seem to be any willingness for that kind of action, if any. General Simatupang, always an admirer of Sjahrir and also a man almost always in the past prominently mentioned among the "pro-PSI officers," wrote after Sjahrir's death, having in mind, so it seems, especially his last few years:

> The history of our Republic till the present time offers few examples of personalities like Sjahrir—emerging to bring high promises and great hopes, but

---

[129] Ibid., April 14, 1962, pp. 206–207.

[130] Sjahrir, "Keadaan dan Tugas," in *Sosialisme, Indonesia, Pembangunan*, p. 209.

[131] Sjahrir's comments on Finer in Sjahrir, "Buku-buku cacatan harian," July 16 to August 16, 1962; Sjahrir, "Keadaan dan Tugas," in *Sosialisme, Indonesia, Pembangunan*, p. 210.

[132] Quoted in Anwar, *Sebelum Prahara*, p. 337 (February 28, 1962).

[133] Sjahrir, "Keadaan dan Tugas," in *Sosialisme, Indonesia, Pembangunan*, p. 208.

[134] Ibid., p. 203.

[135] Quoted in Anwar, *Sebelum Prahara*, pp. 283–84.

then putting a brake on playing their roles before they fulfilled either the promises or the hopes.[136]

Indonesia, in the early 1960s, was by many experts at home and abroad seen as a country almost on the verge of a Communist take-over.[137] Indonesian politics was seen as a triangle of power made up of Sukarno, the army, and the Communists. The "former PSI," as it was carrying on into the early 1960s, was mostly described as a group keeping its identity with difficulty and essentially by being anti-Communist.

For Sjahrir at least, however, and now perhaps even more than before, the Indonesian Communists were not "the real communists." "Leaders of communism in this country," Sjahrir wrote,

> do not keep to Marxism-Leninism ... they accepted that in the framework of "guided democracy," there was no space for the Indonesian Communist Party to move as a real communist party.... As a revolutionary communist party they are paralyzed and impotent.[138]

The Indonesian Communist leaders, Sjahrir also wrote,

> have completely mortified their own militancy, in order that they might, in the framework of the national front, mobilize for the government.... They have ordered workers not to strike.[139]

They have again proved to be just "nationalists," and "their nationalism explains in part, why they are active mainly in Eastern Java."[140] In one of his last texts, Sjahrir wondered if there might be some chance for the mind and body of the Indonesian Communist leaders to revitalize. Sjahrir's answer was negative: the mortification of these Communists' spirit "went too far," Sjahrir wrote, "it is too late."[141]

The current ideology of the Indonesian Communist Party, Sjahrir argued, "is in fact nothing but a 'rationalization' of weakness." "They still read Marx, Engels, Lenin, Stalin, and Mao to themselves"; they perhaps still believed that

> all the humiliation they have subjected themselves to, and all their behaving like nationalists, is merely playing a comedy ... waiting for a right moment.[142]

---

[136] Simatupang, "Apa arti Sutan Sjahrir," p.187; interview with Simatupang, Jakarta, January 4, 1987.

[137] See, e.g., Brackman, *Indonesian Communism, passim.*

[138] Sjahrir on "Khruschev dan kebudajaan" in Sjahrir, "Buku-buku cacatan harian," also Sjahrir "Tinjauan dalam Negeri," 1964 later published in Sjahrir, *Sosialisme, Indonesia, Pembangunan*, pp. 232, 234.

[139] Ibid., p. 206.

[140] Sjahrir's comments on Brackman in Sjahrir, "Tinjauan Buku," 1963, 3: 33.

[141] Sjahrir, "Tinjauan dalam Negeri," in *Sosialisme, Indonesia, Pembangunan*, p. 230; see also Sjahrir, "Buku-buku cacatan harian," August 27, 1963, and 1962, vol. 5, p. 90.

[142] Sjahrir on Brackman, in Sjahrir, "Tinjauan Buku," 3: 33.

But, Sjahrir was sure—and he used the same term he used for the army at the same time—"the Communists lost their compass."[143]

The Indonesian Communists, Sjahrir wrote,

> are seen, by the world outside, as an alternative to the regime of President Sukarno and his "guided democracy," and the military are seen as the third player.

But "the world outside" was wrong.[144] The Communists might still gather some energy, Sjahrir wrote, but "such energy would be transformed into slogans, and the slogans would come out of the mouth of President Sukarno himself."[145]

> The Communists have entrusted the future and their destiny to President Sukarno.... They have forgotten what they learned in Lenin's "State and Revolution."[146]

In October 1962, Sjahrir wrote that "experience may be a handicap," and, in the same paragraph, he talked about some of his generation as about "victims of memory."[147] Of all Solzhenitsyn's portraits from Stalinist Russia, of all the fighters and martyrs of the failed revolution, Sjahrir seemed to be impressed most by an old peasant woman in one of the writer's lesser known short stories: a woman, Sjahrir wrote, for whom "one day was like the other," who "was not connected to time," who "kept to the beliefs of the past [*takhjul kuno*]," and, who could see the purpose of her life as living with "decency and love [*kesusilan dan tjinta*]."[148] "I am inclined," Sjahrir wrote on a different occasion, in August 1963,

> to accept that there is truth in what my wife believes, that there is a '*goddelijke vonkje*' [godly sparkle] in mankind and that we have to adjust our lives accordingly.[149]

It is difficult to find any remnants in Sjahrir's late writing of the disturbing and inspiring notion of the margin and the outside world. Max Weber did not appear to awaken in the Sjahrir of the 1960s—as he did in the Sjahrir of the 1930s—the idea of enterprising Protestantism being not unlike Indonesian Islam.[150] Images of welfare states in the outside world, still so significant to Sjahrir's vision just a few years previously, became gray, too: Indonesia might learn, Sjahrir suggested at one place, from Yugoslavia, Poland, Taiwan, or Japan.[151]

---

[143] Sjahrir on "Bulletin for the Study of the USSR" in Sjahrir, "Buku-buku cacatan harian," 1962, vol. 5, p. 66.

[144] Sjahrir, "Keadaan dan Tugas," in *Sosialisme, Indonesia, Pembangunan*, pp. 206–207,

[145] Ibid., p. 223.

[146] Quoted in Anwar, *Sebelum Prahara*, p. 284 (September 20, 1962).

[147] Sjahrir, "Buku-buku cacatan harian," October 13, 1962.

[148] Sjahrir on Alexander Solzhenitsyn, ibid., 1962, vol. 6, pp. 78–79.

[149] Sjahrir on Dos Pasos in ibid., August 30 , p. 64.

[150] Sjahrir on Max Weber, ibid., vol. 1, p. 276.

[151] Sjahrir on land reform in China, ibid., August 16, 1963, p. 12.

Sjahrir's view of the two superpowers appeared to have softened. Of course, these were the early 1960s, still before the US armed forces landed in Vietnam, and these were the times of Khruschev. Orwell's "1984" will not come, Sjahrir wrote.[152] Yevtushenko's fears that Stalin might rise from his grave were unfounded.[153] Khruschev's reforms were proving that "God made all the men in his own image [*God heeft de mens naar eigen aangezicht geschapen*]," meaning that universal values were finally about to prevail.[154]

Sjahrir was very pleased, so he wrote, by a book by one Walter W. Heller, that somebody had sent him to prison. Sjahrir especially liked the author's idea that, in the US, "there are already tools 'built-in as shock-absorbers and cushions'"—mechanisms, which "delay or limit any tendency towards economic crises or depressions." "I have found here," Sjahrir wrote,

> something for which I had been looking for a long time. . . . I would very much like to have a book like this in my possession.[155]

Reading one of Hans Kohn's texts on nationalism, Sjahrir enjoyed Kohn's view, namely that, in the US, "Freedom, Liberty, Justice, Democracy do in fact already exist."[156] Sjahrir seemed to come to believe, now, that "rough times" in the US were over. On John Kenneth Galbraith's American essays, he noted that he was "afraid" that "Galbraith's attitudes are too polemical."[157]

As before, Sjahrir believed that Indonesia should keep a low profile in world politics. Also this argument had not fundamentally changed, only its emphasis had shifted. Sjahrir wrote, now, almost exclusively about Sukarno's policy of verbal and demonstrative "confrontation" with the pro-British, "neo-colonialist" Malaysia, and, more broadly, with the world imperialist "old declining forces." Sjahrir warned, that if the aggressive policy continued, Indonesia might "suffer embarrassment [*bisa menderita malu muka*]."[158]

Sjahrir still described Sukarno—his style, him as the center—in the terms that he had often used before. He wrote about ostentatiousness and theatricality, living in fantasy (*fantasie*),[159] a lack of rational thinking (*rasionalisme, kalkulasi, perhitungan*),[160] listening to "experts in passion," instead of "experts in thinking," flamboyance as "overcompensation" for an inferiority complex,[161] mystical nationalism, overuse of

---

[152] Sjahrir on John Dos Pasos in Sjahrir, "Buku-buku cacatan harian," August 30, 1963, vol. 14, p. 64.

[153] Sjahrir on "Khrushev dan kebudajaan," in ibid.

[154] Sjahrir "Tentang Golongan Muda," in ibid., August 14, 1963, 1962, vol. 4, p. 77.

[155] Sjahrir on a speech by President Kennedy in ibid., October 25, 1962, vol. 1, p. 316. It is not clear from Sjahrir's text which book by Heller he had in mind.

[156] Sjahrir on Hans Kohn's "American Nationalism" in Sjahrir, "Tinjauan Buku," 2: 12.

[157] Sjahrir's comments on Dos Pasos in Sjahrir, "Buku-buku cacatan harian," p. 63; Sjahrir on Galbraith ibid., July 31, 1962.

[158] Quoted in Anwar, *Sebelum Prahara*, p. 357.

[159] Sutan Sjahrir, "Tinjauan dalam negeri,"[1964] in Sutan Sjahrir, *Sosialisme, Indonesia, Pembangunan*, pp. 219–20; see also Sjahrir, "Keadaan dan Tugas," ibid., pp. 197, 199.

[160] Sjahrir, "Tinjauan dalam negeri," in *Sosialisme, Indonesia, Pembangunan*, pp. 208–9.

[161] Sjahrir on Gunnar Myrdal in Sjahrir, "Buku-buku cacatan harian," September 13–17, 1962, vol. 1, p. 232.

solidarity (*kegotongrojongan*), mixing Hindu-Javanese and nationalist notions (*Ibu Pertiwi*),[162] perpetuating a "system of indifference and ignorance [*sistim masa bodoh*],"[163] a static and hierarchical system.[164] Writing about Sukarno's popularity and about loyalty to Sukarno, Sjahrir still wrote about "deifying the father [*pendewaan bapa*]."[165]

Yet, now, Sjahrir often wrote "state" and meant "nation"; wrote "nation" and meant "people." Now, Sjahrir often seemed to identify his attitude to the "state," to the "nation," and to the "people"—his politics, his dynamism—with "being faithful." The following entry is from Sjahrir's Madiun diary, September 1962:

> To my wife and equally to myself, it is, indeed, amazing that the State could behave to me in the way I am now experiencing. I never have, and I never will expect recognition, and, least of all honors, from my nation and people.... But I have also never dreamed that the State, the nation and the people might suspect me of being unfaithful or not faithful enough [*tidak atau kurang setia*] to my State, nation and people. This is the same, as my wife says, as suspecting me of being unfaithful or not faithful enough to myself, unfaithful or not faithful enough, through my life, to my aspirations and to my consciousness; as if I abandoned the view of life, which I held for the past fifty years, as if, at present, as I am coming closer to my grave, I had no view of life at all.[166]

In June 1963, in prison, Sjahrir read for the first time Herbert Feith' book, which, as we recall, presented Indonesian history after 1949 as a "decline of constitutional democracy." Sjahrir noted about the book in his diary:

> If I were to write about this period, the frame would be different, and also the events and the ideas, which I would emphasize, would very much differ from what is emphasized in this book.... For the time being, in fact, "democracy" for us can not mean a technique of governing, and a citizen-like way of life, but mainly the guarantee against tyranny and despotism.... This [democracy], actually, can be achieved through enlightened [*verlicht*] humanistic despotism or humanistic dictatorship. However little the common people understand, feel the need for democratic rights and for representative government, there is a potential in this kind of humanism, to make education of the people, and material and spiritual happiness of the people, into the principles and aims of such a government. So far as such a government truly behaves like a father of the people, like the people's own flesh and own blood, also the preparedness of the people to exercise its

---

[162] Sjahrir, "Tinjauan dalam negeri," pp. 220–21, 234; Sjahrir, "Keadaan dan Tugas," p. 203; Sjahrir on Bryce's(?)"Industrial Development" in Sjahrir, "Buku-buku cacatan harian," also ibid., September 7, 1962, p. 222;.

[163] Sjahrir, "Tinjauan dalam negeri," p. 221

[164] Ibid., pp. 220–21.

[165] Sjahrir on Finer, in 'Buku-buku catatan harian," July 16–August 16, 1962; Sjahrir on an article "Sosialisme di Mesir," in ibid., August 22, 1963, vol. 4, p. 28.

[166] Sjahrir, "Buku-buku cacatan harian," September 7, 1962.

sovereignty [*kedaulatan*], and to have a government based on democratic techniques, may grow.[167]

The stories about Sjahrir's "leniency" towards Sukarno during this time, and about Sjahrir's "not hating Sukarno" even while he suffered in Sukarno's prison, may appear, in retrospect, as a legend created by Sjahrir's friends, and after Sjahrir died. In his wife's recollections, for instance,

> He was sending messages from prison to his friends to continue with their struggle for the well-being of the people and the nation. "Try to overcome sentiments and a passion of revenge," he urged his friends, whose hearts burned [*berontak*] against the tyranny and unjustice. . . . "We have to think of the fate of the people, that people, who has been suffering for so long. If, suppose, the government should ask for help, you give help, give it wholeheartedly [*dengan ichlas*] and without hate. . . ."[168]

Thus, Mrs. Sjahrir told me, Sjahrir, while in prison, sent Soedjatmoko, his brother-in-law, to Sukarno—"not to get freedom for himself, but to offer help."[169]

Sjahrir might sound confusing even to some of his closest followers, indeed, when, for example in the middle of 1962, he let it be known from prison that

> what had been called the 'Sukarno problem [*masalah Sukarno*]' is over, [and] because of that, it is no use retaining a negative attitude towards Sukarno.[170]

A few months later, Sjahrir argued from prison that "Sukarno is in a blind alley," and he instructed

> PSI-men to help Sukarno in case the possibility opens for such help. Let the PSI-men sacrifice themselves, because only thus may decay be prevented.[171]

In a letter smuggled from prison in mid 1963, Sjahrir advised his followers,

> To work on the strengthening of the general feeling that all the present decline and deterioration is caused by the fact that we have not joined [*turut serta*] in the efforts of the present government, and, more than that, are estranged and made opponents.[172]

"Certainly, our attitude," Sjahrir wrote in the same letter, "can not be that of noncooperation." The letter's mood was set, indeed, by repeating words like "to join in

---

[167] Sjahrir on Finer, ibid., July 16–August 16, 1962.
[168] Manuscript of an article in *Archives Siti Wahjunah Sjahrir*.
[169] Interview with Siti Wahjunah Sjahrir, Jakarta, March 15, 1982.
[170] Anwar, *Sebelum Prahara*, p. 356 (April 5, 1963).
[171] Ibid., pp. 276, 337 (November 13, 1962 and February 28, 1963).
[172] Sjahrir, "Keadaan dan Tugas," in *Sosialisme, Indonesia, Pembangunan*, pp. 210–11.

[*turut*]," "to approach [*mendekati*]," and "to avoid a clash as much as possible [*dengan sebanjak mungkin menghindarkan clash*]."[173]

In April 1963, while in the military hospital in Jakarta, Sjahrir talked to Soedjatmoko about *Deklarasi Ekonomi*, the "Economic Declaration," a new economic program being prepared by the government. According to what Sjahrir was reported by Soedjatmoko to have said, the Economic Declaration was

> a superb [*ulung*] political job by Sukarno.... Sukarno included things demanded by the Indonesian Communist Party ... for instance the whole opening part sounds like the jargon of Aidit.... Neither did Sukarno ignore the wishes of the army.... The Declaration also might be seen as an effort by Sukarno to open himself anew to the West.... The Declaration builds a new space for Sukarno.... Now, Soedjatmoko and his friends should approach and help [*turut membantu*] Soebandrio [by now Sukarno's first deputy] with the follow-up of the Declaration.[174]

Anak Agung, who spent months in Madiun prison together with Sjahrir, wrote and let his wife smuggle letters to Hatta, complaining that "Soedjatmoko, inspired by Sjahrir, believes in phantoms as if they were a reality"; that people in Sjahrir's circle, under Sjahrir's prompting behave as if they might any minute "be called by Sukarno [*dipanggil Boeng Karno*]."[175]

As before, Sjahrir saw the center—and Sukarno's way of power—as "chaotic [*katjau-belau*]," its components "entangled [*simpangsiur*],"[176] and Sukarno himself

---

[173] Ibid., esp. pp. 211–12.

[174] Quoted in Anwar, *Sebelum Prahara*, p. 356 (April 5, 1963). According to Hatta, as he wrote to Anak Agung early in 1964, "In fact, I know, the Economic Declaration originates from Koko[Soedjatmoko]. Soebandrio asked him for proposals for solving the economic problem when efforts by the group of 13 under Djuanda failed. Koko sent two sets of proposals. From this basis emerged what became the Economic Declaration. The plan itself, according to my view, is complete nonsense (*nonsen*). It did not attack the root of the problem, but only the branches." Hatta to Anak Agung, February 10, 1964, in Hatta and Agung, *Surat-menjurat*, p. 34.

[175] Anak Agung to Hatta, August 1964; this quote is from the original draft of the letter Anak Agung showed me in Wassenaar, October 1986. This tone recurs in several letters published later. E.g., Anak Agung to Hatta on February 20, 1964 (Hatta and Agung, *Surat-menjurat*, pp. 28–29) wrote about the "wishful thinking" of Sjahrir's friends; in a letter of June 30, 1964, he wrote about Soedjatmoko "living in the world of daydreaming"(ibid., p. 71); or in the letter of September 28, 1964 (ibid., p. 94), where Anak Agung asked: "How could they—they are not green in politics, they have so many experiences—make interpretations that miss the point so much!" Hatta answered, e.g., by writing: "the analysis by Sjahrir you wrote me about [is] fancy (*angan-angan*)." (Hatta to Anak Agung February 10, 1964.) In the same letter Hatta wondered, "from where is Sjahrir getting the reports," on which he was building all this. In a letter of September 17, 1964, Hatta wrote that he "does not differ" from Anak Agung's view that "Koko inspired by Sjahrir believes in phantoms as if they were reality" especially when behaving as if he might be "called by Sukarno any moment now." (Ibid., p. 91.) On the same issue, see also Lubis, *Cacatatan*, January 27, 1963, p. 221; Lubis describes in that place his conversations with Anak Agung in Madiun prison on the matter. On February 12, 1965, Mochtar Lubis noted in his diary that "several men of the PSI are prepared to sacrifice themselves and to cooperate with Sukarno." (Ibid., p. 337.)

[176] Sjahrir on Herbert Feith in Sjahrir, "Buku-buku cacatan harian."

"stuck [*zit vast*]."[177] But it was almost impossible, now, to discover, in the vision Sjahrir expressed in his prison diaries and other late writing, anything apart from the center. "To call for another general election," Sjahrir wrote to his friends, "is to cry in the middle of a desert."[178] The dynamics, the power, the potential for a change, the future, now seemed to have no other point of reference, but the center and Sukarno. Soedjatmoko told me years later about a talk he had with Sjahrir in prison:

> Sjahrir, occasionally, might be prophetic, indeed. "Sukarno shall end badly," he told me, "and we must be prepared to pick up the pieces."[179]

3. THE DEATH

Late in 1964, the painter Salim, Sjahrir's friend from the 1920s onwards, exhibited his latest works in Gallery M. L. de Boer in Amsterdam. Salim's exhibition was received "enthusiastically" by the Dutch press, and Salim's life was compared with the lives of Jongkind, van Gogh, and van Dongen, "all of whom reached the apex of their career outside the borders of their native countries."[180]

In Indonesia, at the same time, Sukarno had stepped up his all-absorbing revitalization of the revolutionary spirit. Among many actions of the regime, in July 1964, Sukarno's minister of education and culture instructed all the section heads in his ministry no longer to permit "a hair style *à la Beatles*" among the Indonesian youth, and to act strongly against any fashion "not adjusted to the Indonesian identity." Also,

> names like Fransje, Mieke, Mientje, Miesje, and calling one's parents *mammie* or *pappie*, *mammy* or *daddy*, names sweet to Dutchmen and Englishmen, perhaps, but certainly disharmonious to the Indonesian spirit,

were officialy disapproved of.[181]

After a second serious stroke, and the complications which followed, Sjahrir was no more able, by the spring of 1965, to communicate either in speech or in writing. Early in the summer, Poppy Sjahrir arranged for a detailed medical opinion and sent it to Sukarno, with a request that her husband be permitted to go abroad for the treatment not available in Indonesia. Whether because he himself was aging or because he now also believed that Sjahrir was harmless, Sukarno agreed. Only, in the margin of the letter permitting Sjahrir to leave the country, Sukarno, reportedly, added a qualification: "Not to Holland."[182] The choice, then, for some reason, was between Sweden and Switzerland. Mrs. Sjahrir told me that, because she "knew a bit of German," it was to be Switzerland.[183]

---

[177] Quoted in Anwar, *Sebelum Prahara*, p. 225.

[178] Sjahrir, "Tinjauan dalam negeri," in *Sosialisme, Indonesia, Pembangunan*, p. 232.

[179] Interview with Soedjatmoko, Jakarta, November 6, 1987.

[180] Yazir Marzuki, *Pelukis Salim*, p. 57.

[181] Putu Wijaya, "Barat, Timur, Salim," *Majalah Tempo*, September 21, 1974, p. 30; Anwar, *Sebelum Prahara*, p. 81.

[182] The alleged or real original of the document is reproduced as an apprentix to Sutan Sjahrir, *Sosialisme, Indonesia Pembangunan*.

[183] Interview with Siti Wahjunah Sjahrir, Jakarta, November 15, 1987.

No change in Sjahrir's status was required. Switzerland became only another place wherein he was to be restricted.[184] Still a prisoner, or an internee, perhaps, Sjahrir was to travel at government expense. Soebandrio was instructed to get him a diplomatic passport.[185] Sjahrir, his wife, and their two children, left on July 21, 1965, from *Kemayoran* airport in Jakarta. Few friends came to say good-bye, and most of them, on that occasion, saw Sjahrir for the last time.[186] In the words of Mavis Rose:

> No sooner had Sjahrir left than Sukarno himself became seriously ill, a team of Chinese doctors warning that his condition was grave. This medical bulletin seemed to bring to a head [the Communist-army confrontation]....[187]

The apartment prepared for Sjahrir in Switzerland was on the outskirts of Zurich, "quite a nice place, two bedrooms, a living room, a kitchen, a balcony with a view of the lake, rather far away, but visible."[188] There were visitors, family, PSI friends. Idham's wife came; Hamid Algadri stopped by on a business trip to Europe. Soemitro, in exile since the time of the PRRI/Permesta, also came to see Sjahrir. Simatupang came, on his way to the World Congress of Churches, just for a few hours, taking a taxi from the airport:

> We had a dinner and I chatted for a while with *Zus* Pop [Poppy Sjahrir]. Sjahrir could not talk, but we could see that he listened with a great deal of interest to what we were talking about. He also watched television.
> When I was about to leave, *Zus* Pop told Sjahrir to stay at home. But Sjahrir took a coat, a hat and a shawl. Evidently he wanted to go also to see me off. Thus all three of us walked towards a bus stop.
> A picture of Sjahrir who could no longer speak and stood beside *Zus* Pop on the sidewalk as the bus moved on, still sticks in my mind.[189]

Hamid Algadri visited Sjahrir a few days after the "September 30, 1965, affair," when six top army generals were killed, the Indonesian Communist Party was implicated, and the whole system of "guided democracy" was shaken in its fundamentals. "I came to Sjahrir's apartment sometime around October 6," Hamid Algadri recalled,

> there were newspapers all around the place, and Sjahrir was picking up one or several of them at a time, pointing out for me a report, a picture, a commentary. But I could not make out what he really wanted to tell me.[190]

---

[184] *Penpres no.3.thn.1962* stated that Sjahrir should be placed at "suatu tempat tertentu sebagai tempat berdiam sementara dan membawanja kesitu atau melarang untuk sementara orang tersebut bertempat tinggal dalam suatu daerah atau sebagian suatu daerah tertentu dalam wilajah Indonesia." (typescript) *Archives of Siti Wahjunah Sjahrir.*

[185] Thalib, *Karya dan tjita*, p. 5.

[186] Maria Ullfah, "Bung Sjahrir" in *Mengenang Sjahrir,* ed. Anwar, p. 95; interview with Maria Ullfah, Jakarta, March 4, 1982; Anwar, *Sebelum Prahara*, pp. 523–25 (July 21, 1965).

[187] Rose, *Indonesia Free*, p. 204.

[188] Interview with Siti Wahjunah Sjahrir, Jakarta, October 10, 1987; also J. H. W. Veenstra, "Sutan Sjahrir. Het leven van het slachtoffer," *Vrij Nederland,* April 16, 1966.

[189] Simatupang, "Apa arti Sutan Sjahrir," pp. 193–94; interview with Simatupang, Jakarta, January 4, 1987.

[190] Interview with Hamid Algadri, Jakarta, December 13, 1987.

On March 11, 1966, Sukarno, gravely compromised by his real or alleged complicity in the September 30 affair, gave in "effectively, though not formally";[191] a new leader, army general Suharto, de facto stepped into Sukarno's place. Poppy was in the kitchen, and Sjahrir was watching German television as usual, when the news about the Indonesian "new coup d'etat" came in:

> Sjahrir ran to the kitchen, took my hand hurrying me to the television set so that I could hear the rest of the news. He certainly was very excited. And he certainly tried very much to tell me something. What exactly, I could not be sure of.[192]

He watched the television, read the newspapers, listened to the radio, Mrs. Sjahrir says, "till the last moment." The last moment came a few weeks after the events just described, in April 1966. Signs of extremely high blood pressure made Poppy rush Sjahrir to the Zurich hospital. Doctors diagnosed a brain hemorrhage, and gave no hope. Sjahrir was seven days in a coma. Poppy stayed two days in the hospital, then went home, but she could not sleep: there were long-distance telephone calls all night; it was daytime in Indonesia, and people were curious. She went to stay in the hospital again, and there, on April 9, she witnessed her husband's quiet end.[193]

The funeral of Sjahrir, in a way, is still a part of this story. It was a curious affair, a mixture of tragedy and farce, sadness and triumph, and irony, most of all. Perhaps this was how a *perantau*'s return to his homeland should properly happen.

A medical bulletin about Sjahrir, published in Jakarta on April 3, took great pains to explain Sjahrir's whereabouts over the last several years. This made sense, because, besides occasional rumors which, moreover, had not spread very far, it was the first time the Indonesian public learned that Sjahrir had been arrested four years previously and, for the matter, that he was still alive. Some of those, who might have been able to tell more about Sjahrir's last years—Subadio, Mohamad Roem, Anak Agung, Mochtar Lubis, who was arrested later—were still in prison when the news came. What had happened several times before in the Republic's history, happened again: Roem, at least, recalled that they first heard the news of Sjahrir's death on *Radio Nederland* from Hilversum.[194]

On the morning of April 15, 1966, six days after Sjahrir died, the Indonesian state radio, press, and television broadcast a presidential decree signed by Sukarno, who was still formally in office. The decree was dated the day of Sjahrir's death.

> In connection with services he rendered to the State and Nation through his life, either as a leader of the national movement in colonial times, or as the

---

[191] Legge, *Sukarno*, p. 403.

[192] Interview with Siti Wahjunah Sjahrir, Jakarta, March 15, 1982.

[193] Ibid.

[194] Roem, "Tragedi Schermerhorn dan Sjahrir," *Budaya Jaya* 10, 111 (August 1977): 457; Lubis. *Cacatan Subversif*, April 10, 1966, p. 471; also Lubis, "Pejuang, pemikir dan peminat," p. 213. Already in April 1965, it was rumored that Sjahrir had died. According to the rumors, Minister Leimena even, amidst the confusion, sent flowers and a note of consolation to Sjahrir's wife. Ibid., April 3, 1965, p. 350.

prime minister of the republican cabinets at the time of the physical revolution,

the presidential decree declared Sjahrir a "national hero," and ordered for him a state funeral with full honors.[195]

At the same time "An Opinion by General A. H. Nasution" was published, declaring:

> The name and merits of Sjahrir can not be separated from the history of our revolution. As far as the steps taken against Sjahrir by the government in the last years are concerned, these were "security measures taken by the Supreme Military Administrator during the time of the West Irian campaign, and after the State of War and Siege [Staat van Oorlog en Beleg] was lifted, through the extraordinary powers of the President, Supreme Commander, Great Leader of the Revolution, and on the basis of the presidential decree carried out by the Attorney General."
>
> In this case, the Supreme Military Administrator, as far as I know, did not find any proof of [Sjahrir's] wrongdoing.[196]

"We got a letter in Zurich," Mrs Sjahrir told me during an interview in Jakarta in 1987,

> when Sjahrir died, from Minister Dr. Leimena, who was to be the funeral's "Inspector," that Sjahrir had been made a hero, and asking if we agreed to the state funeral. We both—Soedjatmoko, who came to Zurich during Sjahrir's last days, and I—cried. What a change, a few days ago a prisoner, and now a hero![197]

Soedjatmoko, at the same time, a few hours after Sjahrir's death, wrote to George Kahin from Zurich:

> In a very real sense I realize that his failure in politics really signifies his greatness as a man and a human being... his death, now at this stage of Indonesian history, dramatizes the values that he has tried to uphold, even at the cost of continued [loss of] political power.[198]

Poppy agreed to the state funeral.[199] Besides the state committee, Sjahrir's friends organized a private "Committee for Sjahrir's Burial": Jusuf Jahja was its chairman, Rosihan Anwar served as spokesman, Dr. Soedarsono, Maria Ullfah Subadio, Ali Boediardjo, Sudarpo Sastrosatomo, Wibowo, Dr. A. Halim, Hamid Algadri,

---

[195] Anwar, ed., *Perdjalanan terachir*, p. 33. It may be mentioned that Tan Malaka had also become a "national hero," three years before Sjahrir, and also through a presidential decree by Sukarno (No.53/1963). Jarvis, ed., *From Jail to Jail*, 1: cxxvii. (Later he seems to have been again removed from this position.)

[196] Salim, ed., *Bung Sjahrir*, p. 60.

[197] Interview with Siti Wahjunah Sjahrir, Jakarta, November 15, 1987.

[198] Letter from Soedjatmoko to Kahin, Zurich April 10 (?), 1966

[199] Interview with Siti Wahjunah Sjahrir, Jakarta, November 15, 1987.

Djuir Mohammad, Idham, Sutan Sjahsam, Ali Sjahrir, Achmad Fauzy, Sjahrul, Muher, and Omar Tusin were the committee's members.[200]

Some people from Egypt called and, with representatives of the Moslem community in Switzerland, asked for permission to perform Moslem rites for the dead: the ceremonies took place in a special room in the Zurich hospital.[201] Then, Sjahrir's remains were taken on the plane, and his journey back east led first through Holland. "We gathered at the airport, a few Indonesian and Dutch friends," Beb Vuyk wrote in Sjahrir's obituary.[202] Schermerhorn spoke over the coffin: "Sjahrir and I are friends in defeat," he said.[203] Then, through Frankfurt, Cairo, and Bangkok, first on a KLM plane and then on a plane of Indonesian *Garuda* airlines, the party reached Jakarta, *Kemayoran* airport, on April 17.[204]

In the photos taken upon arrival, there is the coffin covered with the Indonesian flag, a small crowd at the plane, Soedjatmoko, and a terribly pale Poppy with the children. From the airport they went to Sjahrir's house on *Tjokroaminoto* 61. There, "on initiative of the members of the family living in Jakarta"—probably Sjahrizal Djoehana, Sjahrir's sister and Noer Alamsjah, Sjahrir's brother—a night of Moslem prayers, *malam tahlilan*, was performed by the dead body.[205]

The next morning, the young people supporting the new regime of the army and general Suharto, the organizations KAMI and KAPPI, built a small "symbolic barricade" in front of the house of mourning. The placard on the barricade read: "Our Father St. Sjahrir Departed From This World." *Tjokroaminoto* street was closed to traffic. Yellow jackets and yellow caps, the color of the University of Indonesia, prevailed (according to one foreign observer they seemed to be the symbol now as *pici*, the black velvet caps, and *bambu runcing*, the sharpened bamboo spears, were the youth symbols during the 1920s and the Revolution of 1945).[206]

One hour before noon, a van stopped in front of the house, and a small group of prisoners from *Keagungan* Street—let out only for the occasion and instantly returned behind bars after the ceremony ended—stepped out and entered the house to pay homage to Sjahrir:

> An old teakwood easy chair was ceremoniously brought into the house by the youth of the "1966 Generation," the easy chair Sjahrir used to sit in, while in prison, during afternoons, to read and to listen to the radio.[207]

By order of the government, for the three days following April 18, flags were to be flown at half-mast. According to Rosihan Anwar, the spokesman for the Commit-

---

[200] *Antara* quoted in Anwar ed., *Perdjalanan terachir*, p. 31.

[201] Interview with Siti Wahjunah Sjahrir, Jakarta March 15, 1982.

[202] Beb Vuyk "In memoriam Soetan Sjahrir, *Trouw*, April 16, 1966; also Beb Vuyk, "Mengenang Sjahrir" in *Mengenang Sjahrir*, ed. Anwar, p. 271.

[203] Quoted in Roem, "Tragedi Schermerhorn dan Sjahrir," p. 457; Anwar, ed., *Perdjalanan terachir*, p. 30.

[204] Interview with B. M. Diah, who was, at the moment of Sjahrir's death, Indonesian Ambassador in Bangkok, Jakarta, December 8, 1987.; Salim, ed., *Bung Sjahrir*, p.48

[205] Anwar, ed., *Perdjalanan terachir*, p. 30; Roem, "Tragedi Schermerhorn dan Sjahrir," p. 457.

[206] Douglas, *Political Socialization and Student Activism in Indonesia*, p. 180.

[207] Salim, ed., *Bung Sjahrir*, p. 50; on the prisoners from *Jalan Keagungan* being present see also Lubis, *Cacatan Subversif*, April 19, 1966, pp. 478–81.

tee for Sjahrir's Burial, 250,000 people attended the funeral procession; the correspondent for the *Washington Star* estimated the crowd at "more than 90,000."[208] Reportedly, the front of the funeral procession had already reached the cemetery in the *Kalibata* outskirts of Jakarta, while the last people in the procession were still near the *Hotel Indonesia*, in the city's center. "I do not think that Jakarta has ever seen so many people accompanying a dead body," Anak Agung wrote.[209] In another opinion offered at the time, it was "the biggest crowd since October 5, when they buried the six generals."[210] In yet another view, it was something comparable only to the funeral of Mohammad Hoesni Thamrin, in 1939, except that "then the thousands walked to the cemetery, and now they rode in cars."[211]

This was a comment by Soewarsih Djojopoespito:

> Flowers and flower petals were spread from a helicopter.... A funeral like for a hero, like for a king, carefully organized. Why had nobody raised a voice to get this man free?

"We followed far behind the convoy of cars," Soewarsih wrote,

> in a microbus, old people, his friends and comrades, sixteen altogether, old, rheumatic, full of memories of the dead, silent and depressed. It was a very long line of cars, jeeps and buses....[212]

As the guard of honor with the coffin arrived at the cemetery, a heavy rain started. "To Indonesians," a foreign observer explained to his readers, "this was a blessing by God onto Sutan Sjahrir. *Rachmat tuhan* they call it...."[213] The open grave as prepared, adjoined the graves of the six generals killed eight months previously.

> "Inspector" for the ceremony, presidium chairman Dr. Leimena offered a wreath on behalf of the government. Other wreaths were presented by general Suharto, the Sultan of Jogjakarta and Dr. Hatta, and all the wreaths brought rippling murmurs of appreciation from the crowd.[214]

Afterwards, flowers from the family were placed on the casket; Mahroezar, the younger brother of Sjahrir, is seen in pictures, at that moment.[215] The music corps of the Jakarta army command played *Gugur Bunga*, "Fallen Blossom." Speeches were read:

---

[208] Anwar, ed., *Perdjalanan terachir*, p. 62; *Washington Star*, April 20, 1966 quoted in ibid.

[209] Anak Agung, "Reminiscences" (typescript); *Archive of Siti Wahjunah Sjahrir*, n.p.

[210] Harry Goldberg, "In Memoriam Sutan Sjahrir," typescript, p.1. *Archives of Siti Wahjunah Sjahrir*.

[211] I. J. Kasimo, "Bung Kecil dalam pandangan saya," in *Mengenang Sjahrir*, pp. 173–74.

[212] Soewarsih Djojopoespito, "De thuiskomst van een oud-strijder," p. 44.

[213] Mary Vance Trent, Jakarta 1966 (typescript), *Archive Siti Wahjunah Sjahrir*.

[214] Ibid.

[215] Salim, ed., *Bung Sjahrir*, p. 51.

Hatta Speaking at Sjahrir's Grave

Hatta, who had not spoken in public since his resignation in 1956, delivered an oration pointing out that the first prime minister of Indonesia had "died a victim of tyranny."[216]

"Our microbus finally moved forward," we read further from Soewarsih's recollections,

> but when we arrived at the cemetery, it was almost seven, and it was dark even when the rain did stop for a while. Many cars were already on their way back. It made no sense still to try to see the grave.[217]

---

[216] Harold A. Crouch, *The Army and Politics in Indonesia* (Ithaca: Cornell University Press, 1978), p. 370. Anak Agung in his letter to Hatta sent on April 12, 1966, suggested that Hatta's speech would be "something like what, in the time of ancient Greece, the speech of Pericles was above the grave of a friend (known as a *Funeral Oration*)." (The italicized words were in English. Hatta and Agung, *Surat-menjurat*, p. 417.
[217] Soewarsih Djojopoespito, "De thuiskomst."

EPILOGUE: ON MEMORY

One is reminded of what Jacques de Kadt once wrote, and what was quoted above, that it has always been very difficult to find a good photograph of Sjahrir. Sjahrir is remembered in contemporary Indonesia. Men and women on the streets of Jakarta, Bandung, Yogyakarta, or Bukittinggi, wherever I have tried this, still late in the 1980s reacted in a lively way to Sjahrir's name, as lively, in fact, as to no other political name of the past, perhaps except that of a local leader and of Hatta and Sukarno. Many of the common people (one tends to talk on the street most frequently to tradesmen, naturally) might say first that he was "a Padang man," by which they mean a Minangkabau; in most cases, they would locate his name in the time of Revolution. The memory of the gigantic funeral, a "shock of recognition," as one Westerner has called it,[1] seems to make many of the men on the street somehow identify Sjahrir with the six generals killed in 1965. Several of the people I talked to even believed that he was one of the life-size bronze figures on the generals' monument standing now in Jakarta.

Sjahrir remains misplaced. He became the only one of the Big Three of the Revolution—after all the marginality he had lived through—who was buried at the center-stage, state-heroes' cemetery. Neither Sukarno nor Hatta lies there. Hatta, at the time of Sjahrir's funeral reportedly told Sjahrizal Djoehana, Sjahrir's sister, that he would never let anybody do this to him.[2] Hatta also made it public, shortly after Sjahrir's funeral, that he wanted his grave to be in his "homeland," which was Minangkabau, "at a cemetery for common people."[3] Sukarno, when he died in 1970, four years after Sjahrir and ten years before Hatta, was permited by the new regime only a private grave, in Blitar, East Java, thus also in "his homeland."

Children's books were written about Sjahrir after his death. One of them, published in 1986, tells Indonesian children learning English:

> Oom Sjahrir became the first prime minister of Indonesia and was prime minister three times. But he had his sad days too. In 1966 Oom Sjahrir got very sick. By that time he was married and had two children of his own. He was taken to Switzerland. There he died on April 9, 1966, at the age of fifty-seven. He was buried by the Indonesian government in the Kalibata Nation-

---

[1] Harry Goldberg, "In Memoriam Sutan Sjahrir," typescript, p. 4; *Archives of Siti Wahjunah Sjahrir.*

[2] Interview with Sjahrizal Djuhana, Bandung, March 7, 1982.

[3] Hatta, *Bung Hatta Antwoordt*, p. 194.

al Cemetery in Jakarta. He was named one of the Indonesian National Heroes.[4]

There are some streets in Indonesia that bear Sjahrir's name—one street in Ujung Pandang, Sulawesi, as far as I know, another, a very nice street in Jakarta, close to the place where he last lived. There used to be one Sjahrir Street in Padang Panjang, West Sumatra, Sjahrir's birthplace, but its name was later changed. There is no place with Sjahrir's name where it might be expected most, in Bandung.[5]

Rumors about the "PSI conspiracy" were also kept alive. Why were the PSI-men "in love with plotting [*gandrung pada makar*]," a confidential white paper asked in the early 1970s—a document circulated first at cabinet level, and later published in a slightly revised form.[6] There were, so the publisher complained, several vaguely explained delays, before a posthumous volume of Sjahrir's writing, on July 15, 1967, was eventually cleared for publication by the Indonesian Attorney General.[7]

In contrast to the PSI, however, the dead Sjahrir is, by and large, absolved by the authorities. Sjahrir's failure in politics, indeed, signifies his greatness. Or, expressed in a slightly different way, in the political memory of present Indonesia, "Sjahrir is a forgotten statesman."

More than a quarter of a century after his death, Sjahrir's admirers remain loyal. "The curious thing is," a friend wrote me in 1982, "that only Sjahrir and Sukarno have genuine 'cults' among the political public." Indeed, whenever I interviewed the group, there was always a copy of *Indonesische Overpeinzingen*, either in the Dutch original or in Indonesian translation, an ancient copy of *Daulat Ra'jat* or *Perdjoeangan Kita* on the shelf and ready. They seemed to be able to quote from the right places.

Sjahrir's photographs hung on the walls in the rooms where my interviews took place. The aging survivors of Sjahrir's circle, so they told me, were still in contact with the younger generations, and I, in fact, also met some of these younger people. It is tempting for a biographer to think that his hero—and thus his story—might reach beyond the hero's physical death. In the case of Sjahrir, however, the legends and myths seem to be made out of immediate contacts, actual living together. In all probability, they will not last after the generation who knew Sjahrir personally passes away. A process, which, as I am writing, is already well under way.

I was repeatedly advised, by Subadio Sastrosatomo, Poppy Sjahrir, Listyo, or Soedjatmoko when he still lived, that in my search for Sjahrir I had to visit Banda Neira. It became a place of pilgrimage—they themselves used the term—for Sjahrir's admirers after Sjahrir died. Hatta went to Banda Neira, in 1972. He wanted it to be a private visit, but the local government made it very official.[8] Virtually all the well-known former-PSI men and women, who could put that amount of money together,

---

[4] M. Budianta, *Sjahrir and the Children of Banda Neira* (Jakarta: Gramedia, 1986), p. 26.

[5] To make the last reference to Tan Malaka in this story, also in his case "no monuments or highways bear his name: I have [Helen Jarvis writes] found only an alleyway in South Jakarta and a back street in Padang." Jarvis, ed., *From Jail to Jail*, 1: cxxvii.

[6] Marzuki Arifin, *Peristiwa 15 Januari 1974* (Jakarta: Indonesia, 1974); Donald K. Emmerson. *Indonesia's Elite: Political Culture and Cultural Politics* (Ithaca: Cornell University Press 1976), pp. 253–54.

[7] Introduction to Sutan Sjahrir, *Sosialisme, Indonesia, Pembangunan*, p. vi.

[8] Siti Wahjunah Sjahrir, "Bung Hatta, beberapa catatan," in *Bung Hatta*, ed. Swasono, p. 484.

have visited Banda Neira at one point or other during the last more than two decades.

Des Alwi, Sjahrir's adopted son from Banda Neira, has been very much the person behind the pilgrimage. He returned to Banda Neira in 1970, built a house there "comparable to the planters' homes around." Out of the old Baadillah mansion where Sjahrir lived with the children, Des Alwi made a museum. He started his own *Merpati Airlines*, which fly twice a week between Ambon and Banda Neira with a good connection to Jakarta. He built two small hotels in the place.[9]

Des Alwi feels that he is acting as a true Bandanese son of Sjahrir—that his business is truly done in the spirit of dynamism and pragmatism that Sjahrir had always preached so well. Des Alwi feels, too, that by helping to rehabilitate Banda Neira through the development of tourism he is opening the place to the world as Sjahrir always would like it to be opened. Des Alwi pointed out to me, and he was correct in this, that some of the island's inhabitants even call him *raja Banda*, "the king of Banda."

Des Alwi also moved into the movie business, and he has made a feature film on Banda Neira among other things. The movie is called *Cucu*, "Grandson," and is about a boy, who returns home from overseas to salvage an heirloom (*harta warisan*) which his grandfather had left, and bad people have stolen. The principal role in the movie is played by Des Alwi's twelve-year old son; thus, by Sjahrir's grandson.[10]

One of the small islands off Banda Neira, the one, in fact, where Sjahrir used to have picnics with his Bandanese children, is now called *Sjahrir*. Another island nearby is *Hatta*. According to one of Des Alwi's info folders:

> Visitors staying in either *Maulana Inn* or *Laguna Inn* can rent airtanks, weightbells, some scuba gear, diveboats, speedboats etc. At Neira one can dive at *Malele Beach*, *Tanah Rata* and in front of the *V.O.C.* governor palace. . . . *Sjahrir* island is a very good place for more professionally minded divers, but the best diving areas are at *Hatta*.[11]

Memory travels curious paths. And it is perhaps right that it should end in nostalgia, a farce, a myth, and a forgetting. This may be culturally inevitable. Culture, perhaps, in order to survive, should remain opaque. This may, indeed, be the noblest task of a *perantau*, too: to test the way, to cross the borders, to be exposed, emulated or ridiculed, misunderstood and forgotten, so that new innocents may be born to the culture, and the same way may be foolishly tried again.

---

[9] Siegel and Tsuchiya Kenji, "Invincible Kitsch or As Tourists in the Age of Des Alwi"; interview with Des Alwi, Jakarta, December 3, 1987. See also Hanna, *Kepulauan Banda*, pp. 144–45.

[10] Interview with Des Alwi, Jakarta, December 3, 1987.

[11] *Maulana Inn Tourist Folder* (Jakarta: P.T.Avisarti Corporation), n.d., n.p

BIBLIOGRAPHY

1. DOCUMENTS IN THE ALGEMEEN RIJKSARCHIEF, THE HAGUE

Ministerie van Koloniën (Ministerie van Overzeese Gebiedsdelen, Minog)

Correspondence, reports, and minutes organized as "Verbaal," "Secret Verbaal," "Mail Report," or "Secret Mail Report."

Memorie van Overgave

S. van der Plas (Sumatra's East Coast, July 2, 1917); H. J. Grijzen (Sumatra's East Coast, February 1921); C. J. van Kempen (Sumatra's East Coast, September 10, 1928); G. F. E. Gongryp (Sumatra's West Coast, December 31, 1934); van Suchtelen (Sumatra's East Coast, April 17, 1936).

Politiek-politioneel overzichten van Nederlandsch-Indië (1927–1938)

Archieven Procureur-Generaal bij het Hooggerechtshof van Nederlandsch-Indië

Archieven Algemene Secretarie te Batavia

Private Papers

J. W. Meyer Ranneft, E. Gobée, Jhr. B. C. de Jonge, Ch. O. van der Plas, H. J. van Mook, Warners, W. Schermerhorn, A. S. Pinke, P. J. Koets, P. Sanders, H. N. Boon, L. J. M. Beel, S. H. Spoor, Romme, C. J. van Kempen

2. DOCUMENTS ELSEWHERE

Archief van de Sectie Krijgsgeschiedenis, Hoofdkwartier van de Koninklijke Landmacht. MS SEAC (The Hague)

Archief van het Ministerie van Buitenlandse Zaken (The Hague)

Indonesië in de V. R.; Ambassade Brussel, 1948; Ambassade Parijs, 1945–1951; Ambassade Chungking-Nanking, 1948; Inlichtingen Sjahrir

Private Papers

Nishijima Collection (Tokyo-Jakarta), Archives Siti Wahjunah Sjahrir (Jakarta), Archives "Gedung Pemuda" (Jakarta), Archives George McT. Kahin (Ithaca, NY), Nehru Smarag (New Delhi)

3. MAJOR INTERVIEWS

Paramita Abdurrachman, Ali Algadri, Hamid Algadri, Ali Boediardjo, Burhanuddin, Des Alwi, B. M. Diah, Mohammad Akbar Djoehana, Prof. Dr. R. Muh. Wiradikarta Djoehana, Sjahrizal Djoehana, Go Gieu Tjwan, Hamdani, Suzanna Hamdani, Hazil Tanzil, Idham, Kartamuhari, Listyo, Aboe Bakar Loebis, Mochtar Loebis, Hans van Marle, Jossine W. L. Meijer, Miral Manan, Shizuo Miyamoto (letter), Moerad, Murwoto, Mohammad Natsir, Shigetada Nishijima (letter), Jos Riekerk, Roestam Anwar, H. Rosihan Anwar, Mohammad H. Said(letter), Yusuf Said, Shizuo Saito(letter), Salim, Leon Salim, Sastra, Maruli T.

Silitonga, T. B. Simatupang, L. M. Sitoroes, Maria Duchâteau Sjahrir, Siti Wahjunah Sjahrir, Violet Hanifah Sjahroezah, Minarsih(Mien) Soedarpo-Wiranatakoesoema, Soedarpo Sastrosatomo, Subadio Sastrosatomo, Soedjatmoko, Lily Gamar Sutantio, S. Takdir Alisjahbana, Judith Tas, M. L. Tobing, Maria Ullfah Soebadio, Usman Gunadi, Beb Vuyk.

4. BIBLIOGRAPHY OF SJAHRIR'S WRITING

"De vervolgingen in Indonesië: het proces Soekarno c.s.," *De Socialist*, November 8, 1930, p. 6.

"Het vonnis van Bandoeng: Een rede van kam. Sjahrir," ibid., January 30, 1931, pp. 12–14.

"De vernietiging der PNI: Het slotstuk," ibid., April, 24, 1931.

(Sidi). "De Indonesische beweging op een dood punt: De outweg," *De Nieuwe Weg* 6 (August 1931): 237–40.

(Sy.). "Sekedar tentang azas, taktik dan strategie perdjoeangan kita," *Daulat Ra'jat* 1, 3, October 10, 1931.

"Kaoem intellectueel dalam doenia politik Indonesia," ibid., 1, 6, November 10, 1931.

(Sd.). "Konperensi Medja Boendar di Londen," ibid., 1, 7, November 20, 1931.

"'Schorsing' Mohammad Hatta," ibid., 1, 9, December 10, 1931.

(not signed). "Faham persatoen didalam strategi dan taktik perdjoeangan, I: sepandjang strategie," ibid., 1, 14, January 30, 1932.

"Faham persatoen didalam strategi dan taktik: sepandjang taktik I," ibid., 1, 15, February 10, 1932.

"Faham persatoen didalam strategi dan taktik: sepandjang taktik II," ibid., 2, 16, February 20, 1932.

(not signed). "Barisan persatoean baru: eenheidsfront," ibid., 2, 17, February 29, 1932.

(not signed). "Kapital dan boeroeh di Deli," ibid., 2, 26, May 30, 1932.

"Pertjobaan atas PNI: Penangkapan! Penggrebegian! Saudara-saudara Djawoto, Semeo dan Hadimoeljo didalam Tahanan!" ibid., 3, 49, January 20, 1933.

(Sj-h). "Perdjoeangan kita dalam pengertian perdjoeangan Sosialistis Oemoem," ibid., 3, 55, March 20, 1933.

Pergerakan Sekerdja. Batavia: Daulat Ra'jat, 1933.

"Vaderlandsche Club-Swadeshi-Soekarno," ibid., 3, 66, July 10, 1933 (reprinted in *Menjala* 2, 21–22, [July 1933]).

"Pergerakan Indonesia Menoempoeh saat jang penting," ibid.

('S' dated Bukit Tinggi, July 1933), "Djalan dan toedjoean dalam perdjoeangan," ibid., 3, 67, July 20, 1933.

(Sj). "Pengaroeh Psychologis dalam pergerakan haroes disingkirkan," ibid., 3, 73, September 20, 1933.

(Sj-h). "Sekedar tentang so'al kapitalisme," ibid., 3, 74, September 30, 1933.

(Sj). "Boeroeh dimasa ini," ibid.

(Sj-h). "Djerman dan volkenbod," ibid., 3, 76, October 20, 1933.

(Sj-h.). "Reformisme, opportunisme dan radikalisme," ibid., 3, 79, November 20, 1933.

(Sj-H.). "Strategie dan taktik perdjoeangan," ibid., 3, 80, December 10, 1933.

(Sj-H.). "Soal persatoean," ibid., 3, 81, December 10, 1933.

and Soebagio. "De honderdvijftig vraagstukken," *Secret Mail Report 1934*, no. 300.

(not signed). "Friedrich Engels: Soeatoe biograpfie dikarang oleh Gustav Mayer," *Ilmoe dan Masjarakat* 1, 1 (September 1936).

"Friedrich Engels dan zaman kita," *Ilmoe dan Masjarakat* 1, 3 (November 1936).

"In de schaduwen van Morgen (Dikarang oleh Huizinga)," *Ilmoe dan Masjarakat* 1, 4 (December 1936).

(S. van de Garde). "Friedrich Engels en Onze Tijd: Een verdediging der dialektiek," *De Nieuwe Kern* 3, 1936–1937, pp. 136–45.

(not signed). "Samenwerking tusschen Nederland en Nederlandsch Indië," (March 1938), *Secret verbaal 20 December 1939–I55*.

"Kesoesasteraan dan Rakjat (Banda Neira, May 1938)," *Poedjangga Baroe (nomor peringatan 1933–1939)* 7, 1 (July 1939); reprinted in Sutan Sjahrir. *Pikiran dan Perdjoeangan*. Jakarta: Poestaka Rakjat, 1947, pp. 79–90.

"Kritiek dan oekoeran J. E. Tatengkens (Neira, June 1939)" ibid., pp. 10–16.

"Brief aan een broer (Banda Neira, November 7, 1941)," *Criterium* no. 8/9 (August/September 1947): 469–78.

Perdjoeangan Kita. Jakarta: Pertjetakan Republiek Indonesia, 1945.

"Before the Mike," *Voice of Free Indonesia* 3, December 1945 (also *Inzicht* 1,2, January 26, 1946).

(Sjahrazad). *Indonesische Overpeinzingen*. Amsterdam: De Bezige Bij, 1945.

Onze Strijd. Amsterdam: Vrij Nederland, 1946.

Mendirikan Negara Kerakjatan dalam Revolusi Kerkjatan (Pidato diutjapkan pada pembukaan konperensi Pamong Pradja di Solo. (February 7, 1946) Yogyakarta: Kemper, 1950 (2nd edition) (also in *Inzicht* 1, 2, February 16, 1946).

"Political Purification in Indonesia," *The Voice of Free Indonesia* 25, July 13, 1946.

"Rede van Premier uitgesproken op de 18de Agustus 1946 voor Radio Indonesia te Djakarta," *Inzicht* 1, 31, August 17, 1946.

"Adakah kolaborasi di Indonesia?" *Sadar*, November 5, 1946.

"Radiorede," (November 19, 1946) *Dagblad*, November 20, 1946.

"Pidato P. M. Sutan Sjahrir disidang KNIP, Malang 1947," typescript in *Archives Siti Wahjunah Sjahrir*.

Renungan Indonesia. Translated by H. B. Jassin. Jakarta: Poestaka Rakjat, (May) 1947.

"Speech by Sjahrir," *Security Council Official Record*, 2nd year, 184th meeting, August 14, 1947, pp. 2002–2003.

"Speech by Sjahrir," Security Council Official Record, 2nd year, 187th meeting, August 19, 1947, p. 2075.

"Speech by Sjahrir for the Asian Relations Organization, New Delhi, November 25, 1947," typescript in *Archives Siti Wahjunah Sjahrir* (for a slightly different version: "Press release," in *Archief Buiten. Zaken: "Inlichtingen Sjahrir"*).

Pikiran dan Perdjoeangan. Jakarta: Poestaka Rakjat, 1947.

Pergerakan Sekerdja Sarekat Boeroeh (re-edition of *Pergerakan Sekerdja* of 1933). Yogyakarta: Badan Penerangan Poesat SBPI, 1947.

Interviews with George McT. Kahin (Batavia/Jakarta, July 27 and August 1, 1948; Yogyakarta, September 30 and November 21, 1948; Batavia/Jakarta, February 15 and 26 and April 19, 1949. *Archives of George McT. Kahin*.

"Indonesia in the Future," translation of a text written for *Sikap*, February 14, 1948. *Archives of George McT. Kahin*.

"Political Conditions in Indonesia. Written at the beginning of 1948" (March 1948), typescript in *Archives of George McT. Kahin*.

"17 Agustus," *Sikap* 1, 1, August 17, 1948.

"Nasionalisme dan Internasionalisme," *Siasat*, August 22, 1948.

"Usaha luar negeri," *Sikap* 1, 4, September 8, 1948.

"Urusan luar negeri," ibid., 1, 5, September 15, 1948.

Out of Exile. (Translated by Charles Wolf Jr.) New York: John Day, 1949.

"Membangun Negara didalam dunia jang runtuh," *Sikap* 2, 5, February 12, 1949.

"Soal kerakjatan," *Sikap* 3, 12, December 27, 1950.

"1 Mei 1951," *Suara Sosialis* 3, 8, May 1, 1951.

Typescript of travel diaries, 1951, in *Archives of Siti Wahjunah Sjahrir*.

"Pidato pembukaan pada kongres ke-1 PSI di Bandung" (February 12, 1952), *Suara Sosialis* 4, 2, April 15, 1952.

"Sedikit Pemandangan Tentang Kongres Kita," ibid.

"Perajaan Mei Dulu dan Sekarang," ibid., 4, 3–4, June 15, 1952.

"Sosialisme di Eropa Barat," part I, *Suara Sosialis* 12 (November 1952); part II, ibid. 13 (December 1952); part III, ibid. 14 (January 1953).

"Kesulitan-kesulitan dalam masa peralihan sekarang dititik dari sudut sosiologi," *Symposion tentang kesulitan-kesulitan zaman peralihan sekarang* (1953), pp. 13–38, 75–80.

"Pengaruh suratkabar atas Bahasa kita dewasa ini," *Pedoman*, November 28, 1953.

"Sosialisme di negeri kita," *Suara Sosialis* 6, 2, February 12, 1954.

"1 Mei 1955," ibid., 7, 4–5, May 1, 1955.

"Internationalisme dalam adjaran dan gerakan sosialis," *Pedoman Sosialis* 1, 1 (June 1955), pp. 5–11.

"Kongres kita jang ke-II," *Suara Sosialis* 7, 7–8, July 25, 1955.

In *Wawantjara dengan Tokoh-tokoh oleh Star Weekly* (August 13, 1955).

"17 Agustus 1955," *Sikap* 8, 28–29, August 15–22, 1955.

"Pemilihan Umum untuk Konstituante," ibid., 8, 40, December 5, 1955.

(Realpolitieker). "Pemilihan Umum jang Pertama di Indonesia," *Suara Sosialis* 8, 1, January 7, 1956.

"Menghadapi Keadaan Baru," *Sikap* 9, 16, April 16, 1956.

"Problems the country faces," *Atlantic* 107, 6 (June 1956).

Indonesian Socialism. Rangoon: Asian Socialist Publishing House, 1956.

Nationalism and Internationalism. Rangoon: Asian Socialist Publishing House, 1956.

"Sosialisme sekarang" (Bombay, November 6, 1956) published in five parts in *Sikap* 10, 1 (January 9, 1957); 10, 2 (January 16, 1957); 10, 3 (January 23, 1957; 10, 4 (January 30, 1957; 10, 5 (February 6, 1957).

"Masa depan sosialisme kerakjatan," *Sikap* 10, 7, February 20, 1957.

"Sosialisme," *Bunga Rampai Sosialisme Kerakjatan*. Jakarta: Dewan Pimpinan Pusat Gerakan Mahasiswa Sosialis, 1957, pp. 9–17.

Sosialisme dan Pimpinan; tjeramah dalam peringatan Dies Natalis Gerakan Mahasiswa Sosialis di Bandung, tgl.16 Oktober 1957. Jakarta: Sekretariat Dewan Partai, 1957 (also in *Sikap* 10, 35; 11, 36 and 38, November 7, 14, and 28, 1957).

"Keadaan negara kita dewasa ini," *Suara Sosialis* 9, 11 (December/January 1958).

"PSI Sepuluh Tahun," *Pedoman*, February 12, 1958.

"Ulang Tahun ke–10 Partai Sosialis Indonesia," *Suara Sosialis* 10, 1–2 (February–March 1958).

"Hadji Agus Salim Sebagain Diplomat" in Salam Solichin. *Hadji Agus Salim: Hidup dan Perdjuangannja*. Jakarta: Djajamuri, 1961, pp. 19–22.

"Buku-buku cacatan harian" (variously dated, Madiun, 1962–1963) in *Archives Siti Wahjunah Sjahrir*.

"Tinjauan Buku" (variously dated, Madiun 1962–1963, Jakarta, 1963–1964, parts I, II, and III) in *Archives Siti Wahjunah Sjahrir*.

"Tinjauan dalam negeri" [1964], in Sutan Sjahrir. *Sosialisme, Indonesia, Pembangunan: Kumpulan Tulisan*. Jakarta: Lembaga Penunjang Pembangunan Nasional, 1982, pp. 213-35.

Sosialisme dan Marxisme: Suatu kritik terhadap Marxisme. Jakarta: Djambatan, 1967.

Nasionalisme dan Internasionalisme. Jakarta: Panitia Persiapan Yayasan Sjahrir, 1968.

Our Struggle (Translated with an Introduction by Benedict R. O'G. Anderson). Ithaca: Cornell Modern Indonesia Project, 1968.

Sosialisme, Indonesia, Pembangunan: Kumpulan Tulisan. Jakarta: Lembaga Penunjang Pembangunan Nasional, 1982.

et al. *Sosialisme Indonesia.Prawoto, Sjahrir, Idham Chalid, Trimurti: Empat Pendapat*. Jakarta: Nusantara, 1960.

5. Selected Books, Articles and Editions of Documents

Abdulgani, Ruslan. *Nationalism, Revolution and Guided Democracy: Four Lectures*. Clayton: Monash University, 1973.

Abdullah, Taufik. "Adat and Islam: An Examination of Conflict in Minangkabau," *Indonesia* 2 (October 1966): 1-24.

———. *Schools and Politics: The Kaum Muda Movement in West Sumatra (1927-1933)*. Ithaca: Cornell Modern Indonesia Project, 1971.

Abeyasekere, Susan. *One Hand Clapping: Indonesian Nationalists and the Dutch, 1939-1942*. Clayton: Monash Papers on Southeast Asia no. 5, 1976.

———. "The Soetardjo Petition," *Indonesia* 15 (April 1973): 81-107.

Abu, Rifai and Abdullah Suhadi. *Chatib Suleiman*. Jakarta: Depertemen Penerangan dan Kebudayaan, 1976.

Anak Agung, Ide Gde Agung, see also Hatta-Agung

———. *'Renville' als kernpunt in de Nederlands-Indonesische onderhandelingen*. Alphen: Sijthoff, 1980.

Alamsjah, St. Rais. *10 orang besar Indonesia terbesar sekarang*. Jakarta: Bintang Mas, 1952.

Algadri, Hamid. *Sukaduka dan Latar Belakang Seorang Perintis Kemerdekaan*. Jakarta: Kantor Wilayah Departemen Sosial, 1980.

———. "Soekarno dan Sjahrir sesudah proklamasi," in "Memoirs" (unpublished typescript, 1987?).

Ali Sastroamidjojo (Ali Sastroamijoyo). *Milestones on My Journey*. St. Lucia: University of Queensland Press, 1979.

Anderson, Benedict R. O'G. "The Language of Indonesian Politics," *Indonesia* 1 (April 1966): 89-116.

———. *Java in a Time of Revolution: Occupation and Resistance, 1944-1946*. Ithaca: Cornell University Press, 1972.

——— and Ruth McVey (with the assistance of F. P. Bunnell). *A Preliminary Analysis of the October 1, 1965, Coup in Indonesia*. Ithaca: Cornell Modern Indonesia Project, 1971.

Anderson, David Charles. "Military Politics in East Java: A Study of the Origins and Development of the Armed Forces in East Java between 1945 and 1948." Ph.D. thesis, London School of Oriental and African Studies, 1977.

Bachtiar, Harsja W. "The Development of a Common National Consciousness Among Students from the Indonesian Archipelago in the Netherlands," *Majalah Ilmu-Ilmu Sastra Indonesia* 6, 2 (May 1976): 31-44.

Balfas, M. *Dr. Tjipto Mangoenkoesoemo: Demokrat Sedjati*. Jakarta: Djambatan, 1952.

Bank, J. T. M. *Katholieken en de Indonesische Revolutie*. Baarn: Ambo, 1983.

F. E. A. Batten and D. de Vries (ed.). *Aan D. M. G. Koch op zijn 75ste verjaardag van zijn vrienden*, The Hague: van Hoeve, 1956.

Beekman, E. M. "Dutch Colonial Literature: Romanticism in the Tropics," *Indonesia* 34 (October 1982): 17–39.

Benda, Harry Jindrich, *The Crescent and the Rising Sun: Indonesian Islam under the Japanese Occupation, 1942–1945.* The Hague: van Hoeve, 1958.

—— and Ruth T. McVey (eds.). *The Communist Uprisings of 1926–1927 in Indonesia: Key Documents.* Ithaca: Cornell Modern Indonesia Project, 1960.

Blom, J. C. H. *De muiterij op de Zeven Provinciën: Reacties en gevolgen in Nederland.* Bussum: van Dishoek, 1975.

Bondan, Mohamad. *Genderang proklamasi di luar negeri.* Jakarta: Kawal, 1971.

Boon, H. N. *Dagelyksche notities vanaf 11 December 1946 tot einde 1947.* Collection H. N. Boon.

——, see also Wiebes, Cees and Bet Zeeman (eds.).

Bos, Jone. "Tien jaar democratisch-socialisme in de Republiek Indonesië 1945–1955." Ph.D. thesis University of Amsterdam, 1979.

Bouman, Hendrik. *Enige Beschouwingen over de Ontwikkeling van het Indonesisch Nationalisme op Sumatra's Westkust.* Groningen: Wolters, 1949.

Braat, L. P. J. (ed.). "De brieven van Soeleiman," *De vrije Katheder* 6, 1, May 3, 1946.

Brugmans, I. J. *Geschiedenis van het onderwijs in Nederlandsch-Indië.* Groningen: Wolters, 1938.

Budianta, M. *Sjahrir and the Children of Banda Neira.* Jakarta: P. T. Gramedia, 1986.

Bunga Rampai Soempah Pemoeda. Jakarta: Balai Pustaka, 1978.

Castles, Lance. "The Political Life of a Sumatra Residency Tapanuli, 1915–1940." Ph.D. thesis, Yale University, 1976.

Clerkx, Lily E. *Mensen in Deli: een matschappijbeeld uit de belletrie.* Amsterdam: University of Amsterdam, 1961

Coast, John. *Recruit to Revolution: Adventure and Politics in Indonesia.* London: Christophers, 1952.

Colijn, H. *Koloniale vraagstukken van heden en morgen.* Amsterdam: De Standaard, 1928.

Cribb, Robert B. "Jakarta in the Indonesian Revolution, 1945–1949." Ph.D. thesis, London School of Oriental and African Studies, 1984.

Crouch, Harold A. *The Army and Politics in Indonesia.* Ithaca: Cornell University Press, 1978.

Dahm, Bernhard. *Sukarno and the Struggle for Indonesian Independence.* Ithaca: Cornell University Press, 1969.

Diah, B. M. *Angkatan Baru '45: Lembaga Perjuangan Pemuda menentang Jepang, mendorong Proklamasi kemerdekaan Indonesia.* Jakarta: Masa Merdeka 1983.

Djaja, Tamar. *Orang Besar Tanah Air.* Bandung: Kolff, 1951.

——. "Sitti Rohana," *Buku Kita* 1, September 9, 1955, pp. 387–90.

——. "'Rohana Kudus: Srikandi' Islam Sebelum Kartini," *Hikmah* 9, 13 (April 7, 1956): 16–18.

——. *Orang-orang besar Indonesia.* vols.1, 2 and 3. Jakarta: Pustaka Antara, 1975.

——. *Rohana Kudus, Srikandi Indonesia: Riwajat Hidup dan perjuangannya.* Jakarta: Mutiara, 1980.

Djajadiningrat, R. T. *Herinneringen van een Vrijheidsstrijder.* The Hague: Nijhoff, 1974.

Djoyoadisuryo, Ahmad Subarjo. "Events leading up to the proclamation of Indonesian Independence," *The Indonesian Review of International Affairs* 1, 5 (1975): 71–100.

——. *Kesadaran nasional; sebuah otobiografi.* Jakarta: Gunung Agung, 1978.

Djojohadikusumo, Margono. *Herinneringen uit drie tijdperken: Een geschreven familie overlevering.* Amsterdam: Nabrink, 1970.

Djojopoespito, Soewarsih. *Buiten het Gareel: Indonesische roman. Met een inleiding van E. du Perron.* Utrecht: de Haan, 1940.

———. "In memoriam E. du Perron," *Kritiek en Opbouw*, August 16, 1940, pp. 192–93.

———. "Du Perron dan pengaruhnja," *Pudjangga Baru* 13, 1–2 (1951).

———. "De thuiskomst van een oud-strijder," *Tirade* 21, 221 (January 1977): 38–47.

Dokumentasi Pemuda: sekitar Proklamasi Indonesia Merdeka. Yogyakarta: Badan Penerangan Pusat SBPI, 1948.

Drees, W. *Zestig jaar levenservaring*. Amsterdam: De Arbeiders pers, 1962.

Drooglever, Pieter Joost. *De Vaderlandsche Club 1929–1942: Totoks en de Indische politiek*. Francker: Werer, 1980.

Dutilh, Margriet. "Het koloniaal Beginselprogram van de SDAP, 1919–1930." Ph.D. thesis, University of Leiden, 1971.

Empatpuluhlima Tahun Sumpah Pemuda. Jakarta: Gunung Agung, 1974.

Encyclopaedie van Nederlandsch-Indië. The Hague: Nijhoff, 1917–, I–

Feddema, H. and O. D. van den Muijzenberg, "Was de Utrechtse Indologie-opleiding een petroleumfaculteit?" *Amsterdams sociologisch tijdschrift* 3 (1977): 465–77.

Feith, Herbert. *The Decline of Constitutional Democracy in Indonesia*. Ithaca: Cornell University Press, 1962.

Foulcher, Keith. "Perceptions of Modernity and the Sense of the Past: Indonesian Poetry of the 1920s," *Indonesia* 23 (April 1977): 39–58.

Garde, S. van de, see Sjahrir, Sutan.

Geertz, Clifford. "Primordial Sentiments and Civil Policies in the New States" in Clifford Geertz (ed.). *Old Societies and New States*. Chicago: Free Press, 1963, pp. 105–157.

Gellhorn, Martha. "Java Journey," *Saturday Evening Post*, June 1, 1946.

Goedhart, see 't Hoen, Pieter.

Graves, Elizabeth E. *The Minangkabau Response to Dutch Colonial Rule in the Nineteenth Century*. Ithaca: Cornell Modern Indonesia Project, 1981.

Goes van Naters, M. van der. *Met en tegen de tijd: Een tocht door de twintigste eeuw*. Amsterdam: De Arbeiderspers, 1980.

Halim, Abdul. *Di antara hempasan dan benturan: kenang-kenangan dr.Abdul Halim, 1942–1950*. Jakarta: Arsip Nasional, 1981.

Hamka. *Adat Minangkabau Menghadap Revolusi*. Jakarta: Tekad, 1963.

———. *Kenang-kenangan Hidup*, I–IV. Kuala Lumpur: Pustaka Antara, 1966.

Hanifah, Abu. *Tales of a Revolution*. Sydney: Angus and Robertson, 1972.

———. "Revolusi Memakan Anak Sendiri: Tragedi Amir Sjarifuddin," *Prisma* 6, 8 (August 1977): 86–100.

Hanna, Willard A. *Kepulauan Banda: kolonialisme dan akibatnja di Kepulauan Pala*. Jakarta: Gramedia, 1983.

Hansen, Erik. "Marxists and Imperialism: The Indonesian Policy of the Dutch Social Democratic Workers Party, 1894–1914," *Indonesia* 16 (October 1973): 81–104.

———. "The Dutch East India and the Reorientation of Dutch Social Democracy, 1929–1940," ibid 23 (April 1977): 59–85.

Harvey, Barbara S. *Permesta: Half a Rebellion*. Ithaca: Cornell Modern Indonesia Project, 1977.

Hatta, Mohammad. "De hetze tegen de 'Perhimpeonan Indonesia': Stokvis 'breekbare waar'," *De Socialist*, October 5, 1929.

——— (M.H.). "Drie jaar Digoel-Schande: Het rapport van W. P. Hillen," ibid., September 12, 1930.

———. *Kumpulan Karangan*. Jakarta: Penerbitan dan Balai Buku Indonesia, 1953.

———. *Sekitar Proklamasi*. Jakarta: Tintamas, 1969.

———. *Portrait of a Patriot: Selected Writings*. The Hague: Mouton, 1972.

———. *Memoir*. Jakarta: Tintamas, 1978.

———. *Bung Hatta Antwoordt*. Jakarta: Gunung Agung, 1979.

———. *Indonesian Patriot: Memoirs*. Singapore: Gunung Agung, 1981.

———. *Pendidikan Nasional Indonesia: A Speech Presented to a Reunion of Members of the Pendidikan Nasional Indonesia, Probably 1968*. Brisbane: Griffith Center of Southeast Asia Studies, 1985.

———, see also Swasono, Meutia Farida.

Mohammad Hatta and Anak Agung. *Surat-menjurat Hatta dan Anak Agung*. Jakarta: Sinar Harapan, 1987.

Hazil Tanzil. "Pelukis Salim: Barat atau Timur," *Indonesia* 2, 4 (1951): 16–20.

——— (ed.). *Seratus Tahun Haji Agus Salim*. Jakarta: Sinar Harapan, 1984.

Holt, Claire (ed. with the assistance of Benedict R. O'G. Anderson and James Siegel). *Culture and Politics in Indonesia*. Ithaca: Cornell University Press, 1972.

't Hoen, Pieter. *Terug uit Djokja*. Amsterdam: Het Parool, 1946.

Ingleson, John. *Perhimpunan Indonesia and the Indonesian Nationalist Movement, 1932–1928*. Melbourne: Monash Center for Southeast Asian Studies, 1975.

———. *Road to Exile: The Indonesian Nationalist Movement, 1927–1934*. Singapore: Heinemann, 1979.

Iwa, Kusuma Sumantri. *Sedjarah Revolusi Indonesia*. Vols. 1–3. Jakarta: Iwa Kusuma Sumantri, 1969.

———. "Autobiography dari Prof. H. Iwa Kusuma Sumantri," typescript dated May 1971.

James, K. A. "De Negeri Kota Gedang," *Tijdschrift voor het Binnenlandsche Bestuur* 49 (1915): 185–95.

Jamin, Muhammad. *Tan Malacca, Bapak Republik Indonesia: Riwajat politik seorang pengadjar revolusioner jang berfikir, berdjoeang dan menderita membentoek negara Repoeblik Indonesia*. Jakarta: Beriat Indonesia, 1946.

Jansen, L. F. *In deze halve gevangenis: Dagboek van mr dr L. F. Jansen, Batavia/Djakarta 1942–1945*. Franeken: Van Wijnen, 1988.

Jarvis, Helen (ed.). *From Jail to Jail. Tan Malaka* 1–3. Athens: Ohio University Southeast Asian Series, 1991.

Josselin de Jong, P. E. *Minangkabau and Negeri Sembilan: Socio-Political Structure in Indonesia*. Djakarta: Bhratara, 1960.

———. *Social Organization of Minangkabau*. Leiden: University of Leiden Institute for Cultural Anthropology, 1975.

Jong, L. de. *Het koninkrijk der Nederlanden in de tweede Wereldoorlog*. vols. 11a, 11b, 11c. Leiden: Nijhoff, 1984–1986.

Jonge, B. C. de. *Herinneringen van Jhr.Mr.B. C. de Jonge*. Groningen: Wolters, 1968.

Jonkman, J. A. *Het oude Nederlands-Indië: Memoires*. Assen: van Goreum, 1971.

———. *Nederland en Indonesië beide vrij: Memoires*. Assen: van Goreum, 1976.

Joustra, M. *Van Medan naar Padang en terug; reisindrukken en ervaringen*. Leiden: van Doesburgh, 1915.

———. *Batakspiegel* (1st edition 1910). Leiden: van Doesburgh, 1926.

Kadt, J. de. "De vermolmde etagere: over de leegheid, onbuikbaardheid en schadelijkheid der dialektiek," *De Nieuwe Kern* 3 (1936–1937), part 1, pp. 161–71, part 2, pp. 201–8.

———. "Soetan Sjahrir: Indonesia's Prime Minister," *The Voice of Free Indonesia* 3, December 1945, pp. 1–4.

―――. *De Indonesische tragedie: Het Treurspel der gemiste kansen.* Amsterdam: van Oorschot, 1949.

―――. *Uit mijn Communistentijd.*Amsterdam: van Oorschot, 1965.

―――, "Sjahrir: Poging tot plaatsbepaling. Benevens een paar persoonlijke herinneringen," *Tirade* May 1966, pp. 460–78.

―――. *Politieke Herinneringen van een randfiguur.* Amsterdam: van Oorschot, 1976.

―――. *Jaren die dubbel telden: Politieke Herinneringen uit mijn 'Indische' jaren.* Amsterdam: van Oorschot, 1978.

Kahin, Audrey. "Struggle for Independence: West Sumatra in the Indonesian National Revolution, 1945–1950." Ph.D. thesis, Cornell University, 1979.

――― (ed.). *Regional Dynamics of the Indonesian Revolution: Unity from Diversity.* Honolulu: University of Hawaii Press, 1985.

Kahin, George McTurnan. *Nationalism and Revolution in Indonesia.* Ithaca: Cornell University Press, 1952.

Kanahele, George Sanford. "The Japanese Occupation of Indonesia:Prelude to Independence." Ph.D. thesis, Cornell University, 1967.

"Kartini Ketjil dari Minangkabau: Sitti Rohana binti Maharadja Soetan dari Kora Gedang sebagain perintis djalan bagi poetri di Minangkabau," *Pandji Islam* 12, May 19, 1941, pp.9054–9055, 9080–9087.

Kato, Tsuyoshi. "Change and Society in the Minangkabau Matrilineal System," *Indonesia* 25 (1978): 1–16.

―――. "Ranta Pariaman: The World of Minangkabau Coastal Merchants in the Nineteenth Century," *Journal of Asian Studies* 39, 4 (1980): 729–52.

Kertapati, Sidik. *Sekitar Proklamasi 17 Agustus 1945.* Jakarta: Pembaruan 1964.

Khatib, Sudarman. "Riwajat Hidup dan Perjuangan Almarhum Chatib Suleiman." Padang Panjang (typescript), 1973.

Koch, D. M. G. (M.K.). "De 'Ziekte der beschaving'," *Kritiek en Opbouw,* March 1, 1938, pp. 30–31.

―――. "H. J. van Mook," *De Nieuwe Stem* 13 (1958), pp. 295–99.

―――. *Batig Slot.* Amsterdam: De Brug, 1960.

Kwantes, R. G. (ed.). *De Ontwikkeling van de Nationalistische Beweging in Nederlandsch-Indië,* vol. 1–4, Groningen:Wolters-Noordhoff, 1975, 1978, 1981, 1982.

Langenberg, Michael van. "National Revolution in North Sumatra: Sumatra Timur and Tapanuli." Ph.D. thesis, University of Sydney, 1976.

―――. "Class and Ethnic Conflict in Indonesia's Decolonization Process: A Study of East Java," *Indonesia* 33 (April 1982): 1–30.

Last, Jef. *Zo zag ik Indonesië.* The Hague: W.van Hoeve, 1954.

Legge, John D. *Sukarno: A Political Biography.*New York: Preager, 1972.

―――. "Daulat Ra'jat and the Ideas of the Pendidikan Nasional Indonesia," *Indonesia* 32 (October 1981): 151–68.

―――. *Intellectuals and Nationalism in Indonesia: A Study of the Following Recruited by Sutan Sjahrir in Occupation Jakarta.* Ithaca: Cornell Modern Indonesia Project, 1988.

Lekkerkerker, C. *Land en volk van Sumatra.* Leiden: Brill, 1916.

Lev, Daniel S. *The Transition to Guided Democracy: Indonesian Politics, 1957–1959.* Ithaca: Cornell Modern Indonesia Project, 1966.

Locher-Scholten, Elsbeth B. *Ethiek in fragmenten: vijf studies over koloniaal denken en doen van Nederlanders in the Indonesische archipel.* Utrecht: HES, 1981.

———. "De Stuw, tijdtekening en teken des tijds," *Tijdschrift voor Geschiedenis* 84, 1(1971): 36–65.

———. "Kritiek en Opbouw (1938–1942). Een rode splinter," *Tijdschrift voor Geschiedenis* 89, 2 (1976): 202–27.

Lubis, Mochtar. *Twilight in Djakarta*. New York: Vanguard Press, 1963.

———. "Van dingen die ik me nog herinner," *Tirade* 19 (1975): 518–40.

———. *Het land onder de regenboog: De geschiedenis van Indonesië*. Alphen: Sijthoff, 1979.

———. *Cacatan Subversif*. Jakarta: Sinar Harapan, 1980.

Lucas, Anton. "The Bamboo Spear Pierces the Payung: The Revolution Against the Bureacratic Elite in North Central Java in 1945." Ph. D. thesis, Australian National University, 1980.

Lukisan Revolusi Indonesia: Indonesia, 1945–1950. Jakarta: Kementerian Penerangan Republik Indonesia, n.d.

Lusink, M. J. *Kroniek 1927: Oostkust van Sumatra*. Amsterdam: Oostkust van Sumatra Instituut, 1928.

McMahon, Robert J. *Colonialism and Cold War: The United States and the Struggle for Indonesian Independence, 1945–1949*. Ithaca: Cornell University Press, 1981.

McVey, Ruth T. *The Rise of Indonesian Communism*. Ithaca: Cornell University Press, 1965.

———. "Nationalism, Islam and Marxism: the Management of Ideological Conflict in Indonesia," introduction to Soekarno. *Nationalism, Islam and Marxism*. Ithaca: Cornell Modern Indonesia Project, 1969, pp. 1–32.

——— (ed.). *Southeast Asia Transitions: Approaches through Social History*. New Haven: Yale University Press, 1978.

"Maleische democratie en padangsche toestanden," *Sumatra Bode*, March 27 and 28, 1907.

Malik, Adam. *Mengabdi Republik*. 2 vols. Jakarta: Gunung Agung, 1978, 1979.

Manganaldarolam, see Sjahbuddin and Syahbuddin.

Mangoenkoesoemo, Soejitno. "Nog iets over 'ons Indonesiërs'," *Kritiek en Opbouw*, March 16, 1939, pp. 39–42.

———. "E. du Perron: Een persoonlijk woord," ibid., August 16, 1940, pp. 187–88.

———. "Brief van een Indonesiër aan E. du Perron (March 22, 1940)," *Criterium* no. 8/9 (August/September 1947), pp. 489–502.

Mangunwijaya, Y. B. "Dilema Sutan Sjahrir: Antara Pemikir dan Politikus," *Prisma* 6, 8 (August 1977), pp. 24–42.

Mansoer, M. D. et al. *Sedjarah Minangkabau*. Jakarta: Bhratara, 1970.

Manusama, A. Th. *Komedie Stamboel of de Oost Indische opera*. Weltevreden: Favoriet, 1922.

Marzuki, Yazir. *Pelukis Salim*. Jakarta: Djambatan, 1983.

Medan Area Mengisi Proklamasi. Medan: Biro Sedjarah Prisma, Badan Musjawarah Pejuang Republik Indonesia, 1976.

Mengenang Sjahrir. Edited by H. Rosihan Anwar. Jakarta: Gramedia, 1980.

Ranneft, J. W. Meijer. "Over Sjahrir," *Libertas* 17 (February 1946).

Mitchell, Istulah Gunawan. "The Socio-Cultural Environment and Mental Disturbance: Three Minangkabau Case Histories," *Indonesia* 7 (April 1969): 123–37.

———. "Points of Stress in Minangkabau Social Life," *RIMA* 6, 2 (1972), 96–115.

Mook, Hubertus Johannes van. *Indonesië, Nederland en de wereld*. Batavia: De Brug-Opbouw, 1949.

———. *The Stakes of Democracy in Southeast Asia*. New York: Norton, 1950.

Mrázek, Rudolf. *The United States and the Indonesian Military, 1945–1965: A Study of an Intervention*, vol. 1 and 2 (Prague: Academia, 1978).

---. "Tan Malaka: A Political Personality's Structure of Experience," *Indonesia* 14 (October 1972): 1–47.

Mulder, Gerard and Paul Koedjik. *H. M. van Randwijk: Een biografie.* Amesterdam: Nijgh en Van Ditmar, 1988.

Murad, Anda. *Merantau: Outmigration in a Matrilineal Society of West Sumatra.* Canberra: ANU, Department of Geography, 1980.

Murwoto. *Autobiografi selaku perintis kemerdekaan.* Jakarta: Departemen Sosial, 1984.

Naim, Mochtar. *Merantau: Causes and Effects of Minangkabau Voluntary Migration.* Singapore: Institute of Southeast Asian Studies, 1971.

Nasution, A. H. *Memenuhi Panggilan Tugas* 1, 3, 5. Jakarta: Gunung Agung, 1982, 1983, 1985.

Nasution, Ida. "Het Indonesisch, zijn groei en ontwikkeling," *Criterium* no. 8/9 (August/September 1947), pp. 555–58.

Niel, Robert Van. *The Emergence of the Modern Indonesian Elite* (second impression). The Hague: van Hoeve, 1970.

Nieuwenhuys, Robert. *Oost-Indische Spiegel; wat Nederlandse schrijvers en dichters over Indonesië hebben geschreven, vanaf de eerste jaren der Compagnie tot op heden.* Amsterdam: Querido, 1972.

Noer, Deliar. *The Modernist Muslim Movement in Indonesia.* Singapore: Oxford University Press, 1973.

Nord, Max. "Du Perron's afscheid van Indonesië," *De Baanbreker*, December 8, 1945.

Officiële bescheiden betreffende de Nederlands-Indonesische betrekkingen 1945–1950.(vols. 1–9 edited by S. L.van der Wal; vols. 10ff. edited by J. S. Drooglever and M. J. B. Schouten). The Hague: Nijhoff, 1971– .

Oey, Hong Lee. *War and Diplomacy in Indonesia, 1945–1950.* Townsville: James Cook University Press, 1981.

Orang Indonesia jang terkemoeka di Djawa. Jakarta: Gunseikanbu, n.d.

Overdijkink, G. W. *Het Indonesische probleem: De feiten 1946.* The Hague: Nijhoff, 1946.

Petrus Blumberger, J. Th. *De nationalistische beweging in Nederlandsch-Indië.* Haarlem: Willink, 1931.

---. *Politiek partijen en stroomingen in Nederlandsch-Indië.* Leiden: Leidsche Uitgeversmaatschappij, 1934.

Papanek, Hanna. "Note on Soedjatmoko's Recollections of a Historical Moment: Sjahrir's Reaction to Ho Chi Minh's 1945 Call for a Free People Federation," *Indonesia* 49 (April 1990): 141–44.

Penders, C. L. M. "Colonial Education Policy and the Indonesian Response, 1900–1942." Ph.D. thesis, Australian National University, 1968.

du Perron, E. *Het land van herkomst.* Amsterdam, 1935.

---. "Notities bij het artikel van Sjahrir," part 1–2, *Kritiek en Opbouw*, June 16, pp. 138–40, and July 1, 1939, pp. 154–56.

---. "Een brief aan een Indonesiër," ibid., August 16, 1939, pp. 195–97.

---. *Indies Memorandum.* Amsterdam: De Bezige Bij, 1946.

Piliang, Burhan. "Tentang teater baru Indonesia dan perkembangannya di Medan," *Budaya Jaya* 9, 100 (September 1976): 561–67.

Pringgodigdo, A. K. "Toelating van niet-Europeese leerlingen tot de ELS," *Koloniale Studiën* 24 (1940): 406–24.

---. *Sedjarah Pergerakan Rakjat Indonesia.* Jakarta: Pustaka Rakjat, 1950.

Pringgodigdo, Soewarni. "Du Perron dan Pengaruhnja kepada kaum intelek Indonesia, 1936–1939," *Pudjangga Baru* 13, 1–2 (July 1951): 29–35 (as reprinted in *Sikap* 4 [1952]: 33–37).

———. "Over du Perron en zijn invloed op de Indonesische Intellectuellen (1936–39)," *Cultureel Nieuws* 16 (January 1952), pp. 135–49.

Postel-Coster, Els. "The Indonesian Novel as a Source of Anthropological Data" in Ravindra K. Jain (ed.). *Text and Context: The Social Anthropology of Tradition*. Philadelphia: Institute for Study of Human Issues, 1977.

Poeze, Harry A. *Tan Malaka, Strijder voor Indonesië's vrijheid: Levensloop van 1897 tot 1945*. The Hague: Nijhoff, 1976.

——— (ed.). *Politiek-politioneele overzichten van Nederlandsch-Indië*, vol. 1 (1927–1928). The Hague: Nijhoff, 1982.

——— (ed.). *Politiek-politioneele overzichten van Nederlandsch-Indië*, vol. 2 (1929–1930). Doordrecht: KITLV, 1983.

Radjab, Muhamad. *Tjatjatan di Sumatra*. Jakarta: Balai Pustaka, 1949.

———. *Semasa kecil dikampung, 1913–1925: Autobiografi seorang anak Minangkabau*. Jakarta: Balai Pustaka, 1974.

Raffael, Burton (ed.). *Anthology of Modern Indonesian Poetry*. Berkeley: University of California Press, 1964.

Raliby, Osman. *Documenta Historica: Sedjarah dokumenter dari pertumbuhan dan perdjuangan negara Republik Indonesia*. Jakarta: Bulan-Bintang, 1953.

Ranuwijaya, Rachmat. "Sutan Sjahrir: peranan dan pikiran politiknja dalam tahun 1926–1948." Ph.D. thesis, University of Indonesia, 1975.

Rasjid, Zainal. *Riwajat orang-orang politik*. Medan: Bakti, 1952.

Rasjidi, Khalid. *Pengalaman Perjuangan Jaman Jepang Sampai Proklamasi*. Jakarta: Yayasan Idayu, 1976.

Reid, Anthony J. S. *Indonesian National Revolution, 1945–1950*. Hawthorn: Longman, 1974.

———. *The Blood of the People: Revolution and the End of Traditional Rule in Northern Sumatra*. Kuala Lumpur: Oxford University Press, 1979.

Resink, G. J. "Rechtshoogeschool, jongereneed, 'Stuw' en gestuwden," *BKI* 130, 4 (1974): 428–49.

Ritman, J. H. "Soetan Sjahrir: Synthese tuschen Oost en West," *Uitzicht* 2, 14/15 (April 9, 1947): 14–15.

Roland Holst, Henriëtte van der Schalk. *De revolutionnaire Massa-actie*. Rotterdam: Brusse, 1918.

Rose, Mavis. *Indonesia Free: A Political Biography of Mohammad Hatta*. Ithaca: Cornell Modern Indonesia Project, 1987.

Rosihan Anwar, H. (ed). *Perdjalanan terachir Pahlawan Nasional Sutan Sjahrir*. Jakarta: Pembangunan, 1966.

———. *Kisah-kisah zaman revolusi; kenang-kenangan seorang wartawan, 1946–1949*. Jakarta: Pustaka Jaya, 1975.

———. *Kisah-kisah Jakarta setelah Proklamasi*. Jakarta: Pustaka Jaya, 1977.

———. *Kisah-kisah Jakarta menjelang Clash ke-1*. Jakarta: Pustaka Jaya, 1979.

———. *Sebelum Prahara: Pergelakan Politik Indonesia, 1961–1965*, Jakarta: Sinar Harapan, 1981.

See also Mengenang Sjahrir.

Roegholt, Richter F. *De geschiedenis van De Bezige Bij, 1942–1972*. Amsterdam: De Bezige Bij, 1972.

Roem, Mohamad. *Bunga Rampai Dari Sedjarah*, vol. 1, 2, 3. Djakarta: Bulan-Bintang, 1972, 1977, 1983

———. "Tragedi Schermerhorn dan Sjahrir," *Budaya Jaya* 10, 111 (August 1977): 457–70.

———. "Memimpin adalah Menderita: Kesaksian Hadji Agoes Salim," *Prisma* 8 (1977): 43–56.

Rutgers, S. J. "Soetan Sjahrir spreekt tot zijn volk," *De Vrije Ketheder* 5, 46 (March 1, 1946): 566–67.

Said, Mohammad H. *Suatu Zaman Gelap di Deli: Koeli Kontrak Tempo Doeloe*. Medan: Waspada, 1977.

"Salim-een militante-artiste-peintre," *Het Inzicht* 1, 25 (July 6, 1945): 3–4.

Salim, Hadji Agoes. "De Perhimpeonan Indonesia en de Indonesisch Nationalistische beweging," *De Socialist*, October 19, 1929.

———. *Djedjak langkah H. A. Salim: Pilihan karangan*. Djakarta: Tintaman, 1954.

Salim, Chalid I. F. M. *Limabelas tahun Digul: kamp konsentrasi di Nieuw Guinea-tempat persemaian kemerdekaan Indonesia*. Jakarta: Bulan-Bintang, 1977.

Salim, Leon (ed.). *Bung Sjahrir: Pahlawan Nasional*. Medan: Masadepan, 1966.

———. *Chatib Suleiman*. Typescript, n.d., n.p.

———. "Inspektur Belanda Memanggilnja Tuan," *Fokus* 2, 28, January 19, 1984.

———. *Prisoners at Kota Cane*. Ithaca: Cornell Modern Indonesia Project, 1986.

Salmon, Claudine. "Presse féminine ou féministe?" *Archipel* 13 (1977): 157–91.

Schermerhorn, W. *Het dagboek van Schermerhorn. Geheim verslag van prof.dr.ir. W. Schermerhorn als voorzitter der commissie-generaal voor Nederlands-Indië. 20 september 1946–7 october 1947.* 1–2. Groningen: Wolters-Noordhoff, 1970.

Schmidt, P. J. "De 'Perhimpoenan Indonesia' en mij Repliek," *De Socialist*, August 6, 1931.

———. *Buitenlandsche politiek van Nederland*. Leiden: Sijthoff, 1945.

Schoonheyt, L. J. A. *Boven-Digoel*. Batavia: de Unie, 1936.

Shiraishi, Takashi. "Islam and Communism: An Illumination of the People's Movement in Java, 1912–1926." Ph.D. thesis, Cornell University, 1986.

———. *An Age in Motion: Popular Radicalism in Java, 1912–1926*. Ithaca: Cornell University Press, 1990.

Siegel, James. *Shadow and Sound: The Historical Thought of a Sumatran People*. Chicago: University of Chicago Press, 1979.

——— and Tsuchiya Kenji. "Invincible Kitsch or As Tourists in the Age of Des Alwi, " *Indonesia* 50 (October 1990): 61–76.

Simatupang, T. B. *Report from Banaran*. Ithaca: Cornell Modern Indonesia Project, 1972.

——— and A. B. Lapian. "Pemberontakan di Indonesia: mengapa dan untuk apa," *Prisma* 7, 7 (1978): 3–13.

Sitoroes, L. M. "Laporan Organisasi dari Pebruari 1950 sampai 12 Pebruari 1952," *Suara Sosialis* 4, 2, April 15, 1952.

Sjahbuddin Mangandaralam. *In memoriam Sutan Sjahrir; perdjuangan dan penderitaanja*. Bandung: Panjasakti, 1966.

See also Syahbuddin.

Sjahrazad, see Sutan Sjahrir.

Sjarifoeddin, Amir (A.Sj). "De toekomst der Indonesisch-nationale scholen," *Kritiek en Opbouw*, November 22, 1941, pp. 327–28.

Slamet, Mas. *Japansche Intriques: De nasleep van de Japansche bezetting*. Amsterdam: Buijyen en Schipperhuijn, 1946.

Smail, John R. W. *Bandung in the Early Revolution, 1945–1946: A Study in the Social History of the Indonesian Revolution*. Ithaca: Cornell Modern Indonesia Project, 1964.

Smit, C. *De liquidatie van een imperium: Nederland en Indonesië, 1945–1962*. Amsterdam: De Arbeiderspers, 1962.

Sneevliet, H. "De nieuwste explosie van koloniaal macht-misbruik in Indonesië," *De Nieuwe Weg* 5 (1930): 8–17.

———. "Indonesië en het probleem van het Verre Oosten," ibid. 9 (1934): 327–37.

Snouck Hurgronje, C. *Nederland en de Islam*. Leiden: Brill, 1911.

———. *Colijn over Indië*. Amsterdam: Brecht, 1928.

Solichin, Salam. *Hadji Agus Salim: Hidup dan Perdjuangannja*. Djakarta: Djajamuri, 1961.

Squire, Clifford William. "Britain and the Transfer of Power in Indonesia, 1945–1946." Ph.D. thesis, School of Oriental and African Studies, n.d.

Stikker, Dirk U. *Memoires*. Rotterdam: Nijgh en Van Ditmar, 1966.

Stoler, Ann Laura. *Capitalism and Confrontation in Sumatra's Plantation Belt, 1870–1979*. New Haven: Yale University Press, 1985.

Subadio Sastrosatomo. *Masa muda saya: Indonesia 1940–1942*. (Vol. 1 of memoirs, typescript).

———. *Perjuangan Revolusi*. Jakarta: Sinar Harapan, 1987.

Soedjatmoko. "Tentang masalah kebudajaan jang benar dan jang tidak benar kepada Prof. Mr. Dr. Supomo," *Gema*, May 1949, pp. 217–24.

———. "The Role of Political Parties in Indonesia" in Philip W. Thayer (ed.). *Nationalism and Progress in Free Asia*. Baltimore: Johns Hopkins Press, 1956, pp. 128–40.

Sukarma. *Sosialisme (kata pendahuluan oleh Sjahrir)*. Djakarta: Dewan Partai Sosialis Indonesia, 1951.

Sukarno. *An Autobiography as Told to Cindy Adams*. Indianapolis: The Bobbs-Merrill, 1965.

Sukarno. *Dibarawah Bendera Revolusi*.

Sukma, Ratu. *Tan Malaka*. Bukittinggi: Pustaka Rakjat, 1948.

Soemargono, Farida Labrousse. "Cultural Life in Yogyakarta during the Period of Independence, 1945–1950." Yogyakarta, mimeo, 1974

Sundhaussen, Ulf. *The Road to Power: Indonesian Military Politics, 1945–1967*. Kuala Lumpur: Oxford University Press, 1982.

Surjo Dediono, R. *Peristiwa Tjikini*. Djakarta: Soeroengan, 1958.

Sutherland, Heather. "Pudjangga Baru: Aspects of Indonesian Intellectual Life in the 1930s," *Indonesia* 6 (1968): 106–27.

Sutjia Tiningsih, Sri (ed.). *Tokoh Nasional:Chairil Anwar*. Jakarta: Departemen Pendidikan dan kebudayaan, 1979.

Suwarna, P. J. "Pedjuang-pedjuang serta gerakan Indonesia pasa saat-saat terachir pendudukan Djepang," *Basis* 18, 11 (April 1969): 368–75.

Swasono, Meuria Farida (ed.). *Muhammad Hatta: Pribadinja dalam kemanusian*. Jakarta: Sinar Harapan, 1980.

Swift, Ann. *The Road to Madiun: The Indonesian Communist Uprising of 1948*. Ithaca: Cornell Modern Indonesia Project, 1989.

Syahbuddin Mangandaralam. *Apa dan Siapa Sutan Syahrir*. Jakarta: Rosda Jayaputra, 1986.

See also Sjahbuddin.

Symposion tentang kesulitan-kesulitan zaman peralihan sekarang. Djakarta: Balai Pustaka, 1953.

Takdir Alisjahbana, S. *Indonesian Language and Literature. Two Essays*. New Haven: Yale University Southeast Asian Studies Cultural Reports Series, 1962.

———. *Indonesia's Social and Cultural Revolution*. Singapore: Oxford University Press, 1966.

———. "Sjahrir dan sikap dan struktur politik yang diperlukan untuk dunia yang sedang tumbuh, "*Ilmu dan Budaya* 3 (July 1981): 263–78.

Tan Malaka. *Politik*. Jogjakarta: Badan Oesaha Penerbitan Nasional Indonesia, 1945.

———. *Moeslihat*. Bukit Tinggi, Nusantara, 1945.

―――. *Rentjana Ekonomi*. Jogjakarta: Badan Oesaha Penerbitan Nasional Indonesia, 1946.

―――. *Dari pendjara ke pendjara*. vol. 1. Djakarta: Widjaja, n.d.

―――. *Dari pendjara ke pendjara*. vol. 2. Jogjakarta: Pustaka Murba, n.d.

―――. *Dari pendjara ke pendjara*. vol. 3. Djakarta: Widjaja, n.d

―――, see also Jarvis, Helen.

Tanner, Nancy. "Disputing and Dispute Settlement among the Minangkabau of Indonesia," *Indonesia* 8 (1969): 21–67.

Tas, Sal. "Het Sexuele Vraagstuk: Een Protest," *De Nieuwe Kern* 2, 6 (March 1936): 171–80.

―――. "Souvenirs of Sjahrir," *Indonesia* 8 (1969): 135–54.

―――. *Wat mij betreft*. Baarn: Ten Hare, 1970.

―――. *De onderontwikkelde vrijheid. Indonesia toen en nu*. Baarn: Ten Hare, 1973.

―――. *Indonesia: The Underdeveloped Freedom*. New York: Pegasus, 1974.

Tatengkeng, J. E. "Kritiek dan eoekoeran sendiri," *Poedjangga Baroe* 6, 10 (April 1939): 157–61.

Tauchid, Moch. *Mengenang Pahlawan Sjahrir*. Jogjakarta: Jajasan Sjahrir, 1966.

Taylor, A. M. *Indonesian Independence and the United Nations*. Ithaca: Cornell University Press, 1960.

Teeuw, A. *Modern Indonesian Literature* 1, 2. Leiden: KITLV, 1986 and 1979.

Tesis Sedjarah Perdjuangan Pemuda Indonesia. Djakarta: Biro Pemuda, Departemen Pendidikan Dasar dan Kebudajaan, n.d.

Thaib, Maisir. *Sjahrir Pegang Kemoedi*. Boekittinggi: Penjiaran Ilmoe, 1946?

Thalib, Ibrahim. *Karya dan tjita Sutan Sjahrir*. Djakarta: Photin, 1966.

Thomas, Lynn L. and Franz von Benda Beekman (eds.). *Change and Continuity in Minangkabau: Local, Regional and Historical Perspectives on West Sumatra*. Athens: Ohio University Press, 1985.

Tichelman, Fritjof. *Henk Sneevliet, 1883–1942: Een politieke biograpfie*. Amsterdam: Van Gennep, 1974.

―――. *The Social Evolution of Indonesia: The Asiatic Mode of Production and its Legacy*. The Hague: Nijhoff, 1980.

Tobing, M. L. *Perdjuangan Politik Bangsa Indonesia: Linggadjati*. Jakarta: Gunung Agung, 1986.

―――. *Perdjuangan Politik Bangsa Indonesia: Renville*. Jakarta: Gunung Agung, 1986.

Trisno Sumardjo. "Salim diantara Kita," *Zenith* 1, 6 (1951): 330–35.

Tuijl, Peter van. "Mijn positie is helaas niet erg benijdenswaardig: Nico Palar en de koloniale politiek van de Nederlandse sociaal democratie, 1930–1947." Ph.D. thesis, University of Amsterdam, 1985.

Veenstra, J. H. W. *Diogenes in de Tropen*. Amsterdam: Vrij Nederland, 1947.

―――. "Sutan Sjahrir. Het leven van het slachtoffer," *Vrij Nederland*, April 16, 1966.

Veer, Paul van 't. *De strijdlustige amateur*. Amsterdam: De Arbeiderspers, 1973.

―――. "Sjahrir en Schermerhorn," *Holland Maandblad* 18, 347 (October 1976): 10–17.

Velde, J. J. van de. *Brieven uit Sumatra, 1928–1949*. Francker: T. Werer, 1982.

Verhoeven, F. R. J. "Enige notities over vormen van culturele samenwerking," *Indonesië* 2 (1948–1949): 364–71.

Verslag van het Congres-Indonesië gehouden door de Partij van de Arbeid. (September 7, 1946). Amsterdam: De Arbeiderspers, 1946.

Vollenhoven, C. Van. *Het Adatrecht van Nederslansch-Indië*, vol. 1. Leiden: Brill, 1918.

Vries, D. de. *Culturele aspecten in de verhouding Nederland-Indonesië*. Amsterdam: Vrij Nederland, 1947.

——— . "Twee vaderlanden," *Orientatie* 5 (February 1948): 22–30.

Vuyk, Beb. "Eddy du Perron," *Kritiek en Opbouw*, August 16, 1940, pp. 188–89.

——— . "Verhaal van een toeschouwer (In memoriam Ida Nasoetion)," *Oriëntatie* 31 (April 1950): 6–22.

——— . "In memoriam Soetan Sjahrir," *Trouw*, April 16, 1966.

Waal, G. De van Ackeren, "Maleische Democratie en Padangsche toestanded," *Sumatra Bode*, March 27 and 28, 1907.

Wal, Simon L. van der (ed.). *Het Onderwijsbeleid in Nederlandsch-Indië, 1900–1942.* Groningen: Wolters, 1963.

——— (ed.). *De opkomst van de nationalistische beweging in Nederlandsch-Indië.* Groningen: Wolters, 1967.

See *Officiële bescheiden*.

Wehl, David. *The Birth of Indonesia.* London: Allen and Unwin, 1948.

Weinstein, Franklin B. *Indonesian Foreign Policy and the Dilemma of Dependence: From Sukarno to Soeharto.* Ithaca: Cornell University Press, 1976.

Wellem, Frederick Djara. *Amir Sjarifoeddin: Pergumulan Imannya dalam Perjuangan Kemerdekaan.* Jakarta: Sinar Harapan, 1984.

Wertheim, W. F. *Nederland op den Tweesprong: Tragedie van den aan traditie gebonden mensch.* Arnhem: Van Loghum Slaterus, 1946.

——— . *Indonesië van vorstenrijk tot neo-kolonie.* Amsterdam: Boom Meppel, 1978.

Wiebes, Cees and Bert Zeeman (eds). *Indonesische dagboek notities van Dr. H. N. Boon.* Houten: De Haan, 1986.

Willinck, G. D. *Het Rechtsleven bij de Minangkabausche Maleiers.* Leiden: Brill, 1909.

——— . *De Indiën en de Nieuwe Grondwet: Proeve tot vaststelling van normale staatsrechtelijke verhoundingen tusschen het moederland en de koloniën.* Zutphen: van Belkum, 1910.

Wolf, Charles, Jr. *The Indonesian Story: The Birth, Growth and Structure of the Indonesian Republic.* New York: John Day, 1948.

See Sjahrir, Sutan.

Woodman, Dorothy. *The Republic of Indonesia.* London: Cresset Press, 1955.

Yamin, M., see Jamin.

Yong Mun Cheong. *H. J. van Mook and Indonesian Independence, 1945–1948.* The Hague: Nijhoff, 1982.

Zorab, A. A. *De Japanse bezetting van Indonesië en haar volkenrechtelijke zijde.* Leiden: Universitair Pers, 1954.

INDEX

In some collective and personal names, instead of the new "u," the old spelling of "oe" is followed according to the prevailing norm.

Abdoelgani, Roeslan, 297, 438, 444, 447–48, 459–60
Abdoelmadjid, 62, 285, 313, 323, 326, 345–46, 364, 369
Abdullah, Basuki, 331
Abendanon, J.H., 245
Abikoesno Tjokrosoejoso, 315
Abu Hanifah, 336, 339, 374, 384
Acehnese, 7n, 138, 186, 188, 256, 431, 444
Affandi, 296, 301, 326
Afghanistan, 358
Aidit, D.N., 432, 488
Algadri, Ali, 363
Algadri, Hamid, 226–27, 230, 238, 363, 399, 413, 462, 465, 472, 490, 492–93
Algemeen Democratisch Bond, "All-Democratic Union," 163
Algemene Middelbare School, AMS, "General Intermediate School," 33–34, 37–40, 42–44, 47, 59, 65, 120, 174, 194, 479
Algemeene Studieclub, "General Study Club," 50
Ali, see Sastroamidjojo, Ali
Ali, see Sjahrir, Ali
Aliarcham, 134
Alimin Prawirodirdjo, 325
Allies, see United Nations
Ambonese, 282–83, 286, 301–2
Amir, see Sjarifoeddin, Amir
AMS, see Algemene Middelbare School
Amsterdam, 1, 3, 56–81 passim, 166, 198–99, 283, 291, 298, 300, 345, 349n, 362, 399, 417–18, 429, 489
Anak Agung Gde Agung, 386, 461–64, 466–68, 488, 491, 494
Anderson, Benedict, 256, 261, 264, 266, 272, 275, 278, 283, 296, 302, 311–12, 315, 318
Angkatan Baroe, "New Generation," 256
Anwar, Chairil, 245, 258, 296, 299–301, 326, 362, 415–16, 424
Anwar, Rosihan, 227, 298–300, 326, 415, 450n, 465, 467, 470, 481–82, 492–94
Apin, Mochtar, 326
Apin, Riwai, 326, 362
Arabian Nights, 8, 30, 185
Arabs, 183, 185–89, 191, 206
Asbeck, F.M. van, 290
Asia Raja, 251–53, 256

Asian Relations Conference, 334–36, 359
Asmara Hadi, 221, 243
Asrama Indonesia Merdeka, "Ashram of Free Indonesia," 248, 250–51, 266, 303
Asaat, 382
Atkinson, T., 287, 289
Attlee, C., 288
Aung San, 336
Australia, 210, 240, 350, 352–54, 360–61, 364–65, 391

Baadilla, 191–92, 195, 499
Baanbreker, 291, 298
Baars, A., 151
Badan Pusat Intelijen, "Central Intelligence Organization," 462
badminton, 468
Baharoeddin, 296, 298, 301, 326
Bali, 461–63
Banda Neira, 143, 160–207 passim, 209–12, 218, 221, 224, 238–39, 245, 248, 275, 280, 283, 357, 362, 413–14, 416–17, 423, 468–69, 476, 498–99
Bandung, 33–55 passim, 56, 58, 61–65, 67–68, 70–71, 77, 82–83, 85–87, 90, 92, 95–96, 100, 103, 108, 114, 116, 118, 120, 144, 154, 158, 161, 174, 160n, 198, 210–11, 214–16, 219, 227–28, 231–34, 237–38, 240, 254, 256, 270–71, 285, 287–88, 299, 410, 413, 418–19, 422–23, 453, 466, 479, 497–98
Barisan Pelopor, "Vanguard Corps," 265
Basoeki Rebowo, 245
Bataks (Mandailing), 7, 30, 188, 201
Batovis, Bandoengse Toneel Vereeniging van Indonesische Studenten, "Indonesian Students' Bandung Theater Company," see theater
Bauer, O., 61
Beatles, 489
Beel, L.J.M., 348
Beerling, R.F., 340
Beethoven, L. van, 152, 175
Belgium, 354
Benda, H.J., 421
Benteng Republic, "Fortress of the Republic," 344, 352, 371–72
Bergman, I., 363
Bergson, H., 126
Bessem, E., 48

Bevan, A., 288
Bevin, E., 355
Bible, 118, 120, 123, 189
Bibliotheek voor Nederlands-lezende Inheemsen, "Library for Dutch-reading Natives," 26
Bidault, G., 357
Blum, L., 244, 292, 343
Boedi Oetomo, 68, 72n, 73n, 155
Boediardjo, Ali, 230, 236–37, 253–54, 335, 365, 375, 388, 393, 406, 492–93
Boediono, 41–42
Boeke, J.H., 343
Boetonese, 183–84
Bogaerdt, A. Th., 332
Boheme, 59, 480
Bohr, N.H.D., 477
Bondan, M., 91, 117–18, 139
Boon, H.N., 344
Boon, J. (Vincent Mahieu, Tjalie Robinson), 413
Borobudur, 53n, 149, 298, 393
Bos Atlas, 130, 207
Boven Digul (Tanah Merah, Tanah Tinggi), 63, 118, 122, 125, 128–53 passim, 157, 165–66, 168, 170, 172, 174, 176, 185, 191–92, 194, 197, 240, 253, 287–88, 290, 341, 349, 460, 467, 469
Brackman, A., 441, 448
British, 199, 273, 280, 286–90, 295–96, 299, 306, 314, 327, 333–35, 337–39, 341, 344, 347, 349–51, 354–55, 365, 370, 377n, 417, 429, 485
Britten, B., 289
Bruggen, C. van, 29
Buchman's Moral Re-Armament, 356
Buddha, 181
Buddhism, 61, 63, 158, 289, 337, 373, 392
Bukittinggi, (Fort de Kock), 13–14, 65, 99–100, 103, 366–68, 380, 420, 446–47
Burhanuddin, 41–42, 86–87, 103, 115–16, 118, 139, 148, 153, 233, 288
Burhanuddin, see Harahap, Burhanuddin
Burma, 335–37, 339, 363, 372
Buru, 139, 211
Business School, Rotterdam, 66, 78, 127n, 288

Cairo, 97, 99
calisthenic, 468
Campbell, A.J., 377n
Carr, E.H., 477
China, 275–76, 335, 367n, 429
Chinese, 30, 37, 58, 103, 136, 183, 188–89, 206, 296, 365, 429, 466, 490
Christians, 123–24, 135, 138, 151, 171, 187, 190, 205–6, 283, 288, 276, 393, 477
Cipanas, 219, 239
Cipinang, 118, 120–28 passim, 165, 197
Cipto, see Mangoenkoesoemo, Tjipto
CKBI, see Congres Kaoem Boeroeh Indonesia
Coast, J., 288–89, 336, 338, 364n, 373, 375, 399–400, 405, 408
Cochran, M., 394–95
Cole, G.D.H., 74
Colijn, H., 48, 53–54, 64, 154, 157, 166n
Committee of Good Offices, 354
Communist International, 180
Communist Party of Holland, 79, 155

Communist Party of Indonesia, see Partai Komunis Indonesia
Communist uprisings, 1926–1927, 40, 91–92, 97, 129, 134, 137, 369
Congres Kaoem Boeroeh Indonesia, CKBI, "Indonesian Workers' Congress," 93–94
Contact Commissie, "Liaison Commission," 253, 323n, 326
CORPS 226
Court, J.F.H.A. de la, 342–43, 356
creoles, see Eurasians
Cripps, Sir Stafford, 288
Critchley, T. K., 391
Croce, B., 293

D'Annunzio, G., 126, 152
Damais, Ch., 241
dancing, 25, 36n, 39, 62, 227, 288
Dante, 152
Darmasetiawan, 390–91
Darwis Thaib, 99, 104
Daulat Ra'jat, 74, 78–79, 84–104 passim, 114, 123, 147, 157–58, 234–35, 278, 309, 318, 412, 425, 476, 498
Defoe, D., 136, 144
Deklarasi Ekonomi, "Economic Declaration," 488
Deli, see Medan
Des Alwi, see Sjahrir, Des Alwi
Deventer, C.Th. van, 24
Dewan Banteng, "Wild Buffalo Council," 445–46, 448–49
Dewan Perdjuangan, "Struggle Council," 446
Dewantoro, Ki Hadjar, 342
Dhani, Omar, 340
Diah, Burhanuddin Mohammad, 252, 256, 264
Dimitrov, G., 244, 313
Diponegoro, 88
djaksa, see jaksa
Djalil, 306
Djaliloeddin, T.M., 292
Djawoto, 95n
Djilas, M., 429
Djoeanda, 365, 488n
Djoehana, Heda (Hedda), 203, 214
Djoehana, M.A. "Aki," 57, 203, 214, 245, 293, 296, 340, 362
Djoehana, R.M.W. Dr., 30, 32, 34, 56, 58, 83
Djoehana, Siti Sjahrizal, 23, 27, 32, 34, 56–58, 62–63, 77, 83, 142, 203, 214, 219, 245, 493, 497
Djohan, see Sjahroezah, Djohan
Djojobojo, see Joyoboyo
Djojohadikoesoemo, Margono, 364n, 400n
Djojohadikoesoemo, Soebianto, 226, 229, 245, 263–65, 273, 288, 298
Djojohadikoesoemo, Soemitro, 288, 364n, 377n, 400n, 403, 406, 413, 439, 445–46, 448–50, 453, 460, 490
Djojopoespito, Soegondo, 83n, 161, 202n, 270, 285, 368, 381, 419
Djojopoespito, Soewarsih, 83, 154–56, 161–63, 197–98, 202, 225, 494–95
Domei press agency, 261–62, 270
Don Quixote, 26, 123, 195
Dongen, K. van, 489
Douwes Dekker E., see Multatuli

Douwes Dekker, E.F.E., 151, 202n
Drees, W., 385–86, 428, 464
Duchâteau, Maria, 59, 81, 88, 111–12, 117, 120–21, 123–26, 128, 139, 141–42, 144–48, 151, 176, 179, 181, 185, 189, 191, 194–97, 199, 212–14, 291, 302, 339–40, 374, 399, 418, 420, 439, 469
Dutch social democracy, see also Social Democratic Labor Party, 291–93, 323, 326–27, 345, 353, 357–58, 379n, 428
Dutch East India Company, 130, 140, 463
Dutch language, 18, 20, 30, 43, 46–48, 51, 110n, 115–16, 188–89, 195, 221, 227, 229, 243, 263, 287, 291, 293, 296, 298–99, 324, 327–28, 388, 413–14, 417, 430, 437–38, 440, 478, 489

Egmont, L. Count of, 293
Egypt, 335–36, 350–51, 358, 417, 493
Einstein, A., 427, 477
Eliot, T.S., 293
ELS, see Europeesche Lagere School
Engels, F., 61, 161n, 173, 185, 199, 421–22, 473–76, 479–80, 483
English language, 30, 37, 42–43, 106, 134, 146–47, 163, 194, 216, 240–41, 263, 269, 287, 301, 336, 352, 363, 383–84, 387, 397, 399, 417, 430, 436–38, 489, 497
"ethical," 16–33 passim, 37, 40–41, 48, 50–52, 59–67 passim, 70, 74, 78, 108–9, 116, 120, 124, 126, 133, 135–37, 147. 149, 152–53, 156, 169, 172, 174, 188, 200, 215, 240–41, 244, 253, 283, 290–92, 310, 380, 394, 406, 413, 422, 440
Eurasians, 8, 30, 135n, 169, 181–82, 189–90, 206, 211, 215–19, 224, 228, 244, 255, 270–71, 282–83, 286, 296, 299–302, 315, 405, 413, 426, 438–39
Europeesche Lagere School, ELS, "European Lower School," 23–24, 26, 30, 35, 50, 65, 165

Fabianism, 230n, 408
Fakkel, 201, 241
Fascism, 108, 155, 163, 198–204, 221, 227, 230, 277–78, 281–82, 285, 291n, 326, 448, 455
Fauzy, Achmad, 493
Feith, H., 402–9 passim, 435, 438, 440–42, 444, 447, 449, 486
Fimmen, E., 62, 69, 107
Floria, J., 300
Fort de Kock, see Bukittinggi
Fox, M., 364n
France, 103, 106, 276, 326, 353, 357, 414, 417, 429, 439
Franklin, B., 397
French language, 37, 42–43, 106
Freud, S., 126
Fries, Ch.C., 126
Fruin–Mees, W., 26
Fujinkai, 251

Galbraith, J.K., 485
gamelan, 52, 58, 134n
Gandhi, M.K., 149, 173, 337, 339
Gani, A.K., 156n, 321, 330, 342, 364
Geertz, C., 404, 438, 443–44
Gelanggang, 326
gelisah, 259–61, 267
Gellhorn, M., 300

General elections, 1955, 430–42 passim, 447
Generation 1945, 298, 301, 415, 424
Generation 1966, 459, 493
Gerakan Hidoep Baroe, "Movement of New Life," 251–52
Gerakan Mahasiswa Sosialis, GMS, "Socialist Movement of Students," 411
Gerakan Pemuda Sosialis, GPS, "Socialist Movement of Youth," 411
Gerakan Rakjat Indonesia, Gerindo, "Movement of the Indonesian People," 155–56, 201, 210, 248, 284, 368–69, 372
Gerakan Tani Nasional, GTN, "National Movement of Peasants," 411
Gerakan Tigapuluh September, "September 30 Movement," 490–91
Gerakan Wanita Sosialis, GWS, "Socialist Movement of Women," 411
Gerindo, see Gerakan Rakjat Indonesia
German language, 39, 42–43, 106, 311, 417, 489
Germany, 1, 9, 35, 126–27, 146, 199, 201, 212, 253, 491
Gobée, E., 52n, 116, 292, 356
Goedhart, F., 291–92, 300–1, 343, 345, 356
Goedhart, J.A.G., 292
Goethe, J.W., 152, 174–75, 473–74
Gogh, V. van, 489
Golongan Merdeka, "Free Groups," 77–78, 83
Gomperts, H.A., 357
gotong royong, 371–72, 448
Graeff, A.C.D. de, 40, 48, 88, 135
Graham F., 370n, 394
Great Depression, 94, 97, 108
Greek classical culture, 37n, 126–27, 152, 163, 174–75, 426, 473–74, 477, 480, 495n
Guild Socialism, 74

Halim, Abdoel, 236, 345, 368, 402, 406, 492–93
Hamdani, 34, 38n, 42, 86–88, 103, 117, 161n, 211, 231–32, 236–38, 270, 285, 413, 460, 466
Hamdani, Suzanna, 336
Hamengku Buwono IX, sultan of Yogyakarta, 342, 389, 393, 396, 401, 403, 406, 408, 456, 494
Hamid II, sultan of Pontianak (Kalimantan), 332, 386, 461–64, 467–69, 472
Han Suyin, 300
Harahap, Burhanuddin, 445–46
Harahap, Parade, 22, 114n
Haroen Moein, 158n
Hartini, 437
Hatta Island, 499
Hatta, Mohammad, 2, 10, 19, 33, 50n, 58, 65–81 passim, 84–85, 87–89, 91–124 passim, 129, 131, 135, 137, 139–207 passim, 209–12, 214, 216–17, 220–25, 231, 234, 242, 245, 247–49, 251, 255, 257–68 passim, 269, 271–74, 278–80, 285n, 286–87, 288, 295–96, 299, 303–4, 311–12, 313n, 315, 317, 319, 319–20n, 323n, 324, 329–32, 341–43, 347, 358, 361, 365n, 366–69, 372–74, 376–77n, 378–82, 384–85, 386–92, 394–408 passim, 432–34, 444–46, 448–49, 453, 461–62, 465, 471, 488, 494–95, 497–99
Hazeu, G.J.A., 20n, 63–64, 169
Hazil Tanzil, 27, 83, 275–76, 413
HBS, see Hogere Burgerschool
Heine, H., 65

Helfrich, C.E.L., 341, 346
Heller, W. W., 485
Hemingway, E., 300, 363
Hendra, 296, 326
Hendraningrat, Latief, 266
Heymans, C., 126
Hilferding, R., 61
Hindu, 96, 149, 158, 163, 170–71, 339, 342, 392, 486
Hitler, A., 204, 243, 263, 451
Ho Chi Minh, 312
Hoge Veluwe, conference at, 316, 323n
Hogere Burgerschool, HBS, "Citizen's High School," 24, 50, 59, 194, 227, 245
hoofddjaksa, see jaksa
Horthy, M., 243
Huizinga, J., 343
Humphries, P., 287, 289
Huxley, J., 357

I Po Gown, 296
Idham, 363, 413, 470, 472, 491, 493
Idrus, 415
Ilmoe dan Masjarakat, 161n
Independent Labour Party, British, 271, 287, 289
Independent, 287, 289–90
India, 333–50 passim, 352–54, 356, 359–60, 372, 380, 388, 392, 429, 438, 451
Indische Partij, "Indies Party," 151, 181, 202n
Indonesia Moeda, "Young Indonesia," 226
Indonesia Raja, 413
Indonesia Raya (anthem), 45, 196n, 252, 401, 417
Indonesian language, 20–21, 24, 27, 31, 37–8, 42–43, 45–47, 53, 68, 106, 115–16, 188–89, 201, 216, 227–29, 239–40, 245, 258–59, 263, 311, 388, 413–14, 426–27, 430, 461
Indonesisch Vrouwen Studenten Vereeniging, IVSV, "Union of Indonesian Studying Women," 226
Indonesische Overpeinzingen, 291, 326, 498
Inggit Garnasih, 437n
Inoe Perbatasari, 38n, 49n, 77, 86–88
Institute of Pacific Relations, 356
International Transport Workers' Federation, ITWF, 61–62, 69
Inzicht, Het, 296–99, 325, 340
Iraq, 336, 358
Irian, see New Guinea
Isa Anshary, Kijaji, 464, 466
Isaacs, H., 475
Iskandardinata, Oto, 251–52
Iskaq, see Tjokrohadisoerjo, Iskaq
Islam, 11–12, 26, 35, 52, 74, 96–100, 102, 104–6, 112, 120–21n, 148–49, 158n, 180, 185–87, 201–2, 205–6, 220, 304, 308, 313, 338–39, 361, 343, 351, 358–59, 390n, 402–3, 405, 410, 417, 420, 422–23, 426, 434–36, 441, 470–72, 477, 484, 493
Ismail, Oesmar, 299
Ismoedikarta, Anwar, 232
Istri Sedar, "Conscious Woman," 86
Italy, 417, 429, 449

jago, 204, 256, 299, 307, 309, 324, 343, 389, 436
Jahja, Daan, 226–27, 229, 238, 245, 273, 399, 466, 481–82
Jahja, Ibrahim, 227, 244, 413

Jahja, Jusuf, 492
jaksa (djaksa, hoofddjaksa), 14, 16, 20, 27, 190
Jamin, Muhammad, 73n, 156n, 311–12, 315, 319, 376–77n
Jani, A., 466
Jansen, L.F., 241, 245
Janssen, C.W., 29
Japanese, 30, 114, 199, 205–68 passim, 269–88 passim, 297, 300, 302–3, 310, 320, 333, 335, 337–38, 352–53, 358, 368–69, 375, 387–88, 390, 393, 399, 406, 412, 484
Jassin, H.B., 245, 326
Javanese, 11, 19, 30–1, 35, 53n, 53–54, 68, 73n, 74n, 87–90, 94–96, 101n, 127n, 137–38, 148–49, 155, 158, 164–65, 170–71, 180–84, 186, 188, 251, 256, 288, 295, 300, 309–10, 313, 321, 324, 328, 334, 342, 352, 361, 371, 379n, 392–96, 405, 408–9, 413, 425–26, 435–36, 441, 443–45, 449, 454, 456–57, 486
Javanese language, 90, 312
jazz, 134, 138, 227, 239, 297
Jefferson, T., 397
Jesus, 181
Jinnah, M., 338, 350, 359
Jodjana, 127
Joesoef, T.M., 292
Jones, H. P., 456
Jong Indonesie, "Young Indonesia," see Pemoeda Indonesia
Jong Islamietenbond, "Young Moslems' Union," 54
Jong Soematranen Bond, "Young Sumatrans' Union," 65
Jonge, Jhr. B.C. de, 108–10, 112–13, 115–16, 122, 152–53, 163
Jongkind, J.B.L., 489
Jonkman, J.A., 351
Josselin de Jong, J.P.B. de, 12
Joyoboyo (Djojobojo), 330, 408n, 441
Juffrouw Cresa, see Mulder, Malia
July 3, 1946 Affair, 318–21, 326, 403

Kadt, J. de, 81, 145n, 199, 202, 215–16, 219, 221, 230n, 253, 271, 287, 291–92, 294, 296, 343, 356, 497
Kafka, F., 1–2, 49
Kahin, A., 378
Kahin, G. McT., 250, 262n, 304, 345–46, 372n, 376, 392, 395, 421, 430–31, 434, 456, 492
KAMI, see Kesatuan Aksi Mahasiswa Indonesia
Kamigayo (anthem), 221, 252
Kant, I., 126–27, 173–75
KAPPI, see Kesatuan Aksi Pelajar–Pelajar Indonesia
Kartamoehari, 232, 234, 285
Kartini, Raden Ajeng, 21
Kautsky, K., 61
Kearah Indonesia Merdeka, "Toward Free Indonesia," 100, 103, 106, 234, 240
Kerensky, A.F., 292
Keretaapi Loear Biasa, KLB, "Special Train," 300–2, 309–10, 314, 323, 332, 401
kesatria, 181
Kesatuan Aksi Mahasiswa Indonesia, KAMI, "Action Unity of Indonesian [university] Students," 493

Kesatuan Aksi Pelajar–Pelajar Indonesia, KAPPI, "Action Unity of Indonesian [secondary–school] Students," 493
Khruschev, N.S., 485
Killearn, M.L., 327–31 passim, 334, 338–39, 349–50, 360, 367
Kipling, R., 29
KLB, see Keretaapi Loear Biasa
KNIL, see Koninklijk Nederlandsch Indisch Leger
Kleffens, E.N. van, 351–53
KNIP, see Komite Nasional Indonesia Pusat
Koch, M., 51n, 108, 154, 271, 340–41
Koestler, A., 343, 414
Koets, P.J., 355–56
Kohn, H., 485
Koiso, K., 248, 250
komedie stambul, see also theater and wayang, 8–9, 26, 38–39, 134, 138, 463
Komisi Bahasa Indonesia, "Commission for Indonesian Language," 245, 258–59, 273n
Komite Nasional Indonesia Pusat, KNIP, "Central Indonesian National Council," 269, 272, 274, 305, 314, 322, 324–25, 375n
konfrontasi, 466, 485
Konfrontasi, 413–14
Koninklijk Nederlandsch Indisch Leger, KNIL, "Royal Netherlands Indies Army," 190, 282, 286, 301–2, 340, 405, 468
konsepsi, 438, 440–41, 445–46
Koperasi Rakjat Indonesia, Korindo, "Indonesian People's Cooperatives," 233–34, 244
Koperasi Rakjat Indonesia, KRI, "Indonesian People's Cooperatives," 234, 244
Korindo, see Koperasi Rakjat Indonesia
Kota Gedang, 12–15, 18, 21–22, 35, 55, 420
Kramer, H., 292
KRI, see Koperasi Rakjat Indonesia
Kritiek en Opbouw, 162–63, 197–98, 201–2, 211, 215, 225, 271, 341, 413
Kusumasumantri, Iwa, 165, 175–86, 189, 201–2, 248–49, 318n, 319n
Kwan-yin, 61, 63

Labour Party, British, 245, 355
Last, J., 61–63, 77, 189, 251, 343, 357–58, 413
Law School, Batavia, 151, 221, 225–26, 229–30, 241–42, 245, 271, 274, 288, 290
League against Imperialism and Colonialist Oppression, 75–76, 92, 169n
Lefebvre, W., 169, 292, 413, 421
Legge, J., 227, 406–7
Leiden, 1, 56–81 passim, 82, 109, 116, 169, 180, 241, 251, 288, 291–92, 399, 417, 438
Leimena, J., 391n, 491n, 492, 494
Lenin, V.I., 276, 317, 483–84
Leninism, 370, 483
Lev, D., 453
Liaison Commission, see Contact Commissie
Liga Demokrasi, "Democratic League," 447–48
Lincoln, A., 397
Linggadjati agreement, 321–34 passim, 338, 340–42, 344, 352–53, 355, 358, 366
Linton, R., 473
Listyo, 159n, 227, 419–20, 498

Loebis, Aboe Bakar, 226–28, 297, 326
Loebis, Hamid, 148
Loebis, Mochtar, 238, 241, 245, 326, 413–15, 419, 435, 461, 468n, 488n, 491
Loebis, P., 292
Logemann, J.H.A., 269, 290–94, 316, 356
Lukman, M.H., 146n, 432
Luxemburg, R., 61, 476

Macdonald, R., 132–33, 292
Macmillan, H., 451
Madilog, 302
Madiun Affair, 361–80 passim, 410, 452
Maeda, T., 220, 248–51, 261–62, 266–68, 327n
Mahabharata, 149, 163, 171–72, 198
Maharadja, Datoek Soetan, 21
Mahieu, V., see Boon, J.
Mahroezar, Soetan, 23, 111, 127, 145n, 160, 494
Maklumat X, "Declaration X," 274
Malaka, Tan, see Tan Malaka
Malay language, see Indonesian language
Malaya, 8, 10, 335–36, 349, 460
Malaysia, 466, 485
Malik, Adam, 93n, 242, 270–74 passim, 305–6, 310–12, 316, 318–19
Malraux, A., 162
Man, H. de 61
Mandailing, see Bataks
Mangoenkoesoemo, Soejitno, 161–63, 210–12, 217–18, 230, 236, 248, 271, 362
Mangoenkoesoemo, Tjipto (Cipto), 45, 49n, 165, 175, 178, 181–82, 189, 191, 194, 200–3, 211–12, 217–18, 220, 224–25
Manifesto Demokrasi, "Democratic Manifest," 245–47
Mao Tse-tung, 275–77, 429, 483
Maramis A.A., 321, 364, 397
Maria Duchâteau, see Duchâteau, Maria
Maria Ullfah, see Ullfah, Maria
Maroeto, see Nitimihardjo, Maroeto
Marshall Plan, 363
Marsman, H., 417
Marx, K., 61, 93, 173–75, 297, 304, 421, 473–76, 479–80, 484
Marxism, 74, 85, 102, 163, 169, 174, 249, 313, 370–71, 374, 408, 411, 421–23, 432, 475, 483
Masjumi, 313, 315, 319n, 320–21, 328n, 336, 338, 343, 346, 366, 368, 371, 374, 378, 395–97, 402–3, 405, 407, 410, 434–35, 440–41, 445–47, 449, 453, 464, 466, 482
Maskoen, 86–88, 118, 240
May, K., 26, 29
Medan (Deli), 14–16, 22–32 passim, 35, 46, 52, 55, 56, 59, 69, 96, 99, 111–12, 144, 148, 160n, 180, 188, 195, 233, 382, 388, 418, 420, 479
Medical School, Batavia (STOVIA), 13n, 30, 226, 229, 236, 243–45, 259, 264
Meer Uitgebreid Lager Onderwijs, MULO, "Advanced Elementary School," 24, 26, 30, 32–33, 37, 47, 59, 65, 194, 479
Menadonese, 138, 148, 151, 189, 282–84
Menon, Krishna, 354, 356–57
Meyer-Ranneft, J.W., 290, 292, 397

military, Indonesian, 276, 315, 319, 328, 373, 377n, 378, 380, 390, 392–93, 407, 437, 442–48, 454–56, 465–66, 481–84, 488, 490–91, 493–94, 497
militia, 204, 455
Minangkabau, 1–2, 5–34 passim, 38, 40, 46, 52n, 53, 57, 65–66, 68–70, 73n, 74–75, 78, 95–106 passim, 120–21n, 128, 131, 137–38, 148–49, 154, 158n, 169–70, 186, 194–95, 220, 232–33, 235, 259, 278–80, 292, 302, 305, 307, 309–11, 332, 364n, 378, 420, 435, 444–45, 449, 459, 469, 497
Minimum Program, 311–12
Moechtar, 161
Moeharto, 227
Moelia, T.G.S., 283
Moeljono, Joke, 362
moepakat (mufakat), 19, 21
Moerad, T.A., 158n, 161n, 234, 240, 413, 460
Moerdianto, 227
Moeslihat, "Strategy," 307–09, 372–73, 385
Moeso Manowar, see Muso Manowar
Moewaladi, 285
Moewardi, 265, 320
Mohammad, Djuir, 493
Montesquieu, Ch. L., 309
Mook, H.J. van, 118, 269, 286–87, 288n, 289–96 passim, 316, 319–20n, 331–32, 334, 341–44, 347, 362, 380, 394
Moslem League, Indian, 338
Mountbatten, L., 286, 334–35, 338–39, 359
movies, 36, 87, 112, 134, 136, 221, 251, 357, 415, 499
mufakat, see moepakat
Mulder, Malia ("Juffrouw Cresa"), 188–90, 194, 205, 357
MULO, see Meer Uitgebreid Lager Onderwijs
Multatuli (E. Douwes Dekker), 24, 169
Murwoto, 42, 77, 86–88, 103, 116–17, 118n
music, 8, 25, 29–30, 35, 39, 62, 111, 134, 333, 415
Muso Manowar, 369, 376–78, 380
Myrdal, G., 476

Naar de Republiek, "Towards the Republic," 310
nafsu, 104, 423, 441, 452–53
Nahdatul Ulama, 403, 432, 435, 441, 447, 456
Nasoetion, Ida, 245, 296, 298n, 299, 325, 340, 362
Nasoetion, Jahja, 93n
Nasution, A.H., 407n, 446n, 447, 455, 462n, 463, 481, 492
Nasution, Yunan, 464, 466, 472
Natal, 6–7, 9, 14, 146
Natsir, Mohammad, 47n, 368, 391n, 402–3, 405–8, 419, 441, 445, 450, 451–52
Nederlandse Indische Guerrilla Organisatie, "Guerrilla Organization for the Netherlands Indies," 462
Nederlandsen Verbond van Vakvereenigingen, "Netherlands Trade Union Federations," 69
Nehru, I., 339
Nehru, J., 175, 334–37 passim, 339, 350, 356, 359, 362, 380, 386, 451, 465
Nenni, P., 429
Netherlands Indies Civil Administration, NICA, 301

Netherlands Indies Government Information Service, NIGIS, 240, 253
New Guinea (Irian), 400, 402, 427, 462–63, 465–66, 492
News from Indonesia, 287, 289–90
NICA, see Netherlands Indies Civil Administration
Nietzsche, F., 173–74, 203, 297, 423, 473
Nieuwenhuys, R., 413
NIGIS, see Netherlands Indies Government Information Service
ningrat, 44, 73–74, 91, 101, 137, 162, 181, 277–78, 281, 286, 313n, 324, 337, 408, 422, 424–26, 443–44
Nishijima S., 250, 261, 266–67
Nitimihardjo, Maroeto, 242
Noegroho, see Saleh Mangoendiningrat, Noegroho
Noer Alamsjah, Soetan, 111, 160, 245, 493
nuchterheid, 18, 21, 293, 328, 476–77
Nurul, Siti, 374

OSP, see Onafhankelijke Socialistische Partij
October 17, 1952 Affair, 407
Oesman, 232, 234
Oetojo, 241, 245, 338, 349n, 363, 364n
Ogburn, W.F., 473, 475–76
Oltmans, W.F., 26
Onafhankelijke Socialistische Partij, OSP, "Independent Socialist Party," 107, 110, 116, 202, 253, 428
Oom Bing, see Versteeg, Bing
Opbouw–Pembinaan, 340, 342, 344, 347
Organisatie Kaoem Boeroeh Penganggoeran Indonesia, "Organization of Unemployed Indonesians," 95
Oriëntatie, 413–14
Orwell, G., 485
Out of Exile, 26n, 387

PKI, see Partai Komunis Indonesia
PNI, see Partai Nasional Indonesia
Padang, 12, 22, 233, 446, 451–52, 497
Padang Panjang, 1, 14, 23, 99–100, 233, 498
Pakistan, 359, 363
Palar, L.N., 94, 292, 323
Pamoentjak, Soetan Nazir, 351, 358
Pane, Sanoesi, 249
Paras, see Partai Rakjat Sosialis
paréwa, 307, 309
PARI, see Partai Repoebliek Indonesia
Parindra, see Parta Indonesia Raja
Parkindo, see Partai Kristen Indonesia
Parman, S., 227n
Parool, Het, 291–93, 300, 343, 357
Parsi, see Partai Sosialis Indonesia
Parta Indonesia Raja, Parindra, "Party of Great Indonesia," 155, 160n, 204n, 434–35
Partai Buruh Indonesia, "Indonesian Labor Party," 325
Partai Indonesia, Partindo, "Party of Indonesia," 72–73, 78, 89–91, 94, 106–10, 115–16, 154–55, 180, 211, 225, 249, 251, 277, 313, 369
Partai Katolik, "Catholic Party," 435, 441, 447

Partai Komunis Indonesia, PKI, "Communist Party of Indonesia," 62–63, 76–77, 91–92, 102n, 115, 118, 231, 240, 249–50, 285, 303, 313n, 325, 342, 368–72, 376, 378–79, 400, 406, 410, 432, 434–35, 442–43, 447–57 passim, 466, 483–84, 488, 490
Partai Kristen Indonesia, Parkindo, "Party of Indonesian Christians," 435, 447
Partai Nasional Indonesia, PNI, "Indonesian National Party," 49–55 passim, 68, 70–73, 313, 315, 321, 330, 336, 347, 366, 369, 378, 395, 403, 405, 407, 409–10, 434–35, 447, 449, 456
Partai Rakjat Sosialis, Paras, "People's Socialist Party," 286
Partai Repoebliek Indonesia, PARI, "Party of the Indonesian Republic," 92, 131, 137, 161n, 303
Partai Sarekat Islam Indonesia, PSII, "Party of Indonesian Islamic Union," 131, 137, 435, 441
Partai Sosialis Indonesia, Parsi, "Indonesian Socialist Party," 284, 286, 368
Partai Sosialis Indonesia, PSI, "Socialist Party of Indonesia," 368–70, 372–75, 379, 395, 400, 402–3, 406–13, 416, 418–19, 422, 424, 426, 430–32, 434–37, 439–42, 445–54, 460–61, 464, 466, 471, 481–83, 487, 490, 498
Partai Sosialis, PS, "Socialist Party," 286, 306, 313, 322–23, 346, 368, 410, 453
Partij van de Arbeid, PvdA, "Labor Party," see Dutch social democracy
Partindo, see Partai Indonesia
Pasteur, L., 427
Pasundan, see Sundanese
Patnaik, Biju, 335, 349
Patriae Scientiaeque, "Motherland and Science," 38, 42, 44, 49, 62
Patterson, W.R., 273
Patty, A.J., 296
Pearl Harbor, 205
Pedoman, 416, 435, 451
Pembela Tanah Air, PETA, "Fatherland Defense Force," 255, 265–66
Pemerintah Revolusioner Republik Indonesia, PRRI, "Revolutionary Government of the Indonesian Republic," 446–47, 449, 452–53, 455, 460–61, 466, 472, 490
Pemoeda Indonesia (Jong Indonesie), "Indonesian Youth," 39–47 passim, 62, 64, 83, 86
Pemoeda Sosialis Indonesia, Pesindo, "Indonesian Socialist Youth," 320
Pemoeda Sumatra, "Sumatran Youth," 54–55
pencak, 138
Pendidikan Nasional Indonesia, "Indonesian National Education," 79–125 passim, 131, 138–39, 141–44, 148, 153, 157–61 passim, 181, 188, 203, 206, 211, 216, 231–35, 237, 239–40, 242, 244, 248, 251, 253–54, 256, 259, 263, 270, 285–86, 288, 303, 322, 333, 363, 367–68, 371, 375, 387–88, 406–8, 411–12, 422, 425, 435, 448, 460
Penjoeloeh–Torch, 240
Perdjoeangan Kita, "Our Struggle," 274–83, 287, 289, 291, 302, 311–12, 336, 355, 427, 498
Perdjuangan Semesta, Permesta, "Common Struggle," 446–47, 453, 455, 460, 472, 490

Perempoean Bergerak, 22
Perhimpoenan Indonesia, (Perhimpunan), "Indonesian Association," 50n, 65–81 passim, 92, 115n, 155, 162, 248, 253, 288, 292, 313n, 323n
Perhimpoenan Peladjar–Peladjar Indonesia, PPPI, "Association of Indonesian Students," 93, 226, 242, 377n
perkeniers, see planters
Permesta, see Perdjuangan Semesta
Permi, see Persatoean Moeslimin Indonesia
Permoefakatan Perhimpoenan2 Politik Kebangsaan Indonesia, PPPKI, "Federation of Indonesian Political Associations," 54, 68
Perron, E. du, 162–63, 197–99, 202, 211–12, 215, 225, 230n, 241, 291, 298, 340–41, 343, 413, 417, 420
Persatoean Bangsa Indonesia, "Union of the Indonesian Nation," 73
Persatoean Moeslimin Indonesia, Permi, "Union of Indonesian Muslims," 98–99, 102, 116, 131, 137, 154
Persatoean Perdjoeangan, "Fighting Front," 312
Pesindo, see Pemoeda Sosialis Indonesia
PETA, see Pembela Tanah Air
Petrus Blumberger, J.T., 244
Philippines, 244, 257, 335, 413, 449, 460
Picasso, P., 414
Pinke, A.S., 341, 346
Planck, M., 477
planters (perkeniers), 28–31, 127, 165, 178–79, 183, 187, 499
Plas, Ch.O. van der, 53n, 118, 240, 273, 290–92, 294, 341
Plato, 126, 152, 163, 175
Poedjangga Baroe, "New Writer," 156, 169, 171, 197, 245, 249
Poetri Indonesia, "Daughters of Indonesia," 40–41, 51
pokrol bambu, 191
Poland, 417, 484
Poppy, see Saleh Mangoendiningrat, Siti Wahjunah
Postel–Coster, E., 459
PPPI, see Perhimpoenan Peladjar–Peladjar Indonesia
PPPKI, see Permoefakatan Perhimpoenan2 Politik Kebangsaan Indonesia
Prawoto Mangkusasmit, 46, 466–69
Pringgodigdo, Abdoel Karim, 77, 83n, 161–62
Pringgodigdo, Gafar, 382
Pringgodigdo, Soewarni, 51, 83n, 89, 161–63, 197–98, 202, 413, 420
prison, 118–28 passim, 138, 160, 165, 176, 197, 423, 463–76, 478–81, 485, 487–89, 493
priyayi, 408–9
PRRI, see Pemerintah Revolusioner Republik Indonesia
PS, see Partai Sosialis
PSI, see Partai Sosialis Indonesia
PSII, see Partai Sarekat Islam Indonesia
PTTR, trade unions, 233, 237
pubertus, 185, 204, 280, 424
PvdA, see Partij van de Arbeid

Rabiah, Siti, 6–9, 14, 27, 30, 134, 146, 160n, 189

Radena, 14, 27, 34, 83–4, 93, 117, 142
Radio Camp, 241, 245, 287, 338, 353
radio, 187, 206, 214, 227, 239–45 passim, 253, 255–56, 261–64, 270, 289, 297, 299, 307–8, 317, 320–21, 344–45, 358, 362, 369, 388, 464, 469, 491, 493
Radjiman Wediodiningrat, 257
Ramalan, 326
Randwijk, H.M. van, 356
rantau, 9–15, 17–18, 20–1, 27, 31, 33–34, 38, 55, 65, 81, 92, 97, 107, 128, 186–87, 196, 279–80, 310, 426, 491, 499
Rasad, Mohammad gelar Maharadja Soetan, 12, 14–16, 20–31 passim, 56–58, 65–66, 191
Rasjid, St. Mohd., 122n, 449–50
Ratna, 14
Ratu Adil, 87–88, 90, 96
Renville agreement, 365–68, 370n, 380n, 392
Resink, G.J., 340
Riekerk, Jos, 59, 63–65, 77, 81, 145n, 169, 253, 413
Rodie, 241
Roem, Mohammad, 97, 391–92, 395–97, 403, 408, 461–62, 464, 466–69, 491
Roesbandi, 38n, 62, 66–67
Rohana Kudus, Siti, 14, 21–23
Roijen, J.H. van, 395–97
Roland Holst, H., 50n, 61, 134–35, 298, 417
Romein, J., 244, 292, 343
romusha, 247–48
Ronkel, Ph.S. van, 22
Roosevelt, F.D., 200, 360n
Rose, M., 432–33, 490
Rostow, W., 474
Round Table Conference, 1949, 395, 397–400, 402, 405, 437
Rousseau, J.-J., 48, 309
rumah tunjuk, 6–7, 9, 11, 14, 128, 279

Sacco, N., 124
Said Ali, Soetan, 133
Saigon, 258–60
Sajap Kiri, 346
Saleh Mangoendiningrat, Miriam, 227, 245
Saleh Mangoendiningrat, Noegroho, 296
Saleh Mangoendiningrat, Siti Wahjunah (Poppy), later Sjahrir, 226–27, 245, 321, 332, 335, 339–40, 367, 397–99, 417–18, 420, 459, 461, 467, 469–71, 489–93, 498
Saleh Mangoendiningrat, Soedjatmoko, 226–31, 236, 238, 243–45, 296, 332, 335, 349n, 360n, 363, 387, 413, 417, 442, 463, 466–67, 469–70, 487–89, 492–93, 498
Saleh, Chaerul, 242, 264–66, 270, 274
Salim, Abdul Chalid, 31, 128, 137, 141, 148, 151–52
Salim, Hadji Agoes, 31, 50n, 69–70, 75, 83, 97, 122, 148, 161n, 185, 201, 242, 335–36, 350–51, 353, 355–56, 358, 362, 365, 382–84, 397, 408
Salim, Leon, 99, 122n, 232, 285, 367, 413, 435, 461
Salim, painter, 59, 82, 84, 127–28, 160n, 326, 357, 362, 399, 414, 439, 480, 489
Salomons, A., 29
Samsoeddin, Raden, 38n, 42
Sanders, P., 330–32
Santoso, Iwan, 226, 244

Santoso, Raden Soeria, 244–45, 247, 253, 273n, 340
Sardjono, S., 240
Sarekat Islam, "Islamic Union," 31, 68, 71
Saroso, 364n
Sartono, 72–73, 78, 89, 156n, 251–52, 274, 313
Sastra, 91–92, 206n, 211, 231–32, 237, 254, 256–57, 285, 303, 413
Sastroamidjojo, Ali, 272, 321–22, 336, 365, 369, 403, 406, 437
Sastrosatomo, Subadio, 226–30, 236, 243–45, 247, 253, 258–59, 263–65, 267, 270–72, 285, 296, 312–13, 345, 360n, 368, 407, 412–13, 434, 436, 451, 462–64, 466–68, 470–71, 491–93
Sastrosatomo, Sudarpo, 227, 229, 230–31, 236, 237n, 238, 243–45, 325, 340, 348, 362–63, 365, 368, 390n, 450n, 492–93
satria, see kesatria
Saudi Arabia, 358
Scandinavia, 417, 429
Schermerhorn, W., 253, 323n, 326–34, 335–38, 340, 343–44, 347–48, 351, 353, 358, 366, 379, 394, 493
Schmidt, P.J., 76n, 107, 253, 288, 343, 353, 365–66
Schumpeter, J., 474
SDAP, see Social Democratic Labor Party
Semaoen (Semaun), 88
Sendja Djakarta, "Twilight in Jakarta," 414
Sentral Organisasi Buruh Seluruh Indonesia, SOBSI, "All-Indonesia Federation of Labor Organizations," 270
Seratus Limapuluh Tanja Djawab, "150 Questions and Answers," 100–3, 106, 234
Setiadjit Soegondo, 253, 292, 323, 325, 336, 341, 347–48, 364
Shakespeare, W., 152, 163, 474
Siam, see Thailand
Siasat, 325–26, 335, 387–90, 395–97, 400, 411, 414–15, 417–18
Sikap, 412–13, 432, 450–51
Simandjoentak, Cornel, 299
Simatupang, T.B., 236–37n, 238, 244, 285, 370n, 380, 393–94, 396, 435, 470, 482, 490
Simbolon, M., 446, 472
Singapore, 36, 82, 87, 92, 241, 287, 335–36, 338–39, 349, 354, 360–61, 363, 364n, 365–67, 373, 378–79, 397, 417, 445, 446n, 449, 450n, 460
Singer sewing machine, 22, 195, 219
Singgih, Pandji, 249
sini sana, 106, 109
Siregar, Amir Hamzah, 229–31, 236, 241
Sitoemorang, Sitor, 298, 326
Sitoroes, Lintonmg Moelia, 226, 230–31, 250n, 285, 296, 313, 419–20, 430, 450n
Sjafroeddin Prawiranegara, 47n, 380, 385, 390, 396, 403, 445–46, 452
Sjahrazad, 291, 343
Sjahrir, Ali, 195, 207, 209, 214, 219, 349, 384, 467, 479, 493
Sjahrir, Bujung, 461, 467
Sjahrir, Des Alwi, 191–95 passim, 207, 224, 263, 399, 449–50, 460, 499
Sjahrir, Does, 191–95 passim
Sjahrir Island, 499

Sjahrir, Lily, 176, 191–95 passim, 207, 209, 214, 218, 384, 467, 471
Sjahrir, Mimi, 191–95 passim, 207, 217, 349, 361, 399, 417–18
Sjahrir, Poppy, see Saleh Mangoendiningrat, Siti Wahjunah
Sjahrir, Siti Wahjunah, see Saleh Mangoendiningrat, Siti Wahjunah
Sjahrir, Upik, 461, 467
Sjahrizal, see Djoehana, Siti Sjahrizal
Sjahroezah, Djohan, 27, 83–84, 93, 123–24, 127, 143n, 145n, 160–61, 199, 211, 241–43, 248, 264, 270, 275, 285, 303, 306, 307n, 335, 368, 413, 418–19, 439, 450n, 471
Sjahsam, Soetan, 23, 128, 160n, 197, 374n, 418, 420, 439, 493
Sjarifoeddin, Amir, 2, 156n, 157, 201, 210–11, 225, 229–30, 241–42, 244, 248, 270, 274–75, 283, 286, 295, 312–13, 315–16, 319–25 passim, 330, 336, 342–43, 346–47, 362, 365–67, 369, 371, 375–76, 378–79, 390, 408–10, 453
Sneevliet, H., 151
Snouck Hurgronje, C., 63–64, 169, 241
SOBSI, see Sentral Organisasi Buruh Seluruh Indonesia
soccer, 25–26, 28, 36, 38, 42, 48, 82–83, 134, 144–45, 193, 195
Sociaal Democratische Studenten Club, "Social Democratic Students' Club," 58–59, 61–62, 76–77
Social Democratic Labor Party, SDAP, see also Dutch social democracy, 61, 76, 94 107, 253
Socialist, De, 61–64, 69, 71, 76–77, 81, 107, 169, 253, 288
Soebagio Mangoenrahardjo, 38n, 41–43, 82–83, 87, 100–6 passim, 206n, 231–32, 234, 285, 413
Soebakat, 92n
Soebandrio, 336, 343, 349n, 354–56, 363, 412, 462–64, 488, 490
Soebandrio, Tien, 340, 343, 362
Soebardjo, Achmad Djoyoadisuryo, 248–52, 266–67, 304, 308, 318n, 403, 462n
Soebianto, see, Djojohadikoesoemo, Soebianto
Soedarso, 326
Soedarsono, Dr., 42n, 234, 263, 270, 306, 322, 333, 363–64, 388, 492–93
Soedirman, General, 319–20, 328, 393–94, 396
Soediro, 320
Soedjadi, 78
Soedjatmoko, see Saleh Mangoendiningrat, Soedjatmoko
Soedjojono, S., 197, 245, 296, 326
Soegondo, see Djojopoespito, Soegondo
Soegra, 271, 285, 306, 413
Soehadi, 91
Soeharto, Dr., 258
Soejitno, see Mangoenkoesoemo, Soejitno
Soeka, 86–88, 116–17, 240
Soekaemi, 86, 248, 413
Soekarni Kartodiwirdjo, 242, 265, 267, 274, 305–6, 311, 315
Soekarto (Sukarto), 91
Soekiman Wirjosandjojo, 319n, 403, 408, 434
Soekoer, Abdullah, 66
Soeleiman, Chatib, 99, 232, 235
Soemantri, Raden Mas, 38n, 41–42

Soemarman, 227, 238
Soemarno, 161n, 232
Soemitro Reksodipeotro, 285
Soemitro, see Djojohadikoesoemo, Soemitro
Soempah Pemoeda, "Youth Oath," 45
Soenarjo, 251–52
Soenting Melajoe, 20–21
Soepardan, 234
Soepeno, 285, 345, 368, 373
Soepomo, Prof., 387, 390, 391n
Soerat Warisan, "Testament," 304, 312, 388
Soeripno, 288–89, 336, 369, 376
Soeroto Koento, 245, 264
Soeryadarma, 382
Soetardjo, Kartohadikoesoemo, 155, 201
Soetomo Tjokronegoro, 245, 247, 259
Soetomo, Dr. Raden, 72n, 73, 93–94, 95n, 108
Soewandi, 245, 247, 283, 387–88
Soewarsih, see Djojopoespito, Soewarsih
Soewirjo, 332
Solo–Valley scenario, 310–11
Solzhenitsyn, A., 484
Sombart, W., 144
Somerset Maugham, W., 178
Soviet Union (Russia), 241, 280, 359–60, 370–71, 376, 376–77n, 406, 427–29, 456, 480, 484
Spoor, S.H., 341
Stalin, J.V., 76n, 483–85
Starkenborgh Stachouwer, A.W.I. Tjarda van, 154, 214
Stokvis, J.E., 51n, 54n, 66, 343
STOVIA, see Medical School, Batavia
Stuw, 116, 133, 162–63, 240, 290–92, 342, 351, 355, 380, 397
Suara Sosialis, 409–10, 412, 431, 439
Subadio, see Sastrosatomo, Subadio
Subroto, Gatot, 369n
Sudarpo, see Sastrosatomo, Sudarpo
Suharto, General, 491, 493–94
Sukarno, 33, 40, 49–55 passim, 68, 70–73, 77, 79, 87–90, 93–94, 106–10, 114–15, 122, 143, 154, 156, 173n, 180–81, 188, 196n, 211, 218, 221–25 passim, 243–45, 247–51, 255–68 passim, 269, 271–75, 277, 280, 284, 287, 294–96, 299, 303–5, 311–24 passim, 328–32, 336, 341–43, 346–47, 349, 352, 358, 361–62, 364–66, 369, 371–73, 378–97, 401, 403, 405, 408–9, 411–12, 414, 429, 432–34, 437–53 passim, 456–66, 482–91, 497–98
Sumual, H.N. "Ventje," 472
Sundanese (Pasundan), 43, 46, 53–54, 90, 163–64, 251, 431, 444
Sundhaussen, U., 466
Supandi, 470
Surio Soemarto, 391n
Suwarto, 466
Sweden, 489
swimming, 145, 467–68, 470
Switzerland, 429, 489–90, 493, 497
Syahrir, see Sjahrir
Syria, 335–36
Szekely–Lulofsz, M., 29

Tabrani, M., 72n
Taiwan, 484

Takdir Alisjahbana, Soetan, 33, 163n, 245, 247, 258, 340, 387–88, 413–14
Taman Siswa, 43n
Tambu, Charles, 241, 245, 287, 289, 353, 363, 413, 460
Tamin, Djamaluddin, 92n, 137, 319
Tamzil, 285, 364
Tan Ling Djie, 313, 346, 376
Tan Malaka, 2, 36n, 50n, 78n, 92–93, 114, 131, 161n, 173n, 180, 205n, 215n, 239n, 242, 250, 257, 269n, 302–20 passim, 376, 388–90, 492n, 498n
Tanah Merah, see Boven Digul
Tanah Tinggi, see Boven Digul
Tandiono Manu, 238
Tapanuli, 6–7, 9, 31
Tas, S., 58–59, 61–65 passim, 76–81, 104, 107, 111–12, 116, 145n, 174, 176, 192, 199, 202, 253, 275, 283, 291–92, 298, 343, 356, 387, 412, 420–21, 432, 463, 480
Tatengkeng, J.E., 171, 413, 416
Technical College, Bandung, 34, 40–41, 50
tennis, 36, 42, 48, 134, 301, 461, 468, 470
Terauchi, H., 258–59
Testament, see Soerat Warisan
Thailand (Siam), 288, 335, 337–39, 363, 364n, 373, 493
Thalib, Ibrahim, 259
Thamrin, Mohammad Hoesni, 201, 494
theater, see also wayang and komedie stambul, 35, 38, 42, 44, 47–48, 54, 59, 62, 66, 71, 134, 138, 149
Theosophical Society, 66
Tichelman, F., 408–9
Tito, J.B., 429
Tjahja Volksuniversiteit, "Radiance People's University," 42–44, 46, 62, 86, 103
Tjalie Robinson, see Boon, J.
Tjipto, see Mangoenkoesoemo, Tjipto
Tjoetjoen, Roesni, 232, 285
Tjokrohadisoerjo, Iskaq, 365
Tolstoy, L.N., 173
Tom Mix, 26, 29, 134
Trevor-Roper, H., 477
Trilling, L., 475–76
Trotskyist, 313, 376

Uitzicht, Het, 340
Ullfah, Maria, later Santoso, later Subadio, 62, 251–52, 387–88, 471, 492–93
Unitas Studiosorum Indonesiensis, USI, 226–27, 229–30, 271
United Malay Nationalist Organization, 336
United Nations (Allies), 239, 244, 253, 255, 258, 269, 273, 287, 289, 304, 306, 339, 350–53 passim, 360, 363–65 passim, 384, 386, 393–95 passim
United States, 124, 280–81, 337, 346–47, 350–54, 359–60, 362, 364–66, 370–71, 377n, 394–95, 406, 427–29, 442, 446n, 453, 456, 465, 475, 485
United States of Indonesia, 400–2
USI, see Unitas Studiosorum Indonesiensis

Vaderlandsche Club, "Patriotic Club," 109
Vanzetti, B., 124

Verenigde Ondergrondse Corps, VOC, "United Underground Corps," 463
Versteeg, Bing, "Oom Bing," 189–90, 205
VOC, see Verenigde Ondergrondse Corps
Volksraad, 50n, 324, 405
Volksuniversiteit, see Tjahja Volksuniversiteit
Vollenhoven, C. van, 63–65, 241
Vonk, G., 290
Vries, D. de, 230n, 413
Vuyk, Beb, 211–12, 214, 217–19, 271, 296, 362, 413, 416–17, 438–39, 493

Washington, G., 397
Watt, J., 302
wayang, see also komedie stambul and theater, 134, 149, 181, 256, 264, 299, 414
Webb, B., 230n
Weber, M., 473–74, 484
Weinstein, F., 275
welfare states, 429
Welter, Ch.J.I.M., 154, 157
Wertheim, W.F., 221, 271, 290, 292, 294, 340, 343, 356
Westenenk, L.C., 22
Wibisono, Jusuf, 407
Wibowo, 226, 481, 492–93
Wigoena, Pandoe Karta, 242, 306
Wijono, 322–23
Wikana, 156n, 248–49, 266–66, 346
Wilhelmus (anthem), 214, 401
Wilopo, 403, 406
Wittfogel, K., 473, 476
Wolf, Ch. Jr., 26n
Wongsonegoro, K.M.R.T., 304
Woodman, D., 288–89, 336, 355, 373

Yemen, 358
Yevtushenko, Y., 485
Yugoslavia, 417, 429, 484

Zainal Abidin, Andi, 227, 230
Zainal Zain, Soetan Mohammad, 288, 364n
Zainal Zain, Yeti, 336
zakelijk, 51, 348, 440, 476–77
Zeggelen, M. van, 26
Zeven Provinciën, 112–13
Zilliacus, K. Konni, 429

www.ingramcontent.com/pod-product-compliance
Lightning Source LLC
Chambersburg PA
CBHW080922300426
44115CB00018B/2912